The natural history of man

The natural

Prentice-Hall, Inc., Englewood Cliffs, N.J.

history of man

Carl P. Swanson

University of Massachusetts

To: Mike and Ruth   Ann and Ed

who justify confidence in the future of man

Prentice-Hall Biological Science Series

William D. McElroy and Carl P. Swanson, editors

Library of Congress Cataloging in Publication Data

Swanson, Carl P
  The natural history of man.

  (Prentice-Hall biological science series)
1. Human biology. 2. Human evolution.
I. Title. [DNLM: 1. Adaptation, Biological.
2. Anthropology. 3. Evolution. GN 24 S972n 1973]
GN60.S96 573 72-6494
ISBN 0-13-610022-8

Picture consultant: Frances L. Orkin

Illustrations by Graphic Spectrum Systems, Inc.

Design by Walter Behnke

10 9 8 7 6 5 4 3 2 1

Prentice-Hall International, Inc., London
Prentice-Hall of Australia, Pty. Ltd., Sydney
Prentice-Hall of Canada, Ltd., Toronto
Prentice-Hall of India Private Ltd., New Delhi
Prentice-Hall of Japan, Inc., Tokyo

Acknowledgments

Chapter 1

pp. 2, 20, 22: From W. Beck, *Modern Science and the Nature of Life.* © 1957 by William S. Beck. Reprinted by permission of Harcourt Brace Jovanovich, Inc.

p. 6: From Th. Dobzhansky, *The Biology of Ultimate Concern.* © 1967 by Theodosius Dobzhansky. Reprinted by arrangement with New American Library, Inc.

p. 26: From S. L. Fahs, *Today's Children and Yesterday's Heritage* © 1952 by Beacon Press. Reprinted with permission.

p. 11: From A. Fremantle, *The Age of Belief.* © 1955 by Anne Fremantle. Reprinted by permission of New American Library, Inc.

p. 14: From W. Howells, *The Heathens.* © 1948 by William Howells. Reprinted by permission of Doubleday & Company, Inc.

p. 28: From K. Koch, "Permanently," in *Thank You and Other Poems.* © 1962 by Kenneth Koch. Reprinted by permission of Grove Press, Inc.

pp. 7, 26: From J. W. Krutch, *The Modern Temper.* © 1929 by Harcourt Brace Jovanovich, Inc; © 1957 by Joseph Wood Krutch. Reprinted by permission of the publishers.

p. 13: From V. Lindsay, "The Congo," in *Collected Poems.* © 1914 by the Macmillan Company; © 1942 by Elizabeth C. Lindsay. Reprinted by permission of the Macmillan Company.

p. 6: From J. R. Oppenheimer, *Science and the Common Understanding.* © 1953, 1954 by J. Robert Oppenheimer. Reprinted by permission of Simon & Schuster, Inc.

p. 15: From K. L. Patton, *"Man Is the Meaning,"* in *Hymns for the Celebration of Life.* © 1956 by K. L. Patton. Reprinted by permission of Beacon Press.

Chapter 2

p. 70: From T. S. Ashton, *The Industrial Revolution, 1760–1830.* Reprinted by permission of Oxford University Press.

p. 49: From W. Beck, *Modern Science and the Nature of Life.* © 1957 by William S. Beck. Reprinted by permission of Harcourt Brace Jovanovich, Inc.

p. 69: From J. Bronowski, *Science and Human Values.* Reprinted by permission of Julian Messner, a division of Simon & Schuster, Inc. © 1956, 1965 by J. Bronowski.

Chapter 3

pp. 74, 76: From A. Koyré, *Newtonian Studies.* © 1965 by Harvard University Press. Reprinted with permission.

Chapter 4

p. 124: From I. Stone, *Clarence Darrow for the Defense: A Biography.* Doubleday, New York, 1941. © 1941 by Irving Stone. Reprinted by permission of Doubleday & Company, Inc.

Chapter 5

p. 159: From Th. Dobzhansky, *The Biology of Ultimate Concern.* © 1967 by Theodosius Dobzhansky. Reprinted by arrangement with New American Library, Inc.

p. 142: From E. O. Dodson, *Evolution: Process and Product.* © 1960 by Litton Educational Publishing, Inc. Reprinted by permission of Van Nostrand Reinhold, Inc.

p. 162: From L. Eiseley, *The Immense Journey.* © 1956 by Loren Eiseley. Reprinted by permission of Random House, Inc.

p. 140: From P. F. Russell, "The Eradication of Malaria." *Scientific American,* June 1952, pp. 22–25. © 1952 by Scientific American, Inc. All rights reserved.

Chapter 6

p. 186: From R. Ardrey, *African Genesis.* © 1961 by Literat S. A. Reprinted by permission of Atheneum Publishers and William Collins Sons & Co. Ltd.

p. 187: From R. Ardrey, *The Territorial Imperative.* © 1966 by Robert Ardrey. Reprinted by permission of Atheneum Publishers and William Collins Sons & Co. Ltd.

p. 172: From A. Carr, "100 Turtle Eggs." *Natural History,* August-September 1967. © 1967 American Museum of Natural History. Reprinted by permission of *Natural History* magazine.

p. 173: From E. O. Dodson, *Evolution: Process and Product,* rev. ed. © 1960 by Litton Educational Publishing, Inc. Reprinted by permission of Van Nostrand Reinhold, Inc.

p. 195: From L. Eiseley, "Fossil Man." *Scientific American,* December 1953, pp. 65–72. © 1953 by Scientific American, Inc. All rights reserved.

p. 175: From R. Estes, "Predators and Scavengers." *Natural History,* February-March 1967. © 1967 American Museum of Natural History. Reprinted by permission of *Natural History* magazine.

pp. 183, 189: From E. A. Hooton, *Apes, Men, and Morons.* © 1937 by G. P. Putnam's Sons. Reprinted with permission.

p. 194: From W. Howells, "Homo Erectus," *Scientific American,* September 1966, pp. 46–53. © 1966 by Scientific American, Inc. All rights reserved.

p. 180: From W. Howells, *Mankind in the Making.* © 1967 by William Howells. Reprinted by permission of Doubleday & Company, Inc.

p. 185: From E. Marais, *The Soul of the Ape.* © 1969 by Human & Rousseau Publishers Ltd. Reprinted by permission of Atheneum Publishers and Anthony Blond Ltd.

p. 179: From O. P. Pearson, "The Metabolism of Hummingbirds." *Scientific American,* January 1953, pp. 69–72. © 1953 by Scientific American, Inc. All rights reserved.

p. 171: From H. Smith, *Kamongo: or the Lungfish and the Padre.* © 1932, © 1960 by Homer W. Smith. Reprinted by permission of The Viking Press, Inc.

p. 192: From S. L. Washburn, "Tools and Human Evolution." *Scientific American,* September 1960, pp. 62–75. © 1960 by Scientific American, Inc. All rights reserved.

Chapter 7

p. 206: From H. Beston, *Especially Maine: The Natural World of Henry Beston, from Cape Cod to the St. Lawrence.* © 1970 by Elizabeth Coatsworth Beston. Reprinted by permission of The Stephen Greene Press.

p. 220: From A. Comfort, *The Nature of Human Nature.* © 1966 by Alex Comfort. Reprinted by permission of Harper & Row, Publishers, Inc.

p. 225: From J. Conrad, *The Many Worlds of Man.* © 1964 by Jack Conrad. Reprinted by permission of Thomas Y. Crowell Company.

p. 204: From L. Eiseley, "Mind as Nature," in *The Night Country.* © 1962 by Loren Eiseley. Reprinted by permission of Charles Scribner's Sons.

p. 202: From C. F. Hockett, "The Origin of Speech." *Scientific American,* September 1960, pp. 88–96. © 1960 by Scientific American, Inc. All rights reserved.

p. 226: From E. A. Hooton, *Apes, Men, and Morons.* © 1937, 1965 G. P. Putnam's Sons. Reprinted with permission.

p. 203: From C. Sandburg, "Wilderness," in *Chicago Poems.* © 1916 by Holt, Rinehart and Winston, Inc.; © 1944 by Carl Sandburg. Reprinted by permission of Harcourt Brace Jovanovich, Inc.

p. 213: From S. L. Washburn and I. DeVore. "The Social Life of Baboons." *Scientific American,* June 1961, pp. 62–71. © 1961 by Scientific American, Inc. All rights reserved.

Chapter 8

p. 244: From L. Eiseley, *The Immense Journey.* © 1953 by Loren Eiseley. Reprinted by permission of Random House, Inc.

p. 278: From D. Fabun, *You and Creativity.* Reprinted by permission of Benziger Bruce & Glencoe, Inc., Beverly Hills, Calif., a division of The Macmillan Company. © 1968 by Kaiser Aluminum Chemical Corporation.

p. 261: From R. B. Fuller, *Nine Chains to the Moon.* © 1938, © 1966 by Richard Buckminster Fuller. Reprinted by permission of J. B. Lippincott Company.

p. 240: From D. Kennedy, *The Living Cell:* Readings from *Scientific American.* Freeman, San Francisco, 1966, p. 2. © 1966 by Scientific American, Inc. All rights reserved.

p. 275: From J. W. Krutch, *The Modern Temper.* © 1929 by Harcourt Brace Jovanovich, Inc.; © 1957 by Joseph Wood Krutch. Reprinted by permission of the publishers.

p. 247: From V. A. McKusick, "The Mapping of Human Chromosomes." *Scientific American,* April 1971, pp. 104–13. © 1971 by Scientific American, Inc. All rights reserved.

pp. 250–51: From J. D. Watson, *The Double Helix: A Personal Account of the Discovery of the Structure of DNA.* © 1968 by James D. Watson. Reprinted by permission of Atheneum Publishers and Weidenfeld and Nicolson Ltd.

p. 266: From R. J. Williams, *You Are Extraordinary.* Random House, New York, 1967. © 1967 by Roger J. Williams. Reprinted by permission of Random House, Inc.

Chapter 9

p. 321: From R. Benedict, "The Growth of Cultures," in *Man, Culture and Society,* ed., H. L. Shapiro. © 1956 by Oxford University Press, Inc. Reprinted with permission.

p. 292: From S. R. Binford and L. R. Binford, "Stone Tools and Human Behavior." *Scientific American,* April 1969, pp. 70–72. © 1969 by Scientific American, Inc. All rights reserved.

p. 305: From H. Brown, "Human Materials Production as a Process in the Biosphere." *Scientific American,* September 1970, pp. 195–208. © 1970 by Scientific American, Inc. All rights reserved.

p. 291: From J. Conrad, *The Many Worlds of Man.* T. Y. Crowell, New York, 1964, pp. 107–8. © 1964 by Jack Conrad. Reprinted by permission of Thomas Y. Crowell, Inc.

p. 318: From R. Dubos, *So Human an Animal.* © 1968 by Rene Dubos. Reprinted by permission of Charles Scribner's Sons.

p. 308: From D. Fabun, *The Corporation as a Creative Environment.* Reprinted by permission of Benziger Bruce & Glencoe, Inc., Beverly Hills, Calif., a division of The Macmillan Company. © 1970 by Kaiser Aluminum & Chemical Corporation.

pp. 300, 306: From D. Fabun, *Dimensions of Change.* Reprinted by permission of Benziger Bruce & Glencoe, Inc., Beverly Hills, Calif., a division of The Macmillan Company. © 1970 by Kaiser Aluminum & Chemical Corporation.

p. 312: From D. Fabun, *You and Creativity.* Reprinted by permission of Benziger Bruce & Glencoe, Inc., Beverly Hills, Calif., a division of The Macmillan Company. © 1970 by Kaiser Aluminum & Chemical Corporation.

p. 284: From P. Handler, ed., *Biology and the Future of Man.* © 1970 by Oxford University Press. Reprinted with permission.

p. 318: From E. E. Morison, *Men, Machines, and Modern Times.* © 1966 by The M.I.T. Press. Reprinted with permission.

p. 303: From R. A. Rappaport, "Flow of Energy in an Agricultural Society." *Scientific American,* September 1971, 116–32. © 1971 by Scientific American, Inc. All rights reserved.

p. 323: From L. Smith, *The Journey.* © 1954 by Lillian Smith. Reprinted by permission of W. W. Norton & Company, Inc., and McIntosh and Otis, Inc.

p. 282: From M. Swenson, "3 Models of the Universe," in *Half Sun Half Sleep.* Reprinted by permission of Charles Scribner's Sons. First printed as "Models of the Universe," in *Poetry in Crystal.* © 1963 by Steuben Glass.

pp. 290, 317: From L. A. White, *The Science of Culture: A Study of Man and Civilization.* © 1949 by Leslie A. White. Reprinted by permission of Farrar, Straus & Giroux, Inc.

Chapter 10

p. 351: From D. Fabun, *Dimensions of Change.* Reprinted by permission of Benziger Bruce & Glencoe, Inc., Beverly Hills, Calif., a division of The Macmillan Company. © 1970 by Kaiser Aluminum & Chemical Corporation.

pp. 339, 371, 375: From J. Huxley, "The Future of Man—Evolutionary Aspects." in *Man and His Future,* ed. G. Wolstenholme. Reprinted by permission of Little, Brown and Company and J. & A. Churchill Ltd.

p. 360: From A. MacLeish, "The Great American Frustration." *Saturday Review,* July 13, 1968. © 1968 by Archibald MacLeish. Reprinted by permission of *Saturday Review,* Inc.

p. 338: From S. Mills, "O and All the Little Babies in the Alameda Gardens Yes," in *Ecotatics,* ed. J. G. Mitchell and C. L. Stallings. © 1970 by the Sierra Club. Reprinted by permission of Pocket Books, a division of Simon & Schuster, Inc.

p. 375: From N. S. Momaday, "An American Land Ethic," in *Ecotatics,* ed. J. G. Mitchell and C. L. Stallings. © 1970 by the Sierra Club. Reprinted by permission of Pocket Books, a division of Simon & Schuster, Inc.

p. 348: From J. R. Newman, Book review in *Scientific American,* January 1959, 149–54. © 1959 by Scientific American, Inc. All rights reserved.

Additional acknowledgments and complete references to all quoted material can be found in the *Bibliographic notes* that begin on page 379.

Preface

The title of this book will undoubtedly suggest different things to different people, depending upon the image engendered by the term "natural history." One thinks possibly of that delightful book by Gilbert White, *The Natural History of Selborne*, which since 1789 has passed through more than two hundred editions, or of the more recent volume by Marston Bates, *The Natural History of Mosquitoes*. These volumes deal with a specific place or a specific subject, whereas I, at least at first glance, seem to have attempted the more ambitious task of encompassing a more open-ended subject. Because some thinkers have asserted that man does not have a nature, only a history, this subject may also be controversial. To me, as a biologist, such a distinction introduces a meaningless cleavage into the affairs of man, for if we do not think of him as having a natural history, we throw away the evidence of the past 100 years, and return to a creationist kind of thought. And so I feel comfortable with the title of this book, even though it may be a bit presumptuous.

The natural history of man could very legitimately take off in many directions and have many varied emphases. Whatever man was, is, or might become, whatever he has done, is doing, or might do—all of these fall within the province of his natural history. Similarly, the emphasis could be biological, cultural, behavioral, ecological, technological, or aesthetic, and the central theme could be related to food, energy control, arts and crafts, language, or racial diversity. Any one, or any combination, of these approaches could yield a well-structured image of man, and each would contain a modicum of truth that could withstand close scrutiny. The fact remains, however, that man, in his total dimensions, defies easy and simple categorization; he is like a finely cut gem, with one facet after another gleaming more brightly than the others as the angle of scrutiny is varied. No author,

regardless of breadth of learning or depth of erudition, can hope to deal effectively with all of these facets; the subject is too vast, the information too voluminous. In addition, each of us, unavoidably, wears intellectual blinders that permit us to see only what is directly ahead. We are consequently unable to focus simultaneously on peripheral issues that may be as important, or even more so, in delineating man. Furthermore, the truth and what passes temporarily for the appearances of reality, whether of man or of anything else, are elusive phenomena that at times seem to be within our grasp, at other times merely a hazy mirage on the mental horizon.

Why then attempt to achieve the impossible? I suppose it is simply that every writer feels impelled to seek the truth, however biased and fragmentary his view may be. Each of us, of whatever intellectual persuasion, believes that he knows the rules of the chase and is therefore on the right path, the theologian through revelation and sacred writings, the poet via metaphor leaping over metaphor, the scientist through measurement, experimentation, and quantification. We all believe, as indeed we must if the chase is not to be simply an idle game, that we will recognize reality when it appears, whether this be through a vision, an exquisitely turned phrase, or a carefully executed experiment. So we must continue to search for our *Pietà*s and our *David*s as Michelangelo did within his blocks of Carrara marble. We recognize, however, in our more sober moments, that the ultimate image of man cannot be caught in words of permanence, or even in the cool loveliness of marble; still, the chase pushes us on.

Therefore, it is important that I explain precisely what it is that I am attempting and set down the limited dimensions of my own search for the essence of man. This can be done quite simply: it is my purpose to consider the influence of scientific discoveries on man's changing view of himself and his place in the universe. Science influences our lives, our thoughts, and our philosophies, and to ignore what science has to offer in this regard is to prejudice, perhaps even to falsify, the image at the outset. I subscribe to the view that our knowledge of the biology of man—his natural history, if you will—is our most certain point of departure in constructing an image of man that has some correspondence to reality. I do not believe that we can understand man as a human being unless we know something of his animality and of the biological antecedents out of which his humanity has emerged. I do not believe that we can understand where our journey into an uncertain future will take us unless we have some idea of our orientation in space and time and of the processes that have shaped us and will continue to shape us. I do not believe that we can understand ourselves as individuals or as a species unless we have some appreciation of the roles that myth, magic, religion, and science have played in developing and changing our images of ourselves and of our universe. Whether in the course of these chapters I have, to use a phrase from John Donne, knitted "that subtle knot, which makes us men," only the reader can judge. I have depended largely on biological information and ideas to construct my images because this is the discipline with which I am most familiar. When deemed appropriate, however, I have made use of information from astronomy, geology, and anthropology, and I have not hesitated, when reinforcement was necessary or desirable, to journey into the realms of poetry, religion, philosophy, and history.

A word about the arrangement of the book and a suggestion as to how it might best be read might be useful. The numerous quotations may be found intrusive, disturbing to the flow of thought; this is, in a sense, their purpose. They are designed to make the reader pause and think. I would suggest, however, that the text, with its accompanying illustrations, be read first, this to be followed by a second reading during which the quotations adjacent to the text can be used to create a dialogue with the text and thus enrich and broaden what I have said. Should the reader choose to pursue a given topic further, the references to original literature will serve, hopefully, as an entering wedge. The bracketed numbers that follow the names of the authors of quotations refer to the numbered bibliographies that are arranged by chapter at the end of the book.

The continuous strip of quotations and illustrations above the text is intended to serve a somewhat different purpose, to take the reader out of the field of biology and into broader realms of thought. Biology, particularly that portion of it in which man is a central theme, is not an isolated discipline. At any given point in time, it is, like any other subject, a reflection of the temper of its age. Its goal, like that of all scientific endeavors, is the discovery of order in the universe, but such discoveries have a way of upsetting older orders of thought, thereby creating temporary disorders in the minds of men. Biology is influenced by, and in turn exerts its own influence on, the arts, philosophy, religion, the social sciences, and the other varied affairs of man. Every question has its appropriate time to be asked if a reasonable answer is to be expected. These quotations and illustrations, therefore, are included in an effort to reflect these influences and interactions, to show that there is a web of thought in the history of man, just as in the natural scene there is a web of life through which a flow of energy passes. The web of thought, while real, is not so obvious, so easily disrupted, or so fragile as the web of life. Man is always the central element in this web, with intellectual energy flowing through him in many directions, to be converted to other forms, to mix and blend and emerge in new shapes, and to be stored for future use. In this way we reshape the past for our own ends and are able to grasp nuances and contexts that would otherwise escape us.

All the quotations and illustrations as well as the text reflect my own fragmentary vision of a portion of the web of thought. They also reflect, probably in ways that even I do not detect, my biases and preferences, patterns of chance or deliberate readings, past experiences and future hopes. In their totality, they constitute an attempt to see the biology of man in a broader context of humane learning. The reader can probably add his or her own favorite quotations to the list; in fact, this book should ideally become an annotated version of the reader's own experiences, and may even result in the construction of an image of man that is more appropriate than the one that I offer.

Although this book is a distillation of certain facets of my own knowledge and interest, many other persons have played a role, directly or indirectly, in determining its nature and eventual publication. I should first of all acknowledge the generosity of publishing houses, journals, and individuals in permitting me to use quoted materials or illustrations. A few persons deserve special recognition. John Raina, who was at the time an editor with Prentice-Hall, was respon-

sible for getting the book off dead center and into a state of growth and development. His friendship, encouragement, and editorial expertise during much of the early preparation was constant and invaluable; my only regret is that the book did not appear under his editorship. This would perhaps have been a dubious honor for him, but it would have been a distinct pleasure for me. The particular format of the book was suggested by David Esner, director of Prentice-Hall's Project Planning Department, while Raymond Mullaney, of the same department, edited the text and made the final selection of the quotations and illustrations and determined their placement. It has been my very good fortune to have worked with these gifted bookmen; if there is any uniqueness to the book as a published piece of work, the credit is theirs. Mrs. Janine Sommer, Miss Sallie Hemry, and my daughter Ann transformed my laborious script into pages of clean type. And lastly, I gratefully acknowledge my debt to the students of The Johns Hopkins University and the University of Massachusetts who served as sounding boards for my ideas, and who through written papers, discussion, argument, and often dissent forced me to clarify and refine the manuscript that has become this book. This is their book as well as mine. I alone, however, bear the burden of any errors contained herein.

Carl P. Swanson

Contents

The natural history of man

I WHO SPEAK

I am a human being, whatever that may be. I
speak for all of us who move and think and feel
and whom time consumes. I speak as an
individual unique in a universe beyond my
understanding, and I speak for man. I am
hemmed in by limitations of sense and mind and
body, of place and time and circumstance, some
of which I know but most of which I do not. I am
like a man journeying through a forest, aware of
occasional glints of light overhead, with
recollections of the long trail I have already
traveled, and conscious of wider spaces ahead. I
want to see more clearly where I have been and
where I am going, and above all I want to know
why I am where I am and why I am traveling at
all. I, John Berrill, a self-conscious fragment of
life, want to know; and this book is an
exploration and an inquiry for my own satisfaction
and for any who wish to come with me.

Our scientific age is an age of extension of the
senses by means of instruments, and because of
this torrents of new and novel information pour
in—and we are trying to put it together and to
turn the new searchlights towards our own status,
past, present and future. This need to understand
the nature of things has found expression in the
cosmogonies of the religious creeds of all
mankind and in some form perhaps ever since we
first learned to communicate thought by means of
speech. It is the great conversation, one that
started long before the dawn of recorded history
and that becomes more animated all the time. For
too many the discussion is already closed, with full
acceptance of the dogma of particular religions.
For the rest it is wide open, for the origin, nature
and destiny of man are problems inadequately
solved by the philosophers, religious or otherwise,
of the ancient world, whether or not their answers
survive in contemporary form.

N. J. Berrill, Man's Emerging Mind,
Dodd, Mead & Company, 1955

1

Through a kaleidoscope

Our concern is with man, and therein lies the difficulty: there is no image of him that is universally acceptable. He defies simple description or explanation, although each of us from time to time and for many reasons seeks the answer that never comes, but always must be sought. When we view man biologically, we recognize him by a single name— *Homo sapiens*, "man, the wise one." He is made up of blood and bones, nerves and muscles, appetites and fears. Within this limited and restricted context, he is little different from a hundred other animals, and biological information gained from a study of one of these related species can often be applied directly to man.

But man is also a human being, an animal who invented a culture and who does not exist outside this culture. As

What a piece of work is a man! how noble in reason! how infinite in faculty! in form and moving how express and admirable! in action how like an angel! in apprehension how like a god! the beauty of the world! the paragon of animals!

W. Shakespeare [35]

Fujihira photo, Monkmeyer Press Photo Service

What of man, the organism? What is he? What is his origin, his state, and his destiny? Man, we know, is an animal which, like all animals, seeks food, shelter, and security, mates and reproduces, who fights off the encroachments of a hostile environment until it is possible to fight no longer. Then, like all animals, he dies. But man is unique among animals, for he alone has the ability—and apparently the compulsion—to build cultures. His growth is not completed by reproduction, nor is it fulfilled by death, because the biological pattern of man has made his nature self-surpassing.

Culture is that milieu of ideas, myths, and values which only the human animal can exude. It is the result of man's unique ability to create and respond to symbols. "Without symbols," wrote Lewis Mumford, "man's life would be one of immediate appetites, immediate sensations; limited to a past shorter than his own lifetime, at the mercy of a future he could never anticipate, never prepare for. In such a world, out of hearing would be out of reach, and out of sight would be out of mind." For these reasons, man needs not only bread, but art, ritual, philosophy, science, myth, religion, dance, and drama. When, by ignorance or adversity, he is barred from these symbols of his culture, man is destitute and, thus malnourished, he languishes.

W. Beck [2]

the culture changes, so does he; he shows a thousand, even ten thousand thousand, faces. The colored images in a kaleidoscope have a basic, multifaceted, symmetrical configuration, but when the instrument is turned, the colored fragments within it shift their position, and a new configuration emerges. So it is with man. He too has a basic configuration inherited from his biological past, but as the kaleidoscope of culture is turned, new images of man, and of the world in which he lives, make their appearance. "Who is man?" is a question that has no definitive answer; man is a creature of space and time, of molecules, cells, and tissues, of accomplishments and failures, but also of dreams and visions of reality. He employs every means at his command to answer the question concerning his nature, for he has a deep-seated need to know, and knowledge is the source of security and satisfaction. He has used magic and has constructed myths that fill this need and satisfy him for a while; he has, more recently, sought to discover his identity by applying the methods of science to the stars, the rocks of the earth, and his own biological and social being. And the search continues. As August Kekule, the discoverer of the ring structure of the benzene molecule, once said: "Let us learn to dream, gentlemen, then perhaps we shall find the truth. . . . but let us beware of publishing our dreams before they have been put to the proof of the waking understanding."

Man's intellectual temper

Ever since man began to record his thoughts and his acts for posterity, he has generally claimed for himself the highest position in the hierarchy of living things. As a maker

Through a kaleidoscope

O Lord, our Lord, how excellent is thy name in all the earth!
Who hast set thy glory above the heavens.
When I consider thy heavens, the work of thy fingers,
The moon and the stars, which thou hast ordained;
What is man, that thou art mindful of him,
And the son of man, that thou visitest him?
For thou hast made him a little lower than the angels,
And has crowned him with glory and honor.
Thou madest him to have dominion over the works of thy hands;
Thou hast put all things under his feet;
All sheep and oxen, yea, and the beasts of the field;
The fowl of the air, and the fish of the sea,
And whatsoever passeth through the paths of the seas.
O Lord, our Lord, how excellent is thy name in all the earth!

Psalm 8

---

and user of tools, a successful exploiter of the physical and biological environment in which he exists, a creator of a unique kind of inheritance in the form of culture, and an investigator who, with varying degrees of objectivity, can include himself among the objects worthy of study, his claim has an unchallenged validity. He reigns supreme, and the only threat to his continued dominance arises within himself, a threat that is becoming increasingly more evident as the exploitative success of the human species reveals the limitations of man's environment and, perhaps, of man himself.

The creation myths, hypotheses, and theories of many cultures, both primitive and contemporary, have depicted the creation and organization of the universe, the origin and fashioning of man and other living things, and the establishment of civilizations (see illustration 1.1). Philosophies of life and death, and of the past, present, and future, are variously interspersed among these ideas. They represent the ingenious, profound, often speculative thoughts of man when confronted with the unknown; and the degree to which these ideas approach reality—however reality is defined—depends upon the assumptions, motives, tools, and intellectual approaches utilized in any exploration of this unknown. Only rarely has man given himself a subordinate position. Some peoples consider man to be lower in the scale of being than the gods or angels; others hold that he occupies no special seat of dominance, that he is a part, but not a special part, of the world in which he lives, and that he is actively influenced, as are all living things, by the stars, moon, wind, and rain. According to this philosophy, the boundary lines between animals, men, and gods are fluid and subject to change. In virtually all other cultures, however, man's position of dominance is taken for granted. But history informs

1.1 *Jacopo della Quercia*, The Creation of Man.

Ah, vain are words, and weak all mortal thought!
Who is there truly knows, and who can say,
Whence this unfathomed world, and from what cause?
Nay, even the gods were not! Who, then, can know?

The source from which this universe hath sprung,
That source, and that alone, can bear it up—
None else: THAT, THAT alone, lord of the worlds,
In its own self contained, immaculate
As are the heavens above, THAT alone knows
The truth of what itself hath made—none else!

Hindu Hymn of Creation [*32*]

Michelangelo, David.
Alinari-Art Reference Bureau

---

us that the reasons for dominance have varied with time and that any particular form of belief stems from the intellectual temper of each age.

The basic philosophy of the Far Eastern religions is that the world of life—including all animals and man, but generally excluding plants—consists of a multitude of timeless, nonphysical souls undergoing an endless succession of incarnations and reincarnations. These souls, upon the death of the body, could take up habitation anywhere in the scale of living things, with the particular habitation depending upon the consequences of every previous act of the individual. This system—called the doctrine of karma—is therefore rigidly individualistic, with each person being morally responsible for all his actions and thoughts. Inevitably, this philosophy led to a devaluation of, and a withdrawal from, life in general, for the hope of all men was to escape from the "wheel of karma," the continual cycle of death and rebirth, and to gain either immortality and eventual bliss through absorption into the ultimate being of the universe, or total nonexistence. Although some men might eventually escape the wheel, the world of living things in general had no beginning and no foreseeable end.

Within our own Western culture, a state of ambivalence prevails. Two thousand years of Judeo-Christian tradition affirm that man's position of dominance was conferred upon him by divine decree and design. In Genesis (1:26–28) we are given the following account of the origin of man:

Then God said, "Let us make man in our image, after our likeness; and let them have dominion over the fish of the sea, and over the birds of the air, and over the cattle, and over all the earth, and over every creeping thing that creeps upon the earth." So God created man in his own image, in the image of God created he him; male and female he

1.2   Old Tibetan refugee in Leh spinning his prayer wheel.

Christa Armstrong photo, Rapho Guillumette Pictures

Through a kaleidoscope

4

Man is all symmetry,
Full of proportions, one limb to another,
  And to all the world besides.
  Each part may call the farthest, brother;
For head with foot hath private amity,
  And both with moons and tides.

  Nothing hath got so far
But man hath caught and kept it as his prey;
  His eyes dismount the highest star:
  He is in little all the sphere.
Herbs gladly cure our flesh, because that they
  Find their acquaintance there.

  For us, the winds do blow,
The earth doth rest, heaven move, and fountains flow;
  Nothing we see, but means our good,
  As our delight, or as our treasure;

The whole is either our cupboard of food,
  Or cabinet of pleasure.

  The stars have us to bed:
Night draws the curtain; which the sun withdraws.
  Music and light attend our head.
  All things unto our flesh are kind,
In their descent and being; to our mind,
  In their ascent and cause.

        .   .   .

  More servants wait on man
Than he'll take notice of. In every path,
  He treads down that which doth befriend him
  When sickness makes him pale and wan;
Oh mighty love! Man is one world, and hath
  Another to attend him.

G. Herbert [15]

---

created them. And God blessed them, and God said to them, "Be fruitful and multiply, and fill the earth and subdue it; and have dominion over the fish of the sea and over the birds of the air and over every living thing that moves upon the earth."

Modern science, of course, challenges this point of view, although Western civilization, for the greater part of its time span, has taken this scriptural statement as philosophical justification for human existence and action. It has contributed in large measure, as John Marcus [27] has said, to the mystique that provides an objective and believable reality and is, in substance, "the source and vehicle of the messianic consciousness of history crucial to Western civilization." It gave "coherence to the seemingly unrelated, meaningless and even contradictory manifestations of history"; it gave to the individual "a sense of a meaningful relationship to his world, as well as a plan and a role in the scheme of things"; and it gave to the community of men "a sense of unity in purpose and a continuity in time," a vision of a shared goal and a basis for purposeful action. Such a mystique has a reality of its own, no less real than that derived through the discoveries of science, but clearly different in character.

The thoughts expressed in both Eastern and Western philosophies were a late development in the evolution of man's concept of himself. We now know that 30,000 years ago Neanderthal man of the Mousterian culture buried his dead with food and artifacts, revealing by this act that a mystical view of man's position in nature is a cultural trait that developed long before man began to record his thoughts (see illustration 1.3). There is, in addition, evidence that 400,000 years ago Peking man practiced a form of cannibalism that suggested that he believed in the transference

To the historian thinking broadly about the recent destiny and future prospects of western civilization, it may well appear that our own culture, in which whatever our temperament we are bound to live, is set off from those of Asia, Africa, and the world of antiquity by two fundamental factors. From one of these it emerged: its religious chrysalis was Christianity, investing history with the promise of fulfillment of a sort. The other it produced: the most dynamic, distinctive, and influential creation of the western mind is a progressive science of nature. Only there in the technical realm, indeed, does the favorite western idea of progress hold any demonstrable meaning. No one understands political power better than Machiavelli did. Picasso cannot conclusively be held a better or worse artist than Leonardo was. But every college freshman knows more physics than Galileo knew, whose claim is higher than any other's to the honor of having founded modern science, and more too than Newton did, whose mind was the most powerful ever to have addressed itself to nature.

C. C. Gillispie [14]

1.3 Pyramids and the Great Sphinx at Giza, Egypt. Although Neanderthal man was probably the first to bury food and artifacts with his dead, this practice reached its culmination in the involved funeral practices of ancient Egypt.

TWA

Lawrence Frank photo, Rapho Guillumette Pictures

Transience is the backdrop for the play of human progress, for the improvement of man, the growth of his knowledge, the increase of his power, his corruption and his partial redemption. Our civilizations perish; the carved stone, the written work, the heroic act fade into a memory of memory and in the end are gone. The day will come when our race is gone; this house, this earth in which we live, will one day be unfit for human habitation, as the sun ages and alters.

Yet no man, be he agnostic or Buddhist or Christian, thinks wholly in these terms. His acts, his thoughts, what he sees of the world around him—the falling of a leaf or a child's joke or the rise of the moon—are part of history; but they are not only part of history; they are a part of becoming and of process but not only that: they partake also of the world outside of time; they partake of the light of eternity.

These two ways of thinking, the way of time and history and the way of eternity and of timelessness, are both part of man's effort to comprehend the world in which he lives. Neither is comprehended in the other nor reducible to it.

J. R. Oppenheimer [30]

of spiritual qualities from one man to another. Since 1859, with the publication of Darwin's *Origin of Species,* this view has undergone still more profound changes, and science has provided us with a different vantage point for looking backward into man's past and forward into his future. We can now study man both as an animal and as a human being. Viewed in its entirety, the history of man is the history of an expanding consciousness and self-consciousness, a development that in the course of time drew man apart from his surrounding world and tended to accentuate his conception of his own uniqueness.

Accompanying this self-awareness is a death-awareness. As Theodosius Dobzhansky [6] states it:

Man is burdened with death-awareness. A being who knows that he will die arose from ancestors who did not know. Viewed in evolutionary perspective, self-awareness is primary and death-awareness is secondary; death-awareness is the bitter fruit of man's having risen to the level of consciousness and of functioning ego. Self-awareness has developed as an important adaptation; death-awareness is not obviously adaptive, and it may be biologically detrimental.

Man first became an observer as a result of his separation from nature. As his awareness of his own uniqueness increased and was sharpened, his curiosity drove him to look back at the surroundings from which he emerged, to attempt to explain what he saw in his expanding universe, to alter or affect this universe for his own ends, and ultimately to regard this universe with varying degrees of attachment or detachment, awe or reverence, disdain or affection. These urges, which were of enormous selective value to man in coming to terms with a sometimes incomprehensible and often hostile environment, involve mystical, empirical, and

Through a kaleidoscope

. . . Formerly [man] had believed in even his darkest moments that the universe was rational if he could only grasp its rationality, but gradually he comes to suspect that rationality is an attribute of himself alone and that there is no reason to suppose that his own life has any more meaning than the life of the humblest insect that crawls from one annihilation to another. Nature, in her blind thirst for life, has filled every possible cranny of the rotting earth with some sort of fantastic creature, and among them man is but one—perhaps the most miserable of all, because he is the only one in whom the instinct of life falters long enough to enable it to ask the question "Why?" As long as life is regarded as having been created, creating may be held to imply a purpose, but merely to have come into being is, in all likelihood, merely to go out of it also.

J. W. Krutch [21]

The whole earth's a place of never-ending arrivals and departures; Glad to see you is but the echo of goodbye, Sally, goodbye, Sue. Still the interlude, strange interlude, was a fine and exciting one.

When he thought of all the common routine of life that had to be gone through—to eat, to drink, to sleep, to clothe ourselves, to take time for play, lest we perish of care, to suffer and fight common and uncommon ills, then the achievements of man, in spite of all these, are tremendous indeed.

S. O'Casey [29]

---

intellectual approaches out of which arose the germs of myth, magic, religion, rational thought, and, eventually, the scientific attitude. All of these form a part of man's mental attitudes and help to determine man's view of himself and his environment. In their totality, these elements characterize the temper of any particular culture, society, or age; their impact has led in most instances to a developing isolation of man from his environment. Only lately has he come to realize—perhaps too late—that he cannot be divorced from his environment without suffering serious consequences. He has begun to understand the message of an ancient Chinese proverb: "If one takes no thought for that which is distant, he will soon find sorrow near at hand."

Linnaeus (Carl von Linné 1707–1778) placed the scientific stamp of approval on man's dominance in the biological world; he was a primate (Latin: *primus*, "first"), and among the primates he was clearly in the vanguard. His supposed divinity was slowly being eroded as his antecedents were being unearthed, but his position of dominance was not challenged. Our most certain knowledge of man is that he is an animal and that he has reached the highest peak of dominance attained in the animate world, but science today holds that his dominance is biologically and culturally, not divinely, conferred. No other intellectual position seems tenable or reasonable.

Nevertheless, man's image of himself continues to undergo rapid and continual change, for it is the nature of man not only to see what is but also to project what might be. Man's projective propensities, apart from his intuition and artistically derived value judgments, stem from his adoption of the scientific attitude, reinforced by the discoveries and insights of all of the sciences and by increased

Man, the last and best of created works, formed after the image of his Maker, endowed with a portion of intellectual divinity, the governor and subjugator of all other beings, is, by his wisdom alone, able to form just conclusions from such things as present themselves to his senses, which can only consist of bodies merely natural. Hence the first step of wisdom is to know these bodies; and to be able, by those marks imprinted on them by nature, to distinguish them from each other, and to affix to every object its proper name.

C. Linnaeus [25]

1.4 Excavation at the La Brea tar pits near Los Angeles, California. Bones of many species of animals are found intermingled in this location.

Natural History Museum of Los Angeles County

Standard Oil Co. (N.J.)

It belongs to a highly developed race to become, in a true sense, aristocratic—a treasury of its best in practical and spiritual types—and then to disappear in the surrounding tides of men. So Athens dissolved like a pearl in the cup of the Mediterranean, and Rome in the cup of Europe, and Judaea in the cup of the Universal Communion. . . . Always some great culture is dying to enrich the soil of new harvests, some civilization is crumbling to rubbish to be the hill of a more beautiful city, some race is spending itself that a lower and barbarous world may inherit its stored treasure-house. Although no race may consciously devote itself to the higher ends of mankind, it is the prerogative of its men of genius so to devote it; nor is any nation truly great which is not so dedicated by its warriors and statesmen, its saints and heroes, its thinkers and dreamers. A nation's poets are its true owners; and by the stroke of the pen they convey the title-deeds of its real possessions to strangers and aliens.

G. E. Woodberry [43]

knowledge and communication with other cultures having different points of view. The result is an ever-shifting vantage point for observation and speculation, and the nature of man seems to take on a chimeric and kaleidoscopic aspect with passing time.

How then can one approach rationally the question "What or who is man?" The Roman historian Terence (190?–159 B.C.) said that because he was a human being, all things human were of concern to him. This is an admirable point of view to adopt for a discussion of the natural history of man, but difficulty is immediately apparent—the subject is too vast, and neither the beginning nor the end is clearly defined. Limitations are therefore necessary, and we shall confine ourselves to a consideration, within the particular intellectual framework of our age, of man's knowledge concerning the following: his orientation in space and time, his origin within the animal kingdom, his uniqueness as a species, his uniqueness as an individual, his development of a culture as a consequence of his biological antecedents, his interactions with the environment, and the effects of the environment on him. We should first, however, examine man's changing thought structure and his gradually evolving view of himself as different from all other living things.

Because man is an animal, he is constrained in many of the operations of his daily existence by the same laws of physics and chemistry that affect any other animal. But man's extraordinary evolution has made him a very special kind of animal. He is an energy-consuming, history-recording, data-processing, decision-making animal who can act with design when he chooses, can make use of the lessons of the past in achieving present aims, and can project

Through a kaleidoscope

Francisco Goya, Lo Mismo
(The Same, With or Without Reason).

ideas and plans into the future. He is an animal who lives in what he considers to be a purposeless world, but who injects purpose into his life. He is an animal who creates systems of values, morality, and ethics because he has found, through cultural evolution, that these abstractions have a high survival value. He is an animal who considers it useful to view himself as a machine, even though he has difficulty in defining the kind of machine that he really is. For all these reasons, we shall study man not only as an animal—a vertebrate, a mammal, and a primate—but also as a unique human being.

It can be argued that such a picture of man is a limited one, and the argument, of course, is well grounded. The image of man is as rich and varied as we wish to make it, and the scientific image we choose to examine is only one of many. It is limited because science itself, as it attempts to clarify reality, can provide only a limited validity. When we limit the kind of incoming messages that go to construct the self-conscious image of man that we seek to project, we must inevitably accept a partial image of man, and because science provides a constant stream of new messages for us to assess, our image of man will not have any degree of finality. Rather it is one that is bound to change with time.

We could, for example, base our image of man on the works that he has created. He is the builder of the Salisbury cathedral (illustration 1.5), the Taj Mahal, Angkor Vat, the Pantheon, and the projected Third World of the future; he is also the builder of igloos, the camel-hide tents of the Bedouins, and cities throughout the world. He is the painter of the caves at Altamira, and of pop, op, hard-edge and minimal art. He is also Rembrandt, Paul Cézanne, and Paul

1.5   Salisbury cathedral, England.

Through a kaleidoscope

Man in sooth is a marvelous vain, fickle, and unstable subject.

M. de Montaigne [28]

American Airlines

Klee. He may on occasion exhibit the virtuosity of a Picasso or the single-minded primitiveness of a Grandma Moses. He is the author of the *Psalms,* the *Divine Comedy,* and *King Lear;* of *Pogo* and *Peanuts,* as well as of *Orphan Annie, Fannie Hill,* and the *Tropic of Cancer.* He is the creator and the destroyer of gods and demigods, demons and angels; he is Genghis Khan, Hitler, Gandhi, and Martin Luther King; he is a member of the DAR, the SDS, and the Black Panthers; he is, most meaningfully, yourself. Whatever he has done, and whatever he is, a different image emerges each time we make an assessment. But because scientifically derived information provides us with our most verifiable approach to the reality of man, it will afford a reasonable base for subsequent departures in image formation. Whatever man may have acquired in the form of cultural vestments, he is, as Desmond Morris states, the naked ape, visible for our inspection.

The temper of our age

The past is the source of our identity. It is so in a selective sense, to be sure, for not every organism embraces all of the past in its makeup; but every organism, including man, is tied to the past genetically and historically, however much he may attempt to escape it. The past is all that we know—the future becomes the past the moment that we touch it, and our view of the past keeps changing as we move into the future. To make the past a usable part of our tradition and experience, we need constantly to redo our past in order to give it present meaning. This is easier to do historically than it is genetically. The historian reinter-

Through a kaleidoscope

. . . Though death is the law of all life, man touches this earthen fact with the wand of the spirit, and transforms it into the law of sacrifice. . . .

The vital flow of life has this in common with disease—that it is self-limited; the fever runs its course, and burns away "All thoughts, all passions, all delights," have this history. In the large arcs of social being, movements of the human spirit, however embracing and profound, obey the same law of the limitation of specific energy. Revolutions, reforms, re-births exhaust their fuel, and go out. Races are only greater units of man; for a race, as for an individual, there is a time to die; and that time, as history discloses it, is the moment of perfection.

This is the largest fact in the moral order of the world; it is the centre of providence in history. In the life of the human spirit the death of the best of its achieving elements, in the moment of their consummation, is as the fading of the flower of the field or the annual fall of the leaves of the forest in the natural world; and unless this be a sacrificial death, it were wantonness and waste like the deaths of nature; but man and his works are supernatural, and raised above nature by an imperishable relation which they contain.

G. E. Woodberry [43]

---

prets the past from new vantage points, but biological antecedents, carried in the genes we inherit, are not so easily modified in the light of new conditions. Human engineering, of a genetic sort, is a theoretical possibility, but not yet a manageable actuality. Possibly this is why cultural and biological evolutions move at such different paces, and why we still can be viewed as the naked ape as well as the human being.

The past, to employ Kenneth Boulding's imagery, has designed an ideological filter system through which all incoming messages must pass. In formulating new images of man we can use only those messages that have been selectively transmitted and assimilated. We are now, without question, in an age of science, and we are reasonably attuned to the incoming messages that science pours out. But our filter system is an inherited one, too limited in transmittance and too imperfectly formed to allow only the passage of truth and to screen out all error. The component parts filtering through are variable with each individual and determine collectively the temper of our age. Intellectually, these include the elements of myth, magic, empiricism, and scientific attitude, the latter embracing not only empiricism but also observation, experimentation, and prediction. Each of these has a role in helping to answer the question "Who or what is man?" and in coping with the exigencies of existence.

Primitive, or better prehistoric, man considered himself, from all that can be gathered anthropologically, very much a part of nature. He lived in a world inhabited by spirits; he had not yet developed his exploitive potentialities and was never very far from starvation. Even the early urban civilizations were at best only a few weeks away from starva-

"We are like dwarfs seated on the shoulders of giants; we see more things than the ancients and things more distant, but this is due neither to the sharpness of our own sight, nor to the greatness of our own stature, but because we are raised and borne aloft on that giant mass."

So, in the twelfth century of our era, wrote Bernard of Chartres. This "giant mass" of "famous men and our fathers that begot us" is important to us not genetically and emotionally only. We get from our remote ancestors not just our faces and our frowns, the curve of an eyebrow and the trick of a likeness, but also all our history and our literature, our declarations of independence and our famous slogans. We get, too, our ideas and the very ways in which we think, together with the words we use to think with. Indeed "we have nothing that we are not given," nothing that has not been handed down and used again and again.

And the "giant mass" is made up of specific individuals. "Man" generically—if we admit that "man" exists apart from men, and one of the reasons for reading this book is to discover if we will admit "man" so to exist—has been defined by the "ancients" as "a rational animal capable of laughter." "Man," we know, invented the wheel, the pulley, the arch, the internal combustion engine, the airplane. He discovered electricity and split the atom. Yet who or what was this "man"? Very, very few men have invented or discovered anything; most men, through all the ages, and still today, are dwarfs who couldn't even figure how to set an egg up straight or how to light a fire by rubbing sticks together, unless borne aloft on the shoulders of the giants.

A. Fremantle [12]

Through a kaleidoscope

tion, thus making the siege a most practical strategy of warfare. Food was the main link that tied man to the land, and when an abundance of food was available, as at the end of a harvest or a successful hunt, man naturally assumed that he had been the beneficiary of the forces of nature that he felt but could not comprehend. The sacrifice or sacrament to show his gratefulness as well as his helplessness was a common act among early tribes. That his fate was in the hands of the gods or formless spirits was, and is, a common theme (see illustration 1.6). The transition from this step to present-day formalized rituals, with their inherent concept of a dependence on providence—spelled either with an uppercase or lowercase "p"—has been a continuing evolution. Among these thoughts and practices are the elements of magic and myth, and out of them have emerged, respectively, science and various practices and beliefs of the world's religions.

1.6 The role that spirits and the supernatural played in the life of prehistoric man is shown by this cave painting, known as "The Sorcerer," discovered near Les Trois Frères, France.

American Museum of Natural History

Magic

Magic is a practical art consisting of acts and techniques that bring man in touch with the sources of magic and that are the means to a definite and expected end to follow later on. It therefore presupposes a tappable source of influence that, under the proper circumstances, can be drawn upon, something like a special bank account. It is, in essence, a form of positive thinking to ensure that some desired action, usually some distance removed, takes place. Its utilitarian purpose is to control nature or other individuals by influence rather than by understanding or to alter the course of nature for the magician's own benefit or for the

Then I had religion, *then* I had a vision.
  I would not turn from their revel in derision.
Then I saw the Congo, creeping through the black,
Cutting through the jungle with a golden track.
Then along the riverbank
  A thousand miles
  Tattooed cannibals danced in files;
  Then I heard the boom of the blood-lust song
And a thigh-bone beating on a tin-pan gong.
And *"Blood!"* screamed the whistles and the fifes of the
    warriors;
"Blood!" screamed the skull-faced, lean witch-doctors;
  "Whirl ye the deadly voo-doo rattle,
  Harry the uplands,
  Steal all the cattle,
  Rattle-rattle, rattle-rattle,
  Bing!
  Boomlay, boomlay, boomlay, *boom!"*

Listen to the yell of Leopold's ghost
  Burning in Hell for his hand-maimed host.
  Hear how the demons chuckle and yell
  Cutting his hands off, down in Hell.
  Listen to the creepy proclamation,
  Blown through the lairs of the forest-nation,
  Blown past the white-ants' hill of clay,
  Blown past the marsh where the butterflies play:—
  "Be careful what you do,
Or Mumbo-Jumbo, God of the Congo,
And all of the other
Gods of the Congo,
Mumbo-Jumbo will hoo-doo you,
Mumbo-Jumbo will hoo-doo you,
Mumbo-Jumbo will hoo-doo you."

V. Lindsay [24]

---

benefit of someone for whom he acts. Its efficaciousness requires that the right person—the shaman, the sorcerer, or the witch doctor—exercise the spell, perform the rites, and pronounce the proper incantations (illustration 1.7). When magic works, it is evidence of man's superiority over, but not necessarily his separateness from, nature.

The use of magic is based on fear, anxiety, greed, or helplessness in a hostile environment, and its success and biological importance lie in the assistance it renders when an impasse has been reached between man and his environment or between man and man. Magic helps bridge the gap between man and the rest of nature, a gap developed by man's growing consciousness of himself and his increasing awareness of the complexity of his environment. It supplies man with ready-made rituals and beliefs that optimize his

At an early stage of his intellectual development man deems himself naturally immortal, and imagines that were it not for the baleful arts of sorcerers, who cut the vital thread prematurely short, he would live for ever. But in time the sad truth of human mortality was borne in upon our primitive philosopher with a force of demonstration which no prejudice could resist and no sophistry dissemble. Nevertheless, even if he reluctantly acknowledged the existence of beings at once superhuman and supernatural, he was as yet far from suspecting the width and the depth of the gulf which divided him from them. The gods with whom his imagination now peopled the darkness of the unknown were indeed admitted by him to be his superiors in knowledge and in power, in the joyous splendour of their life and in the length of its duration. But, though he knew it not, these glorious and awful beings were merely . . . the reflections of his own diminutive personality exaggerated into gigantic proportions by distance and by the mists and clouds of ignorance upon which they were cast.

J. G. Frazer [11]

1.7 *A Navaho medicine man has prepared a sand painting on the floor of a hut as part of a ritual designed to cure the sick child held by his mother. The child will be laid upon the painting and then smeared with paint.*

You go to a hospital and maybe once a day the doctor comes around and he stays there, maybe five minutes. He talks a little bit, but he asks you questions. Once in a while they give you a little medicine, just a bit of it. About the only thing they do is put something in your mouth and see how hot you are. The rest of the time you just lie there, but the medicine men help you all the time—they give you lots of medicine and they sing all night. They do lots of things all over your body. Every bit of your body is treated.

A Navaho Indian [42]

There is probably no better example of how a basic religious feeling—a sense of the special, the supernatural—takes form as a religious belief than in the idea of mana. The word itself is from the Pacific, being common to many of the languages of Melanesia and Polynesia, but it has other names in other places. Mana means a kind of force or power which can be in anything, and which makes that thing better in its own special qualities, such as they are, perhaps to the point of being marvelous.

A man who has mana is stronger, or smarter, or more graceful, though mana is not strength or brains or agility. That man's spear or, if he has been civilized, his tennis racket, has mana if it does what is expected of it with particular sureness; but mana is something different from the niceness of balance or the workmanship which has gone into it. At the same time, if the pro who made the spear or the racket consistently turns out first-class spears and rackets, then he obviously has mana of his own, or else he has ways of inducing mana into whatever (spears or rackets) he makes. And there is no difference in the mana which is in the tool, or its owner, or its maker; it simply causes each one to excel in his special way.

. . .

Typically, mana is a sort of essence of nature; it is not a spirit, and it has no will or purpose of its own. It can very well be compared with electricity, which is impersonal but powerful, and which flows from one thing to another, and can be made to do a variety of things, although in itself it remains the same flowing force.

W. Howells [17]

We are two, the world and me. The world is just as I sense it (see it, touch it, taste it, smell it, hear it). The world is like me. In me there is a spirit; in the world as a whole, and in each part of the world that I deal with, there are spirits who rule. I have come to terms with these spirits. I do so by rituals, by magic. *"The superior man is the magician or witch doctor who knows the spirits and how to deal with them."*

D. Fabun [8]

Analysis shows that magic rests everywhere on two fundamental principles: first, that *like produces like,* effect resembling cause; second, that *things which have once been in contact continue ever afterwards to act on each other.* The former principle may be called the Law of Similarity; the latter, that of Contact or Contagion. From the one the magician infers that he can produce any effect he desires merely by imitating it in advance; from the other, that whatever he does to a material object will automatically affect the person with whom it was once in contact. Practices based on the Law of Similarity may be termed Homoeopathic Magic; those based on the Law of Contact or Contagion, Contagious Magic. Both derive, in the final analysis, from a false conception of natural law. The primitive magician, however, never analyzes the mental assumptions on which his performance is based, never reflects on the abstract principles involved. With him, as with the vast majority of men, logic is implicit, not explicit; he knows magic only as a practical thing, and to him it is always an art, never a science, the very idea of science being foreign to his thinking.

J. G. Frazer [11]

control over nature and enhance his faith in himself and in his victory of hope over fear, of confidence over doubt, of optimism over pessimism. Magic, nevertheless, has nothing to do with the meaning of life and can provide no answers to questions that might be asked concerning life.

Magic is difficult to disprove. When it fails, it may simply be that the time was not propitious, that the incantation was improperly said, or that the shaman or sorcerer was out of step with the spirits. Whether it can be disproved or not, magic is a part of the natural history of man. Perhaps it played a larger role in man's life in the past than it does at present, but nevertheless it is still with us. We rap on wood for good luck, have our horoscopes read, avoid passing under ladders, and build hotels without a thirteenth floor. We wear amulets, cross our fingers, and see to it that a black cat does not cross our path.

According to Bronislaw Malinowski [26] magic never originates or is invented; it is always there "residing exclusively in man, let loose only by his magical art, gushing out with his voice, conveyed by the casting forth of the rite." But magic is human-centered not only in the sense that only a properly instructed man can invoke it, but also in the sense that it is concerned exclusively with human affairs. Magic, therefore, adds a new dimension to the world of man, that of pervading essences, forces, or spirits. These may be impersonal, such as the concept of *mana,* the power of the elemental forces of nature, or personal, such as the benevolent or malevolent gods or spirits possessing human attributes. The present disillusionment with science caused by its apparent inability to solve the problems of mankind spurs a rising interest in magic and its practitioners and even the claim that science is simply another type of magic.

Through a kaleidoscope

Myth

Another part of this new dimension is the element of myth, which includes all supernatural religious beliefs and which performs the historical functions of religions. It is similar to magic in that it is frequently associated with the performance of rites, symbolic acts, and ceremonies, but it differs in that it is not basically or necessarily concerned with practical affairs, that is, with a control over nature or man. Rather, the genesis and general acceptance of a myth involve attitudes of submission, devoutness, and reverence, coupled with an uncertainty, even a fear, of the nature of the world "out there," and can be contrasted with the self-assurance and often manipulative certainty that is part of the practice of magic. Every man in every age sooner or later becomes aware of the discrepancies between the inner world of his dreams, hopes, and undefined impulses and the outer world of experiences, uncontrolled happenings, and unembraceable vastness, and so he makes an attempt to harmonize these two facets of existence. It is the function of a myth to establish such connections and to effect a degree of harmony between the inner and outer realms of human experience. In this way fear and uncertainty can be reduced and light is permitted to enter the dark regions of the mind.

Saint Paul said that the invisible must be made visible to be understood. A myth, therefore, is an outward projection of what we sense internally. According to Voltaire, God made man in his own image, and man returned the compliment. As shown by illustrations 1.8 and 1.9, this trend

There are questions which come to every man in feelings of wastelands and loneliness beyond the healing of known companions. For these he has sung a sad song in the day and night and written stories of slaughter and agony. For want of answers his mind has splintered and he has wandered off into the ecstasy of madness. He has sought answers in the arguments of wine and wisdom of opium. Many have stifled the voices, drowning them in hurry and noise. Many have listened unwillingly, and turned away as soon as they could. Some listen again and again, until the yearning unknown is itself known and familiar: the quandaries become remembered faces without names, and the mysteries, silent companions. To them the unanswerables are no longer pools of terrible drowning. These become the depth and body of the sea, the lifting presence beneath the keels of their vessels. They make of the mysteries a song and a story; they are taught the ways of acceptance and peace. Having known the wonder and been wedded unto it, they are secure and unconquerable.

K. L. Patton [31]

Through a kaleidoscope

Ay, but to die, and go we know not where;
To lie in cold obstruction and to rot;
This sensible warm motion to become
A kneaded clod; and the delighted spirit
To bathe in fiery floods, or to reside
In thrilling region of thick-ribbed ice;
To be imprison'd in the viewless winds,
And blown with restless violence round about
the pendant world; or to be worse than worst
Of those that lawless and incertain thought
Imagine howling; 'tis too horrible!
The weariest and most loathed worldly life
That age, ache, penury and imprisonment
Can lay on nature is a paradise
To what we fear of death.

W. Shakespeare [36]

I do not know where to find in any literature, whether ancient or modern, any adequate account of that nature with which I am acquainted. Mythology comes nearest to it of any.

H. Thoreau [41]

1.8   That the Greeks tended to portray their gods in human form is revealed by this bust of the supreme god Zeus.

1.9   The Egyptians preferred to show their gods as animals or bizarre mythical creatures. This bronze sculpture, executed between 900 and 300 B.C., is a representation of Bastet, the Cat Goddess.

toward anthropomorphism, which we have inherited from the Greeks, contrasts sharply with the Egyptian and Mesopotamian practice of peopling their world of the spirit with monstrous creatures, for example, the inscrutable sphinx, a reclining lion with the head of a man, ram, or hawk and the wings of an eagle.

A myth binds men together with a common set of beliefs and is more of a communal affair than an individual practice; however, the ultimate fate of the individual is inextricably involved. A myth is also more effective when formalized and even institutionalized, and an institution is secure to the extent that its dogma is secure. Myth is an essential part of forms of belief; when we feel that we are no longer

God had five children: the gorilla, chimpanzee, elephant, pygmy, and man. Each was given fire, seeds, and tools, and told to go out alone into the world to settle down somewhere. The gorilla went first, and as he traveled along a forest path he saw some delicious red fruit. After he had eaten his fill and returned to the path, he found that his fire had gone out. So he stayed in the forest, living on fruit. The chimpanzee left home next, and he too became hungry as he passed a tall tree in fruit. He climbed up, and when he returned the fire had gone out. So the chimpanzee, like the gorilla, went to live in the forest. The same fate befell the elephant.

The pygmy went much farther than the others and finally cleared away some underbrush, planted his seed, and built a small hut; he did not cut down the tall trees, but he kept the fire going and learned the ways of the forest. Then at last man ventured forth and traveled very far. He cleared a large garden and cut down the trees, and he built himself a large house. He burned the brush and planted his seeds and lived there til the harvest was ripe.

After a time God went out to see how his children had fared. He found the gorilla, chimpanzee, and elephant in the forest living on fruit. "So," said God, "you can never again stand before man, but must ever flee from him." Then God found the pygmy under the trees and he said: "So you will always live in the forest, but no place will be your fixed abode." And finally he came to man and saw his house and his garden and he said: "So your possessions will remain always."

Myth of the Bulu tribe [33]

---

able to define the meaning of life in precise terms, we must satisfy ourselves by describing it in an understandable manner. And the search for the essential image of life goes on continuously even today. At least in the prehistoric societies, myths seem to be intimately connected with those physical and biological crises or phases that confront not only every member of a community as an individual but also the community at large. Among these crises are conception, pregnancy, birth, puberty, breeding behavior, old age, and death on the human level, and storms, floods, fire, and volcanic eruptions in the physical environment. Very early in his career on this planet, man must have recognized a primary and inescapable fact of life: namely, that the processes of birth, life, and death involve an appalling amount of uncertainty, suffering, and pain. Man is the only animal, for example, who exhibits any death-consciousness, who knows the difference between what is and what might be.

Because early man did not understand the nature of these crises, he surrounded them with an aura of mystery and, gradually, with a series of communal rites and ceremonies that were preserved through the ages among various groups (see illustration 1.10). Why should this be so? The answer seems to be that in the presence of a natural environment that seemed capricious, man recognized that social cohesion was necessary for survival at a time when tribal units were small. The tribe could survive better as a group than as single individuals. As Mark Schorer [34] has stated it: "Myths are the instruments by which we continually struggle to make our experience intelligible to ourselves. A myth is a large, controlling image that gives philosophical meaning to the facts of ordinary life. . . . Without such images, experience is chaotic, fragmentary and merely phenome-

The questing mind of man has always asked the eternal "Why?" The creative minds of artists have always spun a literary web of answers in words and ideas. The human animal does not submit supinely either to the harsh demands of the physical world or to the ever-pressing demands of his society and its culture-bound limitations of individual freedom. Reasons are demanded. Reasons are given. . . .

Although primitive mythology is rich in variety, it is truly remarkable to discover how stable is the solid core of basic myths the world over. It would seem that the fundamental myths strike right to the roots of the question as to what is man, how did he come to be, why is life, why death, why evil—and good. Once developed by primitive literary philosophers, refined and shaped through generations of telling and retelling, their appeal became so elemental that they spread smoothly and quickly from primitive hearth to primitive hearth until the whole world was girdled with a pristine web of common stories. . . . The Creation, the Flood, the Fall of Man, the Mark of Cain, the Tower of Babel, and many others are part of a worldwide heritage of ancient myth, part religious, part secular.

E. A. Hoebel [16]

"When I mean religion," declared Parson Thwackum, "I mean the Christian religion; and not only the Christian religion but the Protestant religion; and not only the Protestant religion, but the Church of England."

H. Fielding [10]

The glories of our blood and state,
  Are shadows, not substantial things.
There is no armor against fate,
  Death lays his icy hand on kings,
  Scepter and crown,
  Must tumble down,
And in the dust be equal made,
  With the poor crooked scythe and spade.

J. Shirley [38]

The corpse of the Swede, alone in the saloon, had its eyes fixed upon a dreadful legend that dwelt atop of the cash-machine: "This registers the amount of your purchase."

S. Crane [5]

---

nal. It is the chaos of experience that creates them, and they are intended to rectify it." As each of the crises became a focus for ceremony performed tribally, man eventually invented gods whom he associated with each crisis. The evolution of today's more sophisticated religious, social, and fraternal groups can be traced to these early beginnings, and many of their rites have an ancient lineage. Each of us has probably been initiated into one or more of these groups—a formal church, Rotary, Greek fraternities or sororities, Boy Scouts, even the PTA. We thereby gain a sense of security and solidarity denied to most of us as individuals. Even specific ceremonies have survived to the present day. The balls introducing debutantes to society, for example, can be traced back to ancient fertility rites.

1.10   Torture ceremony, Mandan Indians.

American Museum of Natural History

I weep for Adonais—he is dead!
O, weep for Adonais—though our tears
Thaw not the frost which binds so dear a head!
And thou, sad Hour, selected from all years
To mourn our loss, rouse thy obscure compeers,
And teach them thine own sorrow, say: "With me
Died Adonais; till the Future dares
Forget the Past, his fate and fame shall be
An echo and a light unto eternity!"

P. B. Shelley [37]

Dorothea Lange photo, collection of the Library of Congress

A most important biological principle is recognized in, and fostered by, the very nature of myths and their offshoots. Man is not a loner; he is by nature gregarious and communal, as are most of his primate relatives. The misanthrope is an atypical man. The rites of passage, taking many forms, bring the individual into the communal fold, and other myths gather family and community into cohesive units.

Death is probably the most serious biological crisis for any individual, and in the face of death, man, individually and in a sense communally, is confronted with one of two alternatives—life after death or annihilation and oblivion. Whichever alternative is accepted depends upon one's view of man and of the universe in which he exists. Given a choice in the absence of irrefutable evidence for or against either alternative and basing his decision on the fact that he occupies a lofty seat in the hierarchy of living things, man has most often chosen to accept the existence of an afterlife and has visualized immortality in a wide variety of forms. In this age of science, acceptance of this concept is considered by many to be in the nature of hedging one's bets, but death-consciousness and the consequences of death are part of our evolutionary and intellectual heritage. The acceptance of the concept of an afterlife is an act of faith, and science cannot affirm or deny its validity on present evidence.

As stated earlier, the origin of the concept of immortality in some form can be traced back some 30,000 years to Neanderthal man. The fact that he buried his dead with food and weapons indicates that he had some idea of an afterlife. The concepts of original sin and divine grace, which were later added to ideas of an afterlife, have confounded our assessment of man, because, as will be pointed

Through a kaleidoscope

IBM

Science is an almost grotesquely ambivalent phenomenon: it is at the same time highly systematic in its approach to the real world, yet it is never complete and never reaches final conclusions. It is the model of certainty in its methodology and logic, yet its driving force is deliberate doubt, and its results are probable, never certain. It requires of its workers absolute discipline, yet it is the fountainhead of exciting new ideas and new ways of thought. Though it may be local in origin, its conclusions are universal. For its creators it is a supreme adventure of the spirit, while at the same time it is the sole basis of endless reams of myth and superstition. It is the healer and builder and the propagator of untold suffering and death. Is it any wonder that science, the strong, the promising, the unforeseeable, the anarchical force in our modern world, should be the cause of acute anxiety?

The remedy is understanding and maturity. . . . Because science is not an absolutist doctrine, its position is the hardest to defend in the unending battle with absolutism, and its defenders require a maximum of sympathetic understanding. It is their inability to give this understanding, to make the effort it requires, to find contentment in a world in which all questions have not been answered, which have turned men to theism, transcendentalist metaphysics, cynicism, and struggle.

W. Beck [2]

out later, they became an effective intellectual barrier to the advancement of scientific thought and to our understanding of man as the animal that he is. In the Middle Ages, these concepts led to the abasement of man and his earthly abode and to feelings that this earthly life is worthless. They have indirectly been the cause of bloody religious wars and have engendered our present inability to cope effectively with certain human problems desperately in need of solution, for example, the question of population control.

Science

Magic and myth are two elements that help to shape the intellectual climate of any age, ours included. As has been indicated, their role as stabilizing elements is probably less important today than it was in earlier ages, but they still help man to view his life as something meaningful and inject an element of order into the sometimes chaotic pattern of human existence. They reflect man's attempts to reduce uneasiness and uncertainty in a world that he did not understand and was slow to comprehend. More recently, a third element has been added to man's intellectual equipment. This new factor is probably best defined as a scientific attitude and has a commonality with magic and myth in that it helps to put order into man's experience and structure into his universe. However, it differs from magic and myth in its mode of endeavor. Science is empirical in that it is rooted in experiences and observations from which it attempts to draw logical inferences, but it goes beyond empiricism in that it is enriched by an imagination that groups these experiences, from the level of facts to higher levels

Through a kaleidoscope

Werner Muckenhirn photo,
Nancy Palmer Photo Agency, Inc.

of integration, in a more or less connected and unified view. Science is also extended by a speculative habit that carries it beyond the observational and experimental and into the unknown. Like the magic of divination, science gains force from its predictive qualities and from its use as a basis for decision making. Unlike magic, however, it eschews influence and force in favor of understanding as an end in itself and as a means of controlling nature. It seeks to resolve ambiguities, and it does so by devising critical and decisive tests that can be used to distinguish between alternative points of view. It does not honor minuteness of detail unless there is a means to explain the relation between these details and some wider, more universal concept. Unlike magic and myth, science cannot deal with those things that cannot be observed, measured, tested, and validated. Like art and philosophy, it seeks after truth—truth about reality—but it contents itself with the knowledge that the truths it uncovers may be partial, incomplete, relative, and displaceable by greater truths yet to be discovered. In company with myth and magic, science is responsible for the sensibility, the intellectual climate, of our society, for it is made by people and is a reflection of the style of these people.

In our present context, science has provided a new way to an understanding of man. It is above all a questioning, problem-oriented endeavor, and no areas are off limits to its probing, even though there are realms of human thought and action where science has little or nothing to contribute. By asking the right questions, the scientist can focus on those problems that he has hopes of solving and can isolate them from their metaphysical encumbrances. By doing so, he automatically sets limits to what he can learn from observation and experimentation, but the answers he derives can

Through a kaleidoscope

... The battlefield where the innovator struggles with his age is often within the mind of the scientist. . . . Scientists are men, and, like other men, they are brought up to hold the same views that other people hold. The importance of this fact is that the scientist, like everyone else, is a creature of his times, its prejudices, truths, and assumptions, and when the moment comes to make conclusions from the evidence at hand, the scientist may find it impossible even to conjure up, much less believe, a possible explanation for his data that conflicts with things that, consciously or unconsciously, he has always believed. If such a conclusion should seem inescapable, it may still be easier to believe that some error has occurred than that an eternal truth is false. . . . In other words, the scientist in making this first crucial decision is acting under the influence—or tyranny in many cases—of his times. Despite everything, his freedom of action is severely limited. He is, in fact, an individual interacting with his culture, its values and strictures, and what comes out of this interaction is of decisive importance for the course of science.

This is understandable and to some extent desirable. Yet, had such paralysis of the imagination afflected all men of science, the world would have known no Copernicus, Galileo, Newton, Darwin, or Pasteur. Each of these pulled down an ancient temple of truth because the evidence made it necessary to do so and, in turn, each changed the course of history.

W. Beck [2]

But while science has this much in common with magic that both rest on a faith in order as the underlying principle of all things, . . . the order presupposed by magic differs widely from that which forms the basis of science. The difference flows naturally from the different modes in which the two orders have been reached. For whereas the order on which magic reckons is merely an extension, by false analogy, of the order in which ideas present themselves to our minds, the order laid down by science is derived from patient and exact observation of the phenomena themselves. The abundance, the solidity, and the splendour of the results already achieved by science are well fitted to inspire us with a cheerful confidence in the soundness of its method.

J. G. Frazer [11]

be stepping stones to further questions and, in pyramidal fashion, to further solutions. In addition, he admits that metaphysical questions are incapable of solution and so legitimately disregards them.

The strategy of modern science was slow in maturing. It gained its logicality from the Greeks and from the earlier Eastern civilizations that had contributed to Greek thought. There then followed a long hiatus before a reawakening took place in the sixteenth century, first in northern Italy during the Renaissance and later in France and Elizabethan England. This rebirth of science gave rise eventually to what is now known as the scientific revolution. Linked with the rise of humanism and reacting against the stultifying Scholasticism of the Middle Ages, the scientific revolution was a genuine mutation in scholarship, a shift from an arbitrary, intuitive, often anthropomorphic view of the world to one in which single events could be isolated, studied, and eventually understood in physical terms. In its initial phases, science, as we now understand it, was not firmly disassociated from magic and myth, and Francis Bacon's requirement that the scientist should put nature to the question was not adopted as an integral part of the strategy of science—except by a limited number of individuals—until the nineteenth century, when it became clear that in the future little in the way of reliable and consentient information could be added to man's knowledge of himself and his environment except by employing the methods and tools of science.

The crucial elements of the strategy of science, in addition to a prerequisite curiosity, are the following: (1) conducting directed observations, (2) grouping these observations into some systematic order, which is itself a selective

Through a kaleidoscope

. . . Men of science do not pledge themselves to creeds; they are bound by articles of no sort; there is not a single belief that it is not a bounden duty with them to hold with a light hand and to part with it, cheerfully, the moment it is really proved to be contrary to any fact, great or small. And if in course of time I see good reasons for such a proceeding, I shall have no hesitation in coming before you, and pointing out any change in my opinion without finding the slightest occasion to blush for so doing. So I say that we accept this view as we accept any other, so long as it will help us, and we feel bound to retain it only so long as it will serve our great purpose—the improvement of Man's estate and the widening of his knowledge. The moment this, or any other conception, ceases to be useful for these purposes, away with it to the four winds; we care not what becomes of it!

T. H. Huxley [19]

---

act, (3) explaining the meaning of this order by means of conceptualization, and (4) testing this explanation by means of experimentation that bridges the gap between the empirical and the theoretical. The object of an experiment must always be to overthrow the hypothesis, to search out and account for ambiguities that might exist in most ideas. Only in this manner can one arrive at the simplest statement that will hold together the varied facets of our experience.

Man, of course, has always been an observer of nature (see illustration 1.11); he had to be to exist and evolve in the world from which he extracted his living. He had to be able to read the heavens, to judge the seasons, to know the ways of animals, to distinguish one plant from another, to recognize himself as a functioning organism. Because he is an imaginative, curious creature who takes nothing for granted and who requires answers to his questions, he could not help but build up an impressive store of information that was coupled with ideas that embodied his view of nature and of himself. The richness of early man's folklore and myths reveals his keenness of observation and the fertility of his imagination in putting his observations into frames of reference meaningful to himself.

The power of the scientific method is not that it keeps any one of us from error but that by mutual criticism and persuasion we gradually clarify and correct each other's intuition, until they become part of the canon of the subject. . . . To understand scientific knowledge, we must not only understand scientific ignorance; we must also understand scientific error. . . . The scientific system . . . makes allowances for individual error, and it has techniques for checking and correction. . . . The only arbiter of truth is Nature, interrogated by experiment. . . .

J. Ziman [45]

1.11   Stonehenge, Salisbury Plain, Wiltshire, England. Evidence suggests that this structure was probably used in connection with some form of sky worship and thus represents early man's attempts to observe nature in a systematic way. The stones are aligned on significant risings of the sun and moon and could have been used as a counting device for predicting solar and lunar eclipses.

As I view my contribution to the writing of our times, it seems to me to consist of a double affirmative, saying first that an awareness and experience of Nature is necessary to Man if he is to have his humanity, and saying in the second place that same awareness must have something of a religious quality, the Italian pietàs, if you will. . . .

Nature is a part of our humanity, and without some awareness and experience of that divine mystery man ceases to be man. When the Pleiades and the wind in the grass are no longer a part of the human spirit, a part of very flesh and bone, man becomes, as it were, a kind of cosmic outlaw, having neither the completeness and integrity of the animal nor the birthright of a true humanity.

H. Beston [4]

Only in more recent times, and particularly since the beginning of the scientific revolution, has man become a conscious experimenter with deliberate goals in mind. To become so, a change in thinking had to take place. The hard, irreducible fact, not the idea, had to become the stable point of reference, although man had to recognize that an isolated piece of information, unrelated to an idea, was totally useless. Attention turned, therefore, to the details of nature, to the nitty-gritty of everyday phenomena, to the realm of weights and measures, to heartbeats and dissections, to chills and fever, to moving bodies and growing plants, to questions whose answers could be agreed upon. This is obviously not the realm from which answers to the larger philosophical questions can be drawn, and the questions asked of nature took a different form. If one believes that man is divinely created, one does not ask questions about the mode of creation or the origin of man. The new questions being asked were more limited in scope and hence more readily answerable. Truth began to take on a different face, one that is limited, provisional, and sometimes ephemeral.

This transition could not have taken place unless man first assumed that he was a reliable observer of nature, and second that his probings, properly planned and executed, could penetrate behind appearances to discover hidden meanings. Gradually, he also came to realize that appearance and reality were not necessarily the same and that even as an observer he possessed a built-in fallibility, a subjectivity that made any observation provisional, but nevertheless the best at the moment. As Kenneth Boulding emphasizes, just as a painter never approaches his painting with an "innocent eye," so we never receive "raw data"; these data come to

In invention, the creative process *forms* an original pattern; in discovery, the creative process *reveals* one. Discovery constantly adds to the number of things from which new patterns can be made; new patterns, particularly in technology, enable new discoveries to be made. The two—discovery and invention—are phases in the creative process that are in resonance, each reinforcing the other.

Creativity is a state of mind, and it is most widely expressed by very young children, because their confrontation with their environment is constantly made up of original discoveries and inventions. In time, through social pressures to conform and the repetition of experience, most of them lose this sense of wonder and become less and less creative, trapped in a concrete mold not of their own making.

D. Fabun [8]

---

us only through a filter system whose structure is determined partly by each of us as individuals and partly by the particular age in which we exist. Curiosity about an observation, not the observation itself, is the starting point of science, and curiosity is individually and culturally determined.

Reliance on observations, and the grouping of these observations into larger and larger concepts, also implies that there is an orderliness to nature, that this orderliness is discernible, and that what is true in the particular is likely to be true in general. The ordering of experiences into conceptual schemes becomes a meaningless practice unless it is assumed that the ordering is a reflection of reality and a basis for further action. Because science can never be certain that it has discovered the truth for which it has been searching, it continually reexamines its observations, tests its hypotheses, and weighs the generality of its laws. Error, whether of observation or of conceptualization, cannot remain hidden for long, and dogma and absolutes are always viewed with suspicion.

The act of conceptualization, in science as in any other human endeavor, is a creative act; it is also indispensable, provided it is kept under rigid control. Science, as an intellectual process, could not exist if its vast load of detailed information were not tied up into convenient packages, namely, hypotheses, theories, and laws. Some two million research papers in science and technology are published annually in some 30,000 specialized journals, and to remember the details contained in even a limited number of these papers is an enormous task. The specialist must of course know the details of his area of interest—its ambiguities, confirmations, and extensions, as well as its basic facts—but enormous economy is achieved by the formula-

The clear light of science, we are often told, has abolished mystery, leaving only logic and reason. This is quite untrue. Science has removed the obscuring veil of mystery from many phenomena, much to the benefit of the human race: but it confronts us with a basic and universal mystery—the mystery of existence in general, and of the existence of mind in particular. Why does the world exist? Why is the worldstuff what it is? Why does it have mental or subjective aspects as well as material or objective ones? We do not know. All we can do is to admit the facts.

J. Huxley [18]

The universe revealed by science, especially the sciences of biology and psychology, is one in which the human spirit cannot find a comfortable home. That spirit breathes freely only in a universe where what philosophers call Value Judgments are of supreme importance. It needs to believe, for instance, that right and wrong are real, that Love is more than a biological function, that the human mind is capable of reason rather than merely of rationalization, and that it has the power to will and to choose instead of being compelled merely to react in the fashion predetermined by its conditioning. Since science has proved that none of these beliefs is more than a delusion, mankind will be compelled either to surrender what we call its humanity by adjusting to the real world or to live some kind of tragic existence in a universe alien to the deepest needs of its nature.

J. W. Krutch [21]

Some beliefs are like pleasant gardens with high walls around them. They encourage exclusiveness, and the feeling of being especially privileged. Other beliefs are expansive and lead the way into wider and deeper sympathies. Some beliefs are like shadows, darkening children's days with fears of unknown calamities. Other beliefs are like the sunshine, blessing children with the warmth of happiness. Some beliefs are divisive, separating the saved from the unsaved, friends from enemies. Other beliefs are bonds in a universal brotherhood, where sincere differences beautify the pattern. Some beliefs are like blinders, shutting off the power to choose one's own direction. Other beliefs are like gateways, opening up wide vistas for exploration. Some beliefs weaken a child's selfhood. They blight the growth of resourcefulness. Other beliefs nurture selfconfidence and enrich the feeling of personal worth. Some beliefs are rigid, like the body of death, impotent in a changing world. Other beliefs are pliable, like the young sapling, ever growing with the upward thrust of life.

S. L. Fahs [9]

tion of a concept that embraces more and more of experience within its limits. Complexity is reduced and simplicity introduced, at least so far as the management of details is concerned, but concepts have the added value of introducing comprehensiveness because their usefulness often extends beyond the known into the unknown, but only until their usefulness is called into question by too many ambiguities. Comprehensiveness has, therefore, a predictive value, providing as it does a basis for belief as well as for action.

Concepts are not without their dangers, however. Commitment to any scheme in an unyielding way is the most certain way to dogma and authority, to intellectual rigidity, and to a stifling of imaginative innovation. Yet temporary allegiance, or at least tentative adherence, to a scheme is necessary as a base of operation; within its sphere of reference and influence it sets the temper of science, defines the problems worthy of exploration, and gives its adherents a comfortable and psychologically satisfying base of belief.

A concept, of course, must be reasonable in relation to its time if it is to gain and retain acceptability. But how does one judge reasonableness? A scientist must, of necessity, know the solidly based facts from which a concept arose; he must also be aware of existing ambiguities that have brought the validity of the concept into question. He must, if he is clever enough, conceive of other concepts that might embrace both the facts and the ambiguities, but to be successful these must be testable, open-ended in that they can include other facts still to be unearthed, and predictive. The untestable and closed hypothesis leads only to dead ends. Science exists only because there are gaps of knowledge still to be filled and many unknowns still to be explored.

Through a kaleidoscope

> The most beautiful thing we can experience is the mysterious. It is the source of all true art and science.
>
> *A. Einstein* [7]

> A modern poet has characterized the personality of art and the impersonality of science as follows: Art is I; Science is We.
>
> *C. Bernard* [3]

Science and the arts

The kaleidoscopic nature of man is revealed through his art and his other cultural achievements probably more so than through the methods, practice, and results of science. It is through the arts that the full diversity of man as a thinking and feeling animal gains visible expression. His folklore, language, literature, architecture, and music are tangible evidence of his attitude toward nature and his concept of himself. They indicate what man deems important and what trivial, what sacred and what profane, and what necessary for the inner as well as for the outer man. These expressions reflect his integration with, as well as his alienation from, nature and the degree to which he has accommodated to, and made use of, a particular environment. The sand paintings of the Navajo Indians, the soapstone and bone carvings of the Eskimo, the Gothic cathedrals of Western Europe, and the multimedia of the artist of today tell us as much of man as does a knowledge of his muscles and bone, fossil teeth, and racial characteristics.

The separation between the sciences and the arts is not, of course, a clean one, and should not be, because both are the products of the imagination and inventiveness of man. But, as indicated in C. P. Snow's *Two Cultures*, their distinctiveness has been made more evident with the passage of time. Each discipline, as it matured acquired its own groups of practitioners, its own set of roles, and its own mystique. However, the pervasiveness and indeed the primacy of science continues to influence the arts today, not only in terms of language and imagery but also through use

1.12 The full diversity of man is revealed in every aspect of his existence. Variety is present even in limited elements of a single culture, as a comparison of the Philadelphia Orchestra and the Jefferson Airplane shows.

RCA Records

RCA Records

Through a kaleidoscope

27

One day the Nouns were clustered in the street.
An Adjective walked by, with her dark beauty.
The Nouns were struck, moved, changed.
The next day a Verb drove up, and created the Sentence.

Each Sentence says one thing—for example, "Although it was
    a dark rainy day when the Adjective walked by, I shall
    remember the pure and sweet expression on her face until
    the day I perish from the green, effective earth."
Or, "Will you please close the window, Andrew?"
Or, for example, "Thank you, the pink pot of flowers on the
    window sill has changed color recently to a light yellow,
    due to the heat from the boiler factory
    which exists nearby."

In the springtime the Sentences and the Nouns lay silently on
    the grass.
A lonely Conjunction here and there would call, "And! But!"
And the Adjective did not emerge.

As the adjective is lost in the sentence,
So I am lost in your eyes, ears, nose, and throat—
You have enchanted me with a single kiss
Which can never be undone
Until the destruction of language.

K. Koch [20]

The process of envisaging facts, values, hopes
and fears underlies our whole behavior pattern;
and this process is reflected in an extraordinary
phenomenon found always, and only, in human
societies—the phenomenon of language.
Language is the highest and most amazing
achievement of the symbolistic human mind. The
power it bestows is almost inestimable, for
without it anything properly called "thought" is
impossible.

S. Langer [22]

of the scientific method to solve problems of an essentially nonscientific nature. The difference between these two endeavors of man, taking many forms and leading to diverse results, can perhaps be appreciated by a study of the language of each, using poetry as an example of the arts.

Language is perhaps the greatest single gift and achievement of the human organism, and what we do with language is never indifferent for it is one of the most effective forms of power. It is the means whereby we dissect our world and our experiences within this world. In science and in the literary arts, words powerfully and inevitably shape and reflect our thinking, our attitudes, and our actions. Words also define the limits of our experience, for words are the only tool we can use to describe experience. When we encounter new worlds, we must invent new words to describe them or else invest old words with new meaning.

Language, of course, is a form of symbolism, and as such it can be a trap as well as an aid. The symbol itself may come to stand for the aspect of reality that it originally was employed to represent, thereby distorting our sense of reality and alienating ourselves from it.

The language of science is meant to convey facts and ideas, not emotions. Within any single scientific context, words should have but a single meaning in order to eliminate uncertainty and ambiguity of interpretation, and the language should not contain metaphors or analogies that would tend to diffuse rather than to sharpen images. The goal of science is a consensus of reasonable opinion over the widest possible field. Science, however, is constantly conveying messages. If scientific progress is not to come to a standstill, its language must be capable of being modified, enlarged, limited, and transformed, reflecting what is recent and per-

Through a kaleidoscope

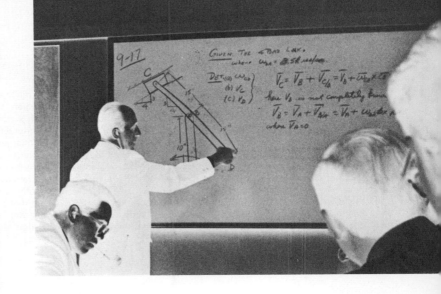

haps provisional while retaining that which is sound and viable. If the language becomes rigid and turns into a system that claims to be self-sufficient, the mind that operates in such a system will go on working inside it forever, cut off from the reality that the concepts that it deals with are supposed to represent. We need only compare our language of today with that of twenty-five years ago to realize to what extent science has altered and enriched our daily conversation and our range of expressions, but all of us, whether we are scientists or not, realize that the compactness as well as the newness of much of the language of science—the so-called scientific jargon—is responsible in part for the barrier that exists between the scientist and the layman. But what most nonscientists fail to realize is that the jargon peculiar to each discipline is designed for the linguistic economy that is necessary for precise communication.

The biological term "gene" can be cited as an example of a word that has undergone change with time and with the maturation of the science of genetics. When first used around the turn of the century to replace the word "factor," a less precise Mendelian term, gene referred that abstract "something" that was inherited in a predictable manner and that determined in an unknown way a delineated character in an organism. Its physical reality, however, was long questioned until experimental evidence demonstrated that the gene was located in a particular region of a particular, microscopically visible chromosome. As a result the gene became less abstract and more tangible. Scientific investigation during the last several decades has shown also that the gene is a particular kind of molecule having a known dimension, a regular internal structure, and a specific mode of action. Our image of the gene is consequently sharper,

. . . A piece of scientific writing offers to every man the same studiously unequivocal message; as far as the writer is consistently scientific, his terms have only an intellectual value, put only the mind into play, and guide all minds through the same routine of syllogism and inference to an inevitable conclusion. In contrast with this uniformity in the appeal of science is the infinite variableness and adaptability of literature. Every piece of literature is a mimic piece of life that tempts the reader to capture from it, with mind and heart and imagination, an individual bliss; he may, in some measure, shape it as he will—work out his own destiny with it. . . .

L. E. Gates [13]

Through a kaleidoscope

The thinking poet does not walk down the finely swept path of formally developed and sequent series of logical postulates. He advances by metaphor, which is a form of leaping. The philosopher, the historian, the scientist move as snails on a slate and leave behind them a glistening trail that we can follow with even an unpracticed eye. The poet moves like a ground squirrel; where he is now gives no promise or assurance of where he will be next. . . . So the poet, like the child, is forever interrogating his universe and forever rejecting the answers that logical thinkers are only too eager to give him. Sensing reality for what it is, he has always known that the answers that man invents are imposed on reality and not contained in it. Truth stands in this and in this alone. So the poet understands that the chase is a false hunt and that man at his best can only construct fitting inquiries about the isolated experiences that he has chosen to call reality. This is the end of poetical thinking and the wisdom that is poetry.

D. C. Allen [1]

1.13 *A page from the original manuscript of* Alexander Pope's Essay on Man. *A poem is a very personal expression of very personal feelings and emotions, and the poet may revise his work over and over again until his words convey his emotions perfectly.*

The Pierpont Morgan Library

It is impossible to dissociate language from science or science from language, because every natural science always involves three things: the sequence of phenomena on which the science is based; the abstract concepts which call these phenomena to mind; and the words in which the concepts are expressed. To call forth a concept, a word is needed; to portray a phenomenon, a concept is needed. All three mirror the same reality.

A. L. Lavoisier [23]

Many a man, when I tell him that I have been on to a mountain, asks if I took a glass with me. It was not to see a few particular objects, as if they were near at hand, as I had been accustomed to see them, that I had ascended the mountain, but to see an infinite variety far and near in their relation to each other, thus reduced to a single picture. The facts of science in comparison with poetry, are wont to be as vulgar as looking from the mountain with a telescope.

H. Thoreau [41]

and the word is more than simply an operational figure of speech. It has been progressively shorn of its fuzziness as it has been limited in connotation.

The sciences, therefore, in their striving for preciseness and economy of expression, have in a sense impoverished our language. Indeed, the general laws of nature will ultimately be reduced to mathematical formulas, the most concise form of language that we possess. The language of the poet, however, serves a different purpose, even though it too undergoes change with time. Its purpose is not to make a specific statement of fact, but rather to broaden and deepen man's range of personal experience and to release his finer emotions. This is accomplished through new words and new juxtapositions, through rhythms and patterns, metaphor and analogy, passion and sensuousness (see illustration 1.13). The relationship between man and his fellow men, and between man and his environment, is heightened and enriched. Although science does somewhat the same thing as it strives to extend man's knowledge of himself and his world, the procedure is much more impersonal.

The poet is not so much concerned with an approximation to reality, that is, with the truth or falsity of his statement, as he is with the construction of an image that is well suited for the achievement of his experiential or emotional goal. Ambiguities may be exploited rather than avoided, and metaphor may be piled on metaphor. The poet asks only that his images be consistent with one another and with the form in which they are presented. We may question Tennyson on the correctness of his physical interpretations when he writes, "Let the great world spin for ever down the ringing grooves of change," but we accept the aptness of his imagery as it relates to his conceptual goal.

The Man of science seeks truth as a remote and unknown benefactor; he cherishes and loves it in his solitude; the Poet, singing a song in which all human beings join with him, rejoices in the presence of truth as our visible friend and hourly companion. Poetry is the breath and finer spirit of all knowledge; it is the impassioned expression which is in the countenance of all Science. Emphatically it may be said of the Poet, as Shakespeare hath said of man, "that he looks before and after." He is the rock of defence for human nature; an upholder and preserver, carrying everywhere with him relationship and love. . . . Poetry is the first and last of all knowledge—it is as immortal as the heart of man. If the labours of Men of science should ever create any material revolution, direct or indirect, in our condition, and in the impressions which we habitually receive, the Poet will sleep no more than at present; he will be ready to follow the steps of the Man of science, not only in those general indirect effects, but he will be at his side, carrying sensation into the midst of the objects of science itself. . . . If the time should ever come when what is now called science, thus familiarized to men, shall be ready to put on, as it were, a form of flesh and blood, the Poet will lend his divine spirit to aid the transfiguration, and will welcome the Being thus produced, as a dear and genuine inmate of the household of man.

W. Wordsworth [44]

The Metropolitan Museum of Art, Gift of Charles Bregler, 1941

A multiple exposure photograph by Thomas Eakins (1844–1916) showing George Reynolds pole vaulting.

The difference between scientist and poet is that—
One, gathering proof systematically
all around the perimeter, goes.
The other sits still in the center,
as if listening, and knows.
One isn't any better than the other, and they need each other.

M. Swenson [40]

Both the scientist and the poet interrogate man and nature, the scientist through deliberate experiment, the poet more like a questioning child. Both see man and nature clothed in his own way, in the precise and formal vestments of knowledge or in the rainbow garments of emotion and imagery. Both broaden the horizons of man and expand his sensibility of himself and of the world in which he lives. But neither the scientist nor the poet can provide a total view of man in all his varied aspects; both are needed to complete the picture.

Summary

In a kaleidoscope it is the bits of colored glass—reds, yellows, greens, and blues—falling into particular patterns that yield the images we see. Each image is unique and fleeting, for as the pieces of glass shift, so too does the image. Only the multifaceted configuration persists. So it is with man, seeing himself in the kaleidoscope of history. Time, place, and circumstance turn the tube, tumbling elements of human invention, imagination, and discovery, of magic myth, experience, science, and the arts into new configurations and new images. As we grasp the import of these images, we become aware that man has a history and that his relation to himself, to society, and to the earth and the universe undergo change as his knowledge of, and response to, himself and his surroundings increases. It is science that provides much of this knowledge today, just as dogma, revelation, and authority provided it in the past. But the kaleidoscope continues to turn, the future becomes the past, and new images of man continue to appear.

Through a kaleidoscope

2

A new course is charted

Those changes in thinking and action that gave rise to modern science—and all that this implies in present outlook, knowledge, terminology, methodology, technology, our thoughts about man, and the constantly accelerating dynamics of change—have been referred to as a mutation in scholarship. The term "mutation," in its present biological sense, means a change in the physical structure or relationship of a transmissible molecule of inheritance (a gene) that leads to a discernible and heritable change in an organism. A mutation in scholarship is no less a departure in form and subsequent expression. In this instance, changes in a traditional system of thought provided the Western world with a new image of itself and of its potentialities. It is axiomatic that the more rigidly structured a system,

There is another form of temptation, even more fraught with danger. This is the disease of curiosity. . . . It is this which drives us on to try to discover the secrets of nature, those secrets which are beyond our understanding, which can avail us nothing, and which men should not wish to learn. . . . In this immense forest, full of pitfalls and perils, I have drawn myself back, and pulled myself away from these thorns. In the midst of all these things which float unceasingly around me in my everyday life, I am never surprised at any of them, and never captivated by my genuine desire to study them. . . . I no longer dream of the stars.

St. Augustine [2]

Innovation would seem to result from two types of cause, the first being internal elaboration of purely traditional substance. The scholastic method [of the Middle Ages], so frequently dismissed as sterile, was in fact peculiarly apt to produce this type of innovation. Its typical instrument, the *quaestio* form of commentary, by the very fact that it began with a statement—however perfunctory—of the arguments *against* an accepted or orthodox position was bound in certain minds to provoke an interest in the arguments *for* the radical or heterodox position. And in time this speculative interest was likely to ripen into veiled and even overt conviction. . . . Masking itself with irony as a protection against ecclesiastical condemnation, the skepticism flourished in fourteenth-century Paris and Oxford, and persisted in the fifteenth century at Padua and the other Italian universities. . . .

D. B. Durand [17]

At his most characteristic, medieval man was not a dreamer or a wanderer. He was an organizer, a codifier, a builder of systems. He wanted "a place for everything and everything in the right place." Distinction, definition, tabulation were his delight. Though full of turbulent activities, he was equally full of the impulse to formalize them. War was (in intention) formalized by the art of heraldry and the rules of chivalry; sexual passion (in intention), by an elaborate code of love. Highly original and soaring philosophical speculation squeezes itself into a rigid dialectical pattern copied from Aristotle. Studies like Law and Moral Theology, which demand the ordering of very diverse particulars, especially flourish. Every way in which a poet can write (including some in which he had much better not) is classified in the Arts of Rhetoric. There was nothing which medieval people liked better, or did better, than sorting out and tidying up. Of all of our modern inventions I suspect that they would most have admired the card index. . . . In their most sublime achievements . . . we see the tranquil, indefatigable, exultant energy of passionately systematic minds bringing huge masses of heterogeneous material into unity. The perfect examples are the *Summa* of Aquinas and Dante's *Divine Comedy;* as unified and ordered as the Parthenon or the *Oedipus Rex,* as crowded and varied as a London terminus on a bank holiday.

C. S. Lewis [23]

whether intellectual or organismic, the more unlikely it is that a mutation will bring about a permanent change of expression; the mutation will probably be lost or suppressed before it attains general visibility. It is equally clear that the environment in which a mutation arises determines its reception, persistence, and the rapidity of its spread. But mutations of ideas, once in print, are usually permanent, even though their impact and influence may be delayed. In the present context, the historical roots of the mutation that eventually led to the rise and full expression of modern science stretch back not only to the Middle Ages but also to much earlier Greek thought. As it gained in effectiveness and general acceptance, this mutation profoundly altered the natural history of man and increased our understanding of where man resides in space and time and how he came to occupy his present position of biological dominance.

It is significant that printing and modern science have developed together and at comparable rates. In the fifteenth century, Johann Gutenberg spent 5 years, close to 2.5 million minutes, casting the type for his now-famous Bible, the

2.1   The Gutenberg Bible.

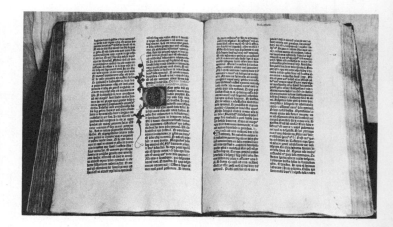

... The Middle Ages depended predominantly on books. Though literacy was of course far rarer then than now, reading was in one way a more important ingredient of the total culture. ... They were indeed very credulous of books. They find it hard to believe that anything an old *auctour* has said is simply untrue. And they inherit a very heterogeneous collection of books; Judaic, Pagan, Platonic, Aristotelian, Stoical, Primitive Christian, Patristic. Or (by a different classification) chronicles, epic poems, sermons, visions, philosophical treatises, satires. Obviously their *auctours* will contradict one another. They will seem to do so even more often if you ignore the distinctions of kind and take your science impartially from the poets and philosophers. ... If, under these conditions, one has also the great reluctance flatly to disbelieve anything in a book, then here there is obviously both an urgent need and a glorious opportunity for sorting out and tidying up. All the apparent contradictions must be harmonized. A Model must be built which will get everything in without a clash; and it can do this only by becoming intricate, by mediating its unity through a great, and finely ordered, multiplicity.

C. S. Lewis [23]

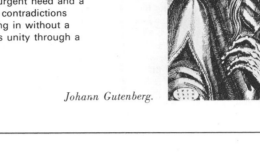

Johann Gutenberg.

---

first printed book in the Western world. It took an additional 3 years to produce two hundred copies of it. Today, by means of advanced computer techniques, the same Bible can be set into type in 77 minutes. Science has had a similar growth rate.

This change in scholarship gained social visibility, the first indication of its eventual spread, and a congenial environment during the revival of learning that is generally characterized in history as the Italian Renaissance, from about 1450 to 1550. But the Renaissance was much more than simply a revival of ancient learning; it was an intellectual ferment, abetted by a wide variety of other factors, that came to affect virtually every facet of European life. The reason why the effects of the Renaissance were so widespread is that society is a superorganism, and a perturbation in one part of the system makes itself felt throughout the whole, just as it does in an individual organism. The results, thus magnified, become more discernible than the initial disturbance itself.

The Renaissance was characterized by confusion, excitement, transition, and future promise. Constantinople had fallen to the Turks in 1453, and elements of Greek and Near Eastern learning were filtering westward toward the continent of Europe, and particularly toward northern Italy. Increasing secularization of the Papacy and the economic power of the Roman Church were leading to an inevitable lessening of ecclesiastical authority and the escape of the universities from clerical control. The feudal system of Europe was nearing an end, and the artisans, the source of technological innovations at the time, had gained a sense of identity and strength through the growing importance of medieval guilds. The spirit of geographical exploration, fos-

Existence was regarded by the medieval man as a cosmic drama, composed by the master dramatist according to a central theme and on a rational plan. Finished in idea before it was enacted in fact, before the world began written down to the last syllable of recorded time, the drama was unalterable either for good or evil. There it was, precisely defined, to be understood as far as might be, but at all events to be remorselessly played out to its appointed end. The duty of man was to accept the drama as written, since he could not alter it; his function, to play the role assigned. That he might play his role according to the divine text, subordinate authorities—church and state—deriving their just powers from the will of God, were instituted among men to dispose them to submission and to instruct them in their proper lines. Intelligence was essential, since God had endowed men with it. But the function of intelligence was strictly limited. Useless to inquire curiously into the origin or final state of existence, since both had been divinely determined and sufficiently revealed. Useless, even impious, to inquire into its ultimate meaning, since God alone could fully understand it. The function of intelligence was therefore to demonstrate the truth of revealed knowledge, to reconcile diverse and pragmatic experience with the rational pattern of the world as given in faith.

C. L. Becker [6]

A new course is charted

This humanist is a great rebel . . . a great individualist—he wants to be himself. . . . [The humanists] were men who dared to be themselves, because they trusted in their own natural powers, in something inside themselves. . . . The Renaissance was the age of the hero, the hero as artist, the hero as soldier of fortune, the hero as explorer, the hero as scholar, even the hero as poisoner. If you were less than a hero, you were a failure. . . .

Perhaps at bottom humanists . . . were rebelling because they felt the familiar, but to sensitive men and women never comfortable, gap between the ideal and the real had in late medieval times reached an excessive degree of obviousness. That gap, always pretty plain throughout the Middle Ages, was by the fifteenth century almost too wide for the most ingenious explanations to close. The ideal was still Christian, still an ideal of unity, peace, serenity, organization, status; the reality was endemic war, divided authority even at the top, even in that papacy which should reflect God's own serene unity, a great scramble for wealth and position, a time of troubles. . . . This complex movement is a very conscious rebel, a rebel against a way of life it finds corrupt, overelaborated, stale, unlovely and untrue. The humanists seem to be opening a window, letting in the fresh air, and doing a lot of other pleasant things.

C. Brinton [8]

It is generally admitted that the 17th century underwent, and accomplished, a very radical spiritual revolution of which modern science is at the same time the root and the fruit. . . .

This scientific and philosophical revolution . . . can be described roughly as . . . the disappearance . . . of the conception of the world as a finite, closed, and hierarchically ordered whole, . . . and its replacement by an indefinite and even infinite universe which is bound together by the identity of its fundamental components and laws, and in which all these components are placed on the same level of being. This . . . implies the discarding by scientific thought of all considerations based on value-concepts, such as perfection, harmony, meaning and aim, and finally the utter devalorization of being, the divorce of the world of value and the world of fact.

A. Koyré [22]

tered by Portugal, Spain, Holland, and England, but infecting all of Europe, was enlarging the known world, and the diversity of cultures, the increased wealth, and the new plants and animals from Africa, the Far East, and the Americas were having an economic, colonial, and intellectual impact. The introduction of movable type took learning and knowledge out of the monasteries and put them into the open marketplace and led to the development of newspapers and the printing of 20 million volumes during the first hundred years of its use. The artist, who frequently was also an inventor and an engineer, was discovering a sense of perspective and seeing, for the first time, the richness of detail that a minute examination of nature could bring forth. A rediscovery of the classical past, particularly that of Greece, restored to the thinking man a confidence in his own faculties and a sense of the continuity of history and the commonality of man despite diverse patterns of beliefs and customs. There was, in addition, an increase in wealth, which, together with other social changes, accompanied the expansion of the mind and spirit.

The bonds of spiritual, intellectual, political, economic, artistic, and geographical orthodoxy were seriously strained, if not actually broken, during this comparatively short period of history. Men who were formerly characterized by their otherworldliness began to take an interest in the world around them. The realities of this world were beginning to be recognized as entities in themselves, not merely symbols of a world beyond. Human existence was beginning to be viewed as something to be lived as fully as possible on this earth, and not simply and solely as a probation for what might exist beyond the grave. There was, indeed, the hope that consignment to Dante's hell after a life of hard and

A new course is charted

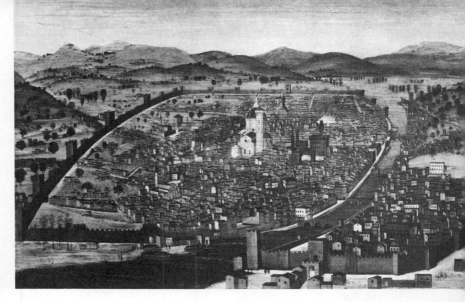

*Fifteenth-century Florence,
by an unknown artist.*

often degrading labor was not a foregone inevitability. A
spirit of inquiry and of correlative criticism was emerging,
and man came to recognize that he was not only free to
judge, but that he was also capable of doing so for himself.
The Renaissance man was fully conscious of contributing
to a changing life style. As many scholars have pointed out,
these attitudes, in their aggregation, constitute the essence
of humanism, the freeing of the mind of man from dogma
and authority; they are also the essence, and a very necessary essence, of the scientific mind. In the final analysis,
they helped man to realize that his position of dominance
was due to his own intellectual strengths, rather than to
any divine decree, and revealed to him the delight to be
found in understanding the details of himself and of the
natural world. In the future, the essence of man would be
sought for in nature and nowhere else.

These changes did not, of course, affect all men in all
stations of life, and they did not occur in all areas of Europe
simultaneously. Unlike the Black Plague that swept Europe
in devastating fashion in the fourteenth century and affected
all men in all places, the virus of intellectual freedom spread
more slowly and selectively. The focus of infection was in
northern Italy in the free city-state of Florence and at the
University of Padua. Florence was the home of the Medicis,
among the first patrons of humanism; Leonardo da Vinci
(1452–1519) was a familiar figure there, as was Michelangelo (1475–1564), Niccolò Machiavelli (1469–1527), and
Sandro Botticelli (1445–1510). Rebelling against the rigidity of medieval Scholasticism, these artists and writers
set new standards of critical scholarship and new patterns
of creativity. Coupled with the Florentine ferment, and
indeed preceding it in time, was the equally important

A new course is charted

Sixteenth-century Padua.

ferment taking place at Padua, the center of emerging experimental thought and methods in the sciences. At Padua, Aristotelianism, the philosophical system based on the writings of Aristotle and espoused by the Scholastics, was recognized as the fallible work of a man rather than an unchallengeable dogma, and so it was open to dissection, discussion, and criticism. Under the rule of the anticlerical state of Venice, Padua harbored such men as Andreas Vesalius (1514–1564), a Flemish anatomist whose discoveries overthrew many of the theories of the second-century Greek physician Galen, William Harvey (1578–1657), an English physiologist who charted the circulation of the blood, and Galileo Galilei (1564–1642), an Italian mathematician, astronomer, and physicist. These men, along with the Polish astronomer Nicholas Copernicus (1473–1543), were among the initiators of modern science, and since their time our views of man and his universe have been unalterably changed.

For present purposes, the year 1543 provides a convenient vantage point for looking backward in time to the old order of things and forward to what was to be. By this time, the Renaissance had run its course and was coming to a close in Italy, pushed into obscurity by the Reformation and the Counter-Reformation; but the seeds of inquiry had already been planted, and the first of the scientific fruits were ready for harvest. It was the year in which two momentous books were published: Copernicus's *De revolutionibus orbium coelestium* [On the revolutions of celestial bodies], and Vesalius's *De humani corporis fabrica* [On the structure of the human body]. Two more dissimilar classics would be difficult to imagine, but each charted a new course for science, one from which it has not deviated.

A new course is charted

For if the Earth be the Center of the World, stand still, and the Heavens move, as the most received opinion is, . . . what fury is that . . . that shall drive the Heavens about with such incomprehensible celerity in 24 hours, when as every point of the Firmament, and in the Aequator, must needs move . . . 176,660 [miles?] in one 246th part of an hour: and an arrow out of a bow must go seven times about the earth whilst a man can say an Ave Maria, if it keep the same pace, or compass the earth 1,884 times in an hour, which is beyond human conceit: fleeter than a dart and a wind-swift arrow. A man could not ride so much, going 40 miles a day, in 2,904 years, as the Firmament goes in 24 hours; or so much in 203 years, as the said Firmament in one minute; which seems incredible: . . . To avoid therefore these impossibilities, they ascribe a triple motion of the Earth.

R. Burton [10]

The influence of Copernicus

Despite the influence of the Renaissance, the world of Copernicus was still basically the world of the ancients, scarcely modified by a millennium and a half of Christian influence. The dominant philosophy, Scholasticism, embodied a reverence of the classical tradition, a belief that the Greeks and even the Romans were "more civilized, more elegant in behavior and expression, more sagacious in the conduct of affairs, and better informed." The field of theology was the only exception. Here, Christian monotheism had replaced the pluralistic paganism of the ancient world. The medieval Christian, using as his guide the writings of St. Thomas Aquinas (1225–1274), accorded piety a more elevated position than knowledge and judged faith to be a more reliable avenue to truth than reason. There was a general belief that this life had no value in itself and was merely a time of preparation for an eternal afterlife. The universe and man were divinely created and God was the first cause and source of all things. There was little reason for inquiry.

The view of the universe that Copernicus was to overthrow had been proposed in its original form some 2,000 years before by the Greek astronomer and mathematician Pythagoras. According to the Pythagorean system, the earth was a perfect, motionless sphere surrounded by eight other crystalline spheres. The five known planets—Mercury, Venus, Mars, Saturn, and Jupiter—and the sun and the moon revolved around the earth on the seven inner spheres, while the stars were permanently fixed to the outer sphere, which marked the edge of the universe. A later Greek

The Renaissance man was one of many legacies, but of them all perhaps the strongest was his optimism. . . . Renaissance optimism was predicated upon a sense of security, the felt existence of order, pattern and sequence; and because the roots of the Renaissance extended so far back into the Middle Ages, it was to the Middle Ages that the Renaissance was indebted for the principle of order by which man could view his world as the manifestation of an omniscient and omnipotent God and himself as that God's special creation. . . .

H. Baker [4]

When I consider the short extent of my life, swallowed up in the eternity before and after, the small space that I fill or even see, engulfed in the infinite immensity of spaces unknown to me and which know me not, I am terrified and astounded to find myself here and not there. For there is no reason why it should be here, not there, why now rather than at another time. Who put me here? By whose order and design have this place and time been allotted to me?

The eternal silence of those infinite spaces strikes me with terror.

B. Pascal [29]

The laboratory of Olaus Roemer,
a seventeenth-century Danish astronomer.

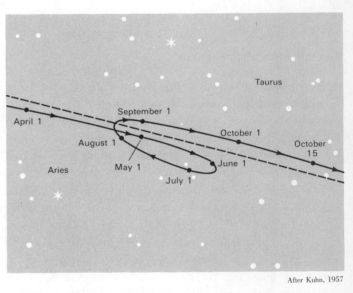

2.2   The apparent retrograde motion of the planet Mars.

astronomer, Hipparchus, noted that although the planets generally moved from east to west across the heavens, this motion was from time to time interrupted by intervals of westward motion (illustration 2.2). To account for this so-called retrograde motion, he devised his system of epicycles. He proposed that the planets move continuously in a small circle, the epicycle, whose central point traveled steadily around the circumference of a second, larger circle, the deferent (illustration 2.3). Five major epicycles were therefore constructed to account for variations in the motion of the five planets. Ptolemy, a second-century Greco-Egyptian astronomer, synthesized and systematized the various data gathered by the early Greek astronomers. In his

A new course is charted

	Hierarchy of Spirits	Physical Universe	Circles of Dante's Hell and Their Occupants
1	Angels	Earth	Limbo—the unbaptized and the virtuous pagans
2	Archangels	Moon	The lustful
3	Princes (Principalities)	Mercury	The gluttonous
4	Virtues	Venus	The hoarders and the spendthrifts
5	Potentates	Sun	The wrathful
6	Dominations	Mars	City of Dis—the heretics
7	Thrones	Jupiter	The violent against themselves, their neighbors, god, nature, and art
8	Cherubim	Saturn	Panders and seducers, flatterers, sorcerers, barrators, hypocrites, thieves, sowers of discord, and falsifiers, simoniacs, and fraudulent
9	Seraphim	Fixed stars	Traitors to kindred, country, guests, and lords

The hierarchies of Spirits, the physical universe, and Dante's Hell.

Almagest, he presented his system of astronomy based on an earth-centered (geocentric) universe—the Ptolemaic system (illustration 2.4).

Most men of the Middle Ages firmly adhered to the Ptolemaic system. They felt that they did indeed live in a physically limited, rigidly structured universe, centered around a motionless earth. This view is readily in accord with what the senses tell us. The motion of the earth spinning on its axis at a rate of 1,600 kilometers (about 1,000 miles) per hour cannot be sensed by man, because he shares this motion with the earth, and motion can be sensed only in relation to other unconnected bodies. The concept of the earth in motion had been considered by Ptolemy, but was rejected because it was assumed that the centrifugal forces produced by the speed of revolution would destroy the earth and all things on it. The assumption that the earth is the center of man's universe is a similarly sensible and appropriate concept. The dome-shaped sky above seems to imply that the earth is centered in a perfect sphere; the regular motion of the planets across the sky apparently means that they are orbiting the earth; and, finally, the notion of concentric spheres harmonized with the Greek ideal of perfection. Even today, modern treatises on navigation, using the fixed stars as guideposts, ask the reader to assume that the earth is stationary.

This pre-Copernican cosmology was aesthetically, spiritually, and psychologically satisfying in the sense that it gave man not only a comprehensible world view, but also a feeling that he existed in a beautifully structured system that was consistent with his own view of himself as a divinely created being. The cosmology of Dante's *Divine Comedy* is Ptolemaic, but Dante added spheres that ex-

2.3 *Two solutions of early astronomers to the problem of retrograde motion. In order to explain the apparent westward motion of planets from point 2 to point 3 shown in (a), early observers of the heavens posited the system of epicycles (b) or a looping deferent (c).*

After Kuhn, 1957

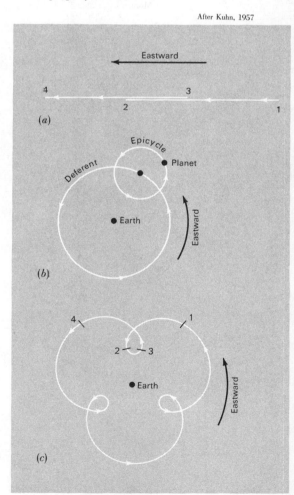

The conception of our infant scientific society can best be assigned to the Renaissance. At that time, men challenged authority and the dogma that had ruled for centuries and questioned the nature of the universe and man's place in it. This spirit of questioning in the Western world occurred on many fronts—in religion and philosophy and political theory, in art and literature, and in science. One important result was the expression in the Declaration of Independence and the Bill of Rights of the Constitution of the idea of individual personal, political, and intellectual freedom as controlling in an organized society. The same forces that liberated men politically, and in other ways, also produced the scientific method. With the growth of freedom of inquiry and the development of techniques for discovery, there began an acceleration of our ideas about nature. And the knowledge gained became highly significant when translated by technologists into tools.

Through our privileged perspective we can see that, given the conditions of the last five centuries, everything that has happened has been virtually inevitable. For the achievement by men of the right to search for truth was the critical breakthrough. When this right was established on a continuing basis, it was only a matter of time until bacteria were discovered, electricity was identified, and nuclear fission was revealed. In a word, modern scientific knowledge and its application are a consequence of the vigorous exercise of the freedoms that arose in Western Europe and America.

G. T. Seaborg [31]

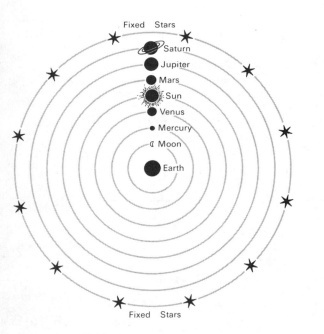

2.4   The Ptolemaic universe.

tended into the earth and provided a physical location for hell (illustration 2.5).

The Ptolemaic universe was invested with meaning as well as being a satisfying physical entity. It was divided into two main sections, an interior sphere for man and a larger, exterior celestial realm. The earth and sublunar space was the abode of man; it was a region of change and often of decay. Beyond this were the revolving crystalline spheres to which the planets, including the moon, were attached, and still further out were the fixed stars, "the flaming ramparts of the universe" as described by the Roman poet Lucretius. In contrast to the earth and sublunar space, this outer region was characterized by immutability, with each orbiting planet and each sphere governed, in the Greek view, by one of their many gods, and, in the Christian view, by a hierarchy of angels. The imaginative Greeks had added two additional spheres beyond the fixed stars: the Primum Mobile, the source of all motion for the inner, orbiting planets, and beyond that, the Empyrean Heavens, the permanent residence of their gods. There was consequently no need to explain the motion of the planets; it was sufficient to know that it was imparted to them by the Primum Mobile. The postulated existence of the Empyrean Heavens interposed a reasonable and comfortable distance between man and his gods.

The Greeks had estimated the visible universe to be about 125 million miles in diameter. Al Fargani, the ninth-century Arabian astronomer, had placed the fixed stars about 75 million miles distant. As Alexander Koyré [22] explains it, the universe "was sufficiently big not to be felt as built to man's measure," its size being more befitting that of the gods. But this did not diminish the significance of the earth

A new course is charted

believed to be located immobile at its center. The earth was different from the celestial regions in character and permanence, but it was still, in the eyes of man, "the reason for which the rest was made." By way of contrast, we now know that the nearest star to earth, Proxima Centauri, is 4 light years distant, a light year being 6 trillion miles.

Even the introduction of the epicycle by Hipparchus could not bring complete order into astronomical charts, and as time went on epicycles were added to epicycles. There were approximately eighty of them in the Ptolemaic universe in addition to the major deferents. The exterior sphere of the two-sphered universe was becoming crowded, and the universe of the ancients was in danger of collapse under the burden of improvisations. It was the patchwork complexity of this universe that disturbed the neat, mathematical mind of Copernicus, and he was to bring about a major modification of the system by the simple expedient of exchanging the position of the sun and the earth (illustration 2.6). In doing so, he brought about a revolution in ideas, based upon the "minutiae of astronomical research," and the world of man has never looked the same since that time.

Copernicus was not a rebel in the sense that the Florentine humanists were, or that Galileo, who followed him, was to become. Neither was he, as Thomas Carlyle was to say of Francis Bacon, "in converse with this universe at first hand." He contributed but few observations of his own; rather, his working materials were the astronomical data compiled by those who preceded him. Copernicus was a canon in the Church of Poland and a mathematician rather than an astronomer, and his object was not to revolutionize but to simplify, to render more orderly the astronomy of this day. The inconsistencies in a system built up by cen-

2.5 Dante's Hell.

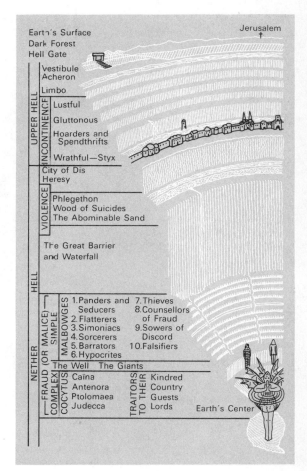

Galileo Galilei.

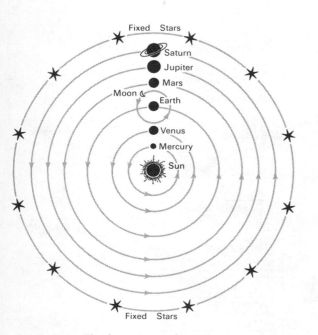

2.6　*The Copernican universe.*

First we must remark that the universe is spherical in form, partly because this form being a perfect whole requiring no joints, is the most complete of all, partly because it makes the most capacious form, which is best suited to contain and preserve everything; or again because all the constituent parts of the universe, that is the sun, moon, and the planets appear in this form; or because everything strives to attain this form, as appears in the case of drops of water and other fluid bodies if they attempt to define themselves. So no one will doubt that this form belongs to the heavenly bodies.

N. Copernicus [12]

turies of astronomical accretions of various sorts and the practical necessity of developing a reliable calendar based on celestial phenomena were sufficient reasons for reconsidering and recomputing, over a period of 30 years, the passage of the sun and the planets through the heavens. Although he was by temperament more of a Scholastic and an Aristotelian than a true man of the Renaissance, Copernicus lived, however, in an age when the old notions of geography, politics, and cultures were yielding to newer visions and broader horizons. And when old ideas in one area of thought or experience are successfully challenged, it is easier similarly to attack old ideas in another realm of thought.

Judged, as he should be, within the circumstances of his own century, Copernicus was an innovator who had the capacity to examine meticulously and to recreate new images. He was a genius who could look at old, familiar patterns, penetrate to their essence, and suddenly discern a new import, a fresh direction to follow. Unknowingly, he made reasonable the hope that the mysteries of the heavens could be understood by man in physical and tangible terms. Despite his conservatism, Copernicus was clearly aware of what he was proposing as the new astronomy, and what its reception was likely to be. He was prepared for the rejection of his ideas at the same time that he was equally prepared to defend them on the basis of mathematical consistency. But as he more or less expected, his book, published in the year he died, created no immediate stir; dedicated to Pope Paul III, it was fully understandable only to a handful of mathematicians like himself. Most of the contemporary astronomers were not sufficiently well versed in mathematics to realize the full impact of his ideas. It would remain for others who followed him to expose the meaning of his ideas, and thus to cause a profound shift in the direction of scientific thought. In fact, it was not until 1616 that the Church, now keenly aware of the incompatibility between Copernicanism and the biblical account of the fall and redemption of man, placed *De revolutionibus* on the *Index liborum prohibitorum*, the list of books that the Roman Catholic Church prohibited its members from reading.

In transposing the positions of the sun and the earth, proposing thereby a heliocentric universe as a replacement for the older, geocentric one of Ptolemy, and in claiming that the earth not only rotates on its axis but also makes an annual orbit of the sun, Copernicus introduced a number of innovations. The earth was now a moving planet, losing its pristine uniqueness, and the moon became a planet of the earth, not of the sun. The five major planetary epicycles were shown to be superfluous, and the temporal irregularities of the planets in their passage around the ecliptic were explained. Retrograde motion was demonstrated to be an apparent, not a real, motion, an illusion to an observer on one revolving sphere watching the movements of another sphere as both circle the sun in different orbits and at different speeds (illustration 2.7). Copernicus, however, did not move the earth far off center; common sense observations of the heavens demanded that the earth be somewhat centralized. Only Venus and Mercury—the inferior planets—lay between the sun and the earth. Displacement of the earth required a somewhat larger universe than that previously calculated, but Copernicus's world was still bounded by the fixed stars, and the orbits of the planets remained perfectly spherical. Copernicus, furthermore, did not concern himself

2.7   The true explanation of retrograde motion, in this case of Mars. Both Earth and Mars move around the sun in an eastward direction, but because their orbits and orbital speeds are different, Mars seems to move in a westward direction at times. As the diagram shows, this motion is only apparent.

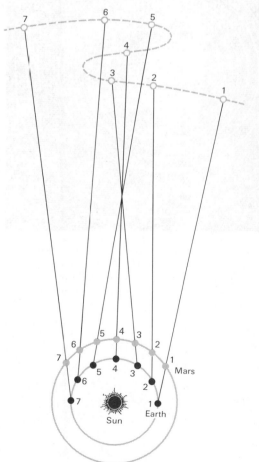

Why was it, then, that a century after [Copernicus's] death his work became the centre of one of the most violent intellectual controversies that the world has known? The reason was that, though apparently simple and harmless, it in fact gave the death-blow to the whole medieval system of thought, for it touched that system at its most vital spot. It is hard for us to realise today, when so many quite dissimilar departments of knowledge surround us on all sides, that medieval thought was essentially a unity. The subjects we know as astronomy, physics, chemistry, theology, psychology, physiology, and so on, were then all fused together in a single system. Above the outermost sphere of astronomy was the heaven of theology, pictured in the same diagram. The stars were not remote globes of gas; they affected men's temperaments and to some extent controlled their destinies. The planets had affinities with the earthly metals. Human bodies represented the universe on a smaller scale.

H. Dingle [*13*]

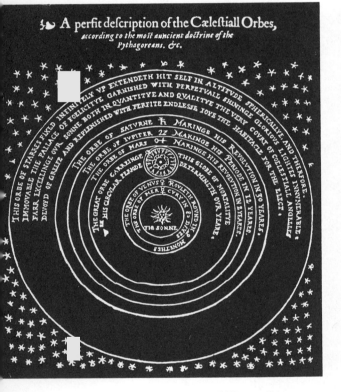

2.8 *The infinite universe of Thomas Digges. Digges broke the circle of fixed stars that Copernicus had set up as the border of the universe and proposed instead that the universe was infinite in extent.*

with ideas of motion other than to state that it is the natural function of perfect spheres to rotate.

The Copernican system was a conceptual vision and was of no greater practical use to the everyday astrologer or navigator than was the Ptolemaic system, which it sought to displace. The new system was exciting to those men who used these theories and concepts as the springboard to further experimentation and discovery. Thomas Digges (d. 1595) and Giordano Bruno (1548–1600), the latter to die at the stake for his beliefs, took the closed world of Copernicus and expanded it into an infinitely open system, thereby destroying the celestial spheres and initiating an erosion of heaven (illustration 2.8). Johann Kepler (1571–1630), who in his search for the harmony and music of the spheres (heard only within his soul) had rejected the idea of an infinite universe, elongated the planetary orbits into ellipses and formulated the basic laws of planetary motion, altering thereby the beautiful sphericity of both the Ptolemaic and Copernican universe. Galileo used his telescope—the first truly scientific instrument for extending the senses—to open up a new world of science, demonstrated the validity of the Copernican concept through his study of the phases of Venus (illustration 2.9) and the moons of Jupiter, and showed that sensory appearance could be deceiving and that it is our own limitations of perceptions and reason that place boundaries around our world. Isaac Newton (1642–1727) demonstrated that the forces of gravitation linked all material bodies in an immense universe and showed that these bodies moved in accordance with strict mathematical laws and that in things diverse—the fall of an apple, the trajectory of a cannon ball, and the motion of a planet—there existed a beautiful unity. God was still

A new course is charted

	Mean Distance from the Sun, Astronomical Units	Length of Year, Earth Units	Rotation, Earth Units	Equatorial Diameter, Kilometers (1 Kilometer = 0.62 Mile)	Mass, Earth = 1
Sun	—	—	25–35 days	1,390,000	332,000
Moon	1.00	365.26 days	27.3 days	3,475	0.012
Mercury	0.39	87.97 days	58.64 days	4,830	0.05
Venus	0.72	224.70 days	243 days	12,108	0.82
Earth	1.00	365.26 days	23.9 hours	12,750	1.00
Mars	1.52	686.98 days	24.6 hours	6,800	0.11
Jupiter	5.20	11.86 years	9.93 hours	143,000	317.8
Saturn	9.54	29.46 years	10.23 hours	121,000	95.1
Uranus	19.18	84.02 years	10.8 hours	47,000	14.5
Neptune	30.06	164.79 years	15.3 hours	45,000	17.2
Pluto	39.5	248.4 years	6.39 days	6,000 (?)	0.8 (?)

The planetary constants as known today.

the Creator, but he had a thorough knowledge of mathematics and engineering.

Gone was the comfortable, finite, two-sphered universe in which man occupied a central position. Man might still exercise dominion over his earth, but the earth was now but another planet, no different apparently from the others,

2.9 Galileo strengthened the Copernican view of the universe by explaining that the phases of Venus, which he had observed through his telescope, depend on the relative positions of Earth and Venus as both orbit the sun.

What I prophesied twenty-two years ago, as soon as I found the heavenly orbits were of the same number as the five (regular) solids, what I fully believed long before I had seen Ptolemy's Harmonies, what I promised my friends in the name of this book [*Harmony of the World*, 1619] which I christened before I was sixteen years old, I urged as an end to be sought, that for which I joined Tycho Brahe, for which I settled at Prague, for which I have spent most of my life at astronomical calculations—at last I have brought to light, and seen to be true beyond my fondest hopes. It is not eighteen months since I saw the first ray of light, three months since the unclouded sun-glorious sight burst upon me. Let nothing confine me: I will indulge my sacred ecstasy. I will triumph over mankind by the honest confession that I have stolen the golden vases of the Egyptians to raise a tabernacle for my God far away from the lands of Egypt. If you forgive me, I rejoice; if you are angry, I cannot help it. The book is written; the die is cast. Let it be read now or by posterity, I care not which. It may well wait a century for a reader, as God had waited six thousand years for an observer.

J. Kepler [21]

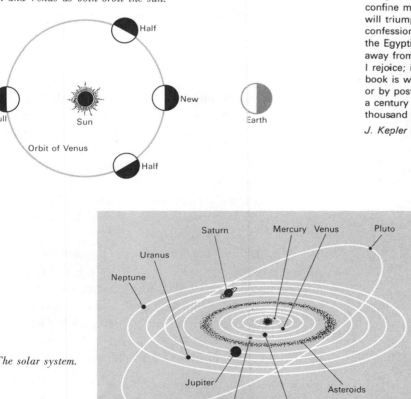

2.10   The solar system.

Is it not evident, in these last hundred years (when the study of philosophy has been the business of all Virtuosi in Christendom), that almost a new Nature has been revealed to us?—that more errors of the school have been detected, more useful experiments in philosophy have been made, more noble secrets in optics, medicine, anatomy, astronomy, discovered, than in all those doting ages from Aristotle to us?—so true it is, that nothing spreads more fast than science, when rightly and generally cultivated. . . .

I am sufficiently sensible of my weakness; and it is not very probable that I should succeed in such a project, whereof I have not had the least hint from any of my predecessors, the poets. . . . Yet we see the art of war is improved in sieges, and new instruments of death are invented daily; something new in philosophy and the mechanics is discovered almost every year; and the science of former ages is improved by the succeeding.

I hope I shall not be thought arrogant when I enquire into their errors [i.e., the errors of the ancients]. For we live in an age so sceptical, that as it determines little, so it takes nothing from antiquity on trust; and I profess to have no other ambition in this *Essay,* than that poetry may not go backward, when all other arts and sciences are advancing.

J. Dryden [*16*]

2.11 *The title page of the first edition of Vesalius's* De humani corporis fabrica.

revolving ceaselessly in a space that knew no bounds. Man's divinity had been diminished.

Among the small, but growing group of seventeenth-century thinkers, Blaise Pascal (1623–1662) most appreciated the significance of the new discoveries and described man's new status in poignant terms. Pascal recognized, however, that if man was diminished in this newly found world, there were compensations. Man gained stature in his own eyes, a stature acquired by reason of his success as an observer and as a conceptualizer and by virtue of his newly found knowledge that he, and he alone, was to be the judge of the nature of reality.

The influence of Vesalius

In no small measure, but for entirely different reasons, Vesalius was also to contribute to a strengthening of man's confidence in himself as an observer, and he shares with Copernicus the honor to have consolidated, in book form, the spirit of inquiry and the pleasure of discovery that characterized the developing sciences and that distinguished them so vividly from the practices of the ancients and medievalists who valued ideas so highly that they ignored even the obvious fact.

It would be difficult to imagine two men of the sixteenth century who contrasted more sharply than Copernicus and Vesalius, a contrast that includes not only their personal lives but also their mode of scholarship, the character of their two books, and the impact that each had on succeeding generations. They are similar in that they both were transitional figures, each bound by the prevailing, but for each

Des fanguicus blůt
Go.xxx. iarn ein mã
So man das erwelen důt
Das felbbig fol man hon

An illustration from H. Brunschwig's Pestbuch (1500). The seated man is being bled while an attendant holds his arm.

National Library of Medicine

---

different, forms of authoritarianism, yet each unknowingly opening separate doors that would lead to the scientific revolution of the seventeenth century and eventually to the present age of science. Each would contribute substantially to the developing natural history of man.

Copernicus was a dying man when his book was published in 1543. His book was the product of 30 years of laborious mathematics, written largely in obscurity, and concerned with the removal of internal consistencies in prevailing astronomical thought. It was an exercise in conceptualization. In it Copernicus looked at data from a different vantage point and dealt with ideas rather than with new observations. Insofar as the natural history of man is concerned, it seriously disturbed the interrelatedness of theology and astronomy and was to widen the crack that eventually separated science from philosophy and made the former into a distinct discipline.

When his book was published, Vesalius was 29 years of age, a young, popular, and ambitious lecturer in medical anatomy at the University of Padua. Although teaching in an environment where criticism and analysis of the ancients were openly practiced, Vesalius, nevertheless, was not free from the authoritarianism of Galen and of Avicenna (980–1037), the Arabic scholar who further popularized Hellenistic medicine. As Vesalius wrote: "I cannot sufficiently marvel at my own stupidity, I who have so laboured in my love for Galen that I have never demonstrated the human head without that of a lamb or ox, to show in the latter what I could not find in the former."

De fabrica is, in a modern context, a descriptive textbook on human anatomy. Its significance today is not in the text as such, which tended to follow previous writings and,

It is difficult to fathom the real nature of Vesalius's contribution, for one can scarcely imagine why the world had to wait so long for a man who could write down what his eyes perceived. Vesalius was not the first to dissect the human body. Dissection and the witnessing of surgery became part of the curriculum of the Italian medical schools as early as the eleventh century, and by the middle of the thirteenth century the practice was fairly well organized in the universities of Salerno, Bologna, and Padua. One might suppose that the misleading errors of Galen could have easily been corrected by several hundred years of firsthand dissecting experience. But though the old editions of Galen became encrusted with marginalia, the medieval respect for classical authority knew no limit. Progress, it seems, was not to take place.

W. Beck [5]

A new course is charted

Now there had been executed on that spot a noted robber, who, since he deserved more than ordinary hanging, had been chained to the top of a high stake and roasted alive. He had been roasted by a slow fire made of straw, that was kept burning at some distance below his feet. In that way there had been a dish cooked for the fowls of heaven, which was regarded by them as a special dainty. The sweet flesh of the delicately roasted thief they had preferred to any other; his bones, therefore, had been elaborately picked, and there was left suspended on the stake a skeleton dissected out, and cleaned by many beaks with rare precision. The dazzling skeleton, complete and clean, was lifted up on high before the eyes of the anatomist, who had been striving hitherto to piece together such a thing out of the bones of many people, gathered as occasion offered. This was a flower to be plucked from its tall stem.

Mounting upon the shoulders of his friend, and aided by him from below, young Andreas ascended the charred stake, and tore away whatever bones he found accessible, breaking the ligaments which tied the legs and arms to the main trunk. The trunk itself was bound by iron chains so firmly to the stake, that it was left there hanging. With stolen bones under their clothes, the two young men returned to Louvain.

But in the evening Vesalius went out alone to take another walk, did not return in haste, and suffered the town gates to close against him. He had resolved to spend the night afield under the stars; while honest men were sleeping in their beds, he meant to share the vigil of the thieves. There was the trunk of the skeleton yet to be had. At midnight none would dare to brave the spectacle of fleshly horrors, to say nothing of such ghostly accidents as might befall them among corpses of the wicked, under rain, moon, stars, or flitting night clouds.

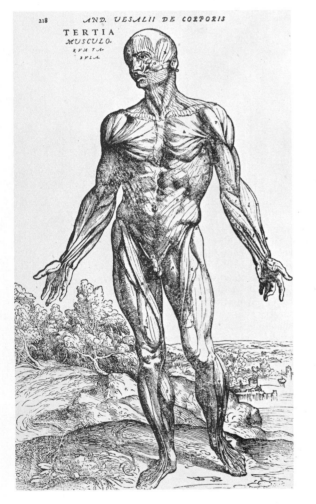

2.12   An illustration from De fabrica.

indeed, perpetuated some of the older errors, but rather in the character of the illustrations, reputedly done by a student of Titian, which required minute attention to detail to ensure accuracy (illustration 2.12). It is in the illustrations that Vesalius's powers of observation, freshly reinforced from work at the dissecting tables, were graphically recorded, gradually revealing the discrepancies existing between what was supposed to be as opposed to what the eye could actually see. Galen and Avicenna were apparently discouraged, if not actually prevented, from carrying out free dissection of the human body by the strictures of society, but Vesalius, in the freedom of Renaissance Padua, had no such imposed restrictions. *De fabrica* did not add a single new conception to the body of science, but it contributed immensely in observational detail.

It is of some interest to point out that the naturalistic movement in art, the desire to depict the actual rather than the idealized figure, played a significant role in the advancement of science, with Vesalius a beneficiary. The works of Leonardo da Vinci, Raphael, and Michelangelo reveal this trend. It is probable that they all performed illicit dissections; there is, in fact, a suggestion in Michelangelo's writings that he did a bit of grave robbing to secure corpses for dissection. The interest of these artists was primarily in surface anatomy, but they fully realized that the underlying musculature and bone structure contributed to visible appearances. Furthermore, improvements in the art of making woodcuts demanded similar improvements in minute detail, and there seems little doubt that this artistic trend, coupled with the improved art of printing, had its influence on the preparation of anatomical drawings in Vesalius's text; at least the drawings were often more accurate than the text.

A new course is charted

Certain, therefore, that no man would come to witness his offence, Vesalius at midnight again climbed the tree to gather its remaining blossom. By main force he deliberately wrested the whole set of bones out of the grasp of the great iron fetters, and then having removed his treasure to a secret spot, he buried it. In the morning he returned home empty-handed. At leisure then, and carefully, he smuggled through the gates, day after day, bone after bone. But when the perfect skeleton was set up in his own house he did not scruple to display it openly, and to demonstrate from it, giving out that it had been brought by him to Louvain from Paris. The act of plunder was, however, too bold to escape attention. Vesalius afterwards was banished from Louvain for this offence.

H. Morley [26]

The second edition of *De fabrica* also shows that Vesalius was growing more confident in his capacity of an observer. As the errors of the past were being revealed and corrected, the authority of the past was being inevitably undermined.

The influence of William Harvey

In his 1906 Harveian oration, Sir William Osler said that "By no single event in the history of science is the growth of truth, through slow states of acquisition, the briefer period of latent possession, and the for us glorious period of conscious possession, better shown than in the discovery of the circulation of the blood."

Osler was referring principally to the discoveries of William Harvey, the Padua-trained, English physician who was not only the father of modern human physiology, but also the one who broke the back of Galenic authoritarianism. Whether Osler's sweeping generalization can be accepted without qualification is a moot point, but the story of the discovery of the circulation of blood serves a purpose here in a number of ways. First, it epitomizes that amalgam of talents—rarely found in any single individual—needed to bring about the solution of any complex problem. Second, it involves the art of conceptualization encountered in Copernican thought, that is, the ability to see old problems with fresh eyes and from other points of view, with the result that new avenues to discovery are opened up. Third, it is tied in closely with that Vesalian "converse with nature at first hand" that leads to the factual details that support or refute any conceptualization. Finally, it involves the experimental approach that was distinctly Harveian. William

It was a humanist of the stamp of Leon Battista Alberti who launched the notion that a "scientific conception of art" was the basis by which mathematics (i.e., theory of proportions and theory of perspective) is the common ground of the painter and scientist: "I would like a painter to be as learned as he can in all the liberal arts, but first I desire that he know geometry. Our rough sketches from which is expressed all the perfect art of painting, will be easily understood by the geometer, but he who is ignorant of geometry will not understand those nor any other method of painting: consequently I affirm that it is necessary that a painter undertake the study of geometry." Painting is a science, and the perspective view used by painters, is also a science: "Hence painting would be naught else but the intersection of the visual pyramid, according to a given distance, once the center is situated and the lighting established with lines and colors in a certain surface artificially represented."

P. Rossi [30]

Thus far I have spoken of the passages of the blood from the veins into the arteries, and of the manner in which it is transmitted and distributed by the action of the heart; points to which some, moved either by the authority of Galen or Columbus, or the reasonings of others, will give in their adhesion. But what remains to be said upon the quantity and source of the blood which thus passes, is of so novel and unheard-of character, that I not only fear injury to myself from the envy of the few, but I tremble lest I have mankind at large for my enemies, so much doth wont and custom, that become as another nature, and doctrine once sown and that hath struck deep root, and respect for antiquity influence all men: Still the die is cast, and my trust is in my love of truth, and the candour that inheres in cultivated minds.

W. Harvey [20]

Galen's career presents a unique phenomenon in the history of science and one perhaps unique in cultural history as a whole. Nearly every exhibition of human activity seems to go through a process of development, flowering, and decline. The Ancients, even the most scientific of them, were not generally great hands at experiment, and Galen represents the climax and flower of the experimental spirit in antiquity, certainly so far as the biological disciplines are concerned. He brought experimental physiology to a very high standard indeed, but he was quite without successors. There is no fading out of physiological activity. It simply disappears. Yet Galen was no solitary worker; he was constantly demonstrating his experiments to large audiences of colleagues and he had many pupils, but he had no followers or imitators. Ancient science fell dead with Galen.

C. Singer [*35*]

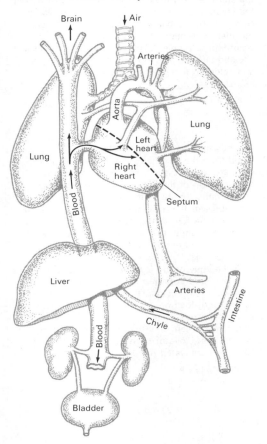

2.13 The Galenic view of circulation.

Brain

Air

Arteries

Aorta

Lung

Left heart

Right heart

Lung

Blood

Septum

Liver

Arteries

Intestine

Chyle

Blood

Bladder

Harvey was a problem solver. He was able to see a particular problem in isolation, to pose possible answers, and to develop a planned experiment to test alternative hypotheses. Coupled with these modes of thought, and indeed inherent in them, was the ability to ask the kind of question of nature, freed from philosophical import, for which reasonable answer was possible. Such questions will always yield answers limited in their applicability, but because the answers are verifiable within the limits of the techniques available, they provide the stepping stones to further advances.

The problem of circulation was an involved one and was concerned with the roles of the liver, heart, and lungs as operative parts of the system and with the character of venous and arterial blood. The anatomy of these organs, including the valves in the blood vessels, was well known even if their function was not. Harvey was to add no significantly new anatomical information bearing on the problem, although he stressed the need to study all animals and their functions in order to appreciate and understand the human body. The Galenic view of circulation (illustration 2.13) was that it was an ebb-and-flow phenomenon and that the venous and arterial systems were separate and distinct from each other. According to Galen a flow of materials from the stomach and intestines, consisting mainly of digested food (chyle), passed through the portal vein to the liver, where the chyle was transformed into blood. The liver, in the Galenic view, was therefore a "first heart," which produced blood. The blood then passed through the hepatic vein to the *vena cava* (now known to be the main venous vessel leading to the heart) and was distributed by two branches to the upper and lower parts of the body. Because the stomach and intestines also had need for his newly

A new course is charted

Galen.

formed blood, enriched by "natural spirits" in the liver, the portal vein carried blood from the liver to the stomach at certain times of the day. The portal vein, therefore, was viewed as a one-way street, but the direction of flow was determined by the needs of traffic.

When the ascending portion of the *vena cava* reached the thorax, a part of the blood passed into the right side of the heart, the "second heart" in Galenic terms, where a cardiac contraction sent some of it to the lungs, these being large organs needing a substantial supply of blood. The same contraction pushed a part of the blood to the left side of the heart through the septum, a membrane that divided the two parts of the heart and which was said to contain "pores" for the purpose of blood transfer. The liver-venous system was thus a complete unit, with the liver producing the blood from chyle, and the veins distributing this blood to each organ throughout the body. Each organ evaporated the excess blood remaining after its needs were met.

The liver-venous system, which provided nourishment, was not sufficient, however, for proper functioning of the body; a "vital spirit" supplied by the arteries was also required. It was believed that this "vital spirit" was obtained from air taken into the lungs and passed, via the pulmonary vein, to the left side of the heart, where it was mixed with venous blood squeezed through the septum. Arterial blood was then distributed to the organs of the body, including the lungs, where it was either used or evaporated. The lungs, in this view, were a source of "vital spirits," and the left side of the heart was a mixing device in which a small amount of venous blood was converted into arterial blood. The function of respiration was to provide the "vital spirits"

Which motions [of the blood] we may be allowed to call circular, in the same way as Aristotle says that the air and rain emulate the circular motion of the superior bodies; for the moist earth, warmed by the sun, evaporates; the vapours drawn upwards are condensed, and descending in the form of rain, moisten the earth again; and by this arrangement are generations of living things produced; and in like manner too are tempests and meteors engendered by the circular motion, and by the approach and recession of the sun.

And so in all likelihood, does it come to pass in the body, through the motion of the blood; the various parts are nourished, cherished, quickened by the warmer, more perfect, vaporous, spiritous, and, as I may say, alimentive blood; which, on the contrary, in contact with these parts becomes cooled, coagulated, and, so to speak, effete; whence it returns to its sovereign the heart, as if to its source, or to the inmost home of the body, there to recover its state of excellence, or perfection.

Here it resumes its due fluidity and receives an infusion of natural heat—powerful, fervid, a kind of treasury of life, and is impregnated with spirits, and it might be said with balsam; and thence it is again dispersed; and all this depends on the motion and action of the heart.

W. Harvey [20]

A new course is charted

By what way thou art made immortal, know.
Thou art too narrow, wretch, to comprehend
Even thyself, yea, though thou wouldst but bend
To know thy body. Have not all souls thought
For many ages that our body's wrought
Of air and fire and other elements?
And now they think of new ingredients,
And one soul thinks one, and another way
Another thinks, and 'tis an even lay.
Know'st thou but how the stone doth enter in
The bladder's cave and never break the skin?

Know'st thou how blood which to the heart doth flow
Doth from one ventricle to th' other go?
And for the putrid stuff which thou dost spit;
Know'st thou how thy lungs have attracted it?
There are no passages; so that there is
(For ought thou know'st) piercing of substances.
And of those many opinions which men raise
Of nails and hairs, dost thou know which to praise?
What hope have we to know ourselves, when we
Know not the least things which for our use be?

J. Donne [15]

*2.14   The title page of William Harvey's great
work on circulation.*

for the blood on inspiration, and to remove impurities from the venous blood on expiration.

Prior to Harvey, however, the Galenic view had been subject to criticism. The porosity of the septum of the heart was seriously questioned. Vesalius, for example, expressed uncertainty in the first edition of *De fabrica:* "None of these pits penetrate," so far as he could see, "from the right ventricle to the left; therefore, indeed, I was compelled to marvel at the activity of the Creator of things, in that blood should sweat from the right ventricle to the left through passages escaping sight." In the second edition of the same work he took a stronger stand, saying that because he could not find the pores, he doubted their existence and questioned the function of the heart as a mixing device. Andrea Cesalpino (1519–1603) had correctly postulated an outward movement of the blood through the arteries and a return via the veins, with connections between the two systems at their extremities, but his grasp of the entire circulatory system was inadequate to gain acceptance of his views because they were not backed up with convincing and substantiating evidence. Matteo Colombo (1516?–1559), successor to Vesalius at Padua, had also correctly described the passage of blood from the right side of the heart to the lungs, and thence back to the left side of the heart, but he retained, on the other hand, some aspects of the ebb-and-flow concept of Galen. Michael Servetus (1511–1553), a Spanish theologian and physician, had similarly pointed out the course of the "lesser," or pulmonary, circulatory path and had viewed the lungs as the mixing site of venous blood and "vital spirits," but he made the mistake of joining his physiology with his heretical theology, and John Calvin, who liked neither, had him burned at the stake in Geneva.

A new course is charted

The Black Death.

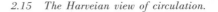

Harvey, like his predecessors, was an empiricist, a practical man of medicine accustomed to making observations and using them as a basis for his decisions. His success in solving as much of the problem of circulation as was possible in his day was due, however, to a number of steps that, in aggregate, were to carry him around a blind corner and allow him to see the problem in a new light. He had, above all else, that happy faculty that all geniuses display, the faculty of selectively remembering those facts that served his purpose while recognizing, however vaguely, the unknown into which he was venturing. He visualized circulation as an isolated problem in hydraulics, the flow of liquids from one place to another; he analyzed the role of each part in the flow system, having what appeared to be a clear notion that the structure and function of an organ must be consistent with each other; he quantified the system of flow as he visualized it; and finally, he tested his hypotheses with simple but convincing experiments, convincing, that is, to himself and his immediate colleagues, although he pointed out—with a surprisingly contemporary view—that he did not expect anyone over 40 years of age to accept his views.

Harvey's explanation of circulation (illustration 2.15) began with the heart and its rhythmical beating. The muscularity of the heart and of the great aorta seemed to him to be more pronounced than would be necessary if their sole purpose were simply to prevent the escape of "vital spirits," as had been suggested. He asserted that it was more likely that the heart was a pumping organ designed to push fluids through a conducting system. He concluded, therefore, that blood was forced out of the heart during systole (contraction), that it filled up during diastole (expansion), and, further, that the essential function of the heart was

2.15   The Harveian view of circulation.

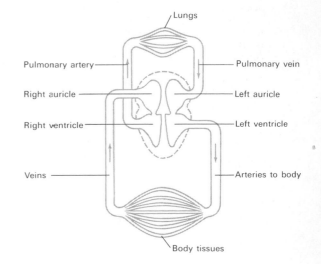

Macabre beauty of the skeleton
   Endures his lonely inquest, head to foot:
Flexions, articulations, one by one
   He tries as sensitively as his lute.
The silverpoint states very preciously
   Pronation, supination, what you will:
Of bones like finely carved ivory
   It redes the riddle with a Chinese skill.
Like dahlia-flowers most implicate and rich
   The intimate clots of life he can expose,
Even the poor heart, so vulnerable, which
   He draws as delicately as a rose—
Then, smiling, lets his sinister hand unglove,
   Startling, bizarre, the Anatomy of Love.

R. Taylor [38]

. . . if any individual desire, and is anxious not merely to adhere to, and make use of, present discoveries, but to penetrate still further, and not to overcome his adversaries in disputes, but nature by labor, not in short to give elegant and specious opinions, but to know to a certainty and demonstration, let him, as a true son of science (if such be his wish), join with us; that when he has left the antechambers of nature trodden by the multitude, an entrance may at last be discovered to her inner apartments. And in order to be better understood, and to render our meaning more familiar by assigning determinate names, we have accustomed ourselves to call the one method the anticipation of the mind, and the other the interpretation of nature.

. . . Yet it is but just that we should obtain this favor from mankind (especially in so great a restoration of learning and the sciences), that whosoever may be desirous of forming any determination upon an opinion of this our work either from his own perceptions, or the crowd of authorities, or the forms of demonstrations, he will not expect to be able to do so in a cursory manner, and whilst attending to other matters; but in order to have a thorough knowledge of the subject, will himself, by degrees, attempt the course which we describe and maintain; will be accustomed to the subtlety of things which is manifested by experience; and will correct the depraved and deeply-rooted habits of his mind by a seasonable, and, as it were, just hesitation: and then, finally (if he will), use his judgment when he has begun to be master of himself.

F. Bacon [3]

the transference of blood from the veins to the arteries. He showed also that the course of blood was from the *vena cava* to the right auricle, thence to the right ventricle, lungs, left auricle, left ventricle, and, finally, aorta. He asserted that venuous blood was exhausted blood that was restored by passage through the lungs, but he could not explain why, for oxygenation had yet to be discovered. The function of the valves in the heart was to prevent backward flow during contraction, the liver played no role in the formation of new blood, and the postulated pores in the septum of the heart were an imagined and unnecessary part of the system. The arterial walls were constructed in a way that made them tough enough to withstand the force of pressure but elastic enough to expand when the blood was forced through. The meaning of the pulse became evident. The walls of the veins were thin because the blood was simply flowing back to the heart, and the valves in the veins were intended to keep the flow unidirectional.

A determination of the volume of blood flowing through the system reinforced his views. Harvey calculated that each time the heart contracted and emptied itself, two ounces of blood was pushed out of the left ventricle and into the main aorta. Because the heart of a man at rest beats seventy-two times a minute, it pumps 144 ounces of blood each minute, 540 pounds each hour, and more than 6 tons each day. It was therefore absurd, when the problem was visualized in this way, to think that the body could produce that much blood in the liver, to be used by the various organs or evaporated. There could be but one answer—the circulatory system was a closed one, the blood circulates in continuous flow, and the heart keeps the flow moving.

A new course is charted

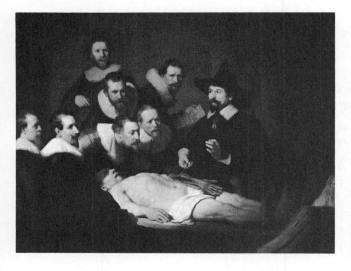

Rembrandt, The Anatomy Lesson.

The auricles are loading pumps for the ventricles, and the ventricles are forcing pumps that send blood either through the lungs or out into the arteries.

Harvey's logic, moving from inference to inference and bolstered by quantitative considerations, seems irrefutable, but he was well aware of the fact that a similar use of logic had also established the Galenic view of circulation, and he knew this view to be incorrect. Straightforward empiricism was insufficient to establish in the eyes of others the validity of what he so strongly felt to be true. He realized that he had to test his conclusion by performing the convincing experiment. Harvey subscribed to the Baconian rather than to the Galilean view of experimentation. Bacon had stated that "nature should be put to the test," and he viewed an experiment as a means of judging the merits of an idea and as a "remedy for ignorance." Galileo, on the other hand, placed a greater emphasis on the significance of the abstract idea, with the experiment being a useful means of supporting the abstraction, but second in importance to it. Harvey used experimentation for step-by-step confirmation of his inferences, recognizing that each experiment has limited applicability, but that each one provides firm ground for proceeding to the next one.

To test his ideas concerning blood flow and the function of venous valves, Harvey tied a cord about a man's arm, making sure that the cord was sufficiently tight to cut off the flow of blood in the veins but not in the arteries. A doctor or nurse does the same thing today when a blood sample is to be taken. With each beat of the heart, Harvey pointed out, the veins below the cord become more and more distended. The rhythmic beating of the heart, sending

There are and can be only two ways of searching into and discovering truth. The one flies from the senses and particulars to the most general axioms, and from these principles, the truth of which it takes for settled and immoveable, proceeds to judgment and to the discovery of middle axioms. And this way is now in fashion. The other derives axioms from the senses and particulars, rising by a gradual and unbroken ascent, so that it arrives at the most general axioms last of all. This is the true way, but as yet untried. . . .

Those who have handled sciences have been either men of experiment or men of dogmas. The men of experiment are like the ant; they only collect and use; the reasoners resemble spiders, who make cobwebs out of their own substance. But the bee takes a middle course; it gathers its material from the flowers of the garden and of the field, but transforms and digests it by a power of its own. Not unlike this is the true business of philosophy; for it neither relies solely or chiefly on the powers of the mind, nor does it take the matter which it gathers from natural history and mechanical experiments and lay it up in the memory whole, as it finds it; but lays it up in the understanding altered and digested. Therefore from a closer and purer league between these two faculties, the experimental and the rational, (such as has never yet been made) much may be hoped.

F. Bacon [3]

---

blood through the arteries, is also forcing it into the veins; the connection between arteries and veins is, therefore, established. With the flow of blood cut off by the cord, the portion of the vein above the cord collapses. The blood, therefore, does not flow back toward the heart at any time through the arteries, nor did it flow from the veins into the arteries; the valves prevented this movement, and their anatomy was such as to permit flow in one direction only. An ebb-and-flow phenomenon was impossible.

There were many questions that remained unanswered in spite of Harvey's experiments. It was not until 30 years later that the Italian anatomist Marcello Malpighi (1628–1694) demonstrated that the arteries and veins were connected by beds of fine capillaries; the microscope would be needed to reveal these fine connections. Still later, Richard Lower (1631–1691), an English physician and physiologist, showed that the heart continued beating only if connected with the nerve that provided a flow of "spirits" to it; the heart was being viewed more and more as a mechanical device.

It might be assumed that Harvey's discoveries, in spite of unanswered questions, would be readily accepted by the medical-biological world, but the canons of taste, scientific or otherwise, are not so readily altered, and the role of experimentation in understanding reality was grasped by only a few men. Harvey's ideas did not, in fact, gain wide acceptance for another quarter of a century. But the seeds of future science had been planted. Even if they were to grow slowly for some time, they had a tenacious hold and were eventually to free themselves from historical and philosophical entanglement.

A new course is charted

And I confess I could heartily wish, that philosophers, and other learned men (whom the rest in time would follow) would by common (though perhaps tacit) consent, introduce some more significant and less ambiguous terms and expressions in the room of the too licenciously abused word nature, and the forms of speech, that depend upon it; or would, at least, decline the use of it as much as conveniently they can; and where they think they must employ it, would add a word or two, to declare in what clear and determinate sense they use it.

R. Boyle [7]

Gateway to the present

Harvey is but one representative, although a most important and central one so far as biology is concerned, of the new breed of seventeenth-century men whose endeavors and attitudes towards themselves and their subject matter made the scientific revolution a reality. Robert Boyle (1627–1691) was equally important in the chemical sciences. It will be well to look backward again, from the vantage point of the accomplishments of Harvey, in order to grasp the change that had taken place and to isolate in some small measure the conditions that promoted or hindered the establishment of science as a legitimate, meaningful, and respected occupation of learned men.

Ancient and medieval science was, without question, subordinate to theology and philosophy as a discipline. This was true in the medieval universities, and even the scientists—the term "scientist" was first coined by the Reverend William Whewell in the nineteenth century—who held chairs in the universities aspired to the more prestigious chairs of philosophy. Students, to be sure, were taught science, or natural philosophy as it was called, but they gained no serious commitment to it as a worthwhile occupation. Botany and zoology, possessing no theoretical base, were adjuncts of medicine, and the Renaissance student of medicine had also to be versed in astrology. The practical worth of science, upon which its continuity would depend, remained to be established as a social need even though Francis Bacon and some of his medieval predecessors had

Once more let it be noted that the relation between a flourishing natural science and the degree of individual or group freedom from legal or moral restraints in a given society is by no means clear and simple. It would be pleasant to hold that there is a direct correlation, the more freedom (as we Americans understand freedom) the greater scientific advancement. Now it is clear, of course, that in a society where all novelty is forbidden there can be no science, since science depends on someone's producing something new. But such despotic societies exist only in imagination, at least in the Western world. The actual record shows that science grew up in a Europe for the most part ruled by absolute monarchs, and that it owed much to the patronage of these monarchs and their ministers. Indeed, as science slowly proved itself useful in adding to man's command of his material environment, the possessing classes were persuaded of its value to themselves, and were delighted to endow and protect scientists. After all, the discovery of the law of gravitation did not endanger in any obvious way their interests. Freedom for scientific investigation is by no means the same thing as freedom for artistic, philosophical, political, or moral experimentation. No doubt scientists need some kinds of freedom, but most of all they need freedom from the dead weight of custom and authority *in their own fields*.

C. Brinton [8]

Cannibal feast in Brazil, an illustration from De Bry's America *published in Frankfurt early in the seventeenth century.*

The scientists of the seventeenth century swept away the miserable universe of death, famine, and torture of human beings in the name of God. They took a world that had been peopled with demons and devils, and that superstition had thronged with unseen terror at every side. They cleansed it with clear words and plain experiment. They found an ethic that advised people to renounce their desires, and to cultivate in a hostile universe the humility which befitted their impotence, and they taught men instead to take pride in their human status, and to dare to change the world into one which would answer more fully to their desires. . . . Empiricism was the expression of a confidence in one's senses; the eyes and ears were no longer evidence of human corruption but trusted avenues to a knowledge of nature. The body was not the tainted seat of ignorance, but the source of pleasures and the means for knowledge. Human energies, hitherto turned against themselves, could reach out beyond concern for exclusive self.

L. A. Feuer [18]

advocated this point of view. Science, even today, is basically a middle-class occupation, and the relative absence of this class of students in the medieval universities and their preference, when opportunity presented itself, for commerce, law, politics, or theology did not encourage the formation of an unencumbered body of knowledge having an intrinsic worth and interest. The privileged amateur or the recipient of princely patronage might engage himself in science, and the growth of trade and navigation and the changing needs of warfare might put a premium on improved technology, but science had not yet acquired an air of respectibility. The time was not yet ripe when, as Blaise Pascal in his *Pensees* was to state, "simple workmen [would be] capable of convicting of error all great men who are called philosophers." The value of the simple fact, discovered, understood, verified, and acted upon by man, was not yet appreciated as a step towards a broader generalization.

Furthermore, an open-ended society would be a necessary condition for the development of science. There had to be developed what Lewis Feuer [18] has called an "ethic of freedom," a "liberation of curiosity," which would alter men's view toward nature and give men the joy of discovery, the mastery of control, and the sense of intellectual competition that is so often the spur to further discoveries. The Renaissance, of course, contributed to this ethic of freedom with its emphasis on learning. So did the Protestant Reformation, which broke the authority of the Roman church in northern Europe and then never consolidated its own form of authority because of diverse and individual interpretations of sacred writings. And so too did the discoveries in the Age of Reconnaissance, which so vastly broadened and enriched the world for man.

A new course is charted

This said, the whole assembly gave consent
To drawing up th'authentic Instrument,
And, for the nation's gen'ral satisfaction,
To print and own it in their next Transaction:
But while their ablest men were drawing up
The wonderful memoir o'th'telescope,
A member peeping in the tube by chance,
Beheld the Elephant begin t'advance,
That from the west-by-north side of the Moon
To th'east-by-south was in a moment gone.

. . .

But when, at last, they had unscrew'd the glass
To find out where the sly imposter was,
And saw 'twas but a Mouse, that by mishap
Had catch'd himself, and them, in th'optic trap,

S. Butler [11]

The new spirit of freedom and curiosity in science in the seventeenth century is best reflected, perhaps, in the founding and proliferation of new academies of learning. These were not connected with either the churches or the universities, but became, in essence, competing institutions that brought together men of common interests who sought pleasure in the advancement of knowledge, who gained stimulation from a discussion of ideas, and who competed, often acrimoniously, with one another for new discoveries. Galileo was the fifth member of the *Accademia dei Lincei* in Rome, whose patron was a naturalist of noble birth; other institutions included the *Accademia dei Cimento* of Florence, which numbered Evangelista Torricelli (1608–1647) discoverer of the vacuum barometer, among its members, and which not only brought men together for a discussion of Galilean thought, but also established a priority of problems in physics to be solved experimentally; the French *Académie Royale des Sciences*, founded in 1666 by Jean Baptiste Colbert (1619–1683), a society that required its members to be "curious about natural things, medicine, mathematics, the liberal arts, and mechanics"; and the *Royal Society of London for Improving Natural Knowledge*, which was founded earlier but was formally chartered by Charles II in 1662. Listed among its early members were many notables. Newton was its president from 1703 until his death in 1727; Robert Hooke (1635–1703), the discoverer of cells, was its first secretary and principal demonstrator; Christopher Wren (1632–1723) the architect of St. Paul's Cathedral, delivered one of the first lectures on astronomy; John Evelyn (1620–1706) the diarist, composed its motto; and the poet John Dryden (1631–1700) helped to formulate the rules for simple scientific exposition, which

Their [the members of the Royal Society] first purpose was no more, then onely the satisfaction of breathing a freer air, and of conversing in quiet one with another, without being ingag'd in the passions, and madness of that dismal Age. And from the Institution of that *Assembly,* it had been enough, if no other advantage had come, but this: That by this means there was a race of young Men provided, against the next Age, whose minds receiving from them, their first Impressions of *sober* and *generous knowledge,* were invincibly arm'd against all the inchantments of *Enthusiasm.* But what is more, I may venture to affirm, that it was in good measure, by the influence, which these Gentlemen had over the rest, that the University it self, or at least, any part of its Discipline, and Order, was sav'd from ruine. And from hence we may conclude, that the same Men have now no intention, of sweeping away all the honor of Antiquity in this their new Design: seeing they imploy'd so much of their labor, and prudence, in preserving that *most venerable Seat* of antient Learning, when their shrinking from its defence, would have been the speediest way to have destroy'd it. . . . Their purpose, is, in short, to make faithful *Records,* of all the Works of *Nature,* or *Art,* which can come within their reach: that so the present Age, and posterity, may be able to put a mark on the Errors, which have been strengthened by long prescription; to restore the Truths, that have lain neglected; to push on those, which are already known, to more various uses: and to make the way more passable to what remains unreveal'd.

T. Sprat [36]

A new course is charted

. . . If one reads Sprat's *History of the Royal Society* carefully, it becomes clear that Sprat was commissioned to write it by members of the Society, greatly concerned with the public attitude toward their scientific work. They were clearly less worried about the attitude of men of religion than they were about the "Restoration Wits." . . . On the surface, Charles II, who had chartered the Society, remained its patron, but behind the scenes his attitude was different. Pepys tells of an evening when the King attended an aristocratic party and spent an hour and a half laughing at the Virtuosi. Why? Because, said His Majesty, those silly men had spent their time, ever since their foundation, in "weighing the air," and doing nothing else. . . . On the stage too were sly digs at the absurdities of the new science, culminating a few years later in the comedy of Shadwell's *Virtuoso,* the most extensive, drastic, and amusing stage criticism of the Royal Society in which the name character, Sir Nicholas Gimcrack, epitomizes all that seemed absurd in science. He not only weighed the air, but bottled it up and kept it in his wine cellar, like fine champagne, to open in his chamber when he desired a change of climate. Each of Gimcrack's discoveries and experiments had its source in a real experiment or discovery by a member of the Royal Society, as the audience well knew. As Shadwell satirized them, they sound as silly as Boyle's weighing the air did to the King and his courtiers. . . .

M. H. Nicolson [27]

was to be free from high-flown phrases and ambiguities. Two Dutchmen, Christiaan Huygens (1629–1695), who formulated a theory of light, and Antony van Leeuwenhoek (1632–1723), who perfected the microscope, were regular correspondents to the Royal Society, while Huygens was an elected member of the French Academy. Science had early acquired an international aspect, which it continues to retain. The Royal Society also initiated and published its own scientific journal, the *Philosophical Transactions,*

2.16 *The title page and table of contents of the first issue of the* Philosophical Transactions.

PHILOSOPHICAL
TRANSACTIONS:
GIVING SOME
ACCOMPT
OF THE PRESENT
Undertakings , Studies , and Labours
OF THE
INGENIOUS
IN MANY
CONSIDERABLE PARTS
OF THE
WORLD·

Vol I.
For *Anno* 1665, and 1666.

In the *SAVOY,*
Printed by *T. N.* for *John Martyn* at the Bell, a little without *Temple-Bar* , and *James Allestry* in *Duck-Lane*,
Printers to the *Royal Society.*

Presented by the Author May. 30ᵗʰ 1667

(1)   *Numb.* 1.
PHILOSOPHICAL
TRANSACTIONS.

Munday, March 6. 166⁴⁄₅.

The Contents.
An Introduction to this Tract. An Accompt of the Improvement of Optick Glaffes at Rome. *Of the Obfervation made* in England, *of a Spot in one of the Belts of the Planet* Jupiter. *Of the motion of the late Comet predicted. The Heads of many New Obfervations and Experiments, in order to an Experimental* Hiftory *of* Cold; *together with fome* Thermometrical *Difcourfes and Experiments. A Relation of a very odd Monftrous* Calf. *Of a peculiar Lead-Ore in* Germany, *very ufeful for Effays. Of an* Hungarian *Bolus, of the fame effect with the* Bolus Armenus. *Of the New American Whale-fifhing about the* Bermudas. *A Narative concerning the fuccefs of the* Pendulum-watches at Sea *for the* Longitudes ; *and the Grant of a Patent thereupon. A Catalogue of the Philofophical Books publifht by* Monfieur de Fermat, *Counfellour at* Tholoufe, *lately dead.*

The *Introduction.*

Hereas there is nothing more neceffary for promoting the improvement of Philofophical Matters, than the communicating to fuch, as apply their Studies and Endeavours that way, fuch things as are difcovered or put in practife by others ; it is therefore thought fit to employ the *Prefs,* as the moft proper way to. gratifie thofe, whofe engagement in fuch Studies, and delight in the advancement of Learning and profitable Difcoveries, doth entitle them to the knowledge of what this Kingdom, or other parts of the World, do, from time to time, afford, as well

A   of

If any town should engage in rebellion or mutiny, fall into violent factions, or refuse to pay the usual tribute, the King hath two methods of reducing them to obedience. The first and the mildest course is by keeping the island hovering over such a town, and the lands about it, whereby he can deprive them of the benefit of the sun and the rain, and consequently afflict the inhabitants with dearth and diseases. And if the crime deserve it, they are at the same time pelted from above with great stones, against which they have no defence but by creeping into cellars or caves, while the roofs of their houses are beaten to pieces. But if they still continue obstinate, or offer to raise insurrections, he proceeds to the last remedy, by letting the island drop directly upon their heads, which makes a universal destruction both of houses and men.

J. Swift [37]

---

in the 1660s and continues without interruption to do so today (see illustration 2.16). The scientific revolution was truly a mutation in scholarship.

Science today is a social institution supported and encouraged by both public and private sectors of society. It is recognized as the evolving base of national and international economy, prestige, and preeminence and as that force which, if properly controlled and directed, can assist materially in permitting every man to live out his life in dignity, free of want and drudgery. Such visions of utopia have always appeared, miragelike, as man tried to look beyond the present and into the future. Their central theme of idealistic existence is a reflection of the aspirations of the particular age. *The City of God,* written by St. Augustine (354–430), and *Utopia,* by St. Thomas More (1478–1535), depicted societies that were based on religion, while Francis Bacon's *New Atlantis* was one of the first books on which a scientifically based utopia was set forth (see illustration 2.17). The socialization of science, with its implicit promise of utopian progress and its even greater promise of practical worth, the latter made obvious through the improvement of mechanical devices that reduced the labors of the individual while yielding greater profits, had its beginning in the seventeenth century. The role of the academies and their fostering of scientific journals, the new-found ethic of freedom arising from many sources and reflected in diverse literary works of the period, and the expanding industrial and colonial enterprises—all contributed to an environment congenial to the growth of science as an incipient social force.

Because science is but one of many social phenomena, it influences, and in turn is influenced by, the cultural

2.17   *The island of Utopia.*

Gloucester. These late eclipses in the sun and moon portend no good to us: though the wisdom of nature can reason it thus and thus, yet nature finds itself scourged by the sequent effects: love cools, friendship falls off, brothers divide: in cities, mutinies; in countries, discord; in palaces, treason; and the bond cracked 'twixt son and father. This villain of mine comes under the prediction; there's son against father: the king falls from bias of nature; there's father against child. We have seen the best of our time: machinations, hollowness, treachery, and all ruinous disorders, follow us disquietly to our graves. Find out this villain, Edmund; it shall lose thee nothing; do it carefully. And the noble and true-hearted Kent banished! his offence, honesty! 'Tis strange.

Edmund. This is the excellent foppery of the world, that, when we are sick in fortune,—often the surfeit of our own behaviour,—we make guilty of our disasters the sun, the moon, and the stars: as if we were villains by necessity; fools by heavenly compulsion; knaves, thieves, and treachers, by spherical predominance; drunkards, liars, and adulterers, by an enforced obedience of planetary influence; and all that we are evil in, by a divine thrusting on: an admirable evasion of whoremaster man, to lay his goatish disposition to the charge of a star! My father compounded with my mother under the dragon's tail; and my nativity was under Ursa major; so that it follows, I am rough and lecherous. Tut, I should have been that I am, had the maidenliest star in the firmament twinkled on my bastardizing.

W. Shakespeare [32]

The utopian, as thinker, is irrational and logical at the same time. Once he constructs his imaginary commonwealth (sometimes even an imaginary world with laws of physics different from ours), once he takes the big leap into another system of thought, he proceeds with strict logic, leaving nothing to chance. His human beings behave, or are made to behave, like automata; the organization of their lives never changes as they perform with clocklike precision the tasks assigned by the central authority. Precisely because he has established his own fundamental thought-system, the utopian thinker's people are no longer bound by human nature and its rich variations as we know human nature; the utopian has authorized himself to deal with his *dramatis personae* much more freely than a novelist or a playwright. His characters, their umbilical cord with mother earth and ordinary humanity severed, are puppets, quasi-zombies, lacking historical dimension, bereft of freedom and choice.

T. Molnar [25]

circumstances in which it is rooted. In this sense, it is not appreciably different from a biological mutation whose expression is determined by the genetic background in which it arises. An examination of the field of literature can perhaps provide a reasonable index of the temper of the times and can reveal the changing patterns of thought and expression through a study of the use and style of language, the ideas being explored, and the subject matter discussed. Through literature, the evolving views of man on man are most clearly revealed. Mention has already been made of *The Divine Comedy*, with its pre-Copernican concept of the celestial universe linked with a mirror-image of earthly spheres extending inward until hell is reached at the earth's center. Dante had no visions of the new cosmology to be; his world was spherical and finite, and the realm of Heaven was known. One might normally suppose that a good deal of the new thinking would be reflected in at least some of the plays and sonnets of William Shakespeare (1564–1616), but, oddly enough, he was apparently unconcerned with these changes taking place in science around him. Hamlet, Macbeth, Gloucester, and Lear might search for guidance from the stars or place the onus for their lot on the heavens, but so too did every other man of that time. However, some of Shakespeare's characters, for example, Edmund in *King Lear*, take a more scientific attitude. Nevertheless, Shakespeare was more concerned with the audience seated before his stage, and the daily lives of people, real or imagined, was of more importance to them than the retrograde motions of the planets or the rotation of the earth.

It was John Donne (1573–1631) who saw more clearly than most of his contemporaries the significance of the new discoveries to the meaning of man. The richness of his poetic

A new course is charted

And new Philosophy calls all in doubt,
The Element of fire is quite put out;
The Sun is lost, and th'earth, and no man's wit
Can well direct him where to looke for it.
And freely men confesse that this world's spent,
When in the Planets, and the Firmament
They seeke so many new; then see that this
Is crumbled out againe to his Atomies.
'Tis all in peeces, all cohaerance gone;
All just supply, and all Relation.

J. Donne [*14*]

Tavern and coffeehouse around 1700.

---

language and allegorical symbolism is similar to that of Shakespeare and of John Milton (1608–1674), but he differed sharply from Shakespeare in exhibiting a remarkable sensitivity to the new astronomical ideas of the day. The discovery of two new stars during Donne's lifetime had disturbed the tranquility of the fixed heavens, and Galileo's writings had stirred his restless imagination. His philosophical reaction was one of deep doubt. He saw the comfortable certainty of the here and the hereafter, with its proportionate order and unity and its immutable heavens, shattered by Copernicus and Galileo, and he knew intuitively that man's place in the scheme of things would never be the same. Like Pascal, he also saw the role of man in the infinities of space significantly diminished, but cleric though he was, he could not, as did Pascal, dismiss the relevancies of science and continue to find unquestioned certainty in a Christian faith:

Doubt wisely; in a strange way
To stand inquiring right is not to stray;
To sleep or run wrong is.

In keeping with the growing edge of science, Donne's approach was analytical and his themes abstract. The anniversary of the death of his patron's daughter provides him with a convenient point of departure for examining the new anatomy of the world and, doubt engendered, the moral predicament of man who has fallen from his once secured station.

Milton, on the other hand, is a confused literary figure insofar as he reflects the science of his day. As he states in *Areopagitica:* "I enrol myself among the number of those who acknowledge the word of God alone [the Scriptures]

A new course is charted

Man is only a reed, the weakest to be found in nature; but he is a thinking reed. It is not necessary for the whole of nature to take up arms to crush him: a puff of smoke, a drop of water, is enough to kill him. But, even if the universe should crush him, man would still be more noble than that which destroys him, because he knows that he dies and he realises the advantage which the universe possesses over him. The universe knows nothing of this.

All our dignity, then, consists in thought. It is upon this that we must depend, not on space and time, which we would not in any case be able to fill. Let us labour, then, to think well: this is the foundation of morality.

. . . It is not in space that I should look to find my dignity, but rather in the ordering of my thought. I would gain nothing further by owning territories: in point of space the universe embraces me and swallows me up like a mere point: in thought, I embrace the universe.

B. Pascal [*29*]

. . . Poetry gained in clarity of meaning and precision; the thing uttered had one meaning, clear and unambiguous. Poetry also gained a greater sense of form through its respect for regularity and well-marked boundaries. It has been said that neoclassical poetry is like a formal garden, proportion, order, and discipline counting for so much. Most important of all, poetry had gained a sense of social responsibility. Under the influence of science it began to respect objective truth, to mirror external nature less distorted by the poet's imagination. . . .

The picturing of external nature and external man was perhaps the greatest gain to poetry, as it was also its greatest loss. It made possible a comprehensive view; it called attention to general truths about man and the world he lived in. It revealed things in proportion, the larger facts getting more attention than lesser details. Human intelligence revealed its superiority in shaping a world for man's use, a world classified and pyramided, with human and social values at the top. Man was confident and self-assured; he saw clearly what he had trained himself to see, and he was blissfully unaware of the human depths and metaphysical distances on which he had turned his back.

R. L. Sharp [*34*]

as the rule of faith." He was fully aware of the astronomical knowledge of his time, but in *Paradise Lost* and *Paradise Regained* his universe was a poetic collage consisting of whatever he chose to include from Copernican or pre-Copernican concepts; he appropriated and accommodated both the new and the old for his own poetic use. His cosmos is Ptolemaic in structure, with the sun and the planets arranged above the central earth and circling at prodigious speeds. Milton's Hell, situated far below the floor of Heaven and with the earth and solar system suspended between them on a golden chain, can be viewed as allegorical fancy, but, in keeping with older philosophies, he viewed the irregularities of the planets as a disorder introduced by God after the fall of man from grace. He allowed the archangel Raphael to give an astronomical lecture to Adam in which he states that it is difficult to tell "Whether the Sun, predominant in Heaven? Rise on the earth, or Earth rise on the Sun"; he had Satan swim for "Nine Times the Space that measures Day and Night to mortal men," through the immensities of space that Galileo revealed, that terrified Pascal, and that suggested distances that we now calculate in the light years of modern astronomy. He was, furthermore, both pre-Copernican and Keplerian in his treatment of the harmony of the spheres, reflecting the same uncertainties expressed by Robert Burton in *The Anatomy of Melancholy.*

Shakespeare, Donne, and Milton are representative of the age of great poetry, an age that shared the Elizabethan and Renaissance exuberance of style, language, and theme, but still carried with it remembrances of what Rabelais called the "Darkness of Gothic night." It eventually gave way, at least in England, to an equally important age of great

A new course is charted

When I consider every thing that grows
Holds in perfection but a little moment,
That this huge stage presenteth nought but shows
Whereon the stars in secret influence comment;
When I perceive that men as plants increase,
Cheered and check'd even by the self-same sky,
Vaunt in their youthful sap, at height decrease,
And wear their brave state out of memory;
Then the conceit of this inconstant stay
Sets you most rich in youth before my sight,
Where wasteful Time debateth with Decay,
To change your day of youth to sullied night;
   And all in war with Time for love of you,
   As he takes from you, I engraft you new.

W. Shakespeare [33]

---

prose and poetry of a less metaphysical character. Donne is clearly the transitional figure; his sermons, in particular, stripped away metaphors and allegorical references from the English language and prepared the way for John Dryden who gave "grace and suppleness" to the English tongue and who, as a member of the Royal Society, helped to establish the style of exposition appropriate for scientific writing. The *Tatler* and *Spectator Papers* of Addison and Steele continued to simplify the language, brought it closer to the idiom of the people and took the affairs of men, including science, out of the cloisters and academies, out of the hands of the select few, and put them into the coffeehouses and the open market place. In the eighteenth century, William Blake, an English artist and poet, might condemn science as "the Tree of Death," but the interrelations between science and literature were numerous and profound, and science had an intense impact on the analytical and critical aspects of literature as well as on its stylistic expression. Newton, for example, gave a new world of color to the poets and consequently a rich metaphor for the philosophical consideration of light and darkness in the minds of men. In his *Opticks* he had shown that white light could be disassembled into the colors of the spectrum and recombined again into white light by means of another prism. In his *Essay on Man,* Alexander Pope (1688–1744) wrote, "God said, 'Let Newton be'; and all was Light," but the same writer added, "So Darkness strikes the sense no less than Light."

Pope and Jonathan Swift (1667–1745) were the chief satirists during the age of prose. Both saw the dangers of science when it was in the hands of men less capable than Newton. Pope worried about the role of the dunces (those who knew too much, not too little) in guiding the arts and

A new course is charted

By means of this loadstone, the island [Laputa] is made to rise and fall, and move from one place to another. For with respect to that part of the earth over which the monarch presides, the stone is endued at one of its sides with an attractive power, and at the other with a repulsive. Upon placing the magnet erect with its attracting end towards the earth, the island descends; but when the repelling extremity points downwards, the island mounts directly upwards. When the position of the stone is oblique, the motion of the island is so too. For in this magnet, the forces always act in lines parallel to its direction.

J. Swift [37]

2.18 The Brobdingnagians, an illustration from the 1727 edition of Gulliver's Travels, *by Jonathan Swift.*

sciences, whereas Swift denounced unmercifully everyone and everything that came within his ken, and there was little that he overlooked. There seems little reason to doubt that his knowledge of the telescope and the microscope provided points of departure for his descriptions of Gulliver's travels to Brobdingnag, land of giants (illustration 2.18), and to Lilliput, land of tiny men. Swift's description of the Grand Academy of Lugado and of "The Arts wherein the professors employ themselves" could be variously interpreted as a biting satire on Bacon's *New Atlantis,* the universities of England, or the men of the Royal Society and their experiments. The members of the Grand Academy extracted sunbeams from cucumbers, returned human excrement to its original state as food, developed a device for ploughing the fields with hogs who simultaneously fertilized the fields with their droppings, manufactured colored silk from spider webs, and perfected a breed of naked sheep. The Flying Island of Laputa, which could "rise and fall, and move from one place to another" by manipulation of a "loadstone of prodigious size," presumably derives its inspiration directly from William Gilbert's studies on magnetism.

Science, to be sure, was only of peripheral and incidental interest to Swift and his literary contemporaries, and neither these men nor the natural philosophers could use the fragmentary and unconnected odds and ends of scientific discoveries to construct a picture of the future. Man was their central theme and focus, and science was but one of the many forces reshaping not only their age, but also their view of man and his place in nature. Nevertheless, it was a period when nothing was taken on trust, and independence of thought and freedom of expression were their badges of

A new course is charted

68

*Gemini VII photographed by the crew of
Gemini VI, modern versions
of the Flying Island of Laputa.*

NASA

emancipation. If the details of nature were there to be explored by the scientists, and if their findings could be reported with impunity, it was only natural for others to do the same in their own areas of competence. In doing so, they often translated the results of science to a broader reading public. Thus, in 1686, the Frenchman Bernard de Fontenelle (1657–1757) wrote his *Plurality of Worlds,* one of the first works whose deliberate purpose was to bring science to the general reading public. It is interesting to note that the popularity of the microscope among the leisure class as a source of entertainment—even Samuel Pepys, the London gadabout and diarist, had one—was such that as a scientific instrument it fell out of favor among the scientists and probably thereby delayed the development of cellular studies for almost a century.

The interest in science shown by literary figures of the seventeenth century was consciously and deliberately exploited by the industrial and political segments of society. It gave rise to what the contemporary economist Robert Heilbroner, has called "a philosophy of optimism . . . toward the future" as a "historical attitude." This new attitude eliminated man's feeling of total subservience to nature, with only a vision of the hereafter to alleviate the harsh realities of existence, and made him aware that he could control nature, a prospect that carried with it the promise of human betterment and a brighter future.

In the world of industry, each new discovery, particularly in the area of the mechanical arts and in what we might now refer to as "industrial technology," emphasized the significance and promise not only of a systematic exploitation of nature, but also of a systematic investigation into

At the time of the Scientific Revolution in the sixteenth century, and for two centuries after it, most self-made men got their wealth by trade (in which I include the support of trade by insurance and banking), and often by oversea trade. As *The Merchant of Venice* reminds us, this is how the great fortunes in North Italy, in Holland and in England were made. It was therefore natural that science in these two centuries was agog with problems of trade, and particularly of navigation. The Industrial Revolution in the eighteenth century shifted the source of wealth from trade to manufacture; and manufacture has needed more and more mechanical energy. Science has therefore been preoccupied in the last two centuries with problems which center on energy—practical problems from the heat engine to the electromagnetic field, and theoretical problems from thermodynamics to atomic structure. Now that we are in sight of having as much energy as we can need, the interest of scientists is moving from the generation of energy to its control, and particularly to the automatic control of power processes, whose tools are the valve, the semi-conductor and the computer. A characteristic invention of the Scientific Revolution was the telescope, of which Galileo heard from Holland, and which he presented to the Doge after a demonstration in the port of Venice in the presence of the Senate in 1609. The characteristic invention of the Industrial Revolution was the power machine which does the routine work of the human muscle. The characteristic invention of the second Industrial Revolution through which we are passing is the control mechanism which does the routine work of the human brain.

J. Bronowski [9]

A new course is charted

Invention appears at every stage of human history, but it rarely thrives in a community of simple peasants or unskilled manual labourers: only when division of labour has developed, so that men devote themselves to a single product or process, does it come to harvest. Such division of labour already existed when the eighteenth century opened, and the industrial revolution was in part cause, and in part effect, of a heightening and extension of the principle of specialization.

Invention, again, is more likely to arise in a community that sets store by things of the mind than in one that seeks only material ends. The stream of English scientific thought, issuing from the teaching of Francis Bacon, and enlarged by the genius of Boyle and Newton, was one of the main tributaries of the industrial revolution. Newton, indeed, was too good a philosopher and scholar to care whether or not the ideas he gave to the world were immediately "useful"; but the belief in the possibility of achieving industrial progress by the method of observation and experiment came to the eighteenth century largely through him. Natural philosophy was shaking itself free from its association with metaphysics and—again the application of the principle of division of labour—splitting up into the separate systems of physiology, chemistry, physics, geology and so on.

T. S. Ashton [1]

the productivity of common labor. The invention of the windmill, wheeled plough, and horse collar, all of which eased the labors of man, had occurred during the Middle Ages, but now the rising tempo of discovery and the increased understanding of mechanical forces and instruments were rapidly beginning to transform the arts of mining, weaving, potting, steel making, agriculture, and navigation. Man had learned how to manufacture power as well as things, and the industrial revolution of the eighteenth century was underway. Capitalism developed along with industry, and the growing colonial empires served not only as a source of raw materials, but also as a new and expanding market for the growing flood of manufactured products.

An increasingly large middle class of society accompanied, and in a sense was caused by, these changes, and a new social force was generated. Along with the acquisition

2.19 Abraham Darby was the first iron maker to use coke in a blast furnace, thereby making iron available in large quantities for the first time. In this view of Coalbrook Dale, England, in 1758, four coke ovens used by Darby are shown along the river at lower right.

British Information Service

For, indeed a change was coming upon the world, the meaning and direction of which even still are hidden from us, a change from era to era. The paths trodden by the footsteps of ages were broken up; old things were passing away, and the faith and the life of ten centuries were dissolving like a dream. Chivalry was dying; the abbey and the castle were soon together to crumble into ruins; and all the forms, desires, beliefs, convictions of the old world were passing away, never to return. They cannot come to us, and our imagination can but feebly penetrate to them. Only among the aisles of the cathedrals, only before the silent figures sleeping on the tombs, some faint conceptions float before us of what these men were when they were alive, and perhaps in the sound of church bells, that peculiar creation of the middle age, which falls upon the ear like the echo of a vanished world.

A. Froude [*19*]

The tomb of Duke Henry the Lion and his wife Mathilde, Braunschweig Cathedral, Germany.

Stadtbildstelle, Braunschweig

---

of material benefits go personal aspirations, and these became more evident as the future became the present. David Hume (1711–1776) set forth his views of government as man-given and man-removed and thus vitiated the divine right of kings and shattered the barriers of privilege. As Heilbroner expresses it: "At the bottom it was the spread of political ideas from mind to mind, of economic pressure from market to market, of scientific advance from laboratory to laboratory which provided the metabolism of social growth and change." No one, of course, could yet foresee that the ideas of progress and the brightness of the future would be still further advanced by the nineteenth-century concept of evolution, only to end in the disillusionments and problems of the late twentieth century.

Summary

The sixteenth and seventeenth centuries, following close upon the heels of the Italian Renaissance, the subsequent Protestant Reformation, and the discoveries of the New World, were years of tremendous change in the ways in which men viewed themselves and the world around them. Mutations took place in virtually every aspect of intellectual, artistic, religious, political, and economic life, with the sciences contributing new information and new methods that reoriented man in space and provided a new approach to an understanding of the ways of nature and of man. In the process, dogma and authority gave way to a reliance on continued observation, measurement, and experimentation, with the individual man acquiring a growing confidence in himself as a trustworthy surveyor of natural phenomena.

A new course is charted

For twice a thousand years the sciences stood where they did and now remain almost in the same condition, receiving no noticeable increase, but on the contrary, thriving most under their first founder, and then declining. Whereas in the mechanical arts, which are founded on nature and the light of experience, we see the contrary happening, for these (as long as they are popular) are continually thriving and growing, as if the breath of life inspired them—at first rude, then convenient, afterwards adorned, but at all times advancing.

F. Bacon [3]

It was a period of many great men, each one of whom looms large in the intellectual history of the West. As the heavens were rearranged by Copernicus, the earth lost its pristine centrality and became just another planet. Kepler, Galileo, and Newton, working out the laws of motion of the planets and earthly bodies, revealed the mechanical nature of the universe as well as its vast dimensions. Vesalius and Harvey brought man into this mechanical scheme, and the supernatural became more impersonal and faceless. Inevitably, man's view of himself underwent revision. Displaced as he now was in a much larger, imperfect, and not strictly circular celestial system, man began to question whether the earth was created for his use and delight, whether permanence was not an illusion, and whether he was not just a part, and an insignificant part at that, of an impersonal and constantly changing universe.

Change was clearly in the air, and as is so often the case when this is so, the direction of change, particularly as it related to an understanding of man, was not readily apparent. What was missing, as we now see in retrospect, was a sense of time and of history, as well as understanding of the relation of man to other living things; these things would come slowly.

A new course is charted

3

Of time and variation

It was said that the world had been described "favorably, piously, and by an Englishman." The reference is to Sir Isaac Newton whose mathematical description of the force of gravity was a crowning achievement of the scientific thought of the seventeenth century, an achievement that still provides the basis for a good part of classical physics, particularly mechanics. The universe, infinite though it might be, was a world-machine, and astronomers and physicists, bolstered by mathematicians, had shown it to be complex, but beautifully ordered and precisely regular. The identity of terrestrial and celestial mechanics was established, thus breaking down any lingering vestiges of doubt that these two domains were governed by different sets of conditions and by different laws. The tides, the regularity of the equi-

Our days have been the happiest time of the eighteenth century. Emperors, kings, and princes step down from their feared heights, and, as friends of men, scorn pomp and glitter and become fathers, friends, and confidants of their people. Religion tears off its popish garb and stands forth in its divinity. Enlightenment advances with giant steps. Thousands of our brothers and sisters who previously spent their lives in holied idleness are given back to the community. Hatred born of dogma and the compulsion of conscience sink away; love of man and freedom of thought gain the upper hand. The arts and sciences blossom, and our vision into the workshop of nature goes deep. Artisans approach artists in perfection; useful skills flower at all levels. Here you have a faithful portrait of our time. Look not proudly down upon us, should you stand higher or see farther than we, but rather recognize from this picture how with courage and strength we raised and supported your standard. Do the same for those who come after you and rejoice!

Anonymous

Thus it seems to me that I have the right to assume that when we are speaking about Newton and Newtonianism we know more or less what we are speaking of. More or less! Somehow this very expression used in connection with Newton strikes me as improper, because it is possible that the deepest meaning and aim of Newtonianism, or rather, of the whole scientific revolution of the seventeenth century, of which Newton is the heir and the highest expression, is just to abolish the world of the ''more or less,'' the world of qualities and sense perception, the world of appreciation of our daily life, and to replace it by the (Archimedean) universe of precision, of exact measures, of strict determination.

. . .

The Newtonian law of attraction according to which its force *diminishes* in proportion to the square of the distance is not the only law of that kind that explains the facts but, besides, is the only one that can be uniformly and universally applied to large and small bodies, to apples and to the moon. It is the only one, therefore, that it was reasonable for God to have adopted as a law of creation.

A. Koyré [13]

noxes, the orbits of comets, the elliptical paths of the planets, and even the known perturbations of the moon were accounted for by the same general laws of nature that would also account for the fall of an apple or the flight of an arrow or a cannonball. The key to unlock nature and force her to reveal her inner workings seemed to be the art of precise quantitative measurements and the incorporation of these measurements into general mathematical expressions. Newton, in fact, delayed publication of his findings because his calculations of the path of the moon relative to the center of the earth did not coincide exactly with the observed path, but a later refinement of terrestrial measurements by others showed his thesis to be correct.

The nature of gravitation, as distinct from the Newtonian description of it, remains to be fully explained even today, but the ability to deal with a phenomenon, even if only in an abstract fashion, provides a measure of confidence in what one is doing, an economical means of communication and an inspiration for further exploration. We still ask, as

3.1   *The 200-inch Hale telescope at the Mount Wilson and Palomar Observatories.*

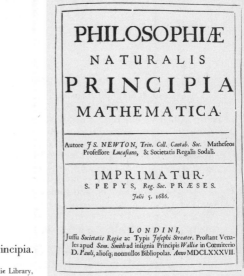

The title page of Newton's Principia.

did the jesting Pilate, "What is truth?" but the discoveries made by Newton and his contemporaries helped to generate a scientifically-based luxury of certitude comparable to the religiously-based certitude of the Middle Ages.

The seventeenth century was a period rich in the discoveries of physical and mathematical relationships, paralleling changes of comparable magnitude in the social, economic, political, and cultural world. The emergence of a new and fruitful concept—the ideas of Copernicus, Galileo, Kepler, and Newton are examples—or the invention of new instruments to aid and extend the range of the senses, for example, the telescope and the microscope, opens the floodgates for other inventions and discoveries. A momentum is generated, and a chain reaction sets in. In the field of mathematics, John Napier (1550–1617) had somewhat earlier developed his logarithms and made use of the decimal point, thereby greatly lessening the time and labor of reckoning. Gottfried Leibniz (1646–1716) and Newton developed the notations of the calculus; René Descartes, (1596–1650) constructed his analytical geometry and system of coordinates; and Pascal devised his theory of probability.

A similar enrichment took place in the field of mechanics. Galileo formulated his laws of motion and acceleration; Gilbert experimented with magnets, discovered that they had poles, came to the conclusion that the earth was a magnet with its own magnetic poles, and constructed a primitive kind of compass needle; Olaus Roemer (1644–1719), a Danish astronomer, measured the speed of light with surprising ingenuity and accuracy; Huyghens visualized light as a series of waves (Newton conceived of it as a stream of particles, and both theories are still in use today) and invented the reflecting telescope; Torricelli made use of the

What, then, was *discovery* to Galileo? It was the perception of cohesive, mathematical structure within the buzzing detail of experience. For him, every falling coin, every wind-blown leaf, every new moon was a special kind of anomaly, an occasion for inquiry. Phenomena like these, familiar but not understood, were the windows through which the anatomy of the universe could be witnessed, if one but focused the appropriate mathematical lens. Through lenses of his own design Galileo had seen the moon as terrestrial. So also he viewed dynamical events through algebraic lenses ground by his own intellect. To have perceived that all of nature was visible through such lenses—more, to have urged that its capacity to be so viewed was the defining characteristic of what we are entitled to call "Nature"—*there* is the synoptic discovery of this visionary student of the facts. All his other findings are subordinate to, and supportive of, this one brilliant insight.

N. R. Hanson [11]

Of time and variation

Yet there is something for which Newton—or better to say not Newton alone, but modern science in general—can still be made responsible: it is the splitting of our world in two. I have been saying that modern science broke down the barriers that separated the heavens and the earth, and that it united and unified the universe. And that is true. But, as I have said, too, it did this by substituting for our world of quality and sense perception, the world in which we live, and love, and die, another world—the world of quantity, or reified geometry, a world in which, though there is place for everything, there is no place for man. Thus the world of science—the real world—became estranged and utterly divorced from the world of life, which science has been unable to explain—not even to explain away by calling it "subjective."

True, these worlds are every day—and even more and more—connected by the *praxis*. Yet for *theory* they are divided by an abyss.

Two worlds: this means two truths. Or no truth at all.

This is the tragedy of modern mind which "solved the riddle of the universe," but only to replace it by another riddle: the riddle of itself.

A. Koyré [13]

3.2 The warrant for the hanging of Bridget Bishop, an alleged witch, at Salem, Massachusetts, in June of 1692.

Courtesy, Essex Institute, Salem, Massachusetts

vacuum in the invention of the barometer; Boyle showed that the volume of a gas exhibits a precise relationship to temperature and pressure; and Harvey, as previously discussed, demonstrated that the circulation of the blood could be treated as a problem in hydraulics, with the heart an amazingly effective pump. It was little wonder that Descartes, with transparent enthusiasm, could exclaim: "I have come so far that I am confident I shall be able to account for the place of every star." There seemed to be no room in this physical world for unaccountable variations.

Man was a part of this mechanical and mathematical order. If there had been any doubt, Harvey's study of the heart removed it. It is true, to be sure, that man's position in the universe had been decentralized and that, in the process, he had lost some of his unique relation to a world once believed created for his use and dominion, but he was nevertheless part of a larger world of even greater perfection and orderliness. The world was a perfected piece of art and, as such, demanded a master craftsman and engineer as its creator. In the sense that science was revealing the extent of this perfection, the results of scientific thought and investigations were, nevertheless, but footnotes to theology. Even Newton, so much the genius of his century and so far advanced in his mathematical thinking, was very much the traditionalist in other ways; he saw his great work *Principia* as revealing the order of a universe set in motion and governed by a creator. Physics and metaphysics were still comfortably embraced by "natural philosophy," and metaphysics provided the frame of reference within which all concepts of man and his universe would fit.

"Faith," as St. Paul says, "is the substance of things hoped for, the evidence of things not seen." The cosmology

Of time and variation

The exaltation of the faculty of reason in the Puritan ethos—based partly on the conception of rationality as a curbing device of the passions—inevitably led to a sympathetic attitude toward those activities which demand the constant application of rigorous reasoning. But again, in contrast to medieval rationalism, reason is deemed subservient and auxiliary to empiricism. . . . It is on this point probably that Puritanism and the scientific temper are in most salient agreement, for the combination of rationalism and empiricism which is so pronounced in the Puritan ethic forms the essence of the spirit of modern science.

The Puritan insistence upon empiricism, upon the experimental approach, was intimately connected with the identification of contemplation with idleness, of the expenditure of physical energy and the handling of material objects with industry. Experiment was the scientific expression of the practical, active and methodical bents of the Puritan. This is not to say, of course, that experiment was derived in any sense from Puritanism. But it serves to account for the ardent support of the new experimental science by those who had their eyes turned toward the other world and their feet firmly planted on this. . . .

R. K. Merton [21]

of the ancient and medieval world had been shattered, but the newly conceived, impersonal, abstract order of things, with its mathematical purity of operation, was to become an adequate, if, for some, a somewhat sterile, substitute for the personal earth over which man had been given dominion. Nevertheless, accommodation to the new order brought about a restructuring of the thoughts of men, posed new questions to be answered, and directed the activities of men into other channels. Witches dabbling in black magic might still be hanged or burned at the stake (in Salem, Massachusetts, the last witch was hanged in 1693), but freedom of inquiry, at least in the academies of science, was not frowned upon, and novelty of discovery and interpretation, particularly in the physical sciences, was not forbidden by church or state (illustration 3.2). Most importantly, old beliefs had been successfully challenged, with the result that the question of the essence of man and his place in the scheme of nature—the perennial problem of philosophy—demanded reexamination with a greater urgency now that man had been cast adrift in solar orbit. Pascal might argue that the mundane facts and interpretations of science were irrelevant to the spiritual needs of a Christian, but even Christians were thinking men. Their horizons were being vastly broadened, intellectually by their own writers and philosophers and physically by the adventurers who were opening up new lands for colonization and exploitation.

When beliefs are being questioned, an uneasiness, a restlessness, even a belligerency, prevails among those who ask questions. Montaigne (1533–1592), a man ahead of his time, prods his readers with skepticism: "I am prepared to hate even probable things as soon as someone tries to impose them on me as infallible." Sir Thomas Browne (1605–

Natura nihil agit frustra, is the only indisputable axiome in Philosophy; there are no *Grotesques* in nature; nor any thing framed to fill up empty cantons, and unnecessary spaces; in the most imperfect creatures, and such as were not preserved in the Arke, but having their seeds and principles in the wombe of nature, are every-where where the power of the Sun is; in these is the wisedome of his hand discovered: Out of this ranke *Solomon* chose the object of his admiration, indeed what reason may not goe to Schoole to the wisedome of Bees, Ants, and Spiders? what wise hand teacheth them to doe what reason cannot teach us? ruder heads stand amazed at those prodigious pieces of nature, Whales, Elephants, Dromidaries, and Camels; these I confesse, are the Colossus and Majestick pieces of her hand; but in these narrow Engines there is more curious Mathematicks, and the civilitie of these little Citizens more neatly sets forth the wisedome of their Maker; Who admires not *Regio-Montanus* his Fly beyond his Eagle, or wonders not more at the operation of two soules in those little bodies, than but one in the trunck of a Cedar? I could never content my contemplation with those generall pieces of wonder, the flux and reflux of the Sea, the encrease of Nile, the conversion of the Needle to the North, and have studied to match and parallel those in the more obvious and neglected pieces of Nature, which without further travell I can doe in the Cosmography of my selfe; wee carry with us the wonders we seeke without us: There is all *Africa* and her prodigies in us; we are bold and adventurous piece of nature, which he that studies wisely learnes in a *compendium,* what others labour at in a divided piece and endlesse volume.

T. Browne [4]

Of time and variation

The emergence of the new type of scientist has thus been linked to the rise of new social classes interested in a more open social structure and a more empirically oriented education on the one hand and to Protestantism on the other. It must be emphasised, however, that the only thing which this explains is the enhancement of the *status* of science and the change in the *role* of the scientist-scholar who now can openly and respectably become a scientist without having to be primarily something else. The change in status helped to increase scientific activity and the change in the definition of the role contributed similarly to the increased systematisation, clarity and boldness of scientific thought.

J. Ben-David [3]

Undoubtedly, the works of Sir Thomas Browne are already lacking in solid content, and verge into the pure emotionalism of music; yet they are saved in the end by the writer's sturdy regularity of life and by the great tradition which hung upon the age. Wonder with him was a wholesome elation of spirit, substituting dreams, it may be, for the laws of the solid earth, but still a tonic and not a narcotic to the law of character. "Now for my life," he exclaims in the most famous passage of his *Religio*, "it is a miracle of thirty years, which to relate were not a history but a piece of poetry, and would sound to common ears like a fable; for the world, I count it not an inn but an hospital, and a place not to live but to die in. The world that I regard is my self; it is the microcosm of my own frame that I cast my eye on; for the other, I use it but like my globe, and turn it round sometimes for my recreation." Here, if I may repeat, is no harsh opposition of spirit and matter, but an attempt to interpret and estimate the law of nature by the law of a man's inner life. For this protest of the pure imagination against an all-invading rationalism the book was carried over Europe, accepted the more readily because the window of escape into the *O altitudo* was opened by one who had standing in the schools of the new science.

P. E. More [22]

1682), in *Religio medici,* asks why it is that horses, "that necessary creature," are not found in the New as well as the Old World. Bacon urged the philosophers and scientists to "put nature to the question." And Harvey, Newton, Hooke, and Boyle demonstrated the value and success of experimentation and independence of thought in revealing the order and unity that existed in nature.

But these men were products of their time as well. However comfortable they might feel in destroying the old order of the heavens and in constructing a concept of nature based on orderly laws of motion and energy and interpreted in mechanistic and mathematical terms, they were nevertheless bound by the strictures of a sacred history that they could not easily and comfortably discard. The Judeo-Christian writings provided man with historical perspective and gave his life meaning and purpose. A single philosophy that would embrace both the mechanistic world and divinely created man was possible only by viewing everything in theistic terms. The major past events of this accepted history were the original creation, the inundation of the entire world by the great Flood, and the repopulation of the earth by the descendants of Noah. The single future event of consequence was the final conflagration that would consume the earth and its inhabitants and be followed by a hoped-for redemption and everlasting life.

The development of historical geology

It would take another revolution in thinking to make this history unacceptable, a revolution that would have as its basis the examination and eventual understanding of the

Of time and variation

Amid all the revolutions of the globe the economy of Nature has been uniform, and her laws are the only things that have resisted the general movement. The rivers and the rocks, the seas and the continents, have been changed in all their parts; but the laws which direct those changes and the rules to which they are subject have remained invariably the same.

J. Playfair [24]

mundane events daily experienced by man. Just as the Copernican revolution depended on the "minutiae of astronomical data," so the revolution to come would have its origin in geology and evolution, in the role played by wind, rain, and frost in changing the face of the earth, and in the study of variation in barnacles and differences in beaks and feeding habits of birds inhabiting neighboring islands. There would unfold, gradually but surely, a new concept of the age of the earth and its inhabitants. Change, not permanence, would be found to be the most characteristic feature of life, including man; and chance, not design, would have to be taken into account. These would have to be woven into the fabric of thought before the theory of evolution, with its enormous implications for an understanding of man, could provide a new frame of reference to engage the thoughts of man and eventually remold science, philosophy, and social affairs. A static world would give way to a dynamic one where change would follow change, ceaselessly and inexorably. Man would find that he too was the product of change and chance and time. In the process, every triumph of science was taken to be a defeat of, or a challenge to, the major tenets of established religions.

As a modern and well-defined science that is based on processes of rock formation, as well as descriptions of different kinds of formations, geology makes no sense unless it is invested with historical perspective. The Grand Canyon of the Colorado (illustration 3.3) is an awesome and beautiful spectacle of nature, but the impression made on all but the insensitive viewer is heightened by the knowledge that he is seeing, in the exposed strata of sedimentary rock, the cutting action of millions of years of flowing water. superimposed upon the added millions of years during which the

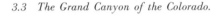

3.3 *The Grand Canyon of the Colorado.*

American Airlines

Of time and variation

In the six hundredth year of Noah's life, in the second month, on the seventeenth day of the month, on that day all the fountains of the great deep burst forth, and the windows of the heavens were opened. . . .

The flood continued forty days upon the earth; and the waters increased, and bore up the ark, and it rose high above the earth. . . . And the waters prevailed so mightily upon the earth that all the high mountains under the whole heaven were covered; the waters prevailed above the mountains, covering them fifteen cubits deep. And all flesh died that moved upon the earth, birds, cattle, beasts, all swarming creatures that swarm upon the earth, and every man; everything on the dry land in whose nostrils was the breath of life died.

Genesis: 7

---

sediments were laid down. One may gaze upon such scenes of majesty, and upon the "everlasting hills," and gain only an impression of changelessness. But by studying the processes that erode a land and muddy a river after a hard rain, that transform limestone into marble, that produce granite under one set of circumstances and basalt under another, and that leave rock strata upended and exposed to sight, one can have some sense of the forces involved and the time during which such forces act. The significance of these processes to an understanding of man is that such mundane knowledge removed all pretense that the history of the earth could be deduced from sacred writings and made man aware that the history of the earth and the history of man on earth were not coincident in time. We can now see that such knowledge also demonstrated that the legend of Noah, one of the most effective barriers to progressive thought because of its limited time scale, was based on a local inundation that affected a local population. This further showed that fossils were the remnants of past worlds of life.

The early Greeks recognized that sedimentary rocks containing marine fossils were once under the sea, even though some of these rocks were found in mountainous regions. Vast floods of the past, some of them covering the entire earth, were assumed to be the cause for the extinctions that resulted in these fossils, although no satisfactory hypothesis

3.4 A portion of a large group of fossil turtles discovered in Uinta County, Wyoming. These fossils are over 40 million years old.

Smithsonian Institution

Leonardo da Vinci, Deluge.

was advanced to account for the disposal of the receding waters. This concept of the origin of fossils was disputed however. The sacred writings of Judaism, Christianity, and Islam did not lend themselves to such an interpretation, for it could hardly be argued that what was divinely created could so callously be made extinct. Avicenna, a tenth-century Arabian physician, explained that fossils were due to a creative force which could change the inorganic into the organic; in fossils, the form was there, but life was absent. Robert Hooke, of the Royal Society, remained skeptical: "Nature does nothing in vain, and nothing could be vainer than imitating living organisms in stone." The usual explanation, prior to the eighteenth century, was the old view that a succession of devastating floods accounted for the presence of fossils, but the fallacies in this view were equally apparent. Floods would have little effect on marine animals, and, as Hooke pointed out, the 40 days and 40 nights of Noah's flood was too short a period for laying down thick beds of fossil-bearing rock. Not until the nineteenth century, however, was the true nature of fossils fully understood and widely accepted.

Painstaking field studies provided the clues to geologic processes. Abraham Werner (1749–1817), of Freiburg, and Jean Guettard (1715–1786), among others, were instrumental in formulating basic ideas reinforced with sound evidence. Werner, although an advocate of successive inundations, the so-called Neptunist view, demonstrated that the structure of the earth's crust had a logical order. It was not an unintelligible jumble of rocks. In undisturbed stratified rocks, the order of position was the order of formation— the youngest on top, the oldest at the bottom. Guettard was concerned with the volcanic origin of basalt and with the

The passage of time works against fossil preservation. Different conditions of environment have existed and each change has possessed the capabilities of destroying a previously well preserved fauna. Uplift of parts of the earth and the exposure of rocks to the forces of weathering and erosion, or ground water and the elevated temperatures associated with volcanic activity, are only a few of the geologic processes which have been operating for five billion years of earth history. Most of the history of life has been learned from rocks less than 600 million years old, and the uncertainty associated with fossils which have been described from older rocks is amplified by the continual destructive work of geologic processes. In spite of the rigorous requirements for preservation and the abrading effect of geologic processes, numerous fossils have been preserved and the history of life of the past is becoming well understood.

D. L. Clark [7]

Of time and variation

The face of places, and their forms decay;
And that is solid earth, that once was sea;
Seas, in their turn, retreating from the shore,
Make solid land, what ocean was before.

Ovid [23]

NOAA

Surely, if there is in the system of nature wisdom, we may look for compensation between the destroying and repairing operations of the globe. But why seek for this compensation in the *rest* or immobility of things? Why suppose perfection in the want of change? The summit of the Alps was once the bottom of the sea; the existence of our land depended then upon the change of seas and continents.

J. Hutton [12]

Hutton was impressed with the tremendous role that fossils played in making up the bulk of the earth's strata. He accepted the conclusion that calcareous strata were composed of the remains of sea animals, and that these remains were the relics, not of one catastrophe, but of a quiet deposition over vast periods of time. These strata, then, had resulted from the destruction of a succession of former worlds, and Hutton made the process of decay his first principle in the operation of the earth-machine. On the bottom of the sea, the detritus was consolidated by the pressure of the water above and, he conjectured, by the heat of the earth coming from below the sea bed. This same heat also, in some manner, elevated the consolidated strata, giving rise to new worlds, and thus repairing the decay of the old ones. The renovation process was Hutton's second principle. Hutton postulated a world always in existence as his third principle, although the present world is actually undergoing both decay and repair continuously.

In the destruction of a world, Hutton made clear, "we are not to suppose, that there is any violent exertion of power, such as is required to produce a great event in little time; in nature, we find no deficiency in respect to time, nor any limitation with regard to power."

F. C. Haber [10]

existence of long-extinct volcanoes. He showed that basalt was of igneous, and not of sedimentary, origin and that it resulted from a rapid cooling of molten lava. This was in contrast to granite, whose visible crystal structure developed as a result of a slow cooling rate. Confirmation by others was obtained in the laboratory, actually in an iron foundry, where rocks of various natures were melted and cooled, some slowly, others rapidly. The conversion of limestone to marble under high temperature and pressure was similarly demonstrated. It seemed clear to Guettard that the interior of the earth was quite hot, with volcanoes being safety valves to relieve the pressures caused by high temperature.

Guettard also initiated the practice of geological surveys. His maps showed that one type of formation in France traversed the English Channel and reappeared in England. An English engineer, William Smith (1769–1838), would add further evidence to the growing volume of geological data. He established the principle that the geological ages of sedimentary rock could be identified and assigned by their fossil content, and that similar strata in widely separate places were formed at the same time.

James Hutton (1726–1797) is to geology what Galileo and Newton were to physics and what Darwin would be to biology. He tied the odds and ends of geologic data into a single unifying principle. His four-volume treatise, *Theory of the Earth, with Proofs and Illustrations,* laid down the principle of uniformitarianism, the concept that the forces of nature operating today have operated through all time. He pointed out that stratified rock is laid down in water, changed by heat, and elevated by pressure, that earthquakes and volcanoes are part of the continuing operation of nature, and that organic decay and erosion by wind and water go

Of time and variation

There rolls the deep where grew the tree.
  O earth, what changes hast thou seen!
  There where the long street roars hath been
The stillness of the central sea.

The hills are shadows, and they flow
  From form to form, and nothing stands;
  They melt like mist, the solid lands,
Like clouds they shape themselves and go.

But in my spirit will I dwell,
  And dream my dream, and hold it true;
  For though my lips may breathe adieu,
I cannot think the thing farewell.

A. Tennyson [*31*]

---

on, as he stated, "with no vestige of a beginning. no prospect of an end." It was these forces that sculptured, and continue to sculpture, the face of the earth.

But acceptance of the principle of uniformitarianism meant that the earth must have existed for a much longer time than was previously thought, a length of time that was sufficient to allow for the extensive terrestrial changes that had taken place. Archbishop James Ussher, who in 1654 had asserted that man and the earth were created in 4004 B.C., was clearly in error. Georges Louis Leclerc, comte de Buffon (1701–1788), the great French naturalist, postulated that the earth was about 168,000 years old, a figure he thought necessary to account, at least in part, for the degree of salinity of the oceans. Hutton increased the age of the earth by several orders of magnitude, to millions of years. At the beginning of the twentieth century, the earth was still estimated to be only about 50 million years old, and it was not until the discovery of radioactivity and its usefulness as a geologic chronometer that the present estimate of 4.5 billion years was reached.

Charles Lyell (1797–1875) consolidated and made widely acceptable the principle of uniformitarianism. His three-volume work, *Principles of Geology*, published in the early 1830s, ranks with Newton's *Principia* and Darwin's *Origin of Species* as one of the most influential pieces of scientific writing. He clarified and extended Hutton's ideas, and his volumes, as well as his friendship and counsel, had a profound effect on the young Darwin. Darwin's theory of evolution, in essence, was the application of the principle of uniformitarianism to the organic world, although the processes that Darwin described were of a somewhat different character.

I must reply to a kind of objection which has already been made to me on the very long duration of time. Why throw us, it has been asked of me, into a space as vague as a duration of 168,000 years? Because, according to the view of your plan, the earth has aged 75,000 years, and organic nature must still subsist for 93,000 years: is it easy, is it even possible to form an idea of all or of the parts of so long a course of centuries? I have no other reply than the exposition of the monuments and the consideration of the works of nature: I will give the details of this and the dates of the epochs which follow from it, and it will be seen that, far from having increased the duration of time unnecessarily, I have probably shortened it far too much.

And why does the mind seem to get lost in the space of duration rather than in that of extension, or in the consideration of measures, weights and numbers? Why are 100,000 years more difficult to conceive and to count than 100,000 pounds of money?

Buffon [*5*]

3.5 *A newly emerged volcano in eruption off the south coast of Iceland in 1964.*

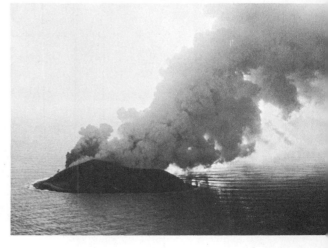

Of time and variation

Coal mine, England, 1785.

Radio Times Hulton Picture Library

There is but one first cause, and foure second causes of all things; some are without efficient, as God, others without matter, as Angels, some without forme, as the first matter; but every Essence, created or uncreated, hath its finall cause, and some positive end both of its Essence and operation; This is the cause I grope after in the workes of nature, on this hangs the providence of God; to raise so beauteous a structure as the world and the creatures thereof, was but his Art, but their sundry and divided operations, with their predestinated ends, are from the treasury of his wisedome.

T. Browne [4]

The maturing of biology

Biological science achieved a separate and distinct identity a good deal more slowly than did the physically and mechanically oriented sciences. There are a number of reasons for this delayed development and separation, all of which tended to keep biology in a subordinate position even though a substantial amount of descriptive and experimental studies were conducted and reported. The botanists and zoologists of the seventeenth century were well acquainted with the substantive and philosophical changes taking place in the physical world and with the maturing art of measurement, and they sought to apply these discoveries to the world of living things. New relationships and new principles, peculiar to the living world, were the inevitable result. For example, Jan van Helmont (1577–1644), a physician and chemist, showed that a willow plant increased its weight by 164 pounds over a 5 year period, whereas soil in which it was growing weighed only 2 ounces less than it originally did. All of the added weight, though distinct from water, was believed to be derived from it. Stephen Hales (1677–1761) would similarly seek to relate the growth of plants to the mechanico-physical laws of the day. His studies on the movement of water in plants, on transpiration from leaves, and on the contribution of air to growth were ingenious and meticulous. Harvey, in addition to his studies on circulation, was also intrigued by the problems of growth and made the point, novel and brilliant for its time, that all living things are derived from eggs that have been fertilized.

Of time and variation

Look Nature through, 'tis neat gradation all.
By what minute degrees her scale extends!
Each middle nature join'd at each extreme,
To that above it, join'd to that beneath.
   . . . But how preserv'd
The chain unbroken upwards, to the realms
Of Incorporeal life? those realms of bliss
Where death hath no dominion? Grant a make
Half-mortal, half-immortal; earthy part,
And part ethereal; grant the soul of Man
Eternal; or in Man the series ends.
Wide yawns the gap; connection is no more;
Check'd Reason halts; her next step wants support;
Striving to climb, she tumbles from her scheme.

E. Young [32]

Vast chain of being! which from God began,
Natures aethereal. human, angel, man,
Beast, bird, fish, nsect, what no eye can see,
No glass can reach; from Infinite to thee,
From thee to nothing.

A. Pope [25]

Biology, however, had as yet no theoretical structure peculiar to itself and to which the details of old and new observations could be referred. This was particularly true as regards man. Harvey might well demonstrate that certain aspects of man's physiology could be viewed and studied in a mechanical way, but it was quite another matter to withdraw from man his divinely conferred status of being created in the image of his creator. Secondly, until a discipline could assure its potential practitioners of an opportunity to follow their calling, it could not attract to it the bright young minds of the day. A student might gain some training in biology, but only through the available medical schools or, indirectly, through lectures at the several academies of science or through the sporadic writings of academicians. There was no biological curriculum in the universities. The student's botanical exposure was related to pharmacology, and his knowledge of zoology was human oriented. A third, although delayed, factor was the industrial revolution. Beginning in England in the latter half of the eighteenth century, it transformed industry from an agrarian base to one driven by power machinery, but it had little or no effect on biology at the same time that it provided a powerful impetus to the physical sciences through its demand on improved technology.

More important, however, than any of the factors just discussed was the existence of a genuine conflict in the minds of the biologists of that period, a conflict that had its origin in two incompatible elements: the classification of every living thing in some kind of hierarchical order, a Middle Age tradition as well as a useful end in itself, and the recognition, from actual experience with living plants and animals, that although species show varying

The manticore, a mythical animal described in Topsell's History of Four-footed Beasts (*1658*).

Porta developed his theory in detail [in 1588] and pushed it to great lengths. He supposed, for example, that long-lived plants would lengthen a man's life, while short-lived plants would abbreviate it. He held that herbs with a yellow sap would cure jaundice, while those whose surface was rough to the touch would heal those diseases that destroy the natural smoothness of the skin. The resemblance of certain plants to certain animals opened to Porta a vast field of dogmatism on a basis of conjecture. Plants with flowers shaped like butterflies would, he supposed, cure the bites of insects, while those whose roots or fruits had a jointed appearance, and thus remotely suggested a scorpion, must necessarily be sovereign remedies for the sting of that creature. Porta also detected many obscure points of resemblance between the flowers and fruits of certain plants, and the limbs and organs of certain animals. In such cases of resemblance he held that an investigation of the temperament of the animal in question would determine what kind of disease the plant was intended to cure. It will be recognised from these examples that the doctrine of signatures was remarkably elastic, and was not fettered by any rigid consistency.

A. Arber [2]

degrees of natural affinity with one another, they do not display any clear-cut relationships of a hierarchical nature. The former view is static; the latter, on the other hand, embodies a lineal and a temporal relationship, an evolutionary connection between things, and as such conflicts with the idea of each species having a distinct creation. The ambiguities were readily apparent to most observers although their resolution was not.

The medical herbals and pharmacopeias of the period constitute an intriguing chapter in the history of biological writings and aid us in understanding and appreciating the nature of the conflict. In the herbals appears the curious doctrine of signatures, the notion that the Creator, in His wisdom, has aided man in making wise use of the flora by stamping each species with an unmistakable sign to indicate its purpose to man. Thus the bloodroot, so named because of the blood-red sap which exudes from an injured root, was deemed beneficial in curing maladies of the blood and the circulatory system. The lobed leaves of the liverwort were considered to be a sign that the plant could be used in curing, or at least alleviating, malfunctions of the liver. Nevertheless, there were many species having similar "signatures" that were of no value either medicinally or nutritionally. Why were they so constructed?

Throughout these writings runs the theme that all species were preserved in the same state in which they were at the time of creation. This was the doctrine of special creation. Ideas of evolution have been expressed in one form or another throughout recorded history, but the single persistent concept, going back to Aristotelian thought and sanctified in sacred writings, was that species were constant through time. Furthermore, the adaptation of organisms to

Of time and variation

This is called savory. It is hot and dry in the fourth degree. Seethe it in wine or water and drink it, and it purgeth the reins, the bladder, the menstruosity in the bowels, and it purgeth the lungs and looseth the great humors and compelleth and putteth them out by the mouth by spitting; therefore it is burning, and stirreth him that useth lechery; therefore it is forbidden to use it much in meats. Also, soak it in vinegar or in wine and drink it, and that shall make thee a good meek stomach. Also, when it flowereth it should be gathered and dried, and powder made thereof. Also, take the powder of savory and boil it with clarified honey and use to eat thereof or boil it in wine and drink it, and it will loose tough phlegm in the breast. Also, for fretting in the belly, drink powder of it in warm wine, and thou shall be whole. Also, if ye take the less savory, it hath the same virtue and strength that the other savory hath. Also, make gruel with water and flour and powder of savory and eat thereof, and that shall cleanse all the spiritual members of a man.

An old herbal [17]

---

their environment, evident to any careful observer, reinforced the doctrine; plants and animals seemed to belong where they were found, and such wisdom was to be expected of the Creator.

The doctrine of special creation was a reasonable scientific theory, appropriate for its time and consistent with what was known scientifically. It was derived from, and in return gave stability to and provided support for, the religious philosophy of the Western world. It gave meaning to man and his existence and to his view of his place in nature by its insistence on permanence and design, and all aspects of the natural world could be referred to it with assurance. It was a comfortable doctrine in that it made questions of origin, diversity, and variation unnecessary. Like the legend of Noah, however, it delayed an understanding and an

3.6 *The male and female mandrake, an illustration from* Dalechamps's Historia generalis plantarum (1586). *The male plant is at left.*

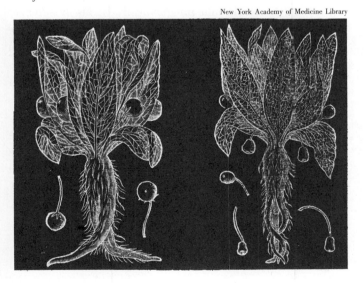

We would urge men of University standing to spare a brief interval from other pursuits for the study of nature and of the vast library of creation so that they can gain wisdom in it at first hand and learn to read the leaves of plants and the characters impressed on flowers and seeds. Surely we can admit that even if, as things are, such studies do not greatly conduce to wealth or human favour, there is for a free man no occupation more worthy and delightful than to contemplate the beauteous works of nature and honour the infinite wisdom and goodness of God. We are sure that the pursuit of plants can appeal to the young; for we have seen many sons of Trinity College finding in it both bodily exercise and mental satisfaction. Of course there are people entirely indifferent to the sight of flowers or of meadows in spring, or if not indifferent at least pre-occupied elsewhere. They devote themselves to ball-games, to drinking, gambling, money-making, popularity-hunting. For these our subject is meaningless. We offer a hundred banquets to the Pythagoreans or rather the true philosophers whose concern is not so much to know what authors think as to gaze with their own eyes on the nature of things and to listen with their own ears to her voice; who prefer quality to quantity, and usefulness to pretension: to their use, in accordance with God's glory, we dedicate this little book and all our studies.

J. Ray [28]

. . . the number of true species in nature is fixed and limited and, as we may reasonably believe, constant and unchangeable from the first creation to the present day.

J. Ray [28]

3.7 John Ray.

appreciation of the dynamic and changing nature of the living world.

The doctrine of special creation was fully set forth in the writings of John Ray (1627–1705). A clergyman by training, Ray turned to natural history when his refusal to submit to the anti-Puritan directives of Charles II of England ended his prospects of securing a pulpit. While traveling and collecting specimens through Holland, France, and Italy, he met virtually all of the men who were contributing to the scientific revolution of the seventeenth century. On his return to England, he joined Hooke, Boyle, Wren, and, later, Newton in the affairs of the Royal Society. He was fully conversant with the changing state and methods of scientific thought, and his many volumes on plants and animals soon established him as one of the foremost natural historians of his age. He laid the foundations of systematic biology that Linnaeus would later strengthen and expand, and his influence persisted until the publication of Darwin's *Origin of Species.*

Ray's science and his theology were inseparable. Both are set forth clearly and unequivocally in his *Wisdom of God Manifested in the Works of the Creation.* The philosophy expressed was not only a reaffirmation of Christian doctrine in a large sense; it also defined the relations between God, man, and nature, delved into the purpose of science, or "experimental philosophy" in his terminology, and clarified the meaning of knowledge to a Christian audience. This volume epitomized the thinking not only of his own time but also of the two following centuries. More importantly, however, the frame of reference it provided determined the kinds of questions that could legitimately be asked of nature and of man. There could, for example,

Of time and variation

"... but tell me your name and business."

"My *name* is Alice, but—"

"It's a stupid name enough!" Humpty Dumpty interrupted impatiently. "What does it mean?"

"*Must* a name mean something?" Alice asked doubtfully.

"Of course it must," Humpty Dumpty said with a short laugh: "*my* name means the shape I am . . ."

"When I use a word," Humpty Dumpty said, in a rather scornful tone, "it means just what I choose it to mean—neither more nor less."

"The question is," said Alice, "whether you *can* make words mean so many different things."

"The question is," said Humpty Dumpty, "which is to be master—that's all."

L. Carroll [6]

"Man is created for this purpose, that there might be someone to regard God's work, and the things brought forth by Him, and that while he admires the creation, even learns to know the Creator." It is these words of the eminently learned Ray, which especially egged me on to observations, so that I now with all my heart desire to investigate nature.

C. Linnaeus [19]

---

be no questions raised concerning the origin of living things because origin and divine creation were synonymous. Adaptation, an understanding of which would be crucial in Darwinian thought, was in Ray's view a static fact, not a dynamic result of interaction between organism and environment. The meaning of variation could not arise, because the constancy of species was assured. Ray was too observant a naturalist, however, not to recognize the existence of variation, even within species, but he viewed them only as deviations from a fundamental species plan that was flexible but sharply limited in scope. But it would be these same variations that, in the minds of later scientists, would demand a more satisfying explanation, an explanation that emerged only when the great length of the history of the earth was made apparent.

Carolus Linnaeus (Carl von Linné, 1707–1778) was the great systematist of the eighteenth century. His avowed aim, derived from the methods of Ray and built around his philosophy, was to arrange and label every natural object so that an intelligent catalog could be constructed for man's use. In his own words, he wanted to develop "an index of the book of nature." Implicit in Linnaeus's thinking was the idea that a natural system of classification was possible, and that such a system should depend upon discernible patterns of difference. Philosophically, this idea had long been known as the great chain of being, or the *scala naturae*, an archetypal plan of gradually increasing complexity from the simplest atom to the most complex organisms, ascending, as Sir Thomas Browne had said, "in comely order," with man at the apex of living things, and with only the several orders of angels existing between man and God. This was a static chain of being with no transi-

There was for [Ray] nothing incongruous in seeing the objects of his study, the order of the universe, the life of plants and animals, the structure and functioning of nature, as the manifestation of the Mind of God. Indeed the wonder with which he regarded the works of creation, and the thrill which accompanied his growing insight into the processes of their growth and function, were to him, as to mankind in general, essentially religious. He found in this new approach to the physical world the awe and reverence, the release and inspiration which psalmists, poets, thinkers and explorers have always found; and though it was difficult to reconcile his discoveries with the formulae of Christian tradition it was impossible not to find in them a profound religious and indeed Christian significance.

. . . He worked, here as elsewhere, within the framework of contemporary Christian thought, but with a loyalty to experiment and observation and a faith in the unity and rationality of nature which contributed powerfully to the abandonment of that framework and stimulated the quest for a truer and more scientific interpretation of the data of physical studies. It is as absurd to suggest that he foreshadowed the concept of evolution or adopted the categories of a modern scientist as it is to blame him for not doing so. But in drawing attention to the unity of nature, to the problems of form and function, to adaptation, and to a great number of strange and in some cases still unexplained phenomena he gave the first strong impulse to the scientific movement of to-day. A good case could be made for assigning to the successive editions of the *Wisdom of God* a primary place in the development of modern science.

C. E. Raven [26]

O, yet we trust that somehow good
  Will be the final goal of ill,
  To pangs of nature, sins of will,
Defects of doubt, and taints of blood;

That nothing walks with aimless feet;
  That not one life shall be destroyed,
  Or cast as rubbish to the void,
When God hath made the pile complete;

That not a worm is cloven in vain;
  That not a moth with vain desire
  Is shriveled in a fruitless fire,
Or but subserves another's gain. . . .

Are God and Nature then at strife,
  That Nature lends such evil dreams?
  So careful of the type she seems,
So careless of the single life,

That I, considering everywhere
  Her secret meaning in her deeds,
  And finding that of fifty seeds
She often brings but one to bear, . . .

"So careful of the type?" but no.
  From scarpéd cliff and quarried stone
  She cries, "A thousand types are gone;
I care for nothing, all shall go. . . ."

A. Tennyson [*31*]

The importance of Linnaeus' portrait of nature lay in its originality and creative simplicity. All species of organisms were to be grouped into three levels of higher categories, the genera, orders, and classes, each category to be given one-word names. Previous authors had used a mixture of single words and phrases to designate more or less informal categories. Linnaeus described each category with a very brief diagnostic phrase which was designed to distinguish it from other categories of the same rank, instead of giving the usual relatively aimless description. Coupled with this rigid formality in structure was the poetic precision and fire of Linnaeus' writing, whose aptness persuaded the reader that the author had complete control of his materials.

U. Lanham [*16*]

3.8 Linnaeus.

tional stages, and with each category created separately and independently from that above or below it in complexity. Certain groupings, such as quadrupeds, worms, flowering plants, and ferns, were discernible, but these were viewed as the plan of original creation, not as a dynamic relation traceable to a common ancestor. To suggest in the eighteenth century that man and worms, redwoods and fungi, represented divergent lines of descent from some distant ancestor would have been the height of intellectual absurdity.

Linnaeus's great work *Systema naturae*, published in 1753, set forth the binomial system of nomenclature in use today. According to this system, each plant or animal is given a two-word Latin name. The first name designates the genus to which any living thing belongs. The second word is an adjective that modifies, and hence subdivides, the genus. Although this second element is sometimes called the specific name, the actual species is identified by the combination of the two words. Sometimes a third element is added to the name. This designates the authority who named the species in the first place; thus, all organisms named by Linnaeus are identifiable by the letter "L." In this system, man is *Homo sapiens* L.—man, the wise one, as designated by Linnaeus. Adoption of Linnaeus's system of nomenclature was a step of enormous simplicity and economy. A knowledge of Latin was shared by most intellectuals, whereas the common, nonscientific names of organisms varied widely from country to country, and even from place to place where a single language was being spoken.

Linnaeus attempted to construct his system of classification on the basis of natural affinities, but in the case of flowering plants, for example, his classification based on the number of stamens was as contrived as that used in some

Of time and variation

Man, nature's last and most distinguished servant, to whose advantage and convenience almost all things are subservient, also maintains the balance of nature in many cases. The colossal whales in the ocean can scarcely escape his power; the fierce and ravenous beasts of prey, such as lions and tigers, he is forced to keep within bounds in order that he himself may enjoy peace; wherever there is an abundance of plants, trees, fish, birds and animals, he knows how to use them to his own profit. In this way he maintains a seemly balance, so that nothing which is unprofitable may increase too much. But even man himself is subject to this same natural law, although I know not by what intervention of nature or by what law man's numbers are kept within fitting bounds. It is, however, true that the most contagious diseases usually rage to a greater degree in thickly populated regions, and I am inclined to think that war occurs where there is the greatest superfluity of people. At least it would seem that, where the population increases too much, concord and the necessities of life decrease, and envy and malignancy towards neighbours abound. Thus it is *a war of all against all!*

C. Linnaeus [20]

Albrecht Altdorfer, The Battle of Issus.

---

of the herbals of the Middle Ages, in which plants were divided according to use, for example, medicinal, edible, and poisonous plants. Linnaeus was aware that his system was imperfect, but the discovery of a natural system was, to him, the goal of science. This goal remains with us today, but it is infused with dynamic rather than static relationships.

The question of the meaning of variation among organisms was a more persistent source of concern to Linnaeus than it was to Ray, and he came less and less to take direct refuge in the doctrine of special creation. From an early position of certainty about the constancy of species as a reflection of a predetermined order of nature, he moved gradually to a state of nagging doubt. As Copernicus worried over the "minutiae of astronomical data," so Linnaeus began to question the significance of variations, and he eventually began to speculate on the origin of species, the roles of time and chance in the establishment of new forms, and the possibility that hybridization could alter and make more complex the original plan of creation. Earlier, the English philosopher John Locke (1632–1704) had advanced the idea that species had no separate and distinct reality, that they were merely created in the minds of man for purposes of imposing order on the infinite and overlapping variations of nature. Leibniz, the German contemporary of Locke, had expressed similar views on the unbroken and continuous gradations between organisms, but the pervasive influence of Ray and Linnaeus had turned thinking away from this position and hardened it into a concept of immutability.

Toward the end of his life, Linnaeus's experiments in hybridization caused him to question the concept of constancy, particularly as this related to genera. He wrote in

. . . I demand of you, and of the whole world, that you show me a generic character . . . by which to distinguish between Man and Ape. I myself most assuredly know of none. I wish somebody would indicate one to me. But, if I had called man an ape, or vice-versa, I should have fallen under the ban of all the ecclesiastics. It may be that as a naturalist I ought to have done so.

C. Linnaeus [20]

Of time and variation

The twinflower (Linnaea borealis), *a creeping evergreen shrub named after Linnaeus.*

Henry N. Mayer photo, National Audubon Society

Another of Linnaeus' contributions was his struggle with a question of highest theoretical significance, that of the difference between artificial and natural classification. Linnaeus thought of himself not as creating an ordered classification of living things, but as discovering and describing an order that already existed in nature. He thought that this order was created by God; as he said, "God created, Linnaeus described." An artificial category was one constructed by the classifier that did not match the order that actually existed in nature. There could be any number of artificial classifications of a group of plants. But since a natural classification was one that matched the order existing in nature, there could be only one natural classification, which thus stood as a goal toward which the classifier came ever closer as he perfected his work. Linnaeus thought that the species he had constructed were natural, and that his genera were natural. However, he admitted failure in constructing natural orders and classes; these, he said, were artificial. He thought that natural orders and classes did exist, but that he did not have the knowledge and ability to define them, and that the task was one for botanists of the future to complete.

U. Lanham [16]

A Dissertation on the Sexes of Plants that certain species of South African geraniums "would almost induce a botanist to believe that the species of one genus in vegetables are only so many different plants as there have been different associations with the flowers of one species, and consequently a genus is nothing else than a number of plants sprung from the same mother by different fathers. But whether all these species be the offspring of time; whether, in the beginning of all things, the Creator limited the number of future species, I dare not presume to determine." He could add further, in considering species of *Achillaea* (yarrow), that perhaps one species might have been derived from the other under the influence of climate and environment, a beginning murmur that would grow in volume and would become embodied in both the Lamarckian and the Darwinian views of evolution.

Linnaeus's concept of time was not expressed in precise terms, yet his discussion of fossils leaves no doubt that his idea of the duration of geologic time went well beyond the limitations imposed by the legend of Noah. He recognized forms that had no living counterparts and wondered what had happened to them. He could, on one occasion, state that "we shall never believe that a species has entirely perished from the earth," and on another that fossils were "the only remaining fragments of the ancient world . . . far beyond the memory of history whatsoever." Bound by the Scriptures, however, he never fully succeeded in extending his thinking much beyond that which could be accommodated within the doctrine of special creation.

As a natural historian, Linnaeus shared the European spotlight with Buffon. Their views of nature rarely, if ever, overlapped, and Buffon was one of Linnaeus's sharpest

Of time and variation

Man is by nature a classifying animal. His continued existence depends on his ability to recognize similarities and differences between objects and events in his physical universe and to make known these similarities and differences linguistically. Indeed, the very development of the human mind seems to have been closely related to the perception of discontinuities in nature. . . . Early biologists, such as Theophrastus, and later the herbalists merely wrote down folk taxonomic systems . . . designed, not for information retrieval, but for communicating about organisms with those who already understand the nature of the organisms being discussed . . . In an operational system, especially one that is strictly verbal, the number of names cannot be multiplied beyond meaningful limits; many speakers of the language must be familiar with each name that is passed down from generation to generation as part of that language. As there are more and more names, the names become less and less useful. . . . We have as yet named only about 15 percent of the world's organisms and have no real chance of adding many to the total before the rest become extinct. Despite this, we cling to the naive view of Renaissance man and assume that the extension of those folk principles deeply rooted in our collective psychology is the only appropriate way to deal with this diversity. We implicitly assume that we know as much about a mite from the Amazon Basin as we do about the mallard duck, and reflect this assumption in our presumably scientific but actually folk system of naming the two kinds of organisms.

P. H. Raven [27]

---

critics. Whereas Linnaeus stood for the inviolate and immutable nature of things and felt that the goal of science was to provide an index of things properly arranged, Buffon summarily dismissed the Linnaean system as a matter of artificial contrivance and sought for the causes of diversity through an understanding of the laws of nature. Nature to Buffon was a system of "matter in motion," an old idea that had its origin in Greek atomism. But in Buffon's hands, this concept was not far removed from a biological version of uniformitarianism. Buffon accepted variation as a fact. He felt that it was inexhaustible and was the natural consequence of the laws of nature acting on matter through time and in space. Species, however permanent they might seem to be, were but the results of these natural forces, created, changed, and often annihilated with the passage of time. He saw no final causes and no design, although he was equivocal about the role of permanence in nature, as can be seen from the following statement: "It seems that everything which can be, is: the Creator's hand seems not to have been opened in order to give existence to a determinate number of species, rather it seems to have thrown forth at one and the same time a world of creatures related and unrelated, an infinity of harmonious and contrary combinations, a perpetuity of destructions and renewals." In the endless variety of nature, Buffon saw only forces at work; there was purpose to nature so far as man was concerned, and there were no limits to man's attempts to understand the workings of nature. He viewed the earth as a ceaselessly changing panorama, rather than as simply an abode for man. He studied the effects of the environment on living systems, and looked upon man as augmenting natural forces in his creation of domesticated varieties of plants and animals.

3.9 *Buffon.*

Of time and variation

I met a traveller from an antique land
Who said: "Two vast and trunkless legs of stone
Stand in the desert. Near them, on the sand,
Half sunk, a shattered visage lies, whose frown,
And wrinkled lip, and sneer of cold command,
Tell that its sculptor well those passions read
Which yet survive, stampt on these lifeless things,
The hand that mockt them and the heart that fed;
And on the pedestal these words appear:
'My name is Ozymandias, king of kings:
Look on my works, ye Mighty, and despair!'
Nothing besides remains. Round the decay
Of that colossal wreck, boundless and bare
The lone and level sands stretch far away."

P. B. Shelley [30]

Nature being contemporaneous with matter, space, and time, her history is that of all substances, all places, all ages; and although it appears at first view that her great works never alter or change, and that in her productions, even the most fragile and transitory, she always shows herself to be constantly the same, since her primary models regularly reappear before our eyes in new representations; however, in observing her closer, it will be seen that her course is not absolutely uniform; it will be recognized that she admits sensible variations, that she receives successive alterations, that she even lends herself to new combinations, to mutations of matter and of form; that, finally, much as she seems to be fixed as a whole, she is variable in each of her parts; and if we encompass her in all her extent, we can no longer doubt that she is today very different from what she was at the beginning and from what she became in the succession of time: it is these various changes that we call her epochs. Nature has existed in different states; the surface of the earth has successively taken different forms; the heavens themselves have varied, and all the things in the physical universe, like those in the moral world, are in a continual movement of successive variations.

Buffon [5]

Buffon's trend of thought was clearly far removed from that of Ray and of Linnaeus, and he showed a remarkable insight in anticipating, even initiating, the kind of biological thinking that would lead science forward. He was, in the best sense, a scientific optimist; if an answer to a question was not yet available, he felt that it would come in time as man's knowledge deepened. It was Buffon's mode of thought, not that of Ray or Linnaeus, that paved the way for Lamarck and Darwin. Buffon seemed perennially to be on the verge of enunciating the ideas of natural selection, but somehow this step was never quite taken. As the contemporary historian of science John Greene [9] has stated:

In many ways his ideas were more akin to the speculations of pagan antiquity than to those of modern evolutionists. Although he stressed the variability of nature and recognized that some variants were more likely to endure than others, he never pushed the idea of natural selection to its logical conclusion. He used it to explain how species disappeared but not how they were modified. He saw the elimination of the weak and the mal-adapted as an occasional extraordinary event rather than as a process operating relentlessly within species as well as among species. He viewed change more in terms of degeneration than of improvement. . . . In all these questions, however, his ultimate appeal was to observation and experimentations.

As the nineteenth century dawned in Western Europe, one can see in retrospect the convergence of a number of scientific ideas, ideas that were dissimilar in subject matter and origin but similar in importance when viewed in the light of a theory of evolution not yet enunciated, although dimly apprehended in the minds of some individuals. The union of these ideas was not achieved until overwhelming and irrefutable evidence firmly fixed their relations and interdependence, and inevitable delays occurred because

Of time and variation

Elihu Vedder, The Questioner of the Sphinx.

Museum of Fine Arts, Boston,
Bequest of Mrs. Martin Brimmer

each new theory challenged the biblical concept of the nature of man and his universe. The extension of human knowledge is never direct, and if a view of reality is to be generally accepted, it must be consistent with man's hopes and fears, with his traditions and future prospects. From a scientific point of view, the drag of theology was a heavy one; the theologians and philosophers, some of whom were also scientists, saw the sanctity of man and his relation to his God being badly eroded, and their defense was articulate and determined. The result was not so much a debate that divided scientists and philosophers as it was a question to be decided by each individual. The church, whether Catholic or Protestant, was still a powerful institution of society, and the need to conform and support or to combat a theological position was evident even in scientific writings.

We have already discussed these important issues: the question of time and its bearing on the history of man and of the earth; the nature of fossils and the manner of their deposition in rock strata; and the significance of variations and the legitimacy of species. In developing his concept of uniformitarianism, Hutton might see "no vestige of a beginning, no prospect of an end" for those forces that have shaped the earth, but his views of the physical world were not generally accepted until Lyell's consummate geologic treatise, written between 1830 and 1833, dispelled all doubts, not only because of the reasonableness of presentation, but because of the respect accorded him in his day. Lyell's evolutionary view embraced primarily the physical, rather than the biological, world. Buffon might himself, on occasion, accept variations as a departure point in discussing natural history, but the necessity of adopting an evolu-

Of time and variation

95

. . . would it be too bold to imagine, that in the great length of time, since the earth began to exist, perhaps millions of ages before the commencement of the history of mankind, . . . all warm-blooded animals have arisen from one living filament, which THE GREAT FIRST CAUSE endued with animality, with the power of acquiring new parts attended with new propensities, directed by irritations, sensations, volitions, and associations; and thus possessing the faculty of continuing to improve by its own inherent activity, and of delivering down those improvements by generation to its posterity, world without end?

E. Darwin [8]

If we consider each species in the different climates which it inhabits, we shall find perceptible varieties as regards size and form; they all derive an impress to a greater or less extent from the climate in which they live. These changes are made slowly and imperceptibly. Nature's great workman is Time. He marches ever with an even pace, and does nothing by leaps and bounds, but by degrees, gradations and successions he does all things; and the changes which he works—at first imperceptible—become little by little perceptible, and show themselves eventually in results about which there can be no mistake.

Buffon [5]

tionary point of view was not evident. At the same time, the concept of the fixity of species was not easily dislodged, gaining support as it did from the Greek view of "immutable organic form," from biblical authority, and from wide acceptance among philosophers of the idea of the great chain of being. The latter had embodied within it the principle of continuity of forms, but this could be accepted without invoking the question of descent or familial relationships. The fact that the concept of the fixity of species gained its strength from literary sources rather from field or laboratory studies did not have a major effect on its general acceptability; it was simply more consistent with the intellectual temper of the time. The question concerning fossils was no longer whether they were remains of organisms of past ages, for by the beginning of the nineteenth century, this was a prevalent view. The plaguing question was how they got where they were. Until the "how" was answered, their significance was openly debatable.

Two scientists—Frenchmen, colleagues, and biologists—point up the divergent views that were held in the period just prior to the announcement of Darwin's ideas of evolution. These were Georges Cuvier (1769–1832), a gifted paleontologist and the father of the science of comparative anatomy, and Jean Baptiste Lamarck (1744–1829), a versatile scientist who proposed the first comprehensive, although incorrect, theory of evolution.

Cuvier opposed the uniformitarian views of Hutton and proposed that sudden, terrible catastrophes, including Noah's Flood, were the key to an understanding of the past history of the earth. To his own satisfaction and to that of a great many other intellectuals, he brought the geological and biological sciences into reasonable harmony with a

M. de Lamarck was the last representative of that great school of naturalists and general observers who held sway from Thales and Democritus right down to Buffon. He was the mortal enemy of the chemists, of experimentalists and petty analysts, as he called them. No less severe was his philosophical hostility amounting to hatred for the tradition of the Deluge and the Biblical creation story, indeed for everything which recalled the Christian theory of nature. His own conception of things was simple, austere, and full of pathos. He constructed the world out of the smallest possible number of elements, and with the fewest crises and the longest duration imaginable. . . . Similarly in the organic realm, once he had admitted the mysterious power of life, in as minimal and elementary a form as possible, he supposes it developing on its own, building itself up, complicating itself little by little. Various organs were born of unconscious needs, of simple habit working in the different environments against the constant destroying power of nature. For M. de Lamarck separated life from nature. Nature in his eyes was cinder and stone, the granite of the tomb, death itself. Life intervenes only accidentally, as a strange but singularly industrious intruder, fighting a perpetual battle with some little success, achieving here and there a certain equilibrium, but always vanquished in the end.

C. A. Sainte-Beuve [29]

---

literal sacred history. Working in the Paris basin, with its rich deposits of marine and freshwater fossils interspersed with strata devoid of fossils, he realized fully that the earth was older than the 6,000 years purported in the Mosaic account, and he proposed that periodic and sudden inundations of the sea that wiped out all or most of existing life were followed subsequently by a repopulation either through supernatural intervention or by those organisms that somehow escaped each catastrophe. In his view, there were no transitional forms that linked the fossils of one stratum with those of an adjacent layer, and so he saw no organic connection between successive catastrophes. The fact that a fossil in one stratum might bear a general, but not specific, resemblance to one in another layer merely indicated that nature did nothing by violent transitions in form. Variation, even between strata, had its limits, and evolution was ruled out, even though succeeding creations showed greater advances in structure, complexity, and perfection. Because there were no human fossils in the deposits he examined, Cuvier felt that man must have appeared on the earthly scene only after the latest flood.

Cuvier's antievolutionary stand gained credence not only because it fitted what most people wanted to believe, but also because of his indisputable brilliance as a comparative anatomist. His knowledge of animal structures was so extensive that from a single fossil fragment, such as a leg bone, he could reconstruct, to the astonishment and delight of his audiences, prehistoric organisms whose existence no one had suspected. He believed, consequently, in the extinction of species. It was not until the publication of Lyell's *Principles of Geology* that the concept of the earth that Cuvier had created was finally shattered. As the following passage indi-

Of time and variation

Domestic cat.

Siberian tigers.

Ron Garrison photo, San Diego Zoo

The same species has been given to every collection of similar individuals which have been produced by other individuals like themselves. This definition is correct. . . . But to this definition has been added the supposition that the individuals which make up the species never vary in their specific characters and that consequently the species has an absolute constancy in nature. It is exactly this supposition that I propose to combat.

J. Lamarck [15]

3.10 *Jean Baptiste Lamarck.*

cates, Cuvier in a way wished for some sort of evidence for evolution even though he was an antievolutionist: "Genius and science have burst the limits of space; and a few observations, explained by just reasoning, have unveiled the mechanism of the universe. Would it not also be glorious for man to burst the limits of time, and, by a few observations, to ascertain the history of this world, and the series of events which preceded the birth of the human race?" The heart has reasons which the mind cannot know, even to those who voice them.

Lamarck, on the other hand, took for granted the mutability of species, viewed fossils as evidence of changes taking place through unlimited time, and, most importantly, recognized that the adaptation of an organism to its environment was a dynamic interrelationship. If the environment is changing, Lamarck reasoned, the organism also must change if it is to survive. As a corollary, he saw that if environmental change was in one direction, organismic change must be in the same direction, simply because such change is adaptive. Furthermore, adaptive change takes place when an organism responds to pressures imposed by the environment; the environment does not directly alter the organism, the organism alters itself. To any organism, the shifting environment presents a series of challenges and opportunities to which it must respond or die, and because, according to Lamarck, only living things can act purposefully, the response is from within the organism.

Lamarck, therefore, concentrated his attentions on the process whereby an organism is enabled to elicit a response to an altered situation. In doing so, he separated nature from life. The former had no purpose; it was inanimate and dead. Life, on the other hand, drew its sustenance from nature,

Of time and variation

Perhaps, at some time or somewhere in the universe, the species of animals are, or were, or will be, more subject to change than they are at present in ours; and several animals which possess something of the cat, like the lion, tiger, and lynx, could have been of the same race and could be now like new subdivisions of the ancient species of cats. So I always return to what I have said more than once, that our determinations of physical species are provisional and proportional to our knowledge.

If beings change successively, passing through the most imperceptible nuances, time, which does not stop, must eventually put the greatest difference between forms that existed in ancient times, those which exist today and those that will exist in far-off centuries; and the *nil sub sole novum* is only a prejudice based on the weakness of our organs, the imperfection of our instruments and the shortness of our lives.

G. Leibniz [18]

Bobcat.

and it was stable and continuous so long as the environment was stable. But an organism has needs to meet if it is to adapt to a changing situation, and it was these needs that Lamarck viewed as the driving force of evolution toward greater complexity and adaptability. These needs were felt internally by the organism and led to altered structure and function. If the need were greater, the organs would be enhanced or altered in function, or even created anew; if less, the organ would be diminished, atrophied, and even lost. Because these organ changes were, in Lamarck's view, inherited, his theory of evolution has been associated popularly with the inheritance of acquired characteristics. In all fairness to Lamarck, however, it should be pointed out that the inheritance of acquired characteristics was a prevalent view before his time and that it persisted well into the twentieth century. He simply used the idea to reinforce his view of evolution.

Lamarck's theory has been shown to be incorrect in that it was grounded not in fact, but on intuitive reasoning. Nevertheless, Lamarck rejected outright the idea that literary sources, sacred or not, can form the basis of scientific explanation; he dismissed catastrophes of any sort as major extinctive forces; he viewed adaptation in a thoroughly modern light; and he recognized that the processes of evolution must be known if the history of life is to be understood. In successive editions of *The Origin of Species*, Darwin paid Lamarck the compliment of leaning more and more toward the theory of the inheritance of acquired characteristics as a source of variation and the cause of evolution, even though he was in error on this point. It was not until the founding of the science of genetics that the true basis of variation was discovered.

Oh! how great is the antiquity of the terrestrial globe! and how little the ideas of those who attribute to the globe an existence of six thousand and a few hundred years duration from its origin to the present!

The natural philosopher and the geologist see things much differently in this respect; because, if they consider ever so little, first, the nature of fossils spread in such great numbers in all parts of the exposed globe, either at heights, or at considerable depths; second, the number and disposition of the beds, as well as the nature and order of the materials composing the external crust of the globe, studied in a great part of its thickness and in the mass of the mountains, how many occasions they have to be convinced that the antiquity of this same globe is so great that it is absolutely outside the power of man to appreciate it in any manner!

How much this antiquity of the terrestrial globe will grow in the eyes of man, when he has formed a just idea of the origin of living bodies, as well as the causes of the development and gradual perfecting of the organization of these bodies, and especially when he has conceived that, time and circumstances having been necessary to bring into existence all the living species such as we see them, he is himself the latest result and the present *maximum* of this perfecting, whose end, if there is one, cannot be known!

J. Lamarck [14]

Standard Oil Co. (N.J.)

His parent hand, with ever-new increase
Of happiness and virtue, has adorn'd
The vast harmonious frame; his parent hand,
From the mute shell-fish gasping on the shore,
To men, to angels, to celestial minds,
For ever leads the generations on
To higher scenes of being.

. . .

Once more search, undismay'd, the dark profound
Where Nature works in secret: view the beds
Of mineral treasure, and the eternal vault
That bounds the hoary Ocean; trace the forms
Of atoms moving with incessant change
Their elemental round; behold the seeds
Of being, and the energy of life
Kindling the mass with ever-active flame.

M. Akenside [1]

Summary

A grasp of the dimension of time and of the slow but ceaseless change that accompanies its passage requires perspective, and perspective itself is equally difficult to attain, particularly when the image of man tends to get in the way. But when a picture of the earth's past began to emerge, it came by way of the physical sciences, specifically geology, and through an understanding of the history of the earth as an inanimate object and not as an abode created especially for man. The history of the earth cannot be quantified. It is not subject to those mathematical methods used by early astronomers in studying the heavens or by Harvey in dealing with the flow of blood through the heart. However, in the immense perspective of geologic time, the daily changes in the earth's crust can be translated into mountain building and erosion and into the formation of vast deposits of fossil-bearing rocks. The history of the earth and of man must be interpreted according to different time scales.

So too with variation. Once the idea was broached, examples to reinforce the concept were there for the observant eye to detect. Change in living things and the earth merged with the passage of time and provided a new and different image, a shifting panorama on an expanded stage.

In the process some of man's cherished ideas ceased to serve as frames of reference within which man could see himself. The time was ripe for a comprehensive theory that would embrace the inanimate and animate worlds and portray them not as static images, but as shifting views that slowly changed as the kaleidoscope of time was turned.

Of time and variation

4

Of change and chance

The publication in 1543 of *De revolutionibus orbium coelestium,* by Copernicus, and *De humani corporis fabrica,* by Vesalius, marked a turning point in intellectual history. In 1859, the publication of another book had a similar impact on man's thoughts about his nature, his past, and his future. That book was *On the Origin of Species by Means of Natural Selection, or the Preservation of Favoured Races in the Struggle for Life,* and its author, Charles Darwin (1809–1882), was destined to become one of the preeminent figures in the history not only of biology but of all human thought. As Julian Huxley has said: "After Darwin it became necessary to think of the phenomenal world in terms of process, not merely in terms of mechanisms, and eventually to grasp that the whole of reality is a single process of evolution."

The *Origin* was the cataclysm that broke up the crust of conventional opinion. It expressed and dramatized what many had obscurely felt. More than this: it legitimized what they felt. Coming from so unexceptional a source, with all the authority of science and without the taint of ulterior ideology, it became the receptacle of great hopes and great fears. Those who were already partial to the mode of thought it represented—which could mean anything from a mild naturalism or deism to a belligerent atheism—often fastened upon it as the symbol and warrant of their belief; if they later loosely spoke of it as the cause of their conversion, the error is understandable, the leap from justification to cause being all too easily effected. Similarly, those who had already committed themselves to the other side, finding naturalism uncongenial or unpersuasive, tended to look upon the *Origin* as the incarnation of all that was hateful and fearful. There were, to be sure, some who experienced a genuine crisis of faith upon reading it, as there were also some who came to it with an open mind and left unconverted; if the former have been more publicized, it may be because the loss of faith is a more dramatic affair than the retention of faith. For most men, however, the *Origin* was not an isolated event with isolated consequences. It did not revolutionize their beliefs so much as give public recognition to a revolution that had already occurred. It was belief made manifest, revolution legitimized.

G. Himmelfarb [17]

To have lived when this prodigious truth was advanced, debated, established, was a rare privilege in the centuries. The inspiration of seeing the old isolated mists dissolve and reveal the convergence of all branches of knowledge is something that can hardly be known to the men of a later generation, inheritors of what this age has won.

J. Fiske [14]

4.1   *Portrait of Charles Darwin by Julia M. Cameron.*

Smithsonian Institution

Thomas Henry Huxley (1825–1895), a prominent English biologist and Julian's grandfather, became Darwin's champion, seeing to it that the theory of evolution by natural selection was explained, as it needed to be, to audiences of many persuasions. When Darwin's views were made known to him, Huxley's supposed reaction was: "How extremely stupid not to have thought of that." It was the normal reaction of one who has stared at familiar, age-old patterns of biological unity, diversity, and continuity, and who now unexpectedly sees them with fresh insight and new import. New patterns of belief were beginning to unite the physical, biological, and human worlds into one grand scheme of change operating through time.

Joseph Hooker (1817–1911), Britain's foremost botanist and confidant of Darwin, reported that the volume "created a tremendous furore on all hands" when it appeared. Man's view of himself was challenged as it had never been before, and few who thought seriously about such things could remain neutral. In 1876, when T. H. Huxley gave the inaugural address at The Johns Hopkins University in Baltimore, the local newspapers referred to him as a disciple of the devil and predicted that the future augured no good for a university that had chosen him as a spokesman and that, in addition, had no prayer at the ceremonies that marked its opening.

In 1900, nearly a half-century after the publication of *The Origin of Species*, a London newspaper asked its readers to list the ten most influential books that had appeared in the nineteenth century. As one might well imagine, the lists varied widely, depending upon reading habits, preferences, and backgrounds, but Darwin's book was on virtually every list. Probably not all the respondents had

Of change and chance

The voyage of the Beagle has been by far the most important event in my life and has determined my whole career; . . . I have always felt that I owe to the voyage the first real training or education of my mind. I was led to attend closely to several branches of natural history, and thus my powers of observation were improved, though they were already fairly developed. . . .

Therefore, my success as a man of science, whatever this may have amounted to, has been determined, as far as I can judge, by complex and diversified mental qualities and conditions. Of these the most important have been—the love of science—unbounded patience in long reflecting over any subject—industry in observing and collecting facts—and a fair share of invention as well as of common sense. With such moderate abilities as I possess, it is truly surprising that thus I should have influenced to a considerable extent the beliefs of scientific men on some important points.

C. Darwin [10]

---

read the book, and many who had read it questioned its conclusions, but there certainly was no doubt about its great significance. It dealt with the question of biological change, and in a later book, *The Descent of Man*, Darwin applied the same thinking to the origins and evolution of the human species. But the impact of Darwin's writing extended well beyond the limits of biology, and there were few aspects of life—social, economic, philosophical, and religious, as well as scientific—that were not profoundly influenced. As assessed by Richard Lewontin, Darwinism "was the percussion cap for a charge already set." It was the culmination of a century or more of materialistic and mechanistic thought that had acceptably explained the physical universe and that now was being applied to a study of the living world and man. A world of design and stability was giving way to a purposeless universe of random change and blind chance. Today we view evolution by means of natural selection as a scientific fact, reinforced as it is by a wide variety of observations and experiments. Purpose, if any, is not inherent in this system of change, but rather is injected into it by man. Because man now understands the process, he can, if he chooses, direct and control his own future and that of any other living species.

Darwin was 22 years old when he signed on the naval survey ship H.M.S. *Beagle* as a naturalist. He had thoughts of becoming a clergyman, and his religious views were orthodox and his interpretation of Scripture literal. He must have known of the writings of his grandfather Eramus Darwin on the subject of evolution and the mutability of species, but there is no indication that these writings had any effect on his thinking then or later. He had, however, developed a strong, if undirected, interest in natural history,

It is difficult for us to understand that during more than half a century paleontologists saw clearly the evidence of successive faunas leading continuously to higher organization, and yet did not sense or admit the obvious implication. . . . Charles Darwin in 1859 furnished the key that arranged all the facts of paleontology in sensible order. The doctrine of evolution acted like a blood transfusion; it changed paleontology from a rule-of-thumb technique into a science with a firm philosophic foundation.

C. L. Longwell [22]

4.2 H.M.S. Beagle, *the ship on which Darwin journeyed to South America, off Rio de Janeiro, July 5, 1832.*

Bahia, or San Salvador. Brazil, Feb. 29th.—The day has passed delightfully. Delight itself, however, is a weak term to express the feelings of a naturalist who, for the first time, has wandered by himself in a Brazilian forest. The elegance of the grasses, the novelty of the parasitical plants, the beauty of the flowers, the glossy green of the foliage, but above all the general luxuriance of the vegetation, filled me with admiration. A most paradoxical mixture of sound and silence pervades the shady parts of the wood. The noise from the insects is so loud, that it may be heard even in a vessel anchored several hundred yards from the shore; yet within the recesses of the forest a universal silence appears to reign. To a person fond of natural history, such a day as this brings with it a deeper pleasure than he can ever hope to experience again. After wandering about for some hours, I returned to the landing-place; but, before reaching it, I was overtaken by a tropical storm. I tried to find shelter under a tree, which was so thick that it would never have been penetrated by common English rain; but here, in a couple of minutes, a little torrent flowed down the trunk. It is to this violence of the rain that we must attribute the verdure at the bottom of the thickest woods: if the showers were like those of a colder clime, the greater part would be absorbed or evaporated before it reached the ground. I will not at present attempt to describe the gaudy scenery of this noble bay, because, in our homeward voyage, we called here a second time, and I shall then have occasion to remark on it.

C. Darwin [10]

The glories of the vegetation of the Tropics rise before my mind at the present time more vividly than anything else. Though the sense of sublimity, which the great deserts of Patagonia and the forest-clad mountains of Tierra del Fuego excited in me, has left an indelible impression on my mind. The sight of a naked savage in his native land is an event which can never be forgotten. Many of my excursions on horseback through the wild countries, or in the boats, some of which lasted several weeks, were deeply interesting; their discomfort and some degree of danger were at that time hardly a drawback and none at all afterwards.

C. Darwin [10]

4.3 *Picton Island, Tierra del Fuego region.*

and his activities as a collector in new and strange lands soon convinced him that he should pursue a scientific career.

Darwin carried the first volume of Lyell's *Principles of Geology* (1830) with him in his sea chest. This had been urged upon him by one of his professors at Cambridge, who admonished him, however, not to accept the views advocated in it. But as Darwin said himself, the reading of this book "altered the whole tone of one's mind," even though he eventually rejected Lyell's view of organic evolution. What the volume did give him, in addition to geologic information, was a sense of the enormousness of time, a dimensional feature necessary for the development of any evolving system, physical or biological. He gradually came to realize that the eons of time that were available for geological processes to sculpture, slowly and inevitably, the face of the earth were also available for changing the character of the organisms that inhabited the earth.

Darwin also became acquainted with Lyell's assertion that the apparent progression of organisms toward greater and greater complexity, as postulated by Cuvier, had no firm basis in the fossil record and that discontinuities in the fossil record were an illusion, not evidence for successive catastrophes. When the conditions for fossilization were absent, no fossils could be formed, but this did not mean discontinuities in the fauna and flora of the world. The stream of life continued from one geologic age to another without gaps. Lyell, nevertheless, could not reject the idea of a design in nature, with each species being specifically created for the environment in which it existed (the so-called "creationist" theory). He pointed out that species in a diversified environment might show more variation than one

Of change and chance

in a physically restricted niche and that some species might even become extinct as the environment became altered and uninhabitable, but this was as far as he would go. He could not apply the principle of uniformitarianism to the living world as he had applied it to the world of rocks. In later years, Darwin said that his own writings were, in large part, an extension of Lyell's thinking, but he continued to resent the fact that Lyell could not accept the theory of lineal descent through modification. Darwin fully realized that the acceptance of his theories was retarded by the opposition of so eminent a scientist as Lyell and voiced his bitterness: "You cut my throat, and your own throat; and I believe you will live to be sorry for it."

During the 5 years that he was aboard the *Beagle,* Darwin's views concerning evolution did not undergo any major change, if we are to judge by his account of his journey in *The Voyage of the Beagle.* He was, however, a meticulous observer and an inveterate collector; he saw organisms in relation to their environment, and with an eye to geographic distribution. He pointed out that much of what he observed would be "of equally great interest to the philosophical naturalist," but except for his continual attempt to compare the various data that he had gathered, an attempt that is recorded throughout *The Voyage,* he had not yet acquired a strong speculative mode of thought. The origin of species was uppermost in his mind, nevertheless, and he began, soon after his return to England, a series of notebooks in which he amassed everything bearing on this topic. By 1837 he had the main outlines of this theory of evolution worked out. His lengthy essay of 1844, privately circulated, contained the gist of his arguments,

The Sea of Faith
Was once, too, at the full, and round earth's shore
Lay like the folds of a bright girdle furled.
But now I only hear
Its melancholy, long, withdrawing roar,
Retreating, to the breath
Of the night wind, down the vast edges drear
And naked shingles of the world.

M. Arnold [2]

It is impossible to reflect on the changed state of the American continent without the deepest astonishment. Formerly it must have swarmed with great monsters: now we find mere pigmies, compared with the antecedent, allied races. If Buffon had known of the gigantic sloth and armadillo-like animals, and of the lost Pachydermata, he might have said with a greater semblance of truth that the creative force in America had lost its power, rather than that it had never possessed great vigour. The greater number, if not all, of these extinct quadrupeds lived at a late period, and were the contemporaries of most of the existing sea-shells. Since they lived, no very great change in the form of the land can have taken place. What, then, has exterminated so many species and whole genera? The mind at first is irresistibly hurried into the belief of some great catastrophe; but thus to destroy animals, both large and small, in Southern Patagonia, in Brazil, on the Cordillera of Peru, in North America up to Behring's Straits, we must shake the entire framework of the globe. An examination, moreover, of the geology of La Plata and Patagonia, leads to the belief that all the features of the land result from slow and gradual changes. It appears from the character of the fossils in Europe, Asia, Australia, and in North and South America, that those conditions which favour the life of the *larger* quadrupeds were lately co-extensive with the world: what those conditions were, no one has yet even conjectured.

C. Darwin [10]

whereas *The Origin of Species* presented the wealth of evidence upon which his theory was based. Darwin's great work was forced into early publication because in 1858 Alfred R. Wallace, a zoologist studying the fauna of Malaya and the islands of the East Indies, submitted a manuscript to Darwin in which he had, in the brief space of some twenty pages, spelled out an exact duplicate of the theory of descent via the natural selection of better adapted forms. One can imagine Darwin's dismay when Wallace asked him to see to the publication of his essay if he thought that it had sufficient merit. Taking what was perhaps the only ethical route out of this situation, Darwin permitted his own views and those of Wallace to be presented in the form of a joint communication to a meeting of British naturalists in July 1858. In November of the following year, *The Origin of Species* was published.

Both Darwin and Wallace had "conversed with nature at first hand." Neither was an armchair philosopher; both drew the same conclusions from their diverse observations. Accepting variation among individuals of a species as a starting point, both saw that species tended to produce more offspring than the environment could support, that inevitably a struggle for existence among individuals must ensue, and that, as a result, those variations that were better adapted to a given situation would have a greater probability of survival and continued propagation. Neither the theory of evolution nor, indeed, the theory of natural selection was original with either of them. In this sense, Darwin and Wallace were the "inheritors, not the creators" of an acceptable theory of evolution. But, most importantly, they answered the question of *how* evolution proceeded and, at

Certainly no conclusion from the natural sciences can be more important to men than that which concerns Genesis: for to place this book in the class of fables would be to throw into deepest ignorance that which it is most important for them to know; their origin, their duty, and their destination.

J. A. Deluc [12]

There cannot be a design without a designer; contrivance without a contriver; order without choice; arrangement without anything capable of arranging; subserviency and relation to a purpose, without that which could intend a purpose; means suitable to an end, and executing their office in accomplishing that end, without the end ever having been contemplated, or the means accommodated to it. Arrangement, disposition of parts, subserviency of means to an end, relation of instruments to a use, imply the presence of intelligence and mind.

W. Paley [25]

The fixed laws of science can supply natural religion with numberless illustrations of the wisdom, the beneficence, the order, the beauty that characterize the workmanship of God; while they illustrate His infinity by the marvellous complexity of natural combinations, by the variety and order of His creatures, by the exquisite finish alike bestowed on the very greatest and on the very least of His works, as if size were absolutely nothing in His sight.

F. Temple [31]

---

least in the case of Darwin, backed up the idea, cogently and accurately, with an impressive body of evidence derived from a wide variety of sources.

Intellectuals were sharply split over the Darwin-Wallace theory of evolution. There were few neutrals among the scientists, and the debate was often acrimonious and personal. As Gertrude Himmelfarb has said: "Darwin's friends were as quarrelsome as his enemies." Thomas Bell, president of the Linnaean Society of London, blandly summed up scientific progress in the year 1858 in these words: "The year passed without being marked by any striking discoveries such as revolutionize the science in which they occur." But subsequent history does not bear him out. The theories proposed by Darwin and Wallace in July of that year were to lead to the publication of *The Origin of Species*, one of the most influential books ever written, regardless of subject matter; the science of biology and of man would never be the same.

Darwin knew how to assemble information in support of a theory, and he did this superbly well in proposing his theory of evolution. Some of the data was well known to others in the field of natural history; much of it he collected himself on his *Beagle* voyage or at his country home; other information he garnered from plant and animal breeders and from voluminous correspondence. Whatever its source, Darwin marshaled the data into meticulous order and stamped it with his own indelible mark of interpretation. Throughout his assessment of data is the acceptance of change as a characteristic of life, with the added corollary that the present array of living organisms is the result of continuous change from some previous past state.

Of change and chance

The Lord let the house of a brute to the soul of a man,
  And the man said, "Am I your debtor?"
And the Lord—"Not yet: but make it as clean as you can,
  And then I will let you a better."

If my body comes from brutes, my soul uncertain, or a fable,
  Why not bask amid the senses while the sun of morning shines,
I, the finer brute rejoicing in my hounds, and in my stable,
  Youth and health, and birth and wealth, and choice of women and of wines?

⋅ ⋅ ⋅

If my body come from brutes, though somewhat finer than their own,
  I am heir, and this my kingdom. Shall the royal voice be mute?
No, but if the rebel subject seek to drag me from the throne,
  Hold the scepter, Human Soul, and rule the province of the brute.

I have climbed to the snows of Age, and I gaze at a field in the Past,
  Where I sank with the body at times in the sloughs of a low desire,
But I hear no yelp of the beast, and the Man is quiet at last
  As he stands on the heights of his life with a glimpse of a height that is higher.

A. Tennyson [32]

4.4 *Similarity of the skeletal structure of the wrist among various animals. (a) Water tortoise; (b) some primates; (c) man, gorilla, chimpanzee, and some lemurs.*

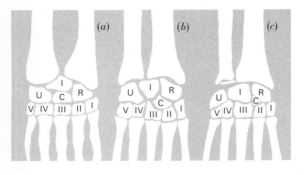

Unity of structures

The similarity of organisms, one to another, in related groups was a widely known and accepted, but variously interpreted, phenomenon. The reproductive organs of the flowering plants are basically similar in morphology, although infinitely varied in small details. Similarly, among animals, a comparable unity of plan can be seen externally in the characteristics of ears, nose, eyes, and legs, internally in the skeletal structures (illustration 4.4), and more obscurely, as we now know, in the character of organs, cells, blood, and molecular building blocks. How one interprets these features of similarity depends upon one's prior assumptions. The concept of the great chain of being included the idea that such unity was the "comely order" of progression leading to man at the apex, but acceptance of this view did not necessarily mean the acceptance of any theory of organic evolution. As Cuvier, who developed the science of comparative morphology, had pointed out, nature did not take sudden leaps from one successive geologic age to the next, and such unity was simply the retention, with slight change, of a previously determined design.

Darwin had a different view. In *The Origin of Species* he wrote:

What could be more curious than that the hand of a man, formed for grasping, that of a mole for digging, the leg of the horse, the paddle of the porpoise, and the wing of the bat, should all be constructed on the same pattern, and should include similar bones, in the same relative positions? . . . Nothing could be more hopeless than to attempt to explain this similarity of pattern in members of the same class by utility or

Of change and chance

by the doctrine of final causes. . . . If we suppose that an early progenitor . . . of all mammals, birds, and reptiles, had its limbs constructed on the existing general pattern, for whatever purpose they served, we can at once perceive the plain significance of the homologous construction of the limbs throughout the class.

The mode of life of an organism, however different and remote it may be from a related species (for example, mole and porpoise) cannot disguise and obscure the basic similarity of structures. Such a resemblance, in Darwin's view, was interpretable and understandable only on the assumption that at some time in the past, a divergence from a common ancestor took place. A group of related species has, therefore, a history, traceable to the past as a branching system of divergences, some of which may have persisted to the present, while others may have become extinct. The degree of similarity of structure becomes, as a result, a measure of their ancestral affinity.

A century earlier, Linnaeus had expressed the thought that the goal of science was the development of a natural system of classification. The Darwin-Wallace concept of descent through modification, but with evidences of affinity through unity of structure, brought Linnaeus's goal closer to realization and changed the science of classification from a static to a dynamic state of being.

Again, the sheep and the cow have no cutting-teeth, but only a hard pad in the upper jaw. That is the common characteristic of ruminants in general. But the calf has in its upper jaw some rudiments of teeth which never are developed, and never play the part of teeth at all. Well, if you go back in time, you find some of the older, now extinct, allies of the ruminants have well-developed teeth in their upper jaws; and at the present day the pig (which is in structure closely connected with ruminants) has well-developed teeth in its upper jaws; so that here is another instance of organs well developed and very useful, in one animal, represented by rudimentary organs, for which we can discover no purpose whatsoever, in another closely allied animal. The whalebone whale, again, has horny "whalebone" plates in its mouth, and no teeth; but the young fetal whale, before it is born, has teeth in its jaws; they, however, are never used, and they never come to anything. But other members of the group to which the whale belongs have well-developed teeth in both jaws.

T. H. Huxley [19]

Similarity of development

Development includes all the progressive and cumulative changes that occur during the life history of an individual. These processes occur at all levels of biological organization

A man said to the universe:
"Sir, I exist!"
"However," replied the universe,
"The fact has not created in me
A sense of obligation."

S. Crane [6]

and affect everything from small molecules to complex organs and organ systems; they also occur sequentially, one stage of development following another in predictable and orderly fashion. Development, therefore, is the gradual ac-

4.5 *Stages in the embryonic development of four species. Although it is somewhat difficult to distinguish the species at an early stage of development, this task becomes easier in more advanced stages.*

Man	Pig	Salamander	Chicken

Not Time affects me—I am Time, old, modern as any,
Unpersuadable, relentless, executing righteous judgments,
As the Earth, the Father, the brown old Kronos, with laws,
Aged beyond computation, yet ever new, ever with those mighty laws rolling,
Relentless I forgive no man—whoever sins dies—I will have that man's life:
Therefore let none expect mercy—have the seasons, gravitation, the
    appointed days, mercy? no more have I,
But as the seasons and gravitation, and as all the appointed days that forgive not.
I dispense from this side judgments inexorable without the least remorse.

W. Whitman [35]

---

quisition of adult form and function as the individual changes from a fertilized egg to its mature proportions, and then on into its stages of senescence.

Darwin was fully aware of the studies carried out, particularly by German zoologists, on the embryos of various species. Among the vertebrates, for example, the earlier the embryonic stage, the more difficult it is to determine the species of which it is representative. As the embryo grows, however, it takes on features that are characteristic of its own species. The embryos of such dissimilar species as a fish, a bird, and a man are virtually indistinguishable at an early stage. They all display gill pouches, a fact that suggests that man and birds share a common ancestry with the fish. The barnacles, a group of invertebrates about which Darwin published four monographs, were once classified with the mollusks (snails, clams, and so on). The discovery, in 1830, that they have a larval (embryonic) stage, known as a nauplius, led to their reclassification with the crustaceans (crabs, lobsters, and shrimp).

Comparing embryonic stages of organisms is, in principle, no different from comparing the anatomy of adult forms (see illustration 4.5). Embryos are simply younger and more labile forms, and they display a unity of structure that is equally revealing of natural affinities. When a visible variation appears in a mature organism, this must mean that a variation had been introduced somewhere during the course of development; the earlier in embryogeny the variation, the more drastic the change in an adult, because time and growth would tend to magnify the change. Darwin interpreted these embryonic similarities and dissimilarities in terms of unity or diversity, of lineal continuity or branching

As all the organic beings, extinct and recent, which have ever lived, can be arranged within a few great classes; and as all within each class have, according to our theory, been connected together by fine gradations, the best, and, if our collections were nearly perfect, the only possible arrangement, would be genealogical; descent being the hidden bond of connexion which naturalists have been seeking under the term of the Natural System. On this view we can understand how it is that, in the eyes of most naturalists, the structure of the embryo is even more important for classification than that of the adult. In two or more groups of animals, however much they may differ from each other in structure and habits in their adult condition, if they pass through closely similar embryonic stages, we may feel assured that they all are descended from one parent-form, and are therefore closely related. Thus, community in embryonic structure reveals community of descent; but dissimilarity in embryonic development does not prove discommunity of descent, for in one of two groups the developmental stages may have been suppressed, or may have been so greatly modified through adaptation to new habits of life, as to be no longer recognisable. . . . As the embryo often shows us more or less plainly the structure of the less modified and ancient progenitor of the group, we can see why ancient and extinct forms so often resemble in their adult state the embryos of existing species of the same class. Agassiz believes this to be a universal law of nature; and we may hope hereafter to see the law proved true.

C. Darwin [11]

His work gives the impression of one Who moves slowly, tentatively, as it were, feeling his way, to some dimly foreseen end by the use of instrumentalities not thoroughly mastered; the process is apparently characterized by many setbacks, by unfulfilled promises, roads that seem to have been built a certain way and abandoned. Although, viewed as a whole, the process is seen to be a grand ever-expanding movement upward on the scale of being, there is also an immense amount of destruction and incidental waste; there is much conflict and much suffering on the part of creatures so constituted as to be capable of great happiness. In short, the God of evolution appears to be one Who, like ourselves, is beset with limitations over which he triumphs by the use of infinitely varied appliances and adjustments.

J. LeConte [20]

---

divergence, for he regarded no stage of life to be free of change.

He would interpret vestigial organs in the same manner. In some snakes the vestiges of the pelvic girdle are still formed although they perform no function; in other snakes they are completely absent. In man, the vermiform appendix, a vestigial part of the digestive system, is a nuisance because it tends to become infected and at times must be removed surgically. The human coccyx at the lower end of the spine is the evolutionary remnant of an ancestral tail. Lamarck would have agreed with Darwin that these vestigial organs were once functional in previous ancestral forms, but he would have proposed that disuse was the cause of their functional and structural atrophy—the species no longer needed the particular organ and so it atrophied like an unused muscle. On the other hand, Darwin would have postulated that variations had occurred in the nature of these organs and that natural selection had favored those forms in which a reduction in function, paralleled by a change in morphology was taking place. In speaking of birds, he wrote in *The Origin of Species:* "There is no greater anomaly of nature than a bird that cannot fly; yet there are several in this state. We may believe that the progenitor of the ostrich genus had habits like those of the bustard, and that, as the size and weight of its body were increased during successive generations, its legs were used more and its wings less, until they became incapable of flight." There are overtones of Lamarckianism in this statement, for Darwin was not entirely freed from a use-and-disuse position, but, generally speaking, the main thrust of his argument was based on variations that occurred randomly and were perpetuated selectively.

I find myself after reasoning through a whole chapter in favor of man's coming from the animals, relapsing to my old views whenever I read again a few pages of the ''Principles'' or yearn for fossil types of intermediate grade. . . . Hundreds who have bought my book in the hope that I should demolish heresy, will be awfully confounded and disappointed. As it is, they will at best say with Crawford, who still stands out, ''You have put the case with such moderation that one cannot complain.'' But when he read Huxley, he was up in arms again.

My feelings, however, more than any thought about policy or expediency, prevent me from dogmatising as to the descent of man from the brutes, which, though I am prepared to accept it, takes away much of the charm from my speculations on the past relating to such matters. . . .

What I am anxious to effect is to avoid positive inconsistencies in different parts of my book, owing probably to the old trains of thought, the old ruts, interfering with the new course.

But you ought to be satisfied, as I shall bring hundreds towards you, who if I treated the matter more dogmatically would have rebelled.

I have spoken out to the utmost extent of my tether, so far as my reason goes, and farther than my imagination and sentiment can follow, which I suppose has caused occasional incongruities.

C. Lyell [23]

Geologic record

As pointed out earlier, Darwin was profoundly influenced by Lyell, and he collected fossils whenever the opportunity was present. While on his voyage, he unearthed in Patagonia a fossil glyptodont that was 4 meters (13 feet) long and recognized that it was an ancestral form of the present-day armadillo. He was not disturbed by the absence of transitional forms between related species. If one could accept the principle of uniformitarianism as it applied to rocks, he could see no reason why it could not be applied to the fossils contained within the rocks. As Darwin put it in *The Origin of Species:*

With respect to the finer shades of transition, . . . no one has any cause to expect to trace them in the fossil state, without he be bold enough to imagine that geologists at a future epoch will be able to trace from fossil bones the gradations between the short-horns, Herefordshire, and Alderney breeds of cattle. . . . Rising islands, in the process of formation, must be the best nurseries of new specific forms, and these points are the least favorable for the embedment of fossils. . . . Periods of subsidence will always be most favorable to an accumulation of great thicknesses of strata, and consequently, to their long preservation. . . . Hence many more remains will be preserved to a distant age, in any region of the world, during periods of its subsidence than of its elevation.

Although Darwin had no difficulty in bridging the gaps between geologic periods and in accepting the fact that ''missing links'' were inevitable, others, following Cuvier, were not so convinced. The fossil record at that time was incomplete, as indeed it still is, and it was not until a decade

The readiest way, perhaps, of persuading the reader that we may dispense with great and sudden revolutions in the geological order of events is by showing him how a regular and uninterrupted series of changes in the animate and inanimate world must give rise to such breaks in the sequence, and such unconformability of stratified rocks, as are usually thought to imply convulsions and catastrophes. It is scarcely necessary to state that the order of events thus assumed to occur, for the sake of illustration, should be in harmony with all the conclusions legitimately drawn by geologists from the structure of the earth, and must be equally in accordance with the changes observed by man to be now going on in the living as well as in the inorganic creation. It may be necessary in the present state of science to supply some part of the assumed course of nature hypothetically; but if so, this must be done without any violation of probability, and always consistently with the analogy of what is known both of the past and present economy of our system.

C. Lyell [23]

Forward, backward, backward, forward,
  in the immeasurable sea,
Swayed by vaster ebbs and flows than can be known
  to you or me.
All the suns—are these but symbols of innumerable man,
Man or Mind that sees a shadow of the planner or the plan?
Is there evil but on earth? or pain
  in every peopled sphere?
Well, be grateful for the sounding watchword
  "Evolution" here,
Evolution ever climbing after some ideal good,
And Reversion ever dragging Evolution in the mud.
      . . .

Many an aeon moulded earth before her highest, man, was born,
Many an aeon too may pass when earth is manless and forlorn,
Earth so huge, and yet so bounded—pools of salt,
  and plots of land—
Shallow skin of green and azure—chains of mountain,
  grains of sand!
Only That which made us meant us to be mightier by and by,
Set the sphere of all the boundless heavens
  within the human eye,
Sent the shadow of Himself, the boundless,
  through the human soul:
Boundless inward in the atom, boundless outward in the Whole.

A. Tennyson [33]

American Museum of Natural History

*4.6 The fossil cast and restoration
of Archaeopteryx.*

*4.7 Opuntia cactus and Palo Santo
on the island of Santa Cruz in the Galapagos.*

Eugene Gordon photo, Nancy Palmer Photo Agency

after the publication of *The Origin of Species* that the discovery of the fossil *Archaeopteryx* (illustration 4.6) provided scientists with an indisputable link between the prehistoric flying reptiles and the modern species of birds. Darwin's confidence in the meaning and significance of the fossil record has, of course, been vindicated completely, particularly by the elucidation of the history of the horse, a history that spans 60 million years and passes through approximately thirty distinct species.

Geographical distribution

It was the seemingly inexplicable distribution of plants and animals over the globe that first stimulated Darwin to ponder over the origin of species. Mention has been made

Of change and chance

The natural history of these islands is eminently curious, and well deserves attention. Most of the organic productions are aboriginal creations, found nowhere else; there is even a difference between the inhabitants of the different islands; yet all show a marked relationship with those of America, though separated from that continent by an open space of ocean, between 500 and 600 miles in width. The archipelago is a little world within itself, or rather a satellite attached to America, whence it has derived a few stray colonists, and has received the general character of its indigenous productions. Considering the small size of these islands, we feel the more astonished at the number of their aboriginal beings, and at their confined range. Seeing every height crowned with its crater, and the boundaries of most of the lava-streams still distinct, we are led to believe that within a period, geologically recent, the unbroken ocean was here spread out. Hence, both in space and time, we seem to be brought somewhat near to that great fact—that mystery of mysteries—the first appearance of new beings on this earth.

C. Darwin [10]

---

of the fact that he considered rising islands to be the best nurseries for the development of new specific forms, and well he might, for the Galapagos Islands played a large role in the development of his theory of evolution. Earlier, during his voyage, he made note of certain rodents of the South American pampas and observed how they differed from one region to another, even though it was obvious that they were closely related forms. The nearer together such forms were geographically, the less they differed. There was a gradation through space, but marked differences if one compared distantly separated forms.

The Galapagos Islands are on the equator about 960 kilometers (some 600 miles) west of Ecuador and are of relatively recent volcanic origin. In Darwin's day, the flora and fauna of the islands were different from, although closely similar to, comparable groups on the mainland of South America. Surprisingly, there also were distinct forms endemic to each of the islands. The island inhabitants, for example, could determine from which island a particular giant tortoise came by examining certain peculiarities of the shell. But it was the finches of the Galapagos that intrigued Darwin. They were similar to those he had seen recently in Peru, but each island had its particular inhabitants. Some were larger or smaller than the Peruvian form, but what struck Darwin most was "the perfect gradation in the size of the beaks, . . . from one as large as that of a hawfinch, to that of a chaffinch, and even to that of a warbler. . . . One might really fancy that from an original paucity of birds in this archipelago, one species had been taken and modified for different ends." Because the beaks are related to feeding habits, this too had undergone change. Some thrived on seeds, others on insects, and one, having the woodpecker's

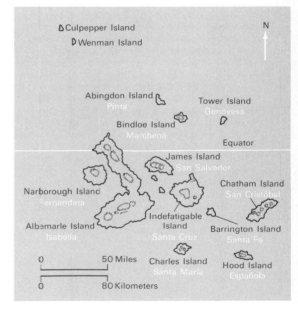

4.8 *The Galapagos Islands as they were known in Darwin's day. The islands' current names are in white.*

The distribution of the tenants of this archipelago would not be nearly so wonderful, if, for instance, one island had a mocking-thrush, and a second island some other quite distinct genus;—if one island had its genus of lizard, and a second island another distinct genus, or none whatever;—or if the different islands were inhabited, not by representative species of the same genera of plants, but by totally different genera, as does to a certain extent hold good; for, to give one instance, a large berry-bearing tree at James Island has no representative species in Charles Island. But it is the circumstance, that several of the islands possess their own species of the tortoise, mocking-thrush, finches, and numerous plants, these species having the same general habits, occupying analogous situations, and obviously filling the same place in the natural economy of this archipelago, that strikes me with wonder. . . .

C. Darwin [10]

4.9 *Variations in the beak structure of four of Darwin's finches. The shape of the beak is related to feeding habits. Shown here are (a) a warbler finch; (b) an inhabitant of the mangrove swamps; (c) an insect-eating finch; (d) a large, seed-eating ground finch.*

(a)   (b)

(c)   (d)

habits but not a woodpecker bill, used a cactus spine as an aid in its search for grubs within rotting wood (see illustration 4.9).

As would be expected according to the creationist theory, each of the finches seemed admirably adapted to its island niche. But because the ten islands of the Galapagos group were similar in all respects, why was there a different grouping of species on each one? Furthermore, as Darwin was aware, the Cape Verde Islands off the coast of Africa are also equatorial and of recent volcanic origin. Why did their flora and fauna differ from that of the Galapagos and resemble rather that of Africa? A more reasonable answer, consistent with all other evidence, was that the islands were invaded by one or more pairs of animals, or by plants through seed dispersal. These plants and animals then increased in number and became diversified by the appearance of variations. Finally, the process of natural selection permitted the survival of only the favored groups. Having viewed different animals in other lands, Darwin or Wallace could see no other possible answer.

Variation and natural selection

Crucial to the theory of evolution through natural selection is the existence within any species of a pool of heritable variations that can be passed on from one generation to the next; evolution, regardless of mechanism, cannot take place in an unvarying species. There must be alternatives from which to choose. Darwin knew that variations existed, but he did not, and could not, know their origin. He was equally uncertain about the mechanism of inheritance and, as time

Of change and chance

The capacity of improvement in plants and animals, to a certain degree, no person can possibly doubt. A clear and decided progress has already been made, and yet, I think it appears that it would be highly absurd to say that this progress has no limits. In human life, though there are great variations from different causes, it may be doubted whether, since the world began, any organic improvement whatever in the human frame can be clearly ascertained. The foundations therefore, on which the organic perfectibility of man rest, are unusually weak, and can only be considered, as mere conjectures. It does not, however, by any means seem impossible, that by an attention to breed, a certain degree of improvement, similar to that among animals, might take place among men. Whether intellect could be communicated may be a matter of doubt: but size, strength, beauty, complexion, and perhaps even longevity are in a degree transmissible. The error does not seem to lie in supposing a small degree of improvement possible, but in not discriminating between a small improvement, the limit of which is undefined, and an improvement really unlimited. As the human race however could not be improved in this way, without condemning all the bad specimens to celibacy, it is not probable, that an attention to breed should ever become general; indeed, I know of no well-directed attempts of this kind, except in the ancient family of the Bickerstaffs, who are said to have been very successful in whitening the skins, and increasing the height of their race by prudent marriages, particularly by that very judicious cross with Maud, the milkmaid, by which some capital defects in the constitution of the family were corrected.

T. Malthus [24]

---

went on, fell back to the Lamarckian idea of the inheritance of acquired characteristics. It was not until the twentieth century that geneticists identified both the source of variations and their mode of inheritance.

Darwin, meticulous observer that he was, detected variation in all the organisms he examined, from man to the barnacles. He was particularly impressed by what man had done with his domesticated plants and animals. He familiarized himself with a vast amount of breeding information and bred pigeons to test the efficacy of selection procedures. It became clearly evident that change could be brought about by rigorous selection of a particular variant. Such changes were also heritable, and a race could be made to breed true for that variant. In this way, a breeder could establish a purebred herd of cattle or a flock of pigeons that differed from the original stock on which selection was begun. The many breeds of dogs, for example, are traceable to a common ancestry and owe their existence to this method of selection.

Such selection, Darwin recognized, was artificial; man was the selector, and the result was breeds within a species, not new and different species. Much could be achieved in a short time, as he observed in his experiments with pigeons. Could the same results be brought about under natural conditions? The variations, of course, were present; otherwise the products of domestication would be inexplicable. And these variations, Darwin pointed out, were not sudden, dramatic changes in structure or behavior; they were small, cumulative shifts that eventually could be used to distinguish one species from another. Although a breeder could fix these variations in a given population by determining breeding patterns, natural, unsupervised breeding was random and

I say that the power of the population is indefinitely greater than the power of the earth to produce subsistence for man . . . [for] population when unchecked increases in geometrical ratio, subsistence only increases in an arithmetic ratio. A slight acquaintance with numbers will show the immensity of the first power in comparison with the second.

Throughout the animal and vegetable kingdom nature has scattered the seeds of life abroad with the most profuse and liberal hand. She has been comparatively sparing in the room and nourishment necessary to rear them. The race of plants and the race of animals shrink under this great restrictive law. And the race of man cannot by any effort of reason escape from it. Among plants and animals its effects are waste of seed, sickness and premature death. Among mankind, misery and vice.

T. Malthus [24]

tended to diffuse rather than concentrate existent variants, and no obvious selective agent seemed available to channel and accumulate these minute variations until they became sufficiently visible for a taxonomist to recognize the existence of a new species. Darwin realized that no man could live long enough to witness the formation of a natural species, but he also was aware that vast stretches of time, measured in geologic terms, were available for it.

The answer to the nature of a selective mechanism came to Darwin, and to Wallace as well, not through biological observations or speculation, but by the reading of a sociological essay by Thomas Malthus (1766–1834), an English clergyman. Malthus's *Essay on the Principles of Population* (1798) was an answer to an earlier book by the Marquis de Condorcet (1743–1794), a French revolutionary and philosopher who advocated a social utopia in which all men, regardless of birth, privilege, or prestige, were to be equally assured of freedom and opportunity, either by law or by custom. A condition of social perfectibility would, therefore, come into being. Malthus, without necessarily arguing against the desirability of such goals, pointed out that they were impossible to attain. Human populations have unlimited potentialities for growth, but inevitably, if numbers continue unchecked, the food supply will become limited. In fact, argued Malthus, the more prosperous and secure a nation, the greater the increase in population, because each individual lives longer as a result of improved conditions. The demands placed on a limited food supply by an ever growing population would cause a return of poverty and consequent inequality and conflict. Condorcet's utopia was not possible unless a rigorous check on population increases was instituted, and Malthus saw no hope of this.

Of change and chance

Life flings us out randomly like seeds into all sorts of crevices, high and low. Some fall on rocks and some among thorns, while others have the still worse fate of being overnourished and overprotected. But the evolutionary hope is that every seed, by its very combination of accidents, will find in itself some new potentiality for development that will enlarge the experience of the whole race. We have regarded the survival of the fittest as a cruel doctrine; but it is a doctrine of life as much as a doctrine of death. It means the survival of wing and brain, of the most adaptable, the most enduring, the most anticipatory the most enjoying, the most diversely communicating with the universe. The picture of man's evolution is not that of a huddled community waiting to be eaten, but that of explorers always learning how to live beyond the fringes. In the rock itself, one tough flower may find a hard niche that in a time of storms preserves the species. What seemed catastrophe becomes the single hope of salvation.

J. R. Platt [26]

The Condorcet-Malthus controversy has a familiar ring today, but Malthus's argument was the stimulus to Darwin and Wallace when viewed against the background of other biological information. Both realized that species produce more offspring than reach maturity; a struggle for existence must, therefore, take place. If the offspring vary among themselves, then any favored individual or race would have a greater probability of surviving and reproducing. Each generation would differ slightly from the preceding one, and the harsher the environment the more rigorous would be the selective process, channeling change in a given direction. The food supply need not be the only limiting factor; physical factors such as temperature, soil condition, and the amount of moisture and light and biological factors such

4.10   *The height at flowering time of* Achillea lanulosa, *a species of yarrow, indicates how altitude affects the habit of growth.*

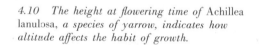

Jens Clausen, Carnegie Institution of Washington

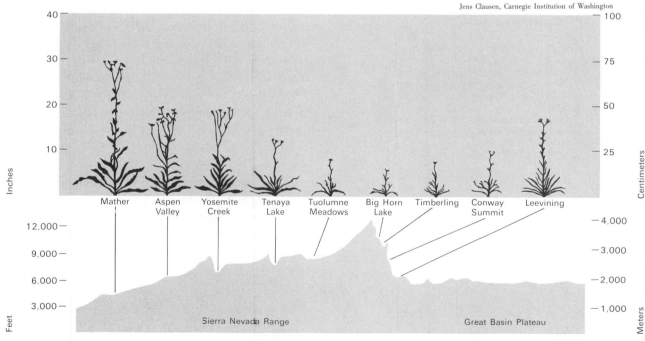

Paul Almasy photo,
World Health Organization

In February 1858 . . . the problem [of evolution] presented itself to me, and something led me to think of the positive checks described by Malthus in his Essay on Population, a work I had read several years before, and which had made a deep and permanent impression on my mind. These checks,—war, disease, famine and the like,—must, it occurred to me, act on animals as well as man. Then I thought of the enormously rapid multiplication of animals, causing these checks to be much more effective in them than in the case of man; and while pondering vaguely on this fact, there suddenly flashed upon me the idea of the survival of the fittest,—that the individuals removed by these checks must be on the whole inferior to those that survived. I sketched the draft of my paper . . . and sent it by the next post to Mr. Darwin.

A. R. Wallace [*34*]

as presence or absence of competition and resistance or susceptibility to disease can be similarly influential (see illustration 4.10).

The environment, consequently, provides the mechanism for natural selection. It makes understandable a number of major biological problems. In the first place, adaptation, or the relation of a species to its environment, is the result of a dynamic interaction between organisms and their physical and biological surroundings, not the product of an all-wise Creator. Furthermore, because environments undergo ceaseless change, so too must a species, otherwise migration becomes necessary or extinction results. Persistence of a species is an indication of its ability to cope with whatever vicissitudes confront it. Secondly, both Darwin and Wallace recognized that, despite the production of offspring, populations in a given environment tend to be stable in numbers. The predator-prey relationship illustrates this. For the past 15 years, on Isle Royale in Lake Superior, the herd of moose has remained stabilized at about six hundred head; the vegetation will not support a greater number through the harsh winters. A stabilized pack of about fifty wolves prey on the moose, culling out from the herd the young, the sick, and the aged. An overproduction of moose would strip the island of vegetation and lead to the ultimate starvation of the entire herd; an overproduction of wolves would decimate the moose herd and cause starvation of the entire pack. A dynamic equilibrium between prey and predator comes into play, not guided by design or purpose, but governed by the rigors of existence.

The theory of evolution through natural selection rests, therefore, upon a broad and varied base of information, much of it observational but supplemented, in more recent

Of change and chance

"In harmony with Nature?" Restless fool,
Who with such heat dost preach what were to thee,
When true, the last impossibility—
To be like Nature strong, like Nature cool!

Know, man hath all which Nature hath, but more,
And in that *more* lie all his hopes of good.
Nature is cruel, man is sick of blood;
Nature is stubborn, man would fain adore;

Nature is fickle, man hath need of rest;
Nature forgives no debt, and fears no grave;
Man would be mild, and with safe conscience blest;

Man must begin, know this, where Nature ends;
Nature and man can never be fast friends.
Fool, if thou canst not pass her, rest her slave!

M. Arnold [3]

---

years, by sound experimental data. The resistance of flies and mosquitoes to DDT and of pathogenic bacteria to specific antibiotics are examples of how organisms can react and accommodate themselves to a drastically altered environment simply because they possess an inherent variability. The variability was not developed in anticipation of changed situations—pesticides, many of them not found in a natural state, could not have been anticipated—but was present because organisms, both within and between species, are variable. The list of species that have become extinct or endangered within the historical present, and as a result of man's activities, grows yearly; man himself has altered the environment for these species, and they have not been sufficiently variable to accommodate successfully to new changes.

No other theory of evolution can encompass and make reasonable this same mass of data in as satisfactory a manner. Therefore, the scientific world now accepts evolution as a fact, natural selection as its main driving force, and adaptation as a goal, a goal not in the sense that it is predetermined and purposeful but rather in the sense that adaptation is the equivalent of sustained existence and successful reproduction. Adaptation, or "fitness," however, is a relative and not an absolute state. If an organism cannot adapt, it does not exist; adaptive changes are, therefore, evolutionary changes. But evolutionary changes are not necessarily adaptive changes for all time; if they were, no species would ever become extinct. What, broadly speaking, does a commitment to Darwinian evolution imply? Without any attempt at completeness, a number of conclusions follow, filtered to be sure by the current intellectual climate, but arguable in reasonable fashion.

4.11 The carved letters on this gravestone become outlines as a result of the growth of lichens. The depressions become miniature water reservoirs, or microenvironments, that enable the lichens to gain a foothold in an otherwise inhospitable habitat.

Courtesy of Dr. Paul Barrett

Of change and chance

"Teleology," remarked von Brücke . . . , "is a lady without whom no biologist can live; yet he is ashamed to show himself in public with her." . . . The important thing to do is to develop aright evolutionary teleology, and to present the argument for design from the exquisite adaptations in such a way as to make it tell on both sides; with Christian men, that they may be satisfied with, and perchance may learn to admire, Divine works effected step by step, if need be, in a system of nature; and the anti-theistic people, to show that without the implication of a superintending wisdom nothing is made out, and nothing credible.

A. Gray [16]

First, the universe is purposeless and nonteleological, governed by the laws of nature that have operated through all time and will continue to operate in the future. The principle of uniformitarianism is as applicable to the biological world as Hutton and Lyell had shown it to be in the physical realm of the earth's surface. Purpose, morals, ethics, and values are themselves by-products of evolutionary change, but were injected into the picture by man as he achieved a cultural self-consciousness. If there is any guiding force behind the operation of the universe other than the laws of nature, this has not been demonstrated scientifically. There may be other roads to truth, and man may operate on the basis of intuitive judgments, but evolution is a scientific explanation of events, and science cannot progress on negative evidence.

Second, instability is characteristic of this universe. Galaxies, stars, and planets have undergone inexorable change in the past, and will continue to change in the future. It has been estimated that in another 5 billion years the sun,

4.12 *Flood damage in an olive orchard in central Tunisia, 1971. The fact that the trees were unable to adapt to the sudden change in their environment has resulted in the destruction of the entire orchard.*

Florita Botts photo, Nancy Palmer Photo Agency

the earth's ultimate source of life-originating and life-sustaining energy, will become a dead star, and life on earth will cease. A similar instability in the hereditary materials of organisms has led to the present diversity on this planet, and will lead to future diversity, the nature and results of which are not predictable except in those circumstances where man exercises the degree of control of which he is capable.

Third, evolution is a short-term, limited, and opportunistic process. It is *short-term* in the sense that it is non-anticipatory of the future needs of a species, because natural selection acts continuously on all stages of the life cycle and because the length of a generation is brief. The first criterion of evolutionary success is survival, just being alive, and the second is the propagation of one's own kind. Evolution is *limited* because, at any given time, the potentiality for heritable variations is limited, and because the environments to which a species can adapt are not infinitely variable or available. It is *opportunistic* in the sense that a species, to be continually successful, must be sufficiently variable to seize environmental opportunities when they arise. Suitable variations and suitable environments must coincide in time, and this is a matter of pure chance. We have no way of knowing the kind and number of variations that appear inopportunely and hence do not enter the evolutionary pool. Variations, when they do arise and are expressed, must pass environmental muster, but their appearance is not, as a rule, environmentally determined. A plant may give rise to a variation that makes it drought-resistant, but if its roots are continually in water, the variation is useless to itself although it may be passed on to its offspring for use at some future time and place.

Be it enacted by the general assembly of the state of Tennessee that it shall be unlawful for any teacher in any of the universities, normals and all other public schools of the state, which are supported in whole or in part by the public-school funds of the state, to teach any theory that denies the story of the divine creation of man as taught in the Bible and to teach instead that man has descended from a lower order of animals.

Section One, Anti-Evolution Law, Tennessee, 1925

. . . (Clarence) Darrow declared the Anti-Evolution Act to be as "brazen and as bold an attempt to destroy learning as was ever made in the Middle Ages. . . . The state of Tennessee, under an honest and fair interpretation of the constitution, has no more right to teach the Bible as the divine book than that the Koran is one, or the book of Mormons or the book of Confucius or the Buddha or the Essays of Emerson or any one of the ten thousand books to which human souls have gone for consolation and aid in their troubles.

"I know there are millions of people in the world who derive consolation in their times of trouble and solace in times of distress from the Bible. I would be pretty near the last one in the world to do anything to take it away. . . . But the Bible is not one book. The Bible is made up of sixty-six books written over a period of about one thousand years, some of them very early and some of them comparatively late. It is a book primarily of religion and morals. It is not a book of science. Never was and was never meant to be. . . ."

I. Stone [30]

Natural Selection acts exclusively by the preservation and accumulation of variations, which are beneficial under the organic and inorganic conditions to which each nature is exposed at all periods of life. The ultimate result is that each creature tends to become more and more improved in relation to its conditions. This improvement inevitably leads to the gradual advancement of the organisation of the greater number of living beings throughout the world. But here we enter on a very intricate subject, for naturalists have not defined to each other's satisfaction what is meant by an advance in organisation. Amongst the vertebrata the degree of intellect and an approach in structure to man clearly come into play. . . .

. . . But we shall see how obscure this subject is if we look, for instance, to fishes, amongst which some naturalists rank those as highest which, like the sharks, approach nearest to amphibians; whilst other naturalists rank the common bony or teleostean fishes as the highest, inasmuch as they are most strictly fishlike, and differ most from the other vertebrate classes. We see still more plainly the obscurity of the subject by turning to plants, amongst which the standard of intellect is of course quite excluded; and here some botanists rank those plants as highest which have every organ, as sepals, petals, stamens, and pistils, fully developed in each flower; whereas other botanists, probably with more truth, look at the plants which have their several organs much modified and reduced in number as the highest.

C. Darwin [11]

Fourth, all living things share a common ancestry. From bacteria and viruses to man, the biochemical processes of life are remarkably similar, and unity of function at this level is indicative of ancestral affinities. It is popular to assume that man is more complex than a bacterium or even a fish, but the comparison breaks down when it is realized that there is no clear-cut relationship between structural complexity and the heritable information possessed by an organism, and that bacteria can perform many synthetic reactions of which man is incapable. The family tree of life, then, has many branches. Some of these branches have been terminated as a result of extinction, but many others, representing the species alive today, are still growing. The important point is that once life began, it was never interrupted or snuffed out entirely.

Fifth, at some distant time in the past, about 2 or 3 billion years ago to judge from fossil evidence, the spark of life arose when a favorable and chance grouping of organic molecules occurred. It is probable, but not certain, that this occurred only once and, further, that each species has arisen once, and only once, and in a given locale. The limited or widespread geographic distribution of a species is a function of its migratory potential, not an indication of multiple origins. The flora of eastern North America, for example, is remarkably similar to that of eastern Asia; some species occur in both regions. Proponents of the creationist theory could explain this by positing separate and distinct creation events, but geologic evidence reveals that a continuous flora once extended across the Northern Hemisphere, that land bridges were once present where only water now exists, that the discontinuity in distribution was brought about by advancing ice sheets that wiped out the

Of change and chance

Clarence Darrow pleading at the Scopes trial, July 10, 1925. John T. Scopes, wearing a white shirt and no jacket, is seated at the table behind Darrow, with arms interlocked.

Culver Pictures

flora in the intervening areas, and that the exposed land was repopulated by other, more aggressive and better adapted species as the ice retreated.

Sixth, man is as much a product of natural selection as is any other living thing. He is, to be sure, a product also of a cultural evolution, but a culture was possible only because he had the antecedent biological equipment necessary to create such a system of existence.

As was pointed out earlier, neither Darwin nor Wallace shed any light on the source of variations. Darwin's insistence on the significance of small variations as the source of change was a serious deterrent to the immediate acceptance of his ideas by all scientists. Each small variation, in his view, could, if favorable, confer only a small advantage to its possessor in the struggle for existence, but many small variations, accumulated through time, could, in aggregate, confer a decided advantage. This conflicted with the then current view of inheritance, which was that the differences between parents would be blended in the offspring. Small variations would tend to be "swamped" and would disappear in the blending process. The argument was difficult to refute, and in the successive editions of *The Origin of Species* Darwin retreated more and more toward the Lamarckian view of the inheritance of acquired characteristics. He was unaware that views of particulate inheritance were extant, views that would have served his purpose admirably, and that have since been shown to be correct. In the eighteenth century, Pierre de Maupertuis, head of the Academy of Sciences in Berlin, had shown, for example, that human variation—polydactyly, in particular—had a particulate basis, that this anomaly did not disappear with time, and that the environment neither produced nor modified it. In

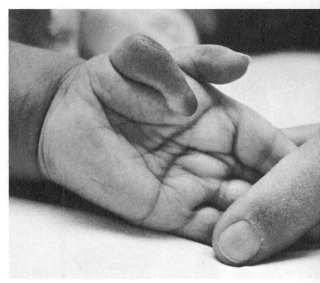

The National Foundation—March of Dimes

4.13 *Polydactyly, an example of human variation.*

Of change and chance

The joining of the Union Pacific and Central Pacific railroads at Promontory, Utah, May 10, 1869.

1865, the Austrian monk Gregor Mendel put particulate inheritance on a firm quantitative and qualitative basis, but Darwin, if he knew of this information, was not alone in failing to recognize its significance. In the early twentieth century, Mendelian inheritance was unearthed and coupled with the then newly discovered behavior of chromosomes in sexual reproduction, providing a solid and readily verifiable foundation for the physical basis of inheritance. In the 1950s, this aspect of inheritance was further refined when the particles of inheritance, or genes, were identified with specific, unique molecules found in each cell of all organisms.

The present-day view of natural selection is basically unchanged from that advanced by Darwin and Wallace although it is now more customary to speak of differential rates of reproduction rather than of a struggle for existence. Population studies have yielded to mathematical solution; modes of inheritance, some of them approaching the bizarre in complexity, adhere nonetheless to a basic pattern throughout the living world. It is now even possible to compute how many variations are required to alter a single character—say, the internal structure of the hemoglobin molecule—in the millions of years that separate man from the ancestral fish. Yet all of these discoveries are consistent with, and can be embraced by, the theory of natural selection.

This theory is a materialistic and mechanistic explanation of the diversity of living organisms. Just as Newton's theory of gravitation described the motion of the planets and stars in their course for all time, so this theory describes and explains the flow of organisms through time as well. Its mechanistic base resides in the nature, action, and altera-

Of change and chance

Whether it be in the development of the Earth, in the development of Life upon its surface, in the development of Society, of Government, of Manufactures, of Commerce, of Language, Literature, Science, Art, this same evolution of the simple into the complex, through successive differentiations, holds throughout. From the earliest traceable cosmical changes, down to the latest results of civilization, we shall find that the transformation of the homogeneous into the heterogeneous, is that in which Progress essentially consists.

H. Spencer [29]

---

tions of genes, and their selective retention or loss in a particular environment. Both theories deal, in the final analysis, with matter and motion, for that is what science is all about. Because science is a human endeavor, the theory of evolution through natural selection is a human construct; if a more satisfactory explanation were advanced tomorrow to account for the character of the living world, the Darwinian view would be discarded without regret.

Evolution and man

The Origin of Species contains only a peripheral reference to man. Darwin merely noted that "Light will be thrown on the origin of man and his history." Earlier, Wallace had asked him if he intended to discuss man, and he answered, by letter in 1851: "I think I shall avoid the whole subject, as so surrounded with prejudices; though I fully admit that it is the highest and most interesting problem for the naturalist." It was apparently more important to gain acceptance of his views first, and he was right, of course, in realizing that a frontal attack on the problem of the origin of man would blind his readers to the implications of his major thesis.

Darwin would return to the human problem in *The Descent of Man,* published in 1871, but *The Origin of Species* left no doubt in the minds of the reading public that the gist of what Darwin advocated was a direct refutation of the biblical account of man's origin. Lyell and Hooker in England and Asa Gray and Louis Agassiz in America, all eminent in their respective fields of natural history, were reluctant to extend Darwinian thought to man.

Even if it be granted that the difference between man and his nearest allies is as great in corporeal structure as some naturalists maintain, and although we must grant that the difference between them is immense in mental power, yet the facts given in the earlier chapters appear to declare, in the plainest manner, that man is descended from some lower form, notwithstanding that connecting links have not hitherto been discovered.

C. Darwin [3]

Of change and chance

My Father's attitude towards the theory of natural selection was critical in his career, and oddly enough, it exercised an immense influence on my own experience as a child. Let it be admitted at once, mournful as the admission is, that every instinct in his intelligence went out at first to greet the new light. It had hardly done so, when recollection of the opening chapter of Genesis checked it at the outset. He consulted with Carpenter, a great investigator, but one who was fully as incapable as himself of remodeling his ideas with regard to the old, accepted hypotheses. They both determined, on various grounds, to have nothing to do with the terrible theory, but to hold steadily to the law of the fixity of species.

E. Gosse [15]

From The Hornet, *London, March 1871. Charles Darwin portrayed as "a venerable orang-outang, a contribution to unnatural history."*

Thames & Hudson Ltd., London

. . . I have stongly maintained on sundry occasions that if Mr. Darwin's views are sound, they apply as much to man as to the lower mammals, seeing that it is perfectly demonstrable that the structural differences which separate man from the apes are not greater than those which separate some apes from others. There cannot be the slightest doubt in the world that the argument which applies to the improvement of the horse from an earlier stock, or of ape from ape, applies to the improvement of man from some simpler and lower stock than man. There is not a single faculty—functional or structural, moral, intellectual, or instinctive,—there is no faculty whatever that is not capable of improvement; there is no faculty whatsoever which does not depend upon structure, and as structure tends to vary, it is capable of being improved.

T. H. Huxley [19]

Only Agassiz rejected Darwinism in all its aspects, although it is said, perhaps apocryphally, that he was converted on his deathbed. T. H. Huxley, Wallace, and Herbert Spencer were not so hesitant to express their views and accepted the antiquity of man without question. Inevitably, man's physical attributes and his mental and spiritual qualities were contrasted, lumped, even totally separated from one another. Wallace, for example, could find no cause for believing that evolution could account for the moral and intellectual nature of man, and even dismissed some physical traits as inexplicable on the basis of natural selection. Huxley and Darwin, however, made no such distinctions, viewing man as a totality. Darwin described his own position in *The Descent of Man.*

Man is liable to numerous, slight, and diversified variations, which are induced by the same general causes, are governed and transmitted in accordance with the same general laws, as in the lower animals. Man has multiplied so rapidly that he has necessarily been exposed to struggle for existence, and consequently to natural selection. He has given rise to many races, some of which differ so much from each other that they have often been ranked by naturalists as distinct species. His body is constructed on the same homological plan as that of other mammals. He passes through the same phases of embryological development. He retains many rudimentary and useless structures, which no doubt were once serviceable. Characters occasionally make their reappearance in him, which we have reason to believe were possessed by his early progenitors. If the origin of man had been wholly different from that of all other animals, these various appearances would be mere empty deceptions, but such an admission is incredible. These appearances, on the other hand, are intelligible, at least to a large extent, if man is the co-descendant with other mammals of some unknown and lower form.

Some naturalists, from being deeply impressed with the mental and spiritual powers of man, have divided the whole organic world into three kingdoms, the human, the animal, and the vegetable, thus giving to man

Of change and chance

The growth of a large business is merely a survival of the fittest. . . . The American Beauty rose can be produced in the splendor and fragrance which bring cheer to its beholder only by sacrificing the early buds which grow up around it. This is not an evil tendency in business. It is merely the working-out of a law of nature and a law of God.

J. D. Rockefeller [27]

I remember that light came as in a flood and all was clear. Not only had I got rid of theology and the supernatural, but I had found the truth of evolution. "All is well since all grows better," became my motto, my true source of comfort. Man was not created with an instinct for his own degradation, but from the lower he had risen to the higher forms. Nor is there any conceivable end to his march to perfection. His face is turned to the light; he stands in the sun and looks upward.

A. Carnegie [4]

---

a separate kingdom. Spritual powers cannot be compared or classed by the naturalist: but he may endeavour to show, as I have done, that the mental faculties of man and the lower animals do not differ in kind, although immensely in degree. A difference in degree, however great, does not justify us in placing man in a distinct kingdom. . . . If man had not been his own classifier, he would never have thought of founding a separate order for his own reception.

Commenting further on man as distinct from other animals, he said:

As man advanced gradually in intellectual power, and was enabled to trace the more remote consequences of his actions; as he acquired sufficient knowledge to reject baneful customs and superstitions; as he regarded more and more, not only the welfare, but the happiness of his fellowmen; as from habit, following beneficial experience, his sympathies became more tender and widely diffused, extending to men of all races, and finally to the lower animals, so would the standard of his morality rise higher and higher.

Further on in *The Descent of Man,* Darwin sums up his point of view after tracing man's relationships within the vertebrate group.

Thus we have given to man a pedigree of prodigious length, but not, it may be said, of noble quality. The world, it has often been remarked, appears as if it had long been preparing for the advent of man: and this, in one sense, is strictly true, for he owes his birth to a long line of progenitors. If any single link in this chain had never existed, man would not have been exactly what he is now. Unless we willfully close our eyes, we may, with our present knowledge, approximately recognize our parentage; nor need we feel ashamed of it. The most humble organism is something higher than the inorganic dust under our feet; and no one with an unbiased mind can study any living creature, however humble, without being struck with enthusiasm at its marvellous structure and properties.

4.14   *Ten years after its publication, Darwin's* Descent of Man *was still the subject of a great deal of satire as shown by this page from* Punch's Almanack for 1882.

MAN·IS·BVT·A·WORM.

Of change and chance

It was a town of red brick, or of brick that would have been red if the smoke and ashes had allowed it; but, as matters stood, it was a town of unnatural red and black, like the painted face of a savage. It was a town of machinery and tall chimneys, out of which interminable serpents of smoke trailed themselves for ever and ever, and never got uncoiled. It had a black canal in it, and a river that ran purple with ill-smelling dye, and vast piles of buildings full of windows where there was a rattling and a trembling all day long, and where the piston of the steam engine worked monotonously up and down, like the head of an elephant in a state of melancholy madness. It contained several large streets all very like one another, and many small streets still more like one another, inhabited by people equally like one another, who all went in and out at the same hours, with the same sound upon the same pavements, to do the same work, and to whom every day was the same as yesterday and tomorrow, and every year the counterpart of the last and the next.

C. Dickens [13]

Sheffield, England, in the nineteenth century.

Whatever the course of social philosophy in the future, however, a few conclusions are now accepted by most humanists: that such biological ideas as the "survival of the fittest," whatever their doubtful value in natural science, are utterly useless in attempting to understand society; that the life of man in society, while it is incidentally a biological fact, has characteristics that are not reducible to biology and must be explained in the distinctive terms of a cultural analysis; that the physical well-being of men is a result of their social organization and not vice versa; that social improvement is a product of advances in technology and social organization, not of breeding or selective elimination; that judgments as to the value of competition between men or enterprises or nations must be based upon social and not allegedly biological consequences; and, finally, that there is nothing in nature or a naturalistic philosophy of life to make impossible the acceptance of moral sanctions that can be employed for the common good.

R. Hofstadter [18]

To meet the criticism of those who could not see man diminished, he added: "Believing as I do that man in the distant future will be a far more perfect creature than he now is, it is an intolerable thought that he and all other sentient beings are doomed to complete annihilation after such long-continued slow progress. To those who fully admit the immortality of the human soul, the destruction of our world will not appear so dreadful."

The inclusion of man in an evolving, purposeless, and directionless system of change would have an effect well beyond the laboratories of science. Europe in the 1850s was in a state of change and rising hopes. The industrial revolution had been going on for a century, the material well-being of nations was greater, even if the working poor were sometimes worse off than before, and the revolution of 1848 on the Continent was an expression of the expectations of the oppressed. A man need not be bound to the wheel or the hoe for the rest of his life, for change carried with it the hope of progress. In fact, Spencer equated change and progress. Darwin's theory of evolution provided justification for what in fact was already being practiced industrially, economically, and socially. A man might piously subscribe to a revealed religion as a personal belief, but laissez-faire economics could most conveniently be embraced within a nature "red in tooth and claw" and could become, as one example, the social Darwinism of late nineteenth century America, when the so-called robber barons accumulated great wealth by applying the law of "survival of the fittest" in their attempt to gain control of monopolies. These changes would have occurred anyway, in all likelihood, but Darwinism provided a stamp of approval in the struggle for existence. Darwin recognized this himself when he said in

Of change and chance

The voyagers scanned the shore. A conference was held in the boat. "Well," said the captain, "if no help is coming, we might better try a run through the surf right away. If we stay out here much longer we will be too weak to do anything for ourselves at all." The others silently acquiesced in this reasoning. The boat was headed for the beach. The correspondent wondered if none ever ascended the tall wind-tower, and if then they never looked seaward. This tower was a giant, standing with its back to the plight of the ants. It represented in a degree, to the correspondent, the serenity of nature amid the struggles of the individual —nature in the wind, and nature in the vision of men. She did not seem cruel to him then, nor beneficent, nor treacherous, nor wise. But she was indifferent, flatly indifferent. t is, perhaps, plausible that a man in th s situation, impressed with the unconcern of the universe, should see the innumerable flaws of his life, and have them taste wickedly in his mind, and wish for another chance. A distinction between right and wrong seems absurdly clear to him, then, in this new ignorance of the grave-edge, and he understands that if he were given another opportunity he would mend his conduct and his words, and be better and brighter during an introduction or at a tea.

S. Crane [7]

---

a letter to Lyell: "I have noted in a Manchester newspaper a rather good squib, showing that I have proved 'might is right,' and therefore that Napoleon is right and every cheating tradesman is also right."

In the field of literature, the naturalistic trend stems from the ideas of evolution, although Marx, Spencer, and Auguste Comte exerted an effect as well. Naturalism is a philosophy based on a deterministic explanation of human behavior, that is, a law of causation. It is an objective search for truth, amoral and pessimistic in attitude, with no ethical standards for comparative judgment. Ibsen's *Ghosts* is an example of this expression in the dramatic field, and heredity, sexual selection, adaptation, and survival enter into the drama, with the characters caught in a life that is a predetermined trap. Life is to be lived, and with whatever means there are at hand; no moral judgment is exercised. The novels of Thomas Hardy are other expressions of this fatalism, as are the writings of Émile Zola and Gustave Flaubert in France and Stephen Crane, Jack London, Frank Norris, Sherwood Anderson, and Theodore Dreiser in America. As in all periods, the interplay between science, social forces, and art goes on, each reflecting in its own way the temper of the times.

For the naturalists, however, men are "human insects" whose brief lives are completely determined by society or nature. The individual is crushed in a moment if he resists; and his struggle, instead of being tragic, is merely pitiful or ironic, as if we had seen a mountain stir itself to overwhelm a fly. Irony is a literary effect used time and again by all the naturalistic writers. For Stephen Crane it is the central effect on which almost all his plots depend: thus, in *The Red Badge of Courage* the boy makes himself a hero by running away. In *A Mystery of Heroism* a soldier risks his life to bring a bucket of water to his comrades, and the water is spilled. In *The Monster* a Negro stableman is so badly burned in rescuing a child that he becomes a faceless horror; and the child's father, a physician, loses his practice as a reward for sheltering the stableman. The irony in Dreiser's novels depends on the contrast between conventional morality and the situations he describes: Carrie Meeber loses her virtue and succeeds in her career.

The effect of naturalism as a doctrine is to subtract from literature the whole notion of human responsibility. "Not men" is its constant echo. If naturalistic stories had tragic endings, these were not to be explained by human wills in conflict with each other or with fate; they were the blind result of conditions, forces, physical laws, or nature herself.

M. Cowley [5]

Summary

Darwin and Wallace did not offer evolution as a new idea. What they, and Darwin in particular, did, was to take a number of ideas and pieces of information and weave them into a grand theory so meticulously documented and so reasonably argued that refutation had to be made on non-

Then they fell upon each other, like young bulls, in all the glory of youth, with naked fists, with hatred, with desire to hurt, to maim, to destroy. All the painful, thousand years' gains of man in his upward climb through creation were lost. Only the electric light remained, a milestone on the path of the great human adventure. Martin and Cheese-Face were two savages, of the stone age, of the squatting place and the tree refuge. They sank lower and lower into the muddy abyss, back into the dregs of the raw beginnings of life, striving blindly and chemically, as atoms strive, as the star-dust of the heavens strives, colliding, recoiling and colliding again and eternally again.

J. London [21]

scientific grounds. At the heart of the theory was acceptance of the fact that every species was a storehouse of variability and that individuals varied among themselves; that populations generally were stable in numbers over a period of time, despite a reproductive rate that could swell these numbers; and that the environment selected for survival those individuals and species that were most suitably adapted to that environment. Over a period of time species changed, with extinction as well as survival a part of the total picture.

The concept of evolution, as proposed by Darwin and Wallace, has since been enriched by an understanding of the causes and/or basis of variation, by an appreciation of the modes of inheritance, and by population studies of both qualitative and quantitative nature. Although the Malthusian view of competition has been generally displaced by a greater emphasis on differential rates of reproduction, the substance of the theory remains. It forms the basis of all biology today, giving it a sound theoretical structure. In addition, the concept extends from cosmological events to man, and there are few fields of endeavor where the concept does not apply or has not had an influence.

5

Evolution as a process

During the period from 1859 to the end of the nineteenth century, the Darwinian theory of evolution was gradually accepted and strengthened even though there were those who, seeing it in conflict with revealed religion, could not accept it. For a good part of the world of science, however, it provided a plausible direction for thought about, and exploration of, the living world and a rationale for viewing the enormous diversity of life as well as the changing landscape of the physical world. Comparative anatomy, paleontology, classification, and physiology contributed to this growing wave of acceptance, and biology, as a discipline, acquired a significant sense of unity and identity, because it now had a theoretical, even if controversial, frame of reference within which to operate. In this regard, it is of

The armadillo,
an unlikely evolutionary success.

R. F. Head photo, National Audubon Society

. . . as we look back at the events surrounding the publication of the *Origin of Species,* it is all too easy to regard that great advance of understanding as a major discontinuity in the scientific stream, as a titanic revolution of man's thought, taken in isolation and without precedent. At this distance it is all too easy to ignore the scientific matrix from which it sprang, the matrix which, in vague and unformulated intuition, had engaged Erasmus Darwin in his *Zoonomia* more than half a century before the publication of the *Origin,* the matrix from which sprang the independent formulation of evolutionary theory by Alfred Russel Wallace at Ternate, the matrix from which the obscure Edward Blyth was able to correctly outline a theory of evolution in a paper actually preceding the publications of Darwin—though, ironically, his inferences from that theory were precisely wrong, supporting conclusions the very opposite of Darwin's own.

C. P. Haskins [13]

In counting the petals of marsh marigolds also I have found, perhaps, once or twice per thousand heads, an extra petal growing out of the stalk about an inch below the true flower. Abnormal variations thus undoubtedly exist; how many of them exist in such numbers as to be capable of giving rise to a new variety, *how many are indeed fertile at all,* are points which must be fully determined before it can be asserted that evolution is largely the product of such abnormal variation. Every variation, unless frequent, very advantageous or very fertile, is sure to be swamped. The frequency and fertility of normal variations are easily ascertainable, but these are matters wherein the statistics of abnormal variation are at present rather to seek.

K. Pearson [15]

some historical interest to point out that the first professorship in biology in America was made in 1876, with Henry Newell Martin, a student of T. H. Huxley, as the initial appointee.

There remained a nagging element of doubt, however. It stemmed, as earlier emphasized, from the problem of variations. These variations could be seen by any keen observer, but what was their source and their nature? How were they inherited? Many biologists retained, or retreated toward, a Lamarckian point of view, as indeed did Darwin in his later years, and placed a greater emphasis on the role of use and disuse in modifying structures; climate was also stressed in this same Neo-Lamarckian sense. Adding to the doubt was the further problem of speciation. It seemed well and good for man to select rigorously and create new varieties and breeds of domesticated plants and animals, but had he ever produced a new species by these tactics? The answer was clearly a negative one. The species problem was one of paramount philosophical and biological interest at the time, because both the doctrine of special creation and Darwin's theory rested on the nature of species. But it is not always easy to shift one's focus from the obvious and major problem of species to the seemingly lesser problem of variation among individuals in order to gain a larger perspective. But this was what was needed to gain an understanding of the meaning of evolution in all particulars.

Darwin, of course, was well aware of the significance of variation in his whole scheme of evolution; without variation there was no evolution. He saw that variations had little effect individually, but he also realized that they were important for survival, individually or collectively, if they conveyed any advantage to their possessor. He also noted that they

Evolution as a process

Restricted and dark were many of these niches, and equally dark and malignant were some of the survivors. The oblique corner with no outlet had narrowed upon them all. Biological evolution could be defined as one long series of specializations—hoofs that prevented hands, wings that, while opening the wide reaches of the air, prevented the manipulation of tools. The list was endless. Each creature was a splintered fraction of the life force; the greater portion had died with the environments that created them. Others had continued to evolve, but always their transformations seemed to present a more skilled adaptation to an increasingly narrow corridor of existence. Success too frequently meant specialization, and specialization, ironically, was the beginning of the road to extinction. Here was life's final paradox: success was failure. It was the essential theme that time had dramatized upon the giant stage.

L. Eiseley [9]

---

occurred randomly in a population, with no relation to immediate or future needs. The question of whether a variation was advantageous or deleterious was therefore, a matter of time and place; that is, the variation had to occur at a given time and in a given environment, and the combination of time and place determined whether the variation was "good" or "bad" for survival in the long run. But Darwin and his fellow scientists subscribed generally to a blending type of inheritance in which the eggs or sperm produced would be essentially uniform in developmental potentialities. Offspring resulting from the union of these gametes (sexual cells) would be intermediate between their parents, and distinct parental variations would lose their identity. Unlike two different color beads, which when mixed maintain their separate identities, the variations of each parent would blend together, just as a mixture of ink and water does (illustration 5.1). The fact that this was true for such obvious quantitative characters as height and weight and for many of the characters with which plant and animal breeders were concerned—yield of a crop, milk production, quality of wool— made it reasonable to assume that a blending type of inheritance was operative. Not until Mendelian inheritance was understood did geneticists recognize that although characters may or may not be intermediate in expression, the factors that determined these characters retain their singular identity and never undergo blending of any sort.

We will return to the details of Mendelian inheritance in a later chapter, but we wish here to be a bit more specific concerning variation so that our discussion of evolution is not simply an abstract exercise. Mendel stated that certain well-defined characters were governed by "factors" (we now call them genes) and that these were transmitted to offspring

5.1 Blending and particulate inheritance. When two liquids that can be mixed are poured together, the resultant solution is intermediate. If the dark liquid is considered to be the variant solution, additional dilutions would cause the mixture to tend toward the original light solution, and the dark would be diminished rather than expressed. This illustrates a blending type of inheritance. On the other hand, if the inherited variations are thought of as particulate (the lower portion of the illustration), the variant forms could persist without dilution and could emerge and be expressed if circumstances favor their existence.

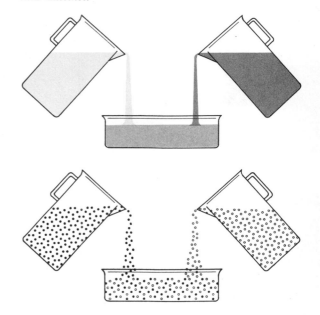

The physical universe is a storehouse of immeasurable treasures, shut up under a combination-lock; particular sciences are the prongs of the key which man adjusts to various tumblers, until he spells out the magic word and opens the lock. How childish, how absurd, to claim that these sciences, or the laws which they combine into a system, made the lock, and stored the treasury! Yet such is the logic of materialism; and that result is possible only to minds that move in the tread-mill of physical laws, till they imagine these to be the final seat and source of power. . . .

J. P. Thompson [23]

We have not been hasty to reach this conviction. We have pondered many a difficulty and raised many a query, but we have seen old difficulties vanishing and new proofs perpetually arising. We have learned more of the wonderful resources of the hypothesis in explaining the current and the exceptional phenomena of life and organization. We now think it far safer to accept the hypothesis than to reject it. If it is safer for the scientist it is safer for religion. It is therefore time for the theologian to seek how to coordinate his essential faith with the impending finality of science . . . .

A. Winchell [26]

by the gametes. By 1875 it was realized that eggs and sperm are true cells, that despite their difference in shape and size they contribute equally to the character of an offspring, and that, as cells, they both possess nuclei. As the nature of cell division came to be understood and the behavior of chromosomes was clarified, it was shown that the abstract "factors" of Mendel were inherited in the same manner as the chromosomes. The factors were therefore located in the chromosomes, and the physical basis of inheritance was established. Refinement of this study in the twentieth century has revealed that a factor is a particular kind of molecule that provides the coded information required by a cell or an organism in order to bring a character into expression so that natural selection can act upon it.

Let us take a further look at adaptation and natural selection. Adaptation can be considered to be a state of being or a process of becoming adjusted to a given set of environmental conditions. Any organism can, of course, carry out its life processes, including reproduction, within a limited range of environmental conditions and may even

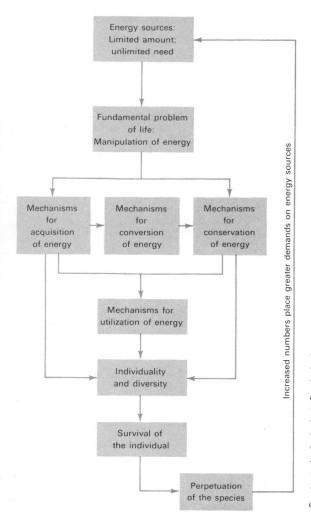

5.2 The success or failure of an organism or a species is determined by how successful it is in extracting energy from its environment for the processes of growth, maintenance, and reproduction. Variations can occur at all stages of this cycle. These variations, which are determined by the information bound up in an organism's inheritance, lead to diversity and, if successful, to greater demands on the environment because of increased numbers and more efficient means of energy manipulation.

Courtesy of Dr. H. H. Hagerman

Evolution as a process

. . . in the mind of the uncivilized man, the great central truths of religion are so densely overlaid with hundreds of trivial notions respecting dogma and ritual, that his perception of the great central truths is obscure. These great central truths, indeed, need to be clothed in a dress of little rites and superstition, in order to take hold of his dull and untrained intelligence. But in proportion as men become more civilized, and learn to think more accurately, and to take wider views of life, just so do they come to value the essential truths of religion more highly, while they attach less and less importance to superficial details.

Having thus seen what is meant by the essential truths of religion, it is very easy to see what the attitude of the doctrine of evolution is toward these essential truths. It asserts and reiterates them both; and it asserts them not as dogmas handed down to us by priestly tradition, not as mysterious intuitive convictions of which we can render no account to ourselves, but as scientific truths concerning the innermost constitution of the universe—truths that have been disclosed by observation and reflection, like other scientific truths, and that accordingly harmonize naturally and easily with the whole body of our knowledge. The doctrine of evolution asserts, as the widest and deepest truth which the study of nature can disclose to us, that there exists a power to which no limit in time or space is conceivable, and that all the phenomena of the universe, whether they be what we call material or what we call spiritual phenomena, are manifestations of this infinite and eternal Power.

J. Fiske [11]

---

tolerate stress conditions for brief periods of time, but it does so through physiological adaptations rather than through short-term heritable changes. Environmental adaptation, on the other hand, as a species characteristic, for example the ability to exist in tropical as opposed to arctic conditions, has a heritable base. It is thus appropriate here to view it as a process, because in an evolutionary context, it is consistent with what we know of the changing character of organisms and environments as they flow through time. An organism, as an individual, or a species, as a collection of individuals, must adapt continuously or die. An organism, for example, can be viewed as a flow chart of energy (illustration 5.2). The sun is the ultimate source of life-giving energy, and green plants trap this energy in the form of light and convert it into chemical energy; animals obtain their chemical energy from various types of food. Variations basically influence the manner in which energy is trapped, converted, stored, and eventually utilized, and the structural features of organisms are consistent with their functional behavior. Ultimately, these variations result in individuality and diversity among organisms, and survival is determined by how well these energy mechanisms permit the species to exist in a particular environment. Continued survival of individuals, generation after generation, determines the continuation of a species, with maintained or increased numbers being a measure of success. However, the numbers cannot exceed the capacity of the environment to sustain them, and so a perpetual interplay between organisms and environment goes on. As improved methods of energy utilization arise through random, inherited variations—improved, that is, in relation to an environment and not to any ideal abstract design—the species undergoes change as certain individuals

There is no exception to the rule that every organic being naturally increases at so high a rate, that, if not destroyed, the earth would soon be covered by the progeny of a single pair. Even slow-breeding man has doubled in twenty-five years, and at this rate, in less than a thousand years, there would literally not be standing-room for his progeny. Linnaeus has calculated that if an annual plant produced only two seeds—and there is no plant so unproductive as this—and their seedlings next year produced two, and so on, then in twenty years there should be a million plants. The elephant is reckoned the slowest breeder of all known animals, and I have taken some pains to estimate its probable minimum rate of natural increase; it will be safest to assume that it begins breeding when thirty years old, and goes on breeding till ninety years old, bringing forth six young in the interval, and surviving till one hundred years old; if this be so, after a period of from 740 to 750 years there would be nearly nineteen million elephants alive, descended from the first pair.

C. Darwin [4]

A group of breaker boys at a coal mine. The photograph was taken sometime between 1909 and 1913 by Lewis W. Hine.

George Eastman House

In order that any great amount of modification should be effected in a species, a variety when once formed must again, perhaps after a long interval of time, vary or present individual differences of the same favourable nature as before; and these must be again preserved, and so onwards step by step. Seeing that individual differences of the same kind perpetually recur, this can hardly be considered as an unwarrantable assumption. But whether it is true, we can judge only by seeing how far the hypothesis accords with and explains the general phenomena of nature. On the other hand, the ordinary belief that the amount of possible variation is a strictly limited quantity is likewise a simple assumption.

C. Darwin [4]

become more favored in the struggle for existence and therefore perpetuate their kind more successfully than others. Adaptation is thus relative, rather than absolute. It is a process of continual adjustment as generations succeed one another, and as different fertility patterns alter the heritable structure of a persisting population.

One generation of a species does not perpetuate itself exactly in the succeeding generation. Furthermore, not every individual of one generation contributes its inheritance to the next one. In a human population, some members die before their reproductive age is reached, some are sterile for one reason or another, while others, through choice, misfortune, or some other kind of exclusion factor, do not become parents. The parents of the next generation are, as a result, "a selected rather than a random sample of a population." If the selected group differs in any way from the population as a whole, and this selective system continues, the species gradually undergoes systematic change (illustration 5.3). Evolutionary change is consequently inevitable. Should the environment undergo systematic change as well, a channeling circumstance arises, and the species follows a given direction. But the direction is purposeless in that changes in organisms and environment occur independently of each other and without prior foresight or intent; natural selection is the result.

Wallace and Srb [25] express this succinctly:

Natural selection does not *cause* the disparity between parents and the rest of the population; it *is* the disparity. Thus, when we say that natural selection results in the adaptation of organisms to their environment and in evolutionary changes in population, we are simply saying that the continual contrast, generation after generation, between reproducing individuals as one group and the remainder of the population

Evolution as a process

as another results in adaptation and evolution. . . . Granted that offspring tend to resemble their parents, that environmental changes do not occur haphazardly, and that differences among individuals govern, at least in part, their relative reproductive success—granted these three conditions, we find that adaptation is an *unavoidable evolutionary change* within populations of living things.

Variations occur by changes within a gene, and a gene is a given type of molecule. Such variations may be beneficial, harmful, or neutral so far as the reproductive potential of the individual is concerned. Harmful genes tend to be eliminated from a population in the long run, but there is no guarantee that a variation will be perpetuated simply because it is potentially beneficial. We will never know, for example, how many beneficial human variations have been lost on the battlefields of the world.

How frequently do variations, or mutations as they are now known, arise? The rate varies from gene to gene, even within a species, but each gene seems to have a characteristic rate of change. In bacteria, resistance to streptomycin occurs in about one out of every billion cells; in man, achondroplastic dwarfism appears at a rate of one instance per 12,000 births. This means one mutation per 24,000 sexual cells, because an offspring results from the union of

5.3 *In a population that remains constant in numbers, a change in the nature of the population is inevitable if individuals differ in their ability to reproduce. In this case, the dark circles are considered to be nonreproducing members, and so the population quickly becomes entirely white. If the dark circles had a lower reproductive capacity than the white ones, the change in the population would take longer. In the block at right, the individuals in the third generation are the survivors of a single individual in the first generation. Small populations, therefore, are more able to bring about change in the nature of a population than are large ones.*

After Wallace and Srb, 1964

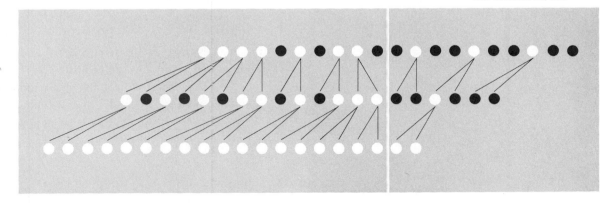

Italy is a model of what can be accomplished with mankind's new weapon against malaria: DDT and such related insecticides as benzene hexachloride. These destroyers of malaria-carrying mosquitoes have at last made it economically feasible to eradicate malaria from a whole nation, instead of trying to control it in a limited area. The special virtue of these insecticides is their lasting effectiveness. Because they remain lethal to mosquitoes for many months after they are applied, they make it possible to wrest a region from the insects and hold it against reinvasion.

DDT has opened a new era in the world's health. But we are still only at the beginning of this era. The story of Italy's conquest of malaria is a great, heartening chapter in human history; what is more, it apparently foreshadows more brilliant chapters still to come.

P. F. Russell [18]

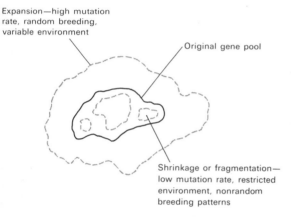

Expansion—high mutation rate, random breeding, variable environment

Original gene pool

Shrinkage or fragmentation— low mutation rate, restricted environment, nonrandom breeding patterns

5.4 The gene pool consists of all the inherited information possessed by a breeding population. It is not a constant feature, and a wide variety of factors influence it through time.

egg and sperm, and two mutated genes of the same sort are required for expression of the trait. Hemophilia and albinism in humans arise at a rate of three cases per 100,000 sexual cells. Cystic fibrosis of the pancreas, one of the most frequently inherited diseases of childhood, occurs in one out of every 3,000 white births, thus suggesting a very high rate of mutation. The reasons for the differences in rates are not known, but the rates in experimental organisms can be increased significantly by X rays, ultraviolet light, and a wide variety of chemicals, some of which are found in various foods.

A species, therefore, possesses, at any given time, a source of variability among its members. This is referred to as its gene pool, which fluctuates with time, because no individual carries all of the variations of a species, and not all of the individuals of one generation contribute equally to the next. Mutations, nonrandom mating, selection, migration, and other factors affect the pool and, consequently, the ability of the species to cope with environmental changes (illustration 5.4).

Simple adaptations

Many of the hospitals of this country are plagued with a strain of staphylococcus (bacterium) that is resistant to antibiotics. Antibiotics and the sulfa drugs were introduced into medical practice in the late 1930s and early 1940s and were viewed as the miracle drugs of the century, as indeed they are. Their ability to counteract bacterial infections was dramatic, particularly under the battlefield conditions of World War II. However, there soon appeared strains of

Evolution as a process

Dusting a potato crop with insecticide.

Grant Heilman photo

pathogenic (disease-causing) bacteria, such as staphylococcus, that were resistant to a particular antibiotic, although susceptible possibly to other kinds of antibiotics. Laboratory studies showed that the resistance was inherited, and that it occurred spontaneously, that is it was not caused by the antibiotic, but was present in the natural gene pool of the population. The antibiotic had drastically altered the bacterial environment, thus killing off the vast majority of the pathogens, but even a single surviving resistant individual could, by continued division, build up a population of pathogens able to withstand the new environment and even thrive in it. The persistent strain of staphylococcus in our hospitals today appears to be multiply resistant, in that it is unaffected by several of the more commonly used antibiotics.

A similar kind of adaptive resistance to DDT, an insecticide, has been found among flies and mosquitoes. Widely used throughout the world, particularly where insects are disease carriers, for example, malaria via mosquitoes, or typhus via body lice, DDT was initially an effective agent of control. But again, resistant individuals survived, and DDT is no longer as effective as it once was in those areas where it has been used repeatedly. This has been especially true when it has been used against those organisms that have a short life cycle.

The growing national and international ban on the widespread use of DDT, however, is an indication that not all organisms can accommodate adaptively to its effect by the acquisition of a heritable resistance. DDT is a persistent chemical that finds its way into the food chain of many animals. Washed from farms, forests, and homes into the lakes, rivers, and oceans, it accumulates first in microorganisms eaten by small fish, and then in larger fish, which

This storage of DDT begins with the smallest conceivable intake of the chemical (which is present as residues on most foodstuffs) and continues until quite high levels are reached. The fatty storage depots act as biological magnifiers, so that an intake of as little as 1/10 of 1 part per million in the diet results in storage of about 10 to 15 parts per million, an increase of one hundredfold or more. . . . One part in a million sounds like a very small amount—and so it is. But such substances are so potent that a minute quantity can bring about vast changes in the body. In animal experiments, 3 parts per million has been found to inhibit an essential enzyme in heart muscle; only 5 parts per million has brought about necrosis or disintegration of liver cells; only 2.5 parts per million of the closely related chemicals dieldrin and chlordane did the same.

One of the most sinister features of DDT and related chemicals is the way they are passed on from one organism to another through all the links of the food chains. For example, fields of alfalfa are dusted with DDT; meal is later prepared from the alfalfa and fed to hens; the hens lay eggs which contain DDT. Or the hay, containing residues of 7 to 8 parts per million, may be fed to cows. The DDT will turn up in the milk in the amount of about 3 parts per million, but in butter made from this milk the concentration may run to 65 parts per million. . . .

R. Carson [2]

Evolution as a process

David Muench photo

The nature of the selective force which has produced industrial melanism is by no means agreed upon. The most obvious explanation is that the melanistic forms are less conspicuous to predators in smoky industrial areas than are the original light forms. Actual counts of moths taken by birds has in some cases substantiated this. Ford, however, believes that melanism is secondary to physiological changes, such as resistance to poisoning by lead salts of industrial smoke. In preindustrial times, melanism failed to spread because the melanistic moths were conspicuous to predators and resistance to lead poisoning was not of value. Both traits, however, proved to be preadaptive to the industrial environments, and hence the recent rapid spread of melanism. Whatever the selective force, here is a well documented case of transformation of species, at least to a subspecific degree, within historical times. As the transformation is associated with a known environmental change (industrialization), it is difficult to doubt that selection has been responsible for the change.

E. O. Dodson [7]

in turn are eaten by birds such as ospreys, pelicans, and eagles. It has been claimed that the declining populations of these species are due to the fact that DDT and other related chemicals similarly used interfere with the formation of the shell of eggs, thereby reducing hatchability to such an extent that these species are now in danger of extinction. Some other chemicals, such as mercury, pose a threat to man as well. Like genes, these chemicals have their "good" and "bad" aspects depending upon the environment, the use to which they are put, and the side effects resulting from their persistence. A balanced use must be sought, with the beneficial and deleterious effects weighed against each other.

Man himself is therefore a serious environmental factor for many organisms. There is, in fact, no single species over which he could not exercise absolute control if he put his mind and talents to work on it. In most instances, however, his effect has been unintentional rather than deliberate. Industrial melanism, the development of a dark variety of moths from a lighter variety because of changing environmental conditions, is a case in point and indicates how a favorable change makes its appearance and then spreads throughout a population. In England, the industrial revolution, beginning in early eighteenth century, rolled on in high gear, with its urban homes and factories fueled by coal. Soot inevitably poured from the chimneys and coated the surrounding neighborhood, blackening tree trunks and, in the process, destroying the lichens that grew on them. These tree trunks were also the resting place of a number of species of moths when not in flight.

Under normal conditions, light-colored moths resting on light, lichen-covered tree trunks are effectively camouflaged

Evolution as a process

. . . If we look at the pine trees which cover the slopes of a high mountain, we notice that those near the summit are much smaller than those near the base, and they are likely to be gnarled and spreading. The same is true of trees and shrubs which grow near the seashore and are exposed to constant winds. We might suspect that these differences result directly from the effects of the severe environment. This is true to a certain extent. Nevertheless, when seeds are taken from trees growing at various altitudes in the mountains, and their offspring are raised in a uniform nursery, those descended from trees growing at the lower altitudes grow faster and become larger than do the progeny of trees which were growing at higher altitudes. Evidently, therefore, natural selection has sorted out genotypes adapted to the conditions of their native environment. . . .

G. L. Stebbins [22]

from predators, mostly birds. On soot-blackened trunks, the light-colored moths are a readily visible prey. In the 1850s, near Manchester, a dark form of one of the moth species was collected and preserved. A comparison of old collections of insects clearly indicated that the dark, or melanic, form was increasing in frequency, not only among populations of the peppered moth (*Biston betularia*), one of the first species in which this form of melanism was observed, but also among the members of about seventy other species in other parts of industrial England (illustration 5.5).

The inheritance of industrial melanism is relatively simple and depends on the accumulation of one or more variations, all of which add up to a dark body color. Each species tested, however, has adapted by a different set of variations, indicating that adaptation to a given set of conditions need not be arrived at by a single route of variation; a number of different genes are apparently in control of coloration. One can ask, on the other hand, whether the camouflage is as effective as it is purported to be. This was tested in the field by H. B. D. Kettlewell, a British biologist. By releasing a known number of light and dark moths in clean and sooty areas and then observing the rates of predation, he established that the rate of survival of the dark form is 17 percent below that of the light form in clean areas, but 10 percent above in soot-blackened regions. In 1850, less than 1 percent of the moths in industrial areas were dark; by 1900 they had increased in frequency to 99 percent in some areas, indicating that the selective advantage was strikingly effective.

Finally, a simple form of adaptation in humans can be mentioned. Many of the natives of tribes in western and central Africa have abnormal red blood cells in that they

5.5 *Industrial melanism. The light-colored moth is the ancestral form.*

S. Beaufoy

Louder and louder yet, it shrieks and cries as it comes tearing on resistless to the goal: and now its way, still like the way of Death, is strewn with ashes thickly. Everything around is blackened. There are dark pools of water, muddy lanes, and miserable habitations far below. There are jagged walls and falling houses close at hand, and through the battered roofs and broken windows, wretched rooms are seen, where want and fever hide themselves in many wretched shapes, while smoke and crowded gables, and distorted chimneys, and deformity of brick and mortar penning up deformity of mind and body, choke the murky distance. As Mr. Dombey looks out of his carriage window, it is never in his thoughts that the monster who has brought him there has let the light of day in on these things: not made or caused them. It was the journey's fitting end, and might have been the end of everything; it was so ruinous and dreary.

C. Dickens [5]

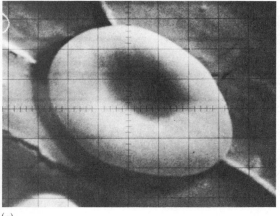

(a)

(b)

5.6   (a) A normal red blood cell (magnification about 7,000×) and (b) sickled red blood cells (magnification about 3,500×).

assume a sickle shape rather then the usual ovoid form when exposed to air (see illustration 5.6). This is caused by an abnormal hemoglobin that is an inefficient oxygen carrier and also causes the cells to collapse partially. Severely affected individuals generally die from anemia at an early age; they have received the mutated gene from both father and mother. Others, receiving one normal gene from one parent and an abnormal gene from the other, have normal red blood cells, although a certain percentage of the hemoglobin is abnormal. These persons are carriers of the trait, but do not show it themselves in any pronounced manner. However, the presence of the gene, even though not visibly expressed, confers a decided selective advantage; its possessor does not contract malaria, the parasites of which can feed only on fully normal hemoglobin. Here then we have a gene that is highly deleterious under some circumstances, highly beneficial under others. Should malaria be wiped out in these regions of Africa, the gene determining the abnormal form of hemoglobin would undergo selective reduction in frequency and possible elimination because of deaths through anemia; in malaria-ridden areas it will be selectively retained, because deaths from anemia would be balanced by deaths of normal individuals from malaria.

Complex adaptations

The adaptations described above are readily demonstrated to be caused by one or, at most, a few gene mutations. We do not know how long the sickle-cell trait has been in existence, but others, such as resistance to DDT, have made their appearance within a relatively brief and recent

A recent social survey of the Lancashire city of Leigh, near Manchester [England], provides a . . . picture of human adaptation to unhealthy and dreary surroundings. The mill dominates the town, the air is gritty, obscured by smog, but human life is not defeated by the murky environment. The sociologists found in Leigh a vigorous, thriving culture, and a deep involvement in community affairs. Everywhere in Northern Europe the people of the industrialized areas have indeed managed to create a way of life that is spirited and emotionally warm despite soot, grit, and gloomy skies. They have remained highly active and productive physically, biologically, and intellectually. Their expectancy of life is not very different from that of people of the same stock and economic status living in uncontaminated areas, nor is their birth rate smaller. Two hundred years of history thus demonstrate that human beings can become adjusted to contaminated and darkened atmospheres. The raping of nature by technology does not necessarily make the environment incompatible with human life.

R. Dubos [8]

---

span of time. Although the mutation leading to such resistance probably appeared many times in the past, it did not persist, because it possessed no selective value at that time. We can well imagine, then, that complex adaptations take place over substantially longer time period and probably involve many different mutations, each one of which, when it comes into existence and gains expression, contributes to the probability of survival and continued reproduction. All of the intermediate steps leading to present states of adaptation do not remain in existence, and so the stepwise progression to the present-day stage cannot be detected. Each adaptive advancement would tend to replace the previous progenitor through competition, as in the case of industrial melanism, and this of course makes the determination of hereditary patterns that much more difficult to unscramble. The most accomplished biologist would find it difficult, even theoretically, to describe every step in the course of evolution of the tail of a male peacock or the structure of an orchid. Nevertheless, if industrial melanism can spread as it has during the course of a hundred years, enormous patterns of divergence are equally possible over the millions of years during which biological evolution has been taking place. The modern horse, for example, took 60 million years to evolve from an original species no larger than a small dog; the fossil record has yielded at least thirty species of the horse and its ancestors, each one of which eventually gave way to a better-adapted type as time passed. Consequently, only the latest species still exists.

Complex adaptations are of endless variety. Mention has already been made of the finches of the Galapagos Islands, whose bills are correlated with feeding habits. The feet of birds are similarly correlated with their habit of life (illus-

To suppose that the eye with all its inimitable contrivances for adjusting the focus to different distances, for admitting different amounts of light, and for the correction of spherical and chromatic aberration, could have been formed by natural selection, seems, I freely confess, absurd in the highest degree. When it was first said that the sun stood still and the world turned round, the common sense of mankind declared the doctrine false; but the old saying of *Vox populi, vox Dei*, as every philosopher knows, cannot be trusted in science. Reason tells me, that if numerous gradations from a simple and imperfect eye to one complex and perfect can be shown to exist, each grade being useful to its possessor, as is certainly the case; if further, the eye ever varies and the variations be inherited, as is likewise certainly the case; and if such variations should be useful to any animal under changing conditions of life, then the difficulty of believing that a perfect and complex eye could be formed by natural selection, though insuperable by our imagination, should not be considered as subversive of the theory. How a nerve comes to be sensitive to light, hardly concerns us more than how life itself originated; but I may remark that, as some of the lowest organisms, in which nerves cannot be detected, are capable of perceiving light, it does not seem impossible that certain sensitive elements in their sarcode should become aggregated and developed into nerves, endowed with this special sensibility.

C. Darwin [4]

Evolution as a process

The most obvious objection [to natural selection] is that which is drawn from the general permanence of known species within the period of human history. Varieties have indeed sprung up under domestication, but in these cases the animals or plants have been placed under conditions very different from those which exist in nature, and the breeds or races thus produced seem gradually to lose their peculiarities when removed from artificial conditions. Among wild species variations occur; but these seem oscillatory, rather than progressive, and introduce no change in the specific type. The descriptions of our best known species given by the most ancient naturalists are as applicable now as then. The figures of animals which have come down to us among the fragments of ancient art, are sufficiently accurate representations of the species with which we are most familiar to-day. And the strength of this argument is greatly increased by the fact that some of our present species can be traced back geologically to a period long preceding the commencement of recorded history. . . . Such facts as these constitute an argument of some force against the theory, but are by no means conclusive. The period of recorded history is too short to be appreciable in the progress of organized nature. And the mere fact of certain species remaining essentially permanent for immense periods proves nothing decisively, for the Darwinian theory involves no rapid or constant change in specific types. On the contrary, Darwin expressly says that ''natural selection always acts very slowly, generally at only long intervals of time, and generally on only a very few of the inhabitants of the same region at the same time.'' Again, ''The periods during which species have been undergoing modification, though very long as measured by years, have probably been short in comparison with the periods during which these same species remained without undergoing any change.''

W. N. Rice [17]

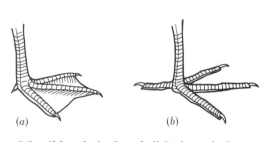

5.7 Although the feet of all birds are built on the same basic plan, there are variations that adapt particular species for a special life-style. This illustration shows the foot of a wading bird (a) and a perching bird (b).

5.8 Protective coloration. Note the almost invisible crab in the center of the photograph.

tration 5.7), yet all are built on the same fundamental plan of structure. The forelimb of the vertebrate group has undergone even more drastic change over the 300-million-year period of its existence. In each instance, the adaptation is consistent with a particular way of life. A look at a perfected organ—for example, a wing of a bird—raises the question of how intermediate stages could have had a selective value, a question not easy to answer. The fossil record provides some clues to intermediate forms of change, but it must be remembered that an individual or a species must always be adapted if it is to survive, and each change leading to a more or less perfected state contributes to adaptiveness.

The coloring of animals shows a remarkable diversity, but the diversity in all instances can be interpreted in terms of selective survival. Mimicry, a superficial resemblance of one organism to another or to natural objects among which it lives, is a form of protective coloration. If an organism's coloration permits it to blend in with its environment, its purpose is concealment; on the other hand, if one species imitates the coloration of another, the intent is usually to advertise the dangerous or unpalatable qualities of the species that is being mimicked.

The striped pattern of a zebra may seem blatantly showy and evolutionarily ridiculous when seen on an open plain or in a public zoo, but in the pattern of light and shade of a shrubby or forest environment, the zebra blends inconspicuously into the background. Among the native birds of America, the ground feeders are patterned in the grays, browns, and blacks of the forest floor, marsh, or stubble field, and this is often coupled with the behavioral trait of remaining immobile when disturbed. Ovenbirds, thrushes, quail, mourning doves, bitterns, and rails differ markedly

Evolution as a process

To this theory Darwin simply adds what he calls the principle of "natural selection," to guide this blind chaotic struggle of the elements to the well-ordered result. But, after all, it does not appear that this principle adds any thing to the scheme except a new name. This natural selection implies no intention, no intelligent purpose, no rational choice; it is only another name for the fact, for the result for which it professes to account. It suggests no real cause. It is in truth no principle at all. The result itself is represented as the result not of any antecedently impressed or inherent law, but merely of the play of circumstances, of the whirl of accident, of the universal conflict and struggle out of which all forms arise, and in which they are preserved or destroyed by virtue of their mutual adaptations or antagonisms. . . .

D. R. Goodwin [12]

from the brightly colored orioles, blue jays, tanagers, cardinals, and grosbeaks, the latter group feeding and nesting in trees where danger from predation is less and maneuverability greater. Conspicuous coloration also has a territorial significance, in that is keeps pairs of breeding individuals evenly spread over available feeding space. Other species as varied as a lizard and a grasshopper possess the shape and coloration of leaves. Anyone who has tried to find the tiny green tree frog, *Hyla,* knows how difficult it is to detect it among the foliage of his perch. Other living things have a similar ability to camouflage themselves (see illustration 5.8).

Warning coloration is a "hands off" display and is not a form of mimicry. The colors employed are those readily discernible: black, orange, red, white, and yellow. The black and white of the skunk and the yellow and black of bees and wasps are familiar examples of animals dangerous to handle, while the orange and black of the monarch butterfly advertises its unpalatable, even poisonous, nature to a predator. Among the highly colored insects, the great majority have been shown to be unpalatable, whereas the neutral colored ones are generally edible.

Mimicry enters the evolutionary realm of warning coloration when palatable and harmless species mimic others that are distasteful or harmful. This has occurred in a number of butterfly species, the mimicking of the monarch by the viceroy being a well-known example (illustration 5.9). The

Mrs. Brower . . . reasoned that if natural mimics are highly effective in deterring potential predators, equally effective mimics could be produced by artificial means. To determine this, she used captive starlings and meal worms, which are their normal food when in captivity. In order to make distasteful "models," she dipped meal worms into a bitter substance, quinine dihydrochloride, and at the same time colored them with a band of green cellulose paint. She made "mimics" by coloring meal worms with the same type of green paint, and dipping them in distilled water. Non-mimetic, edible, painted meal worms were made by using orange paint of the same type and distilled water.

The nine starlings used were each given 160 trials over a period of 16 days. In each trial, a bird was given an orange banded, edible and a green banded meal worm, either a model or a mimic. Different birds were given either 10, 30, 60, or 90 per cent mimics. The starlings ate all of the orange banded meal worms, showing that the paint itself had no effect on palatability, and also that these birds have no instinctive aversion to brightly and conspicuously colored prey. They quickly rejected the bitter, green-banded models, and after having tasted them, avoided the similarly colored "mimics." Eighty per cent of the palatable green-banded "mimics" escaped predation in this manner.

G. L. Stebbins [21]

5.9 Mimicry among butterflies. The Monarch (a) is the model; the Viceroy (b) is the mimic.

American Museum of Natural History

(a)   (b)

The direct influence of climatic or geographical conditions upon animals is, in the main, ignored by the leading exponents of the doctrine of natural selection. . . .

There is, however, a vast amount of unquestionable proof of the direct and constant action of climate and other conditions of life upon animals, and that such geographical variations as the thicker and softer fur of mammals inhabiting cold regions, smaller size and brighter colors at the southward, etc., etc., do not require the action of natural selection, in its strict and proper sense, for their explanation. It is well known, for instance, that a flock of fine-wooled sheep, when taken to a hot climate, rapidly acquire a coarser and coarser fleece, till, in a few generations, it nearly loses its character of proper wool, and becomes simply hair; that the change affects simultaneously the whole flock, and is not brought about by one or two individuals acquiring a coarser fleece and through their descendants modifying the character of the herd. . . .

J. A. Allen [1]

5.10 Members of the phlox family of flowering plants and their pollinating agents. The basic type, from which the others are derived, is pollinated by a bee. The others have undergone modification during the course of evolution, changing their structure and in some cases their color. These alterations are accompanied by a change in pollinating agent.

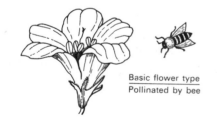

Basic flower type
Pollinated by bee

viceroy has aptly been termed "a sheep in wolves' clothing." The protection afforded by mimicry of this sort is not absolute, but it is sufficient to afford a degree of protection to the mimic, and thus an advantage in survival. Mimicry, however, imposes its own limitations. If the mimic becomes more numerous than the model species that is being mimicked, predators would learn quickly to step up their rate of predation. There must exist an optimum balance in the numbers of the unpalatable model and the palatable mimic, a balance that would make it more probable that the model and not the mimic would be attacked. This differential factor tends to limit the spread of the mimic, because it is restricted to the territory of the model species.

The adaptations described have been related basically to survival of the individual. They determine how well the organism gets on in a world that provides its sustenance but also threatens its existence. But mere survival is not sufficient in an evolving, changing world if the species is to continue. The goal of the chicken is to produce an egg, so to speak; the biological goal of one generation is to produce the next one. So it is not surprising that adaptations at the reproductive level are as numerous and diverse as those found at the gross morphological level. These adaptations involve not only the structure of reproductive organs, mechanisms of fertilization, and dispersal and nourishment

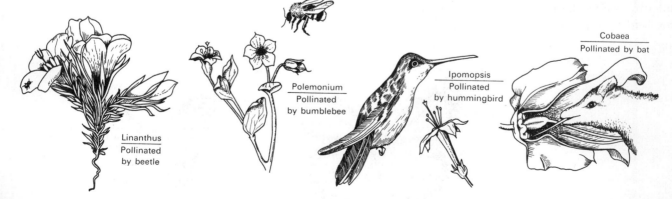

Linanthus
Pollinated
by beetle

Polemonium
Pollinated
by bumblebee

Ipomopsis
Pollinated
by hummingbird

Cobaea
Pollinated by bat

(a)   (b)   Wisconsin Department of Natural Resources

Physiological adaptation. Ptarmigans in summer (a) and in winter (b).

of the young, but also, among animals, patterns of recognition, territorial establishment, and courtship behavior. No one who has witnessed the mating flight of a woodcock in early spring as it hurtles across the face of the moon, or seen the courtship ballet of a pair of great-crested grebes as they skitter across the water, or knows that the female mantis decapitates the male prior to copulation can fail to be impressed by the varied means whereby life ensures continuation of a species.

Death in the early stages of life—eggs, spores, seeds, embryos and larvae of all kinds—is appalling in terms of numbers. These incipient life forms account for a good part of the base of the food chain along with unicellular forms of life. Nature must therefore be recklessly extravagant in production to offset these losses. Only when nourishment is carried through to the weaning stage can an animal species afford to lessen the number of offspring.

We need mention only the flowering plants to illustrate reproductive adaptability. All flowers are constructed on a basic plan, but their diversity of shape and color is intimately related to their mode of reproduction. Wind-pollinated plants—oaks, grasses, ragweed, and so on—are greenish in color, basically odorless, and very simple in form. They have been derived from insect-pollinated forms in which color, taste, and odor help to attract the pollinating agent. Without insects, or in some cases, bats or humming-birds, the transference of pollen could not take place and sterility would, in most instances, result because the great majority of plants in their natural state are self-sterile. A mutual adaptability of plant and pollinator often develops and is sometimes so highly specific that neither can exist without the other (illustration 5.10). Flowers built on the

Very few birds produce less than two young ones each year, while many have six, eight, or ten; four will certainly be below the average; and if we suppose that each pair produce young only four times in their life, that will also be below the average, supposing them not to die either by violence or want of food. Yet at this rate how tremendous would be the increase in a few years from a single pair! A simple calculation will show that in fifteen years each pair of birds would have increased to nearly ten millions! whereas we have no reason to believe that the number of the birds of any country increases at all in fifteen or in one hundred and fifty years. With such powers of increase the population must have reached its limits, and have become stationary, in a very few years after the origin of each species. It is evident, therefore, that each year an immense number of birds must perish—as many in fact as are born; and as on the lowest calculation the progeny are each year twice as numerous as their parents, it follows that, whatever be the average number of individuals existing in any given country, *twice that number must perish annually,*—a striking result, but one which seems at least highly probable, and is perhaps under rather than over the truth. It would therefore appear that, as far as the continuance of the species and the keeping up the average number of individuals are concerned, large broods are superfluous. On the average all above *one* become food for hawks and kites, wild cats and weasels, or perish of cold and hunger as winter comes on. This is strikingly proved by the case of particular species; for we find that their abundance in individuals bears no relation whatever to their fertility in producing offspring.

A. R. Wallace [24]

Evolution as a process

When we see any structure highly perfected for any particular habit, as the wings of a bird for flight, we should bear in mind that animals displaying early transitional grades of the structure will seldom have survived to the present day, for they will have been supplanted by their successors, which were gradually rendered more perfect through natural selection. Furthermore, we may conclude that transitional states between structures fitted for very different habits of life will rarely have been developed at an early period in great numbers and under many subordinate forms. Thus, to return to our imaginary illustration of the flying-fish, it does not seem probable that fishes capable of true flight would have been developed under many subordinate forms, for taking prey of many kinds in many ways, on the land and in the water, until their organs of flight had come to a high stage of perfection, so as to have given them a decided advantage over other animals in the battle for life. Hence the chance of discovering species with transitional grades of structure in a fossil condition will always be less, from their having existed in lesser numbers, than in the case of species with fully developed structures.

C. Darwin [4]

sweet pea plan are dependent on pollination by bees, tubular flowers or those with spurred petals require long-tongued moths or hummingbirds, whereas the Yucca plant, the "Spanish sword" of the deserts in the American Southwest, and the pronuba moth cannot long exist without each other.

Speciation

The first task in the development of any discipline is the description and classification of the units with which one deals; their interrelationships become apparent when the identity of the units is recognized and defined. Biology has many such units, but the one most readily comprehended is the species. The living world, despite its diversity, is not a continuum, with all forms blending gradually and imperceptibly into all other forms. Darwinian evolution is predicated on the thesis that such a continuum must have existed in the past, for species can only arise gradually from other species, but today there are distinct gaps between species, even those closely related to one another, and these gaps are rarely traversed by one species breeding with another. If this were true, species distinctions would break down, and the art of classification would be made impossible by the presence of intermediate forms.

All of us recognize that dogs belong to a single species, even though man, through domestication and selection, has produced many distinct and recognizable breeds. But if a collie and a wirehaired terrier were bred together, the offspring would be a mongrel; it would belong to neither breed, but would show the characteristics of both. The prevalence of mongrels in our dog population indicates that

If you were an early nineteenth-century biologist looking at an animal and trying to decide why it moves, changes color, emits sounds, [or evolves], you would be in the same situation as an early physicist who suddenly had an electric fan dropped on his desk. If he knew a little about electric charges and currents, and had a suitable source of charge, he might get the fan to go. And he might even, by playing around a little, find a neat relation between the breeze made by the fan and the current passed through it. But he certainly would have no idea how electric current can be transformed into mechanical motion. Before the physicist could go any further with the problem of the fan, he would certainly have to discover Faraday's laws. But at the moment we are talking about—with the fan sitting before him, and a nice little empirical equation on paper—can you imagine that he would leave the fan and go to his armchair if he had a screwdriver handy?

This is not a frivolous question. The history of the physical [and biological] sciences illustrates two fundamental principles—techniques, if you will—of explanation. One of them is to use the idea of *parts* and the *relations* between those parts. This tactic of *analysis* begins at the simpleminded level of opening up a fan to find a motor, and taking the motor apart to find coils, armatures, and brushes. But it goes on to the invention of atoms and of parts of atoms—of parts and relations that the naked senses will never be able to detect, and whose existence is established solely by the wide-ranging success of the theories based on them. The refusal to analyze, whether at the level of fans and animals or at the level of insulators and conductors, nerves and muscles, is self-imposed defeat. . . .

J. M. Reiner [16]

---

breeds or varieties do not selectively reproduce within the breed; a dog recognizes a dog, not his pedigree. A breed, therefore, enjoys a precarious existence, preservation of which is maintained only because of man's intervention. The destruction of a breed or variety occurs through outcrossing with other breeds or varieties within the same species. The

On the view that species are only strongly marked and permanent varieties, and that each species first existed as a variety, we can see why it is that no line of demarcation can be drawn between species, commonly supposed to have been produced by special acts of creation, and varieties which are acknowledged to have been produced by secondary laws. On this same view we can understand how it is that in a region where many species of a genus have been produced, and where they now flourish, these same species should present many varieties; for where the manufactory of species has been active, we might expect, as a general rule, to find it still in action; and this is the case if varieties be incipient species. Moreover, the species of the larger genera, which afford the greater number of varieties or incipient species, retain to a certain degree the character of varieties; for they differ from each other by a less amount of difference than do the species of smaller genera. The closely allied species also of the larger genera apparently have restricted ranges, and in their affinities they are clustered in little groups round other species—in both respects resembling varieties. These are strange relations on the view that each species was independently created, but are intelligible if each existed first as a variety.

C. Darwin [4]

5.11 *Through domestication and artificial selection, man has been able to produce families of plants from a single species. The four vegetables shown here, (a) Chinese cabbage, (b) Earliana cabbage, (c) Brussels sprouts, and (d) kohlrabi, have all been produced from a single wild species of* Brassica oleracea.

(a)   (b)   W. Atlee Burpee Co.

(c)   (d)

Photograph of the last living passenger pigeon, 1911.

National Audubon Society

species, however, is constant, a distinct biological entity. The constancy, on the other hand, is relative, for our temporal view covers but a brief span of years, and so a species must also be viewed as a point in time along a route of continual change.

Man, in a similar sense, is also a species. He is composed of many races that came into existence in past ages, but these races are capable of interbreeding without difficulty, and the mobility of man ensures that interracial reproduction will continue at an even faster pace in the future than it has in the past. A pure human race is a rarity today, if it exists at all. But man cannot breed outside the circle of man. He of course exhibits structural, biochemical, and behavioral relationships with other species of the primate group, the order of mammals comprising man together with apes, monkeys, and related forms. It has been said that a man would be a monster if he were either less than or more than a man, but this is a social and behavioral judgment that is unrelated to biological fact. A reproductive barrier separates man from all other species, but the same can be said for most other legitimate species.

A species can therefore be defined as a closed system whose members do not ordinarily exchange heritable materials with members of other similarly closed systems. This is not an absolute situation, for interspecific hybrids are known in nature, and man has caused the formation of others. For example, the Washington Zoo exhibited the fertile offspring of a cross between an Alaskan brown bear and a polar bear, but the natural habitats and behavior of the two are so different that hybridization does not occur in their native environments.

Most or perhaps all the variations from the typical form of a species must have some definite effect, however slight, on the habits or capacities of the individuals. Even a change of colour might, by rendering them more or less distinguishable, affect their safety; a greater or less development of hair might modify their habits. More important changes, such as an increase in the power or dimensions of the limbs or any of the external organs, would more or less affect their mode of procuring food or the range of country which they inhabit. It is also evident that most changes would affect, either favourably or adversely, the powers of prolonging existence. An antelope with shorter or weaker legs must necessarily suffer more from the attacks of the feline carnivora; the passenger pigeon with less powerful wings would sooner or later be affected in its powers of procuring a regular supply of food; and in both cases the result must necessarily be a diminution of the population of the modified species. If, on the other hand, any species should produce a variety having slightly increased powers of preserving existence, that variety must inevitably in time acquire a superiority in numbers. These results must follow as surely as old age, intemperance, or scarcity of food produce an increased mortality. In both cases there may be many individual exceptions; but on the average the rule will invariably be found to hold good.

A. R. Wallace [24]

We need to recognize, however, that varieties and races within a species are the sources of new species. Every new adaptive mechanism is a potential source of separation of one segment of a species from its main population (see illustration 5.12). This is the gist of Darwinian evolution. The process of speciation is intimately connected with the development of isolating mechanisms that, in the course of time, function as effective barriers that separate one group from another within a species. If the total population of a species can freely interbreed through its entire range, the only effective evolution is the replacement of the original form by a more favored race; no isolating mechanism is necessary under these circumstances. It may be thought, for example, that the industrial melanism of moths previously described fits this situation, with the melanic form gradually displacing the original form. But further consideration would show that this could occur only within a portion of the range, that is, the soot-laden areas. Industrial melanism can be viewed as incipient speciation, not yet come to full fruition, but reproductive isolation, resulting from variations independent of coloration and emerging at some possible future time, would have to come into play if a single species were to split into two new ones.

Geographical isolation is an obvious and necessary factor in evolution. An impassable physical barrier, such as a mountain range or ocean, may separate a group of individuals from the main body of the species. This group, no longer free to exchange its variations with the main group, and possibly having within it variations not necessarily characteristic of the species as a whole, will accumulate at random new kinds of variations and will encounter new

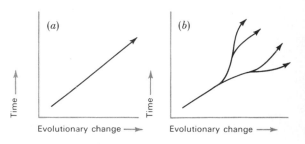

5.12 *Two ways of viewing evolutionary change. (a) The population of organisms undergoes change from one state to another. Darwin referred to this type of change as "descent with modifications"; today it is called "phyletic evolution." (b) The population splits up into distinct entities that will eventually achieve the status of recognizable species. Darwin referred to this form of change as "the origin of species"; today it is generally called "evolutionary divergence."*

The life here is not dramatic on the surface; we don't go down to the sea in currachs, we only go to the creamery with the horse and cart. There are no great forests here or no great lakes or no great deserts to feed the imagination. There are no earthquakes or great floods or hurricanes to remind us that life is wonderful and terrible. It is a land of little fields and of people who lead what seem to be uneventful lives. You think about "the long littleness of life" and in infertile moments you say to yourself "that's this place, all right." But in your secret heart you know you are wrong. You know that under the accretions is the profound life, almost smothered by the inhibitions engendered by a land where there is so little spiritual room, almost worn away by the attrition of living, but always alive and now and then reaching the surface.

Human nature may be the same from China to Peru but the life of a place is powerfully influenced by the shape of the landscape, the color of the sky, the sun and the rain, the history of the people. The life takes on its own unique texture.

Words of a Kerryman

It seems likely that the dominant core of a population or species is rarely primarily involved in the evolutionary process. Presumably reproductive isolation must eventually isolate the evolving group in order for speciation to occur.

Such a behavioral mechanism seems appropriate to explain the evolutionary events that have resulted in the present 14 species of finches in the Galapagos Islands. The original invaders occupied a habitat closest to their original habitat. Subsequently, countless subordinate individuals were driven off into other kinds of habitat, unoccupied by competing passerines. Eventually, a mutation occurred in one of these, which provided improved chances of survival in marginal habitat. The rest of the process logically follows, with successive occupancy of, and adaptation to, other habitats. What is new in this account of the evolution of these finches is the proposed role of socially subordinate birds and their enforced dispersal into marginal habitats.

J. J. Christian [3]

environmental situations out of which will emerge new patterns of adaptation. Should chance, at a later time, permit the intermingling of the group with the main body of the species, the divergence may have become sufficient to prevent their interbreeding again, and the two species, one old and one new, can exist together without loss of identity.

The classic case of finches discovered by Darwin on the Galapagos Islands was mentioned in the previous chapter. We shall discuss these birds in greater detail here because they offer a clear example of speciation. The first finches on the Galapagos were probably chance individuals of a South American mainland species. Previously uninhabited by birds of the finch group, the islands were open to exploitation. Fourteen species now exist. Six of them are tree finches confined to the forests and mangrove swamps and subsisting mainly on insects; another six are ground finches and seedeaters confined the the arid coastal areas; one is an insect-eating warbler finch inhabiting all ten islands; and the last is a solitary species occupying only Cocos Island, about 800 kilometers (some 500 miles) west of the Galapagos. Among both the seedeaters and those subsisting on insects, differences exist as to food preference, differences that are also reflected in beak structure and feeding behavior (see illustration 4.9). The suspected progenitor stock is believed to be a seed-eating form that is similar to the present mainland species in South America. If the Galapagos had been one island, rather than ten, it is likely that only one species would have developed, a species that would have been different from its progenitor, but without the diversity presently evident. However, the islands of the Galapagos group offered isolation and a variety of different environments. Under these conditions of selection and confinement,

Evolution as a process

the isolated populations departed from the mainland type and from one another, with full speciation the end result.

More than geographical isolation is involved. Ecological isolation also exists as shown by environmental and food preferences, both of which lessen competition and reinforce separation. A behavioral isolation also is evident in song patterns, mating characteristics, and nest-building procedures. Even if no reproductive incompatability exists, the other mechanisms, once established, would be sufficient to preserve each species as an entity (see illustration 5.13). Many species can be crossbred in captivity, but do not do so under natural conditions.

If a species, with its varieties and races, extends over a wide and ecologically varied range, and if, as we have discussed, adaptations arise as a result of random variations and ecological challenges, then one can assume that individuals farthest apart are likely to be the most reproductively incompatible in the sense of producing viable and fertile offspring. In a substantial number of species, as widely separate as birds and plants, this has been found to be so, justifying Darwin's original contention that races or varieties are incipient species.

Why has this not occurred in the case of man? At some time in the past, man was split into many races, with sharply defined differences of a physical nature distinguishing one from the other. This presumably occurred when the number of human beings was small, and men were widely dispersed in small, self-contained groups. There is no reason for believing, however, that there exists any racial reproductive incompatibility among the races of mankind, and one can only assume that before such incompatibility developed, the mobility of man brought about racial mixing to prevent it.

5.13 *Steps in the evolutionary divergence within a single parental population that can lead to the eventual formation of two distinct species, or even three species if the parental population continues to exist.*

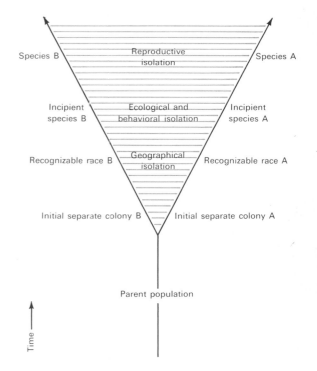

Species B — Reproductive isolation — Species A

Incipient species B — Ecological and behavioral isolation — Incipient species A

Recognizable race B — Geographical isolation — Recognizable race A

Initial separate colony B — Initial separate colony A

Parent population

Time

. . . the alpha hemoglobin in the gorilla differs in only one amino acid from that of man. And that of the chimpanzee is identical to that of man. In an over-all sense, the rate of acceptable mutation in the globins is only about 1 amino acid per 100 residues per 6,000,000 years. For other proteins, such as cytochrome c, the allowable rate proves to be even less: 1 in 20,000,000 years. But a more accurate measure of the possible rate of amino acid replacement *may* be obtained from the fibrinopeptides which appear to serve no other function than to be excised from fibrinogen, when it is converted to fibrin in the formation of a blood clot, and then to be degraded. In these the apparent rate is 1 amino acid change per 100 residues per 1 million years. These numbers are in reasonable agreement with the averaged estimate from nucleotide change—approximately 4 replacements per 100 amino acids per 15,000,000 years.

It is thus possible to suggest that in the last several million years a considerable number of the proteins of man could have undergone mutational changes in one or two amino acids. But a *major* change in a particular protein would be highly unlikely—at least by the mutational processes leading to the changes so far studied.

R. L. Sinsheimer [20]

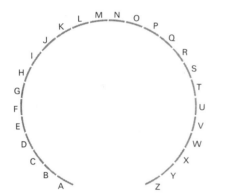

5.14 *The idealized development through time of a race circle (Rassenkreis). Form A can breed with Form B; B with C; C with D; and so on through the circle. Y can breed with Z, but A and Z cannot interbreed. Such breeding systems have been discovered among birds and smaller animals.*

It has been estimated that it may take as long as a million years to produce a species under natural conditions; if this speculation has any validity, man has been here on earth for too short a period to have segmented into species categories.

Rates of evolution

Darwin recognized that the act of speciation could not be witnessed during the lifetime of a single observer; a longer view had to be taken. Bacterial and insect resistance to chemicals and patterns of industrial melanism have taken place within observable limits of time, but these are still intraspecific, not interspecific, changes. Only by turning to the fossil record can we gain an impression of rates of change in particular groups. Just as no two living members of a species are exactly alike, so no two members of a fossil species are similarly exact, indicating that minute changes—microevolution, as it is called—occurred in the past as they are occurring today and that they contributed to evolution in the same manner. Gaps in the fossil record are clearly evident and suggest that evolution may have proceeded by large jumps, but no positive evidence forces the conclusion that macroevolution has played any significant role in speciation. The gaps are more readily accounted for by assuming that not all intermediate forms were fossilized.

Evolution from one group to another taken place at an uneven rate, and the same is true of change within a single group; it may be rapid during one geologic age, slow or nonexistent during others. It might be logical to assume that

Evolution as a process

A subtle chain of countless rings
The next unto the farthest brings;
The eye reads omens where it goes,
And speaks all languages the rose;
And, striving to be man, the worm
Mounts through all the spires of form.

R. W. Emerson [10]

rates of mutation, length of generation, and numbers of individuals produced per breeding parent are major contributory factors in determining direction, speed, and intensity of evolution, but this appears not to be so. Environmental conditions provide the limiting features of evolution. Variation, as laboratory experiments have shown, is always present, but only environmental opportunities can bring about its release for new adaptive change.

An unchanging environment provides few challenges or opportunities to any evolving group. A deep-sea marine shell, *Lingula,* has evolved very little in the past 500 million years; comparable shell forms of shallow marine waters have undergone immense diversification. The opossum has not changed appreciably since the Cretaceous period, some 80 million years ago. It is a forest dweller and has been confined to this kind of environment throughout its existence. The modern horse, on the other hand evolved out of a dog-sized mammal with small head, long tail, five toes, and omnivorous food habits. In 60 million years, thirty or more species evolved, passing through changes that altered its size, character of feet, tail, and skull. The teeth of the various species indicate that feeding habits also changed; as the animals moved out of the forests and onto the dry, grassy plains, they became grazers rather than browsers. Today only a single species of horse is known, the others having suffered extinction.

Among plant groups, those requiring a moist environment during at least part of the life cycle have evolved less than those inhabiting drier territory. Algae, mosses and ferns, all ancient stocks, exhibit far less diversity than the more recent flowering plants. Among the latter, greater diversifi-

If it be granted, as I think it must, that natural selection is an effective factor in most . . . examples of phyletic evolution, the conclusion to be drawn from the rates of phyletic evolution, so slow in terms of human observation and experiment, is that the selective forces involved are indeed very small . . . any selective pressures . . . were slight and arose or increased only as small and gradual changes occurred in the population and its environment. . . . We observe, [however], that a more marked shift in adaptive status, as from browsing to grazing in horses, is accompanied by a definite and measurable increase in the rate of evolution of the organs concerned, and . . . it seems rather obvious that this is a response to increased selective pressures. . . . There is evidence that subspecies, or, at least, clearly differentiated local races may evolve in less than a century but commonly require 10,000 years or so for their evolution, and may evolve for as much as 500,000 years without rising to the specific level. The evolution of a species, full distinct genetically and morphologically, seems usually to require 50,000 years or more in mature groups, and even in groups with fairly rapid average evolutionary rates, such as mammals, some living species are about 1,000,000 years old. . . . Some living invertebrate species are much older than this and in a few cases seem to be as much as 30,000,000 years old.

G. G. Simpson [19]

I heard a thousand blended notes,
While in a grove I sat reclined,
In that sweet mood when pleasant thoughts
Bring sad thoughts to the mind.

To her fair works did Nature link
The human soul that through me ran;
And much it grieved my heart to think
What man has made of man.

Through primrose tufts, in that green bower,
The periwinkle trailed its wreaths;
And 'tis my faith that every flower
Enjoys the air it breathes.

The birds around me hopped and played,
Their thoughts I cannot measure—
But the least motion which they made,
It seemed a thrill of pleasure.

The budding twigs spread out their fan,
To catch the breezy air;
And I must think, do all I can,
That there was pleasure there.

If this belief from heaven be sent,
If such be Nature's plan,
Have I not reason to lament
What man has made of man?

W. Wordsworth [28]

---

cation has taken place in unsettled regions than in those where environmental conditions have remained stable. The eastern United States, for example, possesses a more conservative flora than do the coastal areas of the West. During the past 60 or 70 million years, the West has witnessed mountain building, volcanic activity, and intermittent droughts, with subsequent opening up and wiping out of environmental niches; the East remained relatively stable during the same period, except in those areas covered by glacial ice. Even in the West, however, some small areas remained unaltered; in one of these regions the ancient redwoods continue to cling to existence.

A general principle emerges from the examination of these changes. As Verne Grant has stated: "A population living in a stable environment, once it has reached the highest adaptive level possible, can be maintained at the same adaptive level by stabilizing selection for long periods of time; whereas a population living in a changing environment is exposed to progressive selection, and may respond to this mode of selection by changing in phase with its environment." Further, it would also appear that the greatest diversification arises when a particular group first comes into existence. A new group is readily changeable, not having reached its maximum adaptability, and all environments are challenging and potentially exploitable. Only after such initial explorations does a period of consolidation take place. The history of any major group of organisms, for example, mammals or flowering plants, reveals a large amount of intragroup diversification, with many variations on a theme; but only rarely have changes been so fundamental that a new group results.

Origins

Radioactive measurements of the oldest rocks indicate that the earth is about 4.5 billion years old. The oldest fossil-bearing strata are approximately 3 billion years old, the fossils being bacterial or algal deposits. Younger and younger strata, dated by appropriate radioactive techniques, provide a chronology of the past, and as human history is broken up into convenient blocks of time—the Golden Age of Greece, the Renaissance, the scientific revolution, the Roaring Twenties, and so forth—so the history of the earth and of life has been similarly segmented.

Unless, on the basis of faith, we wish to believe that life was divinely created 3 billion years ago and has followed a predetermined path since that time, we must subscribe to the point of view that life, in some manner, arose spontaneously out of inanimate matter, has evolved gradually to its present state of diversification, and will continue to evolve into the indefinite future. Life cannot arise spontaneously today. Even if the circumstances were appropriate, primitive life, whatever its form, could not compete with existing organisms.

The conditions on earth have not always been as they are today. Air-breathing organisms are adapted to an atmosphere containing 21 percent oxygen, but that oxygen is largely a by-product of plant life, being given off in the process of photosynthesis. It would appear that life originated when the earth was surrounded by a reducing atmosphere, that is, a nonoxidizing one, and when the waters of

In these days of space exploration, the problem of the origin of life has rather suddenly become fashionable. Belief in the existence of extraterrestrial life, and of extraterrestrial rational beings, has a potent romantic appeal. . . . It is almost a pity to oppugn so glamorous a notion. But what are its credentials? Probably the main one is that there must be, conservatively estimated, 100 million planets in the universe whose environments are believed by authoritative astronomers to be tolerably similar to terrestrial ones. And with so many chances available, even an improbable event is like to happen more than once. This would be a strong argument if we knew just how probable, or improbable, the event under consideration really is, but for this we have no secure enough basis for judgment.

The further argument, that once life has arisen it is bound to evolve approximately as it did on earth is less dependable still. At first blush, this may not seem unsound; many of the body structures of existing organisms are adaptations which help to solve the problems of survival posed by the environment, and it may seem that natural selection should bring them into existence wherever they are needed, as it did on earth. This is not necessarily so; in the first place, an adaptive problem may not be solved at all, and the species may become extinct; moreover, and this is crucial, many adaptive problems may be solved in more than one way. The solutions which we know to have been utilized by organisms on earth cannot be guaranteed to have been either the best conceivable ones, or the ones that would occur again in the thinkable . . . situation of the evolution occurring for the second time here, on earth. . . . The flow of evolutionary events is . . . not always smooth and uniform; it . . . contains crises and turning points which, viewed in retrospect, may appear to be breaks of the continuity. The origin of life was one such crisis, radical enough to deserve the name of transcendence. The origin of man was another.

Th. Dobzhansky [6]

Evolution as a process

Hale Observatories

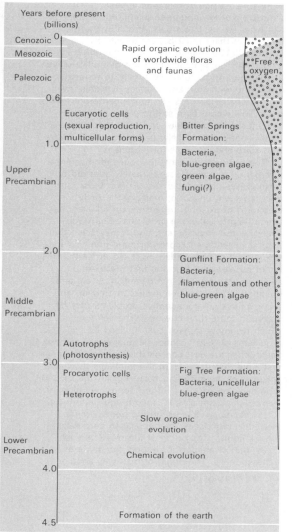

Years before present (billions)			
Cenozoic	0	Rapid organic evolution of worldwide floras and faunas	Free oxygen
Mesozoic			
Paleozoic			
	0.6		
Upper Precambrian		Eucaryotic cells (sexual reproduction, multicellular forms)	Bitter Springs Formation: Bacteria, blue-green algae, green algae, fungi(?)
	1.0		
	2.0		Gunflint Formation: Bacteria, filamentous and other blue-green algae
Middle Precambrian			
	3.0	Autotrophs (photosynthesis)	
		Procaryotic cells	Fig Tree Formation: Bacteria, unicellular blue-green algae
		Heterotrophs	
		Slow organic evolution	
Lower Precambrian		Chemical evolution	
	4.0		
	4.5	Formation of the earth	

the earth were considerably warmer than they are now (see illustration 5.15).

Darwin saw the possibilities with remarkable insight and clarity and included the following passage in *The Descent of Man:*

It is often said that all the conditions for the first production of a living organism are now present, which could ever have been present. But if (and oh! what a big if) we could conceive in some warm little pond, with all sorts of ammonia and phosphoric salts, light, heat, electricity, etc., present, that a protein compound was chemically formed ready to undergo still more complex changes, at the present day such matter would be instantly devoured or absorbed, which would not have been the case before living creatures were formed.

Chemists have shown experimentally that in an environment largely devoid of molecular oxygen, but containing hydrogen, nitrogen, methane, and water in which inorganic salts are dissolved, complex organic molecules such as car-

5.15 *Biological evolution was preceded by a long and complex chemical evolution that led to the formation of molecules of amino acids, sugars, and nucleic acids. These somehow acquired the organization and behavior of replicating living systems, first as cells that derived their energy from the breakdown of chemical substances (heterotrophs), then as cells that could use the energy of the sun through photosynthesis (blue-green algae first, and then green algae). The emergence of the green algae (eucaryotic cells having a nucleus bound by a membrane and generally characterized by sexual reproduction, as contrasted with procaryotic cells, which lacked a membrane-bound nucleus) signaled the beginning of a period of rapid evolution and rapid accumulation of oxygen in the atmosphere. Thus, the great diversity of life as we know it today, and as it is revealed in the fossil record, is primarily the product of the last 600 million years, whereas the steps leading up to this stage took nearly 4 billion years.*

After Barghoorn, 1971

When I heard the learned astronomer,
When the proofs, the figures, were ranged in columns before me,
When I was shown the charts and diagrams, to add, divide, and measure them,
When I sitting heard the astronomer where he lectured with much applause
   in the lecture-room,
How soon unaccountable I became tired and sick,
Till rising and gliding out I wandered off by myself,
In the mystical moist night-air, and from time to time,
Looked up in perfect silence at the stars.

W. Whitman [27]

---

bohydrates, proteins, and nucleic acids can be formed when the mixture is activated by ultraviolet light or electrical discharges similar to those that could have been produced by lightning in a primitive environment. These compounds and their derivatives are found in every living organism today, being the molecular basis of all structures, heritable information, and energy. It is a long step, of course, from these molecules to a complex living cell, the basic unit of organization of all known organisms except viruses, but millions and millions of years of chemical evolution preceded biological evolution. Darwin's principles of variation and natural selection operate chemically as well as biologically, and only the more stable molecules persisted. Even the improbable becomes probable on a statistical basis when sufficient time is available.

Whether life arose once or many times is conjecture, but a number of features of life, from bacteria to man, suggest that life is monophyletic, that is, all life traces back to one point and one ancestor in time. The fluid and chemical state of cells is very similar to that of seawater in which life is supposed to have arisen. Some molecules such as sugars and amino acids exist into two forms which are mirror images of each other (right-handed, or dextro, and left-handed, or laevo). All living things selectively use dextro sugars and laevo amino acids, never their mirror images or mixtures of both. The primary energy source for all cells is adenosine triphosphate, or ATP. The basic informational molecules of all organisms are nucleic acids. These cannot be fortuitous similarities, and the most stable and useful chemical combinations that in aggregate constitute life must have been selected very early in the history of life and have persisted since that time.

It may not strike you as a marvel. It would not, perhaps, unless you stood in the middle of a dead world at sunset, but that was where I stood. Fifty million years lay under my feet, fifty million years of bellowing monsters moving in a green world now gone so utterly that its very light was traveling on the farther edge of space. The chemicals of all that vanished age lay about me on the ground. Around me still lay the shearing molars of dead titanotheres, the delicate sabers of soft-stepping cats, the hollow sockets that held the eyes of many a strange, outmoded beast. These eyes had looked out upon a world as real as ours; dark, savage brains had roamed and roared their challenges into the steaming night. Now they were still here, or, put it as you will, the chemicals that made them were here about me on the ground. The carbon that had driven them ran blackly into the eroding stone. The stain of iron was in the clays. The iron did not remember the blood it had once moved within, the phosphorus had forgot the savage brain. The little individual moment had ebbed from all those strange combinations of chemicals, as it would ebb from our living bodies into the sinks and runnels of oncoming time. . . . Like men from those wild tribes who had haunted these hills before me seeking visions, I made my sign to the great darkness. It was not a mocking sign, and I was not mocked. . . .

L. Eiseley [9a]

Summary

The results of evolution surround us at every hand—the living plants and animals; ourselves as part of the animal kingdom; the varied rocks and soils; the shape of mountains and the outline of the seacoasts; even the stars that shine at night. To the casual eye, there is an immutability to these scenes; tomorrow will be like today, and another year will bring no detectable change. Someone has said that "if you approach a clavichord on its own terms, it has a tremendous amount to give." So it is with the universe around us. It is only when we train the eye to see, when we gain a sense of the variation among seemingly similar things, and then set all of these against the background of time—time that was available and will continue to be available in great blocks of eons and eras—it is only then that we can appreciate the fact that we see ourselves and the universe as a temporary phase in the endless process of change. Today will not be the same as tomorrow, just as yesterday is not the same as today; and neither yesterday nor today can be recovered.

The theory of evolution is the only broad generalization that can help us to understand the scene around us, and ourselves as part of that scene. It is the only theory that pulls together the odds and ends of observations, sees unity in diversity, and embraces variation, adaptation, survival, and extinction within a common frame of reference.

6

Emerging humanity

At a recent convention, a speaker described man as "the cheapest, most reliable, 160-pound computer mass-produced by unskilled labor." The remark was intended to be somewhat facetious, but from an evolutionary point of view it is an accurate description of a living system that can react to an environmental change with speed and precision, a necessary feature for survival in a complex, fluid, and frequently threatening world. Consider, if you will, the following situation. You are driving a modern, high-performance automobile and are approaching a busy intersection. The light changes suddenly from green to yellow. You must make up your mind, with split-second decisiveness, whether you go through on the yellow signal or stop the car and wait for the next change to green again. What are the pieces

I think the computers first made us aware of one of the more evident limitations of the biological brain, its millisecond or longer time scale. Computers flashing from circuit to circuit in microseconds can readily cope with the input and response time of dozens of human brains simultaneously or can perform computations in a brief period of time for which a human brain would need a whole lifetime.

Similarly I believe that we will come to see that our brains are limited in other dimensions as well—in the precision with which we can reconstruct the outside universe, in the nature and resolution of our concepts, in the content of information that may be brought to bear upon one problem at one time, in the intricacy of our thought and logic—and it will be a major contribution of the developing science of psychobiology to comprehend these limitations and to make us aware of them, to the extent that we have the capacity to be aware of them.

For I think it is only logical to suppose that the construction of our brains places very real limitations upon the concepts that we can formulate. Our brain, designed by evolution to cope with certain very real problems in the immediate external world of human scale, simply lacks the conceptual framework with which to encompass totally unfamiliar phenomena and processes. I suspect we may have reached this point in our analysis of the ultimate structure of matter, that in various circumstances we have to conceive of a photon as a wave *or* as a particle because these are the only approximations we can formulate. We, and I mean we in the evolutionary sense, have never encountered and had to cope with a phenomenon with the actual characteristics of a photon.

R. L. Sinsheimer [28]

A physicist friend of mine frequently remarks on how much more difficult it seems to be to teach a 17-year-old a few laws of physics than it is to teach him to drive a car. He is always struck by the fact that he could program a computer to apply these laws of physics with great ease but to program a computer to drive a car in traffic would be an awesome task. It is quite the reverse for the 17-year-old, which is precisely the point. To drive a car, a 17-year-old makes use, with adaptation, of a set of routines long since programmed into the primate brain. To gauge the speed of an approaching car and maneuver accordingly is not that different from the need to gauge the speed of an approaching branch and react accordingly as one swings through the trees. And so on. Whereas to solve a problem in diffraction imposes an intricate and entirely unfamiliar task upon a set of neurons.

R. L. Sinsheimer [28]

of information coming into your mental computer, and how are these acted upon once they are received? You judge your own speed, the distance you are from the intersection, the performance of your car to cover a given distance or to stop if need be, and the length of time the light will be yellow. You appraise visually the relation of other cars to yours: to the right and left, to the rear through a backview mirror, and to the front. You look for possible pedestrians and probably for the possible presence of a traffic policeman. You may even review traffic regulations and your traffic record as all this goes on, and you are making a judgment as to whether you are in a hurry or not. With this input information, you make a decision: to stop or to go ahead, and this involves bringing into play a reaction system that either brakes the car to a stop or presses on the accelerator to keep the car moving. Yet all this is done quickly, generally accurately, and without deliberate conscious effort.

Nearly 3 billion years of evolution, of trial and error, of success and failure, but with the thread of life continuously intact, separate the first tentative beginnings of life from this remarkably responsive and reactive organism called man. All other living organisms have a similarly long and involved history, and each exhibits its own set of novelties that have come into existence through change and chance, and that enable it to exist and to reproduce.

Climbing the primate tree

Man is a vertebrate, a mammal, a primate, and a human being, and the fossil record gives us some idea of when, in the course of time, these successive stages came into

Emerging humanity

Gerstenkorn . . . calculates that the moon after its capture in a retrograde orbit approached the earth as close as 2.89 earth radii before changing its orbit and retreating to its present distance. At that time the tides were 8,000 times higher than at present, attaining amplitudes comparable with the present mean ocean depth. . . .

The erosive power and heating effect of such tides can account for all the phenomena associated with the Infracambrian deposits. . . . The tides would eventually sweep across the interior and, laden with sediment and rock fragments, abrade the land surface and reduce the continents to peneplains. The detritus would fill any existing deep basins and be swept over the edges of the continental shelves and dumped into the oceans.

The tidal friction would raise the ocean temperatures to unprecedented levels, bringing carbon dioxide out of solution to precipitate calcium carbonate. This would account for the anomalous association of coarse, siliceous clastics with thick fine-grained carbonates.

The effect on living organisms must have been drastic. The high temperatures may account for the scarcity of organic remains other than algae in these deposits. Life was not extinguished, but it may have survived only in the cooler arctic areas where tidal effects were minimal.

. . .

The sudden appearance of rich Cambrian life may be explained by the development of a new favorable environment in the warm, shallow seas which covered the scars left by the earth's near encounter with the moon.

The tidal theory for the origin of the Cambrian-Precambrian unconformity may appear to conflict with the Principle of Uniformitarianism by postulating a cosmic accident to account for the observed phenomena. We might do well, however, to examine critically both the glacial and tidal theories to determine which one is better able to explain the facts.

W. S. Olson [23]

---

existence and led gradually to the next step. The first vertebrates appeared about 400 to 500 million years ago in the Ordovician, but this period was preceded by the Cambrian, in which the major groups of invertebrates show up in great numbers as fossils, and the Precambrian, which witnessed the beginnings of life. The Precambrian lasted at least 3.5 billion years and perhaps as much as 4 billion, and evidences of life from this period are not fossils in the sense of identifiable specimens. Rather, the evidence consists of organic remains and chemical "markers" that are judged to have been produced by living creatures: sugars, amino acids and other hydrocarbons found in rocks, calcareous deposits left by bacteria, algae, or their predecessors, skeletal remains of protozoa, and borings produced by worms.

The sudden appearance of a richly diversified and structured life in the Cambrian suggests that life had evolved to the point of producing resistant compounds of calcium and silica that were shaped into exterior shells and skeletons. These lend themselves to ready fossilization and hence identification. The size of organisms seems also to have increased as three-dimensional multicellularity made its appearance. Whether the skeletal systems developed as a response to a size and weight problem or simply appeared by chance, thus permitting greater sizes to be attained, is a moot question.

Some of these Cambrian forms—*Lingula,* for example— have persisted unchanged to the present time, an indication that life does not have to evolve when a suitable, unchanging environment to which it is adapted exerts no pressure on it to respond. This does not mean that mutations failed to make their appearance; rather, it probably indicates that, being well adapted, any chance mutation would in all likeli-

A most significant corollary for the history of life is that, although photosynthetic plants release oxygen as a waste product, animals *require* free oxygen, either in the air or dissolved in water, for respiration. Two atmospheric physicists, L. V. Berkner and L. C. Marshall, have recently suggested that the dramatic expansion of animal life around 600 million years ago marks the point when *free oxygen first became abundant enough to support animal respiration.* This provocative idea would explain the disparity between the long Precambrian record of simple plant life and the late appearance of animals. A major difficulty with the Berkner-Marshall hypothesis is the short time proposed for the development of the advanced early animals. As we have indicated, most paleontologists feel that a rather long Precambrian history of animal life is required to explain the complexity of the Ediacara and Early Cambrian faunas. To get around this difficulty, a paleontologist, A. G. Fischer, has suggested that the first animals might have evolved earlier in "oxygen oases" around concentrations of primitive algae. Such animals would have probably been rare, small, shell-less forms, very spottily distributed and hence unlikely to have been preserved as fossils. Following Berkner and Marshall, Fischer then suggests that the first appearance of widespread animal life 600 million years ago signals the time when high atmospheric oxygen levels first liberated these early animals from their dependence on nearby plants and allowed them to disperse and diversify.

A. L. McAlester [20]

Emerging humanity

. . . A comparatively simple amplification of the theory of natural selection will suffice to explain all of the evolutionary progression toward greater complexity which has occurred. The nature of this amplification will, however, become clearer if some of the facts about evolutionary progression are reviewed first.

The most important of these facts is that the progression from a lower to a higher level of organization has taken place very rarely compared to evolutionary diversification at any particular level. . . . Since the period of time over which this evolution took place was at least three billion years, the average length of time between the ascent to one level and the further progression to the next level was 750 million years.

This hardly seems like steady upward progression. Furthermore, although the fossil record of the early geological ages is very scanty, the record that we have suggests that the second and third levels, those of procaryotes [viruses and bacteria] and unicellular eucaryotes, lasted collectively for about two billion years before multicellular organisms appeared. Even the final level of the animal kingdom, that of warm blooded mammals, lasted for more than a hundred million years before man appeared. During this last period, mammals evolved a great diversity of adaptations to different modes of life without materially altering their organizational complexity.

G. L. Stebbins [30]

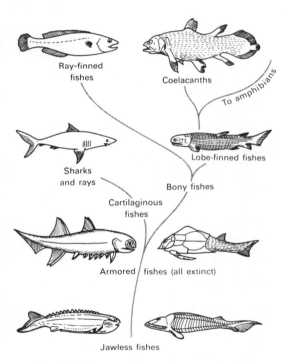

6.1   Evolutionary divergence among the fishes.

hood make these forms less well adapted, and the selection pressure would lead to their elimination instead of their retention. Other species, however, did change, and many flourished only to become extinct at a later time, a fact that shows that the process of evolution varies from group to group and that what is successful or appropriate in an evolutionary sense for one group may not be equally so for another.

The fishes, the first vertebrates, made their appearance in the Late Ordovician and Silurian periods, although their great development took place from the Devonian to the Cretaceous. They evolved out of some invertebrate group, but their ancestry still remains debatable. The acquisition of a dorsal vertebral column was a major innovation. At first cartilaginous and later bony, this column was an internal skeletal feature (endoskeleton) in contrast to the external skeleton (exoskeleton) of many of the invertebrates, and as such provided a means of resisting compression in deep waters and a frame to which segmentally arranged muscles and tendons could be attached. The skeleton could grow as the fleshy parts increased in size, and fishes of larger size made their appearance. The result was enhanced mobility and exploitation of a wide variety of watery niches. But mobility is a complex physical and behavioral activity and is dependent upon a multitude of other changes before full use is evident. Not all of these changes were achieved at once, but each one increased adaptability to the sea and set the stage for further change. Two pairs of appendages, the fins, provided mechanisms for balancing and steering, with the tail contributing the propelling power. Increased mobility put a greater selective pressure on perceptive capability for the pursuit of prey or escape from predators, and

Emerging humanity

The life of the southern High Plains of the United States early in the Miocene as reconstructed from fossil evidence and depicted in a mural by Jay H. Matternes.

Smithsonian Institution

Table 6.1   The geologic time scale*

Era	Period	Epoch	Years before present (millions)	Duration in years (millions)
		Recent began 10,000 years ago		
CENOZOIC	Quaternary	Recent		
		Pleistocene	2.5–3	2.5–3
		Pliocene		13–15
	Tertiary	Miocene		12
		Oligocene		11
		Eocene		22
		Paleocene	68	5–7
MESOZOIC	Cretaceous			72
			140	
	Jurassic			65
			205	
	Triassic			25
			230	
PALEOZOIC	Permian			55
			285	
	Pennsylvanian			40
			325	
	Mississippian			25
			350	
	Devonian			60
			410	
	Silurian			20
			430	
	Ordovician			70
			500	
	Cambrian			100
			600	
PRECAMBRIAN	Upper Middle Lower			

Although many local subdivisions are recognized, no worldwide system of naming has been evolved. The Precambrian lasted for at least 3.5 billion years.

*From W. L. Stokes, *Essentials of Earth History*, 3rd ed. Prentice-Hall, Inc., Englewood Cliffs, N. J., 1973, p. 122.

Of all the individual questions answered by the Theory of Descent, of all the special inferences drawn from it, there is none of such importance as the application of this doctrine to Man himself. As I remarked at the beginning of this treatise, the inexorable necessity of the strictest logic forces us to draw the special deductive conclusion from the general inductive law of the theory, that Man has developed gradually, and step by step, out of the lower Vertebrata, and more immediately out of Ape-like Mammals. That this doctrine is an inseparable part of the Theory of Descent, and hence also of the universal Theory of Development in general, is recognized by all thoughtful adherents of the theory, as well as by all its opponents who reason logically.

But if the doctrine be true, then the recognition of the animal origin and pedigree of the human race will necessarily affect more deeply than any other progress of the human mind the views we form of all human relations, and the aims of all human science. It must sooner or later produce a complete revolution in the conception entertained by man of the entire universe. I am firmly convinced that in future this immense advance in our knowledge will be regarded as the beginning of a new period in the development of Mankind.

E. H. Haeckel [15]

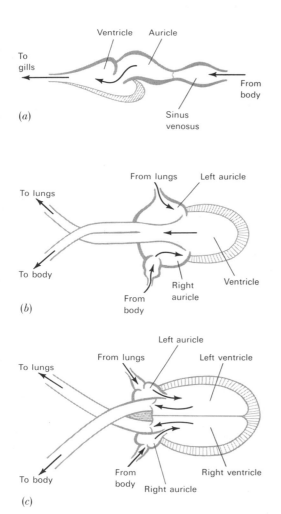

(a)

(b)

(c)

the visual, auditory, and olfactory senses evolved with their appropriate organs, the eye, ear, and nose. The ability to sense pressure changes became concentrated in the lateral line organ, while an air bladder, a pouch pinched off from the digestive tract, allowed adaptation to the pressures at various depths. The blood chemistry and circulatory system provided a more efficient oxygenating system. The simple heart, with one auricle for loading and one ventricle for pumping, kept the blood passing through the gills and skin for gas exchange with seawater and through the tissues for an exchange of oxygen and carbon dioxide (see illustration 6.2). Coordination, large size, and an altered metabolism required a more efficient nervous system and better hormonal control. Localization of the sense organs in a forward position and the development of the brain with the formation of a bony skull for its protection gave rise to the head as we now know it, while the thyroid gland, in primitive form, evolved from cells of the pharynx. The feeding organ was transformed from a mud-grubbing, sucking, toothless, jawless opening to a bony, biting jaw through the modification of supporting arches in the gills, while teeth

6.2 Circulation in a fish (a), an amphibian or reptile (b), and a mammal (c). In the fishes the blood is pumped from the heart to the gills where it is oxygenated, and then to the body tissues, from whence it is returned to the heart. In amphibians the gills do not exist except in a tadpole state, and lungs replace them as the region of oxygenation. Oxygenated blood from the lungs is mixed with unfreshened blood received from the body tissues, but some compensation occurs because oxygenation also takes place through the skin when it is in contact with water; this feature is lost in the reptiles. In mammals all oxygenation is carried out by the lungs, the heart is a dual system, and oxygenated and unoxygenated blood do not mix.

Emerging humanity

The desire of man to inquire into the origin of all things produces daily fresh attempts of ascending the scale leading in that direction. Faith has in this respect an easy task; it builds upon some old myth a system which points to an unknown beyond. The path of science is more rugged, as it must steadily keep to the principle, not to depart from the facts and the limits fixed by observation and experiment. The further back science proceeds, the more necessary is it to use caution in drawing inferences from the facts, and the greater should be the candour in confessing the gaps which are every where met with; not for the reason that no created being can penetrate into the sanctuary of Nature, but simply because the facts and observations are so numerous that they cannot be mastered by one individual.

K. C. Vogt [33]

---

were derived from scalelike structures. A change in diet came with the biting habit, and the digestive tract was altered to handle food in larger pieces instead of in solution. The vertebral column protected the long spinal cord at the same time that it provided support and a point of attachment for the ribs that formed a cage over the internal organs. Scales covered the outer surface for protection, although many of the early forms were armor-plated.

By the Silurian period, some 70 million years after the fishes first appeared, most of the anatomical features now displayed by man were present in the fishes in primitive form and, as we now realize, were capable of subsequent, often drastic, modification (illustration 6.3). The fossil record does not reveal all of the transitional stages, and the structure of soft parts and the chemical composition of internal fluids no longer remain to inform us of subtler changes, but enough is known to reveal the intimations of what was to come. In his bony structure, nervous system, blood chemistry, and embryonic gill slits, man still retains the faint echoes of his fishy ancestry.

The versatility and flexibility of life is indicated by the fact that there are few environmental niches on earth that have not been invaded by some kind of organism. So it was inevitable that life in some form would leave the seas, rivers, and lakes to invade the land. The first to make the move were primitive land plants and air-breathing invertebrates such as wingless insects, millipedes, and mites. The drying up of bays and lakes, brought on by a hotter and drier climate during the Devonian, seems likely to have pressured the movement. The amphibians, requiring a basic change in organization and behavior as they evolved from fishes, followed the land plants, their source of food.

These oldest fragments, dating from a period in the earth's history perhaps 450,000,000 years ago, are not well enough preserved to give us any idea of the nature or appearance of the forms from which they came. It is not until a whole period later, in the late Silurian, that we first find complete skulls and skeletons of these most ancient predecessors of man.

And here we find ourselves in a quaint, bizarre world. These archaic vertebrates were water-living types, with fishlike bodies and tails. But, whereas modern fishes often have naked skins or are covered in many cases merely by thin scales or denticles, these ancient vertebrates were, one and all, armoured with thick plates of bone or bonelike material—scales over the trunk and tail, where motility for swimming was essential, and a solid layer of armour plates over the head region. This armoured condition has led to the present use of the term "ostracoderms" (shell-skinned) for these oldest vertebrates. In their general appearance they were quite unlike the lampreys and hagfishes, in which there is no armour or, indeed, bone of any sort. But when these fishes are more closely examined, it is seen that there are real resemblances to the lampreys, indicating true relationship. Like the cyclostomes, these oldest vertebrates lacked any trace of jaws, the mouth being merely a small hole or crosswise slit; and there are no typical limbs or paired fins, with, at the most, a pair of flaps behind the head region or small spines at the sides of the body. Even in detail there are many resemblances between the ostracoderms and cyclostomes. Many of these old fossils had, as in lampreys, a single nostril high up on top of the head, and casts of such structures as brains and ears show that we are dealing with forms fundamentally similar to the lamprey type.

A. S. Romer [26]

Emerging humanity

Brontosaurus, a large herbivorous dinosaur.

American Museum of Natural History

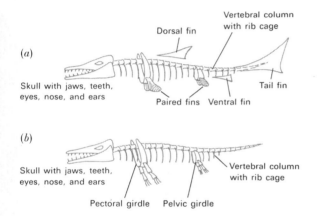

(a)

Dorsal fin

Vertebral column with rib cage

Skull with jaws, teeth, eyes, nose, and ears

Paired fins   Ventral fin

Tail fin

(b)

Skull with jaws, teeth, eyes, nose, and ears

Vertebral column with rib cage

Pectoral girdle   Pelvic girdle

6.3 *The structure of a fish (a) and a land dweller (b). By the time the bony fishes had come into existence, they had all of the features that, through variations on a theme, would lead to the amphibians, then to the reptiles, and finally to the mammals and man. No new features or innovations were added, although no feature remained unmodified as evolution proceeded through the vertebrate groups.*

One can speculate on the many changes that converted the fins of fishes, together with the pectoral and pelvic girdles, into the true limbs of a land dweller, but the other alterations are recorded convincingly in the fossil record. One of the transitional forms was *Ichthyostega*, an animal that displayed a mixture of fish and amphibian features. Its tail still retained the fringelike fin of a fish, and its legs were strong enough only to permit a sprawling posture as it dragged itself along the muddy shores. Its skull was fishlike, bone for bone, and its teeth were much like those of the lobe-finned fishes of today. For about 120 million years the amphibians were the dominant animal form, appearing in many shapes and sizes during the Mississippian and Pennsylvanian periods, when the coal beds were laid down in the great swamp forests.

Amphibians, even today, are restricted to a watery environment at some stage during their life cycle; at best they are only marginally emancipated from the water. Eggs are laid and fertilized in water, and the tadpole stage of frogs, with its gills, is necessarily aquatic. If an animal is to breathe air it must have a lung. This organ is first seen in primitive freshwater fishes in the form of a sac derived from the anterior portion of the gut. Being vascularized, it served as a supplementary respiratory mechanism. A comparable pouch has become the swim bladder of saltwater fishes. An early conversion stage of such a pouch can be seen today in the lungfish, which can exist under conditions of desiccation for prolonged periods of time. Instead of being thin-walled, the air bladder of the lungfish is thick, spongy, and vascularized and functions much as do our lungs for gas exchange. The lungfish, however, like the frog, swallows air in gulps, and cannot expand and contract its chest cavity.

Authors with varying competence have suggested that dinosaurs disappeared because the climate deteriorated (became suddenly or slowly too hot or cold or dry or wet), or that the diet did (with too much food or not enough of such substances as fern oil; from poisons in water or plants or ingested minerals; by bankruptcy of calcium or other necessary elements). Other writers have put the blame on disease, parasites, wars, anatomical or metabolic disorders (slipped vertebral discs, malfunction or imbalance of hormone and endocrine systems, dwindling brain and consequent stupidity, heat sterilization, effects of being warm-blooded in the Mesozoic world), racial old age, evolutionary drift into senescent overspecialization, changes in the pressure or composition of the atmosphere, poison gases, volcanic dust, excessive oxygen from plants, meteorites, comets, gene pool drainage by little mammalian egg-eaters, overkill capacity by predators, fluctuation of gravitational constants, development of psychotic suicidal factors, entropy, cosmic radiation, shift of Earth's rotational poles, floods, continental drift, extraction of the moon from the Pacific Basin, drainage of swamp and lake environments, sunspots, God's will, mountain building, raids by little green hunters in flying saucers, lack of even standing room in Noah's Ark and paleoweltschmerz.

G. L. Jepsen [19]

The circulatory system underwent compensatory change, so that it could send blood to the lungs for aeration as well as to the tissues of the body. A three-chambered heart evolved in the amphibians, with two auricles for loading purposes and a single ventricle as a major pump. Venous and arterial blood mixed in the single ventricle. Although more efficient aeration thereby resulted, it was not as efficient as the system that later characterized the mammals. Land life also required changes in the mode of waste disposal, with nitrogen wastes posing a special problem. Nitrogen wastes result from the metabolism of proteins, with poisonous ammonia (NH_3) a principal by-product. In fishes, ammonia never reaches a high concentration, being lost quickly through the gills and the body wall into the surrounding water or excreted in dilute form along with large amounts of urine. A land dweller solves the problem of nitrogen disposal by converting ammonia into harmless urea, or uric acid, the latter being made up of two molecules of urea, but in order to do so, and to conserve water as well, a major change in kidney development and function had to occur. This transition can be seen in the frog of today. During the aquatic tadpole stage, ammonia is formed and excreted, but metamorphosis into the adult frog brings with it a structural and functional alteration in the kidney and a metabolic change that shifts nitrogenous excretion from ammonia to urea. In addition, a bladder has been added for the storage of urine and for water resorption.

Land dwelling poses still further problems. The typical frog retains a moist skin and is readily desiccated in air, but the toad has a somewhat more impervious outer covering. The skeleton shows rather profound alterations. Feet and the bones of the legs had to be developed from the

When the dry season comes and the swamplands dry out, he [the lungfish] buries himself beneath the mud and engages in a long-time fast. Many animals hibernate in the winter-time when it is cold, but the lungfish goes to sleep in his mud nest, or aestivates, during the hottest months of the year. He is imprisoned there until the rains come again and set him free. The mud around him dries as hard as rock so that he could not, if he wanted it, get anything to eat. So, of course, he has to burn his own tissues for fuel like any other fasting animal, to keep alive. I believe he takes the prize as fasting champion, because he can certainly last for several years, perhaps for five, if he is fat enough when he goes into aestivation. Then, too, he has no water in his earth-bound prison and consequently his kidneys have to stop working. All the products of his metabolism pile up in his blood and tissues—a condition that would kill all other animals that we know anything about in a short time. The dry mud around him and the hot dry air that he breathes tend to steal water out of his body, yet for some reason he doesn't dry up. In short, he goes through an endurance test that no other animal could survive.

H. Smith [29]

Emerging humanity

When a green turtle comes ashore she lays roughly a hundred eggs. Compared to the number of eggs laid by wholly aquatic animals, such as mackerel or lobsters, a hundred is not very many, but it is more than a lizard lays or a setting hen sets on. The eggs are big, round, and white, and they seem a great many when you see them all together.

All sea turtles lay more than once in a season. The usual green turtle comes ashore at least four times during her sojourn at the nesting beach. She often lays a few more than a hundred on her midseason trips ashore and fewer on her first and last trips. But the average is close to a hundred per nest, and there is a great deal of biology packed into that figure. The biology is still mostly unknown, but it is clearly there. The whole race and destiny of the creature are probably balanced at the edge of limbo by the delicate weight of that magic number of eggs. One marvel of the number is how great it is; but another, is how small. When you think of the unpromising future that confronts a turtle egg and the turtle hatchling that comes out of it, you wonder why sea turtles don't give up their stubborn, reckless old way of leaving their new generation on shore and instead carry one big, well-tended egg in a pouch or release myriads of turtle larvae to join the plankton, to swamp the laws of chance with teeming millions of largely expendable progeny.

The answer is that the turtles have already hit on the formula for outwitting predators or, at least, for surviving in spite of them. The formula is simply one hundred turtle eggs. For the green turtle, predation, combined with the other kinds of environmental resistance the race must meet, is measured, in a manner of speaking, as four hundred eggs per season. Any fewer, and the predation prevails and the race wanes. Any more, and the eggs are too heavy to carry in one turtle's belly, or too costly to fill with the right amount of yolk.

A. Carr [4]

6.4   *The general trend of evolution from the lobe-finned fishes to the amphibians. The modern lungfish, a lobe-finned fish, bears the closest resemblance to the earliest ancestor of the amphibians. The salamander represents the final stage of development, whereas the extinct Ichthyostega, the tadpole, and the fully developed frog are intermediate forms.*

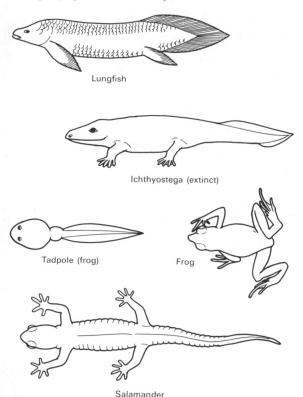

Lungfish

Ichthyostega (extinct)

Tadpole (frog)

Frog

Salamander

fins of the fish, and the pectoral and pelvic regions became modified and strengthened to lift the body off the ground and to give increased stability and mobility. Changes in musculature and nervous control of course paralleled the skeletal changes. Many of the amphibians present in the fossil record developed massive heads, and all acquired a sprawling posture that permitted jumping but not running. It has been suggested that they went into a decline in the Permian because they could not compete with the reptiles, a group that had begun to emerge in the preceding Pennsylvanian period and that dominated the land, sea, and air during the entire Mesozoic era.

The reptiles, evolving out of an amphibian stock, broke the bondage to an aquatic environment. Gills were lost and appeared only during embryonic stages; nitrogen was excreted only in an innocuous form as uric acid, reproductive organs that permitted internal fertilization were acquired, and, most importantly, eggs were laid on land. A. S. Romer refers to this development as "the triumph of the egg," the "most marvelous single invention in the whole history of vertebrate life." To prevent desiccation, the eggs were covered with a tough, flexible outer shell and were laid in a warm, but moist, environment. Inside the outer shell, another thinner membrane encloses a liquid-filled area within which the embryo develops. The reptilian egg, therefore, carries a watery environment within it and, in addition, an embryonic food supply in the form of a yolk. Turtles and crocodiles, to be sure, seem to be aquatic animals, but they lay their eggs on land as do snakes, with the young born capable of maintenance without parental care.

The reptiles dominated the earth for about 125 million years and developed an amazing array of forms. More mobile

Emerging humanity

If we attempt to evaluate the meaning of all the features in the structure of mammals which distinguish them from reptiles, we may perhaps sum them up in one word—activity. The ancestors of the mammals were carnivores, leading lives in which speedy locomotion was a necessity. The limb development has given effectiveness to this potential activity. Brain growth has given it intelligent direction. The maintenance of a high body temperature and the various changes associated with this are related to the need of a continuous supply of energy in animals leading a constantly active life. Even the improvements in reproductive habits, which are a prominent feature of mammalian development, seem related to the needs for a slow maturation of the complex mechanisms (particularly the brain) upon which the successful pursuit of an alert and active life depends.

A. S. Romer [25]

---

than the amphibians, they had more lightly constructed skeletons in relation to their size, although some retained the massive skulls of their ancestors and even elaborated on this plan with bony protuberances of various sorts. The five-toed foot became standardized, and posture gave greater stability and mobility as the body was lifted off of the ground as the legs were moved in toward the center of gravity of the body. Changes in the knees and elbows also permitted the legs to move from front to rear along a line that paralleled the axis of the body. A varied tooth structure gave indication of varied diets, although the crocodile of today has a uniform tooth development suitable only for grasping, with the prey being swallowed whole.

The reptiles invaded all environments except those where low temperatures curtailed their activities. The dinosaurs of giant size are well known, but other reptilian land dwellers ranged down to small lizards and included both carnivores and herbivores. The ichthyosaurs reinvaded the seas to compete with the fishes; they probably gave birth to live young capable of fending for themselves immediately. The pterosaurs, some as small as a sparrow, others with a wingspread of over 8 meters (27 feet), took to the air. Some, for example the pterodactyls, had leather wings, while *Archeopteryx* and others had feathers. The latter type gave rise eventually to the modern birds.

If the Mesozoic can be termed the Age of Reptiles, then the Cenozoic is the Age of Mammals. There is no reliable evidence as to why reptilian dominance declined as the Mesozoic neared its end, but it is likely that the onset of colder and more variable climates brought on an environmental change to which these cold-blooded animals could not readily accommodate. Their environmental range grad-

Adaptive radiation within the class Reptilia has been extremely varied. Three orders returned to the water and again developed specializations appropriate to that habitat. Most extreme of these was the order Ichthyosauria, in which the external form became completely fish-like, but the skeletons prove that these animals were reptiles. The plesiosaurs were less extremely modified. They had turtle-like bodies, and large flippers. The neck was often very long and serpentine in appearance. The third aquatic order is the Chelonia, including the turtles, which are generally adapted to an amphibious mode of life. But, as is well known, some turtles have become exclusively terrestrial and others have become exclusively marine. Representatives of most of the terrestrial orders have also invaded the water. The best known modern reptiles are the snakes and lizards, and these occur in both terrestrial and aquatic forms, and are adapted to predation upon almost every type of animal. The greatest range of adaptive radiation occurred within the several orders of dinosaurs, the ruling reptiles of the Mesozoic era.

E. O. Dodson [10]

Emerging humanity

Female cheetah with her victim, a male reedbuck.

Mark Boulton photo, National Audubon Society

The cerebellum seems to be involved in assessing the body's position in space and in sending out signals that enable you to make rapid corrections of faulty motions. The cerebellum receives information from the cerebral cortex, from sensory organs, and from deep sensations coming from receptors in muscles, tendons, and joints. This deep sense, called *proprioception,* provides information about the position and performance of the limbs and body. Whenever the motor cortex commands muscles to move, it sends information at the same time to the cerebellum. The cerebellum, in turn, sends impulses back to the cerebral cortex (and to other motor centers in the brain) correcting any errors with the outcome that the resulting motion is smooth and well-timed. The cerebellum is able to do this on the basis of information it is always receiving from muscles and joints; that is, it compares the "commands" of the motor cortex with the "performance" of the muscles. The cerebellum does not initiate movements. It acts only to make them precise in time and space.

R. I. Macey [21]

ually became more and more restricted. The plant life on which the herbivorous forms subsisted—the great forests of tree ferns, cycads, and horsetails—went into coincident decline, to be replaced by the conifers and seed-bearing plants that persist today. This shift in plant life very probably restricted the herbivorous reptiles and, in turn, the carnivorous forms that preyed on them. The reptiles, therefore, seem to have been dispossessed not so much through competition with the mammals as by unfavorable climates. The mammals were waiting in the wings of the evolutionary stage, ready to take over when conditions were right and the stage was vacated.

The mammals made their appearance even before the giant reptiles dominated the scene. They evolved out of a small, relatively unspecialized group in the mid-Mesozoic, and by the time the reptiles went into decline, the major mammalian features had been evolved. Originally small, probably nocturnal, and subsisting on a diet of insects and fruits, the mammals were prepared anatomically, physiologically and mentally to occupy the great diversity of niches now available in the developing temperate forests and grasslands. These early forms have been referred to as the "rats" of their time, ever ready to seek an advantage. The features that gave them adaptive selectivity included alterations in posture, dentition, sensory perception, circulation, and reproduction, greater attention to care and feeding of the young, a change from cold-bloodedness to warm-bloodedness, and an increasing brain and hormonal development that is correlated with changed and novel behavior. These features contribute, in their totality, to a characteristic aspect of the mammals, their apparent intelligent activity.

The amphibians and reptiles of today, and those of the

Emerging humanity

It is a matter of adaptive evolution that cats capture their prey through stealth—first stalking or ambushing, then pouncing—and that canids capture theirs by tracking and chasing. These methods are so intimately related to phylogeny that it is possible to reverse the description and say that a carnivore that stalks and pounces on its prey is a cat, and one that trails and runs it down is a canid. The remarkably similar conformation of nearly all cats is thus a proof of basically similar predatory behavior. They are the most anatomically specialized of all the carnivores for a particular mode of predation. The long body; the powerful, quick-reacting (but quickly exhausted) "white" muscles; the relatively short, thick limbs with padded feet and hooked, retractable claws; frontal eyes for good binocular vision; and the short jaws armed with long, stabbing canines are the main specializations that enable cats to stalk so stealthily, to gauge distances accurately, to make a lightning and overpowering surprise attack, and to grip and kill the prey. . . . There is even a specific killing bite common to the cats, directed to the back of the neck. However, leopards and lions, and particularly the cheetah, also frequently kill large prey by gripping the throat until the animal suffocates. In either case it is interesting that all cats direct their attack at the front, whereas canids in general attack large herbivores from the rear.

R. D. Estes [12]

past that gave rise to the mammals, characteristically have their limbs attached in a way that causes them to project from the sides of the body, with their main bulk slung between the legs. The principal joints, therefore, did not bear the full weight of the body, and a sprawling, energy-consuming, sluggish posture resulted. The alligator possesses this posture today, although many of the carnivorous reptiles of the past could move rapidly in search of food or to escape predators, just as lizards can today. In the mammals, however, restructuring of the shoulder and hip girdles brought the limbs inward so that they were beneath the body. The result was that the thrust of weight was down through the limb bones rather than being slung, in essence, between four movable posts. As a consequence, the body is not only lifted off of the ground, but a more efficient and swifter forward locomotion becomes possible (see illustration 6.5). Only at a very much later stage in mammalian development, with the assumption of a bipedal posture, does the clavicle (collarbone) serve to move the forelimbs out to the side of the body once again for increased maneuverability.

Mammalian posture provides for a more active life, but it also introduces a corresponding degree of instability, particularly when the animal is in motion. To make full use of the new posture, an enhanced sense of equilibrium had to develop along with it. This sense resides in the cerebellum, or hind brain, with the inner ear being part of the sensing apparatus. Because the hind brain is part of the autonomic nervous system, positions of disequilibrium are not consciously sensed and are automatically corrected.

The possible sources of food became greatly diversified as the temperate forests and grasslands came into existence. Seeds, nuts, fruits, and foliage of many kinds, as well as

6.5 The transition from a reptilian stance (a) to a mammalian one (b) involved a repositioning of the limb bones so as to move the body off the ground, thus transforming the limbs from simple propelling organs to organs of support as well as of propulsion. The bones were remodeled, and their articulation was changed. In addition, coordinated movement was assured by changes in musculature.

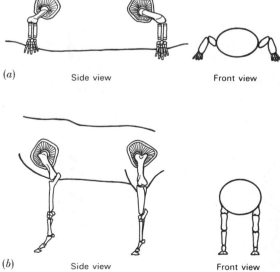

(a)   Side view   Front view

(b)   Side view   Front view

Emerging humanity

In larger buildings the amount of heat needed per room to maintain a comfortable temperature is considerably lower than that needed for smaller buildings. The same applies to various-sized animals who maintain their body temperature by chemical reactions between the food they assimilate and the air they inhale (metabolism). . . . Hummingbirds, who have a very unfavorable surface-to-volume ratio, have to metabolize at a terrific rate, which is, by the way, just about the same as the power production per unit weight in a modern helicopter. On the other hand, large animals can be very economical in their internal heating systems and, in fact, if an elephant metabolized at the same rate as a hummingbird, it would be a roasted elephant, since the temperature of its body would rise to that usually encountered in kitchen ovens. In this connection it is interesting to notice that the rate of "metabolism" inside the sun is extremely low—only a fraction of a per cent of that in the human body. If the heating unit in an electric coffeepot produced heat at the same rate as it is produced in the interior of the sun, the pot would take months to make water boil (assuming, of course, that the coffeepot were perfectly insulated against heat losses). Only the extremely low surface-to-volume ratio of the sun enables its meager rate of energy production to keep its body and surface much hotter than that of a roasted elephant.

G. Gamow [13]

6.6 *Variations in dentition and their relation to function. (a) The alligator, with its undifferentiated dentition, grasps and tears its prey and swallows it whole rather than chews it. (b) Generalized mammalian dentition, with incisors, canines, premolars, and molars for snipping, tearing or grasping, and grinding or chewing. (c) The coyote, with enhanced canines for grasping, reduced incisors, and modified molars for crushing. (d) The horse, with incisors for clipping, no canines, and molars for grinding harsh grasses. (e) The manatee, or sea cow, with molars for grinding aquatic vegetation. (f) The male baboon, with general, all-purpose, primate dentition and exaggerated canines for defense.*

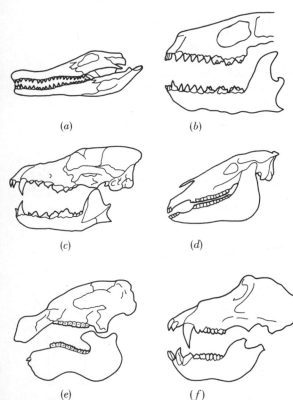

(a) (b)

(c) (d)

(e) (f)

the flesh of other animals, were exploitable sources of nutrition, and the dentition varied with the diet. Man is omnivorous and has a rather generalized dentition, with incisors for clipping, canines for tearing, and molars for chewing or grinding. Other mammals exhibit a varied dentition according to their food habits, and the teeth of the carnivores differ appreciably from those of the herbivores (see illustration 6.6). Among the latter, the horse shows dental changes as it gradually evolved from a browsing state, nipping foliage and twigs from shrubs and trees, to that of a grazing animal of the grassy plains. Grasses, in comparison with leaves and twigs, are harsh fodder, for they contain substantial amounts of silica, and the great grinding surfaces of molars were necessary to reduce the grasses to digestible levels.

Being more mobile, the mammals consequently encountered more variable environmental situations. Therefore, they evolved systems of sensing appropriate to their mode of life, or, conversely, their mode of life placed a premium on the development of sensing systems. All animals must of course be able to appraise an environmental situation if they are to survive, but among the mammals a gradual shift occurred from the basically instinctual behavior of more primitive forms to the more purposeful behavior of later species. This was accompanied and indeed made possible by the development of highly efficient sense organs, by the enlargement of that portion of the brain associated with the dominant sense, and eventually by an increase in the size of the cerebral hemispheres where consciousness, memory, and purposeful action are located. The selective advantage of an enhanced intelligent activity was and continues to be enormous, making it little wonder that the mammals were

Emerging humanity

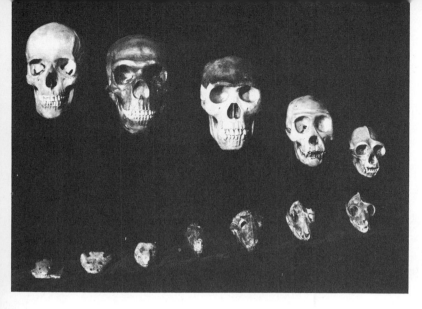

The evolution of the human skull from fish to man.

able to take over when the relatively inefficient reptiles went into decline.

Intelligent activity, however, has far less of a selective advantage when it is subject to control by external environmental factors. The other vertebrates, with the exception of the birds, never rose above environmental constraints for they are cold-blooded, and hence their activities are governed by the temperature of their surroundings, whether air or water. Cold-bloodedness, on the other hand, is less important in a fluid medium, for water temperatures fluctuate less so than those of air. All animals produce heat through the inefficiency of biochemical reactions, but only the mammals and the birds, quite independently of each other, developed means of controlling heat production, retention, and dissipation.

Homoiothermism, or warm-bloodedness, has its disadvantages as well as advantages, although the latter far outweigh the former. The maintenance of a relatively constant body temperature requires that the metabolic fires be constantly stoked, and food consumption has to be stepped up. A snake, for example, requires far less food than a mammal of comparable weight. The smaller the mammal, the greater is the relative amount of food necessary for temperature maintenance; the reason for this is that surface-to-volume ratios increase as size decreases, and heat loss occurs through the surface (see illustration 6.7). The tiny shrew has a voracious appetite, consuming its weight several times over in the course of a day. Its metabolic overturn of food materials is similarly high. It has been calculated that if a man metabolized at the same rate as a shrew, the released heat of metabolism could not be lost rapidly enough, and he would literally roast himself to death.

6.7 *Metabolic rates of various vertebrates. Note the relationship between weight and energy production. The sun produces energy at a very slow rate, but it does not lose its heat as quickly as do the vertebrates. ($10^2 = 1$ followed by two zeroes, or 100, etc.)*

Emerging humanity

Amizilia emerald hummingbird.

Ron Garrison photo, San Diego Zoo

Control of body temperature depends on the *hypothalamus.* It acts as a thermostat and responds to the temperature of the blood bathing it, and to nerve impulses that come from temperature receptors in the skin. It is the front part, or anterior hypothalamus, that responds to heat. We can either stimulate this part electrically or heat it up and get several responses which increase heat loss. These include: 1. sweat secretion, which increases heat loss by evaporation; and 2. dilation of blood vessels in the skin, which causes the surface temperature of the body to approximate the core temperature, with the result that more heat is lost by conduction and radiation. Signals for these responses travel over sympathetic nerves. If we destroy the anterior hypothalamus there will be no response to heat.

The rear portion, or posterior hypothalamus, responds to cold. If we chill the blood surrounding this part of the hypothalamus, any sweating that may be occurring at the time stops. Also, the blood vessels in the skin constrict, minimizing the heat exchange between the core and the cool surface of the body. In addition to preventing excessive heat loss, the hypothalamus is involved in regulating heat production. Chilling, for example, causes shivering and a hormonal discharge which increases body metabolism. These two responses increase heat production.

R. I. Macey [21]

The great significance of homoiothermism, in addition to providing an escape from temperature fluctuations, is that the mammal is potentially ready for action at any time and under virtually all circumstances. If there is any single behavioral characteristic that sets the mammal apart from its reptilian ancestor, it is its restlessness.

Homoiothermism is automatically controlled and consequently requires an array of control mechanisms for efficient operation. The hair of mammals and the feathers of birds assist in keeping warm air trapped close to the body, thus reducing heat loss, but just as an insulated modern home has its thermostats, furnaces, and air conditioners for maintaining an even room temperature, so does the mammal have its internal sensing, heating, and cooling devices. The sensors inform the brain at a subconscious level when rises or falls in temperature depart from optimum ranges, and hormonal and neural regulating devices are set into action. When cold, we shiver, the peripheral blood vessels are constricted, heat loss is reduced, and the body temperature rises as the blood is forced away from the body surface. When hot, we perspire and become flushed. The sweat glands, a mammalian novelty, pour forth fluid, and the heat of evaporation cools the body. The peripheral blood vessels are dilated, and heat loss is stepped up.

Coupled with homoiothermism, and indeed making its evolutionary advent possible, are more efficient circulatory and ventilating systems. The heart is four-chambered, and the venous and arterial blood supplies are separate from each other, being connected only through capillary beds. This makes for a higher compression in the arterial system and a more rapid flow of aerated blood to the tissues, where metabolic demands for oxygen are high and efficiency is

Emerging humanity

The hummingbird wins the honor of living at a rate faster than any other animal at the cost of an enormous food consumption. The bird must devote much of its day to gathering food, mainly nectar and insects. But what happens at night? Hummingbirds are not adapted for night feeding. If their intense metabolism continued undiminished through the night, as it does in other birds, they would be in danger of starving to death before morning.

The trick by which hummingbirds avoid overnight starvation was disclosed by means of a continuous record of their oxygen consumption over a 24-hour period. Each hummingbird was confined in a bell jar with a food supply in a vial. During the afternoon the bird alternately perched and hovered in front of its feeding vial. For an hour before nightfall it indulged in intensive feeding, and much flying and wing-buzzing. During that hour it consumed 24 cubic centimeters of oxygen per gram of body weight. Then the bird settled down for the night.

Twenty minutes later its rate of metabolism had dropped to eight cubic centimeters per gram per hour. By the middle of the night the bird was living at a metabolism level only one fifteenth as rapid as the daytime rate.

Now this is the level at which certain mammals hibernate. The hummingbird at night showed many signs of hibernation. It was completely torpid, practically insensible, scarcely able to move, and when it did stir it moved as though congealed. Its body temperature had dropped to that of the surrounding air—75 degrees Fahrenheit. Hibernation, then, is the metabolic magic by which hummingbirds stretch their food stores from dusk to dawn. Before daybreak the bird's body spontaneously returns to its normal temperature and high metabolic rate. By early morning it is again warm, awake, ready to dart off in search of food.

O. P. Pearson [24]

---

required. The deoxygenated blood can then flow back to the heart through the veins at a more leisurely pace, with movement being aided to a considerable extent by muscular activity rather than by a high compression. The mammalian red blood cell is also a more efficient carrier of oxygen than is the reptilian counterpart. Both, of course, possess hemoglobin, but that of the mammal is able to bind and transport oxygen at more elevated temperatures.

A further modification can be seen in the mechanisms for air intake and exhalation. In reptiles, the movement of air into and out of the lungs is governed by the expansion and contraction of the entire rib cage. This is an improvement over the gulping procedure used by the amphibians, but it is still an energy-consuming activity. This energy expenditure is minimized in mammals by the presence of a diaphragm, a thin, muscular membrane stretching across the body cavity below the lungs. Its contraction and relaxation acts as a bellows, forcing air into and out of the lungs with far less effort.

The mammal gets its name, of course, from the fact that it possesses mammary glands, which apparently are transformed sweat glands. It suckles its young. It also produces its young alive instead of laying its eggs externally, having carried them *in utero* (within the uterus) for varying periods of gestation. This is made possible by an avenue of nutrition between mother and offspring through placental connections, another mammalian first in evolution. A complex hormonal system regulates the entire sequence of events. The advantages of these changes in reproductive processes are several. No shell is necessary for the protection of the egg, and the yolk is dispensable as a nutritive source. The number of eggs produced is sharply reduced because their

Emerging humanity

179

6.8 *A dromedary suckling its calf.*

Ron Garrison photo, San Diego Zoo

That the *Pygmies* of the Antients were a sort of *Apes,* and not of *Humane Race,* I shall endeavour to prove in the following *Essay.* And if the *Pygmies* were only *Apes,* then in all probability our *Ape* may be a *Pygmie;* a sort of *Animal* so much resembling *Man,* that both the *Antients* and the Moderns have reputed it to be a *Puny Race* of Mankind, call'd to this day, *Homo Sylvestris,* The *Wild Man; Orang-Outang,* or a *Man* of the *Woods;* . . .

I will not urge any thing more here, why I call it a *Pygmie;* 'Tis necessary to give it a Name; and if what I offer in the ensuing Essay does not sufficiently Account for the *Denomination,* I leave it to others to give it one more proper. What I shall most of all aim at in the following Discourse, will be to give as particular an Account as I can, of the formation and structure of all the Parts of this wonderful *Animal;* And to make a *Comparative* Survey of them, with the same parts in a *Humane Body,* as likewise in the *Ape* and *Monkey*-kind. For tho' I own it to be of the *Ape* kind, yet, as we shall observe, in the *Organization* of abundance of its Parts, it more approaches to the Structure of the same in *Men:* But where it differs from a *Man,* there it resembles plainly the Common *Ape,* more than any other *Animal.*

E. Tyson [32]

Another vital achievement of the mammals is live birth. The mammal embryo grows in a suit of membranes clearly betraying their origin in those of the reptile egg, to which a new one has been added, the placenta. This is a fat disk of blood vessels through which, from the umbilical cord, runs the blood stream of the unborn young. Through the walls of the placenta and of the womb this blood stream comes so nearly in contact with that of the mother, though without mingling, that the two may exchange all the oxygen, nourishment, and waste products which the life of the fetus demands. Basically, it thus lives by precisely the same things as its parent. It is as good as being out of doors, and takes no effort. The fetus is, practically speaking, a pure parasite on its mother.

Consider the virtues of this system. The warmth and protection it furnishes the unborn are useful, of course, but the birds attain the same ends in other ways. Mainly, there is a much higher limit both to the amount of nourishment this piratical proto-infant can requisition and to the time it takes in the process. In an egg it would eat and grow its way outward to the shell, and then it must hatch or starve; and the size of an egg has practical bounds—ask a hen. Among mammals, on the other hand, perhaps only human beings and a few of their relations, with their overloaded heads, are putting the principle of live birth to any strain. The blank check on time and energy permits the unborn a gradual development to a high level, and a decent size, before it must face the harsh world.

W. Howells [18a]

loss is minimal, fertilization is internal, and the embryos are nourished in the constant temperature bath of the amniotic fluid within the mother's body. Secondly, because the young are suckled, they are not only protected at a vulnerable stage, but also are trained under parental guidance during the period of infancy. By the time of birth, the brain has reached a state where it is ready to be trained, although it continues to enlarge for some time thereafter. Other organs may, in fact, develop more slowly than the brain. The first educational institution in the animal world came into being when the mammalian stock evolved the combined features of live births, a nursing habit, and a prolonged association between young and adults as an apprenticeship for life. The potentiality for success was high, and a continued development of these traits, particularly those of a behavioral nature, led eventually to the evolution of an animal capable of developing a culture.

Our simian ancestors

In the tenth edition of *Systema naturae* (1758), Linnaeus linked man with the great apes, monkeys, and lemurs in the order *Primates,* a classification that remains in effect today. The similarity of man to the great apes in particular was early recognized; the Greeks of the Golden Age were aware of this, and Galen based his anatomical descriptions of man on dissections of monkey and ape species, even though he was physician to the Roman gladiators and was presumably well acquainted with human anatomy. But similarity does not necessarily imply lineal relationships or derivations, and the theory of man's origins from an anthro-

Emerging humanity

An eighteenth-century depiction of two ape-men, a satyr (left) and a pygmy. From C. E. Hoppius, Amoenitates academicae, Erlangen, 1760.

poid stock was first expounded, in unequivocal terms, by T. H. Huxley in his 1863 essays on *Evidences as to Man's Place in Nature*. The lines of descent are still not entirely obvious because of the paucity of fossil evidence—the primitive primates were and continue to be tree dwellers, and a forest is not an ideal place for abundant fossilization—but the broad lines of evolution are reasonably certain.

What is a primate? It turns out that this is not an easy question to answer. While every other group of placental mammals has evolved some specialized attributes that set it apart from other groups, the primates remained structurally generalized as compared to others of the mammalian group. The principal changes that took place involved the progressive enlargement of the brain and alterations in the structure of the hand and the foot and the bones of the thorax and trunk, these related to an arboreal life. But these changes affected those features that enabled man to develop a mode of existence qualitatively different from that of any other animal. As Snowball, the pig in George Orwell's *Animal Farm*, states: "The distinguishing mark of man is the hand, the instrument with which he does all of his mischief."

The fact that the living primates, as a group, are anatomically generalized suggests that they evolved from a primitive group within the mammalian stock. These are the insectivores, shy, unobtrusive insect eaters whose few living representatives include the tiny shrew, the moles, and the European hedgehog. The late Mesozoic and the beginning of the Cenozoic witnessed the rise of a bewildering array of mammalian forms—from the giant whales to the tiniest mouse, and including such diverse forms as elephants, horned and hoofed animals, rodents, and bats—but the

The order Primates consists today of what seems to be a rather heterogeneous collection of types. In fact, it is not easy to give a very clear-cut definition of the order as a whole, for its various members represent so many different levels of evolutionary development and there is no single distinguishing feature which characterizes them all. Further, while many other mammalian orders can be defined by conspicuous specializations of a positive kind which readily mark them off from one another, the Primates as a whole have preserved rather a generalized anatomy and, if anything, are to be mainly distinguished from other orders by a negative feature—their lack of specialization. This lack of somatic specialization has been associated with an increased efficiency of the controlling mechanisms of the brain, and for this reason it has had the advantage of permitting a high degree of functional plasticity. Thus, it has been said that one of the outstanding features of Primate evolution has been, not so much progressive *adaptation*, . . . but progressive *adaptability*. . . . It may also be noted that the evolutionary trends associated with the relative lack of structural and functional specialization are a natural consequence of an arboreal habitat, a mode of life which among other things demands or encourages prehensile functions of the limbs, a high degree of visual acuity, and the accurate control and co-ordination of muscular activity by a well-developed brain.

W. E. Le Gros Clark [6]

Emerging humanity

Until I met the shrew I thought that humans had the greatest catholicity of taste of any living creature, but shrews outdo us. They live up to their class name of insectivore and go far beyond it. Beetles, butterflies, crickets, hoppers, ants, and grubs and centipedes are gulped down as fast as they can be caught. Slugs, snails and earthworms are taken just as fast, and so are mice if they are slow in moving out of the way. Their own weight in meat every three hours is the pace desired, although if meat is scarce they turn to berries, nuts and coniferous seeds. Like a man or a bear a shrew is omnivorous.

Shrew life is short and fast, though far from merry. If not cut off by an owl or hawk or weasel it ends in a sudden senility, a quenching of the blazing little flame, after about fifteen months. Once around the sun, two or three families produced within a leafy nest beneath a log, too much eaten much too fast, and it is over. Prolific, insatiable, poor-sighted and color-blind, with a probing snout and short legs, a shrew above all is of the earth, earthy, a creature of the ground, living in the semidark of logs and leaves and underground spaces, in a world of low-down smells and sudden swooping danger. Is this where we start? I believe so.

N. J. Berrill [3]

6.9   *Three primitive members of the primate family: (a) the common tree shrew; (b) the white-fronted lemur; (c) the tarsier. Compare these photos with the skeletal drawings in illustration 6.10.*

primates do not make a fossil appearance until the Cenozoic. Fossil remains in Paleocene rocks over 60 million years old show a mixture of primate and insectivore features.

The primitive living members of the primates are the prosimians, which include the tree shrews, lemurs, and tarsiers. The tree shrews inhabit the islands of the East Indies and possess a long muzzle with the eyes in lateral orbits (that is, vision is not stereoscopic), five-toed, clawed feet that can be used for grasping, and three pairs of mammary glands. They are nonmenstrual and bear two young as a rule. Their dentition is typically that of an omnivorous primate, consisting of incisors, canines, and molars. The varied dentition is mentioned because so much of man's ancestral beginnings are known only from teeth and jawbones, resistant parts of the body that lend themselves more readily than others to fossilization. Significantly, the tree shrews of today lead an arboreal existence, and it is assumed that the early Cenozoic forms were also tree climbers. This

(a)   San Diego Zoo   (b)   Ron Garrison photo, San Diego Zoo   (c)   Lilo Hess photo, Three Lions, Inc.

I believe that our Heavenly Father invented man because he was disappointed in the monkey.

M. Twain [*31*]

I confess freely to you, I could never look long upon a monkey without very mortifying reflections.

W. Congreve [*7*]

Darwinian Man, though well-behaved,
At best is only a monkey shaved.

W. S. Gilbert [*14*]

---

kind of environmental niche had much to do with the molding of other primate characteristics, but being forest dwellers, the tree shrews and their offshoots were less likely to be found in a fossilized state.

The lemurs are confined largely to the island of Madagascar. Although clearly more primitive than monkeys, they nevertheless exhibit significant primate traits. Arboreal and nocturnal in habit, they possess flexible, prehensile feet, with big toe and "thumb" mobile but not opposable; some digits are clawed, while others are equipped with flattered nails. The face is still long and snout-like, the braincase small, and the eyes lateral although positioned more to the front than those of the tree shrew. They are nonmenstrual, and the young are borne singly.

A significant restructuring of the head occurs in the tarsiers, an animal not much bigger than a large mouse. The insectivorelike snout is now flattened into a face, with the nose greatly reduced in size, the jaws shortened, and the eyes, large and prominent as befits a nocturnal animal, moved still further to the front so that vision is very nearly stereoscopic. The head can be rotated so that the animal can look directly backward, and the brain case is enlarged as a forehead becomes part of the facial features. The digits terminate in nails rather than claws. A menstrual cycle occurs, but is entirely internal, and the young are borne singly, as in the lemuroids.

It is worthwhile, at this point, to reconsider the changes that have taken place in the prosimian group. There is considerable difficulty in determining what is cause and what is effect, what is cart and what horse, but the whole package of modification seems clearly related to the assumption of an arboreal mode of existence. The body of the

Lemurs are omnivorous. Pause and contemplate the advantages of being able to eat almost anything. (If you live in a boardinghouse, you know this already.) In the struggle for existence, it often means survival. Even in human society a good digestion and an ability to eat all kinds of food is better than riches or even intelligence. The modern lemurs have lower incisor teeth which lean forward and are supposed to be used for combing their fur; they have three premolars and three molars. Apparently, when the teeth become differentiated and the diet is generalized, fewer teeth avail the animal. The earliest lemuroids are found in the Eocene in North America—the first of the Tertiary geological deposits. Now we have to look for them in out-of-the-way tropical forests in the Old World.

The tarsioids are little cousins of the lemurs—geologically about as old and in structure almost as primitive, but they were more progressive and upstanding, or rather upsitting. These tarsiers went right on eating everything they could find in the trees and remained unspecialized in teeth, but began to specialize in eyesight, in tactile sense, perhaps even in common sense. At any rate, the habit of hand-feeding, the shorter snout, the better vision and larger brain are all inextricably evolved in the organism of the little omnivorous animal. The tarsier is the infant prodigy of the Primates.

E. A. Hooton [*17*]

*Locomotion patterns of wild gibbons,
a drawing from W. T. Hornaday,*
Two Years in the Jungle, *New York, 1885.*

. . . One of the outstanding features in the evolution of the Primates is the progressive elaboration of the sense of vision, which is reflected not only in the perfection of the structural mechanism of the eye itself, but also in the development and expansion of the visual centers in the brain. This tendency is already manifest in the tree-shrews; herein they show a striking approach to the lemurs, and a corresponding divergence from the true insectivores with which in the past they have usually been associated by zoologists. The superficial appearance of the living tree-shrews gives no indication that the brain is conspicuous for its size, yet, compared with the true insectivores, it shows quite a definite expansion of that part which is related to the more complex cerebral functions (that is to say, the cerebral cortex), particularly those areas concerned with vision. On the other hand, the smell apparatus of the brain shows some signs of retrogression, and here, again, is another indication that they have to some degree followed the same evolutionary trend as Primates generally. There are a number of other curiously lemuroid characters in the tree-shrew which would hardly be noticed except on close examination: for example, the details of the construction of the skull, certain features of the tongue, the nose, and the small bones of the ear, and some items in the anatomy of the muscular system. If all these resemblances to the lemurs are considered, together with the evidence provided by the fossilized records of extinct tree-shrews, there remains little doubt that the tree-shrews are properly to be regarded as exceedingly primitive members of the Order Primates.

W. E. Le Gros Clark [5]

prosimians remains essentially mammalian, but the head and legs are drastically restructured, and behavioral changes accompany the structural modifications.

The airy life of a tree dweller is different from that of an animal scurrying about in the underbrush and calls into play a different combination of talents and behavior. Sensory perception for an appraisal of the environment undergoes a shift as the slow ascent towards man takes place. The insectivore nose, with its long nasal passages, is ideally adapted to a world of odors, and the sense of smell is of primary importance. On the ground, the nose is also a tactile organ, while sight is probably of secondary value. The tree shrews and the lemurs retain the elongated snout, but in the latter, the eyes are being moved slightly forward as sight plays a greater role, along with hearing and touch. In the tarsier, the change is completed, with the snout drastically reduced, and the senses of sight, hearing, and touch acutely developed (see illustration 6.10). Corresponding changes occur in the structure of the brain where these sensations are recorded and managed. Even in the tree shrews and lemurs, the olfactory lobes of the cerebrum (the region of the brain in which the sense of smell is centered) are reduced and the visual, tactile, and acoustic centers enlarged.

The prosimians gradually stopped nosing and sniffing their way through life, and climbed a tree for a better view of the world. The need for a stereoscopic vision is obvious; without it, an animal cannot judge the distance from perch to perch. A faulty judgment could mean a fatal accident, and some genes would be eliminated from the prosimian gene pool. One can speculate that the selection pressure was severe in this regard.

Arboreal life also demands a greater degree of dexterity

Emerging humanity

All transformations in organic matter, all modifications of organ function brought about by natural selection, are specialisations. . . . Every modification is selected to react favourably under certain definite sets of natural conditions, and the organism in which such modification has been selected is limited, as far as that modification is concerned, to the special set of natural conditions which selected it. It is under these conditions only that it confers a real benefit upon the possessor.

. . .

No specialisations in nature are without an attendant number of disadvantages. Whether the specialisation continues and the attendant disadvantages are eliminated by selection of course depends upon their relative values in the struggle for existence. But even the elimination of a disadvantage can only be effected by fresh specialisation. There is no such thing in nature as an organism in perfect accord with its environment. Even the highest adaptations are never ideal. In ultimate analysis, this practical truth rests upon the certainty that all the laws of the inanimate universe are inherently hostile to organic life. The struggle of life is not, as it often appears in popular conception, merely the struggle of the organism against competing fellows. From its inception, an organism struggles against opposing laws of matter which make for dissolution and the hindrance of growth. Organic evolution is at best but the line of least resistance. Selection is not so much the preservation of the fit as it is the destruction of the unfit. For the fit it is not so much a conquering invasion as a lucky escape.

E. Marais [22]

---

and mobility than does ground living, and the kinesthetic and motor centers of the brain are correspondingly developed. Furthermore, arboreal animals are vegetarians, with seeds, fruits, and foliage the main sources of food. Such an arboreal animal needs not only grasping digits to climb and to hold on to branches, but also grasping hands to bring food to its shortened face. Gradually, therefore, the hind legs became the primary means of stability and locomotion, while the forelimbs became more versatile, being locomotive, grasping, and feeding organs as circumstances demanded.

Another aspect of arboreal life worthy of further stress is a reduction in the number of young. One can argue that pregnancy poses its own hazards regardless of habitat, but despite the obvious success of the opossum in rearing its many young, the care of multiple offspring from birth

6.10 *The changing shape of the face among the primitive primates (prosimians): (a) the tree shrew; (b) the bush baby, a lemur relative; (c) the tarsier. As the sense of sight became more important than the sense of smell, the face was shortened from front to back, and the head was positioned more centrally atop the vertebral column. The arrows indicate the point of juncture between the head and the vertebral column.*

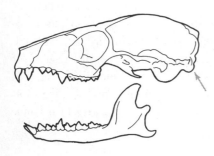
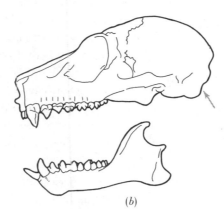
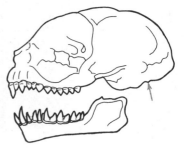

(a)   (b)   (c)

For sheer originality in dealing with [dominance, territory, social survival and sex], one species stands quite alone. None other can rival him in his sorting out of instincts, turning each to his shining advantage. No creature can touch him at turning loose to profit, pain to pleasure, risk to certainty, or wasting struggle to unique satisfaction. Nor can one attribute his soaring triumphs simply to the ascendant primate brain. Others have been so blessed, and many another has fallen. This creature, and this alone, has received in his nature some ingredient of ingenuity beyond present identification. He creates. He pioneers solutions. He negotiates such treaties amongst the instincts that for daring and cunning they will last through the ages. I refer, of course, to the uninhibited, unprincipled, invincible howling monkey.

The howler will stoop to anything. No demands of honour, modesty, reticence, or conformity serve to dilute the effectiveness of his solutions. If he chooses to repel an intruder by defecating on his head, then he will defecate on his head.

And by the ingenuity of his defence, he repels not only the particular invader but all potential invaders who may hear about what happened. . . . He has approached the sexual instinct with the same fine flair for the optimum with which he has approached the territorial drive. . . . Rotating mateship is the term applied by science to the howling monkey's answer. What the term does not quite convey is that in a given howler society all females exert their affectionate demands on all males, that no male competes with another but rather looks on his fellow as a friend in time of need, that sexual frustration becomes something as obsolete as Jurassic reptile eggs, that masculine solidarity takes on the invulnerable overtones of a London club, and that a profound, tightly-woven democracy extends its amiable pattern through the whole society. Every adult gets all the affection that he or she can handle, and every child gets a full complement of fathers.

R. Ardrey [1]

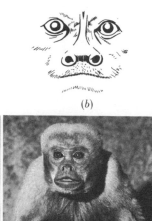

(a)   (b)

Arthur W. Ambler photos, National Audubon Society

6.11 (a) An Old World monkey, an albino toque macaque from Ceylon; (b) a New World monkey, a Humboldt woolly monkey from northern South America. The sketches emphasize the difference in nostril disposition.

through the weaning stage is basically a liability and, to a degree, is incompatible with life in the trees. Ground-dwelling insectivores have many more offspring than the tree shrews to whom they are related, and this number is reduced eventually to one in the higher primates. Twins and triplets are as rare among the monkeys and apes as among humans (the primitive marmoset monkey, however, bears three young as a rule), and the survival rate of multiple offspring through the weaning stage is not high. The undivided time and effort expended on the single offspring from birth to its independence of the mother made more certain its survival and more probable its successful entry into the communal life of the group. This, it can be argued, is a prelude to the later social organization of man.

The remaining members of the primate species are grouped into the Anthropoidea, with the monkeys being the most primitive. Living as they do in tropical forest and savanna areas, their fossil record is quite meager, but their structural features make it certain that they evolved out of a tarsioid or lemuroid line very early in the Cenozoic. The New and Old World monkeys have quite different evolutionary histories, with the New World forms, an early offshoot, bearing no relation to the eventual evolution of man.

The New World group, the Ceboidea, includes the howler, woolly, spider, and squirrel monkeys, plus the capuchin, or organ-grinder monkey. The primitive marmoset is sometimes given a different classification, although it is obviously related to the others. Their faces are peculiarly flat, with the nostrils widely separated and opening laterally instead of downward. They possess true stereoscopic vision, an enlarged braincase, long digits for grasping and feeding, and a prehensile tail that functions, as it were, as a fifth hand.

Emerging humanity

Black howling monkey.

They can, on occasion, walk in an upright, bipedal manner, but their hind feet and pelvic structure do not give them a continuously secure and stable stance in this position. None has achieved the large size of the Old World monkeys or great apes.

Going along with an increased cortical development of the brain is a restless, constantly curious behavior and a well-developed intelligence. The New World monkeys learn quickly to solve problems, and the capuchin, probably the most intelligent of the group, shows some adeptness at tool making. All exhibit a form of social organization. The howler has been most intensively studied from this point of view. The average band consists of three adult males, seven adult females, and a variable number of young, and they occupy and defend an arboreal territory of approximately 300 acres. However, they rarely engage in physical combat with neighboring bands, and confrontation at the edges of territories consists mainly of threats accompanied by clamorous howling. Their social organization, therefore, may be thought of as a simian United Nations, in that it is characterized by a great deal of noise and little combat. Only the young bachelor males remain outside the family groupings.

The existing Old World monkeys, the Cercopithecoidea, are sometimes classified into two major subfamilies and are a highly varied group of over 200 species living in the tropical regions of Africa and Asia. They include the familar macaque, or rhesus monkey of laboratories and zoos, the Barbary ape of Gibraltar, baboons, mandrills, and various langurs. Their nostrils are close together and directed downward as in humans, their tails are not prehensile, and although anatomically generalized, their dentition may include

The howler clan is what I should call a society of most perfect outward antagonism which has achieved a most perfect inward amity. . . . The biological nation spends its aggressive energies on enemies foreign, wastes none on enemies domestic. Within the howler society as within the society of the black lemur there reigns a kind of democratic tranquillity. Leadership is present, but authority is restrained. Differences of opinion are settled with a mumble and a grunt. While the female is never dominant, still her status is remarkably high. And as for offspring, they are the joint responsibility of all adults in the troop. All males, in response to a special cry, will go to the rescue of a young one who falls from a tree; all males with concerted action will defend it against the advance of a predator.

R. Ardrey [1a]

Emerging humanity

A footprint of ancient man preserved in hardened sediment near Dilittepe, Turkey. Its age is estimated at 250,000 years.

Mineral Research and Exploration
Institute of Turkey

6.12   Evolutionary divergence of the primate group during the Cenozoic era. Numerous fossil forms upon which the chart is based are not included, and lines of divergence are tentative.

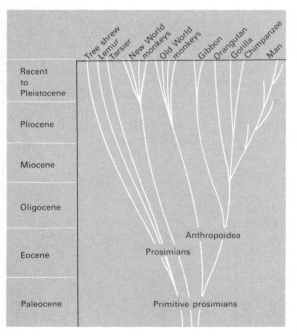

powerful fangs as defensive weapons. The macaque, a destructive pest in India, is a fierce, intelligent fighter. The single patriarch of a harem, with its young, is generally a battle-scarred veteran who must constantly defend his position and his females from the challenges of aggressive, younger males who, like juvenile delinquents, exist outside of the family circle, at least so far as access to the harem females is concerned. Individual macaques vie for social dominance and jealously guard what they regard as their territory, two traits that are also displayed by the baboons of the African plains. The langur of India, on the other hand, is a more solitary animal, with the sexes getting together only for breeding purposes. Others, like the baboon and the mandrill, have abandoned an arboreal existence. Living at the edge of the forests, they have adapted themselves to a shrub and grassy environment, but their locomotion remains quadripedal, rather than upright and bipedal.

The anthropoid, or tailless, apes are the closest relatives of man, but it is now believed that they represent parallel lines of evolution. T. H. Huxley advanced the idea that man arose from an anthropoid stock, and Darwin supported this point of view by stating that the ancestors of man would clearly be classified as apes, but more recent fossil discoveries suggest that both man and the extant apes evolved separately from a common stock. The divergence probably took place in the late Oligocene or early Miocene, some 25 million years ago, but the paucity of fossil remains, particularly of arboreal types, makes any judgment tentative at this time.

The anthropoid apes are divided into two groups, the Hylobatidae, which includes the species of long-armed, acrobatic gibbons, and the Pongidae, which includes the

Emerging humanity

Like leaves on trees the race of man is found,
Now green in youth, now withering on the ground:
Another race the following spring supplies:
They fall successive, and successive rise.

Homer [*16*]

---

orangutan, chimpanzee, and gorilla. The gibbons and the orangutan are arboreal in habit, the other two basically terrestrial. The gibbons have followed a course of evolution different from that of the Pongidae, with their earliest identifiable ancestor being the fossil *Pliopithecus,* a genus that existed throughout Europe during the Miocene and Pliocene. Contemporary with *Pliopithecus,* but spread over Europe, Asia, and Africa, was another variable genus, *Dryopithecus,* out of which the Pongidae and possibly man arose. The basis for this belief, apart from general skeletal features, is the structure of the molars. As with most primates, the grinding surface of the molars is capped by protuberances, or cusps, connected by ridges. The Old World monkeys have four cusps per molar, one at each corner, whereas the lower molars of the anthropoid apes and man have five cusps. *Dryopithecus* shows the five-cusp pattern, indicating that it is a hereditary feature that arose at least 25 million years ago.

The dryopithecine fossils are a variable group, and a variety of names have been assigned to individual specimens, but there seems little doubt that this is the only group yet discovered that appears ancestral to both the great apes and man. One section of the genus is believed to have diverged into a line leading to the apes, whereas another section led to man through the australopithecines, a group that is discussed in the next section. The dryopithecine fossil *Ramapithecus,* discovered first in India but similar to other specimens unearthed in Africa, reveals distinctly human tendencies. The shape of the jaw is more human than apelike in that it is rounded rather than U-shaped, the five-cusp molars are present, the canines are considerably reduced in size, the face is very much foreshortened, and the cranial

On the whole, then, it would appear that the labors of paleontologists, comparative anatomists and psychologists have not yet led to any precise determination of man's relationship to individual genera and species of the primate order. No primate with a properly developed instinct of self-preservation would be willing to entrust his weight to any of their zoological family trees.

For myself, a naive physical anthropologist, the way still seems comparatively straight and plain. I adhere to the old-fashioned belief that the more numerous and detailed the resemblances between two animals the closer the relationship between them. Effects of similarity or difference of habitus can not obscure man's fundamental likeness to the great anthropoid apes, and especially to the gorilla and the chimpanzee. I therefore persist in the opinion that these two apes are our nearest collateral relatives, and as yet am aware of no convincing evidence which conflicts with the theory that the gibbon was an early deviant from a small and primitive generalized anthropoid ape stock; that the main line of anthropoid-humanoid development continued at least into the Miocene period, when giantism began to affect simultaneously the diversifying strains of these arboreal apes. Then it would appear that the ancestors of the orangutan first began their course of evolutionary divergence, leading ultimately to a rigid specialization for slow brachiating. For some time thereafter it seems probable that the ancestors of man and the African apes pursued similar evolutionary courses, until accident or initiative (and I favor the latter explanation) led the protohuman stock to take its chance on the ground.

E. A. Hooton [*17*]

Emerging humanity

189

Were the Australopithecines "men"? This, of course, is a matter of definition. As far as physical structure is concerned, they have been called men from the neck down and apes from the neck up. Their cranial capacity was not much more than that of a chimpanzee; the normal chimp range is about 350–450 cc, that of the Australopithecines 450–550 cc, compared with 1200–1500 cc for modern man. We cannot be sure of their appearance except that they were very low-browed without much of a chin. We do not know whether they were hairy or not, or what their facial features looked like.

We have learned much about their way of life, however, from careful excavations in the Transvaal caves and from Leakey's studies in Tanganyika. Bones associated with the hominid fossils reveal that they hunted many kinds of animals, including baboons and antelope, and it is hard to imagine this kind of hunting except by well-coordinated social groups. Leakey's Tanganyika man, the earliest of them all, clearly used pebble tools, but no stone tools have been found in the somewhat later South African cave deposits. Raymond Dart and his associates, however, are convinced that many of the bones found in the caves were shaped for use as tools, and Dart considers that the Australopithecine way of life was based on the use of bones, teeth and horn—to which he gives the jawbreaking label "osteodontokeratic culture." Whether they had fire or not we cannot determine. Black materials in the caves, at first thought to be surviving traces of hearths, have turned out to be manganese. Nor do we know whether they could talk, or how developed was their vocal communication system. The nature of some of the bone fractures indicates that they had already acquired the very human habit of occasionally killing each other. If not men, then, they were at least well on the way to becoming men.

M. Bates [2]

6.13 *Tentative relationships of modern man and the great apes to some fossil forms.*

capacity is presumed to be substantially enlarged. It is now believed that *Ramapithecus*, or some similar form, was ancestral to both the australopithecines and to man, but the relation of the australopithecines to man is in doubt. Some authorities believe that man arose out of an australopithecine group while others have stated that the australopithecines and man coexisted 2 million years ago, and the one did not give rise to the other.

The coming of man

It is uncertain whether *Ramapithecus* had an upright, bipedal posture; in fact, the origin of the type of structure and method of locomotion can be established only by an examination of pelvic and limb bones, and the earliest of these date from the beginning of the Pleistocene epoch, approximately 2.5 million years ago. *Ramapithecus*, as stated, very probably gave rise to *Australopithecus* (illustration 6.14), but Pliocene fossils that would clearly connect the two either have not been discovered or they have been unrecognized as such. By the beginning of the Pleistocene, however, hominid (human) evolution as distinct from hominoid (ape) evolution was clearly evident.

Human evolution is closely tied to, or coincident with, a drastic alteration in world climate. Beginning about 2 million years ago and continuing to the present time, great continental glaciers have advanced and retreated, covering and uncovering large sections of the Northern Hemisphere with deep layers of ice. The ice sheet that now buries most of Greenland is part of a glacier that began to retreat only a few thousand years ago. These climatic changes brought

Emerging humanity

Australopithecus *in the environment of southern Africa during the early Pleistocene.*

about significant alterations in the distribution of plants and animals. Many of the large mammals became extinct, mastodons, hairy mammoths, and saber-toothed tigers among them. Others, including the ancestors of man, were forced south.

The australopithecines, or southern ape-men, appeared during the latter part of the Pliocene epoch. Their fossil remains have been primarily of African origin, but their presence in Java and China indicates that their distribution was fairly extensive. Dating studies reveal their ages to range from 500,000 to perhaps 5 million years, the latter age being that of a recently discovered specimen from Kenya. The ages of other specimens from the African continent fall in between these extremes. The australopithecine structure places them between the typically apelike individuals and those more obviously human. Their cranial capacity was about 600 cubic centimeters, about the same as a chimpanzee and only about a third as large as that of modern man, whose cranial capacity is generally between 1,400 and 1,600 cubic centimeters. The jaws were powerful and apelike, but the dentition was very close to that of man. Some were nearly as large as a gorilla, others considerably smaller. Most important, however, was that they were upright in stature and made and used tools, indicating an improved use of hands for manipulative purposes. They had not yet discovered the use of fire.

Although a number of animal groups are adept at tool use, the act of making a tool is obviously a human characteristic, and so some of the australopithecines associated with pebble and bone tools were once classified as *Homo habilis,* a member of the family of man, but this classification has now been abandoned. It may well be that the

There is now adequate fossil evidence to indicate, (i) that, from about middle Miocene times, a few widely distributed species of the larger hominoids were present in both Eurasia and Africa and that successive differentiation of these species, through time, has occurred, with little branching or radiation; (ii) that the primary center of speciation among these animals was outside of Europe; (iii) that some dryopithecines in known parts entirely close the slight morphological gap between Hominidae and Pongidae; and (iv) that, if reports as to localities of *Australopithecus* by several serious students be accepted, the data now show that this earliest generally accepted antecedent of man was widely distributed in tropical regions of the Old World in the early Pleistocene. Present archeological evidence does suggest that the use of tools may have occurred first in Africa, but this is not the same as to suppose that the initial species of man differentiated there, unless man be defined solely as a tool-manufacturing primate. To date, the latter supposition is an inference primarily supported by negative evidence—namely, the scanty recovery of australopithecines and of pebble tools in Southeast Asia and China.

E. L. Simons [27]

6.14 A restoration of Australopithecus africanus *by A. Forestier.*

Emerging humanity

Olduvai Gorge, Tanzania, the site of many important discoveries of primitive man and associated animals.

George H. Hansen

The fossil record thus substantiates the suggestion, first made by Charles Darwin, that tool use is both the cause and the effect of bipedal locomotion. Some very limited bipedalism left the hands sufficiently free from locomotor functions so that stones or sticks could be carried, played with and used. The advantage that these objects gave to their users led both to more bipedalism and to more efficient tool use. English lacks any neat expression for this sort of situation, forcing us to speak of cause and effect as if they were separated, whereas in natural selection cause and effect are interrelated. Selection is based on successful behavior, and in the man-apes the beginnings of the human way of life depended on both inherited locomotor capacity and on the learned skills of tool-using. The success of the new way of life based on the use of tools changed the selection pressures on many parts of the body, notably the teeth, hands and brain, as well as on the pelvis. But it must be remembered that selection was for the whole way of life.

S. L. Washburn [34]

6.15 An orangutan using a stick to push candy out of a plastic tube. Many animal groups are adept at tool use; however, tool making as such is essentially a human trait.

Yerkes Regional Primate Research Center of Emory University

australopithecines included both tool makers and those who had not reached this scale of advancement, but it is more generally agreed that *Homo erectus*, appearing about 500,000 to 1 million years ago, was the first to live a distinctly human existence. Whatever the correct sequential interpretation and however fragmentary the fossil record is at present, there is no longer reason to doubt that the evolutionary transformation from apes to man was a gradual one spanning several million years, with a very rapid increase in cranial capacity and intelligence taking place during the latter portion of this period.

H. erectus differs from modern man in his more massive skull, somewhat larger although similarly shaped teeth, and smaller brain (about 900–1,100 cubic centimeters). In cranial capacity, he is therefore intermediate between the australopithecines and modern man. First identified from a skull found in Java and called *Pithecanthropus*, remains of *H. erectus* have been discovered in China (Peking man, *Sinanthropus*) and in a number of African sites. By the mid-Pleistocene, 400,000 to 500,000 years ago, he existed rather widely through Europe and Africa, and as we approach the present, more and more elaborate tools are associated with him. Included among these are stone axes, some equipped with handles, which were made from flint and deliberately sharpened on one side by chipping. A progressive advance in design and finished appearance is evident, indicating that, as his brain increased in size, *H. erectus* was becoming a more and more adept maker and designer of tools.

Tool making requires foresight and planning. As the utility of these tools increased with improved design, that is, utility for hunting and for defense, it is apparent also

Emerging humanity

It is of the utmost importance, in considering hominid evolution, to stress [the existence of] variability between individuals of the same group, and the even greater degree of variation to be expected between different geographical varieties of the same species or different species of the same genus. One gets the impression that some palaeontologists are ignorant of, or perhaps have just ignored, the literature recording such variability, for again and again they have been tempted to create new species or new genera on the basis of single or very fragmentary fossil remains simply because the latter are not *exactly* like other specimens that certainly belong to the same zoological group. It might almost be supposed that they expect individuals of the same species to be equivalent to identical twins! . . .

Probably nothing has done more to introduce confusion into the story of human evolution than the reckless propensity for inventing new . . . names for fragmentary fossil relics that turn out eventually to belong to genera or species previously known. It has been very well said that "rather than filling gaps which exist (in the fossil record), names tend to produce gaps that do not exist," and "it seems that some palaeontologists regard the binominal system as a means of giving every hominid a Christian and surname and for creating phylogenetic schemes like family trees: an activity which starts with the nonsensical premise that the individual and not the population is the unit of evolutionary change."

W. E. Le Gros Clark [6]

---

that the design itself took on an aesthetic importance as man learned to grind and polish stone as well as chip it. The latter aspects of tool making, however, are more characteristic of modern man, *Homo sapiens.* It is probable that *H. sapiens* existed contemporaneously with *H. erectus* for many millennia, but whether *H. erectus* was eliminated by modern man through competition or conquest or simply died out because of an incompatible environment is not known. In any event, man made his appearance very late in geologic history, but quickly established his dominant position among the animals of the earth. Several offshoots, however, would arise and die out before the advent of modern man. A skull recently discovered in a cave in the Pyrenees of southern France, and judged to be 200,000 years old, shows a sharply sloping forehead, massive, prognathous (projecting) jaws with teeth twice the size of modern man, thick eye ridges, and a braincase small and not unlike that of *Sinanthropus.* It is possible that this form evolved into Neanderthal man. It is clearly more primitive than Neanderthal man, who first appeared about 90,000 years ago and had a braincase somewhat larger than present man. Both the Pyrenees man as well as the Neanderthalers were branches from the main line of human evolution and were replaced, or possibly wiped out, by Cro-Magnon man. Where he came from is uncertain, but he occupied an area in southern France and Spain about 35,000 years ago. The generally accepted view is that he represents the first unequivocal appearance of modern man on the evolutionary stage. It should be realized, however, that evidences of man go back still further into prehistory if judgment is made on the basis of tools rather than of skeletons; the dividing line between *erectus* and *sapiens* is uncertain.

6.16 Skulls of the gorilla (a), Australopithecus (b), and man (c) to indicate changes in dentition, shape and structure of the jaw, enlarging cranial capacity, and point of juncture between the head and the vertebral column (arrow).

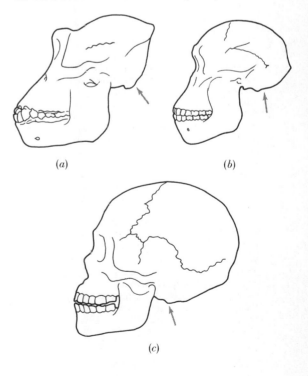

(a)

(b)

(c)

Lioness making run for wildebeest in Ngorongoro Crater, Tanzania.

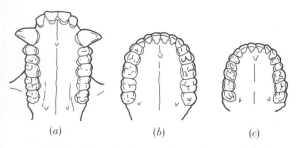

6.17 *Upper dentition of a male gorilla (a), Australopithecus (b), and man (c). Note the change from a U-shape to an arc and the decrease in the size of the canines.*

Where did *Homo erectus* come from? The Swartkrans discovery makes it clear that he arose before the last representatives of the australopithecines had died out at that site. The best present evidence of his origin is also from Africa; it consists of the series of fossils unearthed at Olduvai Gorge by Leakey and his wife and called *Homo habilis*. These remains seem to reflect a transition from an australopithecine level to an *erectus* level about a million years ago. This date seems almost too late, however, when one considers the age of *Homo erectus* finds elsewhere in the world, particularly in Java.

Where did *Homo erectus* go? The paths are simply untraced, both those that presumably lead to the Swanscombe and Steinheim people of Europe during the Pleistocene's second interglacial period and those leading to the much later Rhodesian and Neanderthal men. This is a period lacking useful evidence. Above all, the nature of the line leading to living man—*Homo sapiens* in the Linnaean sense—remains a matter of pure theory.

W. Howells [18]

Both Neanderthal and Cro-Magnon man left behind evidences of cultural development in the form of burials and paintings as well as beautifully fashioned tools. This suggests that a sense of self-awareness had come to man, and that, in their minds, there existed a world of spirits and forces that could be tapped by appropriate techniques of magic; these are cultural elements not too dissimilar from those held by many primitive cultures today or in the immediate past.

H. sapiens would learn to handle metals as well as stone and bone, and to fashion the bow and arrow as well as axes, knives, spears, and needles for sewing. It is of course difficult and sometimes inaccurate to ascertain behavior from fossilized physical remains, but artifacts such as tools imply a certain cultural practice, and one can therefore judge that in prehistoric times, from 100,000 years ago down to the beginnings of man's recorded history, there was a gradual development of a social and cultural organization, initiating thereby another kind of evolution—a cultural evolution—that further separated man from his animal ancestors. In the process, and accentuated, if not initiated, by the demands of cooperative group hunting of large animals, man evolved a language and a system of symbolic words and signs. He also covered and warmed his naked body with clothing, controlled the use of fire, domesticated a number of plants and animals, and initiated systems of agriculture. The remainder is recorded history.

Looking back over primate history we can see, in broad outline, the physical changes that were responsible for the gradual transformation of an insectivorelike animal into the kind of animal we are today. The head was drastically reshaped from front to back. The snout was pushed back

Emerging humanity

If there is one thing that can be stated with absolute certainty today, it is that man arose and went through the main stages of his evolution upon the Old World land mass—Africa, southern Asia and Europe. . . . He arose in a limited area, probably as a quite isolated and rare experiment of nature. But from the beginning he was the most restless of all earth's creatures, and across two million years of time we can dimly make him out venturing on his first experiment: trying to walk and live on the grass.

Now grass, we are accustomed to believe, is even more ubiquitous than man; it seems as fixed as the stars. Nevertheless grass, like man, has had a history, and perhaps even more than man has changed the face of the earth and the course of life. In the closing period of the Age of Reptiles some 100 million years ago, a new form of plant life, the Angiosperms or true seed plants, began to spread over the world with almost explosive rapidity, supplanting the jungles and fern forests. By the Middle Tertiary the grasses, an Angiosperm adaptation, were widely distributed over the

uplands and savannahs of the continents. We can trace the emergence of this new world through the transformations of the animals that got into it. In many areas the old-fashioned shrubbery-eating animals began to disappear. Their teeth were not adapted to the abrasive silica content of grasses. New forms of grazing animals, such as horses, began to evolve in the grass corridors. Then came carnivores adapted to preying upon the grass eaters. Into this new and sunny world, rather late in its history, there ventured a queer, somewhat old-fashioned mammal which had evolved, for reasons still not clearly understood, a fantastically awkward mode of progression. It walked on its hind feet, like something out of the vanquished Age of Reptiles. The mark of the trees was in its body and hands. It was venturing late into a world dominated by fleet runners and swift killers. By all the biological laws this gangling, ill-armed beast should have perished, but you who read these lines are its descendant.

L. Eiseley [11]

---

into a flat face, the eyes were moved forward to give a broader field of vision, the sense of smell was reduced to secondary importance, the dentition was generalized to cope with a varied diet, the head was positioned on top of the spine so as to be consistent with an upright posture, and the braincase was considerably enlarged. The forelimbs, with clawed paws, became the arms and hands of man, with an opposable thumb and an enhanced sense of touch; the hand became not only a grasping mechanism but an instrument of exquisite precision. A restructuring of the thorax, trunk, pelvis, and hind feet made an upright posture not only possible but a position of stability as well, freeing the hands thereby for manipulative purposes. The internal organs were rearranged to conform with bipedalism. All of these changes required a remodeling of bones, a realignment of muscles, and the development of control mechanisms for their coordinated use. Nothing basically new was added during primate evolution, but just as the combination of hydrogen and oxygen give rise to a molecule of water that possesses new qualities, so the combined modifications of existing structures and of behaviors stemming from these changes provided the new basis of adaptation that culminated in the rise of man.

Man is, nonetheless, a most unique and, in some ways, a specialized animal. In a physical sense he can do many things, but none of them exceptionally well. He can run and swim, but he cannot compete with the antelope, the cheetah, or the otter. For a large animal he is relatively weak. He has no claws for offense or defense, and his teeth and jaws are too small and weak for anything but the chewing of food. His back and posture are not such as to permit heavy work or the carrying of heavy loads. Yet he

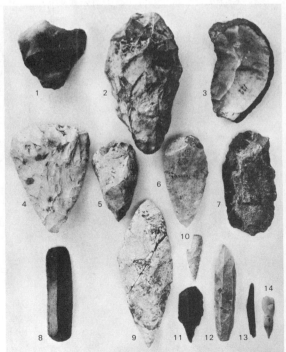

6.18 *Stone tools representing the various phases of the Paleolithic, or Old Stone Age, in Western Europe. Number 1 is the most primitive, 14 the most sophisticated.*

Emerging humanity

The main conclusion arrived at in this work, namely, that man is descended from some lowly-organized form, will, I regret to think, be highly distasteful to many persons. But there can hardly be a doubt that we are descended from barbarians. The astonishment which I felt on first seeing a party of Fuegians on a wild and broken shore will never be forgotten by me, for the reflection at once rushed into my mind—such were our ancestors. These men were absolutely naked and bedaubed with paint, their long hair was tangled, their mouths frothed with excitement, and their expression was wild, startled, and distrustful. They possessed hardly any arts, and, like wild animals, lived on what they could catch; they had no government, and were merciless to every one not of their own small tribe. He who has seen a savage in his native land will not feel much shame, if forced to acknowledge that the blood of some more humble creature flows in his veins. For my own part, I would as soon be descended from that heroic little monkey, who braved his dreaded enemy in order to save the life of his keeper; or from that old baboon who, descending from the mountains, carried away in triumph his young comrade from a crowd of astonished dogs—as from a savage who delights to torture his enemies, offers up bloody sacrifices, practises infanticide without remorse, treats his wives like slaves, knows no decency, and is haunted by the grossest superstitions.

Man may be excused for feeling some pride at having risen, though not through his own exertions, to the very summit of the organic scale; and the fact of his having thus risen, instead of having been aboriginally placed there, may give him hopes for a still higher destiny in the distant future. But we are

---

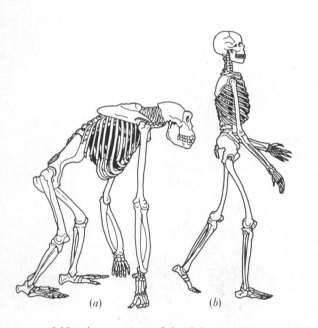

6.19 *A comparison of the skeletons of the gorilla (a) and man (b). The pelvic region of the gorilla is very long and tilts forward, whereas that of man is short and upright. In the gorilla, the vertebral column does not have the typical S-curve found in man, the shoulder girdle is more massive than a man's, the arms are longer than the legs, the feet have no pronounced arches, and the head hangs forward.*

dominates the earth, and it is no exaggeration to say that the continued existence of every other species rests in his hands. He dominates because of his wits and his increased learning ability and retentive memory, the result of an expanded cortical area in our brains, because of his hands, the instruments of his wits, and because of his language, which can express his thoughts and transmit his experiences to others in an economical and enduring fashion.

It is no coincidence that manipulable hands and an enlarged brain evolved together. Tool making occurred early in man's history and when his brain capacity was no greater than that of chimpanzees. But every increase in cortical area with its associative and retentive function takes on a selective advantage when hands are available to be directed and a language can be used for instructive purposes. The rate of increase of brain size, particularly that of the frontal portions, has been spectacularly rapid, increasing about 47 percent in the 300,000 years that separate the australopithecines from *H. erectus* and 45 percent in the last 600,000 years. Despite the fact that this is a rapid change under conditions of natural selection, it is slow when we consider what man can do by exerting severe pressure through artificial selection. The various breeds of dogs are an example of this. Today selective pressure is being exerted primarily by the cultural conditions instituted by man; these will affect him biologically as well as socially. What the results will be only time can tell; we need to remember that our recorded history is only 5,000 years old.

Man is equally peculiar in his social organization when compared even to his closest primate relatives. It has been suggested that this stems, in good part, from his sexual not here concerned with hopes or fears, only with the truth as far as our reason allows us to discover it. I have given the evidence to the best of my ability; and we must acknowledge, as it seems to me, that man with all his noble qualities, with sympathy which feels for the most debased, with benevolence which extends not only to other men but to the humblest living creature, with his godlike intellect which has penetrated into the movements and constitution of the solar system—with all these exalted powers—Man still bears in his bodily frame the indelible stamp of his lowly origin.

C. Darwin [8]

Lowland gorilla.

Ron Garrison photo,
San Diego Zoo

behavior, although cooperative hunting practices must have also played a role. All of the anthropoids—monkeys, apes, and man—are alike in that the females of the group are asynchronous in estrus, so that breeding takes place throughout the year. All except man mate only when ovulation is likely to occur, that is, the female is receptive only when in heat. Man, however, has taken the added step of disassociating mating from ovulation, a step that couples the sexual act with pleasure rather than with reproduction alone. The family relationships are strengthened, for the constant search for mating partners is basically eliminated, social organization is fashioned around the family grouping, and a cooperative form of existence involving all ages is made possible. Communication, the sharing of experiences, and improved learning opportunities are enhanced, and an innovative cultural atmosphere is generated. The many cultures of man are the result.

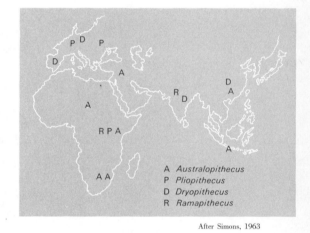

After Simons, 1963

6.20   The regions where fossils of man's ancestors have been uncovered. The fossils of the australopithecines are of Pleistocene age, whereas the pliopithecine, dryopithecine, and ramapithecine fossils are of mid-Pliocene origin.

A   *Australopithecus*
P   *Pliopithecus*
D   *Dryopithecus*
R   *Ramapithecus*

Summary

Some 400 to 500 million years ago the vertebrates appeared on the geologic stage. With few exceptions, these primitive, sea-dwelling vertebrates possessed the basic structures that, through transformation, eventually shaped themselves into modern man. The changes incorporated into the vertebrate system were slow in coming, and not all can be viewed as unequivocal successes, but each change set the stage for subsequent changes, and the trial-and-error process of evolution—of constantly matching a changing organism to a changing environment—finally brought man into being.

Emerging humanity

The Simiadae then branched off into two great stems, the New World and Old World monkeys; and from the latter at a remote period, Man, the wonder and the glory of the universe, proceeded.

C. Darwin [8]

Is man an ape or an angel? I, my lord, I am on the side of the angels. I repudiate with indignation and abhorrence those new fangled theories.

B. Disraeli [9]

The fishes were enormously successful and were the dominant vertebrates for a long period of time. Eventually, one line, the amphibians, invaded the land which was by now populated with an abundance of plant and insect species. The amphibians moved out of the water, but did not really conquer the land; they had to return to water for the reproductive period of their life cycle. The reptiles broke their ties with water by developing a new kind of egg, but failed to conquer the terrestrial environment, because their cold-bloodedness left them at the mercy of the climate. The mammals, with their warm-bloodedness and thermostatic controls, succeeded in conquering the climate and quickly came to dominate the land and even to reinvade the seas. This was accompanied by an increased awareness of, and responsiveness to, a variety of environmental conditions, with restlessness and curiosity characteristic of the entire group. Some assumed an arboreal existence, and a drastic restructuring of the head and the hands took place. Binocular vision was achieved, the visual senses came to be more important than those of smell and hearing, and clawed paws were transformed into nailed hands. A later descent to life on the ground brought on an upright posture and a walking stride, which was made possible by a better positioning of the head, a curved spine, altered pectoral and pelvic girdles, and a double-arched foot. That portion of the brain associated with memory and integration of images expanded rapidly, and the advent of man occurred.

Man is an improbable accident of evolution, the result of a vast number of changes, any one of which, if absent, would have foreclosed the possibilities of his appearance. But he did appear and quickly came to dominate the biological scene.

Emerging humanity

7

The uniqueness of man

When we ask the question "What is man?" the answer will depend upon the context within which the question was raised, upon what the British philosopher Alfred North Whitehead called a "climate of opinion," that particular pattern of thought accepted as a reasonable starting point for discussion and speculation. The biblical view of man as a divinely created being, fully equipped with all physical, mental, and cultural attributes and aspects, was an appropriate medieval concept. Arising out of a combination of Greek thought and the Christian view, it provided an authority and a set of absolutes that dictated and sustained the cosmology, logic, and intellectual frame of reference that is exemplified, for example, in the writings of Dante and Aquinas. Copernicus thought and wrote within this climate

And at last came the monkey, and anyone could see that man wasn't far off now. And in truth that was so. The monkey went on developing for close upon five million years, and then turned into a man—to all appearances.

Such is the history of it. Man has been here 32,000 years. That it took a hundred million years to prepare the world for him is proof that that is what it was done for. I suppose it is, I dunno. If the Eiffel Tower were now representing the world's age, the skin of paint on the pinnacle-knob at its summit would represent man's share of that age; and anybody would perceive that that skin was what the tower was built for. I reckon they would, I dunno.

M. Twain [34]

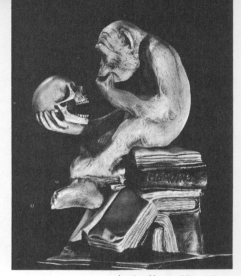

The eighteenth century—"the silver age of the European Renaissance"—virtually begins in the final decades of the seventeenth. When we enter those decades we recognize on all sides the familiar eighteenth century landmarks, lit by the familiar illumination of the time. Glory and loveliness may have passed away, but so also have the fogs and glooms of history; the common daylight which now descends upon a distracted world may be prosaic, but at least it is steady and serene, and has not yet become dark with excessive light. One meets everywhere a sense of relief and escape, relief from the strain of living in a mysterious universe, and escape from the ignorance and barbarism of the Gothic centuries. Nature's laws had been explained by the New Philosophy; sanity, culture, and civilization had revived; and at last, across the vast gulf of the monkish and deluded past, one could salute the ancients from an eminence perhaps as lofty as their own. . . . Nature was the grand alternative to all that man had made of man; upon her solid ground therefore—upon the *tabula rasa* prepared by the true philosophy—must all the religion, the ethics, the politics, the law, and the art of the future be constructed. . . . The laws of Nature are the laws of reason; they are always and everywhere the same, and, like the axioms of mathematics they have only to be presented in order to be acknowledged as just and right by all men. The historic role of "Nature" at this time was to introduce, not further confusion, but its precise opposites—peace, concord, toleration, and progress in the affairs of men, and, in poetry and art, perspicuity, order, unity, and proportion. . . .

B. Willey [39]

of opinion, but his reordering of the planetary orbits and the subsequent efforts of those who initiated the era of modern science shattered this comfortable world and replaced it with a mechanical and material version that the eighteenth-century thinkers believed could be grasped and understood only if reason and science were given free rein. Their faith in natural law revealed by science came from Newton, whereas their confidence in their powers of reasoning stemmed principally from Descartes and Locke. As Clifford Geertz, the anthropologist, has written: "The Enlightenment view of man was that he was wholly of a piece with nature and shared in the general uniformity of composition which natural science, under Bacon's urging and Newton's guidance, has discovered there."

Carrying the mechanistic approach of the new science over into the realm of the mind and the spirit, there was generated, despite the glittering sophistication of the period, an intellectual rigidity as fixed and unvarying as the law of gravity or the structured thought of the Middle Ages. Denis Diderot (1713–1784) the principal editor of the ambitious and influential multivolumed *Encyclopédie*, wrote: "Nothing that exists can be against or outside nature." Nature, it was believed, could be fully understood through the methods of science and reason, and this information would inevitably instruct man to behave naturally and to construct his social institutions in a rational fashion; social progress, happiness, and the ultimate perfection of man would follow as the night follows the day. Out of this period came the philosophies of Hume, Kant, and Locke, Rousseau's noble savage, and the writings of Voltaire and Montesquieu. But as the American historian Carl Becker points out, commenting on the fact that they substituted

The uniqueness of man

What is man in nature? A nothing in comparison with the
Infinite, an All in comparison with the Nothing, a mean
between nothing and everything. . . . What a chimera then is
man! . . . What a contradiction, what a prodigy! . . . The pride
and refuse of the universe.

B. Pascal [25]

Of systems possible, if 'tis confessed,
That Wisdom infinite must form the best,
Where all must fall, or not coherent be,
And all that rises, rise in due degree;
Then in the scale of reas'ning life, 'tis plain,
There must be, somewhere, such a rank as Man.

A. Pope [26]

---

the authority of science and reason for the authority derived
from religious sources, they "demolished the Heavenly City
of St. Augustine only to rebuild it with more up-to-date
materials." This structured rigidity would persist generally
until science was separated distinctly from philosophy and
returned, at least in biology, to a solid factual basis by the
successes of Darwin, the twentieth-century geneticists, and
the anthropologists and cultural sociologists of the last few
decades.

We now recognize that man is, like all living things, a
product of evolution through natural selection. He has a
long vertebrate history, a shorter primate history, and a very
much more abbreviated human history. In making such a
statement, we need to recognize, as Becker emphasizes, that
we have replaced theology with history and philosophy with
science as the most reliable means to an understanding of
man and nature. Only by making use of history and the
methods of science can we grasp man's biological and
human nature and sense his close systematic affinity to the
gorilla and the chimpanzee and his more distant relation
to all other living forms. This intellectual stance provides
us with our only fixed point of departure. As a result of
this approach, we can see that man is also unique among
animals in being a culture former, with all that the term
"culture" implies. Just about the only time one can think
of man as independent of a culture is when one is engaged
in the dissection of an anonymous, formalinized cadaver or
the measurement of a defleshed and bony skull. The essence
of living man is his human nature, and a man disassociated
from his culture is a biological and sociological anomaly.

Because man created his cultures, he has, Clifford Geertz
[13] maintains, "literally created himself. . . . Culture,

George Wesley Bellows, Stag at Sharkey's.

One of the basic principles of evolutionary theory holds that the initial survival value of any innovation is conservative in that it makes possible the maintenance of a largely traditional way of life in the face of changed circumstances. There was nothing in the makeup of the protohominoids that destined their descendants to become human. Some of them, indeed, did not. They made their way to ecological niches where food was plentiful and predators sufficiently avoidable, and where the development of primitive varieties of language and culture would have bestowed no advantage. They survive still, with various sorts of specialization, as the gibbons and the great apes.

Man's own remote ancestors, then, must have come to live in circumstances where a slightly more flexible system of communication, the incipient carrying and shaping of tools, and a slight increase in the capacity for traditional transmission made just the difference between surviving—largely, be it noted, by the good old protohominoid way of life—and dying out. There are various possibilities. If predators become more numerous and dangerous, any nonce use of a tool as a weapon, any co-operative mode of escape or attack might restore the balance. If food became scarcer, any technique for cracking harder nuts, for foraging over a wider territory, for sharing food so gathered or storing it when it was plentiful might promote survival of the band. Only after a very long period of such small adjustments to tiny changes of living conditions could the factors involved—incipient language, incipient tool-carrying and toolmaking, incipient culture—have started leading the way to a new pattern of life, of the kind called human.

C. F. Hockett [18]

rather than being added on to a virtually finished animal, was the central ingredient in the production of that animal itself. The slow growth of culture through the Ice Age altered the balance of selection so as to play a major directive role in his evolution." He adds: "One of the most significant facts about human nature may be that we all begin with the natural equipment to live a thousand kinds of lives and end having lived only one. . . . What man is may be so entangled with where he is, who he is, and what he believes as to be inseparable from them." Stanley Garn, taking a somewhat different point of view, looks upon man's rise to human status as "an example of Predator's Progress." Man's position of dominance in the living world, once believed to have been conferred by divine decree, can now be viewed as having been achieved by dint of pulling on his own biological bootstraps.

Man's physical uniqueness

There are few, if any, physical characteristics of man that he does not share with some other animal group and, at the biochemical level, with plants and bacteria as well, but it is the particular and peculiar combination of traits that makes man uniquely human. Time and circumstance have reshaped him from stem to stern, from his feet to his head, including the parts in between. The many anatomical, physiological, and behavioral changes seen in man have, as a whole, the balanced proportionality and functionality required of any adapted product of evolution. But while it is convenient to speak of the relation of parts one to the other, the patterns of cause and effect remain so intertwined

The uniqueness of man

There is a wolf in me . . . fangs pointed for tearing gashes . . . a red tongue
    for raw meat . . . and the hot lapping of blood—I keep this wolf because
    the wilderness gave it to me and the wilderness will not let it go.

There is the hog in me . . . a snout and a belly . . . a machinery for eating and
    grunting . . . a machinery for sleeping satisfied in the sun—I got this
    too from the wilderness and the wilderness will not let it go.

There is a baboon in me . . . clambering-clawed . . . dog-faced . . . yawping a galoot's
    hunger . . . hairy under the armpits . . . ready to snarl and kill . . . ready to
    sing and give milk . . . waiting—I keep the baboon because the wilderness says so.

O, I got a zoo, I got a menagerie, inside my ribs, under my bony head,
    under my red-valve heart—and I got something else: it is a man-child
    heart, a woman-child heart: it is a father and mother and lover: it came
    from God-Knows-Where: it is going God-Knows-Where—For I am the keeper
    of the zoo: I say yes and no: I sing and kill and work: I am a pal of
    the world: I came from the wilderness.

C. Sandburg [28]

---

that they are impossible to disentangle. As Darwin said,
"Any fool can speculate," but we need here be concerned
not with the sequential order of change, but only with the
fact that the many innovations and modifications arising
during the course of evolution have led to present-day man.

Human walking, or striding, is a gait that is unique in
the animal kingdom, as is prolonged bipedal standing. A
breed of horses known as the Tennessee walking horse
locomotes in an analogous way, but its gait is achieved
artificially by altering its Achilles tendon. The human stride
puts a man in motion, and, when combined with an upright
posture, leaves him teetering continuously on the edge of
catastrophe. Falling is prevented by continual shifting of
the center of gravity of the body from side to side. This
is made possible by the structure and action of the feet,
knees, and pelvis, with the arms and shoulders acting as
auxiliary balancers when necessary.

Gorillas and chimpanzees may occasionally
stand, with bent knees, for *short* periods; but they
do not do so habitually. The same is true of
occasional Old World monkeys. . . . However,
man alone stands with extended knees; and he
alone indulges in prolonged standing. This has
been made possible by an evolutionary bending
backward and upward of the ischium (not, as commonly stated, by a downward
bending of the ilium upon the ischium),
accompanied by a forward tilting of the pelvis
which has produced the lumbar curvature so
characteristic of man. These changes permit
effective action of the hamstring and the gluteal
muscles in the maintenance of an erect trunk
upon a fully extended thigh and leg. This is not
possible in living nonhuman primates, in which
the femoropelvic relations are adapted to a
pronograde, quadrupedal posture. These relations
necessitate a partially flexed femur, producing a
bent-knee gait, when a bipedal posture is
assumed—this in an attempt, so to speak, to
restore effective functional relations between
pelvis and thigh.

W. L. Straus, Jr. [33]

7.1 *Comparison of the foot of man and a gorilla. (a) The left foot
of a man and a gorilla seen from below. (b) The bones of the two
feet seen from the side, with the arch of a human foot indicated by
the arrow. (c) The foot of a man at rest and in motion, with the
points of contact indicated.*

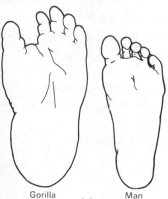

Gorilla   Man
    (a)

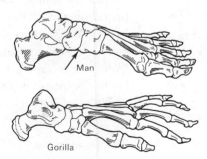

Man

Gorilla
    (b)

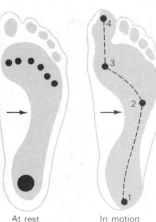

At rest   In motion
        (c)

The evolution of the entire universe—stars, elements, life, man—is a process of drawing something out of nothing, out of the utter void of nonbeing. The creative element in the mind of man—that latency which can conceive gods, carve statues, move the heart with the symbols of great poetry, or devise the formulas of modern physics—emerges in as mysterious a fashion as those elementary particles which leap into momentary existence in great cyclotrons, only to vanish again like infinitesimal ghosts. The reality we know in our limited lifetimes is dwarfed by the unseen potential of the abyss where science stops. In a similar way, the smaller universe of the individual human brain has its lonely cometary passages, or flares suddenly like a super nova, only to subside in death while the waves of energy it has released roll on through unnumbered generations.

L. Eiseley [11]

If our ancestors were knuckle-walkers, then the origin of bipedalism and tool use may be seen in a new way. For a long time I have been puzzled about how a creature could be adapted to partial bipedalism. Man moves so slowly compared to quadrupedal creatures and is so vulnerable without weapons that it has been very hard for me to conceive of a creature any less efficient that could survive at all. A knuckle-walking stage gets around this problem, as shown by the contemporary chimpanzee. The chimpanzee can move very rapidly quadrupedally and then climb out of danger if necessary. The chimpanzee knuckle-walks, climbs for feeding and escape, brachiates, and may walk bipedally for moderate distances, especially when carrying something.

If changed selection pressures favored the bipedal part of the behavior repertoire, then the beginnings of the human kind of bipedal walking and running might evolve while the animal could still move rapidly as a knuckle-walker and escape from danger by climbing. Probably the new selection pressure was for tool use and carrying and, according to this model, the adaptation of climbing for escape could not be lost until weapons had evolved to a level at which they could replace the need for climbing. The human foot must have evolved long after the evolution of simple tools.

S. L. Washburn [37]

Probably the most characteristic feature of man is not his head, but his foot. Two compact arches, at right angles to each other, give stability when a man is at rest and thrust the weight of the body through the ankles to the toes when he is striding. As a man walks, the cushioned heel strikes first, then the ball of the foot takes the weight, and finally the big toe provides a forward thrust, with the rigid arches keeping the points of contact at a minimum (see illustration 7.1). The great apes, having no big toe—the simian "big" toe is actually shorter than the others—and a flexible arch, walk with their ankles, not their heels and toes. The result is a shuffle, not a stride. The perch of man may be precarious, but, compared with the apes, his stride is longer, the action is with a minimum of effort and energy expenditure, and the pace can be substantially faster.

In keeping with the upright posture, the knee can lock into position, thus making a tiring bent-knee stance unnecessary and permitting standing to be a position of rest. When a man is in motion, his pelvis rotates with the stride so that the weight is always on the stance foot, and the lower (lumbar) region of the spine is curved inward for weight distribution. The rib cage is considerably flattened compared to that of a gorilla, the shoulders are moved to the side and are kept in a spread state by the collarbone, and the heavy-boned skull of the ape has been replaced by one that is lighter, has a shorter jaw, and is centrally positioned on top of the spine instead of hanging forward at its tip. Man is thus considerably less top-heavy and more delicately structured than his apish relatives; there is less likelihood of falling forward on his face, or having to use his hands for purposes of locomotion.

Which of these changes came first in the course of evolu-

tion is an open question, but because a fossil of a big toe, a prerequisite both for upright stability and for striding, has been discovered and its age estimated at more than 1 million years, one can surmise that an early ancestor of man developed a human type of stance and locomotion first, after which other structural modifications made their appearance. Neanderthal man, 50,000 years ago, had not acquired all of these changes, for he was barrel-chested, and his skull hung considerably to the front (illustration 7.2). But, although he was clearly in the family of man, he appears to have been an offshoot rather than in the direct line of human evolution.

It can be argued, although with debatable conviction, that the evolutionary pressure leading to a striding habit stemmed from existence in a grassland environment and, possibly, from hunting as a mode of food gathering. Increased endurance, speed, and agility would be obvious adaptive advantages. Because tool use and tool making were also associated with the australopithecines, or with some form coexisting with them, a growing refinement in the manipulative use of the hands would also be expected. In illustration 7.3, the human hand is compared with the hands of other apes. Whatever the sequence of events, it is clear that altered habits went along not only with changes in bone conformation, but also with changes in the size and function of muscles. It took many, closely ordered heritable changes to bring about the structural modifications we now see in man.

The gradual perfection of an upright stature and a striding mode of locomotion as a result of the coordinated action of altered feet, knees, and pelvis, the freeing of arms by displacement to the sides of the body, the increased rota-

7.2 *Comparison of the skeleton of Neanderthal man (a) and modern man (b). Note the shift to an upright posture.*

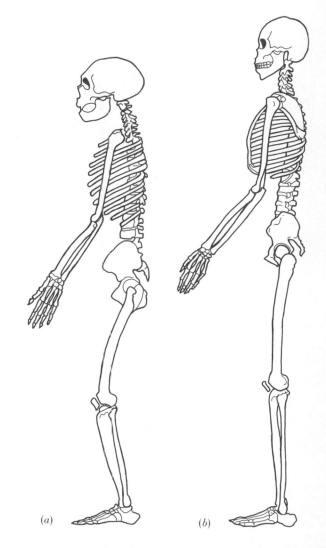

(a)   (b)

The uniqueness of man

In the beginning the world must have been very pleasantly still. The ancient quiet of earth, which is but a vulnerable fragment of the pure silence of space, had not yet gone to hide, like a spirit, in lonely places. Those vast, fantastic fragments that are the continents we know, each ringed with the timeless cadences and confusions of the sea, were full of that inland peace which begins where the ocean murmur dies away. The first sounds to visit human ears were those which are perhaps destined to be the last; that to which we listen, Adam heard. Spacing the quiet, men heard the lovely sounds of earth—rain in the deep woods on dying, late-summer leaves, the stir of trees at sunrise that have been still all night, the fiery snap of lightning, the song of a bird by a lake. A small and local sound of stone struck upon stone, that sharp, complete, integral click without vibration, must have been the first true "made" sound to part the ancient leaves, to be, for ages too vast for centuries to count, the tokening sound of man. Metal with its lengthening vibration then confused the stone, more voices jargoned (for this early world, it would seem, was filling up) the crowd din, and cries of archaic war arose, and presently beginning sounds of the arts and trades intruded with the numbered years.

H. Beston [3]

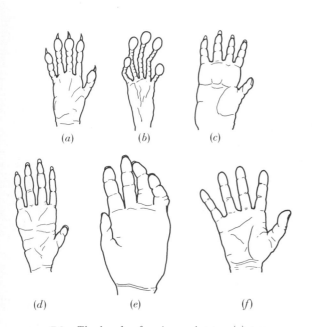

7.3   *The hands of various primates: (a) tree shrew, with the generalized primate pattern and clawed digits; (b) tarsier, with specialized pads at the ends of the digits; (c) baboon, typical of ground dwellers with quadruped stance; (d) orangutan, with long hand and short thumb adapted for arboreal life; (e) gorilla, with short thumb; (f) man, with long thumb and relatively short fingers suitable for opposition.*

bility of the wrist joint, and the transformation of a grasping hand into a mechanism of exquisite precision were accompanied by an increase in cranial capacity. The brain, particularly the cortical region with its capacity for sorting and unscrambling sensory messages and for initiating responsive action, doubled and redoubled in size as human evolution proceeded from a protohuman stock to the present (see illustration 7.4). It requires no great stretch of the imagination to grasp the adaptive advantage of our feet and our hands; a powerful jaw, armed with equally powerful teeth, loses its defensive and adaptive value when discerning eyes and a hand with a club or a spear do the job in better fashion. But what is the adaptive advantage of more brains? We must, of course, being evolutionists, view the brain as we do all other aspects of bodily structure, function, and behavior; it is, to be sure, an instrument for defining reality, for producing poetry, music, and art in all of its forms, and for devising the wheel, the calendar, and the H-bomb, but these are by-products and not the reasons for its early development and continued existence.

Because bigger and bigger brains survived, we must assume that a cortical increase had an evolutionary advantage. Was it because of an increased intelligence? Or because bigger-brained individuals killed off their smaller-brained neighbors, as broken skulls and bones in some fossil deposits would possibly suggest? How much brain capacity is needed under the environmental conditions of 50,000 years ago, the point at which our present cranial capacity had been reached? It is tempting to assume that as our hands became manipulative, a concomitant increase in brain size kept them busy in a directed manner. Stanley M. Garn [12], however, is doubtful: "It is no longer enough to attribute even the

The sources of noise today seem almost limitless. From the kitchen in the modern home comes a cacophony that would require ear defenders in industry to prevent hearing loss. In a series of measurements made in one kitchen, a dishwasher raised the noise level in the center of the kitchen from 56 to 85 decibels, while the garbage disposal raised it to more than 90 decibels. A food blender produces about 93 decibels. Power lawn mowers and leaf rakers, outside air conditioners, and power tools such as saws contribute to the noise in the home. But for most Americans, construction and transportation sources, particularly trucks, motorcycles, sports cars, private airplanes and helicopters as well as commerical jets and military aircraft, are the most serious offenders.

D. F. Anthrop [1]

Jolan Gross-Bettelheim, Assembly Line.

Philadelphia Museum of Art, photo by A. J. Wyatt

---

first increase of hominid brain size to the mere rudiments of technology, and certainly not the second increase that followed *Pithecanthropus.* Surely man did not double and nearly redouble his cerebral volume merely to pick sticks." Rather he sees an increase in cranial capacity going hand-in-hand with an increase in cultural complexity.

Man is a self-conscious animal, and being aware of himself, he is similarly aware of what goes on around him. He had to do so in order to survive. He habitually makes comparisons, forms judgments, and arrives at decisions as a prelude to action. But he is also aware, as no other animals are, that there were men before him and there will be others after him. He is, in addition, an image former, not only of what is but also of what might be. These capacities grow as his culture progresses, and it is inevitable that as social organization becomes more complex, so does the informational input that impinges on his senses. Much of this information is noise, and it therefore becomes necessary to distinguish patterns within this noise if anything useful is to be extracted. Increasing interpersonal contacts add to the amount of noise as well as the tensions of existence, and the need to discern patterns amidst this noise requires elaborate circuitry, which in essence is what the cerebral region consists of (see illustration 7.5).

A large brain, in this view, is a cultural, as well as a biological, product. As Geertz [13] explains it:

> The perfection of tools, the adoption of organized hunting and gathering practices, the beginnings of true family organization, the discovery of fire, and, most critically, the increasing reliance upon systems of significant symbols (language, art, myth, ritual) for orientation, communication, and self-control all created a new environment to which man was obliged to adapt. As culture accumulated and developed, those

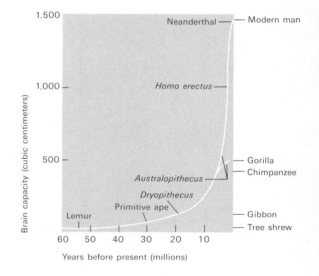

7.4 *Brain capacity, in cubic centimeters, of the various forms leading to man. Extant primates are indicated at right.*

7.5 *A nerve cell (dark area left of center) with its axon extending out from it. The many surrounding fibers—the axons and dendrites of other nerve cells—make up the elaborate circuitry of the nervous system.*

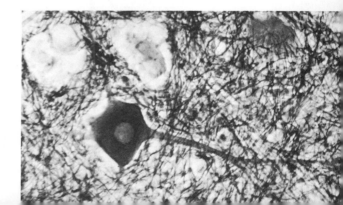

The uniqueness of man

207

Museo delle Terme, Rome   Standard Oil Co. (N.J.)   UPI photo

For a human being, membership in a culture is vital. Lack of a capacity to acquire a culture makes an individual a low-grade mental defective. A fixed capacity to acquire only a certain culture, or only a certain role within a culture, would, however, be perilous; cultures and roles change too rapidly. To be able to learn a language is imperative, but a restriction of this ability to only a certain language would be a drawback. Insect behavior is largely, though not wholly, stereotyped and genetically fixed; human genotype brings about a comprehensive plasticity of behavior. This plasticity is adaptively essential, because culture is wholly acquired in every generation, not transmitted through genes. The connection between genetics and culture is often imagined to consist of the possession by some human populations of genes for this or that cultural trait, or the possession by the human species of genes for this or that "cultural universal," but that is sheer misconception. The biological success of the human species has been due precisely to the genetically secured capacity of every individual free from overt pathology to acquire any or all cultural traits or universals.

Th. Dobzhansky [9]

individuals most able to take advantage of it were better able to survive, and through a process of natural selection the small-brained, protohuman *Homo australopithecus* became the large-brained, fully human *Homo sapiens*. By submitting himself to governance by symbolically mediated programs for producing artifacts, organizing social life, or expressing emotions, man determined, if unwittingly, his own biological destiny. He literally created himself.

Culture-promoting human attributes

The uniqueness of a human being does not reside solely in his anatomical features. However important they might be, and however necessary they are to the eventual development of a culture, they are not sufficient to make the transformation of the human animal into a human being an inevitability. Some prehumans made the grade, others did not. This suggests, then, that there is no such thing as a human nature that is independent of culture. There is an admitted circularity to this argument, however, for evidences of a culture in prehistoric diggings—the chipped stone tools found in the area of australopithecine fossils and the burial of the dead by Neanderthal man—provide criteria for the inclusion of these ancestral forms in the genus *Homo*.

The argument, nevertheless, is a sound one and is backed by observations and experimental data. Culture, to be sure, takes on different meanings in different contexts, but always within the frame of reference of behavior. To the archaeologist, culture consists of the assemblage of material artifacts that appear in repeated patterns or that in successive layers or adjacent sites vary in evolving ways. Whether a stone tool is chipped, flaked, or ground into useful shape, or whether a pottery shard is sun dried, baked, painted, or

The uniqueness of man

"What is man, that thou dost make so much of him,
  and that thou dost set thy mind upon him,
Dost visit him every morning,
  and test him every moment? . . .

"Man that is born of a woman is of few days,
  and full of trouble.
He comes forth like a flower, and withers;
  he flees like a shadow, and continues not. . . .

"For there is hope for a tree,
  if it be cut down, that it will sprout again,
  and that its shoots will not cease.
Though its root grow old in the earth,
  and its stump die in the ground,
Yet at the scent of water it will bud
  and put forth branches like a young plant.
But man dies, and is laid low;
  man breathes his last, and where is he?
As waters fail from a lake,

and a river wastes away and dries up,
So man lies down and rises not again;
  till the heavens are no more he will not awake,
  or be roused out of his sleep. . . ."

Then the Lord answered Job out of the whirlwind:
"Who is this that darkens counsel by words without knowledge:
Gird up your loins like a man,
  I will question you, and you shall declare to me.

"Where were you when I laid the foundation of the earth?
  Tell me, if you have understanding.
Who determined its measurements—surely you know!
  Or who stretched the line upon it?
On what were its bases sunk,
  or who laid its cornerstone,
When the morning stars sang together,
  and all the sons of God shouted for joy?"

Job 7, 14, 38

---

glazed, provide clues that help to define the character of a culture. The anthropologist, on the other hand, although he is aware of, and makes use of, material artifacts, is more concerned with aspects of human behavior, those facets of life that rise above the instinctual level and have to be discovered and learned by each individual. Included within the scope of the anthropologist's concern are those things that in their aggregate determine a way of life—language and logic, myth and magic, codes of ethics and morality, the manufacture of the implements of existence, and the varied means of acquiring and preparing food.

Culture is a societal, not an individual, attribute. The untutored mind, deprived of those experiences that bring the individual into the common fold—society, herd, flock, even a gaggle of geese—is a species monstrosity, a social idiot in the case of humans. Children reared from infancy in the wild—the so-called wolf-children, many of them falsely identified, but some very real—possess only instinctual reactions and are unable to learn the ways of society. And man, in his evolutionary advancement, has lost most of his instinctual reactions, these being replaced by learned responses. The suckling and finger-grasping reactions of newborn humans are instinctual, but precious little else of his animal behavior remains in an unmodified form.

But culture is an adaptation to an environment as well as a feature of the environment to which accommodation must be made, and adaptation, in man no less than in animals, depends upon the physical, mental, and behavioral equipment available for meeting environmental challenges. Man's culture-forming propensities lie buried in his biological past; some of these antecedents are ancient, some more recent, but taken together they brought a prehuman animal

Every separate society has its distinctive culture. The consequent effect is that the characteristic behaviors of the members of every single society are in some respects significantly different from the characteristic behaviors of the members of all other societies. Change the characteristic behaviors of the members of a society and the culture changes with it, effecting a subsequent change in the behavior of the members of that society who follow after. Some general elements of culture are universal among all societies, however, and these make up "the common denominator of culture."

Culture is manifest only in the behavior, beliefs, and attitudes of individuals; yet culture is superindividual and *superorganic* in that each person, as he is born and develops, comes under the sway of preexisting patterns of culture and is molded—or at least influenced—by them.

E. A. Hoebel [19]

7.6 *Remnants of past civilizations, from flakes of stone and tiny pottery chips to this 25-ton Aztec calendar stone tell anthropologists much about the nature of vanished cultures.*

Mexican National Tourist Council

The uniqueness of man

It is a remarkable and little-noticed fact that the two physical organs most concerned with man's intellectual achievements, in other words his great inventions, are represented in disproportionate expanse upon the motor center of his brain. These are the tongue and the hand, particularly the forefinger and thumb. The prelude to man's inventive ingenuity is written into his flesh; there is actually a biological prologue to human culture. Moreover, there exists in these two organs a hint of the distinction which can later be drawn between the inventions which heighten man's sensory perception of his world and the power to wreak his will upon it. Speech breaks up and defines our environment. It projects our minds into past and future time. The hand, by contrast, shapes the tool which the mind proceeds to impose upon nature.

L. Eiseley [10]

7.7 The purple sea urchin, like all radial animals, possesses no head and is therefore automatically eliminated from the list of culture formers. As the text indicates, man alone is capable of forming a true culture.

to the stage in time when a culture emerged and began to evolve. Perhaps our egocentric point of view does not permit us to contemplate the emergence of a culture in any species other than the primate group, but actually it is difficult to imagine a culture in any other group less well equipped than the primates. An upright stature to free the hands for manipulative purposes, with all that this implies in the restructuring of bones, muscles, and other organs, seems, at least in retrospect, a necessary early step, if not the first step. "Look, Ma, no hands" might apply to the riding of a bicycle, but hands are a necessity for the establishment of a culture. The potential usefulness and increasing capability of the hands for manipulative purposes must have preceded the enlargement of the cortex in order that increased brain size would have a selective advantage. This would rule out the immobile plants. They would also be ruled out because they have no nervous system. In addition all radial animals—jellyfish, starfish, and sea urchins, for example—would be eliminated as culture formers because they possess no head. It seems reasonable to suppose that a terrestrial mode of life is also necessary for the formation of culture. Dolphins—the mammal, not the fish—have a large brain, an elaborate system of communication, and a remarkable ability to learn, but a watery environment as a place for the establishment of an ongoing tradition tends to boggle the mind. Warm-bloodedness also seems a prerequisite because it frees the organism from dependence on a major environmental factor, namely temperature. Among cold-blooded animals, the insects are as successful a group as any, and several groups—ants, termites, and bees—have established elaborate social organizations, but they never succeeded in breaking through the rigidity of instinctual

The uniqueness of man

Many of the issues raised regarding individuals and populations, and a society as a collection of organisms or a single epiorganism, come into rather sharp focus in the brain itself; there is a large population, over 10 billion neurons, in the human brain, and they act to give a unity. The early evolution of the behavioral capacities of the brain, probably up to the anthropods and the most primitive vertebrates, depended considerably on improved units—neurons and fibers, receptor and effector cells; but there is little further change in these from primitive vertebrates to man. What is very different is the kind and effectiveness of neuron interactions, the circuitry, if you will, and, still more, the sheer number available. Clearly, neurons collectively constitute a new entity.

More units of the same kind, even interacting in the same way, can do things that fewer units cannot do, things that are actually quantitatively different, so, as a man's mind is more than the sum of neuron minds, so the collective mind of mankind is clearly a very different thing from man's individual mind.

R. W. Gerard [14]

---

bonds, and thus are incapable of purposeful action. The birds must be eliminated also because their forelimbs evolved into instruments of flight.

The circularity of our cultural argument is of course evident; culture and the human status are inseparable, and one cannot be discussed intelligently without presupposing the existence of the other. But despite culture's uniquely human connotations, there are simple precursor elements to be found among other animals. Many anthropologists have dealt extensively with these aspects of culture, but here we

7.8 Certain groups of insects are characterized by elaborate social organization, but because their actions are guided only by instinctual drives, they cannot form what could be called a culture. This portion of a model termitary shows the royal chamber (center), with the queen attended by workers. A developing queen can be seen at the upper left; a winged male ("king") is at the lower right.

Buffalo Museum of Science

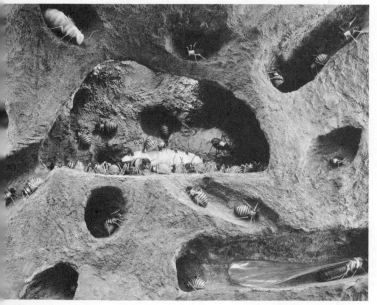

Although culture is considered a unique characteristic of human society, it has simple precursors among some animals. There is no predisposition for culture among chickens; however, learned interactions within a flock may become relatively fixed as social inertia, which has a marked effect on certain biological functions. Rudiments of culture do exist among monkeys. Reports from Japan have shown cultural transmission among free living macaques. The habit of washing food or accepting candy was traced from the practice of one or more individuals to becoming common within the troop. Washburn and DeVore have reported that troops of baboons in Africa set up group territories without intermingling. Each troop has its own characteristic daily routine. The young spend many months in close association with their mothers and are a center of interest for all adults, including the dominant male. Thus traditions become established through generations. Learned behavior integrates the group and very little social strife has been reported among free living monkeys.

Ruth Benedict compared several primitive cultures and showed that they may mold individuals into societies that may have dominant traits of nonaggressiveness, animosity, or extreme rivalry. It is what man develops and learns in his culture that determines his way of life.

A. M. Guhl [15]

Big Daddy [a gorilla] sat hunched by a shrub, motionless, like some unearthly being carved out of granite in the semblance of a man. He reached out with his right hand and bent a branch, which he pushed down under his left foot. Then for five minutes he slowly bent all branches and shrubs within reach and pressed them down without pattern or sequence, rotating slowly until he had constructed the rim of a nest around his body. After that he reclined on his belly with arms and legs tucked under, presenting his massive back to the drizzling rain that had begun to fall. As soon as Big Daddy began to build a nest, several other members of the group did the same. While a female was busy preparing a bed for the night, her infant, about two years old, climbed up seven feet into the crotch of a shrub. The youngster grabbed a branch with one hand and pulled it inward until it snapped. After pushing the branch down into the crotch and stepping on it, it broke in several pieces, all of which were pressed on top of each other until after ten minutes of labor a crude platform was completed. The infant then sat on its nest for about ten minutes and looked around before descending to cuddle close to its mother for the night. Youngsters rarely sleep by themselves until they are almost three years old, but they may build practice nests as early as fifteen months.

G. Schaller [29]

7.9 Among those factors that set the stage for the emergence of a culture is gregariousness. Several members of a troop of baboons are shown here in their East African environment.

Leonard Lee Rue III photo, National Audubon Society

will restrict ourselves to those biological characteristics that set the stage for the emergence of a culture rather than the particular expressions of this or that culture. These characteristics revolve around man's gregariousness, his sexual behavior and physiology, the care and feeding of the young, and the acquisition of a symbolic mode of communication.

Man is a social animal. The terms "misanthrope," "lone wolf," and "hermit" emphasize the antisocial, indeed antihuman, behavior of individuals who shun society or interact with it only peripherally. But gregariousness is a primate character, although not exclusively so, and it has been carried over into the human realm. Troops of baboons, gorillas, and howler monkeys have been extensively studied. The social organization and interpersonal relations vary within such groups and even between groups within a species, but the fundamental grouping, organized primarily, one might argue, for defensive measures, establishes the necessary basis for the development of group behavior and eventually of a learned tradition. Bands of free-living macaques in Japan developed different patterns of traits. One band, for example, initiated the practice of washing its food before eating it, a trait learned from one individual and transmitted to others by example. Other bands never developed the trait, although they were capable of doing so. Learned behavior, therefore, has an integrating influence, and a group acquires a "cultural" distinction.

Several other characteristics reinforce this situation. Man breeds throughout the year, and so the young are an ever-present feature of a social group. This leads to a continuous instead of a seasonal association of the young and the females. The sexual drive is also constant, and the females

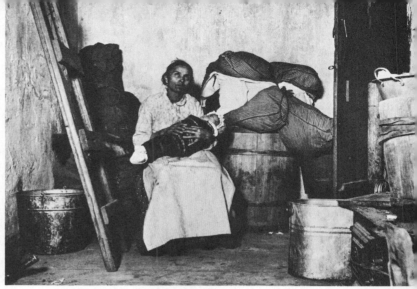

are asynchronously receptive, thus keeping the males a part of the group rather than allowing them to disperse, as would happen at the end of a fixed mating season. As a mammal, the human suckles its young and cares for them until the end of weaning. The nakedness and helplessness of the young, prolonged over a substantially longer period of time than in other animals, requires an equivalently longer period of parental care and protection. Being the focus of much attention, the young spend a substantial amount of time in close association with more experienced members of the group and acquire the traditions of the group through active instruction or imitative repetition. Only through such exposure does an individual learn the habits, skills, and beliefs that make him an integral member of his group. The fact that births are generally single makes such acculturation easier, and some primitive tribes will kill a newborn child

Our observations of some 30 troops of baboons, ranging in average membership from 40 to 80 individuals, in their natural setting in Africa show that the social behavior of the baboon is one of the species' principal adaptations for survival. Most of a baboon's life is spent within a few feet of other baboons. The troop affords protection from predators and an intimate group knowledge of the territory it occupies. Viewed from the inside, the troop is composed not of neutral creatures but of strongly emotional, highly motivated members. Our data offer little support for the theory that sexuality provides the primary bond of the primate troop. It is the intensely social nature of the baboon, expressed in a diversity of inter-individual relationships, that keeps the troop together. . . . It is clear . . . that these bonds are essential to compact group living and that for a baboon life in the troop is the only way of life that is feasible.

S. L. Washburn and I. DeVore [38]

7.10 *The family is the basic unit of social organization among various primate groups. Here, a female proboscis monkey caresses her infant, while the father appears to be watching for intruders.*

Marcel Marceau, one of the world's greatest mimes, speaks with gesture rather than words.

A searching examination needs to step back . . . from the mechanics of human language, and to ask . . . what are the global features that characterize it, and differentiate it from the sharp and immediate messages that are evoked in animals either by their internal state or by their environment. One such characterization is behavioral—human utterances are more detached or disengaged from the stimuli that provoke them than those of animals—and this is a general feature of human behavior. Another characterization is logical—human language relies on an analysis of the environment into parts which are assembled differently in different sentences. (By contrast, the signals of animals are complete utterances, which are not taken apart and assembled anew to make new messages.)

J. Bronowski and U. Bellugi [4]

if its older sibling has not completed the weaning phase. A litter of children would obviously be an evolutionary disaster: they could not be accommodated at their mother's breasts, they would sap a mother's strength and take her out of the economy of the tribe, and they would become literally and figuratively a cultural nuisance. Female sexual physiology, which determines that, as a rule, one fertilizable egg is produced during each menstrual cycle, prohibits the overburdening of a society with helpless and unproductive young. The increasing prolongation of adolescence and dependence of the young today is merely a continued exaggeration of an earlier prehistoric trend.

All of the above traits are biological features built into the genes of man. Each one was probably conservative and not sufficient to disturb seriously a traditional way of life, but each one nudged a group of animals a bit further along the evolutionary path that would lead to man. They were heritable changes and could therefore be acted upon by natural selection. They certainly appeared in less exaggerated form in vertebrate groups antecedent to man, but as they approached human expression they eventually led to a lessening of reliance on instinctual reactions and an increasing dependence on learned responses that become hardened into custom and tradition. The vehicle for the transmission of these cultural features is man's use of a language; it is language that sets man uniquely and unequivocally apart from all other living things.

It has not been possible to reconstruct the evolution of the human language in a satisfactory manner. There are no transitional languages in the sense that they reveal a step-by-step progression from the comparatively closed vocal systems of other animals—the imitative aspects of the myna

The uniqueness of man

It is easy to see why words may be the mark of a man. To illustrate with some extreme examples, what types of persons would frequently use words from each of the following three lists?

1) Square, pad, cool, crazy-man, real gone, far out, the most, chick.
2) Embolism, lacerated, prevent, determine, antibiotic, rest, superficial.
3) Woocide, milprayermachine, friendsin, brainsound, bumfort.

It is obvious what types of people would be likely to use words from the first two lists, and anyone familiar with the neologisms coined by some mental patients will know what type of person would use words from the third. Individual differences in word usage relate not only to obvious differences such as these but also to subtle differences in the ways people learn, perceive, and interact socially.

J. C. Nunnally and R. L. Flaugher [23]

---

bird, mockingbird, and parrot are exceptions of a sort—to the complexity, flexibility, and open-endedness of a human language. Even the most primitive tribes of today have a language as richly symbolic as any modern European tongue. Although a chimpanzee can learn, respond to, and display for its own purposes a wide variety of gestures, attempts to teach a chimpanzee a series of words ended in failure because of the animal's inability to interpret and articulate distinctly different word sounds or to discriminate among the nuances of an intricately and almost infinitely varied and modulated series of vocal sounds. It has been suggested that the great apes lack the language facility of man because they lack the neurological complexity necessary for speech. This is undoubtedly true, but it is equally true that their laryngeal apparatus is incapable of producing the subtle variations of human speech, which depend on coordinated use of tongue, jaws, and lips as well as the larynx. We have no difficulty with such English words as "were," "wear," or "wier," or "gnaw," "new," "know," and "now," but this is not only because we can produce and distinguish these nuances based on vowel sounds, but also because each sound, or combination of sounds, conjures up a different mental image to reinforce the auditory input. Language cannot be disassociated from imagination. As the contemporary English biologist Peter Medawar has expressed it: "Words are not merely the vehicles in which thought is delivered; they are part of thinking."

The vocal systems of other animals have been described as closed rather than open-ended as in man. The limitations, however, are extremely varied. In their attempt to identify various species, experienced bird watchers are as apt to rely on the song as on visual sighting. These sounds are as

7.11 *A yellow baboon vocalizing in a display of aggression.*

Mark Boulton photo, National Audubon Society

The uniqueness of man

Words may be good or bad tools; some outgrow their usefulness, others have to be invented to fill new needs. But the detailed imperfections of words must not blind us to the unique value of words in general. Readers of Helen Keller's autobiography will remember the moving passage when the little creature, blind, deaf and dumb since the age of a year and a half, suddenly realized that, as she put it, "everything has a name." She had already been taught various associations, had learnt to use simple signs, to recognize individual people and places, and to respond to some of the finger language of her teacher. But this day, when those fingers spelt out w-a-t-e-r on one of her hands, while her other hand was held under a spout of water in the well house, she realized that this particular combination of finger signs "*meant* the wonderful cool something" that she was feeling. . . . It was no longer just a sign of wanting or of expecting water; it was a *name*, by which this substance could be mentioned, conceived, remembered, and thought about—a conceptual symbol. This was her first revelation of the meaning of things; it freed her from the prison of her frustrated and under-developed selfhood, and rapidly admitted her to a share in the possibilities of human existence.

J. Huxley [21]

---

specifically unique as are certain musical passages from Vivaldi, Beethoven, or the Beatles. Among the primates, variation is also great, and it is unlikely that the pronounced social organization of primates could have developed in the absence of this vocal repertoire. The Old World monkeys are particularly vocal, although communication among the baboons is accomplished more by gestures than by sounds. Among the great apes, the orangutan emits only an occasional grunt or roar, whereas the gorilla roars impressively and beats his chest when disturbed, although he is generally a quiet animal. The chimpanzee has an amazing repertoire of sounds and gestures to express itself, particularly when young.

As in man, gestures and sounds are a means of communication among animals: for greeting and mating, to signal danger and the presence of food, and to pose threats. A. H. Schultz, a Swiss anthropologist, has referred to gestures as "an intricate and voluminous *silent vocabulary* of great aid in social intercourse." He also states, somewhat facetiously, that "The orgies of noise indulged in specially by howlers, querezas, gibbons, siamangs and chimpanzees, seemingly so repetitious and meaningless, are probably at least as informative to the respective species as most after-dinner speaking is to *Homo sapiens.*"

In the case of man, gestures are subordinate to language as a means of communication and expression. More importantly, however, the human language, coupled to the mind, can convey abstract ideas; it can put into auditory form concepts that may or may not bear a direct relationship to actual experience, concepts that permit man to reach into the past and look into the future and thus provide him with historical reference and patterns for action or thought to

The uniqueness of man

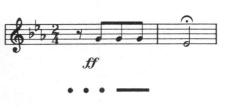

Three ways of expressing the letter V: *Winston Churchill flashing the* V-*sign for victory; the opening bars of Beethoven's* Symphony No. 5; *and the Morse code symbol for the letter* V. *The rhythm of the code matches that of the musical passage.*

come. Because of its open-endedness, human language can be the means for forming and reforming new combinations and patterns of sounds to describe new situations or new feelings. It can also be a means of comparison, projection, analysis, and control, of going from the particular to the general. Finally, it is a vehicle that a group can use to share the individual experiences of all of its members, thus leading to an enormous degree of experiential economy. Verbal signs therefore substitute symbols for objects, emotions, and situations.

Viewed in an adaptive sense, the human language, was a powerful cohesive and integrating force, unifying, molding, and eventually characterizing a group to whom these symbols have meaning and distinguishing this group from others whose verbal signals were different but equally effective. A cumulative tradition was established, a tradition that was transmitted at first from one generation to the next through the medium of folklore and was later made available to all generations of men when verbal signals became written signs. A new form of heredity thus came into existence. The ability to speak and to make use of linguistic expressions is a heritable trait, built into the genes of man. But the components of this new form of inheritance varied from one group of humans to another and thus had to be acquired anew in each individual. In other words they had to be learned as an individual moved from infancy into the ways of the tribe. As with biological inheritance, the elements of cultural inheritance change and evolve, and man therefore, unlike any other living thing, is the combined product of two distinct, but closely integrated, evolutionary systems. We shall deal with these two kinds of evolution in a later chapter.

Language has become far more than a means of communication in man. It is also one of the principal (although far from the only) means of thought, memory, introspection, problem-solving, and all other mental activities. The uniqueness and generality of human symbolization have given our mental activities not only a scope but also a quality far outside the range of other animals. It keeps us aware, to greater extent than can otherwise be, of past and future, of the continuity of existence and its extension beyond what is immediately sensed. Along with other peculiarly human capacities, it is involved in what I consider the most important human characteristic from an ethical point of view: foresight. It is the capacity to predict the outcome of our own actions that makes us responsible for them and that therefore makes ethical judgment of them both possible and necessary.

G. G. Simpson [30]

The uniqueness of man

Standard Oil Co. (N.J.)

On the disadvantages of being human

Like all other animals, man suffers the almost constant trauma inflicted by external agencies and by the wear and tear of his internal organs. He carries within him numerous micro-organisms, some of them pathogenic, and parasites often infect him. He is particularly susceptible to certain diseases, many of which, as far as we know, are unique to him. His cells, particularly late in life, tend to undergo neoplastic and malignant changes. His longevity makes him prone to degenerative diseases, especially of his nervous and cardiovascular systems. Some result from dietary or other excesses and deficiencies, but the causes of other diseases still elude us. Ironically some of the afflictions that beset modern man exist precisely because as *Homo sapiens*, the "wise man," he has managed to some degree to insure the survival and reproduction of individuals whose genetic constitution is so abnormal that they would have perished without his intervention. Some abnormalities alter the development of parts or whole organs and affect their function. Basic (congenital) disturbances in vital biochemical processes are caused by what are known as "inborn errors of metabolism." Failure of man's anatomical construction to meet the demands made on it by his physical pursuits often ends in disaster to the very physical endowments that equipped him to pursue such activities! Perhaps these pursuits too have a genetic background because man's genes make him the particular creature he is. Nonetheless, we consider them as particular attributes that spring from man's particularities. Other mammals, including subhuman primates, occasionally also exhibit certain "abnormal" conditions similar to ours, but we have as yet too little information about these matters.

R. J. Harrison and W. Montagna [17]

Sophocles once said: "Wonders there are many, but there is none so wonderful as man." Our egocentricity would scarcely admit of another opinion, but one likes to think that even an objective and dispassionate evolution would lead to no other conclusion but man. Nevertheless, any number of scientists, engineers, educators, and preachers have maintained that, had they been given the opportunity, they could have turned out a far better product than what has resulted from evolutionary trial and error. Editorial hindsight of course comes equipped with 20/20 vision. Evolution, on the other hand, is short-term, opportunistic, and without foresight, and so it is inevitable that the gradual development of man had "good" and "bad" features. Some of these disadvantageous features are innately biological, others stem from man's cultural aspects.

Many of man's abnormalities of structure and function are confined to individuals and are due to the expression of deleterious genes inherited from one or both parents. Diabetes, certain forms of dwarfism, and color blindness are examples of these. Others, however, are species characteristics. Hairlessness is one of these because it hastens heat loss and consequently sets the stage for an enhanced metabolic activity to counteract this loss. Man of course has learned to equip himself so as to cope with many different kinds of environments, but his hairlessness has required him to supplement his body heat with clothing, particularly outside the tropics and in the temperate zones, where the great advances in culture were made. In the tropics, protec-

The uniqueness of man

. . . And what would it be to grow old? For, after a certain distance, every step we take in life we find the ice growing thinner below our feet, and all around us and behind us we see our contemporaries going through. By the time a man gets well into the seventies, his continued existence is a mere miracle; and when he lays his old bones in bed for the night, there is an overwhelming probability that he will never see the day. Do the old men mind it, as a matter of fact? Why, no. They were never merrier; they have their grog at night, and tell the raciest stories; they hear of the death of people about their own age, or even younger, not as if it was a grisly warning, but with a simple childlike pleasure at having outlived someone else; and when a draught might puff them out like a guttering candle, or a bit of a stumble shatter them like so much glass, their old hearts keep sound and unaffrighted, and they go on, bubbling with laughter, through years of man's age compared to which the valley at Balaclava was as safe and peaceful as a village cricket-green on Sunday. . . .

Indeed, it is a memorable subject for consideration, with what unconcern and gaiety mankind pricks on along the Valley of the Shadow of Death. The whole way is one wilderness of snares, and the end of it, for those who fear the last pinch, is irrevocable ruin. And yet we go spinning through it all, like a party for the Derby. Perhaps the reader remembers one of the humorous devices of the deified Caligula: how he encouraged a vast concourse of holiday-makers on to his bridge over Baiae bay; and when they were in the height of their enjoyment, turned loose the Praetorian guards among the company, and had them tossed into the sea. This is no bad miniature of the dealings of nature with the transitory race of man. Only, what a chequered picnic we have of it, even while it lasts! and into what great waters, not to be crossed by any swimmer, God's pale Praetorian throws us over in the end!

R. L. Stevenson [32]

---

tion against excessive sunlight also requires a form of skin protection; the less pigmented the skin, the greater the protection needed, although it should be emphasized that there is a vitamin D relation to skin color as well. That is, sunlight interacting with the skin leads to the formation of vitamin D, a necessary metabolic chemical involved in calcium absorption and incorporation, but too much of it is as detrimental as too little, and skin color can possibly act as a regulating mechanism. On the other hand, would a fur pelt have served him better than hairlessness? Would such covering have delayed his control of fire for warmth and cooking, and eventually for the smelting of ore and the refinement of metals for weapons and tools? We can only speculate.

Man's anatomical defects are more serious. He has a useless vermiform appendix, tonsils that seem to have but little function, and nasal sinuses that drain poorly; all are subject to frequent and often serious infection. His skull, protecting his all-important brain, is thin and easily damaged; his throat is so constructed that he cannot swallow and breathe simultaneously; and his internal viscera, adapted initially to a quadripedal stance, are not fully rearranged for a bipedal posture. The bony skeleton shows mechanical defects. The thrust of weight of the upper body down through the pelvis places a strain on the lower (lumbar) vertebrae and can cause a rupture of the intervertebral discs; the pelvis is so constructed to make the birth of a large-headed child a hazardous experience; the hip, knee, and ankle joints, no one of them an engineer's model of perfection, are readily subject to sprains and dislocations; and the arches of the feet frequently break down. If these constructions are as poorly conceived as they appear to be, one

7.12 Swollen arthritic hands, evidence of man's anatomical imperfection.

Merck Sharp & Dohme

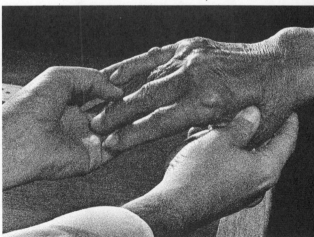

The uniqueness of man

While the subculture of youth has been examined, psychoanalyzed, photographed, deplored and envied, few have wanted even to admit the existence of a subculture of the aged, with its implications of segregation and alienation. Strangely enough, the aged have a lot in common with youth: they are largely unemployed, introspective and often depressed; their bodies and psyches are in the process of change, and they are heavy users of drugs. If they want to marry, their families tend to disapprove. Both groups are obsessed with time. Youth, though, figures its passage from birth; the aged calculate backward from their death day. They sometimes shorten the wait: the suicide rate among elderly men is far higher than that of any other age group.

Time [24]

Ageing is an unpopular process with man—it means that at the height of his status, experience, and skill he gradually finds his strength and health leaving him, until death or invalidism force him out of business. It is a depressing prospect—more so than that of sudden death at an unforeseeable age. Accordingly throughout history one of the favourite human fantasies has been that of getting the better of age. There were legends of physical immortality, and magical ways of getting it. The goddess Aurora prayed for immortality for her mortal lover Tithonus but forgot to pray for eternal youth—Tithonus accordingly lived on and on, becoming more and more senile and decrepit; until he prayed for death. It used to be thought that if only we could control all individual diseases, one by one, the human life-span could be pushed up to 100–120 or more. This has proved a fallacy. The chief characteristic of human ageing is that although one organ may be harder hit than another, there is a general increase in the vulnerability of the whole; cure one disease and another appears. From the changes in the shape of the curve of survival with improved medical knowledge, it seems clear that while in time we might by this means get practically everyone through adulthood to the seventies, nearly all will still be dead by the age of ninety. Improved medicine, moreover, can postpone death without increasing vigour or preventing physical and mental decline, and we have found ourselves producing Tithonuses—kept alive by medicine, but not able to enjoy the extra time given to them.

A. Comfort [6]

must wonder how man made the evolutionary grade. The answer must be that, singly and in combination, the advantage of these features far outweigh their disadvantages. Each, of course, could evolve only through modification of that which preceded it, and, as such, each feature represents a compromise rather than a totally new system or structure devised to meet a specific need.

Many of these defects do not show up until middle and old age, when time exerts its erosive effect on bone, tissues, and mind. Old age, however, does not make postreproductive individuals superfluous members of a tribe; they are valuable in a cultural sense in that they are the repositories of tribal lore and customs, the principal transmitters of culture from one generation to the next. Hence they are stabilizing elements. But at the time when man was emerging from a prehuman past and probably as late as the beginnings of recorded history, old age was reached considerably sooner than it is today. If one defines "senescence" as the increase of one's liability to succumb to the external environment, natural selection at the time of man's emergence was operating on a very differently structured human population than that of today. At present, postreproductive status for women is not reached until they have passed well beyond 40 years of age, and men have a considerably longer reproductive span. Prehistoric man probably had an average life span of 25 to 35 years, less than half that of today.

Man, as a species, is longer-lived than most other mammals, and his average life span is increasing as the result of modern nutrition and medicine (see table 7.1). The perfection of organ transplantation may extend his life span even further, at least for a favored few. Viewed in an evolutionary sense, however, prolonged old age is culturally,

The uniqueness of man

Persons who have led full, active, and productive lives often find that those things that in earlier years gave them pleasure are now suddenly beyond both their physical and mental ability. Some persons in anticipation of retirement years cultivate secondary, less demanding skills for use and enjoyment during the final period of their lives; these are the lucky ones who reap the joy of relaxing with their hobbies. Others are not so farsighted; they assume that their abilities will last forever or, more likely, that they will die in the harness before the onset of physical debilitation. Among the latter are the James Forrestals and the Ernest Hemingways of the world. For these persons a world in which they play no role palls, and they want to get out of it. Are the desires of these persons—persons greatly respected for much of their lives—now to be denied? Are strangers to urge them to reprogram their lives so that they raise flowers as an escape from boredom? If these once active persons argue that death is preferable to sustained boredom, must this attitude be interpreted as a sign of insanity? I cannot believe that it should be so.

B. Wallace [36]

---

perhaps even biologically, disadvantageous. Independent of any humanitarian, religious, or emotional values one may have regarding the sanctity of life and its preservation at all costs, the postreproductive and postproductive individual is a species and a social luxury now that the written word has supplanted the elderly as the transmitter of human lore. This luxury will become increasingly evident as population pressures increase, as automation takes over many of the tasks of our culture, and as resources for living become strained. The industrially developed nations accommodate partially to this situation by prolonging the dependence of the young, thus delaying their procreative and productive possibilities. This is culturally, but not biologically, advantageous. The old are retired early, and the formation of senior-citizen's groups is a compensatory move to offset the loneliness and loss of dignity brought on by an unwanted state of unproductiveness. Biologically, the young are necessary for the continuation of the species, but the old, with few exceptions, are a drain on a limited environment.

Another, uniquely human disadvantage brought on by old age, in this instance peculiar to women, is the phenomenon of menopause. Monkeys and apes continue menstruation beyond reproductive age, when the ovaries have been depleted of viable eggs, but menopause is unknown in these animals. Some physicians view menopause as an unnatural, pathological state; certainly the discomfort, tension, and possible mental instability brought on by changes in hormonal level are evolutionary disadvantages, even though they can be ameliorated by medication. In earlier periods of man's history, when the average life span was 35 years or less, death probably preceded menopause. There is some indication that menopause occurs at a more advanced age

Table 7.1	Maximum life spans of some common vertebrates*	
		Years
Fishes	Common eel	15
	Pike	40
	Rainbow trout	5
Amphibians	Bullfrog	15
	Leopard frog	6
	Spring peeper	7
	Common toad	15
Reptiles	Rattlesnake	22
	American alligator	56
	Nile crocodile	40
	Galapagos tortoise	100
Birds	Common pigeon	30
	Parrot	54
	Crow	69
	Warbler	8
	Duck	19
	Swan	30
Mammals	Elephant	77 (40)
	Dog	34 (13–17)
	Cat	31 (13–17)
	Laboratory mouse	3
	Horse	50 (20–30)
Primates	Gorilla	26
	Chimpanzee	37 (15–20)
	Gibbon	23
	Tarsier	12
	Lemur	25 (7–10)
	Tree shrew	3
	Man	120 (70)

*Most of these records are for animals kept in captivity and free from predation. Comparable records for the same animals in the wild would show lower values. Average life spans, when known, are shown in parentheses.

The uniqueness of man

Sabine Weiss photo, Rapho Guillumette Pictures

The specific purpose of menstruation is obscure. Not least of its imponderables is why it should occur only in certain primates. It would seem to be a waste of tissue and essential substances, such as iron. Several hundred milliliters of blood are lost each month and this is obviously a drain on a woman's reserves and a constant call on her blood-forming bone marrow. Apart from its social disadvantages and discomfort, it often leads to tiredness, bad temper, and anemia. From a biological point of view, menstruation should not occur at all!

R. J. Harrison and W. Montagna [17]

than previously, but it is unlikely that this phenomenon can be viewed today as an adaptive trait. One possible exception to this is that termination of the reproductive cycle after a certain period prohibits child-bearing at a time when the frequency of abnormal offspring is rising, but when the sexual drives have not tapered off in parallel fashion. For example, the frequency of birth of children exhibiting Down's syndrome (Mongolian idiocy) is about six times greater after age 40 than during the earlier reproductive years. This danger could have been avoided, as it is in other higher primates, by ovarian depletion alone, but for some as yet inexplicable reason menopause was inserted into the human life cycle.

Man clings tenaciously to life, as does any other animal, but if cures for heart disease, cancer, and stroke were suddenly to be realized, along with an effective all-purpose antibiotic for infectious diseases, they would constitute, in our present social and scientific state, a disaster of tremendous magnitude unless other degenerative aspects of senescence were also alleviated or overcome. Society would be burdened with an increasing number of unproductive, and unfortunately, unwanted elders. Even though euthanasia is at present morally reprehensible and medically unethical, society may, in the not too distant future, be forced to a serious consideration of death control in the same manner that it is now concerned with birth control. In the past, wars have served traditionally as mechanisms for removing large numbers of young males from the potential breeding pool, thus placing a greater societal value on the older segment of the population, but if war can be eliminated as an intraspecific activity, the youth/age ratios between

The uniqueness of man

Gregor photo, Monkmeyer Press Photo Service

young and old and between the productive and unproductive members of society will undergo significant change.

The development of culture, particularly the aggregation of individuals into larger and larger social groups, generates its own set of problems and undoubtedly influences the biology of man and the direction of his evolution. It seems that man pays a price for communal existence. During the early stages of man's existence, when he moved in small groups as a nomadic hunter, he could, as Garn emphasizes, "outwalk or outrun both parasites and vermin, twin hazards of permanent civilization." The communicable diseases—tuberculosis, smallpox, typhus, typhoid, malaria, cholera, among others—thrive in settled, dense conditions of habitation. The problems of sanitation and waste disposal, brought on by human concentrations, accentuate the spread of disease as disease carriers such as lice, flies, and rats flourish on man's doorstep. Until recently, wars were terminated more often by epidemics among the troops than by the actual conquest of one army by another. As ecological factors, therefore, diseases can have a profound influence on human evolution, with man himself the unknowing agent of dissemination. The white man of Europe, for example, is tolerably resistant to many common respiratory ailments and to smallpox, measles, and tuberculosis; he has lived with them for millennia and has acquired a measure of natural immunity. When he came in contact with the previously unexposed populations of Indians and Eskimos of North America, however, he unwittingly brought his diseases with him and introduced them into a highly susceptible population with devastating results.

Malaria is another case in point, for it is man and his

In this age of specialization we seem to have lost contact with the daily reminders that must have driven home the truth to our ancestors; man cannot live without harvesting plants or killing animals. If plants wither and die and animals fail to reproduce, man will sicken and die and fail to maintain his kind. As individuals we cannot afford to leave our destiny in the hands of scientists, engineers, technologists, and politicians who have forgotten or who never knew these simple truths. In our modern world we have botanists who study plants and zoologists who study animals, but most of them are specialists who do not deal with the ramifications of their limited knowledge. Today we need biologists who respect the fragile web of life and who can broaden their knowledge to include the nature of man and his relation to the biological and physical worlds. We need biologists who can tell us what we can and must do to survive and what we cannot and must not do if we hope to maintain and improve the quality of life during the next three decades. The fate of the world [of man] rests on the integration, preservation, and extension of the knowledge that is possessed by a relatively small number of men who are only just beginning to realize how inadequate their strength, how enormous the task. . . . What is needed is a new discipline to provide models of life styles for people who can communicate with each other and propose and explain the new public policies that could provide a "bridge to the future." . . . Is it man's fate to be to the living Earth what cancer is to Man?

V. R. Potter [27]

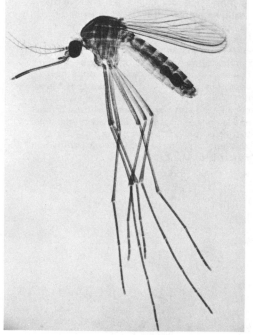

. . . Now the man who has his heart on his sleeve, and a good whirling weathercock of a brain, who reckons his life as a thing to be dashingly used and cheerfully hazarded, makes a very different acquaintance of the world, keeps all his pulses going true and fast, and gathers impetus as he runs, until, if he be running towards anything better than wildfire, he may shoot up and become a constellation in the end . . . . Who would find heart enough to begin to live, if he dallied with the consideration of death? . . . Does not life go down with a better grace, foaming in full body over a precipice, than miserably straggling to an end in sandy deltas? When the Greeks made their fine saying that those whom the gods love die young, I cannot help believing they had this sort of death also in their eye. For surely, at whatever age it overtake the man, this is to die young. Death has not been suffered to take so much as an illusion from his heart. In the hot-fit of life, a-tiptoe on the highest point of being, he passes at a bound on to the other side. The noise of the mallet and chisel is scarcely quenched, the trumpets are hardly done blowing, when, trailing with him clouds of glory, this happy-starred, full-blooded spirit shoots into the spiritual land.

R. L. Stevenson [32]

7.13 *Some disease carriers that plague man:*
(a) *flea;* (b) *Lone Star tick;* (c) Culex *mosquito.*

(a) (b) Carolina Biological Supply Company

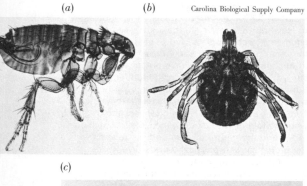

(c)

mode of existence that makes malaria so serious a disease, with an appalling toll of human lives and energy in tropical countries. In Africa, it was the slash-and-burn type of agriculture that opened up the forest areas and provided the breeding places for the malaria-carrying mosquito. Certain abnormal hemoglobins and proteins of man—the hemoglobin responsible for sickle-cell anemia in Africa, the abnormal hemoglobin associated with thalassemia in Europe and the Middle East, and the enzyme (galactose phosphate dehydrogenese) deficiency in red blood cells—owe their persistence in man to the malarial parasite, for it can utilize only the normal hemoglobins in completing its life cycle. It is not the nomad who provides a reservoir of infection, but the settled villager. It is estimated that one-quarter to one-half of Europe's population died from the Black Death in the fourteenth century; such an epidemic, which is only one of many that have swept parts of the earth, cannot but affect the biology of man, particularly his genetic composition, because varying degrees of resistance are present in any population. Settled conditions also promote single-crop agriculture, a practice that leads to protein deficiencies and enhanced susceptibilities to infection and dysenteries. These conditions still persist in many parts of the underdeveloped world, while in more advanced countries, tension and various kinds of pollution, possibly including informational pollution, become evolutionary pressures. We are only dimly aware of the ultimate effect of culture on man's biological nature. Although the road from the protohumans to twentieth-century man has led to man's complete domination of the face of the earth, the development of the human species has not been a sequence of unmitigated blessings.

The uniqueness of man

The races of man

Man belongs to a single species, *Homo sapiens*, but he is a species within which distinct and distinguishable groups of individuals are evident. These are referred to as races. These two categories can be separated on the basis of breeding potentialities. A species represents a closed system; except for very rare exceptions, its members can breed only within the group. Man, for example, cannot interbreed with any other species. The horse (*Equus caballus*) can be bred with the ass (*Equus asinus*), but its offspring, the mule, is sterile. Races, on the other hand, are open breeding systems, and no sterility barrier separates one race from another. It is unlikely that an Eskimo of the Arctic would, under normal circumstances, breed with an Australian aborigine, but we have no reason to believe that they could not breed and produce fertile offspring. Races, however, are incipient species, and the fact that races may be at the beginning or the end of separation from a parental stock, and with many or few shared characteristics, leads to difficulty in classification and definition. These difficulties are increased when cultural as well as biological criteria are used. Breeds are the canine equivalent of races. If the St. Bernard and the Pekingese were the only two breeds of dogs in existence, and if they had been discovered wild instead of being artifically bred by man, they would undoubtedly have been classified as two distinct species. Their size differences alone would have made interbreeding difficult, and although they are known to be interfertile, separation from

A race may be defined as a biologically inbred human group with distinctive physical traits that tend to breed true from generation to generation. For the most part, the traits that are used to differentiate races are the obvious, the visible, the physical qualities that characterize large groups of people. The anthropologist and biologist, therefore, simply take for granted the thousands of more subtle, not-so-obvious, anatomical and biological similarities that exist between races, while highlighting differences. Once we are sure that both horses and cats are mammals, the known similarities underpin a subsequent search for specific differences and the establishment of new categories. Once we know that both men and apes are primates, our attention may turn to the classifiable differences between the two. In cataloging dogs, we implicitly recognize their common caninity, but we explicitly point out breed differences. In like manner, we approach human variation with the realistic acknowledgment that all races have many thousands more biological traits in common than they have traits that distinguish them. Such an acknowledgment does not deny the fact of race; it indicates that the traits we share make us mammals, primates, and humans, whereas the others make us races.

J. Conrad [7]

The uniqueness of man

After the Great Spirit formed the world, he made the various birds and beasts which now inhabit it. He also made man, but having formed him white and very imperfect and ill-tempered he placed him on one side of it where he now inhabits and from whence he has lately found a passage across the water to be a plague to us. As the Great Spirit was not pleased with his work, he took of black clay and made what you call a Negro with a wooly head. This black man was made better than the white man, but still he did not answer the wish of the Great Spirit; that is, he was imperfect. At last, the Great Spirit, having procured a piece of pure red clay, formed from it the Red Man, perfectly to his mind, and he was so well pleased with him that he placed him on this great island, separate from the white and black men; and gave him rules for his conduct, promising happiness in proportion as they should be observed.

Iroquois Myth

Race is not synonymous with language, culture, or nationality. Race is hereditary; language is a cultural acquisition. A Negro may speak English as his native tongue. There is no Aryan race; Aryan is a term applicable only to a family of languages spoken by populations heterogeneous in race, nationality, religion, and other aspects of culture. There is no "French race" and no "German race," properly so-called. Such terms imply nationality, use of a common language, and some degree of conformity to a pattern of culture, but nothing more.

A "pure" race is little more than an anthropological abstraction; no pure race can be found in any civilized country. Racial purity is restricted, at best, to remnants of savage groups in isolated wildernesses. The present races of man have intermingled and interbred for many thousands of years so that their genealogical lines have become inextricably confused. Physical classifications of race merely attempt to delimit groups of approximate physical uniformity, with a restricted assumption of similar heredity.

Each racial type runs the gamut from idiots and criminals to geniuses and statesmen. No type produces a majority of individuals from either end of the scale. While there may be specific racial abilities and disabilities, these have not yet been demonstrated. There are no racial monopolies either of human virtues or of vices.

E. A. Hooton [20]

each other over long periods of time would have led to the development of an actual and potential breeding barrier.

We have very little information concerning the origin of the human races. Such origins must, of course, be based on fossil evidence, and, although it is possible to identify the major races by characteristics of the bony skeleton, the fossil evidence is scanty indeed. Cro-Magnon man of 35,000 years ago had distinctly Caucasian characteristics, whereas skulls of similar age from China are definitely not Caucasian. Skeletal remains in America, considered to date from about 20,000 B.C., are recognizably those of American Indians. Definite Negroid remains are so few as to make the time of their origin uncertain. The time and place of origin of human races must therefore remain unanswered for the moment, and we leave equally unanswered the question of whether the human species arose from one or several ancestral stocks, although the single-stock hypothesis is more likely. Nevertheless, it is reasonable to assume that a considerable diversity had arisen in the human species as long as 50,000 or 100,000 years ago (perhaps even 1 million years ago) and that these differences became accentuated as small groups, moving on foot, came to occupy different environmental regions of the earth and formed isolated breeding groups. Each group had a unique genetic composition that probably differed from that of any other isolated group. It could also have differed from the genetic makeup of the parental stock from which it had broken off. Each group was acted upon by different environmental pressures as natural selection proceeded. These adaptive changes were further reinforced or modified as cultural innovations came into existence at a later time. Spreading out during the brute stage of evolution during which they used only crude stone

The uniqueness of man

Now the whole earth had one language and few words. And as man migrated from the east, they found a plain in the land of Shinar and settled there. . . . Then they said, "Come, let us build ourselves a city, and a tower with its top in the heavens, and let us make a name for ourselves, lest we be scattered abroad upon the face of the whole earth."

And the lord came down to see the city and the tower, which the sons of men had built. And the Lord said, "Behold, they are one people, and they have all one language; and this is only the beginning of what they will do; and nothing that they propose to do will now be impossible for them. Come, let us go down, and there confuse their language, that they may not understand one another's speech." So the Lord scattered them abroad from there over the face of the earth, and left off building the city. Therefore its name was called Babel, because there the Lord confused the language of all the earth; and there the Lord scattered them abroad over the face of all the earth.

Genesis 11

---

implements, each group emerged as a distinct entity with a full panoply of racially characteristic features.

A word needs to be said about the role of isolated populations in the development and preservation of species diversity and in the formation of new species. It is a phenomenon known technically as *genetic drift,* and it illustrates the *founder effect.* When a population of any organism, plant or animal, is so constructed that any member can breed potentially with any other member of the opposite sex, the gene pool—the entire pool from which heritable material is transmitted from one generation to the next—remains essentially intact. It is added to only by new mutations and lessened only by those mutations that are somehow lost. When a segment of the population breaks free of the main group and no longer interbreeds with it, it carries with it only a segment of the gene pool. The smaller the isolated group, the less representative of the larger group it is likely to be. It may carry certain heritable traits that then come to characterize the entire group as a result of inbreeding. For example, all members of the Old Order Amish of Lancaster County, Pennsylvania, trace themselves to three married couples (the *founders*) who came to America from Germany in 1770. The group has stayed intact and has not interbred to any extent with the surrounding population. Comprised now of about 8,000 individuals, they possess a genetic composition that is different from that found among the inhabitants of the German region they left. It also differs from the genetic composition of those who inhabit the surrounding area in Pennsylvania. In particular, one heritable trait, dwarfism accompanied by polydactyly (extra fingers), appears frequently (61 individuals) among its members, whereas the same trait is exceedingly rare in the general

7.14 *Old Order Amish at Hershey Park, Hershey, Pennsylvania. Because the Amish breed almost exclusively within their own group, they have become a classic example of the founder effect.*

Strickler photo, Monkmeyer Press Photo Service

The uniqueness of man

The human species, according to the best theory I can form of it, is composed of two distinct races, *the men who borrow,* and *the men who lend.* To these two original diversities may be reduced all those impertinent classifications of Gothic and Celtic tribes, white men, black men, red men. All the dwellers upon earth, "Parthians, and Medes, and Elamites," flock hither, and do naturally fall in with one or other of these primary distinctions. The infinite superiority of the former, which I choose to designate as the *great race,* is discernible in their figure, port, and a certain instinctive sovereignty. The latter are born degraded. "He shall serve his brethren." There is something in the air of one of this cast, lean and suspicious; contrasting with the open, trusting, generous manners of the other.

Observe who have been the greatest borrowers of all ages—Alcibiades—Falstaff—Sir Richard Steel—our late imcomparable Brinsley—what a family likeness in all four!

What a careless, even deportment hath your borrower! what rosy gills! what a beautiful reliance on Providence doth he manifest, taking no more thought than lilies! What contempt for money,—accounting it (yours and mine especially) no better than dross. . . .

He is the true taxer "who calleth all the world up to be taxed"; . . . His exactions, too, have such a cheerful voluntary air! So far removed from your sour parochial or state-gatherers, —those ink-horn varlets, who carry their want of welcome in their faces! He cometh to you with a smile, and troubleth you with no receipt; confining himself to no set season. Every day is his Candlemas, or his Feast of Holy Michael. . . .

C. Lamb [22]

7.15 *Because of continued inbreeding, albinism occurs more frequently among the San Blas Indians of Panama than it does among more cosmopolitan groups. This tribe holds albinos in special esteem because they are thought to be favored by the gods. In this photo, the albino near the center of the group holds her normal child.*

population. Undoubtedly, one of the founders carried the gene, and it subsequently spread throughout the group. A population of fisherfolk on an island in the St. Lawrence River shows a high incidence of muscular dystrophy, and some isolated villages in the Appalachian Mountains evidence similar frequencies of albinism or idiocies. All are heritable traits and can be traced in all likelihood to one or more members of the founding group. It is a reasonable assumption that when mankind consisted of small nomadic groups, those traits now characteristic of races were present in one or more members of the group and, whether advantageous or not, persisted because of inbreeding. Other traits, although racially characteristic, are more obviously adaptive.

Races are difficult to define simply because they are fluid parts of a species, because, with rare exceptions, the traits present in them are not exclusive possessions, and because classification is a matter of convenience or approach, not simply a reflection of recognizable differences. Human races have been defined on many bases: head shape, hair character, skin color, geography, and blood groups, to name those most frequently used. Some anthropologists have viewed mankind as consisting of three major races—Caucasoids, Mongoloids, and Negroids—with a varying number of subdivisions, while others have defined as many as thirty-two races. The two extremes in classification systems are equally valid; they depend upon different aims and methodology, but they do not call into question the concept of racial distinctions. Despite their fluidity, which today is increasing as a result of greater mobility and interracial marriages, races are a biological reality. They indicate that mankind is genetically diverse and that this diversity is not uniformly spread throughout the world's population. We may subscribe

The uniqueness of man

. . . In the extinction of religions, in imperial revolutions, in the bloody conflict of ideas, there is one thing found stable; it is the mind itself, growing through ages. That which in its continuity we call the human spirit, abides. Men, tribes, states disappear, but the race-mind endures. A conception of the world and an emotional response thereto constitute the life of the race-mind, and fill its consciousness with ideas and feelings, but in these there is no element of chance, contingency or frailty; they are master-ideas, master-emotions, clothed with the power of a long reign over men, and imposing themselves upon each new generation, almost with the yoke of necessity. What I designate as the race-mind—the sole thing permanent in history—is this potentiality of thought and feeling, in any age, realizing itself in states of mind and habits of action long established in the race, deeply inherited, and slowly modified. The race-mind is the epitome of the past. It contains all human energy, knowledge, experience, that survives. It is the resultant of millions of lives whose earthly power it stores in one deathless force.

G. E. Woodberry [40]

to the notion that all men are born equal, but we should recognize this as a cultural goal based on equality of opportunity, and we should not confuse it with the heritable differences that stem from our biological backgrounds. As the geneticist Theodosius Dobzhansky has written: "Equality is not the same thing as identity, and inequality does not necessarily follow from diversity or variety. . . . The differences among people can be seen, measured and studied, . . . equality and inequality are not biological phenomena at all; they are political, ethical or religious principles."

Here we will concern ourselves with four of the major races of man, races that probably had their origins early in the history of man and before cultural innovations stamped man with national, religious, and ethnic identities. These are Eurasians, Africans, Mongoloids, and Australoids.

The Eurasians, also known as the Caucasoids or "white" race, are basically Europeans, but are represented also by peoples of southern India and the Hamitic and Semitic tribes of North and East Africa and the Middle East. Exceedingly diverse in character, they were energetic, far-ranging people, with their diversity due as much to accidental genetic drift as to positive adaptation to environmental conditions. Their original center of dispersal remains unknown, although it

7.16 *Three types of Eurasians (Caucasoids):* (a) *a Danish ferry passenger;* (b) *Ukrainians in native dress;* (c) *an Indian tailor.*

(a) Standard Oil Co. (N.J.) (b) Canadian National Film Board (c) J. Jaquier photo, UNESCO

The valiant pre-historic Aryans
Suppressed all neighboring barbarians.

Their progeny, the Indo-Germans,
Preached culture, using swords as sermons.

From them derived the warlike Teutons
Who cut the Romans up in croutons,

And they begat the Goths and Vandals
Whose raids are celebrated scandals.

From all these strains and many others,
Diverse, yet close as sons and brothers,

Arose our modern Nordic heroes,
To whom all other breeds are zeroes.
        A. Guiterman [16]

7.17   *Two examples of human adaptation to
climate. The long limbs and high surface-to-
volume ratio of the Nilotic Negro facilitates
the dissipation of unneeded body heat, whereas
the short limbs and low surface-to-volume
ratio of the Eskimo aids in its retention.
The epicanthic fold that characterizes the
eyes of Mongoloids is also thought to be an
adaptation to environment, in this case to the
cold and glare of harsh northern climates.*

is likely that man moved out of the tropics into temperate zones only after he invented clothing and learned to control fire. As stated above, Cro-Magnon man was definitely Eurasian, being tall, with a long, narrow skull, a large braincase, thin lips, a straight and prominent nose, a high forehead and prominent chin, all of which gave his face a flat aspect in a vertical plane. Cro-Magnon remains have been found on both sides of the Mediterranean, and skulls with Caucasoid features appear in deposits in the Rift Valley of Kenya. The heavy browridges, powerful jaws, and sloping forehead of the Neanderthal man are missing, but some variant Neanderthal skulls as well as those of the Swanscombe man (England, 250,000 years old) and Steinheim man (Germany, somewhat more recent) show modern features and may be ancestral to Cro-Magnon man.

The large braincases of both the Cro-Magnon and Neanderthal men suggest an intellectual capability of dealing with the drastically changing conditions of the Pleistocene epoch. Their physical features—skin, body build, and length of extremities—are intermediate in nature and were probably adapted to a changing environment rather than to extremes of heat or cold. It should be emphasized, however, that solid evidence in support of the adaptive nature of racial traits is scanty indeed. The Eurasians as a group were still sepa-

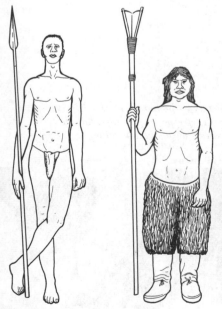

Nilotic Negro   Eskimo

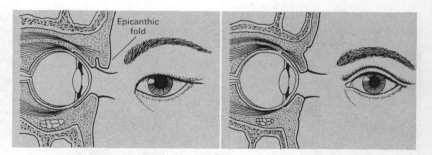

Epicanthic
fold

Mongoloid   Other races

The evidence of history and of prehistory, seen in the light of genetics, is unmistakable. Differentiation within nations has always arisen, so far as we can trace it, from a mixture of races. In Greece and Italy, in Britain and Russia, no less than in India and the Middle East the nuclei of class structure, the foci of discontinuity, have been established from the mingling, friendly or forcible, of different races.

On this view, introduced genetic differences, whether racial or tribal, have sown the seeds of social differentiation and the co-operation of dissimilar individuals out of which the richness of human cultural development has arisen. How have these seeds germinated? All stratified societies that have survived (and there are some to-day which may not survive) have permitted a limited inter-breeding between the stratified groups: slaves could be freed, freemen ennobled and the Brahmin's offspring might sink to a lower social level. Roman Emperors and Indian Kings have by legislation and by direct action controlled these processes with the evident intention of controlling evolutionary change. The development of class society has depended on the slow and controlled mixture of the materials brought together in this way, mixture subject to the processes of mating, promotion and migration, all of them socially selective, and selecting differently in different societies.

C. D. Darlington [8]

---

rated from the Africans to the south by the Mediterranean Sea and the developing Sahara Desert and from the Mongoloids to the east and north by mountain ranges, keeping the races separate until the retreat of the Pleistocene ice some 10,000 years ago.

Basing their opinion on 35,000-year-old skulls bearing incipient Mongoloid features, most anthropologists assert that the Mongoloids originated in northeastern Asia from an ancient white race. Characterized by yellow skin, straight black hair, relatively sparse beard and body hair, round head, flat face with flaring cheek bones, thick-set body, and an epicanthic fold (a prolongation of a fold of the skin) of the eyelids, the Mongoloids have been considered to be adaptations to a cold and harsh northern climate. Two so-called rules derived from a study of animal species, but seemingly applicable to human beings as well, are important in considering the physical appearance of the Mongoloids: Bergman's rule states that the surface-to-volume ratio of those inhabiting colder climates is smaller than that of those who live in the tropics; Allen's rule states that inhabitants of colder climates have shorter extremities—legs, arms, toes, fingers, ears, nose, and so on—than those in the tropics. Both rules relate to the retention or loss of body heat, and an Eskimo, a representative of the early Mongoloids, supports these contentions in that he is short, has a squat build and short extremities, and his body is covered with a subcutaneous layer of fat. An examination of the physical appearance a typical inhabitant of a tropical region would also confirm these two laws (see illustration 7.17).

The early Mongoloids existed prior to the disappearance of the glacial ice, during which time they occupied the Asian coast into inland China and extended their range into North

The adaptations of the Mongoloids provide an excellent example of the rapid alteration of gene frequencies in response to natural selection under severe conditions. Where the climate is favourable, the organism is not taxed and there is no need for change; where conditions are rigorous, however, advantageous mutations have a high selective value.

Of the special adaptations to climate, none is so striking as those for conditions of dry cold. The people who live in the coldest part of the earth are the Tungus of eastern Siberia, where a temperature of −96° F. has been recorded. They are the most extreme Mongoloids, with short, thick-set bodies, flat faces, fat-lidded eyes, coarse black hair and scanty beard and body hair. These features probably developed in response to the extreme cold of the last glacial period, the peak of which was about 25,000 years ago. The people of northern Europe and northern Asia then lived in isolated communities surrounded by ice and either they became adjusted or became extinct. Such conditions were ideal for adaptive changes of an extreme kind. The face became moulded by "climatic engineering." . . . The system of the nasal passage had to be deep to heat the air on its way to the lungs. This meant a forward movement of the cheek-bones, reducing the salient of the nose extending the eye sockets vertically, and a reduction in the brow-ridges. The Mongoloid face, in fact, developed as a result of the flattening of protuberances to reduce the surface area to a minimum. . . . It was then padded with fat to prevent loss of heat. Beardlessness, too, may have some selective value since moisture from the breath would freeze on the beard and so freeze the face underneath.

S. Cole [5]

The uniqueness of man

Eskimo fishermen in northwestern Canada.

Canadian National Film Board

Races of man have, or perhaps one should say "had," exactly the same biological significance as the subspecies of other species of mammals. Widespread animals have local populations that live under diverse conditions and that may become temporarily and in part isolated from each other. They may then more or less accidentally have different proportions of genes (in stricter technical language, of alleles) from other such populations, and if the situation continues long enough, they will almost inevitably evolve somewhat different adaptations to local conditions. Primitive men were relatively few in number and relatively immobile, but they spread over enormous areas—the whole land area of the earth except for Antarctica and a few small islands. They evolved into races or, in better biological terms, into subspecies exactly as any other animal would have under those circumstances. Racial differentiation in man was originally geographic and, for the most part, adaptive.

That was the original biological significance of race. One must say that Negroes were biologically superior to whites, if reference is to prehistoric times, when the races were originating, and to African conditions, to which Negroes were biologically adapted and whites were not. At the present time race has virtually no strictly biological significance because of two crucial changes. First, human adaptation to different environments is now mostly cultural and is directly biological only in lesser part, so that the prehistoric biological adaptations have lost much of their importance. Second, tremendous increases in population size, in mobility, and in environmental changes brought about by man himself have the result that extremely few men are now living under the conditions to which their ancestors were racially adapted.

G. G. Simpson [31]

and South America where they gave rise to the great variety of Indian tribes. The later Mongoloids, after 8000 B.C., gradually fanned out into the Asian continent, Eastern Europe, Malaya, and Indonesia. Their acquisition of the horse about 500 B.C. as a mode of transportation greatly increased their rate of expansion. Those that moved south lost the adaptations to cold—squat bodies, short legs, and body fat—and have acquired, perhaps through intermixture with other races, the more graceful proportions of the Indonesians. The flat face remains, however, as an indication of origin.

The African race includes a variety of Negro types: the typical Negro inhabiting the area south of the Sahara Desert and east to the Indian Ocean, the shorter Bushmen and Hottentots of South Africa, and the still shorter pygmies of Central Africa, India, the East Indies, and the Philippines. The relationship of these groups to one another is uncertain, as is the ancestral stock. They are characterized generally by dark skin, broad nasal apertures, everted lips, woolly hair, sparse beard and body hair, and a large surface-to-volume ratio, which fosters ready heat dispersal. The high surface-to-volume ratio is found among all Negro types despite great height variation, from the very short pygmies to the very tall members of other tribes. The Negroes of North and South America stem largely from inhabitants of west-central and central Africa, who were brought to the New World during the period of slave trading.

The Australoids, the last group to be considered, are thought by many anthropologists to be "archaic whites." Their primitive physical features—prominent browridges, receding forehead and chin, and relatively low cranial capacity—suggest that the Australoids have changed little over vast periods of time and probably date from the late Pleis-

The uniqueness of man

tocene when they possibly coexisted with the Rhodesian and Solo (Java) men of 250,000 years ago. Their culture is still Mesolithic, with few implements and a hunting, nomadic mode of existence. At present they are found primarily in Australia, on some of the neighboring islands, and in Ceylon, India, and Japan, the latter three locations possessing only remnant stocks. Many of the Oceanic islands, first inhabited in post-Pleistocene times, have a racial mixture of Australoid, Mongoloid, and African stocks, and the many microraces suggest that genetic drift has been responsible for their physical differences.

When we view the races as a whole, relying primarily on fossil evidence and being well aware of the paucity of data upon which conclusions are founded, it appears that the Eurasian and Australoid groups are the most primitive and least specialized with respect to climatic adaptations. The Mongoloids, particularly those still inhabiting the upper reaches of the Northern Hemisphere, exhibit specializations that are at least interpretable as adaptations to a cold environment. Their higher metabolic rate is consistent with this view, although such data are to be taken with caution, for the individual, of whatever race, has a capacity for temporary adaptation that could obscure, or be confounded with, racial differences. All varieties of the Negro group are basically tropical people who inhabit the African region where mankind very likely had its early beginnings and possess features that make life in the hot and humid areas tolerable. Many of the racial features, no one of which is peculiar to any race, are governed by complex systems of inheritance; others, such as the several blood types, are inherited in simple fashion, but they too show a distribution that is unequal, thus supporting once again the view that races of

7.18 *This young Hawaiian woman shows the results of racial mixing. Her ancestry combines Hawaiian, Portuguese, Chinese, and English characteristics.*

Hawaii Visitors Bureau

The uniqueness of man

Searching back into prehistory, we find that almost every loss of a life form or species has been caused by one or a combination of three things: Intensive specilization leading to an evolutionary deadend, geological or climatic forces which proved catastrophic, or some other species of fatally inimical life.

It is remarkable that throughout millions of years of evolutionary struggle toward humanity, the life form which was to become man escaped the trap of specialization. This changing, adapting species with its human destiny managed to maintain its options. It also survived the elements.

The third threat—from a strain of hostile life—remains a force to be reckoned with. That threat is man himself.

Man . . . An Endangered Species? [*35*]

men, as with plants and animals, are a product of evolution, with natural selection and genetic drift playing significant roles.

Summary

Uniqueness is not peculiar to the human species; it is that sum of characteristics that enable us to distinguish one individual, one breed or variety, one species from another. There are, consequently, varying degrees of uniqueness, just as there are varying degrees of similarity. In the absence of these features of similarity and dissimilarity, the science of classification and our understanding of evolution would be virtually impossible. On the other hand, when we speak of human uniqueness we are of course viewing the situation from within, but however man-centered our point of view and however much we stress those features of uniqueness that make us more the human and less the animal, we cannot fail to recognize that an enormous gulf now separates us from our nearest relatives in the animal kingdom. In our management of time, communication, symbolism, and the environment and our discovery of self-awareness—all arising out of biological antecedents and all having a high selective value—we are without precedent in the history of life, a new form of organization that has transcended its origins and acquired the ability to direct its own evolution. *Homo sapiens* is the only species that can visualize itself in the frame of reference of space and time and that knows that it knows. On these aspects of uniqueness, as well as on those of structural and behavioral modification, rest the power and the dominance of man.

The uniqueness of man

8

The uniqueness of the individual

In the mechanical, automated world in which we live, crowded as we are by increasing population pressures, we face the growing threat of anonymity, of losing what most of us regard as our most precious possession: our individual uniqueness. From cradle to grave, we go through life tagged by a set of faceless numbers, a set of holes in a computerized punch card, a set of letter grades on an academic transcript. This facelessness tends to be reinforced by conformity that arises from social customs and traditions, from similar environmental influences, from acquiescence to, and acceptance of, current fashions of dress, hair style, and behavior or a set of racial or national traits transformed into categorized cliches. "They are all alike" is a common saying that compresses those embodied by the phrase into a common mold.

It is a familiar observation that the structures of plants and animals are widely variable. Corresponding parts of the same species may seem to present little or no difference if the inspection is merely casual. But many unlikenesses become apparent if the objects are examined closely, and the number of differences increases as attention is directed to more and more minute characters. The philosopher Leibniz contended, as have many others before and after him, that "there are never in nature two beings which are exactly alike, and in which it is not possible to find a difference." Thomas de Quincey relates that Leibniz was once explaining the matter to a royal personage; to give point he turned to a gentleman in attendance with a challenge to produce from any tree or shrub two leaves duplicating each other in venation. The challenge was accepted—but the duplicate leaves could not be found. As with leaves, so it is with finger prints. The London newspaper,

---

If it is a mistake to argue that genetic differences are important between races it is also a mistake to urge, as some people have, that genetic differences between people do not exist or can be ignored. I think we should once and for all realize and admit that people are all different—not Negroes from whites, not slum dwellers from Park Avenue residents, but all individuals are different—there are no two alike. Moreover, we should admit that they are different not only in the lengths of their noses and the color of their hair, they are genetically different in potentialities that really count, for example such special abilities as music, mathematics, and linguistics. But these human differences within a society are not an imperfection of nature or something to regret; quite the contrary. Human genetic diversity is a gift of heaven that can be utilized for the good of mankind to the extent that the society can provide equality of opportunity. It is the equality to develop on the basis of one's special abilities that makes genetic differences meaningful and useful. Where there is inequality of opportunity—as in a rigid class structure in which social position is passed on from father to son—the gift of genetic diversity is squandered.

Th. Dobzhansky [6]

"If you've seen one redwood, you've seen them all" is a politically inspired statement that has inflamed the conservationists, just as the similarly inept "If you've seen one slum, you've seen them all" has inflamed the socially directed egalitarians. Such phrases are thoughtless, often damning, generalities, especially because they are often readily accepted as characterizations of reality. They are an attempt at the economy of expression, but they are uttered in ignorance of sound biological knowledge. If modern biology in general, and the science of genetics in particular, teaches us anything, it is that no two individuals—plant, animal, or human—are likely to be identical. As the American bacteriologist René Dubos has put it: "Each human being is unique, unprecedented, unrepeatable. The species *Homo sapiens* can be described in the lifeless words of physics and chemistry, but not the man of flesh and bone. We recognize him as a unique person by his walk, his facial expressions, and the way he talks—and even more by his creative responses to surroundings and events."

A perceptive glance across a classroom, "along a crowded avenue," as the song goes, or even within the confines of a family circle makes the uniqueness of every individual quickly evident. We may have difficulty in distinguishing one identical twin from another, particularly when they are young, but even twins take on an individuality as time progresses. We may also dislike and rebel against what we consider to be the anonymity of numbers—although even numbers have a uniqueness of their own—but the undeniable fact is that each of us, while possessing similarities that group us into the human race, is indelibly stamped with uniqueness in a physical, chemical, and behavioral sense.

The uniqueness of the individual

News of the World, was quite safe when in 1939 it offered a prize of £1000 to the person having a finger print identical with any one of a series of prints published for the contest . . . Protests may be voiced by some on the basic issue of compulsion, the argument being that fingerprinting is a violation of personal rights and liberties. Such an argument loses force in the face of the obvious fact that fingerprinting is for the benefit of good people, both in its use in combatting crime and in its civil applications. . . . Fingerprint identifications of checks and documents and pocket identification cards already are gaining headway. An article published in 1937 is headed: "Finger Print Everybody? Yes—says John Edgar Hoover." He and many others are still saying "Yes."

H. Cummins and C. Midlo [5]

The fingerprint system of identification is founded on this principle, as is the footprint method used for newborn babies. Other similar systems of identification could be constructed, for example, one based on the immune reactions of our body, but these would be too cumbersome for general use.

Each of us starts life as a fertilized egg, a speck of life no bigger than a tiny piece of dust. The egg itself weighs about one-millionth of a gram; the sperm adds another five-billionths of a gram at the time of fertilization. Under the light microscope, there are no visible differences between one egg and another, nor does the far greater resolving power of the electron microscope reveal any internal suggestions of uniqueness. The most powerful microscope gives no hints of what the egg might become. Yet the fertilized egg is an organism, a unique individual, at its creation. It would not be unreasonable, in the absence of critical information, to assume that uniqueness is impressed upon the organism by the environment as it progresses from the egg to adult stage, but we need only consider the remarkable similarity of identical twins, who develop from a single egg that later splits into two or more independently developing parts, to realize that uniqueness must somehow be present in the egg itself (see table 8.1 and illustration 8.2). This uniqueness, seemingly present in the egg in blueprint form, gradually emerges as development takes place and as the more obvious features of individuality make their appearance. An understanding of the physical basis of this uniqueness stems from discoveries made in the twentieth century, with bits and pieces of the jigsaw puzzle contributed by the sciences of cell biology, genetics, biochemistry, and growth

8.1 *Pain spots on normal hands of two individuals. Spots in solid color are highly sensitive; white ones are insensitive. The other spots are intermediate. Although a system of classification of individuals based on patterns of pain sensitivity would be cumbersome and somewhat imprecise because patient response is involved, such patterns are undoubtedly as unique as fingerprints.*

After Williams, 1967

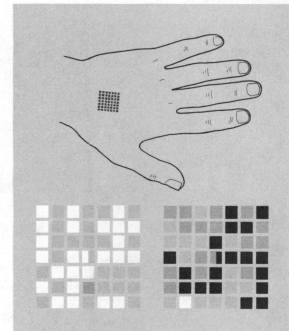

Twins . . . enjoy a special standing among the populations of the Cocopa, Mohave and Yuma. Among the Mohave tribe, twins are supposed to be of supernatural origin and to possess the powers of clairvoyance. ''We have only come to pay you a visit,'' they declare. ''Our parents are up there. Let us live with you a while.''

Not only are Mohave twins favored because of the surprise, admiration and respect that are engendered when the mother gives birth simultaneously to two beings who resemble each other, but also because the event carries with it religious implications and a sense of the supernatural. The Mohave are careful to treat their twins with complete impartiality. They maintain that if more is given to one, the other will grow angry and return whence he came. They also believe that if one twin dies, the other will follow him, even when quite healthy. . . .

Other tribes in California are extremely hostile toward twins. Among the North Pomo and the Kato, both members of a pair are put to death. Often, in the hills of the Northwest Maidus,

even the mother is killed. The Wailaki, the Achomaivi, the Yurok, the Miok and the Pitt Rivers content themselves by killing one of the twins.

Several superstitions support this special kind of infanticide. The North Pomo, for example, believe that twin births are caused by an enemy's malediction, and if the twins were allowed to live they would harm each other. The Yurok's practice is to suffocate one of the twins, generally the female if they are of opposite sex, because they think the two might eventually commit incest. Among the Tolowa tribe, the twins can live if they are of the same sex, but only the first born may live if they are of opposite sex. The reason for killing the second is perhaps the same as that adopted by the Alsea, who say the second twin is not a real person. According to Powers, the Pitt Rivers kill one of the twins because the burden of two children would be too great.

L. Gedda [13]

8.2   *The similarity of these identical twins to each other extends to minute but very obvious likenesses—facial blotches, shortness of the left incisor, and the greater narrowing of the right eye when the twin is smiling.*

Paul Knipping

Table 8.1   Distribution of differences among twins*

Trait and intrapair difference		Identical twins reared together	Identical twins reared apart	Fraternal twins
Height	Under ½ inch	42%	21%	4%
	½–1 inch	40	27	20
	1–1½ inch	16	30	24
	1½ inches and over	2	12	52
Weight	Under 7 pounds	43	43	28
	7–14 pounds	25	21	12
	14–21 pounds	23	24	16
	22 pounds and over	9	12	44
Combined intelligence	0–4 points	44	32	14
	5–9 points	21	30	14
	10–14 points	23	14	14
	15 points and over	12	24	57

*The smallest intrapair differences occur among identical twins reared together, whereas the greatest differences are found among fraternal twins. That the environment exerts an influence is indicated by the fact that identical twins reared apart show greater differences than do those reared together. Data from J. Shields, *Monozygotic Twins: Brought Up Apart and Brought Up Together*, Oxford University Press, 1962.

Growth is defined as an increase in mass. This increase can result solely from an enlargement of cells, but more often it is accompanied by an increase in the number of cells through mitotic divisions. Growth, then, is essentially a process of replication: the original cell takes from its environment the raw materials it needs and converts them into more substance and more cells like itself. Let us consider the human egg. It weighs about [0.000001 grams], and the sperm, at fertilization, adds to it only another [0.000000005 grams]. At birth, however, a child will weigh around 7 [pounds], or 3,200 [grams], which is an increase of about one billion times during the 9-month prenatal period. A newborn child is obviously not simply a mass of cells of comparable size and character to the original cell; if it were, it would be just a ball of cells devoid of human qualities. Nor has its growth rate been uniform throughout its prenatal life. Other processes must act to mold cells into shape, as a potter or a sculptor molds his clay, and to stamp them with character.

C. P. Swanson [40]

---

and development. Our greater understanding of the individual as a unique reacting and acting system comes also from psychology and ethology, the latter being the science of behavior and its formation.

The cellular basis of uniqueness

Cells are the basic unit of organization of all living things. In this sense they are analogous to the symbols of a language. Some symbols, like unicellular organisms, express total meaning without further supporting symbols; other symbols, like cells in a multicellular organism, convey full meaning only when used in combination with others to which it is joined. In another sense, cells are to an organism what atoms are to a molecule: their character, number, and arrangement determine and confer uniqueness. New qualities of structure and behavior often emerge as new combinations are formed.

Because of their small size, cells were not discovered until the invention of the microscope in the seventeenth century. A description and an understanding of subcellular parts had to await the discovery of proper methods of preparation and differential staining, developments that were achieved largely in the nineteenth century. When it became clear that eggs and sperm are also cells, even though they are substantially modified to meet the demands of sexual reproduction, the contributions of cell biology could then be merged with evolutionary concepts, with both of these aspects of biology gaining in dimensions and significance by the merger. That is, it was recognized that a slender bridge of cells spanned generations of organisms and that a continuous and un-

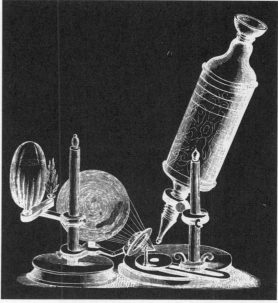

The Bettman Archive, Inc.

8.3   The microscope used by Robert Hooke in his cellular research that led to the discovery of the cork cell. From Hooke's Micrographia, *1665.*

The importance accorded the individual became visible in art early in the Renaissance with the intensification and individualization of facial expressions and gestures. Then in the caricatures of Leonardo da Vinci and Bernini, in Rembrandt's portraits, and in Baroque showpieces for court or church, the imprints of character and the passions on countenance and body were explored and exploited to a far greater degree. With the shift of emphasis from specific details of content to mood or expressiveness, the French Academy issued a handbook which an artist could consult for rendering various expressions.

. . .

The assertion of the worth of the ordinary individual and of

emotionality, which transcended social strata, was in fact implemented earlier in an art closer to nature than was painting—landscape gardening. English writers of the first half of the eighteenth century believed that the clipping of trees, as in the geometric forms of French landscaping, was analogous to the regulation of human impulses by social or traditional influences. In the serpentine paths and artfully contrived "natural" growths of English picturesque landscape gardening, men created an art in which they could actually live in simulation of an existence unfettered by the artificialties of civilization.

G. Pelles [35]

One of the insights that has been most helpful to biologists is the so-called Cell Theory. It is difficult to say precisely what that phrase encompasses. In part, this is because the cellular nature of living systems was revealed not in a dramatic single resolution but rather through a series of clarifications that were developed throughout most of the mid-nineteenth century. The basic postulates of the Cell Theory are, first, that all organisms are composed of subunits resembling one another in the possession of a certain set of organelles and a boundary; second, that these entities arise only through the division of pre-existing cells. . . .

The establishment of the Cell Theory, though attended by far less ceremony than the nearly contemporaneous Darwinian Revolution, has made it possible for biologists to deal coherently with what would otherwise be a hopeless welter of diversity. The doctrine of evolution offered explanations for the enormous breadth of the living spectrum; the Cell Theory offered hopeful assurances that these variations, despite their extent, had a theme, that the theme was the cellular organization of living systems, and that one might hope to comprehend some of the basic whys of life without inspecting an infinite series of special cases.

D. Kennedy [20]

broken chain of cells must have stretched backward through geologic time from species living today to the first cell or cells that arose on earth. Any heritable changes fed into the gene pool of a species must then have occurred first within cells before being incorporated into a group of individuals and acted upon by natural selection. Answers to questions concerning the evolution of organisms, the uniqueness of species and individuals, racial differences, growth, development, aging, disease, and death, and even learning, memory, and image recall must therefore be sought in the varied structure, function, and interrelationships of cells. It might be thought that an answer to the question "What is life?" is to be sought also through cellular studies. The difficulty is that the question is inappropriate today; we do not know enough about cells to begin to frame an answer. What we do know is that a cell, even the simplest one, is an extraordinarily complex molecular machine and that the answer to the question concerning life lies in the manner in which molecules are organized and interact with one another in a dynamic and constantly changing milieu. The laws of physics and chemistry are not violated by cellular systems, and so we are not yet compelled to search for, or to invoke, vital forces to explain their activities. By extension, then, we do not need to invoke such forces to explain man, for whatever else he might be, he is still constructed of cells and cell products.

We earlier described man, or any other organism for that matter, as a processor of energy. Just as an engine, whether idling or running at full capacity, requires a constant input of energy, so too does a living organism. Because organisms are composed of cells, it is the cell, singly or in aggregate, that is the basic manipulator of energy. Its structures are

Frans Hals, Malle Babbe.
The Metropolitan Museum of Art, Purchase, 1871

correlated and consistent with the ways in which energy is received and made available and the uses to which energy is put. Unicellular organisms must of course carry out all of the energy transformations necessary for continued existence. A multicellular organism such as man possesses a variety of cells, some of which are generalized in the sense that they can actually or potentially perform a number of tasks, others of which are specialized to carry out one task efficiently, for example, nerves for the transmission of electrical impulses, muscles for mechanical work, or red blood cells for the transport of oxygen and carbon dioxide. It is during the process of growth and development of an individual that the unicellular egg becomes the multicellular adult, as generalized cells become differentiated into specialized cells as organ systems form and added functions make their appearance.

Organisms, however, especially warm-blooded animals, can function and live only within a limited temperature range. They are not equipped to utilize heat energy for the primary purposes of life. The visible light from the sun, particularly the red and to a lesser extent the blue-violet portion of the spectrum (illustration 8.4), is the principal source of energy for all life. This energy can be trapped only by green plants possessing the photosensitive green pigment chlorophyll, or by the red, brown, and blue-green algae possessing related photosensitive pigments. After light energy is trapped, it is transformed into chemical energy and is bound up in carbohydrates such as sugars and starches. All other forms of life and all activities of life depend upon chemical energy, which resides in the chemical bonds that link atoms into molecules.

A cell is essentially a chemical factory that carries out

Standard Oil Co. (N.J.)

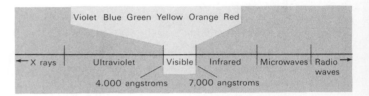

8.4 *The electromagnetic spectrum. Life is dependent only upon a limited portion of the spectrum. We see only a small segment of it because of our limited visual receptivity; we feel part of it in the infrared range in the form of heat; and green plants can trap only selected portions of the visible light for purposes of photosynthesis. Other portions of the spectrum are readily detected by special instruments and are used by man for a variety of purposes, but they play no essential role in the basic business of living. However, the ultraviolet segment may have played an important role as an energy source when life first arose on this planet.*

its transformations within a limited temperature range, with each chemical change being governed by the presence and functional activity of *enzymes,* cellular catalysts that are protein in nature. But a cell is also a unique and closely regulated system. There is little to distinguish the fertilized egg of a chimpanzee from that of a human being; the differences between the two emerge as growth and development proceed. It is now known that what the cell is, what it becomes eventually, and how it functions are all determined by a coded set of information based on molecules of nucleic acid contained within each cell. The uniqueness of every individual is determined by this inherited code and is governed in part by environmental conditions within which it functions. Although the basic nature of the code has been discovered and deciphered, biologists are still only dimly

The uniqueness of the individual

aware of how a complex cell continues to function in an integrated manner. As the biologist André Lwoff [26] has written, the remarkable thing about it all is that "in order to build the immense diversity of living systems" on a cellular basis of organization, "nature has made use of a strictly limited number of building blocks. The problem of diversity of structure and functions, the problem of heredity, and the problem of diversification of species [also, the problem of individual uniqueness] have been solved by the elegant use of a small number of building blocks organized into macromolecules. . . . Each macromolecule is endowed with a specific function. The machine is built to do precisely what it does. . . . If the living system did not perform its task, it would not exist. We simply have to know how it performs its task."

The principal macromolecules are nucleic acids, proteins, carbohydrates, and fats, or lipids, built up, respectively, of the smaller nucleotides, amino acids, sugars, and fatty acids. All of these contribute, singly or in combination, to the intricate architecture and functioning of the cell. The nucleic acids are the source of information, as well as its means of transmission; the proteins, whose unique structure is directly traceable to the nucleic acids, enter into the formation of cellular membranes where they are combined with the fatty acids and, as enzymes, govern the chemical reactions within the cell; carbohydrates are the primary sources of energy; and fatty acids are reservoirs of energy that can be drawn upon when needed. We shall deal with the chemical details of these molecules only to the extent that they help us understand the physical basis of individual uniqueness.

Randomness is an "extensive property"; it doesn't matter how many toothpicks you put together at random—they're still just toothpicks. But if you put together six toothpicks and two corks in a certain way, you can get a figure that looks something like a horse—something entirely new. Order is an "intensive property." This holds throughout science: If you put together protons and neutrons, we get a nucleus—something entirely new. It has new qualities, qualities you can't describe in terms of the constituents. If you then put electrons around this nucleus, you have an atom—again something entirely new, something more than just a nucleus and electrons. Then you can put atoms together into molecules, molecules into macromolecules, macromolecules into organelles, organelles into cells, cells into whole individuals, and individuals into societies. Each time you get something entirely new.

A. Szent-Györgyi [18]

The uniqueness of the individual

Beautiful, angular, and bare the machinery of life will lie exposed, as it now is, to my view. There will be the thin, blue skeleton of a hare tumbled in a little heap, and crouching over it I will marvel, as I marvel now, at the wonderful correlation of parts, the perfect adaptation to purpose, the individually vanished and yet persisting pattern which is now hopping on some other hill. I will wonder, as always, in what manner ''particles'' pursue such devious plans and symmetries. I will ask once more in what way it is managed, that the simple dust takes on a history and begins to weave these unique and never recurring apparitions in the stream of time. I shall wonder what strange forces at the heart of matter regulate the tiny beating of a rabbit's heart or the dim dream that builds a milkweed pod.

L. Eiseley [10]

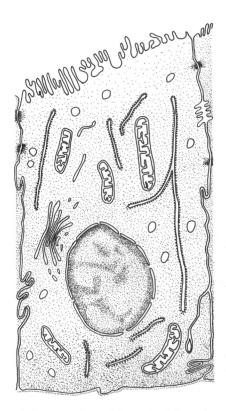

8.5   *A diagram of a cell from the lining of the intestine that reveals features common to most animal cells: a membrane that bounds the cell and separates it from its environment; a nucleus surrounded by cytoplasm; and, within the cytoplasm, mitochondria, the elongated structures with an inner membrane system, stacked and flattened membranes that are concerned, at least in part, with carbohydrate metabolism, and longer, irregular membranes, studded with small projections, that are involved in protein synthesis.*

8.6   *A cell from the root tip of a maize plant, as photographed with an electron microscope (magnification about 6,000×). The elements of the cell described in illustration 8.5 are clearly visible in this photograph. The large central area is the nucleus surrounded by its membrane. Between this membrane and the thick cell wall is the cytoplasm. Mitochondria can be seen at the base of the nucleus. Stacked membranes and those of irregular shape are also visible. The light circular area outside the nucleus at top left is a vacuole, a fluid cavity within the cytoplasm.*

Electron Microscope Laboratory, The University of Texas (Austin)

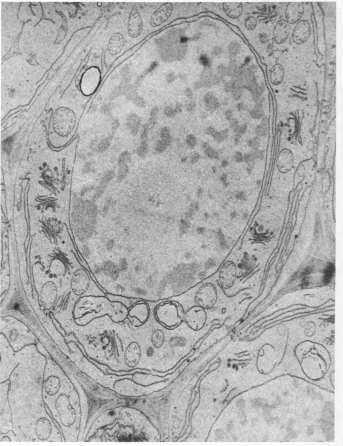

In our laboratories we have for decades observed many wide disparities within groups of highly inbred animals that possess very similar gene pools. These observations led to the experiments with armadillos which normally give birth, after each conception, to a set of monozygous quadruplets, all four of course being of the same sex.

We suspected in the light of our earlier observations that we might find substantial difference within these sets even though the individuals had initially identical complements of genes. This indeed proved to be the case.

We have not used the term "identical quadruplets" nor do we sanction the term "identical twins." These expressions carry the implication that, so far as inheritance is concerned, monozygous quadruplets (or monozygous twins) are the same. This, we now know, is not true.

Within quadruplet sets at birth, we have found anatomical disparities; in brain weights (63%), heart weights (92%), liver weights (49%), spleen weights (2.1 fold), kidney weights (68%), adrenal weights (99%), small intestinal length (70%). Within sets of four, we found extreme variation with respect to hormone levels. The norepinephrine in the brain varied 6.6 fold, in spleen 7 fold, in adrenals 16.6 fold. The epinephrine in the adrenals varied over a 32 fold range! The free amino acids in the brain varied as follows, within sets of quadruplets: aspartate, 5.5 fold; glutamate, 77%, glycine, 3.4 fold; alanine 3.7 fold; γ amino butyric acid, 2.3 fold; taurine 2.7 fold.

These findings bring out the fact that, within quadruplet sets, the individuals may be highly distinctive in their anatomy, physiology, and endocrine patterns and that their central nervous systems may be substantially different biochemically as well as in size.

R. J. Williams [45]

A microscopical survey of the myriad of specialized cells making up the human body reveals a bewildering array of internal structures (see illustrations 8.5 and 8.6). These are important to the specialist seeking answers to specific problems, but it is their common features that concern us here. Each cell has a limiting boundary, a *cell membrane,* that governs what substances enter or leave the cell. Through this membrane the cell interacts with its environment, whether this environment be a closely adjacent and interdependent cell or simply the fluid in which the cell is bathed. Inside the membrane is the *cytoplasm,* a fluid system containing a variety of particulate organelles (a specialized part of a cell analogous to an organ) and membranes. This is basically the work area of the cell where energy is derived from the food taken in, transformed into more usable forms of chemical energy, and utilized for whatever task is being performed. The *nucleus* is the heart of the cell. Surrounded by cytoplasm and engaged in active interchange with it and bounded by a nuclear membrane, the nucleus has been shown, by a wide variety of elegantly definitive experiments, to be the informational center of the cell. It is here that the nucleic acids are found. These acids are linked with protein to form *chromatin,* a complex substance that resolves into *chromosomes* during the course of cell division.

The significance of the nucleus to the ultimate expression of uniqueness, whether this be species or individual uniqueness, is indicated by the fact that the sperm, in the act of fertilization, contributes only a nucleus. Yet the paternal contribution to the resultant individual is as important in a hereditary sense as that of the maternal parent who contributes virtually all of the remaining apparatus of the fer-

The uniqueness of the individual

Plato having defined man to be a two-legged animal without feathers, Diogenes plucked a cock and brought it into the Academy, and said, "This is Plato's man." On which account this addition was made to the definition—"With broad flat nails."

Diogenes Laertius

8.7 *The chromosomes of a garden spiderwort (a), man (b), and a wake-robin (c). The cells of the spiderwort and the wake-robin are from immature pollen grains and contain only one member of each kind of chromosome. That of man is from a cultured leukocyte from the bloodstream and contains all forty-six chromosomes, or twenty-three pairs. The cell is from a male, and one of the smallest chromosomes is a Y, the chromosome concerned with the development of maleness. The X chromosome is of intermediate length and is difficult to pinpoint. Note in each illustration that the chromosomes are constricted at some point, dividing them into two arms. The constriction indicates the position of the* centromere, *an organelle needed by the chromosome if it is to be properly segregated during cell division.*

tilized egg. The character and number of chromosomes found within a cell also stress this importance in a microscopically visible way. Each species, or group of closely related species, is characterized by the number and morphology of its chromosomes. The cells of a normal man or woman, with the exception of sperm and unfertilized eggs, contain forty-six chromosomes, twenty-three contributed by one parent and a similar twenty-three by the other parent. Chromosomes exist, therefore, in pairs in sexually reproducing organisms. In man, each pair of chromosomes is numbered according to length, is recognizable, and is known to contain specific pieces of coded and heritable material in the form of nucleic acid. For example, if one of the

(a)

(b)

(c)

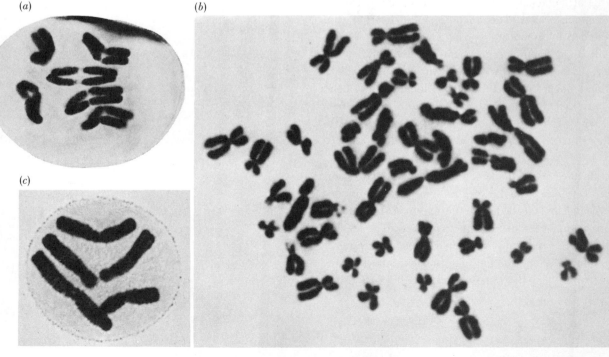

In terms of a metaphor more closely related to cartography, we have a general picture of the various countries (the chromosomes) of the genetic world and have identified many of the municipalities (genes) on the basis of the specific traits to which they give rise. We are still largely in the dark, however, about the location of most of the municipalities, even from the standpoint of deciding in what country they belong. The overall size of the genetic domain (the total number of genes in man) is itself obscure, although we know the number must be very large. More than 1,100 separate enzymes are known, and presumably the structure of each enzyme is specified by at least one gene. Moreover, there are a large number of nonenzymic proteins, each of which is also under genetic control. Besides the structural genes there are other classes of genes controlling various aspects of cell development and activity. Judging from the large number of different gene functions and the known content of DNA in cells, a set of chromosomes must contain many thousands of gene loci.

V. A. McKusick [27]

Table 8.2   Relation between mother's age and frequency of congenital abnormalities*

Mother's age	Frequencies of nervous system abnormalities	Frequencies of mongolism
16–20	1	1
21–25	2.7	0.7
26–30	2.3	1.3
31–35	4.3	3.0
36–40	6.0	9.3
41–45	10.0	34.3
46–50	7.0	146.2
Total number of cases	(144)	(224)

*The nervous system abnormalities may or may not be hereditary. The frequency of occurrence of both kinds of abnormalities is arbitrarily set at 1 for the youngest age group, and other figures are relative to the youngest group. Data from L. S. Penrose, *Annals* of the New York Academy of Science, vol. 57, 1954.

smallest of the chromosomes is present not as a pair but in a triplet state, the individual exhibits Down's syndrome, or mongolian idiocy. He or she is a drastically altered individual, generally incapable of becoming a functional member of society. If another one of the smallest chromosomes has lost a portion of its length, an accident that can occur for unknown reasons, the person possessing this aberrancy will, toward the age of forty, develop chronic myeloid leukemia, a disease that as yet does not respond to medical treatment. The incidence of congenital abnormalities is quite high among children born of older parents, as indicated in table 8.2.

Although most prenatal mortality is very early and is therefore not a large cause of human misery, it is probably a major factor in selection for some human genes. In man, the total embryonic death rate is unknown, since there is no accurate measure of the number of conceptions; but in cattle, sheep, mice, swine, and rabbits, it averages some 30 to 40 percent. It now appears likely that two factors, not previously thought important, are substantial contributors to this death rate.

One factor is chromosome abnormalities. . . . If we consider the large number of chromosomes and the various kinds of errors and rearrangements that are possible, it is likely that these chromosomal abnormalities are a substantial cause of embryonic mortality.

The other newly realized factor in embryonic death is maternal-foetal incompatibility. Apparently, an embryo of blood group A or B with a group O mother has a risk of some 10 percent of dying as an embryo, presumably from antigen-antibody reactions between embryo and mother. On the other hand, in combinations in which no such incompatibilities exist, the group O embryos, and presumably the other homozygous types, are found in deficient numbers at birth and therefore must have died as embryos.

J. Crow [4]

The uniqueness of the individual

Peter Throckmorton photo,
Nancy Palmer Photo Agency

The chemical basis of uniqueness

Research directed toward an understanding of inheritance, evolution, and uniqueness became focused therefore on the nucleus, or, as it happened, on the nuclear equivalent found in bacteria and viruses, because these organisms are simple to manipulate and can be grown by the billions overnight in a test tube. The significance of the problem may be judged by the fact that, in the period after 1940, it attracted a substantial number of the world's most brilliant scientists. The importance of their results is indicated by the awarding to them of a dozen or more Nobel Prizes. The elucidation of the chemical basis of heredity has, without any question, changed and revolutionized biology and given it new insights and direction, in much the same way and with as profound an impact as Darwin's theory of natural selection did in the previous century.

The science of genetics had pinpointed the nucleus and the chromosomes as the critical vehicles of inheritance during the first quarter of the twentieth century, but the chemical quest had its beginnings in a curious experiment carried out by an English bacteriologist, Frederick Griffiths, in 1928 (see illustration 8.8). The pneumococcus bacterium is a pathogen responsible for a form of influenza, and Griffiths had isolated a number of strains, some of which were highly virulent and formed smooth, glistening colonies of cells on culture plates, while others were avirulent (nonpathogenic) and gave rise to rough, irregularly shaped, dull-appearing colonies. If injected into mice, the avirulent strain did not induce influenza symptoms; neither did virulent types that had been killed by heat. However, if the avirulent and the heat-killed virulent types were simultaneously injected, the mice contracted influenza and died. Only virulent bacteria could be reisolated from the dead mice.

Two alternative explanations seem possible: (1) the heat-killed cells had somehow been reactivated by the presence of, or interaction with, the avirulent strain; (2) the avirulent strain acquired something from the heat-killed cells that converted them from a nonpathogenic to a pathogenic state. Subsequently, it was shown that the same phenomenon, now known as *bacterial transformation*, could take place in a test tube, thus eliminating the suggestion that the mice themselves might have had something to do with what happened. It was also demonstrated that the contents of burst virulent cells could produce the same end result. The

8.8 *A diagram of the experiments carried out by Frederick Griffiths that were instrumental in pointing to DNA as the physical and molecular basis of inheritance.*

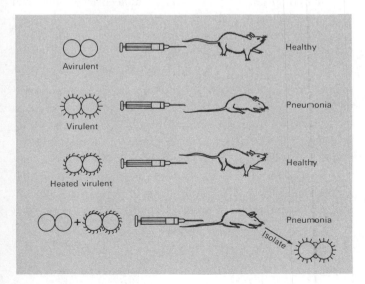

The following morning I felt marvelously alive when I awoke. On my way to the Whim I slowly walked toward the Clare Bridge, staring up at the gothic pinnacles of the King's College Chapel that stood out sharply against the spring sky. I briefly stopped and looked over at the perfect Georgian features of the recently cleaned Gibbs Building, thinking that much of our success was due to the long uneventful periods when we walked among the colleges or unobtrusively read the new books that came into Heffer's Bookstore. After contentedly poring over *The Times,* I wandered into the lab to see Francis [Crick], unquestionably early, flipping the cardboard base pairs about an imaginary line. As far as a compass and ruler could tell him, both sets of base pairs neatly fitted into the backbone configuration. As the morning wore on, Max [Perutz] and John [Kendrew], successively came by to see if we still thought we had it. Each got a quick, concise lecture from Francis, during the second of which I wandered down to see if the shop could be speeded up to produce the purines and pyrimidines later that afternoon.

Only a little encouragement was needed to get the final soldering acomplished in the next couple of hours. The brightly shining metal plates were then immediately used to make a model in which for the first time all the DNA components were present. In about an hour I had arranged the atoms in positions which satisfied both the X-ray data and the laws of stereochemistry. The resulting helix was right-handed with the two chains running in opposite directions. Only one person can easily play with a model, and so Francis did not try to check my work until I backed away and said that I thought everything fitted. While one interatomic contact was slightly shorter than optimal, it was not out of line with several published values, and I was not disturbed. Another fifteen minutes' fiddling by Francis failed to find anything wrong, though for brief intervals my stomach felt uneasy when I saw him frowning. In each case he became satisfied and moved on to verify that another interatomic contact was reasonable. . . .

The next morning I again found that Francis had beaten me to the lab. He was already at work tightening the model on its support stands so that he could read off the atomic coordinates. . . .

---

second of the two alternatives was clearly the correct one, but the nature of the transforming substances was not discovered until 1944. After much fractionation and purification of cell contents, and the testing of each fraction for transformational potency, it turned out that a particular kind of nucleic acid, deoxyribonucleic acid (DNA), was the crucial molecule of transformation and of inheritance as well, because the transformed bacteria can transmit their newly acquired character to their offspring.

Other pieces of evidence supported this conclusion. The amount of DNA per nucleus varied from one species to another; those closely related were similar in DNA content, whereas those remotely related could differ quite appreciably (see table 8.3). Also, it was discovered that sperm had only half the amount of DNA contained in the cells of skin or liver, a fact consistent with the knowledge that sperm contains one-half the number of chromosomes found in other cells of the body. Nevertheless, there was a reluctance to accept this evidence at face value because of a mistaken notion that DNA, despite its large molecular weight and great length, was a molecule of monotonous internal structure. How could such a molecule be responsible, in coded fashion, for the enormous variety of inherited traits that, in aggregate, make a particular species or an individual unique? The proteins, whose structure had been elucidated in the 1950s by Linus Pauling, were infinitely variable because of the way in which the twenty amino acids could be grouped in almost any combination, and so they seemed to be a much more likely candidate as the molecule of inheritance. But by 1952, the biochemist Erwin Chargaff had shown that the old notion of monotonous regularity of DNA was wrong and that internally DNA was nearly as

Table 8.3	Amount of DNA per nucleus in various plants and animals*	
		Billionths of a microgram
Mammals	Man	3.25
	Beef	3.82
	Rat	3.4
	Dog	2.75
	Mouse	3.00
Marsupial		4.5
Birds	Chicken	1.26
	Duck	1.30
	Goose	1.46
Reptiles	Snapping turtle	2.50
	Alligator	2.50
	Water snake	2.51
	Black snake	1.48
Amphibians	Amphiuma	84.0
	Necturus	24.2
	Frog	7.5
	Toad	3.66
Fish	Carp	1.64
	Shad	0.91
	Lungfish	50.0
Miscellaneous	Maize	8.4
	Drosophila	0.085
	Aspergillus	0.043
	Neurospora	0.020
	E. coli	0.0040

*It can be seen that the amount of DNA bears little relation to the evolutionary position of a species or to its morphological, behavioral, or biochemical complexity. The large amounts of DNA in some organisms remains to be explained.

The uniqueness of the individual

[Sir Lawrence] Bragg had his first look late that morning. . . . Immediately he caught on to the complementary relation between the two chains and saw how an equivalence of adenine with thymine and guanine with cytosine was a logical phosphate backbone. As he was not aware of Chargaff's rules, I went over the experimental evidence on the relative proportions of the various bases, noticing that he was becoming increasingly excited by its potential implications for gene replication. . . .

The next scientific step was to compare seriously the experimental X-ray data with the diffraction pattern predicted by our model. Maurice [Wilkins] went back to London, saying that he would soon measure the critical reflections. There was not a hint of bitterness in his voice, and I felt quite relieved. Until the visit I had remained apprehensive that he would look gloomy, being unhappy that we had seized part of the glory that should have gone in full to him and his younger colleagues. But there was no trace of resentment on his face, and in his subdued way he was thoroughly excited that the structure would prove of great benefit to biology.

He was back in London only two days before he rang up to say that both he and Rosy [Rosalind Franklin] found that their X-ray data strongly supported the double helix. They were quickly writing up their results and wanted to publish simultaneously with our announcement of the base pairs. *Nature* was a place for rapid publication, since if both Bragg and Randall strongly supported the manuscripts they might be published within a month of their receipt. However, there would not be only one paper from King's. Rosy and Gosling would report their results separately from Maurice and his collaborators. . . .

Both Rosy's and Maurice's papers covered roughly the same ground and in each case interpreted their results in terms of the base pairs. For a while Francis wanted to expand our note to write at length about the biological implications. But finally he saw the point to a short remark and composed the sentence: ''It has not escaped our notice that the specific pairing we have postulated immediately suggests a possible copying mechanism for the genetic material.'' . . .

J. D. Watson [41]

---

variable as were the proteins. The question then became one of DNA structure. How was the molecule put together so that it could act as the source of coded information that, during the course of growth and development, would guide the development of a fertilized egg so that it would become a man instead of a jellyfish, an oak tree instead of a pine tree?

It is customary to think of research as being associated with the dissection of organisms, with test tubes and shelves of chemicals, and with highly sophisticated instruments. But the fact is that for the most part these are only the means for testing ideas, for trying to distinguish between possible alternative answers, for determining whether this model or that fits all of the facts known at a given time. It was in this way that scientists determined the structure of DNA; as in completing a jigsaw puzzle, the available pieces were fitted together to make a consistent whole, with no piece being forced into a slot unnaturally.

The structure of DNA was announced in 1953 in two brief papers, one by Francis Crick, an English physical chemist, and James Watson, a young American virologist, the other by Maurice Wilkins, an English X-ray crystallographer. The date and the names are as significant to biology as are the year 1859 and the name Charles Darwin.

Several bits of information were known to Watson and Crick as they went about their model building. Chemical analysis of DNA revealed that it was a polymer, that is, a long chain molecule constructed of repeating units. Furthermore, it consisted of three different classes of smaller molecules, and so was unlike such polymers as rubber, starch, or the various plastics, which are composed of a single kind of molecule strung together one after the other.

Though it might surprise the outsider, this emphasis on competition in science will scarcely come as news to working scientists. They know from hardwon experience that multiple independent discoveries are one of their occupational hazards. Since discoveries are typically the temporary culmination of what has been found before, when several scientists are working independently on the same problem, they are apt to move toward the same conclusion. As a result, competition in science is as old as modern science itself.

Watson's beautifully brash account serves to distinguish this competitive motive from the closely allied motive of contest. Competition involves the attempt to win out against the field for the rewards that come with victory; contest involves the directly sportive pleasure of beating particular others. Time and again, Watson records his youthful pleasure in testing his powers against the best there is. He is especially eager to

outstrip the champions—Linus Pauling, "the world's greatest chemist," for one and Erwin Chargaff, "one of the world's leading authorities on DNA," for another. . . .

These elements of competition, contest and reward have made property rights an integral though still ambiguous part of the institution and ethics of science. For if the advancement of knowledge were the only institutionalized motive for scientists, then the concept of property rights would of course make little sense. What matters it who advances our knowledge, providing only that it gets done? Yet property rights have been a gray area in the mores of science for quite some time. More than a century ago, the nonpareil physicist Clerk Maxwell was writing William Thomson: "I do not know the Game laws and Patent laws of science . . . but I certainly intend to poach among your electrical images."

R. K. Merton [30]

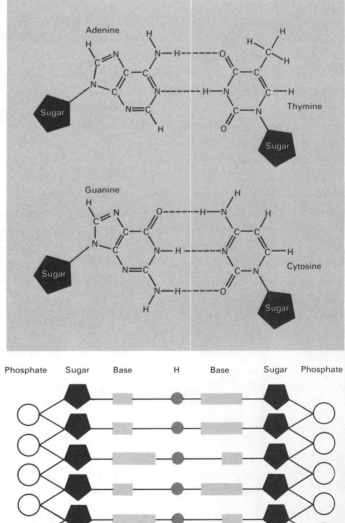

8.9 (a) The chemical configurations of the four bases found in the DNA molecule; they are arranged as base pairs bonded together by hydrogen. (b) The flattened arrangement of a portion of the DNA molecule, with the phosphates and sugars forming the outside of the helix, and the base pairs connecting the two sides. In part (a) the following elements are depicted: hydrogen (H), carbon (C), nitrogen (N), and oxygen (O).

James Watson and Francis Crick, Cavendish Laboratory, Cambridge, England, 1953.

Camera Press, Ltd.

These component molecules of DNA were *phosphoric acid,* a sugar known as *deoxyribose,* and a group of bases. The three kinds of molecules, when linked together, are called *nucleotides.* X-ray analysis had shown that these molecules were linked together so that the bases projected from the sugars, while the sugars were linked together by phosphoric acid. Furthermore, the analysis indicated that the lengthy molecule possessed a helical, or spiral, form, with a diameter of 20 angstrom units (10,000 angstrom units = 1 micron; 1,000 microns = 1 millimeter). The bases were 3.4 angstroms apart, and ten bases, or 34 angstroms, made a complete turn in the helix.

The bases were of four kinds. Two were *purines* (adenine and guanine), and two were *pyrimidines* (thymine and cytosine). These bases are usually represented by their initial letters, A, G, T, and C, and their chemical configurations are shown in illustration 8.9. Additional and earlier chemical analysis of DNA, regardless of its source, revealed three important facts that had to be kept in mind: (1) the number

Table 8.4	*Base ratios in the DNA's of various organisms*[*]			
	A:T Ratio	G:C Ratio	A:G Ratio	T:C Ratio
Man	1.00	1.19	1.47	1.75
Ox	1.04	1.00	1.29	1.43
Turtle	1.03	1.03	1.31	1.31
E. coli	1.06	0.97	1.04	0.95
Wheat	1.00	0.97	1.22	1.62
Gypsy moth virus	1.06	1.07	0.72	0.72

[*]The A:T and G:C ratios are approximately 1:1, but the cross ratios A:G and T:C vary quite widely from one species to another. In the bacterium *E. coli,* the four bases are present in equal proportions, whereas man shows a greater preponderance of A and T, and the gypsy moth virus has more G and C. Genetic diversity, however, is achieved not by the relative amounts of the two base ratios, but rather through the manner by which the base pairs alternate along the length of the DNA molecule.

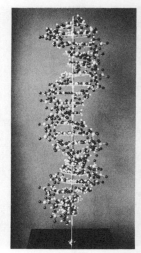

Molecular structure of DNA.

Pfizer, Inc.

(a)

Base pairs

Oxygen

Carbon

Hydrogen

Phosphate

(b)

S	A	H	T	S
P				P
S	G	H	C	S
P				P
S	T	H	A	S
P				P
S	C	H	G	S

(c)

of purines equaled the number of pyrimidines; (2) the number of adenines equaled the number of thymines; and (3) the number of guanines equaled the number of cytosines. Any given kind of DNA can therefore be characterized by its base ratios, that is, A = T, G = C, and A + G = C + T, but A or T does not have to equal C or G. Table 8.4 gives the base ratios for several different organisms.

If we visualize DNA as a source of coded information that the cell can tap as it goes about its business of being alive, we can think of the sequence of bases CATTGCCT as providing one piece of information while another sequence TCCAGTTC provides another, even though the number and kinds of bases are the same. In a very real sense, this is no different from the symbols "team," "meat," and "mate," which possess the same letters but in different sequence, and, as a result, have different meanings.

This does not explain, however, the significance of the one-to-one (1:1) ratios of A to T, or of C to G, nor does it help us understand how, when a cell divides, the two daughter cells have a base composition and arrangement identical to the mother cell from which they arose. Both situations become explicable if it is assumed that the DNA molecule exists as a *double* helix instead of a single one

8.10   The DNA double helix, with three different ways of representing the molecular arrangement. (a) General picture of the double helix, with the phosphate-sugar combination making up the outside spirals and the base pairs the cross bars. (b) A somewhat more detailed representation showing sugars (S), phosphates (P), hydrogen (H), and the four bases, adenine (A), cytosine (C), guanine (G), and thymine (T). (c) Most detailed structure, showing how the space is filled with atoms.

The uniqueness of the individual

When we know more about people, particularly in what specific ways they are alike and in what ways different, we will be incomparably more effective in making and enforcing rules and laws governing their conduct. Whenever we put laws on the statute books that cannot be enforced, which is very often, we create disrespect for law and run the risk of making lawbreakers out of people who would otherwise be law-abiding citizens.

A classic example of a law which we found we couldn't enforce was the Prohibition Amendment, which was placed in our Constitution and then repealed. Thomas Jefferson had said nearly 150 years before, "Tastes cannot be controlled by law," and had in this statement demonstrated great wisdom and insight. *Why* cannot tastes be controlled by law? Because there is a wide diversity of tastes which are not simply trained into people (as is often thought) but are based upon inborn differences of a profound and basic nature. People would have to be changed fundamentally (genetically) before these tastes could be governed by law. If we all had the same tastes or if we were perfectly adaptable in them, one of two things would have happened: either the Eighteenth Amendment would never have been put on the books (we would have agreed on the use of alcoholic beverages), or it would have stayed there and would have been enforced, because we would have adapted ourselves to the new regime.

R. J. Williams [*44*]

(illustration 8.10). The bases could then be paired with one another so that A is paired with T, and C with G, and if the bases are paired, then the two strands of the helix are paired. The two strands are consequently complementary to each other. When a cell divides, its DNA divides as the two strands fall apart, with each strand forming a complementary strand during this process of replication (illustration 8.11). A number of exquisitely executed experiments have proven that this does indeed happen. The Watson-Crick model of DNA has provided us with a precise and workable solution to the question of what constitutes the physical basis of uniqueness. Before we explore how this molecular code is translated into living reality, we need to look into the manner by which inheritance is transmitted.

The mechanics of inheritance

Heredity is basically a conservative phenomenon: like begets like; he is the spitting image of his father; she has her mother's good looks and her father's temperament. But even if like begets like, closer inspection reveals deviations from a pattern. Variations are as much a part of inheritance as are the similarities. The mechanics of inheritance must account for both aspects.

When *The Origin of Species* was published, the patterns of inheritance were generally explained by a blending hypothesis. This concept came into being because the common practice of viewing an organism as a total entity was coupled with the fact that most organisms are either intermediate in appearance between their parents or show a combination of paternal and maternal characteristics. This view delayed

The uniqueness of the individual

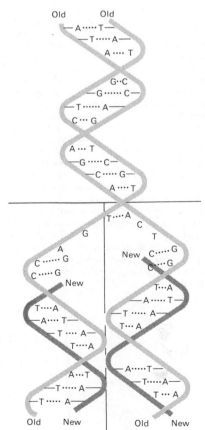

8.11   The replication of DNA is accomplished by the unwinding of the helix from one end and the consequent separation of the halves. The synthetic machinery of the cell then enables each half of the molecule to participate in the forming of a new complementary strand; as a result, two identical strands of DNA are created. It is through the process of replication that the conservatism of inheritance is maintained.

The latest publication of Hugo de Vries: *Sur la loi de disjonction des hybrides* which through the courtesy of the author reached me yesterday, prompts me to make the following statement:

In my hybridization experiments with varieties of maize and peas, I have come to the same results as de Vries, who experimented with varieties of many different kinds of plants, among them two varieties of maize. When I discovered the regularity of the phenomena, and the explanation thereof, the same thing happened to me which now seems to be happening to de Vries: I thought that I had found *something new. But then I convinced myself that the Abbot Gregor Mendel in Brünn, had, during the sixties, not only obtained the same result through extensive experiments with peas, which lasted for many years, as did de Vries and I, but had also given exactly the* same explanation, as far as that was possible in 1866. Today one has only to substitute ''egg cell'' or ''egg nucleus'' for ''germinal cell'' or ''germinal vesicle'' and perhaps ''generative nucleus'' for ''pollen cell.'' An identical result was obtained by Mendel in several experiments with Phaseolus, and thus he suspected that the rules found might be applicable in many cases.

C. Correns [3]

The results which Gärtner obtained in his experiments are known to me; I have repeated his work and have re-examined it carefully to find, if possible, an agreement with those laws of development that I discovered to be true in the case of my experimental plant. However, no matter how hard I tried, I was unable to follow his experiments completely, not in a single case! It is very regrettable that this worthy man did not publish a detailed description of his individual experiments, and that he did not diagnose his hybrid types sufficiently, especially those that resulted from like fertilizations. Statements like: ''Some individuals showed closer resemblance to the maternal, others to the paternal type,'' or ''the progeny had reverted to the type of the original maternal ancestor,'' etc., are too general and too vague to furnish a basis for sound judgment. However, in most cases, it can at least be recognized that the possibility of an agreement with Pisum [garden pea] is not excluded. A decision can be reached only when new experiments in which the degree of kinship between the hybrid forms and parental species are precisely determined, rather than simply estimated from general impressions, are performed.

G. Mendel [29]

acceptance of Darwin's theory of natural selection because the small variations that he insisted were responsible for the gradual change of species through time would have been swamped by blending and would never have an opportunity to be expressed. Darwin himself accepted the blending hypothesis and in later years came to have some doubts as to the significance of small variations.

All of this was changed through the studies carried out by an Austrian monk, Gregor Mendel, who published the results of his hybridization experiments in 1865, but who remained largely ignored for another 35 years. Disregarding the organism as a whole, he concentrated instead on particular traits, traced their patterns of appearance, disappearance, and reappearance through several generations, and came to realize that simple mathematical relationships governed the transmission of these traits. In order to arrive at this conclusion, he made use of precise breeding records.

Mendel experimented with garden peas and noticed that certain traits were mutually exclusive: some plants were tall, others dwarf, but none were intermediate; some unripe pods were green, others yellow; some ripe seeds were round and smooth, others wrinkled. He chose seven pairs of distinct characters and found that all behaved similarly.

The tall versus dwarf character will provide an example of what he did. Mendel knew tall plants, when self-pollinated, gave rise to tall offspring, whereas dwarf ones similarly produced only their kind. When he crossed a tall plant with a dwarf one in a controlled experiment, all of the first-generation (F_1) offspring were tall; the dwarf character was not in evidence. When these F_1 offspring were allowed to self-pollinate, as peas generally do, both tall and dwarf second-generation (F_2) individuals were produced in a ratio

Gregor Mendel.

of three tall plants for every dwarf plant. The dwarf trait, therefore, had not been lost in the F_1 generation, but was merely masked temporarily and reappeared later. Because of this Mendel termed the dwarf trait "recessive" and the tall trait "dominant" and used capital letters to express dominance and lowercase letters for recessiveness.

Mendel tested the F_2 offspring to determine how they behaved. When self-pollinated, the dwarf plants bred true and produced only dwarfs. One-third of the talls also bred true. The other two-thirds of the talls produced tall and dwarf plants, again in a ratio of three talls to one dwarf; they behaved exactly as the F_1 talls had done. Mendel reasoned, therefore, that if the dwarf character could disappear in one generation only to reappear in the next, and if the disappearance and reappearance behaved in a simple mathematically predictable fashion, then there must be a transmittable, discrete entity that is responsible for dwarfness and tallness. He called these discrete entities *factors*; we now call them *genes*. He asserted that they were capable of replacing one another in a breeding system but that they were not contaminated or altered as they were transmitted from one generation to the next. We now know that a given gene can exist in a number of forms as a result of mutations and that the mutated form is transmitted in the same manner as the original gene.

Carrying his reasoning still further, he argued that the sperm carried one factor and the egg another, with both factors being present in the plant itself. A tall plant consequently was *TT* and *homozygous* if it bred true; a dwarf plant was *tt* and *homozygous* also. A tall plant that produced both tall and dwarf offspring when self-pollinated was *Tt* and *heterozygous*. When eggs and sperm were being pro-

The value and utility of any experiment are determined by the fitness of the material to the purpose for which it is used, and thus in the case before us it cannot be immaterial what plants are subjected to experiment and in what manner such experiments are conducted.

The selection of the plant group which shall serve for experiments of this kind must be made with all possible care if it be desired to avoid from the outset every risk of questionable results.

The experimental plants must necessarily—

1. Possess constant differentiating characters.

2. The hybrids of such plants must, during the flowering period, be protected from the influence of all foreign pollen, or be easily capable of such protection.

The hybrids and their offspring should suffer no marked disturbance in their fertility in the successive generations.

G. Mendel [28]

8.12 Mendel's experiment dealing with a single pair of contrasting and mutually exclusive characters depicted in simplified form (a) and in terms of genetic symbols (b).

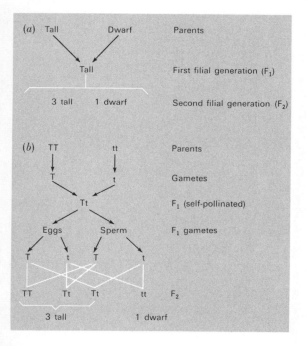

duced in a *Tt* plant, the egg, for example, could contain *T* or *t*, but not both, and the same for the sperm. The random union of eggs and sperm in a *Tt* plant would produce the $3T:1t$ ratio, or to be more exact, a ratio of $1TT:2Tt:1tt$ (see illustration 8.12). Because all traits generally followed the same mathematical rules, it was possible to conduct an experiment with two sets of traits, for example, tall versus dwarf and green versus yellow pods. Although each set of traits, examined by themselves, followed the $3:1$ rule, combined they produced a $9:3:3:1$ ratio because of their independent inheritance. It is of interest to note that Mendel carried out similar studies on bees and hawk weed, but with no success. It happens that these two organisms are unusual in their modes of inheritance. Mendel's choice of the pea was a most fortunate one.

Mendel's ideas were rejected by his contemporaries and were forgotten for 35 years. The blending hypothesis of inheritance was too firmly established to be easily displaced, and the climate of biology was such that his ideas of particulate inheritance could not readily be fitted into the corpus of biological knowledge. The cellular nature of the egg and sperm had not yet been discovered, the method of fertilization was not understood, and the processes and meaning of cell division and the behavior of chromosomes remained to be uncovered. Mendel's factors, despite their precise quantitative behavior, were still abstractions that could not be put on any physical basis that made sense at that time. By 1900, however, the climate of opinion had changed, and when his findings were rediscovered, their relevance to cell and evolutionary theories was immediately apparent.

The uniqueness of the individual

One new and unexpected problem emerging from massive surveys of the chromosomal complements of large segments of the human population is that of management. For example, with the detection at an early age of individuals with sex chromosomal aneuploidy such as 47,XXY and 47,XYY comes the problem of how to treat such individuals and how to counsel their families. There are thousands of aneuploid males living in the United States whose phenotypes, as far as is known now, belie their true sex chromosomal constitution.

About one out of 400 apparent male babies actually has the complement 47,XXY while between one and three per 1000 have the complement 47,XYY. Little is known of the behavioral aspects of this segment of our society, although there is little doubt that males with an extra X or Y are represented more frequently in the prison population than in the general population. The degree of risk that they will display antisocial aggressiveness is quite an unknown quantity, but it must be determined as soon as possible. The legal status of aneuploid individuals who break the law is as yet unsettled. This would appear to constitute a problem which might be advantageously considered jointly by those in the law profession and those in medicine and genetics. The human cytogeneticist therefore appears to be in an unusually important, if unexpected, situation in relation to criminal sociology.

J. German [14]

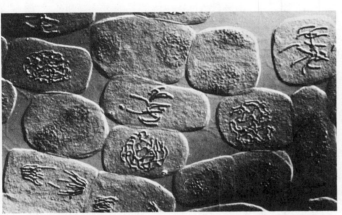

Courtesy of Peter Webster

8.13 Mitosis. In this photograph, the cells of the root tip of the broad bean plant are shown in various stages of the division process.

The science of inheritance can be, and still is, pursued as a study of traits and their mode of transmission from parents to offspring. The inheritance test devised by Mendel remains one of the basic tools of the geneticist. But if we are to explore the relationships between genes and DNA and their connection with the uniqueness of the species and the individual, we need to examine in more detail the relationship of genes to cellular structure and behavior.

Cells increase their number by division, a process called *mitosis* (illustration 8.13). As with any sexually reproducing organism, man begins life as a fertilized egg; repeated division of this original cell, the adherence of cells to one another, and their acquisition of distinctive form and function through cellular differentiation lead eventually to an

In judging Mendel's place in history we have to consider first whether he supplied something which was unique. Such a question can properly apply of course only to his own period, for as the history of discovery shows, in time nearly every major idea is rediscovered. . . . . In the middle of the nineteenth century there is no question that Mendel alone expressed a new and original idea. Its essence was that heredity operates by elements which behave according to definite statistical rules. The main ones were that the transmission mechanism of biological heredity consists of many pairs of alternative characters or elements of which only one member is transmitted by any one reproductive cell; and that in the formation of such cells members of different pairs from the parents enter into all possible combinations with each other. These rules are usually referred to as the principles of segregation and of independent assortment of hereditary elements or genes. The discovery of order where none had been perceived before was of great importance. For the growth of biological ideas, however, the manner of proof was of even greater importance. The rules were demonstrated by simple experiments which anyone could perform. Mendel's paper was throughout an application of inductive reasoning radically applied at a time when general views of biological processes were often reached by deductive processes. Mendel's method of experimental breeding, in which all plants were individually identified and all offspring of deliberately made crosses were classified for each pair of contrasted characters and counted, was simple, but it was original and at that time unique. Moreover the experiments were deliberately designed to test a theory—and this kind of experimental design was new in biology.

L. C. Dunn [9]

Auguste Rodin, The Thinker.

The Metropolitan Museum of Art,
Gift of Thomas F. Ryan, 1910.

adult body composed of thousands of billions of cells, each containing the same amount and kind of DNA and hence of genes. The precise and incredibly accurate quantitative and qualitative duplication and separation of chromosomes ensures that this will be so. The structure of the DNA molecule and the process of cell division make this possible.

Each chromosome has DNA running through its entire length. How this is arranged within the chromosome is not known with certainty, but the double nature of the DNA molecule, its ability to uncoil and to separate into its two complementary strands, the capacity of the cell to resynthesize two double helices once in each cell cycle, each helix being an exact replica of the other, and the formation of a divisional apparatus that segregates the two halves of the chromosome into the newly forming daughter cells, all these traits ensure that all cells of the body are alike in their genetic and chromosomal content. As William Bateson, the great English biologist of an earlier generation, once wrote: "When I look at a dividing cell I feel as an astronomer might if he beheld the formation of a double star: that an original act of creation is taking place before me."

Cell division is a creative process that goes on constantly in our body. Cells have finite life spans, but as they die they are replaced by similarly endowed cells. This is particularly true in the blood-forming tissues, the skin, and the lining of our digestive tract. It is estimated that between 1 and 2 percent of our cells die and are replaced each day. Cell division, therefore, is also a conservative act, preserving, as it does, a genetic uniformity among all cells of the body. The fact that "like begets like" is dependent on this degree of conservatism, which we can trace back to the

The uniqueness of the individual

What is Man?

A self-balancing, 28-jointed, adapter-based biped; an electrochemical reduction plant, integral with segregated stowages of special energy extracts in storage batteries for subsequent actuation of thousands of hydraulic and pneumatic pumps with motors attached; 62,000 miles of capillaries. . . . Millions of warning signal, railroad and conveyor systems; crushers and cranes (of which the arms are magnificent 23-jointed affairs with selfsurfacing and lubricating systems) and a universally distributed telephone system needing no service for 70 years, if well managed. . . . The whole, extraordinarily complex mechanism guided with exquisite precision from a turret in which are located telescopic and microscopic self-registering and recording range finders, . . . the turret control being closely allied with an air-conditioning intake-and-exhaust, and a main fuel intake. . . . Within the few cubic inches housing the turret mechanisms there is room also for two sound-wave and sound-direction-finder recording diaphragms, a filing and instant reference system, and an expertly devised analytical laboratory large enough not only to contain minute records of every last and continual event of up to 70 years' experience, or more, but to extend, by computation and abstract fabrication, this experience with relative accuracy into all corners of the observed universe.

"A man," indeed! Dismissed with the appellation, "Mr. Jones!"

R. B. Fuller [12]

---

replicative nature of the DNA molecule, and the segregative precision of the cell during division.

Each of us is unique, however, an unprecedented, unrepeatable human being. Variation must somehow be introduced into the system; evolution could not take place if things were otherwise, for it cannot proceed in an unvarying situation. Mutations, which, as will be pointed out later, are alterations in the nucleotide sequence of DNA, are the ultimate source of variation, but an additional and more immediate cause of variation is that each of us is heterozygous for many genes, and each of us is the product of biparental inheritance.

As mentioned earlier, the cells of normal human beings contain fourty-six chromosomes. This number is retained generation after generation. But the first act in the creation of a new individual is that of fertilization, during which the nuclei of the sperm and the egg fuse to form the nucleus of the fertilized egg. The chromosome number of the fertilized egg is consequently double that of the egg and the sperm. If no event occurs to offset this trend, unmanageable numbers of chromosomes would be accumulated. A compensatory type of cell division, called *meiosis*, is introduced into the sequence of normal divisions, and in man this occurs in the sex organs as the egg and sperm are produced. Meiosis halves the number of chromosomes, whereas fertilization doubles them (see illustration 8.14). The similarity in the means of transmission of chromosomes and of Mendel's abstract factors is striking, and the quantitative ratios of Mendelian inheritance depend upon the behavior of chromosomes in meiosis and fertilization. It is to Mendel's enduring credit that his laws of inheritance were formulated

The larger and the deeper challenges, those concerned with the defined genetic improvement of man, perhaps fortunately are not yet in our grasp; but they too are etched clear upon the horizon. We should begin to prepare now for their reality.

It is a new horizon in the history of man. Some of you may smile and may feel that this is but a new version of the old dream of the perfection of man. It is that; but it is something more. The old dreams of the cultural perfection of man were always sharply constrained by his inherent, inherited imperfections and limitations. Man is all too clearly an imperfect, a flawed creature. Considering his evolution, it is hardly likely that he could be otherwise. And to foster his better traits and to curb his worse by cultural means alone has always been, while clearly not impossible, in many instances most difficult. It has been an Archimedean attempt to move the world but with the short arm of the lever. We now glimpse another route—the chance to ease the internal strains and heal the internal flaws directly—to carry on and consciously to perfect, far beyond our present vision, this remarkable product of two billion years of evolution. We are, it is true, very young for this task—young in skills, young in wisdom—but also, fortunately, young in heart.

R. L. Sinsheimer [39]

The uniqueness of the individual

Before I was born out of my mother generations guided me,
My embryo has never been torpid, nothing could overlay it.
For it the nebula cohered to an orb,
The long slow strata piled to rest it on,
Vast vegetables gave it sustenance,
Monstrous sauroids transported it in their mouths and deposited
   it with care.
All forces have been steadily employ'd to complete and delight me,
Now on this spot I stand with my robust soul.

W. Whitman [42]

8.14 The stages of meiosis for one pair of chromosomes. In man, meiosis takes place in the ovaries and testicles, producing, respectively, eggs or sperm that are then ready to participate in the act of fertilization. Meiosis is essentially two divisions of the initial cells but is accompanied by only one replication of the chromosomes. Replication of the DNA in the chromosomes takes place as in mitosis, but instead of each chromosome behaving independently of one another, the two members of each pair unite with one another along their entire length, after which they are then segregated to the opposite ends of the cell. The cell is then divided in two by a cell membrane. Each cell, therefore, contains only one member of each pair of chromosomes and so has only twenty-three chromosomes, half the number found in each of man's body cells. A second division in each cell then separates the halves (chromatids) in each chromosome, after which cell membranes form between the newly constituted nuclei. Four cells are thus derived from one original cell, with each having only half the normal number of chromosomes. The union of the egg and sperm in the act of fertilization restores the chromosomes to their original number, forty-six.

After Rhoades, 1950

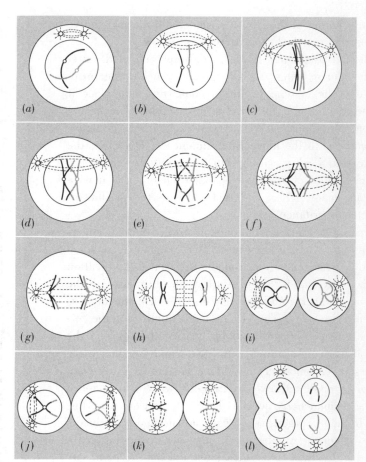

in the total absence of information about chromosomes or cell division.

The chromosomal basis of inheritance can be illustrated in man by a consideration of the inheritance of sex. Male-

The uniqueness of the individual

Thus man's place in the physical universe is to be its master, or at least to be the master of the part that he inhabits, and by controlling the natural forces with his intelligence, to put them to work to suit his purposes, and to build a future world in his own image. It is an exciting possibility. It is what can be done if man has the strength to control his irrational and diversionary tendencies and to develop his strong characteristics. Everything we know implies that the opportunities for future development are unbounded for a rational society operating without war. Man's intelligence,

self-respect, sense of responsibility, and sense of destiny are the qualities which will carry us forward. He must enjoy his role as king of the universe for all this to come true. He must understand that this is his function, he must have enough responsibility to carry it out without causing his own destruction. This, to me, is man's place in the physical universe: to be its king through the power he alone possesses—the principle of intelligence.

W. F. Libby [25]

---

ness and femaleness are mutually exclusive traits having a genetic and chromosomal basis. Man possesses forty-six chromosomes in each cell, but these exist as twenty-three pairs. The first pair is the longest, the twenty-second the shortest; the twenty-third pair is special as we shall see shortly. Both members of the first pair are identical in length, and in the number of genes they contain, although each gene may exist in one form in one chromosome and in another form in the partner. In the garden pea, for example, T would be on one chromosome, t on its partner. These partners segregate from each other during meiosis, one going into one sex cell, the other into another.

The twenty-third pair of chromosomes in man is related to sex determination. In females, this pair consists of identical members called X chromosomes. In males, the members of the pair are unlike. One is an X chromosome, comparable in all respects to the X chromosomes in the female, but the other, known as the Y chromosome, is considerably shorter, is devoid of genes in the usual sense, and is concerned only with the determination of maleness. The chromosomal composition of a female is therefore twenty-two pairs plus XX, a male twenty-two pairs plus XY. The male, in a sense, is heterozygous (comparable to the Tt heterozygous garden pea of Mendel) with maleness dominant. The female is homozygous. Eggs can consequently carry twenty-two chromosomes plus an X, sperm twenty-two chromosomes plus an X or a Y. It is the sperm, therefore, that determines the sex of the offspring.

Hemophilia is an inherited disease characterized by a failure of the blood to clot properly if a vein or an artery is cut. It is sex-linked in the sense that its inheritance is related to the sex chromosomes, the X or the Y chromo-

8.15 (a) A stage of meiosis in a salamander cell, with the chromosomes united in pairs. (b) A single pair of chromosomes, which will undergo the twofold division described in the caption for illustration 8.14.

(*a*)

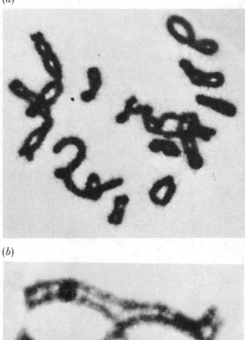

(*b*)

The uniqueness of the individual

. . . It comes as something of a surprise to recall that the very term DNA, and the revolution in our vision of the nature of life epitomized in the concept and the knowledge that genetic information is indeed coded, were largely unknown, except among those professionally concerned with that area of research, less than two decades ago. Yet that frame of reference is now so widely taken for granted that it seems always to have formed the basis for our thinking about the nature of life. And, in the context of the deep and continuous stream of scientific thought that flows beneath its apparent

discontinuities, it is worth recalling that the year 1969 marked the hundredth anniversary of the discovery of DNA by Friedrich Miescher, which he named *nuclein*. . .

But the most sweeping evolutionary questions at the level of biochemical genetics are still unanswered. How the genetic code first appeared and then evolved and, earlier even than that, how life itself originated on earth remain for the future to resolve, though dim and narrows pencils of illumination already play over them. The fact that in all organisms living today the processes both of replication of the DNA and of

the effective translation of its code require highly precise enzymes and that, at the same time, the molecular structures of those same enzymes are precisely specified by the DNA itself, poses a remarkable evolutionary mystery. How can a particular strand of DNA, dependent for its replication on a highly specific enzyme, have possibly evolved the code to direct the information of that same enzyme, given the obvious condition that the evolutionary survival of the organism containing it must have depended on the success of such replication? This question, of course, raises another. Did

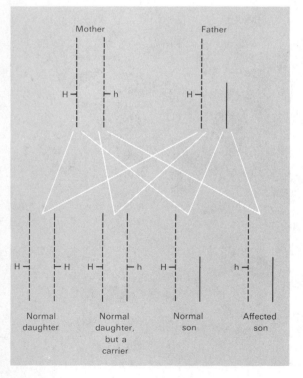

8.16   The inheritance of hemophilia. The long dashed lines signify X chromosomes, whereas the short solid ones denote Y's that are devoid of genes. A normal gene is designated by H, an affected one by h.

somes. The fact that hemophilia is virtually restricted to males might suggest that it is an abnormality associated with the Y chromosome, but it is actually due to a recessive gene located on the X chromosome (see illustration 8.16). The inheritance of hemophilia follows precisely the inheritance of the X chromosomes, permitting us to state, as a result, that a particular gene is carried on a particular chromosome. The general absence of hemophilia in females is due to the fact that hemophiliac males rarely reproduce. Females, therefore, are carriers of the trait in a masked condition, and only pass the trait on to their sons or to their grandsons via their daughters.

There are many more traits and many more genes in man than there are pairs of chromosomes. How many there are is not known but a guess of 10,000 is not an unreasonable one. Each chromosome consists, consequently, of a number of genes, now known to be arranged in linear order. If one were studying the transmission of two genes, both located on the same chromosome, normal Mendelian ratios would not be realized, for the two genes would tend to be inherited together. This would restrict the random segregation of genes, and place a damper on number of variant combinations that can be produced. On the other hand, however, the paternal and maternal chromosomes in an individual, brought in by the sperm and egg respectively, are not inherited together, and the sex cells can come to contain any combination of them possible. The number of combinations is determined by the formula 2^n, with n being equal to the number of pairs of chromosomes. Because in man this is twenty-three pairs, the number of combinations of paternal and maternal chromosomes exceeds eight million. Because any gene can exist in a number of states as a result of

The uniqueness of the individual

the code and the means of translating it appear simultaneously in evolution? It seems almost incredible that any such coincidence could have occurred, given the extraordinary complexities of both sides and the requirement that they be coordinated accurately for survival. By a pre-Darwinian (or a skeptic of evolution after Darwin) this puzzle would surely have been interpreted as the most powerful sort of evidence for special creation. In our day another, but still far from demonstrated (or possibly demonstrable) view seems the only logical one: that a primitive and generalized mode of replication of genetic material arose in evolution either before the existence of these critical enzymes or coordinately with proteins which gradually took on crude and generalized enzymelike functions. Such a tentative hypothesis at least emphasizes once again how far even the most primitive of contemporary single cells have evolved at the most critical biochemical levels—how far, indeed, the exquisite adjustments of such an evolution must have proceeded before anything that in our world we would even recognize as life was possible. By the same token, evidence of that stage in the emergence of life clearly disappeared from our planet long ago, snuffed out by billions of generations of more complex organisms which still must have been far more primitive than anything we now know. So we are left with a real gap in our understanding. New and testable insights into this problem would rank with the greatest of all our advances in evolutionary theory. Indeed, they might well provide innovations for all biological thinking as pioneering and stimulating and important as was the concept of the gene itself in the biology of its day.

C. P. Haskins [17]

---

mutation, and because all sexually breeding organisms are highly heterozygous except when inbred, the process of meiosis, coupled with fertilization, introduces an enormous amount of variation into a population. The number of possible combinations of traits far exceeds the number of human beings that have ever lived.

The realization of uniqueness

A vast amount of information of every description can be stored on computer tapes, ready for recall on a selective basis on receipt of the proper signal. In its coded form, information is only potentially useful; to be useful it must be decoded and translated. The DNA of a cell is analogous to a computer tape. During the course of cell division, it can replicate itself and thus provide other cells with the same memory bank of information, but the messages contained within it are not usable by the cell without prior translation.

In 1941, George Beadle and Edward Tatum discovered that genes, which control heritable traits, exercise their control through the medium of enzymes. Enzymes were known to be highly specific in their action, governing one, and only one, reaction. Thus, if a product P is formed by the series of chemical reactions $A \rightarrow B \rightarrow C \rightarrow D \rightarrow P$, each step in the reaction system is governed by a specific enzyme. If the enzyme governing the step $A \rightarrow B$ is missing or is somehow rendered nonfunctional, the remaining steps in the reaction cannot occur because the intermediate product B would not be formed. Similarly, P would not be produced if the enzymes governing the $B \rightarrow C$, $C \rightarrow D$ or

The uniqueness of the individual

In our crowded world is civilization moving ahead toward the time when tombstones can be mass-produced on an assembly line—all bearing the same epitaph?

HERE LIE THE REMAINS OF A
NORMALIZED STATISTIC

In a statistical age will computers be improved, elaborated and refined so that in the end, instead of our writing programs for them, *they will write programs for us?*

These prospects do not sound alluring; "statistical man" has little to do with you or me or any other real person. But the blame should not be cast on statistics. Rightly used by experts who understand their limitations they are a boon to humanity. But in dealing with *people* they should be used *with care!*

Why? Because a group of people is something like a collection of colorful marbles. In the assortment of marbles all are reasonably round, but they are of different sizes; some are made of pottery, some of glass, some of agate, some of plastic and some of steel. They may be all colors of the rainbow, and individually they may be multicolored, striped, mottled, stippled, translucent, decorated with lustrous flecks and patterned in a multitude of ways.

Try to average these marbles and one comes out with nonsense. Marbles are not made partly of pottery, partly of glass, partly of plastic, partly of agate and partly of steel. Such marbles wouldn't hold together. Try to find the average color of the marbles; mount them on a circular disk, rotate rapidly and observe. The color comes back a dirty gray. But there isn't a dirty-gray marble in the lot! People are as distinctive as marbles, but when we attempt to average them we come up with dirty-gray "man." This doesn't have anything to do with you or me, for we are colorful, interesting specimens more marvelously unique than any marbles. Averaging when applied in this careless way to people can be vicious.

R. J. Williams [46]

The scientific development of genetics in this century started with the rediscovery of Mendel's work in 1900 and gained momentum in the succeeding decades; now it has secured a firm and fixed foundation in our understanding of the physical and chemical bases of heredity. This development, by clearing the mists of fancy and superstition surrounding the very genesis of each of us, has already begun to exert a profound influence on the philosophical and social outlooks of our time. No one would ever again say, as did John Locke, "Let us then suppose the mind of man to be, as we say, white paper devoid of all characters, without any ideas. Then how comes it to be furnished? To this I answer in one word, 'from experience.'" For we now know that in the mind, as in the body, very much is built-in.

We are born with our genes and we are in no small part the product of our genes. We are not born as blank slates—nor are we born equal with equal talents or equal gifts. This is hardly a new or profound thought, but the evasion routes by which men have sought to avoid and to deny this conclusion are now closed.

The role of man on earth is changing. Originally a driven creature struggling for existence in a world he never made, man is now acquiring the knowledge and the power to create his own environment and, literally, to direct his own future. Ours is the age of transition. We may hope that the transition will be such that, to paraphrase Konrad Lorenz, "Man will be seen to be the missing link between the ape and the human being."

R. L. Sinsheimer [38]

D $\longrightarrow$ P steps were missing. The product P, the presence or absence of which would be recognized as an inheritable trait, is therefore controlled by a number of genes, any one of which could interfere with its appearance.

The Beadle-Tatum discovery tells us two things. First, the initial steps in gene action that will lead to the detection of a heritable trait take place at a biochemical level within the individual cell. The trait, however, may be observable only at a much grosser level of detection. For example, albinism, or the absence of the dark pigment melanin in the skin, hair, and eyes, results from an enzymatic failure in the set of reactions that produce melanin as a final product. Second, there must be an intimate connection between enzymes, which function largely in the cytoplasm of the cell, and the DNA located in the nuclei. But enzymes are proteins composed of chains of amino acids, whereas DNA is made up of sequences of nucleotide pairs. Somehow the coded information in DNA must be translated in such a way as to lead to the formation of a specific protein molecule. In the light of present information, we can also draw the conclusion that a gene is a piece of a DNA molecule, and a protein is the product of that gene.

It was known that the proteins not only act in the cytoplasm, but also that they are synthesized there as well. A message must therefore be made in the nucleus and sent to the cytoplasm to be interpreted and translated into a protein of a particular kind. Because everything that happens in a cell depends upon the structure and function of molecules, the message must also be molecular. It turns out to be RNA, a ribose nucleic acid that differs from DNA in that it is single-stranded rather than in the form of a

The uniqueness of the individual

double helix. This RNA is known appropriately enough as "messenger RNA" (mRNA).

DNA therefore has a dual function. It can make more of itself by a process of replication, and it makes RNA by a comparable process of *transcription*. The RNA is complementary to DNA, with but one exception: thymine is replaced by a similar base, uracil (U). Only one of the two strands of the DNA double helix engages in transcriptional activities, the other strand presumably providing the DNA molecule with stability. Thus if the piece of DNA to be transcribed is ATTACGGAC the RNA will be UAAUGCCUG.

The identification of the message is like finding the Rosetta stone; the next problem is to break the code. The question asked was "How does a sequence of nucleotides determine a sequence of amino acids?" The difficulty in answering the question is caused by the fact that there are only four kinds of nucleotides and twenty kinds of amino acids.

A one-to-one relationship between nucleotides and amino acids is clearly insufficient; each nucleotide could specify only one amino acid. Similarly, if two nucleotides specified one amino acid, a 2:1 relationship, this would be similarly inadequate since only sixteen (4×4) of the amino acids could be accommodated. A 3:1 relationship is more than adequate because it gives a potential "vocabulary" of sixty-four words ($4 \times 4 \times 4$), but evidence has shown that the triplet code is correct. Some amino acids are specified by more than one code, and some triplet codes are signals to initiate and stop a message, the equivalent of capital letters and periods of normal sentences. Thus the triplet code AAG specifies the amino acid lysine, and CAU specifies histidine.

The uniqueness of the individual

Now we can define man. Genotypically at least, he is six feet of a particular molecular sequence of carbon, hydrogen, oxygen, nitrogen and phosphorus atoms—the length of DNA tightly coiled in the nucleus of his provenient egg and in the nucleus of every adult cell, 5 thousand million paired nucleotide units long. This store of ''information'' could specify 10 million kinds of proteins. Almost certainly, most of this information controls just when and where some few thousands of proteins will be made—the tendons and enzymes, antibodies, hormones and the like, of which the body is composed.

J. Lederberg [22]

Table 8.5 Triplet codes and the amino acids each code determines*

Code triplets	Amino acid	Code triplets	Amino acid
AAA	Lysine	CAA	Glutamine
AAG	Lysine	CAG	Glutamine
AAC	Asparagine	CAC	Histidine
AAU	Asparagine	CAU	Histidine
AGA	Arginine	CGA	Arginine
AGG	Arginine	CGG	Arginine?
AGC	Serine	CGC	Arginine
AGU	Serine	CGU	Arginine?
ACA	Threonine	CCA	Proline
ACG	Threonine	CCG	Proline?
ACC	Threonine	CCC	Proline
ACU	Threonine	CCU	Proline
AUA	Isoleucine?	CUA	Leucine
AUG	Methionine	CUG	Leucine
AUC	Isoleucine	CUC	Leucine
AUU	Isoleucine	CUU	Leucine
GAA	Glutamic acid	UAA	Gap
GAG	Glutamic acid	UAG	Gap
GAC	Aspartic acid	UAC	Tyrosine
GAU	Aspartic acid	UAU	Tyrosine
GGA	Glycine?	UGA	Tryptophan
GGG	Glycine?	UGG	Tryptophan
GGC	Glycine?	UGC	Cysteine
GGU	Glycine	UGU	Cysteine
GCA	Alanine?	UCA	Serine
GCG	Alanine?	UCG	Serine
GCC	Alanine?	UCC	Serine
GCU	Alanine	UCU	Serine
GUA	Valine?	UUA	Leucine
GUG	Valine	UUG	Leucine
GUC	Valine?	UUC	Phenylalanine
GUU	Valine	UUU	Phenylalanine

*Question marks indicate uncertainty of code specification at the present time, whereas the word ''gap'' represents the end of any message.

CUG, CUC, CUA, and CUU all specify leucine, but with varying degrees of efficiency under varying cellular conditions. Table 8.5 gives the triplet codes and the amino acid each code specifies.

Breaking the genetic code, which along with the elucidation of the structure of DNA is one of the most remarkable discoveries of this century, allows us to determine the size of a gene: it must contain three times as many nucleotide pairs as there are amino acids in the protein that the gene controls. If a protein contains 100 amino acids, the gene controlling it has 300 nucleotides, and, because each nucleotide is 3.4 angstroms long, the gene must be 10,200 angstroms, or just over 1 micron, in length.

A final problem remains: "How is the protein put together?" or to phrase it differently "How is the message translated?" To make a long and complicated story short, the cell contains a set of "readers," one for each triplet code. These are small RNA molecules, called transfer RNA's (tRNA) and also made by DNA, which possess codes complementary to those in the triplets that permit them to find, and pair with, the coded structure of the messenger RNA. At the same time they carry with them specific amino acids. As the message is being translated—and the message is unidirectional as is a sentence made up of words—the transfer RNA's match up in sequence with the triplet codes, and as they do, the amino acids they carry are united to form a growing protein chain. When the end of the message is reached, the protein is completed, after which it is released to perform its cellular function.

As George and Muriel Beadle point out in their book *The Language of Life*, it is difficult not to adopt a "gee-whiz" attitude in describing the many discoveries that in

The uniqueness of the individual

Just as natural mutations had to be stringently sifted by natural selection if a population were to advance or even not to deteriorate, so, in species divided into many small groups, the mutational combinations in each had to be sifted, by a longer-range natural selection, in the interests of the species as a whole. And again, genera with only one species had, other things being equal, less chance of surviving than did multi-specific ones, since any single species is so likely to prove, in the still longer run, to have been a natural error. This is shown by the fact that such a tiny percent of species of the past have turned out to represent lines that persisted. In accord with this principle is the finding that the category with the highest percent of survivals has been that of phyla, and that successively narrower categories have had a correspondingly decreasing survival rate.

In the case of man, it has been intrinsically dangerous for him to have so long existed as just one species. He has been saved not only by his unparalleled advantages but also by having until recently been divided into thousands of tiny bands, of at most a few score members each. In fact, as we have seen, this condition was especially favorable for the genetic enhancement of co-operative traits, including, I might add, those promoting group initiative or even—to use a harsher word—aggression. Until some two hundred generations ago the population pattern remained like this over by far the largest portion of the area inhabited by man. However, the agricultural revolution resulted in larger, denser, fewer groups, and the urban revolution greatly intensified this trend, thus practically preventing further genetic advances based on intergroup competition and even, in all probability, threatening the maintenance of those previously gained.

H. J. Muller [33]

---

their totality provide us with a clear understanding of the physical basis of individual uniqueness. The real wonder, however, is how it came into being through the processes of natural selection, but because the DNA → RNA → protein system, or some variant of it, is operative in all living organisms, we must assume that it came into existence very early in the beginnings of life on earth and that once initiated it had an extraordinarily high selective value. If there are other systems that were given a trial, we know nothing about them.

The nature of mutations

What has been described above implies that a particular protein in a cell is formed by a particular segment of DNA. Some proteins, of which hemoglobin is an example, have multiple subunit sequences of amino acids, and these are controlled by two or more genes. In a functional sense, then, it is the proteins that give us our individuality, and we may readily grasp this by remembering that our blood types, of which there are many kinds, allergies, various immune reactions, and ability to accept or reject transplanted skin or organs are determined by the proteins present in our bodies. If these proteins differ from one individual to another, then a corresponding difference must exist in the DNA's that furnish the code for them. The fact that the geneticist may deal with traits seemingly far removed from the proteins of the cell—the waltzing of certain strains of mice, for example, or polydactyly in man—does not change the situation; there is no doubt that altered proteins are somehow responsible for these departures from normality. Normality,

One must always keep in mind that the biological or Darwinian fitness (also termed adaptive or selective value) is not the same thing as bodily strength, or intellectual capacity, or excellence in human estimation. Neither are they completely unrelated. Understanding of their relationships requires what Wright describes very neatly as research "in the unpopular and scientifically somewhat unrewarding borderline fields of genetics and the social sciences." As a guideline in this research, Wright suggests that the social fitness of a genotype "may be treated in terms of the balance between contribution to the society and social cost" of its carriers. For the bulk of the population, which corresponds very roughly but by no means precisely to the biological adaptive norm, there is an approximate balance between contribution and cost either at relatively modest or at relatively high levels. Where the social contribution is at levels much higher than the average, one may perhaps speak of social excellence and social elite; to what extent this elite is genetically conditioned is, of course, an open question; that it is not identical with the genetic elite as defined in terms of Darwinian fitness is indisputable. Essentially the same problem arises in connection with the genetic load. A lethal genotype which causes death of the embryo before implantation in the uterus has a Darwinian fitness of zero, makes zero social contribution, but incurs little or no social cost. On the other hand, genotypes which cause subnormal health or mental or physical disability are social as well as genetic burdens.

Th. Dobzhansky [7]

---

of course, is a subjective term for that which is most commonly encountered.

Mutations are deviations from normality; that is how they come to be recognized. They may be dominant or recessive in expression and favorable, neutral, or deleterious to the continued existence of an organism or a species. If a gene is a segment of DNA, then mutations must clearly be alterations in the sequence of nucleotide pairs. Such alterations may involve gains, losses, or rearrangements of the nucleotide sequences.

Remembering that the coded message is read unidirectionally (assume that it is from left to right) and by groups of three nucleotides at a time, the following may be presumed to occur:

DNA: ACC   GCA   CCC   TGC   AAC
Transcription: ↓   ↓   ↓   ↓   ↓
mRNA: UGG   CGU   GGG   ACG   UUG
Translation: ↓   ↓   ↓   ↓   ↓
Protein: Tryptophan—Arginine——Glycine—Threonine—Leucine

Let us now assume that the first G has been lost from the DNA sequence. It is now read as follows:

DNA: ACC   CAC   CCT   GCA   AC
Transcription: ↓   ↓   ↓   ↓   ↓
mRNA: UGG   GUG   GGA   CGU   UG
Translation: ↓   ↓   ↓   ↓   ↓
Protein: Tryptophan—Valine——Glycine—Arginine——?

The protein is now different and would either be nonfunctional or would perform in a manner different from that

Inherited metabolic diseases generate research activity of far greater intensity than one might expect from their relatively rare occurrence. This is because genetic disorders afford a unique opportunity to combine the concepts of genetics with the tools of biochemistry to study the metabolism of man, as has been so successfully done for the metabolism of microorganisms. The lesson of genetics is clear: genes contain the code for the structure of proteins; a mutation in a gene will result in an alteration of the specific protein to which that gene holds the code. The result may be benign or disastrous, depending on the importance of the protein to the overall metabolism and on the effect of the structural change on its function. Faced with a disease of genetic origin, the biochemist's task is to identify the altered protein which is specific to that disorder. Success may lead both to practical applications in the management of the disease and to a clearer understanding of normal metabolic processes.

E. F. Neufeld and J. C. Fratantoni [34]

The uniqueness of the individual

Slash-and-burn agriculture in Zambia.

Marc and Evelyne Bernheim photo,
from Woodfin Camp and Associates

*8.17 The sequential development and appearance
of effects resulting from the action of the
sickle-cell gene when present in the
homozygous state. The presence or absence of
the malarial parasite in the environment has
an effect on the degree of retention of the
gene in a population, but within a given
individual the presence of an abnormal hemoglobin
has an effect that extends well beyond that
relating to the character of the blood.*

of the original protein if the changes occurred in a critical part of the molecule. An added nucleotide would induce a similar, but different, alteration of the protein, depending of course upon where the insertion occurred and the kind of nucleotide inserted.

That this reasoning is not fanciful is indicated by known changes that have taken place in the hemoglobin molecule. Proteins can now be "finger-printed," that is, the sequence of amino acids from one end to the other can be determined (an easy statement to make on paper, but an extraordinarily difficult task to perform in the laboratory). Hemoglobins are tetramers, possessing four subunits consisting of two *alpha* chains and two *beta* chains, totaling about 600 amino acids.

After Neel and Schull, 1954

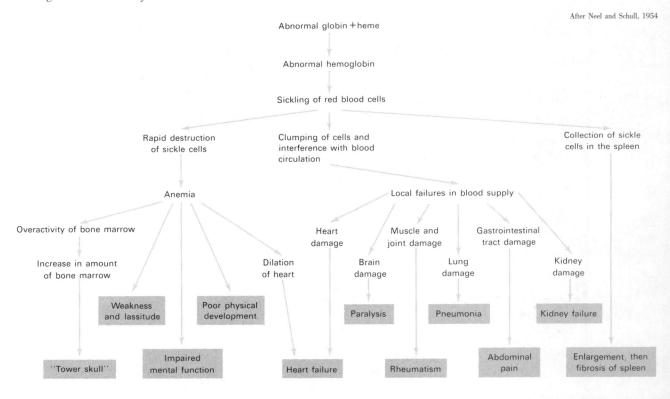

Increases in the man-biting habit of the mosquito have significant effects on the intensity of malaria and hence on the frequency of the sickle-cell trait. In many parts of the world an increase in the mosquitoes' man-biting habit is caused by the displacement or reduction in numbers of cattle or other animals that previously served as hosts for the mosquito. This displacement is caused by growth in human population, so the mosquito must turn increasingly to man as the major host. . . .

The particular agricultural adaptation we have been considering is the ultimate determinant of the presence of malaria parasites in the intracellular environment of the human red blood cell. This change in the cellular environment is deleterious for normal individuals, but individuals with the sickle-cell gene are capable of changing their red-cell environment so that intense parasitism never develops. Normal individuals suffer higher mortality rates and lower fertility rates in a malarious environment than individuals with the sickle-cell trait do, so the latter contribute proportionately more people to succeeding generations.

S. L. Wiesenfeld [43]

A large number of variant hemoglobins, some of them abnormal in function, are known, and they differ in their amino acid sequences, often by only a single amino acid alteration.

The substitution of one amino acid for another, out of the hundreds in the intact molecule, may seem a relatively minor change. However, an individual homozygous for the gene that produces hemoglobin S will very likely die of sickle-cell anemia at an early age; if he possesses a mixture of hemoglobins A and S he is immune to malaria. The change is literally a matter of life and death for those individuals inhabiting a malarial environment; outside this environment, hemoglobin S is a detriment to anyone possessing it, for it is less efficient than hemoglobin A in transporting oxygen.

How can such a mutation, affecting a single amino acid change take place? One possibility is the following, which shows what happens when two possible changes occur in one triplet of the chain that designates hemoglobin A:

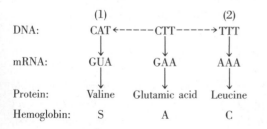

Because glutamic acid can be specified by two triplet codes, valine by four, and leucine by even more, the coded changes indicated above may not be correct in detail; they are, on the other hand, correct in principle.

With no less than, say 1 child in 25 over large parts of Africa having sickle cell anaemia, the rate of elimination of the gene is, of course, relatively enormous; for each time two of the genes come together in a homozygote there is very little chance of their being passed on. A mutation rate high enough to replace them is inconceivable. The reason why so harmful a gene should have become so very common in certain regions of the world must be because the heterozygotes enjoy some advantage over the normal homozygotes. Such an advantage, which may partially, if not wholly, explain the frequency of the gene in those regions, has been found. Heterozygotes are more resistant in infancy and early childhood to malignant tertian malaria. It should be added that it is not only deaths directly due to malaria that are important; malaria predisposes to early death from other causes, so in a community in which the death rate is very high the advantage of the heterozygotes is magnified. There will be in fact an equilibrium. Excess production of the gene owing to the raised reproductive fitness of the heterozygotes is balanced by elimination through the homozygotes.

J. A. F. Roberts [37]

Only 10 or 15 years hence, it could be possible for a housewife to walk into a new kind of commissary, look down a row of packets not unlike flower-seed packages, and pick her baby by label. Each packet would contain a frozen one-day-old embryo, and the label would tell the shopper what color of hair and eyes to expect as well as the probable size and I.Q. of the child. It would also offer assurance of freedom from genetic defects. After making her selection, the lady would take the packet to her doctor and have the embryo implanted in herself, where it would grow for nine months, like any baby of her own.

E. S. E. Hafez [15]

If the average protein is about 100 amino acids in length, then an average gene consists of 300 nucleotide pairs. The possibilities for mutation within even a single gene are astronomical in number when one considers that each nucleotide can be lost or replaced by a different one or that other nucleotides can be inserted anywhere along the length of the gene. When this occurs in a portion of DNA that codes for a nonessential segment of the protein molecule, the mutation may remain undetected because no change in enzyme function occurs. For example, the hormone insulin of swine, cattle, and man differ slightly from one another in amino acid arrangement, but all function similarly. That alterations in nucleotides are not simply idle speculation has been demonstrated by the viral and bacterial geneticists who, with exquisite techniques and precision, have been able to deal with single nucleotide changes and their expression through altered proteins. A suggestion that similar chemical changes are responsible for the mutability of genes in more complex organisms is provided by the data of A. J. Bateman, an English plant geneticist, who identified over 200 forms of the gene governing self-sterility in a rather small population of clover plants.

The wonder is not that mutations occur, but rather than mutations are not more frequent than they are. We can attribute this infrequency to several features: the double helical nature of DNA is such that the nucleotides project inward and are bound in pairs to provide a high degree of stability; the precision of replication is such that during the process copy-errors are reduced; and, as has been more recently discovered, there are within the cell nuclei of many organisms, although not in man and other primates, repair

The world which any consciousness inhabits is a world made up in part of experience and in part of fancy. No experience, and hence no knowledge, is complete, but the gaps which lie between the solid fragments are filled in with shadows. Connections, explanations, and reasons are supplied by the imagination, and thus the world gets its patterned completeness from material which is spun out of the desires. But as time goes on and experience accumulates there remains less and less scope for the fancy. The universe becomes more and more what experience has revealed, less and less what imagination has created, and hence, since it was not designed to suit man's needs, less and less what he would have it be. With increasing knowledge his power to manipulate his physical environment increases, but in gaining the knowledge which enables him to do so he surrenders insensibly the power which in his ignorance he had to mold the universe. The forces of nature obey him, but in learning to master them he has in another sense allowed them to master him. He has exchanged the universe which his desires created, the universe made for man, for the universe of nature of which he is only a part. Like the child growing into manhood, he passes from a world which is fitted to him into a world for which he must fit himself.

J. W. Krutch [21]

---

enzymes that can repair breaks in the molecule and undo mistakes made during the replicative process. These features determine the conservative aspects of inheritance; they ensure species continuity at the same time that they permit diversity, via the mutation route, which is necessary to meet changing environmental conditions. A species, moving through time as a dynamic system, is thus provided with a system of checks and balances to preserve its identity much in the manner that we, as individuals, maintain an internal physiological stability at the same time that we continually process energy derived from food to meet the needs of daily wear and tear and that we, as a social group, maintain cultural stability through our customs, traditions, language, and institutions. No system, whether it is a species, an individual, or a society, can retain identity in the face of a constant and high degree of disorder.

A final word about mutations, in this instance viewing them through geologic time. Our knowledge of the hemoglobin molecule permits us to do this. Beginning with the first appearance of the vertebrates millions of years ago and continuing to the present, the hemoglobins have served as respiratory pigments, carrying oxygen to the tissues of the body and returning carbon dioxide for release through gills or lungs. The overall tetrameric structure of the hemoglobin molecule has not changed a great deal during this very long period of time; only in the primitive lamprey eel and the hagfish does the hemoglobin consist of only one protein chain. We must assume, therefore, that the hemoglobins reached a high degree of perfection very early in vertebrate history and that from then on its evolution has been conservative because it had to retain its respiratory function

Genetics *is* a form of Calvinism—but it is Calvinism with a difference. That there is a sort of predestination at the time of conception is true: what genes an individual has is determined by what sperm unites with what egg. The genes of the gametes become the genes of the zygote, and (by repeated equational division) of all the cells of the adult body. In the formation of the next generation of gametes, chance enters in during the reduction division, in the assorting of the various alternative alleles, but the distribution must always be made from the genes available in the individual as a result of the earlier fertilization. Chance, operating within predestined boundaries, determines the possibilities of the succeeding generation.

G. Hardin [16]

The uniqueness of the individual

Although men flatter themselves
with their great actions, they are not so
often the result of great design as of
chance.

La Rochefoucauld [24]

The most effective avenues of preventing
genetic disease include (1) the primary prevention
of gene mutations, and (2) the detection and
humane containment of the DNA lesions once
introduced into the gene pool. The "natural"
mutuation process in man results in the
introduction of a new bit of genetic
misinformation once in every ten gametes. Most
of the human cost of this "mutational load" is
paid during early stages of fertilization and
pregnancy, where it makes up a fair part of the
total fetal wastage. But about 2% of newborns
suffer from a recognizable discrete genetic defect.
This is just the tip of the iceberg; the heritability
of many common diseases suggests that from
one-quarter to one-half of all disease is of genetic
origin, for there are important variations in
susceptibility to the frankest of environmental
insults.

J. Lederberg [23]

at all times. One can well imagine that severe selection
pressure was operative to maintain an optimal functional
capability, and hence a limit was put on the amount of
change that was permitted to take place.

It is believed that the two genes determining the *alpha*
and *beta* chains of hemoglobin are related, that is, one has
been derived from the other through duplication, and that,
following duplication, they have diverged from each other
in nucleotide sequence as a result of mutations. The tetrameric nature of fish hemoglobin suggests that the duplication took place several hundred million years ago. If we
now compare the amino acid sequences of the human *alpha*
and *beta* chains we find that there are eighty-five single
amino acid differences between the two chains. Taking 500
million years as a round figure separating man from the
fishes, we arrive at a rough figure of one successful incorporation of an altered nucleotide every 6 million years. This
would suggest further that human hemoglobins should not
differ appreciably from those of the anthropoid apes, and
this indeed is so. Human and chimpanzee *alpha* proteins
are identical, whereas that of the gorilla differs by only a
single amino acid. The many variant forms of hemoglobin
in man can be explained by the assumption that the hemoglobin genes mutate frequently and randomly, but their
successful incorporation as a species characteristic is quite
another matter.

The question can be raised as to whether the rate of
amino acid incorporation into hemoglobins is characteristic
of all proteins, or whether each protein—and consequently
each gene governing its formation—has its own intrinsic
rate of change. The latter appears to be the case. Cytochrome C is a protein found in all species of plants and

Henri Cartier-Bresson photo, Magnum

animals and is a basic element of the respiratory cycle within cells. A fingerprinting of the cytochromes from a wide variety of organisms reveals a much slower rate of change than that characteristic of the hemoglobins, with one amino acid alteration per hundred amino acids of chain length occurring once every 20 million years. On the other hand, a far higher rate of change is found among the fibrino-proteins. These are a part of fibrinogen molecules, and when fibrinogen is converted to fibrin during the formation of a blood clot, the fibrino-protein is cut loose and is eventually degraded. It appears to serve no other function and therefore can be judged to play a far less important role in cellular affairs than either hemoglobin or cytochrome C. Its rate of change, calculated on the same basis, is one amino acid alteration per million years.

As indicated, the rate of amino acid substitution in proteins is not to be equated with the rate of mutation in genes governing the formation of these proteins. The rate of mutation of a gene must always be very much higher than the rate of its successful incorporation into the gene pool of a species and the subsequent replacement of its predecessor gene, but the data from the amino acid sequences of proteins give us some sense of the conservativeness, as well as the inexorability, of evolutionary processes. As Dean E. Wooldridge states in his *Mechanical Man:* "The essence of the theory of evolution is the balancing of the near inconceivability of its accomplishments against the correspondingly near inconceivability of its painstaking attention to detail." The data also make evident, as Darwin insisted, that evolution proceeds through the accumulation of many small changes, most of them unnoticed, but each one of which can contribute to the adaptability of the species.

The uniqueness of the individual

We inherit, not through our genes, but through our childhood training, the feeling that what is, is "right." Even the idea of discussing creativity as a human act did not enter the mainstream of human consciousness until the 18th Century. Up until then, it was almost universally held that everything there was, or ever would be, had been formed in one grand act of Creation, and the role of poor mortals was limited to discovering what was already there. We think we know better now; that all of life is a creative process; that the world is constantly new, and that the efforts of human beings to respond to it endlessly create new patterns that shape the environment as it is experienced. . . .

Creativity pervades nature; living things are constantly engaged in the process of combining inorganic elements into new patterns that become cells of blood or bone; new combinations and patterns of inert, primordial things. Through imprinted genetic messages, these originally creative acts tend to become repetitive, and thus are no longer creative. The mollusk can only form shell from calcium; the plant can only make cells from the radiation, air, water and minerals of its environment. Man has similar, built-in, genetic imprints, too, but in addition he has something else, an ability to form new or original patterns of things. What is built-in, in man, is not the response, but the ability to respond in various ways.

D. Fabun [11]

Individuality and culture

Each of us comes into the living world as an unprecedented and unrepeatable individual because of a unique and equally unrepeatable genetic endowment. But we are individually unique in a behavioral sense as well because we are molded, during the processes of growth and development, by the environment in which chance places us, and it is the cultural aspects of that environment, not our genes alone, that give us our humanness. An individual growing up in the absence of a culture is a human animal to be sure, but not a human being capable of exercising the creativity and value judgments that are the essence of culture.

It is difficult, indeed impossible, to separate out, and place a determinative value on, all the influences that mold an individual. We know that the cells of an early embryo, all possessing the same genetic endowment, can be acted upon by position, physical forces, and chemical reactions to become liver, nerve, muscle, or retinal cells, each with a fixed and irreversible nature. In an analogous sense, the individual is equally plastic and malleable, the more so the younger he is. The human individual learns to become the person that he is, and how, what, and when he learns determines the degree of fixity of behavioral responses to cultural situations.

Sigmund Freud laid emphasis on the significance of early exposures of the individual to later behavioral responses; in his assessment of the individual, he generally ignored the role of genetic differences in the development of person-

The uniqueness of the individual

278

ality. But the two cannot be separated. We learn because we have the capability of learning, but what we learn and how this becomes fixed and expressed as response patterns is dependent upon the opportunities we have for learning. To varying degrees, however, we retain a measure of flexibility, of making decisions between alternative situations, and of preserving that which we call freedom of choice, or free will.

Neurobiologists, studying the development of microneuronal connections in the brain, point out that the intricacy of circuitry of nerves in the cortex is related to the corresponding diversity of sensory exposure. Neuronal connections, like any developmental process, are made according to a strict time schedule and with a high degree of specificity, but only if the appropriate environmental signals can act as inductors. If the signal is missing, the connection cannot be made, and will not be made at a later time. In humans, the growing circuitry goes on until a person is about 14 years of age. Just as man created himself out of a prehuman state by the invention of a culture, so each of us creates his own personality out of the genes he possesses and the environmental and cultural circumstances to which he is exposed.

Summary

We can define man as 6 feet of DNA, with its base pairs sequenced in a particular pattern and embedded in the nucleus of every cell. It is this that places each of us in the company of man, and it is within this pattern that each

The uniqueness of the individual

There never were in the world two opinions alike, any more than two hairs or two grains; the most universal quality is diversity.

M. de Montaigne [31]

---

of us acquires uniqueness. There is no uniqueness in being unique, however, for it is a characteristic each of us shares with every other organism, past and present.

The above definition is set in a mechanistic frame of reference, and it would appear that our array of genes, unique though they may be to each of us, programs us in a predetermined manner as physical and chemical processors of materials and energy. There is little doubt that we are what we are because of the genes we possess and the manner in which they function and achieve expression. But just as a house is potentially determined by a prior set of blueprints, so too does it become a home according to the time, place, circumstances, and nature of its occupants. Similarly, we are products of time, place, and circumstance, although we cannot separate the physical body from its human occupant. Genes do not gain expression in a vacuum, but rather in an environment that brings out the potentialities that lie encoded within them. Furthermore, our genes have blessed us not only with the capacity to develop in an entrained manner, but also with the ability to respond creatively to an environment, to make choices and decisions, to manipulate our environment and augment our meager physical resources, to create symbols that emerge as poetry, music, sculpture, and mathematics, as well as an everyday functioning language, and to solve the structure and function of DNA so that we can begin to visualize why we are what we are. We know that we are flesh and bone, the Darwins, Watsons, Cricks, you and I; but within the flesh and bone that is each of us lies the difference, the diversity that spells out our hopes and despairs, our talents and inadequacies, and our future as individuals and as part of the continuing community of man.

The uniqueness of the individual

9

Evolution revisited

In preceding chapters, emphasis was placed on organic evolution, on processes and events that account for the origin and continuity of biological diversity. In relatively recent geological time, these processes brought into being man, an animal who was not only potentially capable of developing a culture but also so plastic in behavior that its future has remained amazingly open-ended and self-manipulable. That potential has been realized and exploited to an extraordinary degree when compared with what has happened among other species. Diversity in the biological world is paralleled by equal diversity in the human sphere of culture. But evolution is not restricted to the biological world; it is characteristic of the entire universe. It occurs at all levels and systems of organization, in all materials,

1 At moment X
  the universe began.
  It began at point X.
  Since then,
  through The Hole in a Nozzle,
  stars have spewed. An
  inexhaustible gush
  populates the void forever.

2 The universe was there
  before time ran.
  A grain
  slipped in the glass:
  the past began.
  The Container
  of the Stars expands;
  the sand
  of matter multiples forever.

3 From zero radius
  to a certain span,
  the universe, A Large Lung
  specked with stars,
  inhales time
  until, turgent, it can
  hold no more
  and collapses. Then
  space breathes, and inhales again,
  and breathes again: Forever.

  M. Swenson [46]

organic and inorganic. The mechanism of evolution varies from one level, or one system, to another, but all share a common characteristic—all exhibit the phenomenon of change with time.

The cosmos, of which we, our earth, and our solar system are a part, is believed to have originated some 10 billion years ago from a primordial mass of enormous density that exploded with unimaginable force and continues to expand as a result of this initial event. This so-called big-bang theory contrasts with steady-state cosmology, a competing theory that postulates a continuous creation of matter throughout time (see illustration 9.1). At the present time, the big-bang theory is the more widely accepted of the two. If we agree with the big-bang theory and the data that tend to support it, we then assume that the universe is expanding, and thus evolving. We can only speculate as to whether this evolving universe is a one-shot affair, or whether, as some propose, it is born, develops, dies, and is then reborn again in cyclical fashion. This view is similar to the Far Eastern philosophy of reincarnation, which relates both to man and the cosmos, but only meager scientific evidence permits us to extend our cosmological thinking so far into the past or the future,

9.1 Two theories of the universe. According to the steady-state theory (a), the galaxies within any given region of space move apart with the passage of time, but new galaxies occupy the vacated regions and thus keep the density of the universe constant. On the other hand, proponents of the big-bang theory (b) assert that no new galaxies are formed as galaxies move apart, and thus the universe is becoming less dense.

From R. T. Dixon, *Dynamic Astronomy*, Prentice-Hall, 1971.

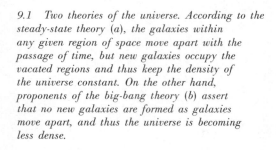

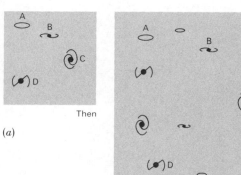

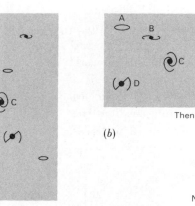

(a)

(b)

Then

Now

and it is faith alone that sustains a belief in a succession of lives on this earth.

The time spans with which we presently deal are enormous, as are the speeds with which the heavenly bodies move away from us through space. Out of the initial primordial mass have come billions of galaxies, each with its own multitude of stars and planets. Each presumably has its temporal existence, and each at some undetermined future date will probably lose its present identity through evolution into something else, what we do not know. This kind of evolution is made possible by gravitational contraction that has an effect on objects of all sizes, but is operative most obviously in cosmological events of great magnitude. Our own solar system, formed by this process, is centered around a minor star, our sun, located at the edge of a galaxy, the Milky Way, which has a flattened lens shape resulting from its rotational behavior (illustration 9.2). The Milky Way is about 900,000 light years in diameter.

Chemical evolution proceeded along with cosmological evolution, with various chemical elements coming into being as neutrons and protons formed nuclear combinations. These then acquired the appropriate numbers of electrons to balance electrical charges. Hydrogen, the simplest element, was the starting point of chemical evolution. One hypothesis is that all the chemical elements were formed within a brief period, perhaps no longer than 30 minutes after the initial explosion of the primordial mass. Supporters of the steady-state hypothesis, on the other hand, assert that the evolution of elements goes on continually in the cosmos. At the molecular level, change occurs constantly, particularly on our earth where water is the universal solvent. This kind of change, with its attendant energy involvements, is of no

9.2 *An artist's conception of the Milky Way.*

All conditions are green
for Mariner, marvelous
through black noons
to Mars.

All systems are go.

It is to be hoped from go
that like a small red salmon
looking for its source
Mariner will thread the right stream
to the red star
and spawn before dying;
not find itself at the wrong spring
and crush its head against a rock
until dead.

U.S. Department of the Interior

In the past, discussions of the orgin of life tended to be speculative exercises, often tinged with superstition. . . . In modern times, the origin of life has become a problem for legitimate inquiry, subject to the same intellectual discipline as are other attempts to understand evolutionary processes—including the requirement for logical elaboration of hypotheses, avoidance of arbitrary assumptions, and recourse to observation and experiment. As with other historical investigations that attempt to reconstruct past events from present evidence, this one is subject to inherent limitations. Our knowledge of the terrestrial environment in the remote past is uncertain and, as the history of the question shows, is liable to drastic revision from time to time as new evidence accumulates. Furthermore, it is impossible to duplicate, or even approximate, the geological time scale, the variety of conditions, and the secular changes in these conditions that occurred during the earth's history. Thus, current discussions of the origin of life adopt the uniformitarian view that the evolution of the earth is a history of gradual change by processes that are still going on. But we cannot exclude the possibility that some unusual event, such as collision with a comet, all evidence of which has been destroyed, played a pivotal role in the origin of life. Because of such constraints, the most one can ever hope to claim for conclusions in this subject is a high degree of plausibility. In this respect, however, studies of the origin of life differ in degree, but not in kind, from other scientific investigations. . . .

P. Handler [26]

quantitative cosmological consequence; life, however, could not have come into being without it.

In our sun, hydrogen is being converted into helium by thermonuclear processes; this is the source of life-giving light and heat on earth. When the solar hydrogen is finally expended, the fires of the sun will die, and it and the earth will pass into eternal darkness. It has been estimated that this will occur about 5 billion years hence. Here on earth, water, pressure, radioactivity, and fluctuating temperatures continue to alter the face of the earth and the elements and molecules within it. About 3 billion years ago, chemical evolution gave rise to a group of molecules that, when the proper organization and behavior were acquired, displayed a totally new quality—life. The atmosphere surrounding the earth was relatively free of oxygen at that time, and laboratory experiments have given us some indication of the formation of those molecules peculiar to living organisms.

The origin of life through chemical evolution introduced a new process into cosmological events; it was, so to speak, a mutation in cosmological processes, but not one that transgressed physical laws. The second law of thermodynamics informs us that the universe as a whole is running downhill, structurally and dynamically. That is, matter is becoming less ordered and energy is becoming more diffuse and more uniformly dispersed. This concept presupposes that there are higher and lower forms of energy, and that energy flow is always toward lower forms. Any unit quantity of energy, however packaged and whatever its form, is endowed with a quality called *entropy*, which is defined as a measure of the degree of disorder associated with the energy. Energy can flow only in such a way that it becomes more and more dispersed or degraded, with entropy increas-

Evolution revisited

Flying to creation.
Swimming to our source.
All conditions are green.

Return to the tree
by the waters of Fort McHenry
    for an encore from the Mockingbird.
Listen to 33 songs
with the whirring and buzzing,
the splicing and throbbing,
the climbing and swooping:
after tentative half-tones
the landing
on the gorgeous stones
    of the whole circle.

The thrills of flight
in any direction
to any zip-coded destination.

On the 12-tone scale of the white noon
none of this
    needs accompaniment.
No accompaniment necessary.
Nobody else necessary.
No other soul, brain, voice
necessary
but everybody welcome.

Interarboreal flight
from star to star
ends the Encore.

Ends the Lesson.
White smoke of Selma & Saigon.
Out of the dark condition of my heart,
Lights.

All conditions are green?
Some conditions are red.
All systems are go?
Some systems are stop.

E. Coleman [12]

---

ing as the dispersal proceeds. For example, the flow would be from gravitational energy, which is the highest form in that it has zero entropy, toward sunlight, a lower form; reverse flow cannot occur. Any conversion process from one form of energy to another is less than 100 percent efficient, with heat energy, a usual by-product, being given off and never recovered.

Life seems to reverse this process. It is a constructive process, creating order out of disorder by selecting from the miscellany of the environment those materials and units of energy that it needs and then concentrating the energy and regrouping the materials into the orderly parts and systems characteristic of each species. Life is, in a sense, the watchmaker of the universe, making use of the carbon atom as the basic substance out of which to build the wheels of life and also repackaging the energy in more usable forms to turn these wheels. Life, indeed, is a continuous experiment in the manipulation and management of matter and energy, and we can, with justification, view evolution as a trend toward increasingly more diversified and often greater degrees of organization, integration, and specialization of structures and functions, all accompanied by a variety of means of energy conversion, concentration, and utilization. But life only postpones the inevitable degradation and dispersal of energy; it does not convert energy from a lower to a higher form. The trapping of sunlight by plants, the first step in energy utilization, has a low order of efficiency, and each step in the food chain, from the green plant to the carnivore, leads to the continual escape of energy through heat loss. Plants as a whole capture solar energy with an efficiency rate of about 0.1 percent, with forests, grasslands, and wetlands substantially more efficient

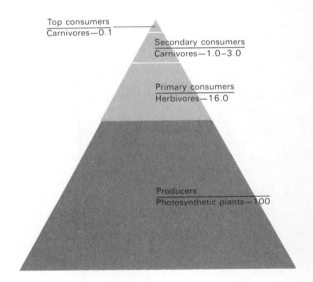

9.3 *The flow of energy from producers to the several levels of consumers. Radiant energy from the sun is the primary source of energy, and the conversion of incident energy by way of photosynthesis is on the order of 0.1 percent, although higher in some systems than in others. From then on, the efficiency of conversion in the form of chemical energy is lower and lower, with much of the loss being in the form of heat. The numbers in the illustration indicate the efficiency of energy conversion from one level to the next in percentages, with the amount of energy derived by photosynthesis being arbitrarily set at 100.*

Evolution revisited

It is easy to sit back smugly in the conceit that we have now reached almost the acme of biological evolution and that, except perhaps for eventually bestowing on everyone the genetic advantages already enjoyed by the most favored, we can hereafter confine our advances to cultural evolution, including the manipulation of things outside our own genetic constitutions. It is true that cultural evolution, in this broad sense, is far more diversified, rapid, and explosive, both figuratively and literally, than biological evolution can be. Moreover, along with the increasing understanding of and mastery over physicochemical forces that our expansion in space and our advances in control over physical energy imply, there will surely be corresponding advances in the physiological, neuropsychological and social realms. Yet all this does not mean that genetic advances beyond the stage represented by the happiest possible combinations of the best endowed of present-day humanity would be either supererogatory, unimportant, or relatively limited.

If the comparatively small genetic difference between apes and men is really as important as it seems to be in determining men's amenability to profit by culture and to contribute to it, why would not beings as far beyond present-day men, genetically, as we are beyond the apes be inordinately better suited still for exploiting the benefits of culture? Do we hastily made-over apes really believe that, having attained our present makeshift form, further steps of this kind are to be despised? Our imaginations are woefully limited if we cannot see that, genetically as well as culturally, we have by our recent turning of an evolutionary corner set our feet on a road that stretches far out before us into the hazy distance.

H. J. Muller [*34*]

With no serious qualifications we can say that all the information needed to produce an adult is found in the tiny amount of DNA enclosed in the nucleus of the zygote. Tiny? Yes, indeed! The weight of the DNA of one fertilized egg is only six picograms [6×10^{-9}]. To use a homely comparison, the amount of zygote DNA needed to specify *all* of the world's population of 3.5 billion people weighs only one-seventeenth as much as one postage stamp. This is microminiaturization of information with a vengeance!

It takes more than information, of course, to make a structure. The DNA of the nucleus is surrounded by the rest of the cell, and in development before birth a steady flow of raw materials must be brought to the fetus, and waste materials removed. After birth, not only the physiological, but also the psychological, needs of the individual must be met. The DNA of the zygote will achieve its ''goal'' of a normal adult human being only if a great deal of love and care is bestowed on the developing human being.

G. Hardin [*27*]

than cultivated fields. Herbivores can convert roughly 16 percent of plant energy, and carnivores, including man, convert the energy of herbivores at a similar rate (illustration 9.3). This continual loss of energy leads to death of the individual and, ultimately, of all life, and the entropy of all systems will continue to increase. The fact that man, as part of the life system, hastens the dispersal of energy in an irretrievable form is illustrated by one of the major problems of modern industrial society; the disposal of waste heat into our environment may set a limit to the levels at which energy can be used and dissipated. In the meantime, "Everything is itself for a while, after which it becomes something else." This is the essence of evolution, from the cosmic to the human phase.

Of the various aspects of life, culture is the element that has appeared most recently. It too is subject to the forces of evolution and is superimposed on the biological, just as the biological was built on the chemical, and the chemical on the cosmological. Just as life resulted from a mutation of chemical processes, so culture arose from a mutation of behavior. Culture is associated with man alone and can be distinguished from other social organizations, such as those of ants, termites, and bees, which are instinctual rather than learned. Culture shares the fundamental characteristic of all evolutionary systems: it changes with time, more slowly here, more rapidly there, but with a pace that, when viewed historically, seems to possess a built-in acceleration factor. Like life itself—we can separate human life from culture only for the sake of convenience—culture is a dynamic process, dependent basically upon the manipulation and management of matter and energy, although possessing

Evolution revisited

Carved objects of unknown use discovered in northwestern Alaska.

American Museum of Natural History

behavioral, attitudinal, and ideological features that constitute its more obviously visible aspects.

Some experts have suggested that the increasing exploitation of energy sources contributes substantially to the acceleration factor. Communication, as one facet of culture, is a case in point. Many animals have developed systems of communication to serve a variety of functions: to signal the presence of food or danger, to pose threats, to keep the community intact and within hailing distance, and to search for mates. Man has elaborated upon this system and has evolved an intricate language, followed by the development of writing, printing, and, more recently, global communication systems making use of electronic devices and space satellites. Energy is required to perform every type of communication, and man has tapped sources of energy so that he can communicate beyond the range of his own voice. He has made more effective use of energy to perfect his means of communication, and the evolution of his system has been accelerated as technology has become more sophisticated. No other species has been able to progress beyond the inherent capabilities of the individual in this regard.

When we view man as an animal, we can trace his evolutionary path by means of the artifacts he has left behind him and the fossil remains of his bones and teeth and, comparatively, through his present anatomy, biochemistry, and genes. He was without doubt tailored physically from apish prototypes by the processes of natural selection, which acted on the heritable variations existing within the ancestral groups that preceded him in geologic time. Millions of years of changes went into the restructuring process, but man, in a real sense, took over the process when he

The rate of change in any social system can be accelerated by two means, or by a combination of both. One is the diffusion of new techniques from one cultural centre to other peoples, and the second is the over-rapid growth of technology towards the climax of a cumulative cycle, such as we live in today. The first is a commonplace of history, the second unique in our own age.

When a peripheral culture area is swamped by the introduction of new techniques, a number of things can happen. A very primitive food-gathering people may be driven into barren wastes, if any are available, as in the case of the surviving South African Bushmen. If there is no escape they succumb to a combination of diseases from which they have no immunity and a neuroendocrinological dysfunction, like that found in animals subjected to crowding. Crowding affects reproduction rates as well as the will to live in a new, incomprehensible, whirling social order, in which old values are discarded and the wisdom of the ancients turned into prattle. To these disorders may be added nutritional shock by the replacement of habitual wild foods by flour, sugar, tea, tobacco, and alcohol. For people subjected to such invasions of privacy and indignities by modern, civilized intruders, there is little hope of genetic survival except by peripheral absorption into the lower fringes of the invading population.

C. S. Coon [14]

Evolution revisited

9.4   *Reconstruction of a Neanderthal family group of about 50,000 years ago.*

acquired those forms of learned behavior that we call his culture. He became, as it were, his own designer, transforming himself from an animal into a human being. In the process, he developed a gradually enlarging informational and behavioral pool that is to cultural evolution what a gene pool is to biological evolution. The biological differences of anatomy, in particular his highly developed and plastic nervous system, that separate him as a species from all other animals made possible the creation of culture, but we cannot state with certainty that these features made culture an inevitability. We only know that an initial small step was taken some time in the past and that, once this step had been taken, the process was irreversible, although future paths remained undefined and optional.

As has been stated, we cannot disassociate man the animal from the culture that makes him human. Culture has made man as much as man has created his culture. It binds men together into a cohesive and identifiable unity and, at the same time, molds and governs the thinking, feeling, and behaving of its constituent individuals. It is that group of communally accepted understandings that provide goals and standards of achievement against which an individual may judge himself. The attainment of these goals is important for the satisfaction of individual and group needs.

A man without a culture does not exist. As an animal, man is indeed physically ill-equipped to exist without a culture. He can run, swim, jump, bite, see, hear, and smell reasonably well, but a host of animals can perform one or more of these feats far better than he. He is a large animal, but his strength and endurance are not commensurate with his size. He would not do well in unarmed competition with many animals smaller than himself, for he has no natural

Evolution revisited

For his successful progress, throughout the savage state, man has been largely indebted to those qualities which he shares with the ape and the tiger; his exceptional physical organization; his cunning, his sociability, his curiosity, and his imitativeness; his ruthless and ferocious destructiveness when his anger is roused by opposition.

But, in proportion as men have passed from anarchy to social organization, and in proportion as civilization has grown in worth, these deeply ingrained serviceable qualities have become defects. After the manner of successful persons, civilized man would gladly kick down the ladder by which he has climbed. He would be only too pleased to see "the ape and tiger die." But they decline to suit his convenience; and the unwelcome intrusion of these boon companions of his hot youth into the ranged existence of civil life adds pains and griefs, innumerable and immeasurably great, to those which the cosmic process necessarily brings on the mere animal. In fact, civilized man brands all these ape and tiger promptings with the name of sins; he punishes many of the acts which flow from them as crimes; and, in extreme cases, he does his best to put an end to the survival of the fittest of former days by axe and rope.

. . .

Cosmic evolution may teach us how the good and the evil tendencies of man may have come about; but, in itself, it is incompetent to furnish any better reason why what we call good is preferable to what we call evil than we had before. Some day, I doubt not, we shall arrive at an understanding of the evolution of the aesthetic faculty; but all the understanding in the world will neither increase nor diminish the force of the intuition that this is beautiful and that is ugly.

T. H. Huxley [31]

---

weapons such as horns, quills, venom, or hooves, no escape mechanisms such as great speed, flight, or camouflage, and no protective outer covering such as fur, feathers, or shell. In one biological sense, man is a very generalized species, adapted and restricted to no special ecological niche; in another sense, he is highly specialized, structurally and behaviorally. Indeed, if he had to depend upon his physical abilities, he would have a difficult time competing for living space in almost any environment. But it is, paradoxically, his very general qualities, coupled with his special mental and manipulative abilities, that permit him to exploit and control a wide variety of environments. He can handle materials with deftness and precision; he can augment his physical powers through the use of energy derived from the environment; he can think, plan, and project into the future; and he can symbolize with impressive inventiveness in order to make understandable and often visible to others the experiences and thoughts of his own individual being. These aspects, cumulative as they are, spell the difference between

Anthropological studies and evolutionary doctrines have suggested useful hypotheses concerning the progressive emergence of the physiological and behavioral characteristics which define each animal species and particularly *Homo sapiens*. Man, it now appears, was not yet fully evolved, either physically or mentally, at the time when he began creating the crude elements from which most of his culture derives. Recent evidence indicates that, one million years ago, very primitive hominids with brains hardly larger than those of anthropoids had reached the stage of toolmaking. The further growth of the human brain apparently coincided with a progressive change in the hominid way of living. . . . Contrary to the old belief that men anatomically like ourselves slowly invented culture, it is probable, in other words, that the increase in the size of the human brain occurred simultaneously with the first phases in the unfolding of human culture. Man and his culture evolved, simultaneously, as it were, through a complex series of feedback processes.

R. Dubos [18]

9.5 Culture binds men together into a cohesive whole and makes possible group action based on communally accepted goals.

Charles Harbutt photo, Magnum

Civilisation is the most highly evolved technique so far discovered by any living organism to ensure the survival of the species, and at the same time to allow it to attain new levels of awareness. The word itself comes from the Latin *civilis,* meaning that which pertains to a citizen, but civilisation today implies much more than mere citizenship. It is a form of biological organisation where mind, which enabled *Homo sapiens* to achieve domination over all other life forms, itself embarks on a process of indefinite expansion. In achieving this expansion it is clear that the laws of mutation and natural selection have applied just as much as they did in the earlier organic phase of evolutionary development.

R. Carrington [8]

Is it human nature to kiss a loved one? If it were, then the practice would be universal. But it is not. There are peoples who do not kiss at all. Some rub noses. Others merely sniff the back of the neck of children. And in some societies a parent or elder relative will spit in the face of a child; saliva is here regarded as a magical substance and this act is therefore a sort of blessing. Among some peoples adult males kiss each other. I once witnessed greetings between men in one of the isolated valleys of the Caucasus Mountains. They kissed each other fervently, pushing aside a thick growth of whiskers to reach the lips. Other peoples regard kissing among adult males as unmanly. Where does human nature enter this picture? It does not enter at all. The attitude toward kissing as well as its practice is not determined by the innate desires of the human organism. If this were so, kissing behavior would be uniform throughout the world as the organism is uniform. But this is not the case. Behavior varies because cultures differ. You will do, or taboo, what your culture calls for.

L. A. White [51]

man and other animals. In their endless expressions in the form of thought, feeling, and behavior, they constitute culture and permit man to exploit his surroundings and to come to terms, very successfully if numbers are a criterion of success, with his environment, with himself, and with others of his own society. But *a* culture specifically, as opposed to culture generically, represents a particular selection of expressions and the exclusion of others, all of which gives one culture its uniqueness and sets it apart of all others. No culture embodies all variants of expression, any more than any human individual portrays all aspects of mankind.

It is often said that in today's world of competition one needs to be a generalist in order not to become outmoded by fast-moving events and technology. Yet it is the specialist who contributes most significantly to this pace, thereby sealing his own doom by his particular, even if narrow, competence. A somewhat similar situation prevails in the arena of evolution, although the time scale is vastly greater.

9.6   In the history of evolution, an organism that specialized in order to better cope with its environment may find itself unable to survive when the environment changes. In a similar way, the specialist of yesterday discovered that his very specialization prevented him from keeping pace with evolving technology.

Ford Motor Company

Chevrolet Motor Division, General Motors Corporation

. . . [the] sense of the kinship of all forms of life is all that is needed to make Evolution not only a conceivable theory, but an inspiring one. St. Anthony was ripe for the Evolution theory when he preached to the fishes, and St. Francis when he called the birds his little brothers. Our vanity, and our snobbish conception of Godhead as being, like earthly kingship, a supreme class distinction instead of the rock on which Equality is built, had led us to insist on God offering us special terms by placing us apart from and above all the rest of his creatures. Evolution took that conceit out of us; and now, though we may kill a flea without the smallest remorse, we at all events know that we are killing our cousin. No doubt it shocks the flea when the creature that an almighty Celestial Flea created expressly for the food of fleas, destroys the jumping lord of creation with his sharp and enormous thumbnail; but no flea will ever be so foolish as to preach that in slaying fleas Man is applying a method of Natural Selection which will finally evolve a flea so swift that no man can catch him, and so hardy of constitution that Insect Powder will have no more effect on him than strychnine on an elephant.

G. B. Shaw [41]

Specialization is one of the first steps toward exploitation of an environment, but it is also a first step toward eventual extinction, because evolution is irreversible and the environment is not stable. Few species have remained flexible enough and sufficiently unspecialized to exist in a wide variety of environments. Man, however, is one of these. He of course possesses all of the general physical features characteristic of a mammal, but no one of these has become so dominant as to subordinate others to it and thus put man on a one-way track. We may well ask why this is so, but any answer is equivocal. The best that we can offer by way of explanation is that man has learned to live by his wits, to use them to respond to environmental challenges not so much by altering his physical aspects, but rather by solving the challenges through cultural cleverness. The mountain, as it were, has been made to come to Muhammad.

Culture, however we wish to define it and whatever elements we wish to include within its limits, is an adaptive mechanism that enables man to hold his own in a competitive world and give meaning to his existence as an individual and as a member of a group. It is as necessary an adaptive mechanism for the emergence and persistence of man as was the appearance of lungs and legs for the invasion of land by the vertebrates. Adaptation, of whatever nature, implies a measure of environmental control, of being able to extract from the environment in selective fashion those things needed for survival and continued reproduction. However, adaptation, so defined, is inadequate in a cultural context; man lives not solely to survive, but also to exist in relative and continuous harmony in his surroundings as he interprets them. Thus, man may acquire and retain certain expressions that are very significant to him as a

Three crucial Paleolithic cultural "breakthroughs"—symbolic speech, tool and weapon making, and fire control and production—allowed man to increase in numbers and to spread all over the world. With these creations he was able to challenge any animal and any environment. In doing so, he discovered that because conditions of life changed constantly, his survival was often directly related to his ability to adjust. What was a cultural asset in the moist tropics might actually be a liability if one were suddenly confronted with a desert situation. A hunting society in an area where game was scarce could save itself through cultural flexibility alone. With man situated in so many locations and conditions about the world it was both necessary and inevitable that his work and its fruit should vary prodigiously. He learned to like many foods, to create many types of clothing and shelter, to enjoy varied luxuries, and to establish and accept different rules for the production, distribution, and accumulation of goods. Some preferences were determined by the environment. Others show clearly man's supple mind and imagination in action. Many early societies perished because they could not adapt rapidly or well enough to variation in environment. Nevertheless, mankind had the key to ultimate survival as our present-day cultural diversity proves. For wherever cultural differences exist, we see the evidence that man at work has successfully met his particular circumstances head on with his creative faculties.

J. Conrad [13]

Evolution revisited

If one goal of prehistory is the accurate description of past patterns of life, certainly it is the job of the archaeologist to explain the variability he observes. Explanation, however, involves the formulation and testing of hypotheses rather than the mere assertion of the meaning of differences and similarities. Many traditionalists speak of ''reading the archaeological record,'' asserting that facts speak for themselves and expressing a deep mistrust of theory. Facts never speak for themselves, and archaeological facts are no more articulate than those of physics or chemistry. It is time for prehistory to deal with the data according to sound scientific procedure. Migrations and invasions, man's innate desire to improve himself, the relation of leisure time to fine arts and philosophy—these and other unilluminating clichés continue to appear in the literature of prehistory with appalling frequency. Prehistory will surely prove a more fruitful field of study when man is considered as one component of an ecosystem—a culture-bearing component, to be sure, but one whose behavior is rationally determined.

S. Binford and L. R. Binford [4]

9.7 An old totem pole discovered in northwest Canada. The totemic symbols generally represent family lineage and may be interspersed with symbols recalling mythical or historical events. These objects are products of a culture and are indicative of man's attempt to order his existence by placing himself in historical perspective.

Canadian Consulate General

self-conscious animal, even though they have neutral, or even detrimental, adaptive value. His varied rites of passage and of burials, for example, have no direct survival value for the living, and the concept of the divine right of kings may have been profoundly detrimental in many instances, but in their time and place they possess a cohesive value; they bind men together. For man this means not only survival as a species, but also survival of man as a cultured species. Culture, however, differs from other adaptive mechanisms in that its controlling aspects consist not of an inheritance having its origin in the physical structure of DNA, but rather of a learned set of habits, thoughts, and patterns of behavior readily suited to a wide variety of physical and social environments.

Culture, like life itself, seems to run counter to the second law of thermodynamics in that it creates order out of disorder. This is merely an illusion, however. Man, from his early beginnings of self-consciousness, seems to have had an innate need for order in his existence, a desire to know who he is and how he fits into both the local and the cosmological scene. He has invested time, effort, and imagination in putting disordered elements into particular patterns that satisfy this need and that provide him with a measure of assurance in an often hostile and frequently capricious environment. Like any other organized system possessing continuity, culture requires energy, and cultural evolution, as we have insisted, depended, and continues to depend, upon the control, manipulation, expenditure, and eventual degradation of sources of energy. Each culture does this in its own way, for while energy is necessary for the existence of a culture, it does not necessarily determine its character. As Leslie A. White [51] has written:

Evolution revisited

Mysterious stone figures on Easter Island.

Eugene Gordon photo, Nancy Palmer Photo Agency

Culture is but a means of carrying on the life processes of a particular species, *Homo sapiens.* It is a mechanism for providing man with subsistence, protection, offence and defence, social regulation, cosmic adjustment and recreation. But to serve these needs of man energy is required. It becomes the primary function of culture, therefore, to harness and control energy so that it may be put to work in man's service. Culture thus confronts us as an elaborate thermodynamic, mechanical system. . . . The functioning of a culture as a whole rests upon, and is determined by, the amount of energy harnessed and by the way in which it is put to work.

Another way of stating the same proposition is that cultural advancement has depended basically upon the ideas and technological innovations that have allowed man to extend his control over the environment and to supplement, from exterior sources, the energy supply of his own body (see illustration 9.8). In this way, man has freed himself, in part, from the constant struggle for daily existence and from the continuing threat of famine, and he is thus able to divert his remaining energy into other cultural channels of an adjustive nature. Earlier we described an individual as the medium through which energy is processed; a culture, large or small, simple or complex, can be viewed similarly. It was through the exploitation of extrabodily sources of energy, and the invention of continuing means of extending this exploitability, that man became the hunter, not the hunted, the farmer and animal husbandman, not the wandering and foraging nomad, and, eventually, the creator of settled villages, cities, and nations. Nothing succeeds like success. The initiation of an energy-based culture—there is no other kind, just as there is no energy-free individual—as distinct from simply a social organization, was an innovative adaptation of unprecedented proportions and undreamed-of potentialities.

9.8   Cultural advancement depends primarily on the success with which man has been able to harness the power of the environment through new inventions and new technology. The windmill, waterwheel, and sail have contributed greatly to the steady evolution of civilization.

The growth of man's dominion over matter through control of energy was, and is likely to be, a long-drawn-out process. It extends back through history and prehistory, to the very beginning of humanity. Every important technical advance in the past has involved some new phase in the control of energy. Steps forward such as the use of tools to redirect human effort to better advantage, control over fire, or control over the energy of horses and other power animals are extremely ancient. Probably these advances were quite obtrusive when first introduced. Although they have turned out to be epoch-making in their outcome, because of their antiquity it is difficult now to reconstruct all the original features of such discoveries. What does persist as obvious, even now, is the need to control energy. This need to achieve dominion over matter inspired these advances and remains perennial. A Robinson Crusoe suddenly abandoned now on a desert island would experience much the same sequence of ideas about how to subjugate the world around him as did the original. In fact, the vocation to control energy in its various manifestations is absolutely basic to human nature.

A. P. Ubbelohde [47]

When we view human settlements as systems of energy mobilized by man—either as basal metabolic or as muscular or, recently, as commercial energy systems—we get new insights. We see man spreading his energy thin in the nomadic phase of his history, then concentrating in one area and using both energy and rational patterns when he organizes his village, where he spends more energy in the built-up part than in the fields. Later we see him concentrating in the small city and using a wider built-up area, where he expends even more energy, and then, when more people are added, we see him spreading beyond into the fields. Finally, when he has commercial forms of energy available and can dispose much more energy without properly understanding its impact on his life and therefore without controlling its relationship to his settlement, man becomes completely confused by his desire for more energy. He suffers because, through ignorance, he inserts this additional energy into the system that he creates in a way that causes problems such as air and thermal pollution.

C. A. Doxiadis [17]

The cultural consequences of energy use

In a scientific sense, energy is the capacity to do work or to overcome inertia by making use of heat, light, radiation, or mechanical and chemical forces. In a broader sense, however, energy can be thought of as the power by which anything or anybody acts effectively to move or change other things or to accomplish any result. It is in the latter sense that the term "energy" is used here, not simply in the sense of that power bound up in the fossil fuels (coal, gas, or oil), in radioactive atoms, or in wind or moving water. It is all of the extrabodily resources that, when brought under control, increase the adaptability or adjustibility of the user. It is the stone ax held in the hand to increase the energy and effectiveness of the wielder; it is the wheat that is cultivated in a field in order to provide a source of food energy that is more reliable and more constant than that provided by the haphazard harvesting of wild plant foods or the hunting of game. Energy is also that force or power that derives indirectly from man's habits: his propensity for accumulating knowledge and broadening the range of uses to which this knowledge can be put; his ability to particularize and to generalize; his sense of time and his ability to connect the past, present, and future; and his power of symbolizing, which leads to experiential economy and permits the conveyance of ideas. Objection may be raised in defining energy in such broad and vague ways, but viewed evolutionarily each new energy acquisition, whether mental or physical, gives man an added differential advantage in

The birth of metallurgy must therefore be seen as the culmination of difficult and scientifically hazy labor, in the course of which men learned to extract a number of metals from their ores by fire and to cast and alloy them. The discovery of metals appears to have begun in the 6th millennium and to have been reasonably well advanced by 2000 B.C. It occurred through an area stretching from western and central Anatolia across the flanks of the Taurus and Zagros mountains to the edge of the central desert of Iran.

The time and place are not accidental. The post glacial epoch in southwestern Asia, particularly after about 8000 B.C., was a time of discovery and exploitation of the material world, during which tribesmen on the flanks of the Taurus, Zagros, and Alborz mountains became arbiters of biological evolution by taming animals and cultivating plants, and instigators of technological revolution by learning the uses of fire and the potential uses of earth.

Archeologists cannot agree on the precise juxtaposition of mountain and plain at which the pastoral arts of Abel, the agricultural arts of Cain, and the metallurgical arts of Tubal Cain were each learned. But it is doubtful today that the earth that yielded Cain's bread was also that which was "turned up as by fire." With some notable exceptions, the rich soils of the Mediterranean littoral or the river valleys of the Fertile Crescent, where agriculture reached its first apogee, are nearly barren of minerals and indeed poor in fuels.

Th. A. Wertime [50]

---

a fight for survival and provides the increased security and stability so necessary for cultural development.

Having forsaken an arboreal existence for life on the ground, man, at the australopithecine stage of development, seemingly lacked, as we have indicated, many of the physical attributes necessary for successful competition for food and living space. Admittedly, we know little of his social habits, but he did not possess a number of attributes found among his simian ancestors: the fierce canine teeth of the baboon; the acrobatic agility of the arboreal gibbon; or the size and strength of the gorilla. He did have the security that comes from living in caves, from organized communal effort, and from the cunning that is his human trademark, and we can surmise that, because man survived, he must soon have reinforced his physical inadequacies by the use of tools and fire. Wooden sticks, clubs, and spears probably preceded the use of deliberately fashioned stone tools by at least a million years. The latter, in the form of crudely flaked hand axes, were once believed to have made their first appearance about 400,000 years ago in the area of China where Peking man existed, but the recent discoveries made by the Leakeys in the Olduvai Gorge in Africa indicate that the australopithecines, or some form coexisting with them, fashioned stone tools of various sorts about 1.7 million years ago. This is the first archeological evidence of the use of an added source of energy—power, if you will—that initiated man's growing dominion over his environment. A sharpened stone ax, either held in the hand or fitted with handle, provided a substantial amplification of energy over that possible from the unarmed hand or clenched fist. Fitted onto a spear or the tip of an arrow, the combined use of

*A page from the Dresden Codex, a manuscript
of still undeciphered Mayan writing.*

stone and wood extended the application of energy at a distance, enhancing the success of the hunter, and broadening the base of defensive and offensive tactics. In fact, as illustration 9.9 indicates, every advance in weaponry, from the thrown spear to our present intercontinental ballistic missiles, has widened the distance between the user and his target, but, when protagonist and antagonist are equally equipped and skilled, this has not enhanced the margin of safety.

The shaping of stone implements for various uses became more and more refined, and stone tools were not replaced by those made of metal until about 5,000 or more years ago. By this time man had advanced culturally in other ways also as he came to exercise a greater degree of control over his environment. Although no fossil evidence can provide us with clues, there is little doubt that a symbolic language

9.9   The evolution of weapons. Every advance in weapons technology as a result of new or more efficient uses of energy has widened the gulf that exists between the user and his target.

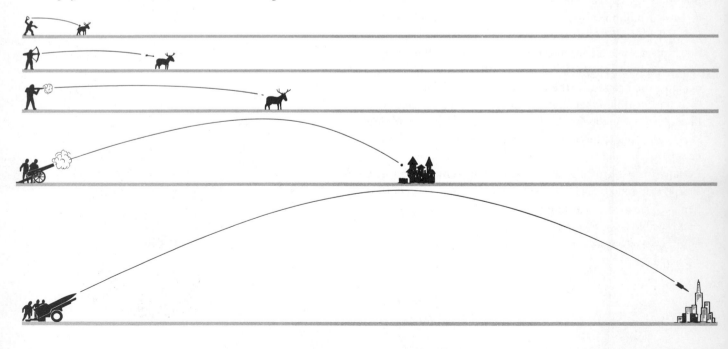

It is difficult to realize the enormously important role that language plays in our social behavior. What would a society without language be like? It would of course have no writing or other means of communication by words, for all these are ultimately dependent on spoken speech. Our means of learning would therefore be greatly restricted. We should be obliged, like the animals, to learn by doing or by observing the actions of others. All of history would disappear, for without language there would be no way of re-creating past experiences and communicating them to others. We should have no means of expressing our thought and ideas to others or of sharing in the mental processes of our fellowmen. Indeed, it is very likely that we should not think at all. Many psychologists maintain that thought itself requires the use of language, that the process of thinking is really talking things over with ourselves.

H. Hoijer [30]

---

of speech and gestures had long been a part of man's culture, for the invention and use of tools seem incomprehensible in the absence of the spoken word. Fire had been under control for at least 400,000 years, first for warmth, protection, and cooking, and, much later, for the smelting of metallic ores and the curing of pottery. Man became more the human being and less the human animal as he learned to supplement his own meager sources of energy through other means and as he became aware of his own powers of manipulation. Indeed, his powers of inventiveness came into play to further his control over nature, and he turned to magic to enhance his chances of success. The stone and clay "Venus" figures (illustration 9.10) that have been found at many excavated sites throughout Europe, some dating from as early as 50,000 B.C., have been interpreted as fertility symbols designed to promote the productivity of the group, whereas the cave paintings of Cro-Magnon man suggest a utilitarian totemism associated with the success of the hunt. The fact that sources of power such as these are false in the sense that they are nonexistent does not mean that they did not serve a practical purpose. In their totality, these tentative attempts at energy manipulation represent the initiation of a gulf between man and nature, a gulf that would widen with time and would emphasize to man his own uniqueness and capabilities and, ultimately, his limitations as well.

For a million years or more, stone tools, supplemented by those of wood and bone, represent the major technological extension of energy use in sustaining the human species. They were apparently sufficient for a nomadic existence and for a wide dispersal of man throughout the Old World and into the New. The fact that many fossil human skulls have

9.10 This fertility figurine, known as the Venus of Willendorf, *is probably over 30,000 years old and is representative of a group of similar statuettes produced by man of the Old Stone age.*

Museum of Natural History, Vienna

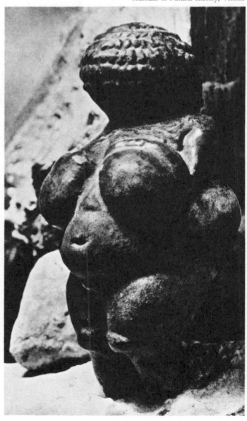

Sedentariness is perhaps the most astonishing biotechnical "invention" and the most successful revolution ever carried through in man's relation to his environment. The conditions for sedentariness are the acquisition of biological knowledge and the faculty of organization of biotic processes. Man creates an artificial landscape, in which fertility and water are preserved by actively fulfilling the rule of return observed in nature. The disturbed cycles of growth are ever-restored by transportation, storage and the use of seed, fertilizers, water, crops and materials. This requires a continual investment of human and material energy to maintain the artifact, implying far-reaching environmental change. By this achievement, man necessarily alienates himself from the ecological context; but he uses his new position to establish a relationship to the land on a new level. . . .

Sedentariness is a cultural achievement, not because it ends the more animal and mobile kind of life and replaces it by another, but because it succeeds in uniting the animal and vegetative trends of environmental relationship in a new spatial order of rest and movement, and because it combines land use with time use in a new pattern of human life. One of the contributions of sedentariness to the quality of man's relationship to environment is that man can identify himself with an environment by feeling that he belongs to it, and by being aware of his obligation to maintain it. It is a central motif of the man-environment relationship, which we shall always endeavour to recover in some form in the course of environmental modification.

A. Glikson [25]

In trying to assess the meaning and significance of palaeolithic art we must at all costs avoid judging it in terms of our own modern culture. Palaeolithic man had no idea of "art for art's sake." If we wish to understand his attitude we must go, not to the modern artist, but to a society like that of the Australian aborigines. Among these people art is not an amusement or a means of self-expression; it is an adjustment to the rites and ceremonies connected with birth, death, fertility and the propitiation of evil forces. When the aborigines of central Australia engrave and paint rocks they do so as part of a ritual that may involve mime, dancing and the recitation of legends, the total aim of which is to reassure society at large and enchance the confidence of its individual members.

The Upper Palaeolithic hunting peoples of western Europe had two great preoccupations: the need for nourishment and the need to perpetuate their kind. They were concerned with their own fertility and with that of the animals on which they so largely depended; and they were concerned, as they might well be, considering the primitive nature of their equipment, with success in the hunt, on which they depended for their only important source of food and clothing. The Upper Palaeolithic cave-dwellers experienced anxieties common to the rest of mankind; their special claim on our attention is the manner in which they sought to resolve them through the medium of art.

G. Clark [11]

cracked domes suggests that early man was cannibilistic, at least in a ceremonial sense. He had, as a hunter, an animal protein base to his diet. and thus food was available in more varied and concentrated form. In this sense man differs from his simian relatives, all of whom have remained basically vegetarian in diet. A hunting existence, however, even though supplemented by wild plant foods of various sorts—berries, nuts, seeds, and roots—does not permit the establishment of stable centers of population, a precondition for a rapidly progressive cultural advancement. A stabilized and continuous food supply was necessary. The archeological record in fact makes it quite clear that no major culture has come into being until it was able to cultivate storable foods. These, in large measure, are the cereal crops, although protein supplements came through the cultivation of leguminous plants such as beans and lentils, which are also storable. Therefore, in order for a culture to progress beyond that possible in a roving society, man had to give up his nomadic way of life and settle down to the more prosaic domestication and cultivation of manageable crops. In this way he could accumulate sufficient excess energy in the form of storable foodstuffs to sustain a small population from one harvest to the next. The plow and the hoe—or their primitive equivalents—took their place alongside the ax, the spear, and the arrow as the principal tools of man. The food producer was thus in a position to produce more than he and his family could use, and the dependent urban centers, which did not produce their own food, could come into being.

The origins of the agrarian revolution—for a revolution it was in cultural terms—which involved the domestication of plants and animals, goes back at least 10,000 years. By

Evolution revisited

The presence of a body of well-instructed men, who have not to labor for their daily bread, is important to a degree which cannot be overestimated; as all high intellectual work is carried on by them, and on such work material progress of all kinds mainly depends, not to mention other and higher advantages.

C. Darwin [16]

When tillage begins, other arts follow. The farmers therefore are the founders of human civilization.

D. Webster [49]

---

this time, Neanderthal and Cro-Magnon man, and possibly others as well, had walked out into the mists of antiquity to disappear forever, although we cannot be certain that their genes are not part of the present human heritable pool. How long it took for the agriculturalist to reach a state of agrarian art that was advanced enough to produce the surplus of food necessary for the establishment of nonagrarian centers of population is uncertain, but there seems good reason to believe that it occurred first in the foothills of the Near East and Abyssinia, with possible extensions later into upper India and western and central China. This is

9.11 On the map, the white dots indicate known and reasonably certain sites of wild grasses—wheats and barleys. The darker, bow-shaped area running from Israel and Jordan north into Turkey and then south into Iran outlines the foothill regions where the grasses were probably first domesticated.

. . . the plants which we grow for food produce only a certain proportion of their substance in the form of starches, sugars, proteins, etc., which we can eat. The rest, apart from water content, consists of fibres which we plough back into the soil, or feed to animals, though occasionally we can use them for textiles or pulp.

The palaeolithic hunter required 10 square kilometres per person to feed himself; the neolithic herdsman, 0.1 square kilometre, or 10 hectares; the medieval peasant two thirds of a hectare of ploughland to produce cereals for subsistence, plus his woodland: the Indian rice grower one fifth of a hectare to produce subsistence; the Japanese one sixteenth of a hectare, or only 640 square metres. It is the growth of population which has provoked these agricultural improvements. But we are still far from the end of the road.

C. Clark [10]

After Harlan, 1951

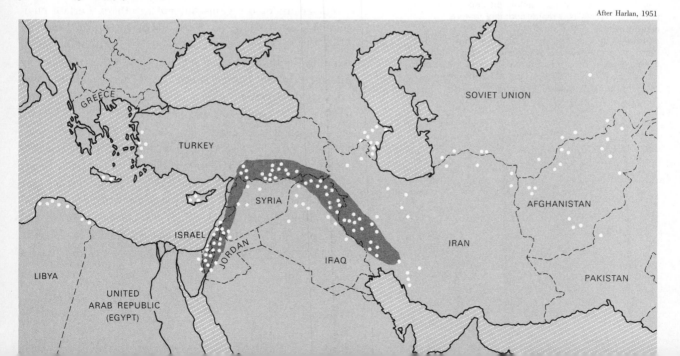

The Industrial Revolution was the product of the Agricultural Revolution, which freed people to leave the land to work in the factories. The feedback from the Industrial Revolution was mechanization of agriculture, thus driving more people off the land to furnish low-cost labor for the factories. The legacy of mechanized agriculture is the big city ghetto. The countries that have managed to create urban ghettoes in this way are called, by a euphemism surpassing belief, "developed." Those which have not seen the light yet are "underdeveloped." Many other factors are involved, but the trek to the cities is, in most countries, the result of mechanized or plantation-type one-crop agriculture. . . .

The true killers of the American heritage were not the hunters' guns but the farmer's herds of cattle, flocks of sheep and goats; most of all, his acres and acres of wheat, corn, potatoes, sugar cane, cotton and tobacco. His seven-league boots had acre-sized soles, and his heels were made of steel.

D. Fabun [22]

Probably the most important of the early cereals was barley. Analyses of archeobotanical material . . . show clearly that the first barleys were two-rowed and resembled rather closely some races of the spontaneously occurring barley found in these regions today. Morphologically, the differences between cultivated two-rowed barley and the spontaneous forms are rather minor. The cultivated forms have a tough rachis that does not break even on threshing, while the wild forms have a brittle rachis that disarticulates at maturity into individual units each containing one seed and two sterile lateral spikelets. While the fragile rachis is a major adaptive feature distinguishing wild from cultivated barley, it is controlled by only two genes. Cytogenetically, there is no difference between wild and cultivated forms. They can be crossed readily; they hybridize rather commonly in nature, and the chromosomes of the hybrids give perfect pairing at meiosis.

J. R. Harlan and D. Zohary [28]

the home of the wild annual grasses from which the cultivated wheats and barleys are derived, the first cereals to be brought under control. As the complex procedures of agriculture were being perfected—sowing, cultivation, harvesting, selection of seed for the next year's crop, storage, and transportation—other plants were brought into the primitive gardens to supplement the cereal diet. In addition, meat from the animal flocks and herds and the fish from the sea, lakes, and rivers were also added. Rice became the staple of the Far East, whereas the inhabitants of the New World came to depend upon maize, supplemented with potatoes and beans. In a sense, these plants domesticated man as much as he domesticated them, for he had to gear his life to their ways if he was to use them effectively.

It is of some interest to ask why settled communities of men, based on a plant or a mixed plant and animal economy, and gradually acquiring a distinctive yet open-ended culture, developed in some regions but not in others. Certain environments are undoubtedly too harsh in climate and too meager in yield to permit any cessation in the unremitting search for food; under these conditions, the nomadic hunting mode of existence cannot readily be changed, and the population is kept rather constant by the food supply. This appears to be true for a number of rather diverse peoples who had shown no change in life styles or numbers until their way of life was interrupted recently by interaction with more modern man. The Eskimo was tied to the land, water, and ice of the Northlands and was unable to alter his way of life until the rifle, motorboat, and snowmobile increased his mobility; he is now caught between two cultures, and his own less diversified culture seems inevitably doomed. At the other end of the Western Hemisphere, the Indians

Grant Heilman

of Tierra del Fuego were caught in an equally restricting environment, and the Australian aborigines were confined by a hot and dry season that at times made food scarce and kept populations from expanding. The character of the climate or terrain cannot provide a total answer, however. A number of groups in seemingly highly favorable environments—lake or riverbank dwellers having access to abundant fresh harvests or those in tropical or semitropical regions with ever-present fruits and roots—were seemingly free from the threat of starvation, but they never advanced beyond a primitive state of culture. In retrospect, it appears that complex cultures tend to develop best in population centers that were located where a long and well-watered growing season alternated with a colder nonproductive period that permitted a diversion of talents into new directions. Such climatic alternations are of course characteristic of the temperate zone and provide both the opportunity and the challenge for a settled mode of existence. Because the earliest civilizations of the Near East and those developing in the higher altitudes of Central and South America were characterized by these climatic conditions, one can assume that the environment was not entirely without influence in this stage of man's cultural development. But this is only an assumption, not a proof.

As a result of all this, the human species was being differentiated into the producers and nonproducers of food, each group providing the other with the necessities demanded by the various cultures. In its earliest stages, it was at best a precarious existence, for in classical civilizations such as Sumer, Egypt, Greece, Rome, and China in the Old World and in the Incan, Mayan, and Aztec cultures of the New World, the surplus, over and above that needed by

There are no miracles in agricultural production. Nor is there such a thing as miracle variety of wheat, rice or maize which can serve as an elixir to cure all ills of a stagnant, traditional agriculture. Nevertheless, it is the Mexican dwarf wheat varieties, and their more recent Indian and Pakistani derivatives, that have been the principal catalyst in triggering off the Green Revolution. It is the unusual breadth of adaptation, combined with high genetic yield potential, short straw, a strong responsiveness and high efficiency in the use of heavy doses of fertilizers, and a broad spectrum of disease resistance that had made the Mexican dwarf varieties the powerful catalyst that they have become in launching the Green Revolution. . . .

The Green Revolution has won a temporary success in man's war against hunger and deprivation; it has given man a breathing space. If fully implemented, the Revolution can provide sufficient food for sustenance during the next three decades. But the frightening power of human reproduction must also be curbed; otherwise the success of the Green Revolution will be ephemeral only.

N. E. Borlag [5]

. . . Judging from ethnological and archaeological evidence, simple natural ecosystems have been most usually and effectively occupied by mobile hunting groups who became intimately adapted to the exploitation of a principal food source, usually seasonally migrant herds of game, such as the bison and guanaco pursued by the mid-latitude grassland hunters of North and South America, or the caribou and sea mammals hunted by the Eskimo of the Nearctic boreal forest and tundra. Such specialized hunters make relatively little direct use of wild plants for subsistence, and, on accout of their highly mobile, game-dependent way of life, they may be precluded as progenitors of plant domestication and cultivation—a conclusion that accords with the lack of archaeological evidence for early agriculture in the simple ecosystems they occupied.

Complex natural ecosystems, on the other hand, have characteristically been occupied by less specialized populations of gatherers, fishermen, and hunters of small and slow game. These forager groups exploit a broader spectrum of plant and animal resources than the specialized hunters; they move less far and less frequently and are normally organized in small bands localized within a circumscribed territory. Historically they have occupied mainly forested and wooded areas and their less mobile existence, coupled with an intimate familiarity with the varied plant life of a limited area, suggests them as the most likely progenitors of plant domestication and cultivation.

D. R. Harris [29]

the producer, probably did not exceed 20 to 25 percent of the total product. Tragedy in the form of starvation was never far off for any early civilization, a situation still existing in some parts of the world today. A failing harvest could signal the end of a civilization. The collapse of the Sumerian culture is said to have resulted from this cause, and the exhaustion of the Italian soils contributed to the downfall of Rome. The slender difference between plenty and starvation made the siege an effective form of early warfare; the Berlin airlift of 1948–1949 indicates that a siege can be broken only with difficulty and with modern means of transportation.

Considered in terms of energy, the storable foods provided a major breakthrough in that they freed man for other pursuits; the glories of the ancient world are eloquent testimony of what was possible in terms of cultural advancement, with slave labor and wood fuel the only other major energy sources. The domestication of cattle, sheep, goats, and pigs, animals native to the same general region as wheat and barley, was of comparable importance to the cultivation of plants. The development of herds freed man from his hunting pursuits and provided wool, hides, and milk, as well as meat. It probably took man well over a million years to progress to an agrarian state, with the agricultural revolution coming into being as the last glacial ice retreated to the north. Thereafter, both a cultural explosion and a population explosion took place. Aided by the development of parallel technological innovations, progress in the arts, industry, and engineering was rapid and spectacular, as table 9.1 indicates. Most members of the human race were still tied to the land and would continue to be so for most of recorded history, but the agricultural revolution converted

Evolution revisited

. . . human intervention tends to reduce the maturity of ecosystems. Both in terms of the small number of species present and of the lack of ecological complexity a farm or a plantation more closely resembles an immature stage of succession than it does a mature stage. Furthermore, in ecosystems dominated by man the chosen species are usually quick to ripen—that is, they are short-lived—and the productivity per unit of biomass is likely to be high. Yet there is a crucial difference between natural pioneer associations and those dominated by man.

Pioneers [plants] in an immature ecosystem are characterized by their ability to survive under unstable conditions. Man's favored cultigens, however, are seldom if ever notable for hardiness and self-sufficiency. Some are ill-adapted to their surroundings, some cannot even propagate themselves without assistance and some are able to survive only if they are constantly protected from the competition of the natural pioneers that promptly invade the simplified ecosystems man has constructed. Indeed, in man's quest for higher plant yields he has devised some

of the most delicate and unstable ecosystems ever to have appeared on the face of the earth. The ultimate in human-dominated associations are fields planted in one high-yielding variety of a single species. It is apparent that in the ecosystems dominated by man the trend of what can be called successive anthropocentric stages is exactly the reverse of the trend in natural ecosystems. The anthropocentric trend is in the direction of simplicity rather than complexity, of fragility rather than stability.

R. A. Rappaport [39]

---

man into a sufficiently proficient producer and manager of storable energy to support a dependent, culture-promoting segment of the population.

Furthermore, if one considers the growing populations of man to be a product of the soil, then the earth was being transformed by man into a more productive environment. Prior to the agrarian revolution, the earth's population was about 10 million, a population that was limited presumably by the food supply and the methods of procurement. Since then, the population rise has followed the exploitation and rising productivity of arable lands. The heavy use of chemical fertilizers and mechanized equipment in the twentieth

Table 9.1   Development of skills*

Skill	Initial use, years ago	Location
Making of stone tools	500,000	Europe, Far East, Africa
Use of fire	500,000	Europe, Far East, Africa
Use of thrown spears	400,000	Europe
Use of bow and arrow	300,000	Europe, Africa
Representational art	100,000	Europe
Domestication of dog	80,000	Europe, Africa
Cultivation of cereal crops	10,000	Near and Middle East
Human portraiture	10,000	Near and Middle East
Domestication of horse, sheep, cattle	9,000	Near and Middle East
Manufacture of cotton	7,500	Europe, Africa, Near and Middle East
Use of iron	6,000	Near and Middle East
Use of the wheel	5,500	Near and Middle East
Cultivation of rice	5,000	Europe, Africa
Manufacture of wool	5,000	Far East
Use of stringed instruments	5,000	Near and Middle East
Use of written word	5,000	Near and Middle East
Use of copper	4,000	Near and Middle East
Making of pottery	2,500	Near and Middle East

*Data from S. Piggott, ed., *The Dawn of Civilization*, McGraw-Hill Book Company, 1961.

century, coupled with better strains of plants and animals and more effective use of land, has led to higher and higher yields per acre and has drastically reduced the number of individuals whose labor is required to feed an expanding population.

No cultural advance comparable to that brought on by the agrarian revolution took place again until the fossil fuels began to yield their bound energies for man's use. Throughout history, coal was used sporadically as a source of power and heat, but it was not until the late eighteenth and nineteenth centuries that the use of coal to fire a blast furnace and to convert water into steam for use in engines became a new and potent source of energy, at least in the Western world. Prior to 1850, wood fuel was the dominant source of energy, a fact to which the stripped hillsides of Greece and Italy bear silent testimony. The increased use of coal eventually resulted in the industrial revolution and played a significant role in converting an agrarian society into one dominated by growing industrial complexes.

9.12 *Total consumption of energy in the United States since 1850 (a) is compared with changing sources of energy over the same period. Note that in 1850 fuel wood accounted for 90 percent of the energy, and coal accounted for the remaining 10 percent. By the year 2000, coal will probably again supply only about 10 percent of the energy, while the other sources will be oil, natural gas, liquid natural gas, hydroelectric power, fuel wood, and nuclear energy. These estimates were made by Hans H. Landsberg of Resources for the Future, Inc.*

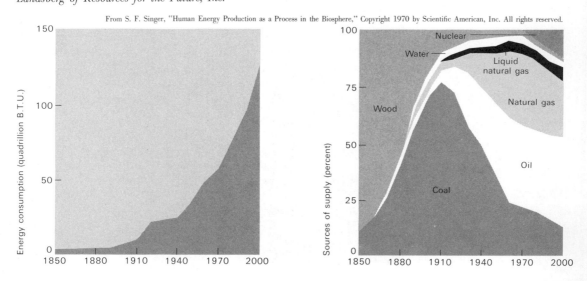

Nature endowed Europe with extraordinarily varied and abundant mineral resources. The conquest of this underground wealth by the Western peoples has been inseparable from the unprecedented power obtained by men in recent centuries over the physical world.

This power has come from the solution of technical problems which earlier civilizations had never seriously faced. Many of these problems first became acute in connection with mining and metallurgy. . . . It was the search for adequate means of draining coal pits that led to the practical use of the force contained in jets of steam, to the invention of the steam engine. As the quantities of minerals dug out of the earth increased, their bulky character exerted increasing pressure on men's minds to discover cheaper methods of carrying them over land and water. It was the difficulty of hauling ores and coal in wagons along rough, soggy ground that led to the invention and development of the railway. The demand for larger quantities of metal for use in war as well as in peace pressed men on to discover methods of treating ores which would reduce the labor and the waste involved in separating and obtaining metals. It was the persistence of western Europeans in exploiting a discovery which had been made by earlier people—that iron ore actually melted when the fires were hot enough—which has produced metal in overwhelming quantities from cascades of liquid flame.

J. U. Nef [36]

The energy of wind and moving water had certainly been exploited earlier. The waterwheel was used before the Christian era and provided power for the great textile industries of Europe before the advent of coal as a common fuel source. However, the use of water for power meant that growing centers could be located only on large rivers. The windmill was introduced into Europe in the eleventh century, and its success and rapid spread is attested to by the fact that the Church, within a short time, placed a tax on its use. The rudder was a ninth-century invention that permitted a navigator to sail an accurate course and eventually made possible circumnavigation of the globe and the consequent discovery of new lands ripe for exploitation. But it was basically coal, coupled with the mechanical devices that made its use feasible and economical, that altered the major cultures of the world. The discovery that petroleum could be used to power machinery accelerated the industrial development and the cultural changes initiated by coal, and the conversion of energy into an electrical form spread the changes over a wider area. Viewed biologically, and in the context of an increasingly more efficient agriculture, these energy sources made possible sharp rises in population density and greater shifts in population to centers that were not engaged in food production, but all this took place at the expense of an environment whose supportive limits are now becoming more and more obvious with each passing year. Illustrations 9.12 and 9.13 contain some important data relative to changing energy sources.

The energy problem remains with us today in an even more crucial and pressing way. The direct trapping of solar energy has not yet proved to be economically or technically feasible except in special circumstances such as the powering

In 1870 horses and mules were the prime source of power on U.S. farms. One horse or mule was required to support four human beings—a ratio that remained almost constant for many decades. Had a national commission been asked at that time to forecast the horse and mule population in 1970, its answer probably would have depended on whether its consultants were of an economic or a technological turn of mind. Had they been "economists," they would in all likelihood have estimated the 1970 horse and mule population at more than 50 million. Had they been "technologists," they would have recognized that steam had already been harnessed to industry and to ground and ocean transport. They would have recognized further that it would be only a matter of time before steam would be the prime source of power on the farm. It would have been difficult for them to avoid the conclusion that the horse and mule population would decline rapidly.

H. Brown [7]

9.13 Changing patterns of work effort in the United States from 1600 to 1960 as a result of increasing industrialism.

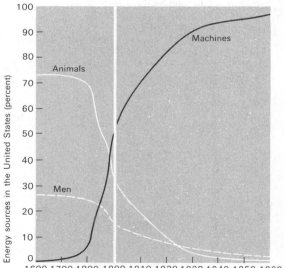

Evolution revisited

What we *are* trying to say here is that the transformation of energy for human use, which has been primarily an engineering and technological problem in the past, will increasingly become an economic, political and moral problem in the next thirty years.

Economic because, with our present technology, most of our energy is produced through the destruction of non-replaceable materials—coal, oil, gas, timber, fissionable elements. We are living off our capital and not our interest. Hydroelectric is not much better; the dams will silt up. The new ones, if we build them, will only replace the ones we've lost. There are inexhaustible sources of energy—the sun, the winds, the tides—but we do not use them. We don't even try to.

Political, because the allocation of available energy is the responsibility of elected officials. Who gets to transform power? Who distributes it? And to whom, and at what cost? These are political questions and to pretend that they are not—that they are a part of the ''natural order'' of things—is to ignore reality in favor of myths. How many myths does it take to turn a turbine?

Moral, because we are not alone. What we extract from the planet, and the sorts of waste we return to it, affects other species, who have as much right to live on this planet as we do. All we have against them is that they don't make money.

If the point of ''producing energy'' is to make money—then God help us; no one else possibly can. Sometime we better start to do some thinking.

D. Fabun [21]

Man stands at the end of a long cycle of energy exchanges in which there is a calculable and irreversible loss of energy at each exchange. A grown adult irradiates heat equivalent to that of a 75-watt bulb. His total energy output, in 12 hours of hard physical work, is equivalent to only 1-kilowatt hour. He requires daily 2,200 calories of food intake, 4 1/2 pounds of water and 30 pounds of air, and he discards 5 pounds of waste. Considered as an energy converter, man is the least efficient link in his particular ''food chain,'' and for this reason the most vulnerable to catastrophic ecologic change. Such a change can be caused by overloading the energy circuit.

D. Fabun [20]

of space vehicles, although future developments may alter this picture. It would appear then that nuclear energy, with its possibilities and its hazards, provides a likely, but uneasy, answer to man's future needs as the fossil fuels become depleted. As Alvin Weinberg, director of the Oak Ridge National Laboratory, has said: "It is my contention, as it was the contention of H. G. Wells and Sir Charles G. Darwin, that our only hope of providing the material needs of the coming billions, and thus buying the time needed to stabilize population by other than a Malthusian catastrophe, is in the development of a cheap and inexhaustible source of energy. From what we now know, this source seems to be nuclear. This, in a nutshell, is the basis for the claim made by nuclear energy technology on this generation's resources." However, the growing per capita consumption of energy, accompanied by an increasing degree of environmental depletion, alteration, and deterioration, makes inevitable some future limit to energy use, although we cannot now say when this will happen.

According to the first law of thermodynamics, energy is neither created nor destroyed, but is conserved. However, energy can be converted into other forms to be used or dissipated, primarily as heat. The successful management of energy for man's use on an ever-expanding basis is therefore related to how man has either redirected his own efforts or developed means for tapping other sources, directly or through conversion. Historically, the process of energy control has been stretched out over many millennia, back to the beginning of the human species. Early steps involved the development and refinements of tools to channel human effort to better advantage, the use of draft animals and human slaves as a source of power, and the control of fire

Evolution revisited

We must have a new industrial revolution even if a few of us have to generate it. Other industrial revolutions have come about unplanned. The first was hailed as a way of ennobling human beings by substituting steam and electrical power for their muscles. This it undoubtedly did, but the generation of power brought with it side effects—including air pollution—which, far from being ennobling, were and continue to be degrading to human existence. In the second revolution the multiplication of ''things'' came about—''things'' that at last could be mass-produced, so that people could have more and more of them. Thus was generated the solid-waste problem.

A third revolution was the tremendous growth in industrial chemistry, and the ability to tailor-make chemicals in vast quantities very cheaply, for all kinds of purposes—for example, pesticides intended to selectively destroy forms of life inimical to various groups of human beings. But these turned out not to be so selective; they have upset the little-understood ecological balance, and have polluted and poisoned the waters.

In preparation for the next industrial revolution, I suggest that we revise our vocabulary. For instance, there is no such thing, no such person, as a consumer. We merely *use* ''things''; and, according to the law of the conservation of matter, exactly the same mass of material is discarded after use. Thus, as the standard of living goes up, the amount of waste and consequent pollution must go up.

I believe we must base the next industrial revolution—a planned one—on the thesis that there is no such thing as waste, that waste is simply some useful substance that we do not yet have the wit to use.

A. Spilhaus [43]

---

and moving wind and water. Stonehenge in England, the Egyptian pyramids, and Angkor Vat in Cambodia could not have been built without slave labor and a sophisticated knowledge of mechanical forces. Indeed, we know of no age of man that did not make use of some kind of machine or tool to augment his physical powers. Technology was, and is, involved at every step; much of it was empirically developed at first and then based later on theoretical and experimentally derived knowledge as the scientific revolution of the seventeenth century moved into high gear. Although the relation of invention to cultural change and to man's altering view of reality is a fascinating topic outside of the scope of this volume, it is inseparable from man's concern with energy. In addition to the increase in knowledge of, or control over, the material world resulting from inventions, each innovation, whether of machines or tools or the ideas giving rise to them, brought cultural changes with it, for each dislocated the old ways of doing things and required accommodation to the new, as the environment changed physically, biologically, and culturally.

Many of the innovations in energy control and use brought on unobtrusive perturbations in the ways of man when they were first introduced. In their aggregate, however, they reinforced man's need or desire for additional energy sources. Although the plow had been invented about 1800 B.C., its true value was not recognized until it was combined 2,700 years later with another simple invention—the horse collar. The union of plow and horse collar made draft animals a far more effective source of power than they had been earlier and brought about significant changes in agriculture. In addition, the horse collar made draft animals an efficient means of transportation. The in-

The arts taken in their ensemble constitute material civilization, and it is this that chiefly distinguishes man from the rest of nature. It is due exclusively to his mind, to the rational or intellectual faculty. That is, it is an exclusively psychological distinction. Civilization, which is human development beyond the animal stage, goes forward under the economics of mind, while animal development takes place under the economics of life. The difference between these two kinds of economics is fundamental. They are not merely dissimilar, they are the direct opposites of each other. The psychologic law tends to reverse the biologic law. This latter law may be briefly defined as *the survival of the best adapted structures.* Those structures which yield most readily to changes in the environment persist. It has therefore been aptly called "survival of the plastic." The environment, though ever changing, does not change to conform to the structures but in the contrary direction, always rendering the partly adapted structures less adapted, and the only organic process possible is that which accrues through changes of structure that tend to enable organic beings to cope with sterner and ever harder conditions. In any and every case it is the environment that works the changes and the organism that undergoes them.

L. F. Ward [48]

The exercise and development of an individual talent in a technological society requires much vaster physical resources than it does in a less technically sophisticated society. For the man who is "good with his hands" to perform economically useful tasks today may require an investment in machinery that runs, for example, as much as $42,000 per worker in the metals industry, $26,000 in the chemicals industry, $77,000 for the petroleum industry. The workman with his simple tool kit or the ditchdigger with his shovel and strong back are vanishing figures in our society. The market analyst needs research materials, surveys, lines of communication and, ultimately, computers to make his work useful. The designer and artist needs more than a drawing board and drawing instruments; to make his work effective requires tons of paper, thousands of dollars of typesetting, plates, and press time. The secretary needs electric typewriters, desks, filing space, communications systems. At every level of endeavor in our society, the development and social use of individual talents requires sophisticated paraphernalia if the effort is to be multiplied into a social or economic value.

D. Fabun [23]

dustrial revolution, based on coal and spurred by the rapidly developing sciences of mechanics and thermodynamics, accelerated the rate of change and revealed the difficulties as well as the rising hopes brought on by the insertion of technological change into a cultural milieu that was often ill-suited to meet the challenge of sudden innovation. It is often said that today the rate of scientific and technological innovation is so great that a comparison with the industrial revolution is only a mental exercise, but it makes all the more pertinent a constant reappraisal of man as a species adapting to a world of precipitous change and shifting values. He is forced to become a student of change if he is to survive. E. E. Morison, in his book *Men, Machines and Modern Times,* and A. R. Ubbelohde, in *Man and Energy,* have dealt with this problem at length. Morison feels that the problem confronting man today, as a species and as a social animal, is not that of being concerned primarily with the mechanical realm and energy manipulation, but rather with "the way we are to deal with all new conditions produced by new machines and ideas. . . . It is not enough to be simply an adaptive society in a time of great change. Means must be discovered for society to keep charge over its own nature and direction." He adds that it is necessary "to take the measure, a little more closely than heretofore, of what man is in the new environment that he has created for himself and to give him the evidence necessary to modify, limit, and organize the developing environment so that he may extend his own range within it."

Any civilization, at a given point in time, has at its disposal a specific amount of tappable energy. It may be marginal in amount, as in nomadic, food-hunting, or herding societies, or readily abundant, as in the highly developed

Evolution revisited

Western cultures. It may be concentrated in restricted forms, for example, in the limited diet and use of fire and clothing by the early Eskimo, or highly diversified—foods and fuels of various kinds, slave labor, draft animals, instruments of energy conversion, storage, and use. But the manner of energy use, the process of deciding how and for what purpose energy is to be used, and the end products of use, all these give to a culture, at least in part, its particular, identifiable characteristic. The larger and the more complex a culture, the more likely it is that the expenditure of available energy is determined by a smaller segment of the society. Hierarchical order becomes established, and the peck order characteristic of chickens, wolves, and baboons finds its counterpart in the human species and in each culture. The irrigated rice culture of early China required pooled community labor and could not have been established except under authoritarian rule. In this aspect, it differs from the early, more loosely organized wheat-based cultures of the Near East. The pyramids of Egypt, Stonehenge, and the vast Gothic cathedrals of Europe represent end products of energy diverted into particular channels for particular reasons, with each reflecting, as well as serving, the needs of a given culture, and each, in the process, giving a culture meaning and shape. Only cultures that had gained reasonable freedom from the continual struggle to obtain necessities of daily survival could afford such visible manifestations of form and style. Leisure, affluence, and independence of thought and action, coupled with the control and directed use of energy, have played significant roles in the evolution of cultures.

The history of life as we know it and the evolution of man inform us in unequivocal terms that man, versatile

9.14 Machu Picchu, the "lost city" of the Incas. Discovered in the twentieth century, this city is believed by experts to have been constructed as a refuge for the Inca Virgins of the Sun. The luxury of channeling energy into projects such as this belongs only to highly developed cultures.

Evolution revisited

Any genetic determinants of human behavior, however great they may appear in certain individual differences, cannot at the present time be ascribed a causative role in cultural differences. It is entirely possible that societies may have genetic differences that are comparable to those of individuals, but such differences are so slight that their existence has never been established, while their role in determining cultural patterns is so infinitesimal that they can be disregarded. A demonstration that genetic factors have shaped cultural patterns will require a rigorous scientific methodology that has not yet been developed.

The assumption that individuals can be bred for a superior culture not only lacks scientific validation of the relation between genetics and culture but presupposes indefensible conclusions concerning the superiority of any culture. There are no ethical grounds for maintaining that modern culture is inherently superior to primitive culture or that either science or philosophy can blueprint a better culture for the future.

J. H. Steward and D. B. Shimkin [45]

though he is as a molder of the environment and as an inventor of culture, can escape neither the constraints of the physical environment in which he lives nor the biological inheritance that has shaped him. He adapts or he becomes extinct. His manipulation of energy has given him a degree of dominance unprecedented in the living world. From what we know of evolution, it appears that those species that were successful were the ones that kept their future options open by means of a diversified gene pool at the same time that they were sufficiently specialized to exist and reproduce in the environment in which they found themselves. Man is now changing more rapidly in a cultural sense than he is in a biological sense. Continued and successful adaptation requires a diversified cultural pool that is enlarged by new ideas, new machines, and new modes of action; but the preservation of the quality of life must remain as important a consideration as the freedom from want and the ensurance of continued reproduction.

Cultural and biological evolution: a comparison

We have sketched very briefly the passage of man through prehistoric and historic times by examining the energy base of culture and by pointing out how this base has changed through the years as man gained greater and greater control of ways of supplementing his own physical capabilities. Accompanying this increased managerial sophistication, and indeed an inseparable and indispensable part of it, has been a growing complexity of ideas and technological innovations, each one of which contributes, actually or potentially, an added increment to an expanding and exploitable pool of

9.15 *The development of grinding implements, an example of cultural evolution.* (a) *Miocene eolith,* (b) *Pleistocene paleolith,* (c) *Recent neoliths.*

American Museum of Natural History

(a)

(b)

(c)

Evolution revisited

To the extent that a species is characterized by occupying a particular position and fulfilling a specific function in an ecological community, man, by virtue of his cultural differences and their development in time, represents (as it were) a multitude of different species. In respect to the environment man is not a consistent biological unit preserving its identity, but an organism in the process of change.

A. Glikson [25]

---

energy which can be tapped in various ways. It should be emphasized again, however, that culture, broadly conceived, is energy-related, but not energy-determined; that is, the amount of energy available does not determine the particular form of a culture, but the kind and amount undoubtedly determines the complexity and productivity of a culture.

The history of man can of course be appraised from other points of view as well. Each view gives only a partial view of the nature of culture and of cultural evolution, and each emphasizes the diverse ways by which man has learned to cope with his universe, his environment, his fellow beings, and himself. However, central to, and independent of, the basis of cultural appraisal is the fact that membership in a culture is vital to man the human being. It releases him from his animality. Central also is the fact that both the biological and cultural evolution of man resulted from forces and events that not only forged new patterns of organization, but also introduced elements of disorganization. This disorganization made its appearance continuously and usually unpredictably, with incorporation or rejection determined by a variety of factors that were not predictable in advance, many being simply accidents of history.

Some anthropologists and sociologists maintain that it is improper to speak of a "cultural evolution," preferring to restrict the use of the term "evolution" to biological contexts. However, because cosmological, chemical, and biological systems, changing with time, have been viewed in evolutionary terms, it seems inappropriate to exclude cultural changes, which have their origin, at least in their initial phases, in biological antecedents. G. Ledyard Stebbins, a contemporary geneticist and evolutionist, has proposed that "evolution is the gradual emergence and adaptive alteration

In the past, many anthropologists who used the term cultural evolution for change in man's way of life believed that this enabled them to arrange all of the diverse contemporary societies into stages of cultural advancement, and on the basis of such seriation to predict the future of cultural systems. Such predictions have not been realized. In addition, a true comparison between the course of organic and of cultural evolution must emphasize the fact that major advances in organic evolution have been so rare and sporadic that no amount of study of those organisms which existed before these major events occurred would have made possible their prediction. For instance, if an intelligent being had been transplanted to the world of life existing in the Triassic period, when the reptiles were in their most active stage of adaptive radiation, he could not possibly have constructed the body plan and behavioral pattern of a bird or placental mammal, much less have predicted that these classes would, several million years later, almost completely displace the dominant reptiles. A social scientist who looks to an organic evolutionist to help him predict what will happen so society in the future, is a blind man seeking help from another who is equally blind.

G. L. Stebbins [44]

We don't know, of course, just where you happen to be at this moment, but chances are that you are in a man-made environment; your office, your home, a school room, library, or public vehicle where you have time to read. Glance about and you will see that almost everything surrounding you has been invented and designed by someone else; some person at some time engaged in a creative act, and the sum total of those acts makes up the world you live in. This applies not only to your physical environment, but your mental one as well—your mind is filled almost entirely by symbols originally formed by creative persons.

D. Fabun [24]

of systems of order that cannot be reversibly destroyed," a definition that embraces the biological and cultural, but would seem to exclude the cosmological and chemical on the basis that adaptation is not a factor in the latter two systems. If, on the other hand, evolution is considered to be gradual, but irreversible, change occurring within ordered systems, we can then compare biological and cultural systems to determine their evolutionary similarities and dissimilarities.

Biological and cultural systems both are characterized by an attempt to create an organized, ordered framework out of the elements of disorder. The two systems, however, are analogous and not homologous. Biological inheritance, and hence evolution, is based on the order and disorder found in the nucleic acid molecules of each cell, which are received from each parent via the germ cells, are unalterable by the individual possessing them, and have an expression that is ultimately limited by the interaction of a given genotype in a particular environment. A culture, on the other hand, is a learned phenomenon acquired during each individual's growth and development and modified profoundly by circumstances of time and place. As pointed out earlier, each of us has the potentiality of living a thousand lives, but each ends up having lived only one.

We can ask, therefore, whether there is a "DNA" of cultural systems that is analogous to the DNA of biological systems. If the answer is in the affirmative, does such a cultural "DNA" exhibit properties and behaviors comparable in any way to those of molecular DNA?

There are at least four features of molecular DNA that contribute to the maintenance and retention of order in biological systems: (1) it is a source of reliable information

Evolution revisited

Indeed it has always, in traditional societies, been the great function of culture to keep things rather stable, quiet, and unchanging. It has been the function of tradition to assimilate one epoch to another, one episode to another, even one year to another. It has been the function of culture to bring out meaning, by pointing to the constant or recurrent traits of human life, which in easier days one talked about as the eternal verities.

. . .

Today, culture and tradition have assumed a very different intellectual and social purpose. The principal function of the most vital and living traditions to-day is precisely to provide the instruments of rapid change. There are many things which go together to bring about this alteration in man's life; but probably the decisive one is science itself.

. . .

The reason for this great change from a slowly moving, almost static world, to the world we live in, is the cumulative character, the firmness, the givenness of what has been learned about nature. It is true that it is transcended when one goes into other parts of experience. What is true on the scale of the inch and the centimeter may not be true on the scale of a billion light-years; it may not be true either of the scale of a one hundred billionth of a centimeter; but it stays true where it was proven. It is fixed. Thus everything that is found out is added to what was known before, enriches it, and does not have to be done over again. This essentially cumulative irreversible character of learning things is the hallmark of science.

This means that in man's history the sciences make changes which cannot be wished away and cannot be undone.

J. R. Oppenheimer [37]

---

encoded in a highly stable molecule; (2) this information can be replicated time and again with a very small margin of error; (3) the information gains expression through the processes of growth and development in a quite predictable and consistent way, as witnessed by the likenesses of identical twins; and (4) the system of which DNA is a basic part tends to suppress or reject gross copy-errors when they arise. These features represent the conservative side of inheritance: like begets like. But not quite alike. If evolution is to take place, diversity or disorder must be present, and the catalysts of change, also having their origin in DNA, are gene mutations, alterations in chromosome structure and number, and the continual recombination of genes and chromosomes during the process of meiosis. Coupled with these, and also contributing to change, are migrations of individuals into, and out of, the gene pool, isolation mechanisms, which tend to fragment the gene pool, and environmental variations, which help to establish different constellations of genes. Retention of species identity requires that the elements of order dominate those of disorder, and this is generally true when long periods of time are considered. But too high a degree of order leads to environmental restriction and can often result in extinction.

The "DNA" of any culture is not a single species of cultural "molecules," but rather an infinitely diverse set of ways of thought, feeling, and behavior possessed by man. These factors determine man's response to himself, to other members of his culture, and to his environment. For lack of a better term, we can refer to these collectively as ideas, or we can think of them as "socio-genes," as compared with "bio-genes." It is these, some only dimly apprehended or articulated, others clearly formulated and expressed, that are

If man is a machine, what becomes of free will? If man is a machine, how can a machine develop a new idea? If a bacterium is a machine whose "intelligence" can be mechanistically explained, can we be sure that our intelligence is not generated in the same way?

I believe the dilemma is solved for man by a highly sophisticated combination of order and disorder. The problem of biological evolution is solved by a built-in "copy-error mechanism" for introducing novelty in DNA molecules in the form of mutations. My theory is that creativity in man is the result of a built-in "copy-error mechanism" in the reproduction of ideas. Our minds operate with a certain built-in amount of disorganization. Our minds are always reshuffling facts and racking them up in new combinations. If the new combinations come too slowly we call a person stupid, and if they come too fast we call him a schizophrenic. Most new ideas do not turn out as expected, but we can weigh them—sometimes subconsciously—in terms of our past experience, rejecting many of them without further test and predicting success for others. A person who does this skillfully is said to have common sense. The scientific method is simply a way of testing our common sense under a rigid set of rules that makes us reject the idea when the facts go against us. It is an acceptance of the fact that the correctness of an idea is not determined by how good the idea makes us feel at the moment of illumination.

V. R. Potter [38]

Evolution revisited

In every culture there are elements of order and disorder. Order helps a culture to maintain its unity and identity; disorder leads to meaningful adaptations.

Jan Lukas photo, Rapho Guillumette Pictures

9.16 Prehistoric man could communicate his ideas only by signals or word of mouth. As more sophisticated communication systems have evolved, one man's ideas can be transmitted instantly to millions of other men over great distances.

American Telephone & Telegraph

reflected in the human language and may constrict, enlarge, and modify it. Ideas become embodied in systems of magic, myth, ethics, and philosophy and, through science and the many forms of art, lead to a growing comprehension of awareness and reality. Through technology, they also give man a growing domination over the environment and a freedom from environmental constraints. It is ideas that enable man to change his environments to suit himself; he is not forced to accommodate to the environment as are other living things. It is ideas that in their totality lead to the "organization of awareness," to the recognition of self at an individual level and of a sense of belonging in a societal sense.

Ideas exhibit the same qualities of order and disorder as does the DNA of living organisms. Ideas are very obviously sources of information—"mental blueprints," if you will. Through word of mouth, example, folklore, writing, printing, and, more recently, computers and global communication systems, ideas can be reproduced (replicated) and can reach wider and wider audiences as communication improves. They also can be expressed in the form of behavior or beliefs. The particular expression is dependent on the cultural milieu in the same way that a genotype may have different expressions in different environments.

These are the elements of order in a culture, and man seems to create and preserve order as best he can, for it is his guarantee of continuing adaptation. Every culture has its frame of reference into which the young are introduced, to which the adults adhere, and out of which have evolved the many systems of law, government, social mores, education, and religions. It is these latter elements that are to regulate the human condition, to determine the relations of

Evolution revisited

man to his fellow beings, to his institutions, and to the cosmos. It is these also that ultimately give meaning to man's existence.

However, a culture cannot evolve when the human condition is static, anymore than life can evolve when diversity of genes and environments is absent. There must be a constant interplay between order and disorder, between organization and disorganization, if a system—a species or a culture—is to retain an identifiable and tangible unity and yet be capable of adapting meaningfully at all times. Just as mutations and gene recombinations are the elements of disorder in biological systems, so mutations in the replication of ideas and the recombination of facts and ideas into new forms provide the disorder of cultures. Copy-error, appearing as mutations, is an inescapable fact at the level of DNA and equally so at the level of ideas. The transmission of ideas from generation to generation by word of mouth, that is, folklore, and the transference of the elements of magic from one shaman to another are highly unreliable when compared with the replicative precision of DNA. This accounts, at least in part, for the rapidity of cultural evolution as contrasted with the biological. In both systems, however, the constant reshuffling of genes on the one hand and of facts and ideas on the other, both within and between interacting cultures, provides new combinations that become subject to natural selection or to cultural choice. Most of this reshuffling leads to diversity within a basic form of organization—Darwin's finches and the many forms of the Christian religion are examples—but occasionally, as in biological systems, new and transcendant forms of ideological organization make their appearance, to replace gradually older forms because the new lead to a greater degree of

These concepts may be formulated into a principle regarding the interaction of biology and culture in man. Where a socioeconomic adaptation causes a change in the environment, the frequency of a gene will change in proportion to the survival value the gene confers on the carriers in the new ecosystem. Increasing frequencies of an adaptive gene remove environmental limitations and allow further development of the socioeconomic adaptation. The environmental conditions crucial to the transmission of malaria are also crucial to the eonomy, but the sickle-cell trait removes a limitation for agricultural development and maintenance by reducing the number of people capable of undergoing intense parasitism and of infecting mosquitoes. The gene frequency and the socioeconomic adaptation continue to develop in a stepwise fashion until either the limit of the gene frequency or the limit of the socioeconomic adaptation is reached.

S. L. Wiesenfeld [52]

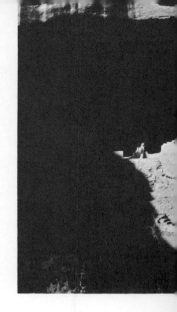

Any society which is to remain healthy through such upheavals as the industrial revolution and the atomic revolution must take out a certain amount of *cultural insurance*. This should consist of ideas, inventions, and legal or constitutional provisions which may appear to be useless or even harmful in the immediate present, but which may form the basis of rapid adjustment to changed conditions. Furthermore, complex societies in a constantly changing world must value and give credit to those of their members who are capable of unorthodox thinking, and who by their vision and foresight can produce and make available the components of this cultural insurance. On the other hand, if all members of society are permitted to have an unlimited range of unorthodox thinking and behavior, the homeostatic stability of the body politic will decline, and its functioning will be seriously impaired. A compromise must be found between blind faith and unbridled free thinking, between mechanical adherance to outworn tools and methods versus reliance upon untried new tools and machines, between unimaginative provision for present needs and idealistic reliance on hoped-for social changes. Most important, as the structure of society and its relationships with other societies becomes more complex, the old compromises, which worked in the past, will no longer do. New compromises must be found before the stability is irreparably lost.

G. L. Stebbins [44]

organization of the elements of human experience. The great role of recombination in the cultural sphere can perhaps best be appreciated by recognizing that the intellectual giants of Western civilization were not so much the discoverers of new facts as they were synthesizers who recast old ideas into new patterns of thought. It is they—the Newtons, Darwins, Watsons, and Cricks—who, unbound by stereotyped thought, could detect the threads of similarity among seemingly unconnected dissimilarities, and who in the process have given us new visions and new ways of thought and action.

An additional element of disorder in a cultural situation, one without parallel in the molecular realm of DNA or even in a nonhuman biological context, is personal detachment of an individual. No member of a society can be totally freed from his culture, either by chance or by design. Brought into a culture as an infant, a time when the choices are not his own and he is basically an authority-acceptor, man's responses are molded and fixed to a greater or lesser degree, and these early influences cannot be erased to the extent that he is able to view his universe with fresh and unclouded eyes. The slate cannot be wiped clean. Nevertheless, because each of us possesses in varying degrees a recognition of self as distinct from a cultural identity, a measure of detachment permits an individual to see himself and his culture in different contexts. Because no individual reflects accurately and completely all facets of a culture, he is only a partial reflection of his culture, exhibiting a selected pattern of responses. Circumstance or accidents of history undoubtedly determine some of these, but choice of a deliberate nature, arising perhaps from new vision, new images, or new arrangement of old elements, determines

Evolution revisited

Abandoned cliff-dwellings, Mesa Verde, Colorado.

American Airlines

others. These may be adaptive, adjustive, neutral, or even nonadaptive in a cultural sense, but they inject novelty into a system and may enlarge the dimensions of a culture, modify it, or even constrict it. Whatever they are, whatever their source, and whatever their influence, they represent the freedom of the individual to act within a system.

There remains, finally, the question of whether there is anything in a cultural system that plays a role analogous to that of natural selection in biological evolution. Differential patterns of growth, survival, and reproduction, operating within heterogeneous groups of plants and animals, can satisfactorily account for the diversity that has been observed, but what processes or circumstances determine what new novelties of culture will broaden, modify, or replace older patterns? Why, within particular cultures, have habits of eating, sleeping, and mating, expressions of filial affection or relationships, patterns of marriage, forms of tools and pottery, or rites of passage or burial become distinctive, even highly stylized? Why, within Western culture and at various times, have we buried, mummified, cremated, or even left to carrion crows the bodies of our dead? Why, for example, do the Hopi Indians of the Southwest have no notion of dimensional time within their conceptual constructs, whereas other, not very distantly related, Indian tribes visualize time much as we do today? The fact is that we do not know, and no Darwin of culture has yet come forth to set things in logical and understandable order. On the other hand, certain things seem evident. We recognize that cultures as a whole, as well as the subordinate elements of a culture, can change with time, or evolve. It is generally accepted that cultural information, whether transmitted by language, gesture, or imitation, is accepted by virtue of

. . . had Whitney died in his cradle the evolutionary process expressed in technology would have produced a machine for ginning cotton. Similarly, although Lincoln is bound historically to the emancipation of slaves and Darwin to the formulation of certain biological principles, the processes of politico-economic evolution would have achieved the one without Lincoln just as evolution of thought would have produced the other without Darwin. The invention of the calculus, which took place almost simultaneously, and independently, in the activities of Newton and Leibnitz, was the logical expression of a developmental process, i.e., it was the emergence of a new mathematical form from previous forms. Just as the invention of the calculus was not dependent upon either Newton or Leibnitz alone, so it was not necessarily dependent upon them both; it would have occurred eventually if both Newton and Leibnitz had died in infancy. The development of mathematics, like the development of technology or medicine, is an evolutionary process: new forms grow out of preceding forms. But in whose person and labors a new form is to appear, and when and where it is to appear is a matter that belongs to the context *history* alone. From the point of view of the evolutionary process every *historical* event is an *accident* and in a sense unpredictable.

L. A. White [51]

Today, the forces at our command, the energy in the technological structure, give shape to virtually all the conditions of life and a rapidly changing shape since we have developed the means by refining the method of invention to change the shape of the technology almost at will.

So the first part of the problem appears to be whether we can now in fact discover the means to close the gap between the changes that destroy the old, which was not bad but is not, in the new dispensation, good and useful, and the developments which are to take the place of the old, but which do not take place fast enough. . . .

And the second part of the problem is like unto it. The point of invention from the earliest days, of fire, iron, and the wheel, has always been to give man some additional advantage over the natural environment. For much of his history the advantages obtained were, on the whole, occasional, small-scale, and, at least in the early stages, local in effect. The conditions of the natural environment, though slowly modified, continued to dominate the condition of man. Now this is changing. With our extensive knowledge and sophisticated instruments we can, in some sort, fix stars of our own in their courses and meddle with the number of days of our years. We are well on the way, in our timeless effort to bring the natural environment under control, to replacing it by an artificial environment of our own contriving. This special environment has a structure, a set of tempos, and a series of dynamic reactions that are not always nicely scaled to human responses. The interesting question seems to be whether man, having succeeded after all these years in bringing so much of the natural environment under his control, can now manage the imposing system he has created for the specific purpose of enabling him to manage his natural environment.

E. E. Morison [33]

Even though all manifestation of life are known to be conditioned by heredity, past experiences, and environmental factors, we also know that free will enables human beings to transcend the constraints of biological determinism. The ability to choose among ideas and possible courses of action may be the most important of all human attributes; it has probably been and still is a crucial determinant of human evolution. The most damning statement that can be made about the sciences of life as presently practiced is that they deliberately ignore the most important phenomena of human life.

R. Dubos [19]

authority and is not subject to test and verification. Furthermore, in contrast to biological inheritance and by virtue of the transmittal of information through language, an individual of a culture has a multiparental rather than a biparental background, with the result that, at a formative and impressionable stage of life, he is the recipient of a broad and blended inheritance, far less restricted than that in a biological system. This fact tends to reduce somewhat the rate of cultural change, and it may be that accidents of history in the form of an occasional, emerging dominant figure of authority play a more significant role in this kind of evolution than do the small, subtle, cumulative alterations that contribute to biological evolution and species formation. At this stage of understanding, we can only state that our knowledge is incomplete.

The role of science in cultural evolution is clearly an ambiguous one. Science proceeds on the assumption that its realm of investigation is an orderly one that is governed by immutable laws that can be discerned in the particular situation but are likewise applicable to the general. The scientific revolution, starting in the Middle Ages and the Renaissance and emerging in visible form in the seventeenth century and expanding since that time, has demonstrated that this orderliness of nature is real and that man is fully capable, eventually if not now, of apprehending and understanding it. A high level of consistency is revealed, and this consistency forms the cumulative, irreversible base of learned things that is the hallmark of science. Where inconsistency and ambiguity are evident, the assumption is that the kind of order that will explain them has not yet been discovered, but will be in the course of time.

Evolution revisited

I have been much concerned that, in this world of change and scientific growth, we have so largely lost the ability to talk with one another, to increase and enrich our common culture and understanding. And so it is that the public sector of our lives, what we hold and have in common, has suffered, as have the illumination of the arts, the deepening of justice and virtue, and the ennobling power of our common discourse. We are less men for this. Never in man's history have the specialised traditions more flourished than to-day. We have our private beauties. But in those high undertakings when man derives strength and insight from public excellence, we have been impoverished. We hunger for nobility, the rare words and acts that harmonise simplicity with truth. In this default I see some connection with the great unresolved public problems—survival, liberty, fraternity.

J. R. Oppenheimer [37]

Science, therefore, is a discoverer of order, but it is the element of discovery that introduces disorder into human situations. As T. S. Eliot has so perceptively stated in *Burnt Norton:* "Human kind cannot bear very much reality." Or as the contemporary biologist V. R. Potter puts it in *Bioethics:* "A large proportion of the human race is psychologically incapable of coping with large doses of disorganization and uncertainty." The great cultures of the past have primarily been concerned with keeping things stable and unchanging, with establishing as it were a state of equilibrium that enables a culture to respond only to a limited extent to the changes taking place around it. But science, emerging as a mutation in scholarship and concerning itself with the perception of order, is, on the other hand, progressive and hence ephemeral. It challenges order at the same time that it reveals order, and in the process exposes new facets of reality that make the old order obsolete, thus dislocating and disrupting the bases of culture and our view of man until new patterns of order are conceived and selected. We of course have the power of choice, but it is easier to hold on to the familiar and comfortable than to adopt the new and exciting.

Science, then, is an instrument of change, and a scientifically-based culture is devoted to the dynamics of change. The socialization of science and, since World War II, the establishment of institutes of research and development have accelerated this process. The very large doses of information, specialized as it is and couched in a jargon that makes difficult its absorption into the common understanding of man, threaten to overwhelm and obscure the stabilizing elements of a culture despite its relevance and intrinsic

9.17 Cultural information, no matter how it is transmitted, is accepted by virtue of authority. This scene, a son listening carefully to the instructions of his father, has been replayed over and over again since the dawn of man.

Standard Oil Co. (N.J.)

The habits of any culture fit the people who learn to use them like well-worn gloves. This fit goes very deep, for their ideas of right and wrong, their selection of human desires and passions, are part and parcel of their whole version of culture. They can react to another people's way of conducting life with a supreme lack of interest or at least of comprehension. Among civilized peoples this often appears in their depreciation of "foreign ways"; it is easy to develop a blind spot where another people's cherished customs are concerned. . . .

Some primitive cultures have not been able to accommodate themselves to contact with the white man. Their whole way of living, when they were brought into contact with modern civilization, has fallen down like a house of cards. The Indians of the United States have most of them become simply men without a cultural country. They are unable to locate anything in the white man's way of life which is sufficiently congenial to their old culture. When the white man first came,

worth. Yet, science basically is a means of putting an end to doubt and ambiguity by permitting man to perceive clearly the elements of order and disorder.

In its evolution, then, culture has shifted its function, particularly in the Western world, from stabilizing the status quo to promoting change. The members of any culture must be students of change, must be functional at a high informational noise level, and must be discriminating in drawing distinctions between "dangerous" and "beneficial" knowledge and between "good" and "bad" technology. This kind of assessment is not easy, but it must come if science is to serve rather than destroy that which has made man what he presently is.

Evolution and progress

One of the plaguing and perplexing questions that has been raised periodically within the context of evolution, but without answer acceptable to all, has concerned the nature of progress. A grand overview of the expanding diversity of living things and of human societies, from the wandering, nomadic tribes to the present megalopolises, brings to light the fact that all things move from the simple to the complex, a situation that seems to justify the use of the term "progress." This word was derived from the Latin *progredior*, "to walk forward," and as such calls to mind qualities or trends such as advancement, proficiency, improvement, and the like. It is also a word that embodies a value judgment, for it has meaning only when used in a comparative sense, in the framework of historical interpretation, and for purposes of establishing rank in serial order.

Evolution revisited

the Plains tribes had a short-lived cultural upsurge when they enthusiastically incorporated the horse into their way of life, and the Northwest Coast Indians had a veritable renaissance of wood carving when they got metal. But closer contact laid bare the great gap between white and Indian values. The Indian cultures could not survive the white man's interference with their tribal ways and the buffalo herds and salmon fisheries on which they depended. Acquaintance with the strange white customs of working for wages and paying for land and conducting private enterprise broke down their old social arrangements without putting anything intelligible in their place. The white man, for his part, was equally unable to see the cultural values which the Indian tribes cherished and which were being broken down and lost forever. Each side was blnd to cultural ideals which to the other were the most real things in the universe.

R. Benedict [3]

Library of Congress

Within the context of evolution, a number of questions pose themselves. Is it justifiable to speak of evolutionary progress? Will the answer be the same when applied to biological evolution and to cultural evolution? Pierre Teilhard de Chardin, a noted anthropologist and theologian, takes an affirmative view in his *Phenomenon of Man*, and he is supported by such eminent evolutionists as Theodosius Dobzhansky and Julian Huxley. Herbert Spencer, in the nineteenth century, used the terms "evolution" and "progress" interchangeably, and R. A. Fisher, the great British geneticist, said: "Evolution is progressive adaptation and consists in nothing else." But is an annual grass an example of progress over a woody tree from which it arose? Were the Aztecs, who sacrificed thousands of human victims to propitiate their gods, more or less progressive than the Mayans or Incas who developed other religious practices? What are the criteria of progress?

A noted historian of science, John Greene, has pointed out that the idea of progress is deeply rooted in the terminology of evolution. The terms "higher" versus "lower," "primitive" versus "advanced," "simple" versus "complex," "more adapted" versus "less adapted" are widely employed, and it is often difficult to ascertain the degree to which teleological thinking, as opposed to mere convenience, enters into their use. When Linnaeus created the class Primates, his intentions were clear; man is highest in the scale of living things, a view proclaimed in Genesis and eloquently defended by John Ray. Can we, however, read progress into the evolution of parasitism? Or are we to agree with Lewis Mumford that "autonomy, self-direction, and self-fulfillment are the proper ends of organisms?" The tapeworm, for example, is an admirably adapted organism, what-

The affluence of the United States, reflected in the consumption of 50 per cent of the world's resources by 6 per cent of the world's population, is to a large degree the consequence of its utilization of energy, roughly one-third of the world's consumption. One may wish to attribute the quality of American life, badly distributed as it is today, to its democratic institutions, to its private and sometimes free enterprise systems and even to its moral fiber, but the fact remains that many of these ideals became realities because there was land with sufficient material and energy resources to support them and their excesses.

The almost unlimited supply of cheap and readily available energy to all segments of the American society has been a major factor responsible for the growth of this nation to the stature it has attained and for the remarkable stability of its political institutions. It follows, therefore, that the potential exhaustion of its energy resources poses a serious threat to its continued vitality and even survival. Thus, the eventual need for a zero rate of growth of consumption of resources also arises from the specter of exhaustion of these resources.

R. F. Beers, Jr. [2]

Evolution revisited

It is hardly possible to exaggerate the importance of this preparation for Darwinism by a vast political and clerical propaganda of its moral atmosphere. Never in history, as far as we know, had there been such a determined, richly subsidized, politically organized attempt to persuade the human race that all progress, all prosperity, all salvation, individual and social, depend on an unrestrained conflict for food and money, on the suppression and elimination of the weak by the strong, on Free Trade, Free Contract, Free Competition, Natural Liberty, Laissez-faire: in short, on "doing the other fellow down" with impunity, all interference by a guiding government, all organization except police organization to protect legalized fraud against fisticuffs, all attempt to introduce human purpose and design and forethought into the industrial welter being "contrary to the laws of political economy." Even the proletariat sympathized, though to them Capitalist liberty meant only wage slavery without the legal safeguards of chattel slavery. People were tired of governments and kings and priests and providences, and wanted to find out how Nature would arrange matters if she were let alone. And they found it out to their cost in the days when Lancashire used up nine generations of wage slaves in one generation of their masters.

G. B. Shaw [41]

ever our human view of its place in the scheme of living things. Are we to use the concept of progress only within a human context, and with whatever value judgment we wish to place arbitrarily upon it, or can it be employed within a broader evolutionary context where change and chance are the rule, and predetermined goals are nonexistent?

The concept of progress as applied to man and his way of life is of course a human invention. It arose in Western Europe during the period of the Enlightenment, having had its origins in the Renaissance and the expanding scientific revolution, and was reinforced by the emerging industrial revolution. Man's growing confidence in himself as an observer and as an assessor of what constitutes reality, and

I believe future generations will think of our times as the age of wholeness: when the walls began to fall; when the fragments began to be related to each other; when man learned finally to esteem tenderness and reason and awareness and the word which set him apart forever from other living creatures; when he learned to realize his brokenness and his great talent for creating ties that bind him together again; when he learned to accept his own childhood and in the acceptance to become capable of maturity; when he began to realize his infinite possibilities even as he sees more clearly his limitations; when he began to see that sameness and normality are not relevant to human beings but to machines and animals; when he learned never to let any power and dictator cut his ties to the great reservoir of knowledge and wisdom without which he would quickly lose his human status; when he learned to live a bit more comfortably with time and space; when he learned to accept his need of God and the law that he cannot use Him, to accept his need of his fellow men and the law that he cannot use them, either; when he learned that "what is impenetrable to us really exists," and always there will be need of the dream, the belief, the wonder, the faith.

L. Smith [42]

his self-awareness of his abilities to better his conditions of life through science and technology inevitably generated the belief that there was no foreseeable end to what man could do. To a most significant degree, this self-confidence has been justified. We are today better fed, housed, and educated, see more art, read more literature, hear more music, and have better and more diversified modes of transportation and communication than at any previous stage in history. All this has been characterized, without question, as progress. But when does progress, as we see it, lose its value and become regression? Progress exacts its price as well as yields its blessings, and when does the price of an advance become too high? The saber-toothed tiger, the Irish elk, and the Scholasticism of the Middle Ages come to mind.

9.18 Broadway, New York City, 1835, and Washington, D.C., 1968. As a means of transportation, the automobile certainly improved upon the horse and buggy, and this technological advance could be termed progress. However, a comparison of these two scenes raises the question of whether progress of this type has truly improved the quality of life for man. When does progress lose its value?

The New York Public Library, I. N. Phelps Stokes Collection

UPI photo

The old saying, "Where there is a will, there is a way," condenses Lamarck's theory of functional adaptation into a proverb. This felt bracingly moral to strong minds, and reassuringly pious to feeble ones. There was no more effective retort to the Socialist than to tell him to reform himself before he pretends to reform society. If you were rich, how pleasant it was to feel that you owed your riches to the superiority of your own character! The industrial revolution had turned numbers of greedy dullards into monstrously rich men. Nothing could be more humiliating and threatening to them than the view that the falling of a shower of gold into their pockets was as pure an accident of our industrial system as the falling of a shower of hail on their umbrellas. Nothing could be more flattering and fortifying to them than the assumption that they were rich because they were virtuous.

Now Darwinism made a clean sweep of all such self-righteousness.

G. B. Shaw [41]

Specialization for purposes of becoming better adapted in a biological sense would undoubtedly have been judged progressive at the time of initiation, but the fossil record shows all too clearly that overspecialization was the first step toward environmental rigidity and eventual extinction. Today, as never before, we are beginning to question our basis of judgment as to what constitutes cultural progress. Is our concept of progress to be equated with the gross national product, one of the great myths of our time, or is it to be judged in terms of the quality of life, a phrase equally difficult to define and certainly more difficult to quantify?

The idea of progress in the biological world has a long and varied history. The concept of a great chain of being began with Aristotle, and life, independent of its assumed mechanism, was viewed hierarchically from simple forms to those more complex, with one stage passing imperceptibly to another "in comely order," as Sir Thomas Browne was wont to say. Lamarck saw this progression as rising from "monad to man," and Cuvier recognized that different rock strata contained comparatively similar forms of past life, but he also noted that more recent strata contained more complex species than did sedimentary rock that was laid down earlier.

Darwin's theory of evolution through natural selection displaced the concept of the great chain of being in the minds of scientists, but he too saw that the origin of more complex forms from simpler ones consisted not of change alone, but included also an improvement in the adaptability of a species to its environment. He was aware of regression as well as progression in some types, but that regression

. . . The history of life on Earth has been one long tale of "taking over." From era to era, different forms of life have proved dominant in one major environmental niche or the other. The placoderms "took over" from the trilobites, and the modern fish "took over" from the placoderms.

The reptiles "took over" from the amphibia, and mammals "took over" from the reptiles.

Mankind looks upon the history of evolution and approves of all this "taking over" for it all leads up to the moment when Man, proud and destructive Man, has "taken over."

Are we to stop here. Is Ouranos to be replaced by Cronos, and Cronos by Zeus, and no more—thus far and no farther? Is Thetis to be disposed of rather than risk the chance of further replacement?

But why? What has changed? Evolution continues as before, though in a modified manner. Instead of species changing and growing better adapted to their environment through the blind action of mutation and the relentless winnowing of natural selection, we have reached the point where evolution can be guided and the Successor can be deliberately designed.

And it might be good. The planet groans under the weight of 3.4 billion human beings, destined to be 7 billion by 2010. It is continually threatened by nuclear holocaust and is inexorably being poisoned by the wastes and fumes of civilization. Sure, it is time and more than time for mankind to be "taken over" from. If ever a species needed to be replaced for the good of the planet, we do.

There isn't much time left, in fact. If the son of Thetis doesn't come within a generation, or, at most two, there may be nothing left worth "taking over."

I. Asimov [1]

---

can also be thought of as a form of adaptation, although adaptation is more frequently thought of as progression toward greater complexity. In a letter to Lyell, Darwin wrote:

Every step in the natural selection of each species implies improvement in that species in relation to its condition of life. No modification can be selected without it being an improvement or advantage. . . . If we look to the whole course of time, the organic condition of life for other forms will become more complex, and there will be a necessity for other forms to become improved, or they will be exterminated; and I can see no limit to this process of improvement.

Improvement, adaptability, greater complexity, increased heterogeneity, and progress become, therefore, almost interchangeable terms in the lexicon of some evolutionists, with the consequent blurring of qualitative differences in meaning. The implication is that natural selection in general favors the gradual, adaptive modification of earlier types with the eventual emergence of newer ones of greater survival capability. But the other side of the coin is that natural selection is mechanical and purposeless and does not guarantee even the survival of a species, let alone its improvement. To apply the term "progress" to the broad sweep of life through geologic time requires that we concentrate our attention on the successes that have survived and forget the vast number of organisms known only from fossil remains or impressions and also those surviving organisms that have regressed to less complicated structures and more simple ways of life.

Specialization, although it is irreversible and foretells future extinction, can of course be viewed as short-term

The one thing we know about a developed society is that it has to inhabit a "Spaceship Earth." It is well recognized that our existing technology is fundamentally suicidal, resting as it does on a linear process which begins with the extraction of exhaustible resources in the shape of ores and fossil fuels and ends in pollution. The great unsolved problem of technology is that of creating what is being called a "looped" economy in which man finds a comfortable life in the middle of the process which is essentially circular, that is, in which the waste products of human activity are all used as raw materials for the next cycle of production. We are still a very long way from this kind of technology, although there are the beginnings of it in, for instance, the Haber process for the fixation of nitrogen from the air (1913) and the Dow process for the extraction of magnesium from the sea. Ultimately, it is clear we will have to use the atmosphere, the oceans and the soil as inexhaustible material resources in the sense that what we take from them we will also put back into them.

K. E. Boulding [6]

According to Pico Della Mirandola, writing in the fifteenth century, we men are somewhere at the midway point of creation, capable of rising toward the angels or of descending toward the beasts. That was the end result of Genesis I. As the Second Genesis approaches, we find our powers to go either way enormously increased. One thing we are not empowered to do is to remain at that midway point, frozen in place like the treasured, timeless figures on Keats' Grecian urn. We live in an evolutionary continuum, a dynamic multidimensional spacetime reality where rest is only a theoretical state. Either we choose to go forward—upward, in Pico's sense, toward a finer tomorrow; or we retreat toward bestiality—a plunge into a sinkhole where indeed no beast would venture.

A. Rosenfeld [40]

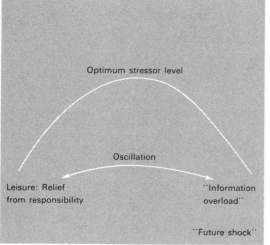

From V. R. Potter, *Bioethics: Bridge to the Future*, Prentice-Hall, 1971.

9.19 Man must continue to adapt if he is to survive. Too much leisure relieves man from the responsibility to adapt, and too much information, or "future shock," makes adaptation impossible. Somewhere between these two extremes lies an area where the environment induces adaptations that are beneficial to man in an evolutionary sense—what biologist V. R. Potter calls the "optimum stressor level."

progress; it permits survival in certain conditions of the environment. But it is of more than passing interest to note that long-term evolutionary change has taken place most frequently and successfully within those groups that remain more generalized in structure and function. It is from such groups that new types of organization emerge. The fishes that gave rise to the amphibians, the amphibians that gave rise to the reptiles, the reptiles that gave rise to the birds on the one hand and to the mammals on the other, and the mammals that eventually gave rise to the primates and to man were all relatively unspecialized representatives of their classes. Generalization may give rise to complexity, but it is not synonymous with complexity. Its value, evolutionarily speaking, is its plasticity, its ability to keep options open and to seize opportunity whenever and wherever it arises. Latent or potential progress seems, therefore, always to be associated with plasticity; actual progress is an evaluative judgment exercised within a given context of time and place and involving standards for judging improvement or regression.

Man, by these standards, is the epitome of evolutionary progress. We, as judges, could hardly think otherwise, although virtually all other species, with the possible exception of human parasites and domesticated forms, would probably consider man to be the most dispensable of species. He is not necessarily the most complex, except in certain ways, but he is without question the most adaptable, occupying a most varied set of habitats even though with little variation in his basic biological features. This stems from three principal interrelated features. The first is sensory. His five senses are adequate, although not exceptional, but they are coupled

Evolution revisited

Last Judgment, *a detail from the west tympanum of Autun Cathedral, France.*

Photographie Bulloz

to a central nervous system that enables man to view the world around him with a greater sense of awareness. The second is manipulative. His hands, doing the bidding of his central nervous system, lead to a greater degree of environmental control, thus freeing man from the purposeless pressures of natural selection. And the last is symbolic. Again the central nervous system, with its yield of symbolic language, has given man that elusive thing called culture, without which he is no longer man, but with which he has virtually shed his animal past.

Some evolutionists have taken the position that there is an inevitability to the process that has led to man and concomitantly that inevitable progress must also be involved. Some have even suggested that man would arrive at a state of perfection if only natural selection were permitted to operate unobstructed by civilization, but this is a highly questionable doctrine. Some channeling, of course, takes place in any evolutionary system. Each change incorporated into a heritable system is not merely irreversible; it also prohibits the exploration of other possibilities. Each incorporated step determines, in addition, what future options for change are possible, and, lastly, each step along the evolutionary path is unique and unrepeatable. Man is as unique as any other species, and if, by some stretch of the imagination, we could conceive of evolution starting over again from some primitive mammalian stock, the probability of man arising as he did would be infinitesimally remote.

We can, in the final analysis, equate biological evolution with progress only if we choose our examples with care and ignore all evolutionary errors. Evolution is a multilinear phenomenon, and we can most clearly detect trends from

There is one striking difference between man and most of the animals. In animals whenever there is competition between two subspecies the one that is better adapted for a specific locality seems to win out. Man, who has reached such a high degree of independence from the environment, is less dependent on local adaptation, and a subspecies of man can quickly spread into many geographically distant areas if it acquires generalized adaptive improvements such as are described by the social anthropologist. Such improvements do not need to and probably often do not have a genetic basis. The authors who have claimed that man is unique in his evolutionary pattern are undoubtedly right. Even though the phyletic evolution of man will continue to go on, the structure of the human species at the present time is such that there appears to be very little chance for speciation, that is, for the division of the single human species into several separate species.

E. Mayr [32]

From its small beginning, science, like other great phyla, has expanded until it is now world-wide in scope and enormously influential. Scientists, indeed, now constitute a "clergy" about as numerous as the religious clergy and certainly better paid and much more powerful. In the 1960 census in the United States, there were 197,000 clergymen. Male chemists, natural scientists and social scientists amounted together to 179,000, and women add another 29,000, just topping the clergy at 208,000 total.

In spite of its successes, science remains a fairly small subculture. The people who think of themselves as scientists, who read scientific journals, who try to keep up with their own field, who teach or do research in some area, do not number much more than one in a thousand of the American population and of course a very much smaller proportion of the world population. Like the clergy, scientists have something of a congregation of laity—the students that they teach, the engineers, doctors, social workers and other professionals who look to one or the other of the pure sciences for the theoretical base of their technology. Even the laity of the scientific "church," however, probably do not amount to more than 1 per cent of the population, whereas the laity of the clergy at least nominally amount to 64 per cent. It is all the more understandable, therefore, that the majority of the population regards science as something wholly outside them, as alien force, even in a sense as an alien religion which they often perceive indeed as something of a threat to their own folk culture.

K. E. Boulding [6]

---

simplicity to complexity, from homogeneity to heterogeneity, if we view the process in the broad sweep of geologic time. Can we apply the same judgment and point of view to cultural evolution? And can we do so with the elements of a culture as well as with culture as a whole?

Culture, as has been emphasized, is both man-made and man-creating. It is similarly multilinear in origin, but each culture does not, as was once supposed, move through distinct and recognizable stages in going from a simple to a complex structure. As we have discussed, increased cultural complexity is related to an increased control over energy sources, but the manner of achieving complexity and of determining cultural content is varied. One can cite arbitrary choice, accidents of history, and, most importantly, borrowings from other cultures, with environmental constraints or opportunities playing impoverishing or enriching roles. Very few cultures, with the possible exception of certain short-lived utopias, have had predetermined goals, although traditions, customs, and institutions are conservative elements once they become established. We can perhaps best view progress, or its absence, in cultural evolution by contrasting or comparing the role of science and art with the process of descent with modification.

The complex cultures that characterize the Western world are based on an expanding technology that today has its roots in a constantly broadening scientific enterprise. Technology arose out of empirical practice and the need of man to solve his problems of living, but since the beginning of the scientific revolution, its relation to science has become more and more intimate and complementary. By providing means of environmental control and energy manipulation, science and technology have influenced every aspect of

Evolution revisited

As to what is strictly "adaptive" and what is not, the usual criterion is the biological one—conduciveness to survival of the species. So far, the passive modifications which gave man a complex brain and an opposable thumb have proven highly adaptive, though his stubborn aggressiveness may eventually bring about his downfall. The utilitarian portion of his cultural achievement has also proven adaptive in helping him to conquer the earth and multiply profusely. His arts, too, can be appraised on this biological basis. Spencer and others have made a good case for music and for art in general as helping to build up social sympathy, communication, and solidarity. They argue that music, dance, and theater have provided recreation, release, and pleasure, thus making life more healthy, attractive, and worth trying to maintain.

The opposite case has also been well argued, especially as to luxurious, civilized art. Ancient philosophers and prophets denounced it for causing war and crime. It has stimulated greed, divided people into hostile religious, political, and racial groups. (Even so, the biologist may insist, the resulting struggles have contributed to natural selection and the survival of the fittest.) Plato and others have said that some kinds of art make people soft, indolent, unfit to serve as soldiers or vigorous leaders. . . . On the other hand, literature and other arts undertake to tell us forcibly of our mistakes: of slums as breeders of crime and disease; of wars as unnecessary evils. Painting at times presents us with symbols of beauty and harmony; at other times with those of anger and anxiety. Art often attempts to improve itself and the civilization around it by negative images and attitudes. It dramatizes evaluative problems and helps us think them out.

T. Munro [35]

---

culture, and they probably will become more pervasive and more influential with the passage of time. Their rate of change determines the rate of change of culture, and it is undeniable that science is cumulative and progressive, building on an established, consentient base and expanding from it. What is shown to be true remains so within its limits; it is the limits that are widened. Newton did not disprove Galileo, nor did Einstein disprove or displace Newton; each added to the structure of physics in his own way. The high point of science today will be still higher tomorrow. The world as we see it and our attitude toward it are constantly being reshaped by science as it moves on. The moon is no longer the same since man has left his footprints on it.

The same cannot be said of art, however central its role in a culture. Art is more a reflection of a culture than it is a molder of its character and a determiner of its content and rate of change. The latter influences are more applicable to science. Art, of course, does change, and it is possible to detect the influences of one age on another and to determine what is original and what derivative in works of art. But the terms "better" or "advanced" or "progressive" are singularly inappropriate except as judged by arbitrary standards of evaluation. The best of African sculpture is not inferior to that of classical Greece, the Italian Renaissance, or the modern school of abstraction, nor is the literature of Elizabethan England, the Romantic Period, or today to be ranked hierarchically; they are simply different from one another and are representative of different styles and different times. Each, when good, is durable, unique, and irreplaceable, but none is cumulative or progressive in the sense that one is higher or lower in a comparative scale.

9.20 Science and technology influence every aspect of culture. The world is constantly being reshaped as science advances. The moon is no longer the mystery it once was now that man has walked upon its surface and brought some of its soil back to earth. Tomorrow, man's technological and scientific expertise may permit him to shape other worlds as he spreads his culture into the depths of space.

NASA

Evolution revisited

In a living room, frozen in an armchair, a young man sits speechless. He has just been asked a terrible question, a question all the more terrifying for its seeming simplicity: Out of all that life can offer, what do *you* want? A silence ensues that seems longer than the uncrossable spaces between galaxies; then, haltingly, he stammers out an answer: "Something—I'm not sure, Yes—I think I want . . . to achieve something that only I could do. I want to fall in love with just one person. To know what it is to bless and be blessed. And to serve a great cause with devotion. I want to be *involved*."

. . . It is the kind of answer that every post-modern man must struggle to find to the anxious question of what he is going to do with his time and space in an ever-changing, expanding universe.

For this is the question that is posed to contemporary civilization: Out of all the possible futures toward which man can direct his continuing evolution, which one does he really *want?* The spectacular advances in basic science which have produced man's accelerating technology have given him almost unlimited power over his environment. What, then, is the kind of world that he really desires? Today almost any kind of future is technically within his reach. Knowing this, post-modern man feels that the greatest adventure into which he can channel his energy is the adventure of inventing the most imaginative and liberating future possible for human life on this planet. And . . . man of the Space Age feels that all individual achievements, all deep relationships with those he loves, find their meaning and fulfillment within this overarching task. And in this task he wants to be *involved*.

W. R. Cozart [15]

Summary

The process of evolution is characteristic of the entire universe. Although the mechanism of evolution varies from one level or system to another, the evolution that has been observed in the biological realm is paralleled by cosmological, chemical, and cultural evolution.

Culture is a dynamic process that is dependent basically upon the manipulation and management of matter and energy. Its behavioral, attitudinal, and ideological features constitute its more obviously visible aspects. Of all living things, man alone is capable of forming a culture, and it is not possible to think of man without also considering his cultural framework.

Energy plays an important role in the development of a culture. New sources or applications of energy give man an added advantage in the fight for survival and provide the security and stability that are necessary for cultural advancement. It should be emphasized, however, that the amount of energy available does not determine the particular form of a culture, but the kind and amount of energy undoubtedly determine the complexity and productivity of a culture.

10

Through a glass darkly

In the preceding chapters we have directly or indirectly dealt with the question "Who or what is man?" It is a question that has many answers, because complete and unbiased objectivity is impossible and because each answer is determined to a considerable extent by the intellectual milieu within which the question is asked. The approach employed here has been primarily that of seeking a consensus of opinion, with consensus resting upon what the several sciences, and biology in particular, have contributed to our understanding of the nature of man. It might reasonably be argued that this approach yields only a partial view of man, that there are other roads to truth, and that insights into man's humanity can be derived equally through his actions and his works, that is, through his systems of myth

Bonnie Freer photo,
Rapho Guillumette Pictures

Finally—what about Man himself, this angel-like creature, this beast, the descent of whom Darwin slowly dared to discuss openly and Mendel as far as we know never tried to analyse? Three most important matters of Man's future are based on a synthesis of Darwin-Mendel principles:

It is the matter of population size and structure—increase, decrease, constitution, and struggle of the human populations.

It is the matter of sufficient food—the nurture of the members of the human species, in relation to plant and animal industry, husbandry, breeding.

It is the matter of social understanding—Man, *Homo sapiens*, is forsooth one species, not many, with all that this implies of interbreeding and gene recombination, of fraternity and mutual help.

What all of us just now desire and what is indeed strikingly needed is not the sudden appearance of a new Linné or a new Lamarck and perhaps not even of a new Darwin or a new Mendel, what we want and what we need is a genius, a combined Darwin-Mendel, whatever his name, nation or colour, who makes the biological unity of mankind etchingly clear to everyone. Will such a genius crop up during our life time?

Å. Gustafsson [18]

and magic, his poetry, painting, music, and architecture, and his role in altering the face of the earth. Few deny that these elements are as important reflections of man as are his peculiarly structured hands and feet, his expanded cortex, and his upright posture.

But we are searching for reasonable certitudes and an agreed-upon point of departure, rather than a kaleidoscopic set of individual judgments. Therefore, two basic facts justify the limited approach we have taken: (1) man's thoughts and actions rest without question on the biological antecedents out of which his culture has grown; and (2) our most reliable sense of reality, including man, derives from the verifiable and repeatable facts of science that stem from observation and experimentation and are tied together by ever more embracing and internally consistent concepts. This position expresses a confidence that our future view of man will not depend upon a devaluation of our present scientific knowledge, but rather will rest upon an expansion of that knowledge, out of which, hopefully, wisdom will emerge and a greater sense of awareness, direction, and potentiality will be manifest. Our feet continue to drag in "biological mud," for we are still animals even though we are men, but where our expanding consciousness will take us as we continue to evolve culturally and biologically will depend upon man himself and his developing ethical character. He must search for answers within himself, not within his created world of spirits, however comforting this realm may be.

Some say that metaphysics, a branch of philosophy that deals with the origin and nature of existence, is an indispensable human appetite. This may well be so, for every known culture has its metaphysical views. But science is

Through a glass darkly

In our explosively changing world it is no longer sufficient to live with philosophies or religions simply handed down from an older generation. We must take up a vital, flexible, and ever-evolving concern about the nature and purpose of man, and about what constitutes a good life and a good society in the light of today's communications, population growth, races, political systems, weapons. We must exhibit a concern with philosophy that is geared to the chain-reacting growth of science, and that is consonant with the impact of science on man's changing conception of himself and his world.

Rather than simply fight for the preservation of the old things that are good, we must plan creatively also to shape the new. We must commit ourselves to dare to build the world we want, knowing that it is possible if we but demand it—and if we use intelligently all the potent forces of science, the arts and the humanities that are at our disposal.

There will always be dangers. But I hold with Thornton Wilder, who said, "Every good and excellent thing stands moment by moment at the razor edge of danger, and must be fought for." To be what we can be, we must be unafraid to place ourselves, our ways of life, our economic systems, in the microscope of science; and, we must have the courage to put into practice the findings that come out, no matter how hard they hit at the patterns of our folkways. To be what we can be, we must first and foremost know what we want to be.

W. O. Roberts [40]

---

also present in every culture although its growth, relatively speaking, was delayed and its impact more recent. But of the two, science has proven the more reliable guide to meaningful existence and will continue to make the future less the fearful unknown and more the hopeful and desired world of man. But the future must be anticipated and planned for, not accepted blindly on an *ad hoc*, exploitable basis.

What we know of man as a human being, beginning with the first stirrings of self-awareness, suggests that he has always lived within, and been guided by, structured systems of thought. These are structures that he invented himself; they have innumerable forms, manifestations, and visible expressions, and they evolve as he lives within them. He seems in fact to be unable to exist successfully in their absence. Biological evolution is not a moral process, but it brought into being a moral and ethical being who has come slowly to realize that instead of being the darling of the gods, free to multiply and to have dominion over all things, he is a self-created organism who, because of his knowledge, must now assume responsibility for himself, his future, and the environment over which he has come to exert an increasing degree of control. He cannot escape this environment even though he can, and has, modified it in manifold ways. He has made this environment extraordinarily productive, but not without cost, and all too frequently without future accountability. We seem to behave, as René Dubos has said, as if we were the last generation to inhabit the earth.

Man's past, in its human phase, has been guided by his mental constructs of who he is and how he should function as an individual and as a member of a society. Most of these

Science has proved that there exists no ethical principle which is, even theoretically, acknowledged by all human societies. Hence ethical values are nothing but functions of the societies in which they originate. The question of what is morally good or morally evil has no meaning except in reference to the moral value system of a given society. There are therefore, no "absolute" criteria by which the value system of a given society can be judged objectively. It may, of course, be judged on the basis of the value system of another society. But there is no possibility of deciding "objectively" which of the two value systems is morally better. If the two societies clash, one can only wait to see which of the two will prevail.

K. von Fritz [47]

Through a glass darkly

Gratiano. Let me play the fool:
With mirth and laughter let old wrinkles come;
And let my liver rather heat with wine
Than my heart cool with mortifying groans.
Why should a man, whose blood is warm within,
Sit like his grandsire cut in alabaster?
Sleep when he wakes? and creep into the jaundice
By being peevish? I tell thee what, Antonio,—
I love thee, and it is my love that speaks,—
There are a sort of men, whose visages
Do cream and mantle like a standing pond;
And do a wilful stillness entertain,
With purpose to be drest in an opinion
Of wisdom, gravity, profound conceit;
As who should say, ''I am Sir Oracle,
And when I ope my lips, let no dog bark!''

W. Shakespeare [43]

10.1   The earth viewed from 22,000 miles away. Modern technology has permitted man to see the earth in perspective and given him the realization that this is the only home he has. The fate of the earth and its resources is closely tied in with the fate of man as a species.

NASA

beliefs and value systems are fictions, images concocted, for one reason or another, in the minds of man, accidents of history that an individual acquires as a result of being born within a given time, place, and race. They therefore can change, albeit slowly, with ethical beliefs changing more slowly than most others. There is little doubt that the future of man will require such change, a reordering of human priorities, a new ethos, a new system of guiding beliefs, that recognizes man for what he is, what he is capable of, and limited by, and what he desires to be in a finite world that is crowding in on him more and more each day. If we ever needed to be reminded that this earth is the only home that man has and that he must live within its constraints or become extinct, the astronauts made this abundantly clear as they viewed the earth from the moon.

We are moving with unrelenting swiftness into a future with which we have no heritage as we do with the past. J. Robert Oppenheimer, as far back as 1954, saw this more clearly than most: "One thing that is new is the prevalence of newness, the changing scale and scope of change itself, so that the world alters as we walk in it, so that the years of man's life measure not some small growth or rearrangement or moderation of what we learned in childhood, but a great upheaval." We are required, whether we wish it or not, to become students of change, but we also must recognize our accountability for future consequences stemming from present actions. There is an urgent need for us to realize that we are a biological species that exists in a physical world in which inner needs and goals must be balanced against an outer reality. This task is enormous and difficult, but it must be carried out if man's humanity is to grow and achieve full stature.

Through a glass darkly

Coming: the control of life, all of life, including human life. With man himself at the controls.

Also coming: a new Genesis—The Second Genesis. The creator, this time around—man. The creation—again, man. But a new man. In a new image. A whole series of new images. What will the new image be?

They will have to be quite different from the images we have known—the images that have led us to Vietnam, to turbulent racial conflict, to nuclear confrontation, to the threat of a polluted and overpopulated planet.

But all these things have come about—have they not?—with man at the controls, more or less. If he is acquiring awesome new powers—and he is—with immeasurably greater controls, does this not accelerate us all, at uncountable G's, toward the inevitable Dead End—a hundred bangs, followed by three billion whimpers?

If we believe so, yes.

But man's new images may offer us surprising alternatives. Their creation will require the energetic projection of the best minds of the race to the farthest reaches of their imaginations.

Future effort?

Anything but. What we believe about man, what we want for man, will profoundly influence what actually happens to man.

A. Rosenfeld [41]

We shall not attempt to define such a system of values—it must evolve as all things evolve—but rather shall discuss those aspects of man and his environment that must be taken into consideration in arriving at an ethos for the future. The nature of man does not alter the fact that he is an animal requiring food, space, and energy in order to live, reproduce, and evolve, but just as a structured system of thought has carried him to the present, a restructuring is now needed for the future. The survival of man as a humane and ethical being is at stake. Potter calls this future ethos "bioethics," Julian Huxley refers to it as "evolutionary humanism," and Dobzhansky has labeled it "the biology of ultimate concern." Regardless of name, its development is crucial and overdue.

Population

Darwin was among the first of the biologists to recognize the facts, consequences, and controls of population increases, and he incorporated this important information into his theory of evolution through natural selection. In *The Origin of Species* he states that "in looking at Nature it is most necessary . . . never to forget that every single organic being may be said to be striving to the utmost to increase in numbers." Malthus had said much the same thing a half-century earlier, and it may well be that Darwin's views were entirely derivative, but the fact remains that the number of offspring capable of being produced by almost any species is large indeed, given enough time. Also, because populations tend to increase in geometric progression,

When man began to travel in vehicles —whether on horseback, raft, or dugout canoe—he began a process of separation which, amplified over the centuries by advances in vehicular technology, broke society into little pieces, and made strangers of us all.

In recent years, this fragmentation has been attributed to the invention of printing, with its formalized breaking down of human experience into standardized bits and pieces that can be arranged into linear sequences. This, it is said, was later transplanted by advancing technology into the standardization of parts (pieces of type), the assembly line for mass production (sentences on a printed page), and the specialized and repetitive actions of workers, which was reflected in the separation of our arts and science; in the compartmentalization of our formal education, and the over-specialization of our economic lives. The result was the breaking down of what had once been the continuous, flowing interaction between organisms, each other, and their environment, into static, standardized bits and pieces. Our intellectual, emotional, social and economic lives had been reduced to a series of "still" pictures which, if sequenced properly and run through the machine at the "right" speed, gave us the illusion of life, but not the feeling of it.

D. Fabun [15]

Through a glass carkly

Now I saw when the Lamb opened one of the seven seals, and I heard one of the four living creatures say, as with a voice of thunder, "Come!" And I saw, and behold, a white horse, and its rider had a bow; and a crown was given to him, and he went out conquering and to conquer.

When he opened the second seal, I heard the second living creature say, "Come!" And out came another horse, bright red; its rider was permitted to take peace from the earth, so that men should slay one another, and he was given a great sword.

When he opened the third seal, I heard the third living creature say, "Come!" And I saw, and behold, a black horse, and its rider had a balance in his hand; . . .

When he opened the fourth seal, I heard the voice of the fourth living creature say, "Come!" And I saw, and behold, a pale horse, and its rider's name was Death, and Hades followed him; and they were given power over a fourth of the earth, to kill with sword and with famine and with pestilence and by wild beasts of the earth.

Revelation 6

Stability and constancy are characteristics of natural populations; in many hosts there are resistant factors that limit any severe attack of feeding species, and most animals feed on living matter. These seemingly diverse factors are related and are the foundation of the mechanism for population regulation which I termed "genetic feedback." Population numbers (herbivore, parasite, or predator) are regulated in this way: high herbivore densities create strong selective pressures on their host-plant populations; selection alters the genetic makeup of the host population to make the host more resistant to attack; this in turn feeds back negatively to limit the feeding pressure of the herbivore. After many such cycles, the numbers of the herbivore populations are ultimately limited, and stability results.

D. Pimentel [38]

that is, 2, 4, 8, 16, and so on, it takes but simple calculations to demonstrate that any species, if allowed to reproduce without any restrictions, could overrun the earth in short order. Such a progression, however, does not occur under natural conditions, although dramatic rises and falls in population numbers have been observed, for example, among rabbits and lemmings. The general tendency is for organisms in an undisturbed environment to preserve a population that is basically stable in terms of numbers, with only minor fluctuations occurring around a relatively fixed mean. Because the potential for a constantly increasing population is present in all species, it is clear that some kind of natural regulatory process must be operative.

Darwin recognized the existence of such forces and postulated four kinds of influences that provide checks to uninhibited increases in numbers. The first was the amount of food available. This sets an absolute limit on numbers, for each species must have the proper kinds of food as well as a specific calorie intake per day if it is to survive. The fact remains, however, that a species in its natural habitat rarely expands its numbers to the point of environmental exhaustion of food; the numbers are generally much below the ultimate capacity of the environment.

The second Darwinian factor was that of predation by other species. Prey-predator relationships have been studied for a number of species, and in virtually all instances, the circumstances reveal the existence of a negative feedback system, that is, an interrelated set of elements, the last one of which serves as a check on the first, thereby keeping the entire system in equilibrium. For example, the moose herd (prey) and wolf pack (predator) on Isle Royale in Lake Superior are in balance with each other, as was mentioned

Through a glass darkly

Albrecht Dürer, The Four Horsemen from the Apocalypse.

in an earlier chapter. The size of the moose herd is kept in check by the wolf pack, and, conversely, the size of the wolf pack is regulated by the number, viability, and availability of the moose herd. Also, and this bears on Darwin's first factor, the amount of browse (shoots, twigs, and leaves) on which the moose feed during the winter months exerts its own regulatory influence on numbers. The moose, the wolves, and the browse comprise, therefore, an interrelated set of factors that maintain a stable population in a stable environment.

When a species is freed for one reason or another from predation, spectacular increases in numbers and a devastation of the environment can occur. This is particularly true in a new, previously undisturbed environment in which an equilibrium has not yet been established. Rabbits, for example, were introduced from England into Australia in 1859, and a dramatic and geometric rise in population occurred very quickly and threatened the agricultural economy of the country because the rabbits had no natural enemies to keep them in check. A similar thing happened when the prickly pear cactus was introduced into Australia and quickly invaded much of the land used for the grazing of sheep.

Darwin's third regulatory factor was the physical environment. Neither a desert nor the Arctic can sustain the great populations of diverse organisms that thrive on a well-watered, temperate plain. Extremes of temperature and moisture generally exert a depressing effect on population density and diversity.

Disease was Darwin's fourth factor. This element tends to be more pronounced either when a disease is first introduced into a new area or when a population has its viability diminished for other reasons. The American chestnut was

. . . the European starling, *Sturnus vulgaris*, . . . has spread over the United States and Canada within a period of sixty years. . . . This subspecies of starling has a natural range extending into Siberia, and from the north of Norway and Russia down to the Mediterranean. We should therefore expect it to be adaptable to a wide variety of continental habitats and climate. Nevertheless, the first few attempts to establish it in the United States were unsuccessful. Then from a stock of about eighty birds put into Central Park, New York, several pairs began to breed in 1891. After this the increase and spread went on steadily, apart from a severe mortality in the very cold winter of 1917–18. But up to 1916 the populations had not established beyond the Allegheny Mountains. . . . By 1954 [however] the process was nearly reaching its end, and the starling was to be found, at any rate on migration outside its breeding season, almost all over the United States, though it was not fully entrenched yet in parts of the West coast states. It was penetrating northern Mexico during migration, and in 1953 one starling was seen in Alaska. This was an ecological explosion indeed, starting from a few pairs breeding in a city park; just as the spread of the North American muskrat, *Ondatra zibethica* over Europe was started from only five individuals kept by a landowner in Czechoslovakia in 1905.

C. E. Elton [12]

Death is finiteness, and Western man rejects finiteness. We long for a limitless supply of everything: air, water, food, wilderness, time, and frontier. But our infinity is linear. We head in a straight, unswerving line for the cosmos, damning any obstacle—even scientific fact—that stands in the way. Sadly enough, as we strive for infinity, we create the irreversible limits. To acquire more electricity and more water, we dam and destroy Glen Canyon for all time. To acquire more food, we deprive the pelican of his—and destroy it, too. For all time. The roster of deaths we have caused in our rush for life is almost endless. And as more of us come into being, more death. . . .

It is not enough to survive, hard as that alone may be. It may not be worth it to survive in a world devoid of humane beings, a world in which man's only aspiration is for biological existence. Quality of life is the concern, and life has not quality without some experience of god. The experience may not even be describable. Can you describe the wisdom of the ecosystem, the flash of awareness that comes when you perceive how the planet functions? Every organism relates to every other. God is an inadequate word. . . .

To aspire to survival and to aspire to humanity are the paths. They are one and the same. For openers, we can turn to the humanity within us, and must to survive. All the logic, precision, and practicality in the world can't save us if we lose our own souls.

The prescription is nothing less than a revolution in consciousness. We are beginning to see it now, and must participate. It takes more than lock-jawed resolution to save a world for all creatures. It takes love and joy. There can be no survival without passion. Passion for humanity, love of the earth, joy of existence, and hope for the future. A very wise man has said that "Pessimism has no survival value." Nor hate, nor elitism, nor puritanism.

S. Mills [33]

10.2 Populations can expand only into those environments that can support them. Neither deserts nor the vast reaches of the frozen north are congenial to living things.

virtually wiped out by a blight introduced from Europe, and the Black Plague killed approximately one-half of the people of Europe during the fourteenth century. During the late 1950s and early 1960s, the rabbit populations of France, England, and Scotland were decimated by myxomatosis, a rather benign disease that is common among Brazilian rabbits. Never having been exposed to this disease, European rabbits were nonresistant. Myxomatosis was purposely introduced into Australia in 1950 to help combat the rabbit plague, but although the initial drop in numbers was phenomenal, the few resistant forms, in the absence of predation, seem once again on the rise to high density levels.

Darwin therefore visualized the population of any species as a balance between an inherent drive to overreproduce and the external resources and forces in the environment that limit the number of individuals capable of being sustained. If this were the whole story, we could expect every species to fill an environment to its ultimate capacity, with external factors responsible for slight fluctuations in numbers. This situation is encountered only rarely. This does not mean that the Darwinian factors are unimportant, but students of ecology and animal behavior have more recently demonstrated that they are more likely to be of secondary importance and that the primary checks on the density of native species are intrinsic to the population itself and not dependent on external controls. Self-regulatory systems govern reproductive and survival rates, and they are more pronounced among species that show high degrees of structural and, most particularly, behavioral complexity. These factors, more so than food, predation, or disease, keep density levels far short of that which would lead to environmental exhaustion or destruction.

Through a glass darkly

Looking back, we see that evolving man has lurched from one crisis to another. Great empires have collapsed, whole civilizations have been violently destroyed; thought has been muzzled, common people cruelly exploited, habitats ruined. One dominant phase of psychosocial evolution after another has reached a limit and has had to crumble and be remodelled or replaced if human advance was to continue. Yet in the long term there has been advance, and new advance has always sprung from new ideas, new knowledge and its applications.

The present phase of the process is rapidly becoming self-limiting and self-defeating. If we fail to control our economic system, we over-exploit our resources. If we fail to prevent atomic war, we destroy civilization. If we fail to control our population, we destroy our habitat and our culture. However, our increasing knowledge is indicating how we might remodel our psychosocial organization and escape from the apparent impasse.

J. Huxley [22]

Self-regulatory mechanisms are basically of two kinds: those that limit the number of adults permitted to breed and those that limit the number of viable young each breeding pair can produce. Each may operate separately or be present in the same species. In the latter case they serve to reinforce each other. Among animal species, both mechanisms have social connotations, both depend upon intraspecific competition, and both operate with feedback as an indispensable element in the system.

These topics need not be dealt with extensively here for they have been treated in the popular press by such authors as Robert Ardrey in his books *The Territorial Imperative* and *The Social Contract* and Konrad Lorenz in *King Solomon's Ring* and *On Aggression*. The territorial systems of various birds and mammals, the limitation of breeding and rearing space, the availability of nesting sites, and the establishment of peck orders, whether these be among chickens or apes, all tend to restrict within a species the right to feed and the right to breed to those individuals who can manage intraspecific competition successfully. The result is that the available food, opportunities for breeding, and space for the rearing of young are distributed over the habitat occupied by a species and crowding is prevented. Dominant individuals maintain their domination by their aggressiveness, and subordinate ones are shunted to the outskirts of the habitat where they may be tolerated, but where they are denied the opportunity to contribute to ongoing generations. Their only hope is emigration to new and unoccupied sites where new competitive situations can be explored and initiated.

These features of population and habitat control based on competition have led V. C. Wynne-Edwards, an English

Research conducted at Aberdeen [Scotland] in the last 8 years has shown how important a factor forced expulsion is in regulating the numbers of the Scottish red grouse. Every breeding season so far has produced a population surplus, and it is the aggressive behavior of the dominant males which succeeds in driving the supernumeraries away. In this case the outcasts do not go far; they get picked up by predators or they mope and die because they are cut off from their proper food. Deaths from predation and disease can in fact be substantially "assisted" under social stress.

V. C. Wynne-Edwards [50]

Through a glass darkly

Some of these activities, like territorial defense, singing, and the arena displays, tend to be the exclusive concern of the males. It has never been possible hitherto to give a satisfactory functional explanation of the kind of communal male displays typified by the arena dances of some of the South American hummingbirds and manakins, and by the dawn strutting of prairie chickens and sharp-tailed grouse. The sites they use are generally traditional, each serving as a communal center and drawing the competitors from a more or less wide surrounding terrain. On many days during the long season of activity the same assembly of males may engage in vigorous interplay and mutual hostility, holding tense dramatic postures for an hour or more at a stretch without a moment's relaxation, although there is no female anywhere in sight at the time. The local females do of course come at least once to be fertilized; but the performance makes such demands on the time and energy of the males that it seems perfectly reasonable to assume that this is the reason why they play no part in nesting and raising a family. The duty they perform is presumably important, but it is simply not credible to attribute it primarily to courting the females. To anyone looking for a population feedback device, on the other hand, interpretation would present no difficulty: he would presume that the males are being conditioned or stressed by their ritual exertions. In some of the arena species, some of the males are known to be totally excluded from sexual intercourse; but it would seem that the feedback mechanism could produce its full effect only if it succeeded in limiting the number of females fertilized at an appropriate quota, after which the males refuse service to any still remaining unfertilized.

V. C. Wynne-Edwards [50]

biologist and ecologist, to propose that "a society is an organization of individuals that is capable of providing conventional competition among its members." The term "conventional" is used because specific systems of behavior are ritualized and lead not so much to bloodshed and death, which would be deleterious to species existence, as to threats of violence and particularized patterns of posture and movement. These social organizations, therefore, have evolved to their present status through the forces of natural selection and are characteristic for each species. Interestingly enough, the competition appears to be based on a male-male interaction, at least in its display phases, although the formation of a bond between male and female follows so that the breeding potential is maintained sufficiently high to ensure species continuation. On this basis, the vocal displays of various species, their differential sexual coloration, and territorial tactics are factors that enter into relations between males prior to the breeding season; they are not designed for the courting of females.

Although Darwinian factors have an effect, and often a crucial one, on population size, further limitation in the number of offspring per breeding pair is a behavioral-hormonal phenomenon dependent upon social pressures brought on by crowding and competition. A study of the vertebrate group beginning with the lower forms reveals a steady decrease in the number of offspring possible during any breeding season, particularly in the mammal group, where close relations between mother and offspring are maintained during the weaning period. Within this broad vertebrate grouping, however, stress conditions that activate the endocrine system lead to reduced litter size, increased intrauterine mortality, abandonment or destruction of the

Through a glass darkly

In the harsh economics of many underdeveloped countries . . . the value of a child works out to be negative. Money spent on birth prevention has a very real economic payout, therefore. The cost of preventing a single birth may be no more than $5.00, far less than the cost of only a single year's schooling. One estimate places the value of $1.00 spent on an effective program to slow population growth as equivalent in stimulating increased per capita income to $100 invested in industrial plant and equipment. [It has been] estimated, too, that a representative newborn baby in India probably will produce goods and services with a present value of only $75 during his lifetime but will consume products with a present value of about $200. Thus India could spend as much as $125 to prevent a birth and wind up ahead economically. And if India could reduce her 20 millions births a year by a fourth, the economic savings would total more than $600 million on an annual national income of about $27 billion.

D. M. Kiefer [25]

young, delayed sexual maturation, inhibition of growth, and lowered resistance to starvation and disease, particularly among the young. Furthermore, these responses to the stress of existence are more prevalent among subordinate members of a social group then among the dominant individuals. Behavior and reproduction are therefore closely intertwined and result in the maintenance of a population well within the limits of environmental capacity and in the retention within the breeding pool of those individuals capable of managing social competition.

What, we may now ask, has this to do with man and his population problems? The question takes on particular significance today because every facet of our present environmental crisis, without exception, stems from, or can be

10.3 Among the mammals, the close relationship between the mother and offspring during the weaning period is a factor that limits the number of offspring produced by each breeding pair. Various behavioral factors help to keep animal populations within the limits of environmental capacity and supplement the Darwinian factors that have been discussed earlier.

Ron Garrison photo, San Diego Zoo

Where should we look for evolutionary pressures today? It is a commonplace observation that people differ in their tolerance for crowding. In large measure these differences are a result of social training, of experience with crowded living. But there may also be a biological basis for them, an innate predisposition for some people to thrive better under crowding than others. This possibility is something biologists have tried to study in animals, and about which much has been written. The selective evolutionary pressure that would favor a crowd-adapted organism is reasonably obvious. If there are innate differences, and if we do face a future of living closer and closer together, evolution would inevitably favor certain

Pieter Brueghel the Elder, Flemish Proverbs.

Dahlem Museum, Berlin

related to, a burgeoning population that threatens to exceed the supporting capacity of the environment. Consequently, there is raised the specter of impending future disaster for the human species unless the demands of the species in terms of number, needs, and aspirations are related in a balanced manner to the finite resources available to it on a sustained basis. The right to feed and the right to breed take on human import, therefore, not so much within the context of natural selection as within the context of a culture where the nonpurposeful forces of evolution are replaced or superseded by subjective value judgments. These are generally conceived and executed by the dominant societies and by the dominant individuals of a society, with the inevitable development of competitive states of existence. Wynne-Edwards describes the problem in this way: "Conventional competition is an inseparable part of the substance of human society, at the parochial, national and international level. To direct it into sophisticated and acceptable channels is no doubt one of the great motives of civilized behavior; but it would be idle to imagine that we could eliminate it." Viewed in another way, a stabilized social system results from the attainment of a balance between the degrees of order and disorder in the human system, with a sufficient degree of order to prevent disintegration, but with an equally sufficient amount of disorder to prevent stagnation and to provide the diversity from which new elements of order are selected and fashioned as the environment itself undergoes change.

If we compare the relative roles of internal and external forces in keeping a population within environmental capacities—that is, the relative roles of the four Darwinian factors and those evolved situations of controlled breeding and

Through a glass darkly

people over others. By the year 2000, of course, nothing measurable will have had time to happen as a consequence of biological evolution. But we ought to know more about the possibilities and implications of such a change. It might be interesting for psychologists to attempt to measure individual differences in tolerance to crowding, and to try to determine whether there are inheritable traits that could serve as a basis for evolutionary selection. When the day comes that we have the necessary facts to support a realistic eugenics program, such information could be valuable.

G. A. Miller [32]

Hester Street, New York City, around the turn of the century.

History Division, Los Angeles County
Museum of Natural History

---

reproduction—it appears that among the higher vertebrates other than man the Darwinian factors are uncontrollable and hence unpredictable forces. These forces can bring on perturbations around a population mean, but, in the long run, they are secondary to the internal forces that keep populations below the maximum sustaining capacity of an environment. The Darwinian factors seem far more applicable to the world of plants and of less sentient animal species, and far less so to the more complex segments of the vertebrate group. In man, even the internal factors seem to have lost their once effective role and must be replaced by others arising out of a cultural awareness of the consequences of overreproduction.

About 10,000 years ago, at the beginning of the agricultural revolution that heralded the initiation of settled populations of man, the habitable portions of the globe were occupied by about 10 million human beings. It has been argued that this was a stable number that reflected the sustaining capacity of an environment of a population that gained its livelihood from hunting and food gathering and that had at its command a limited degree of mobility and a limited source of external energy in the form of fire and stone tools. These groups of early man were undoubtedly small in number and probably were never far from starvation. The control of additional energy through the use of agricultural methods and the buildup of surplus and storable foods led to an expansion of the population in limited areas of the temperate zone. The earth became a more productive planet both in terms of people as well as of food. By the beginning of the Christian era, the earth's inhabitants had reached a total estimated to be between 250 and 300 million. By 1650, the population doubled to an estimated 500

The population density and distribution of primitive man varied in relation to natural conditions according to the normal or Gaussian curve, reaching a peak under optimum conditions and tailing off toward both maximum and minimum limits of physiological tolerance for environmental extremes. Shelford's law of tolerance is a generalization of these relations between abundance, physiological comfort, and environmental factors applicable to all organisms. Modern man has skewed the curve somewhat by this fabrication of artificial home and working environments but the law still applies.

Liebig's law of the minimum and Blackman's limiting factors state that the growth, activity, or even existence of an organism is determined or regulated by that essential factor or condition in shortest supply. Modern man has developed methods of distributing essential elements or products to alleviate local deficiencies, but when his transport system breaks down or in areas where it has not been perfected, the working of this law is apparent. . . .

The laws of Nature apply to man as they do to animals. There are no exceptions. If he can come to understand what they are and how they work, he will know better what to anticipate concerning their effects on himself. He cannot ignore the dynamic forces of the environment with impunity, but being blessed with an intelligence far above that of other animals, he can guard against them or alleviate their effects to his own advantage.

C. S. Kendeigh [24]

Through a glass darkly

The current 2% per year may not sound like an unusual rate of growth. However, . . . Markert has shown that if this rate had existed from the time of Christ until the present time, . . there would be over 20 million individuals in place of each person now alive or 100 persons for each square foot. At our present rate of 2% per year there would be over 150 billion people within two centuries.

We are on the logarithmic phase of a typical growth curve after a long lag period. In nature no animal, plant, or bacterial population has ever maintained a logarithmic phase of growth for very long. The major factors that slow this rate of growth are exhaustion of food supply, accumulation of toxic products, decimation through disease, or the effects of some outside lethal agent which kills a high proportion of the population. Any one or all of these factors will force the population back into a lag phase. I leave it to your imagination which of these factors might apply to the human population. Of course, you will say that humans have intelligence and can intentionally modify some of these factors whereas a bacterial population cannot. I wonder if the present evidence does not support arguments to the contrary.

Some feel that the battle to feed the world population is now lost, and that it is a foregone conclusion that by 1985 we will have world-wide famines in which hundreds of millions of people will starve to death. I must admit that at this time I see no major crash program which would lead me to disagree with this conclusion.

W. D. McElroy [28]

million, despite wars, famines, and devastating plagues. The population of the earth stood at 1 billion in 1850, 1.5 billion in 1900, 2 billion in 1925, 2.5 billion in 1950, 3 billion in 1960, and 3.5 billion in 1968. Projecting this rate of increase into the future, the population will double to 7 billion by the year 2000, 10 billion by 2018, and 20 billion by 2068, and 358 billion by 3068, or eleven persons per acre uniformly spread over the 33 billion acres of the earth's land surface. This, of course, is playing games with future numbers, for the last figure would scarcely leave standing room, but the figures also dramatize why the terms "population bomb" and "population explosion" are not solely figments of someone's imagination. They are real indeed!

There are other ways of viewing this kind of population growth. The successively smaller amount of time between each doubling of the population vindicates Malthus' contention that the rise is geometric and not arithmetic. The early rate of growth from the time of emergence as a human species to the time of the agricultural revolution—a period covering hundreds of thousands of years—was about 2 percent per 1,000 years. Today it is 2 percent per annum, a thousandfold increase in rate. In actual numbers and at the present time, this means 132 additional human beings per minute, 200,000 per day, 6 million per month, and over 70 million per year. There is no apparent end in sight, and future prospects are dismal indeed if the rate of growth continues (see illustration 10.4).

The data suggest that the world population of the human species follows a typical growth curve. Such a curve, however, obscures the fact that the growth has not been uniform either in time or across the face of the earth. In a temporal sense, the rate of growth has accelerated each time man

Through a glass darkly

Every year we list tuberculosis, leprosy, enteric diseases, or animal parasites as the "cause of death" of millions of people. It is well known that malnutrition is an important antecedent of death in all these categories; and that malnutrition is connected with overpopulation. But overpopulation is not called the cause of death. We cannot bear the thought.

People are dying now of respiratory diseases in Tokyo, Birmingham, and Gary, because of the "need" for more industry. The "need" for more food justifies overfertilization of the land, leading to eutrophication of the waters, and lessened fish production—which leads to more "need" for food.

What will we say when the power shuts down some fine summer on our eastern seaboard and several thousand people die of heat prostration? Will we blame the weather? Or the power companies for not building enough generators? Or the econuts for insisting on pollution controls?

One thing is certain: we won't blame the deaths on overpopulation. No one ever dies of overpopulation. It is unthinkable.

G. Hardin [20]

---

has gained control over a new source of energy. There are four identifiable, major turning points in the history of man: the advent of tool making, which occurred more than a million years ago; the agricultural revolution around 8,000–10,000 B.C., which led to settled communities that could rely upon surpluses of storable foods; the scientific revolution, which began in the sixteenth and seventeenth centuries and which continues at an ever-increasing pace today; and the industrial revolution, which was initiated in the eighteenth century in Western Europe. Like the scientific revolution, the industrial revolution continues today at an accelerated rate. The third and fourth stages, as pointed out in the previous chapter, are based on an increased understanding of nature, the exploitation of the fossil and nuclear fuels, the conversion of energy into electrical form for widespread dispersion, and an accompanying technology of amazing sophistication. Each system of energy control enhanced the productivity of the individual and transformed and enhanced the productivity of the environment, thus enlarging its carrying capacity in terms of numbers of individuals by stepping up the yield of foods per unit of cultivated ground. The first two stages, both covering long periods of time, showed evidence of a leveling off of the growth curve, possibly because the supportive capacity of the environment had been reached. The last two stages, continuing through the present, reveals no signs of abatement in population growth as the human species moves into an uncertain future. But one thing is certain; the earth is a finite body, its resources are not limitless, and neither is its habitable surface. Given man's scientific knowledge and technological ingenuity, there is no question that the earth can sustain a population considerably greater than the present one. It

Through a glass darkly

10.4 World population growth from 6000 B.C. to A.D. 2000, together with an indication of the average density of persons per square mile at different points in history.

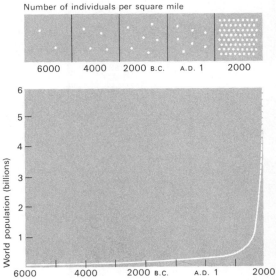

The mere increase in the number of people on our planet, if they were evenly distributed over the land areas, would not in itself produce a powerful force for change. But when people are concentrated in a small space, the force for cultural, social, and technological change increases, in much the same way that, if gases are pumped into a container, the number of collisions between the atoms or molecules in the gas will tend to rise.

Seen in this way, the city is an instrument for accelerating change. It creates an environment in which dense concentrations of people of varying backgrounds can come into contact every day. The product of these contacts is accelerated cultural and social change.

D. Fabun [13]

---

has been projected that the earth's population will level off at somewhere between 10 and 50 billion. Illustration 10.5 gives estimates of future population growth for the United States and the developing countries. But the question is not simply one of how many human beings can survive on this planet, but rather how large can the population grow without destroying the quality of life to be lived by each individual. The humaneness and rising aspirations of our culture are on a collision course with our reproductive and exploitative extravagances.

The unevenness of population growth is geographical as well as temporal. Little is known for certain concerning population distribution in prehistoric periods, but, paradoxically and tragically, the highest rates of growth today are in those areas where the amenities of life are the least attainable and existence is at a bare subsistence level. Affluence and technological sophistication go along with

10.5 Population predictions relative to family size. (a) Population growth for the United States based on a 2-child or 3-child family. (b) Population growth for the developing countries based on the date at which 2-child families can be the established norm. In many developing countries—Brazil, Mexico, Colombia, and the Philippines—the rate of growth exceeds 3 percent per year, a far cry from the zero growth rate represented by 2-child families. Today, the lowest growth rates are found in the Scandinavian countries, with Sweden having the lowest rate—0.3 percent.

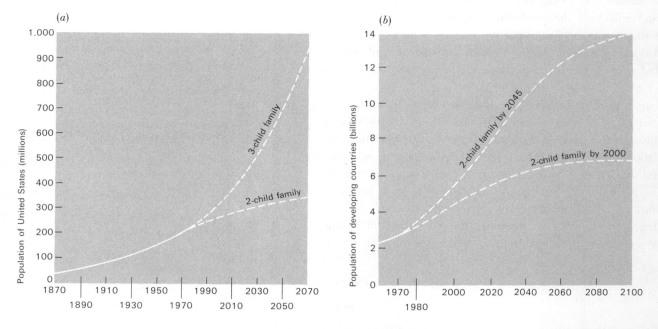

Artist's sketch of proposed Battery Park City, New York.

lower, not higher, rates of population increase. During the last 10 years, for example, approximately 600 million individuals were added to the world's population, with every four out of five being in those areas judged "poor" and "underdeveloped" by Western standards—Central and South America, Puerto Rico, India, Southeast Asia, and Taiwan among them. The rates of growth have in fact been such that, despite the introduction of technological methods for increasing the nutritional productivity of these areas, the population has increased faster than the ability to produce, a situation that has led to even more widespread malnutrition and cultural degradation. This seems to suggest a positive correlation between low calorie intake and fertility,

10.6 Chinese refugees in Hong Kong. The highest rates of population growth today are in those regions of the world where the amenities of life are least attainable.

United Nations

Various kinds of concern are expressed about the "population explosion." Some people seem concerned about sheer physical space and cite figures to show that there will be "standing room only" at some future date. Others see the increase as outrunning food resources or as hastening the end of our nonrenewable resources. Some are convinced that the increase spells genetic disaster, others are esthetically revolted by human crowding, and still others see it as a cause of wars. All such arguments, while they may have some truth, have serious limitations and in any event have had little impact on policy makers in underdeveloped areas: It is demonstrable that current rates of population growth are slowing down economic development and that a reduction in the rate of growth would have substantial salutary consequences for the economy. This argument does not imply that population control is a substitute for the usual ingredients of modernization—education, industrialization, technological development, and so forth—but that it will enable underdeveloped countries to take full advantage of such developments and make it possible for them to add to their per capita wealth and productivity.

J. M. Stycos [45]

Man is our main concern, and he is suffering because settlements impose on him an inhuman life and tend to crush him. Sitting near the source of the Kastalia, in Delphi, I was intrigued by Pindar's desire to hear the dance-step of men. I then remembered a famous Chinese dancer who once visited a temple upon a hill. He climbed the stairs and then ran down them. He climbed up carefully again and then asked why two steps were missing. When the monks told him that no steps were missing, he asked them to dig; and they found two missing steps covered by the soil. There were people moving in dance-steps, and some civilizations built their shells in a way corresponding to these dance-steps. Now we build highways, we allow cars to enter our homes, dining rooms, and offices; we have protected only our bedrooms. We have seen the birth of the new centaur, half man and half car; and we are gradually turning into legless species.

We need our legs and our whole body, we need our senses and our nervous system to operate properly, because, for the time being at least, we need man as we know him at his best. But we do not help him when he commutes for hours in ugly, unhealthy surroundings; we only increase his nervous stresses, and we finally break him. . . . Have we ever thought how many of our phobias are due to the fact that we start our lives held by the hand in order not to be killed by monsters controlling our surroundings, and that life in the jungle may be less dangerous for an uninformed child than is the life in a big city to which he is not adapted? Have we ever thought of the cost of our so-called adaptation to all sorts of sense and nervous-system stresses and the impact of all sorts of magnetic and electrical waves on us?

C. A. Doxiadis [*11*]

Abortion is an ancient practice, but even in antiquity it provoked sharp differences of opinion. Plato, in the *Republic,* approved abortion to prevent the birth of incestuous offspring; Aristotle, always a practical fellow, looked upon it as a useful Malthusian governor. The Hippocratic oath, on the other hand, contains the words "I will not give to a woman a pessary to produce abortion"; Seneca and Cicero condemned abortion on ethical grounds; and the Justinian Code prohibited it. There seems little doubt, however, that in the Roman Empire and the Hellenistic world abortion was, as one authority has stated, "very common among the upper classes." The Christian Church took a stern stand against this "pagan attitude," and pronounced abortion a sin. In many states the law followed church doctrine and made the sin a crime. But in Anglo-Saxon law abortion was considered "an ecclesiastical offense only."

J. R. Newman [*36*]

10.7 *A birth control clinic in India.*

but all physiological evidence points to the contrary. High reproductive rates must relate to other factors, and these are primarily cultural.

A stable population has a growth rate of zero; losses through death are compensated for by a comparable frequency of births, and, occasionally, by recruitment from outside. Any number of factors can affect this growth rate, but our present burgeoning population seems to indicate that the human species is no longer subject to the checks and balances of internal and external forces that tend to restrain the growth of other animal species. Wars, famine, and disease have taken a frightful toll of human lives throughout recorded history, and presumably prior to this time as well, but in the long run they have served to impose only temporary setbacks rather than to prevent a positive growth rate from operating. The human species has also escaped the pressure of internal, evolved forces, or perhaps more accurately, these forces of male-male competition have been redirected into other channels and away from its original reproductive role. Human fertility rates in this century have remained high under conditions of stress and crowding that would have imposed severe constraints on other animal species and on human populations prior to the agricultural revolution. Man made the earth a far more productive place of habitation. Cultural aspects have therefore come to dominate the biology of man. If fertility rates are to be subject to control in such a manner as to maintain an optimum population level, these controls must also be cultural rather than biological.

Population changes, with few exceptions, are very largely a matter of balance between birth rates and death rates. The rapid climb in population levels in this century can

Through a glass darkly

Modern humanitarianism seems to take the form of keeping each individual alive and without pain as long as possible even though he has little to live for. Brochures urge the donation of funds for research to eliminate almost every cause of death. Since every man must die sooner or later, the effect of this research is primarily to postpone death and possibly to make the prolonged life somewhat more pleasant. If these protective and avoidance patterns are greatly extended in the future, one can imagine a society that allows widespread use of drugs to prevent pain and anxiety, brain surgery to prevent both suffering and any aggressive actions by individuals, and extensive use of monitoring equipment to restrict individual behavior with a destructive potential. By such devices, it would certainly be possible to reduce unpleasant subjective experiences and to reduce greatly the impact of interpersonal aggression. In spite of the fact that such a society would undoubtedly produce weak individuals incapable of meeting new threats from the environment, there are indications in our present society that suggest trends in this direction.

G. C. Quarton [*39*]

---

be attributed to a control of death rates without a corresponding change in birth rates. The National Academy of Sciences' report, *The Growth of World Population*, points out why this is so. In 1800 in Western Europe, the average life expectancy was 35 years or less, the birth rate was thirty-five per thousand of population, the death rate was from twenty-five to thirty per thousand, and women gave birth to an average of five children. Today the life expectancy approaches 70 years, the birth rate is from fourteen to twenty per thousand, the death rate is from seven to eleven per thousand, and average number of births is two to three. Both birth rates and death rates declined, but the fall in the death rate was substantially greater and can be attributed to a whole complex of changes taking place in society, with better nutrition, sanitation, and modern medicine having major and direct impacts, particularly on infant mortality. The fall in birth rate is attributable to a deliberate and voluntary reduction in fertility by making use of a variety of birth control methods, such as abstention, abortions, late marriage, as in Ireland, and contraceptive devices.

The fall in infant mortality has two significant consequences: the number of individuals surviving to reproductive age is greater, and the average age of the population is younger, with a greater proportion being nonproductive in terms of consumable food or goods. Conversely, reduced birth rates would lead to a decrease in the number of individuals entering the breeding pool and an increase in the average age of the population. The death rate, as a consequence, would increase, because of the greater proportion of older people in the population.

In less developed countries, where education is minimal and industrialization is not as widespread or as intensive

. . . Norman Himes's *Medical History of Contraception* abundantly establishes the point that people in every culture have tried to control the size of families. Many cultures could come up with nothing better than abortion and infanticide—but not for want of trying. Just run your eye over this small sample of the immense roster of substances and procedures employed by one culture or another: okra seed pod, tannic acid, seaweed, lemon-juice douche, root of spotted cowbane, castor beans, marjoram, thyme, parsley, lavender, rosemary (what is this? a recipe for a cake?), crocus, myrtle, camphor, black hellebore, ball of opium, elephant dung, crocodile dung, camel dung, (no, it's not a recipe), olive oil, cedar oil, copper sulfate, willow, fern root, cabbage blossoms, a piece of bark tied in three knots, gunpowder tea, foam from a camel's mouth, stepping three times over a grave, and holding your breath. Some of these were no doubt partially effective—the lemon-juice douche, for example; but it is doubtful if any of them were as effective as this simple recipe, recorded in the medical literature as long ago as 1888: "Before going to bed, drink a glass of cold water *and don't touch another thing all night*." Effective, but not popular.

G. Hardin [*19*]

Through a glass darkly

Famine had been commonplace throughout European history prior to 1800. Malthus confidently predicted that hunger would become increasingly common in the future.

Subsequent history seemed to prove Malthus wrong. When Malthus was writing England and Wales had a population of about 9 million. Today their population numbers 49 million. Yet it is better fed than ever before. Malthus' "positive checks" of famine and disease have been largely mitigated. Even so, population is not growing at the rate he expected. The growth has been checked by social changes, such as tendencies to postpone marriage or practice contraception, rather than by the catastrophic means Malthus had envisioned.

Malthus missed on two fundamental points. Writing during the years when the Industrial Revolution was only getting under way, he did not foresee how technological innovation in agriculture and business would improve living conditions. Nor did he envision that birth rates would fall drastically as society became more urbanized and industralized, even as mortality also was declining. Malthus' positive checks were removed, but population growth slowed nevertheless. . . .

But Malthus has never been completely discarded. His theories, updated, repolished, and cast in a more modern and sophisticated mold, appropriate to new worldwide conditions, probably have more adherents now than at any time since he died. Many economists, viewing the hurtling growth of population in the nonindustrialized world, have become convinced that Malthus was a prophet before his time. His schedule may have been upset by technical and social changes that he could not foresee, but his basic conclusions were no less valid. The basic factors of food needs and the reproductive powers of a population must be filled into any equation of economic development.

D. M. Kiefer [25]

The most disquieting aspect of the food issue is the fact that, with few exceptions, the scientific and technical community has been signaling a green light to mankind when a stop sign would have been far more appropriate. Recent statements by leading Western scientists in almost all disciplines reveal a shocking disregard for the abject conditions which enclose almost three-fifths of the human race.

It is indeed macabre to witness the present game of calculating how many people the world *could* nourish—*if*. The figures soar beyond 7 billion to 10 billion and even more. Yet, scandalously, the world has failed to provide satisfactorily for even half the 3.5 billion people alive *now*. To give our current population a minimally sound diet would require the immediate doubling of world food production. Thus, whatever else happens and whatever urgent measures are taken, food is going to be the overriding issue of the next 30 years.

G. A. Borgstrom [3]

as in the highly developed ones, the birth rate remains high, while the death rate has dropped precipitously. Economic and social conditions may have changed but little in these areas of relative deprivation, but the importation of modern and low-cost health practices has produced a major population shift. Both infants and older persons survive with greater frequency, but the survival of the young is far more pronounced. Thus, a great proportion of the population consists of young people who produce a great number of offspring because marriage takes place at an early age and contraceptive practices are not well known or not employed because of social and religious prohibitions. The movement of these areas toward cultural modernization is thereby hindered, and in some instances set back, because the population rise is so great that the capacity to feed the inhabitants is being reduced in terms of calories per capita.

Food

Using the primitive weapons at his command, Stone Age man required a substantially greater territory to feed himself than did his agriculturally oriented successor. In his competition with other large mammals for sustenance, Stone Age man's intellectual talents and tools gave him an adaptive advantage, but they were unable to raise him appreciably above bare subsistence levels. The invention of agriculture brought a new dimension to man's existence. The cultivation of cereal crops provided a more certain and continuous food supply and tended to shift the omnivorous and largely carnivorous diet toward a starchy plant base. Experts have estimated that a given area can provide ten times as much

Through a glass darkly

Unemployed in a breadline during the 1930s.

Brown Brothers

plant as animal food. If true, this would make possible a tenfold increase in population density in cultivated areas. Can an increasingly more efficient agriculture sustain the expanding population today? Several estimates have indicated that a world population of 50 billion could be supported, assuming the cultivation of all arable land, more productive crops, improved cultivation practices, and better storage and distribution systems. Central to the problem are the land and the organisms it can produce on a sustained basis. Even more central is the kind of future world in which these teeming billions are to live out their existence. Numbers are meaningless unless they are related to the quality of life one wishes to have, but for a substantial portion of the world's population today a definition of the quality of life would include survival and little else.

Man can cause the deserts to bloom, as he has done in the Near East and in the Imperial Valley of California. He can also do the reverse. Areas of India and Pakistan that were once fertile are now stirred only by the winds raising dust clouds; the forested hills of Greece were barren and could not retain moisture even in Plato's time; and our own dust bowl of the 1930s serves as a vivid reminder of man's role in changing the face of the earth (illustration 10.8). Land, particularly to an expanding population, is a limited and precious commodity. The amount of arable land is diminishing as cities and industrial complexes expand into the countryside, and as highways, railroads, power cables, and pipelines spider-web their way across the landscape with little regard for the productivity of the acreage covered by concerte or asphalt or claimed for rights-of-way. Only rarely does a cultural change increase available acreage; one such change was the substitution of machines for draft animals.

If you were to go down to your backyard or an empty lot and mark off a square yard, stretch a gauze net over it, and then remove all the plants, insects and animals in that little square, you would learn at least two things. First, there is a great amount of life going on there—much more than you would have thought. Second, if you divide your "harvest" up into species (by numbers) there always are a number of other species. Nature has stocked each square of earth with a sufficient diversity of genetic "alphabets" so that if there should be a change in the environment, some of the "minority" groups will probably survive. If you were to try this same experiment on a square yard of man-cultivated land, the story would be different. Constant cultivation, and drenching with herbicides and insecticides, will have wiped out all but the dominant species. Such man-made environments—like stands of corn or wheat, or paddies of rice, or even your own rose garden—are highly vulnerable to environmental change. The dust bowls of North America, the ravaged, bare hillsides of Southern Europe, the deserts around the Mediterranean—all were largely caused by man's agricultural and industrial "progress." Now repeat the square yard experiment on a freeway, a parking lot, or the roof of a building and you'll see where we're headed. There's nothing left to count.

D. Fabun [14]

10.8 *Dust storm, Oklahoma, 1934.*

U.S. Department of Commerce

Through a glass darkly

10.9 *Productivity per acre of corn in the United States beginning with the period from 1920 to 1924. The dramatic increase in productivity beginning in the early 1930s resulted from the introduction of hybrid strains and the more widespread use of chemical fertilizers.*

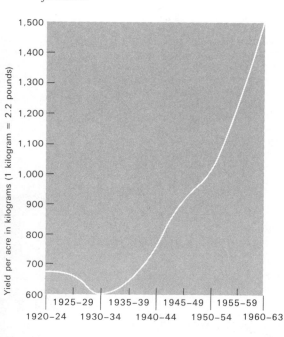

The acreage necessary for the upkeep of animals was freed to be used for man's subsistence in a more direct manner.

Less than three billion acres of the earth's surface yield crops at any given time, and these vary in productivity, depending on soil type, climatic factors, cultivation practices, and kinds of crops. Grain crops occupy 71 percent of this area, other edible plants 22 percent, and nonfood fiber crops, notably cotton, 7 percent. The North American acreage is by far the most productive, with a threefold increase in yield occurring since the 1930s. Better strains of grain, more efficient land use, and extensive applications of chemical fertilizers have made this possible (illustration 10.9). Other regions of the world could also be made more productive with improved agricultural practices and greater capital expenditures, and to this could be added acreage brought into a cultivable state, particularly through adequate water use. However, even the most optimistic estimates of future improvement in acreage and yield leave little doubt that such measures are only palliative and short-run at best and that the last decade of this century is likely to witness famine on a substantial scale if the population does not level off.

The plants and animals that man uses today in his cultivated fields and pastures bear little resemblance to the wild ancestors from which they were derived. They are as far removed in appearance and behavior as the miniature French poodle is from the wild dog, or that egg-laying machine, the White Leghorn, is from the wild jungle fowl of Malaysia. The major crop plants are literally designed and engineered by man through genetic manipulation, with selection being made not only for yield and nutritional value, but also for special localities, marketability, stor-

Through a glass darkly

Few areas of the world have provoked greater agricultural fantasies than the Amazon Basin, which is itself larger than any other Latin American country. Various schemes have been advanced to turn this steaming jungle into a "breadbasket" for the continent. Few of these master-plans have adequately taken into account the fragile ecosystem of the tropical rain forest, which supports a profusion of plant and animal species but which erodes with stunning suddenness under the slash-and-burn cultivation that is now so tragically on the increase. While scientists have not yet defined the precise relationship between mycorrhizal fungi and tree roots which enables the jungle to thrive on very poor laterite soil, they do agree on one vital point: this incredibly lush jungle, where the rainfall averages over 80 inches a year, is ecologically only a few steps removed from a wasteland. If the forest vegetation were to be cleared, says Colombian geologist Carlos Eduardo Acosta, the Amazon Basin would become "a desert like the Sahara."

W. E. Moran, Jr. [35]

---

ability, and, in the case of some, for machine harvesting. Most of these crops could not compete successfully if left to themselves; they are dependent upon man and are as domesticated as man is himself. They are a product of the scientific revolution and of a knowledge of biology; as such, they are characteristically found on the farms of Europe and North America, less so in the rest of the underdeveloped world. Even so, recently developed high-yielding strains of rice and wheat promise to bring about substantial increases in cereal productivity—the so-called green revolution—in the Asian and Latin American nations, and one can only assume that the plant breeder can bring about comparable changes in other plants, including increases in the amount of protein, the lack of which is a major source of malnutrition even in developed countries.

Grain crops, either directly or indirectly, constitute the principal source of food energy for man today. Rice and wheat provide 20 percent of the total calorie intake, other grains provide 33 percent of the total, while much of the remaining 47 percent come from grains indirectly in the form of meat, eggs, milk, and animal fat. This energy is derived from captured solar radiation, but the process is a most inefficient one as we noted in Chapter 9 (see illustration 9.3).

Diets the world over differ widely in calorie intake and food preferences. The consumption of starchy foods, for example, varies from 24 percent in North America to 74 percent in Asia. Some cultures shun meat and meat products, despite their high protein content, whereas others, such as the hunting Eskimos, exist almost exclusively on seal, walrus, fish, and birds. Personal preferences, cultural traditions, religious dictates, and regional distribution of food

The 2 quarts or so of water which a man needs daily for drinking is a requirement obvious to anyone. Less obvious is the equally vital but much larger volume of water needed to sustain a man's food chain from soil to stomach. . . . All this water represents a rather rigid requirement for human life, and it is water which is consumed, in the sense that it is removed from the hydrosphere and returned to the atmosphere.

. . .

. . . let us assume what might be called a simplified but generous American diet of 1 pound of animal fat and protein (beef) and 2 pounds of vegetable foods (bread) per day. It takes about 2 years to raise a steer. If butchered when it is 2 years old, the animal may yield 700 pounds of meat. Distributed over the 2 years, this is about 1 pound of meat per day. It may be seen, therefore, that this diet requires a steady-state situation of about one steer per person.

A mature steer consumes between 25 and 35 pounds of alfalfa a day and drinks about 12 gallons of water. Alfalfa has a transpiration ratio of 800, hence 20,000 pounds of water are required to bring 25 pounds of alfalfa to maturity. In other words, a little over 2300 gallons per day per man are required to introduce 1 pound of beef protein and fat into a person's diet. Add to this the 200 gallons necessary to round out his diet with 2 pounds of vegetable matter and we have a total water requirement of about 2500 gallons per day per person for a substantial American diet.

C. C. Bradley [4]

Through a glass darkly

We forget that the measure of the value of a nation to the world is neither the bushel nor the barrel, but mind; and that wheat and pork, though useful and necessary, are but dross in comparison with those intellectual products which alone are imperishable.

W. Osler [37]

products all play a role in forming dietary habits, but these are likely to undergo change as the agriculture of the world shifts more and more toward the high-yielding cereal crops, as the sea becomes farmed systematically instead of being haphazardly exploited as it is today, and as algae farms are established to yield high-protein dietary supplements. Dietary habits will not be changed willingly or easily, but 80 percent of the world's population has never had the luxury of choosing its meals from a menu. Whether food intake in the year 2000 will be generally uniform through the world, and hence more monotonous, is a debatable point, but it is evident even today that one-crop agriculture, with possible crop rotation, has altered substantial portions of the globe. Primitive man found his food where he could, and it was as varied as the locale he inhabited would afford. He survived in increasing numbers, but to do so he had to know nature in intimate detail. Our few open spaces today still contain a wide variety of plants and animals that served man well, and they could continue to do so today. The rice paddies of the Far East, the vast wheat fields of Russia, and the unending corn fields of our Middle West

10.10 In spite of improved agricultural methods and increasing yields per acre, the world's food supply has not been able to keep pace with unbridled population growth.

International Harvester Company

Standard Oil Co. (N.J.)

Caron/Gamma photo, UNICEF

are far more productive than primitive man could possibly have imagined, but in becoming one-croppers we not only have altered the face of the earth, but also have cropped our minds to what exists about us. We have become more impoverished spiritually, as we have become more affluent materially.

The food and population problems are intimately intertwined. Adequate food for all peoples is an obvious humanitarian goal; poverty and starvation should be the lot of no man. The goal is also politically and industrially desirable, for the alleviation of suffering and malnutrition lessens the threats to peace and promotes the marketability of the by-products of culture. However, adequate and equitable nutritional standards the world over have been extraordinarily difficult to achieve, even with improved techniques, more productive strains of plants and animals, and better distribution. As happens in any population of organisms, added food has led to greater population levels, which in the end have offset nutritional gains and often lowered standards of living. The world will continue to improve its productivity, but if this involves the production of people as well as food, the global crisis will persist or become even more evident. Any population reaching an environmental maximum will inevitably bring the Darwinian factors of constraint into play.

The recent destruction of megafauna in New Zealand, Madagascar, and the West Indies followed from the activities of agricultural man rather than of hunters. This points up a meaningful dichotomy of human societies in terms of their effect on the environment. The contrast between ''prehistoric'' and ''modern'' man in this connection is not of much value. The ''modern'' Plains Indians and African Bushmen have had a very different effect on their environments than did the simple grain farmers of the Eastern Mediterranean some eight or ten thousand years ago. Agriculturally based societies differ from one another only in the degree to which they disturb the natural environment, while they all differ in kind from hunting and gathering societies.

G. S. Krantz [27]

Resources and energy

A culture that has passed beyond subsistence levels inexorably enters a regime of existence that tends, with accelerated rates, to exploit and eventually to deplete the en-

Through a glass darkly

I have looked rather carefully into this matter of terminating man, with a surprising result; namely, it appears to be a hard job to shake him off. He is an ingenious critter, and in his relatively large forebrain he may figure out escapes from extinction—escapes from what appears to be coming to him soon and inevitably—soon, on the cosmic time scale.

No one of us who has thought about it expects man as we know him to be on this planet a million years from now. Let's base our speculations on the much better chance that he could still be here, in spite of hell and high water, ten thousand years from now—that is, one hundred centuries from this epoch. Our dealing with the future will take both logical analysis and imaginative poetry—it will take science *and* the humanities intermingled.

Life on this planet now depends completely on the sun for its continuity, as it depended on the sun some three or four thousand million years ago for its origin. To meet our need, the sun must stand by for one hundred centuries and remain steady. Explode the sun and you expire the biology of this planet. Dim the sun and you damn the man.

The sun's fuel supply of hydrogen is very great. At the present rate it will shine benevolently for billions of years, rather closely thermostated throughout that time. The stars are so remotely scattered from one another that a lethal star-sun collision is out of reason for much longer than our ten thousand years. If the nearest star, Alpha Centauri, were aimed directly at us, which it isn't, and were approaching as fast as one hundred miles a second, which it isn't, it still could not get to us in one hundred centuries—stars, you see, are so isolated in the ocean of space. Also, the sun is of a calm variety, with no likelihood of explosion.

The earth moves in a stable orbit. There is no chance, our celestial mechanics tell us, that it will break loose, escape from the sun, and freeze to death out in empty interstellar space.

---

vironment's natural resources and alter its natural characteristics. In this respect, man differs from all other species of life in the diversity and intensity of his energy requirements, most of which are culturally related or determined. Each step in the acquisition and control of additional energy has been at the expense of natural resources and has placed a greater demand on them. With increasing population and no less equally rising expectations and needs generated by the complexity of society, the utilization of these resources is expected to spiral upward at an extraordinary rate. It began with the first tentative shaping of stone tools, and today, in the developed countries of the West, finds its most dramatic expression in machines that can level mountains, in highly automated industries, in space trips that have permitted man to walk on the moon, and in the destructive instruments of war. But for the vast majority of mankind, these resources can serve a far more basic need, the need to rise above bare subsistence levels, to obtain more adequate food, clothing, and shelter, and to expand educational opportunities; in short, to reach the level of humanity of which each man is capable.

Civilization is a complex affair embodying many peoples, diverse activities, varied dreams and goals, and manifold directions, no one of which is independent of the others or of the environment. The uses of resources are similarly complex and interdependent. Only rarely is a single resource used by itself. As someone has said, we take pleasure in the soft glow of candlelight only when other more adequate sources of illumination are available. Most resources, indeed, are not ready for human use in a natural state except those that were used by nomadic man. Furthermore, the resources of the environment are distributed in uneven fashion

Through a glass darkly

And there is no chance that it will spiral into the sun and perish of temperature. Equable climates for the next hundred centuries—this is my forcast.

We see no way, therefore, of clearing the earth of *Homo sapiens* through the misbehavior of stars, of sun or of earth.

· · ·

I am glad to report that it looks pretty safe on this planet for ingenious man—safe, that is, but for one horrible threat. Man has a deadly enemy at his throat—one that may succeed in returning the planet to the clams, kelp and cockroaches.

The enemy is, of course, himself. Man's worst foe is man. We all know how, with man-made bomb concussions, with radiations and poisons, that cruel enemy can carry out his lethal enterprise. Poor *Homo!* It would be so wasteful to do him in. He is such a nice animal, so kind of heart at times, so cute, so remarkably put together, with opposable thumbs that have created art, and roving eyes that have provided posterity; with his sweet vocal cords, his powerful forebrain. It *would* be too bad, for he is so well-equipped to appreciate the universe—its beauty and its cosmic music.

On happier planets, which circle stars in grander galaxies, the most highly sentient beings may have solved this problem of suicide or survival. I wonder if we could do something about it by giving heavy thought to the matter. I wonder if we shouldn't do something. At least we might start programs that aim specifically at our retaining possession of the planet for the remainder of this century—programs that aim to let us hold on long enough to provide that our near, dear posterity may enjoy something of what we have enjoyed.

H. Shapley [44]

---

throughout the crust of the earth, they are not inexhaustible, and the industrial societies exert a disproportionate drain on them. And lastly, the environment from which these resources are drawn, particularly its biological components, is itself a dynamic complex of interacting and interrelated elements that are so interdependent that the alteration of one feature, intentionally or otherwise, can jeopardize the functioning, usefulness, or survival of the whole. The human species, if it is to survive, cannot continue its present assault on the store of natural resources. Resources that were produced over billions of years are being depleted during the brief span of man's existence. If the present trend continues, man is not likely to survive for long in his present state of culture.

Some natural resources are renewable and, with proper management of withdrawal and growth, can be maintained on a continuous and sustained basis for the foreseeable future. These include the following: forests, which not only yield timber for building, fuel, and paper products, but also add humus to the soil and strengthen its water-holding capacity; the organisms of the world, which vary widely in their usefulness to man; water, which is continuously cycled through the atmosphere, the land, and the lakes, rivers, and oceans, and which, if polluted, can be cleansed; land. which yields the foodstuffs for mankind, and which, with sound practice, can be maintained in top productive capacity; and the oceans, which, although largely unexploited at present except in selected ways, are immense and very varied in their products and possibilities of yield.

The resources of a nonrenewable nature include the ores, minerals, and energy-yielding fossil fuels, to which can be added the fissionable materials as further sources of energy.

Modern industrial society is based on the assumption that it is both possible and desirable to go on forever providing more and more goods for more and more people. Today that assumption is being seriously challenged. The industrial nations have come far enough down the road to affluence to recognize that more goods do not necessarily mean more happiness. They are also recognizing that more goods eventually mean more junk, and that junk in the air, in the water, and on the land could make the earth unfit for human habitation before we reach the 21st century. In short, the terms of the contract between industry and society are changing. Industry has succeeded by specializing in serving one narrow segment of society's needs. We have bought labor and material and sold goods, and we have assumed that our obligations were limited to the terms of the bargain. Now we are being asked to serve a wider range of human values and to accept an obligation to members of the public with whom we have no commercial transactions. We are being asked to contribute more to the quality of life than mere quantities of goods.

H. Ford [16]

Through a glass darkly

The revolution brought about by the magnificent union of science and technology is now threatened by a massive counter-attack driven, I believe, by real and justified fears of its power and consequences, and, perhaps still more, of its unpredictability and the present lack of control over it.

This counter-attack has already noticeably decreased the capabilities and the funding of research and development in the United States. This kind of counter-attack has been powerful for several decades in some of the countries of Western Europe. It is my opinion that it is to a considerable extent responsible for the "technological gap" which reportedly exists between Western Europe and the United States. . . .

Will we—and can we—take action to meet the very real problems that are raised by this enormous power, or will we attempt to escape that responsibility? . . .

This is the test. Will we meet the challenge or will we escape it and slow the progress of our technology? This test of societies is analogous to many of the tests that individuals face in growing up. Dangerous times occur when children are first entrusted with harmful devices. The responsibilities that go with increased power are essential parts of the growth process. When these responsibilities are avoided, the individual escapes both the inevitable growing pains and the growth. I believe that technological progress has been one of the prime movers in our society's growth through the centuries. We must not allow those who would escape this challenge to dominate the thinking of young people.

A. Kantrowitz [23]

10.11 Strip mining. Some argue that this form of mineral extraction is necessary in order to supply increasing energy needs. Others call it criminal destruction of the environment. This is only one facet of the complex question of how to meet the seemingly insatiable demand for energy, while at the same time preserving natural resources and the environment.

Should it be possible to control the nuclear fusion process, that is, the conversion of hydrogen into helium as occurs in the sun, man would have an unlimited source of energy for an indeterminable length of time. As it is now, oil and gas are in shortest supply; fissionable materials, such as uranium and plutonium, are readily exhaustible, but may be enhanced by the development of appropriate breeder techniques; and coal, even at the rate used today, will last for several thousand years. Of the major ores, iron, copper, lead, zinc, and aluminum are mined in huge tonnages, with industry turning more and more to low-grade deposits as extraction techniques are improved and the demand rises.

This is not the place for an assessment of each resource and its role in human cultures, now and in the future. The demands by future generations cannot be predicted with

. . . I want to look at environment in ecological terms. The first step is to make energy the common denominator for all processes involving the transfer or transformation of matter. In ecological systems, a general rule states that as energy (or food) is passed from one organism to another in food chains (plants being eaten by little animals that in turn are eaten by bigger animals, *et cetera*), a significant amount of energy is lost (as heat) at each successive link in the chain. The greater the length of the chain, the greater is the amount of energy dissipated, and thus the greater the inefficiency of the transfer process. In natural systems, the length of these chains is surprisingly short—generally only about two to six links (or species)—owing to these constraints in the transfer of energy.

Already we have a loose framework in which to view and contrast life in New York City and life in, say, rural Vermont. The latter is analogous, at least potentially, to an animal low down in a food chain (close to the primary energy source), and therefore relatively efficient, while the inhabitant of Manhattan is many links distant from his source of sustenance. As energy is transferred from the steer in Texas to the slaughterhouse to the packer to the shipper to the distributor to the local butcher to the consumer in New York, energy is consumed and lost; the greater inefficiency is due in part to the obvious increase in handling, but also to increased spoilage (the hypothetical Vermont farmer grows and harvests only what he can eat or preserve within fairly narrow limits). From an energetic point of view, life in the city is more expensive than life on a small country farm.

P. L. Marks [30]

---

certainty because of the variables involved: population growth, national and international output, income, leisure, and scientific and technological discoveries, to name a few. Even with the best recycling techniques, however, and with substitutes and more efficient uses provided by man's ingenuity, a continued depletion is inevitable. A forest cannot be grown in a generation, and it would be difficult to put asphalted roads back into cultivation even if some other means of transportation were found. As the American biologist Marston Bates has said, man cannot be expected to freeze when he is sitting on a coal mine, although in the end he may condemn his children to do so.

Every resource available to us is either a heritage of the past or a product of man's inventiveness. The sea and the land can be made more productive, and better use can be made of renewable assets. The ores and fossil fuels are a geologic heritage, the result of millions of years of concentration through weathering, leaching, and transforming processes. We are spending this heritage freely and lavisly, but once gone, these materials cannot be replaced within a period of time that bears any significant relation to man's existence. Yet we recognize that their use has permitted man's cultural evolution to its present state; without them, existence on earth of the human species would have had to be organized on a different and undoubtedly less elaborate basis.

Man is endowed with perennial optimism. He sees that life is good, he wants it to be better, and he has come to rely on science and technology to improve his lot and permit him to solve the problems that arise. Clearly this philosophy has gotten us into difficulty; our technological, scientific, and informational sophistication has outstripped our social

To me then, the job and the purpose of science and technology remain overwhelming: to create a more livable world, to restore man to a state of balance with his environment, to resolve the remaining elementary and primitive suffering of man—hunger, disease, poverty, and war. These are not small tasks, nor are they new ones; that in science and technology we have the possibility of dealing with them is an article of faith of all who have committed themselves to the scientific way of life. It is the height of irrationality to turn our backs on all this, as is urged by the more radical of the scientific abolitionists. For rationality and science there is no simple or cheap substitute. Should science die under the onslaught of the nihilists, it could be only a temporary death. That human rationality and human good sense will prevail in the long run we take for granted. It is up to us, members of the older scientific-technological establishment, to persuade our younger impatient scientific nihilists that ours is the course of reason, and that in our arduously built scientific-technological tradition lies our best chance of ultimate survival.

A. M. Weinberg [48]

Through a glass darkly

In the distant past, we may conjecture, man thought of himself as part of nature, at the mercy of natural forces and invented divinities. In the West this view slowly changed, spurred no doubt by the Greek invention of humanism and the Jewish invention of monotheism. The result was the belief that man was at the center of the universe both astronomically and metaphysically. . . . The Christian God was conceived to be exclusively and benevolently concerned with the human condition.

We all know how this position eroded, bit by bit. First, the earth was removed from the center of the universe, then a mechanistic philosophy launched by the Newtonian discoveries removed God from his intimate concern with man, and as a final blow, the divine creation gave way to natural evolution from, of all things, primeval slime. . . .

A few months ago one of the greatest of living scientists told an international gathering composed of other scientists: "We must not ask where science and technology are taking us, but rather how we can manage science and technology so that they can help us get where we want to go." It is not reported that Dr. René Dubos was shouted down by his audience, and yet what he was asserting was precisely what we as a people seem to have dismissed as unthinkable: that "we," which apparently means mankind, must abandon our modern practice of asking where science and technology are "taking *us*," and must ask instead how *we* can "manage" science and technology so that they will help us to achieve *our* purposes—our purposes, that is to say, as men. . . .

A curious automatism, human in origin but not human in action, seemed to be taking over. Cities were being built and rebuilt not with human purposes in mind but with technological means at hand. It was no longer the neighborhood which fixed the shape and limits of the town but the communications system, the power grid. Technology, our grandfathers said, "advanced" and it was literally true: it was technology which was beating the tambours, leading the march. . . .

Wildness and silence disappeared from the countryside, sweetness fell from the air, not because anyone wished them to vanish or fall but because throughways had to floor the meadows with cement to carry the automobiles which advancing technology produced first by the thousands and then by the thousand thousands.

A. MacLeish [29]

management of these forces. The situation was perhaps most clearly defined many years ago by Herman Melville in his novel *Moby Dick*. The white whale was the symbol of all of the powers that lay beyond man and that might curtail his activities in any way, and Captain Ahab drove himself, his crew, and his ship to destruction in his effort to destroy the whale. As the climax approaches, the driven Ahab states, with illuminating insight: "All my means are sane; my motives and object mad."

Wastes and pollution

When a plant or animal dies, its body usually disintegrates and its substance is recycled through the environment by being used by some other organism. Wastes, whether they be dead bodies or offal, are returned to nature as food; life draws from the environment and returns its substance to it. In the Bible, the author of Ecclesiastes acknowledged this when he wrote "dust to dust returneth"; the biologist sees it as the "web of life" or the "balance of nature," even though the process of recycling goes on slowly and is not generally visible. There is little waste, except for the heat produced by metabolic reactions, for what is waste to one species is food to another. Only in coal beds, peat bogs, oil fields, and limestone rock do we find modified accumulations of organic remains in significant proportions. In human terms, however, these cannot be considered wastes—quite the contrary—and they cannot, again in human terms, be equated with the garbage heaps that are as much a symbol of civilization as are skyscrapers and industrial complexes.

Human existence is dignified by the term "culture," but

Through a glass darkly

But still there was something left for man. He might be insignificant cosmically, he might have originated in slime. But here at home on his planet he was boss. The same scientific discoveries that tumbled him from his throne gave him the power to exploit his own planet and to make life easier, richer and abundant for far more people than had ever dreamed of this even fifty years ago.

. . .

The promise of abundance has proved an empty one, since the quest for it requires an exponentiating material affluence. In the course of this quest, in the past ten years, the cruelest blow was struck. Man is not really boss of his planet. Instead he is a slave, fettered to it, condemned forever to exist on what is available. He cannot dump offal into his rivers, lest his children have no water to drink. He cannot push his highways into the wilderness if he wants to preserve the wilderness for his heirs. And he cannot drive one of his three cars into the city because a) there will be a monster traffic jam in the approaches, b) the exhaust of cars will make his eyes burn, and c) when he gets into the city he cannot walk around because the crime will get him.

All of a sudden we have passed from the ownership of a planet into bondage; man's view of himself must undergo yet another change, yet another step down in a previously divine hierarchy. He is thrown back on the limited resources of his planet and his own understanding.

A. Zucker [51]

---

culture, as it moves forward in time and changes its degree of complexity without full knowledge of cause-and-effect relationships, leaves behind its accumulated debris in a form and an amount that precludes recycling within reasonable lengths of time. Man, alone among living forms, thereby gains the dubious distinction of having escaped involvement in the natural process of recycling to such an extent that if there were a global ethos over and above man and concerned with a clean environment, it would view the departure of man from the earth as the most desirable event of the future. Isak Dinesen, the Danish novelist, has perceptively said that the human being is an "ingenious machine for turning, with infinite artfulness, the red wine of Shiraz into urine." Paul Bohannan refers to this as a "reverse Midas syndrome."

Although we hear much about pollution today, prompted most effectively by Rachael Carson's *Silent Spring*, it is not a recent phenomenon. What is new is the realization that

10.12 *When this photograph was taken about 25 years ago, the general public gave little thought to the dangers that wastes and pollution posed for the environment. In the past decade, environmentalists have spurred government and industry to take measures to protect the earth's resources, but only time will tell whether action was taken soon enough.*

Standard Oil Co. (N.J.)

The shore is an ancient world, for as long as there has been an earth and sea there has been this place of the meeting of land and water. Yet it is a world that keeps alive the sense of continuing creation and of the relentless drive of life. Each time that I enter, I gain some new awareness of its beauty and its deeper meanings, sensing that intricate fabric of life by which one creature is linked with another, and each with its surroundings.

The shore at night is a different world, in which the very darkness that hides the distractions of daylight brings into sharper focus the elemental realities. Once, exploring the night beach, I surprised a small ghost crab in the searching beam of my torch. He was laying in a pit he had dug just above the surf, as though watching the sea and waiting. The blackness of the night possessed water, air, and beach. It was the darkness of an older world, before Man. There was no sound but the all-enveloping, primeval sounds of wind blowing over water and sand, and of waves crashing on the beach. There was no other visible life—just one small crab near the sea. I have seen hundreds of ghost crabs in other settings, but suddenly I was filled with the odd sensation that for the first time I knew the creature in its own world—that I understood, as never before, the essence of its being. In that moment time was suspended; the world to which I belonged did not exist and I might have been an onlooker from outer space. The little crab alone with the sea became a symbol that stood for life itself—for the delicate, destructible, yet incredibly vital force that somehow holds its place amid the harsh realities of the inorganic world.

R. Carson [6]

Affluent societies have also been labeled "effluent" societies. That man is a highly adaptable species that can live in polluted environments, in extremely crowded conditions, in situations of acute malnutrition, and in some of the most depressing of environments is well exemplified today. But why should he? And how much lower can he sink and still survive as a "successful" species?

Mushrooming with the population are pollution and litter. We produce 70% of the world's solid wastes but have only 10% of the world's population. There is a need to make the reuse and disposal of rubbish more economical.

W. E. Howard [21]

the human species and its way of life are threatened by the magnitude of its waste products. Prior to this century, mankind could coexist with its wastes, although not without occasional disaster. The Romans, in the first century, B.C., recognized the dangers of waste and built one of the first municipal sewerage disposal systems, the *Cloaca Maxima*. Venice in its early days depended upon the tides to flush its canals of human wastes twice daily, but any visitor to Venice today is aware of, and revolted by, the inadequacy of its disposal system. John Evelyn, the seventeenth century English diarist, criticized the perennial smog that hung over London, and laws were enacted to cut down the emission of smoke from the soft coal fires and chimney pots of England. The plagues that periodically swept through Europe and Asia—typhus, typhoid, diphtheria, and cholera—can be directly attributed to poor sanitation procedures that permitted the harboring of disease and disease carriers, thereby assuring its ready transmission through a dense population.

Some forms of waste and pollution are readily apparent: the smog of our cities, the dead and dying waters of our lakes, the industrial wastes of large manufacturing centers, oil spills, and automobile graveyards. Other forms are more subtle and less visible, but nonetheless they are invidious and dangerous to living forms. Consider, if you will, the trunks of trees in the city and in the forest. Those in the city are free of lichens. These organisms are especially sensitive to the presence of sulfur dioxide, a pollutant derived from the burning of fossil fuels and present in city smogs.

The pesticides are another highly publicized form of pollution. DDT is of inestimable value to malaria-ridden

Through a glass darkly

David Muench

I was driftwood
in the pool, but the waves
of bitterness
have washed me back ashore.

M. Seami [42]

populations, and its usefulness lies not only in its immediate and fatal effect on disease vectors but also in its persistence. It is nonbiodegradable and can continue to act for a long time. Although it is not metabolized, it finds its way into organisms at the bottom of the food chain and becomes more and more concentrated in those species at or near the top of the food chain. What is true for DDT is also true for a wide variety of similarly used chemicals; their effect on many species of wildlife is known and is suspected in many other cases. The unfortunate fact is that their influence does not remain local; the movement of water carries them around the world, even to the penguins of the Antarctic, an area where pesticides have never been applied.

DDT is a pollutant and a waste product only after its initial role is past; as an insecticide it is effective and useful even though resistance to it can develop in certain insect species. It is, therefore, representative of a wide variety of chemicals entering the environment, whose uncertain detrimental effects will appear only after a long lag period. Social and environmental assessments of future consequences of these substances are not made except on a short-run basis. Indeed, the ability to make such assessments is not always present, and even when known, a judgment has to be exercised on the basis of known good versus probable detriment. Even the highly beneficial chemical fertilizers, one of the chief causes of the high productivity of this country's farms, are not without their deleterious effects. The excess nitrates and phosphates, leaching from the soil into rivers and lakes and reinforced by similar nutrients derived from human wastes and detergents, have promoted the bloom of algae to a degree that oxygen is depleted, thus killing off aquatic life. There is some question whether highly polluted Lake

United Nations

10.13   Waste disposal is a worldwide problem as these dead fish in the polluted Tiber River in Italy attest.

Through a glass darkly

Wide World Photos

Many of the deleterious side effects of technology are actually due to the unbalanced development of technology, often the lag of technology in the public sector behind that in the private sector. For example, aircraft development has outpaced air-traffic-control technology. Technology for effluent suppression in both automobiles and central station power plants has lagged behind the growth of the primary technologies. Progress on underground electrical transmission, which is not of much benefit to the individual consumer, has been much slower than other progress in power technology. Waste-disposal technology for nuclear power plants has lagged behind progress in nuclear power itself. In a broader context progress on population-limitation technology may be said to have lagged behind progress in public-health measures and agricultural technology, contributing to the population explosion. Perhaps a better system of technology assessment would have earlier redressed these imbalances in technological development.

It is my view that unless we very soon develop better measures for technology assessment, it is likely that ill-considered political reaction against technical progress will produce a crisis in our society which will make the environmental crisis look tame by comparison. Thus I regard technology assessment as essential to the continued technological progress which in turn I regard as essential to the survival of human civilization.

H. Brooks [5]

Erie can ever be salvaged to the point where it would again be useful for anything other than shipping.

The threat today of wastes and pollutants to man and to other forms of life is very real indeed. A certain amount of waste is inevitable in any civilization. The kitchen middens (refuse heaps) of earlier cultures provide archaeologists and anthropologists with a partial view of what transpired in these now dead cultures, but we are running out of space for future kitchen middens. The remaining living space is too precious to be used for this purpose. Recycling of reclaimable waste will help, as will a reduction of obviously dangerous pollutants, but if man is not to be buried by his garbage or poisoned by the air and water upon which he so depends, the physical assault on the environment must

10.14 Mountains of tin cans await recycling at the Elizabeth, New Jersey, plant of M&T Chemicals, a subsidiary of American Can Company. Recycling programs undertaken by many industries offer hope that the problem of waste disposal can eventually be solved.

M&T Chemicals, Inc.

The way our economy is organized is an essential cause, if not the essential cause, of air and water pollution, and of the ugly and sometimes destructive accumulation of trash. I believe it is also an important element in such dangerous human ecological interventions as changes in the biosphere resulting from the wholesale use of inorganic fertilizers, of the accumulation in various dangerous places such as the fatty tissue of fish and birds and mammals of incredibly stable insecticides. We can properly attribute such adverse effects to a combination of a high level of economic activity and the use of harmful technological practices that are inconsistent with such a high level.

The economist would say that harmful practices have occurred because of a disregard of what he would call *externalities*. As externality is defined as a consequence (good or bad) that does not enter the calculations of gain or loss by the person who undertakes an economic activity. It is typically a cost (or a benefit) of an activity that accrues to someone else. . . . Air pollution created by an industrial plant is a classic case of an externality; the operator of a factory producing noxious smoke imposes costs on everyone downwind, and pays none of these costs himself—they do not affect his balance sheet at all. This, I believe, is the basic economic factor that has a degrading effect on the environment: we have in general permitted economic activities without assessing the operator for their adverse effects. There has been no attempt to evaluate—and to charge for—externalities. As Boulding says, we pay people for the goods they produce, but do not make them pay for the bads.

To put the same point more simply: environmental deterioration has arisen to a large extent because we have treated pure air, pure water, and the disposal of waste as if they were free. They cannot be treated as free in a modern, urban, industrial society.

A. J. Coale [7]

---

be brought into line with the quality of life he chooses to lead. Man is a decision-making animal, and he is now faced with one of the thorniest problems of his long history. Alternative routes of action must be known, and the consequences of elected options must be appraised with as small a margin of error as possible. The fact that our ecological crisis has its roots in the growth of the human population and the technological character of its civilization has led to the repeated suggestion that a moratorium on science and technology be declared. But our knowledge of the intricate interdependencies of man and his environment is at a state where more, not less, science is needed in order to enhance our capabilities of prediction and control. The source of our dilemma is not science, but rather the uses to which we put science. New information derived from science must be used with wisdom and in the light of human values. We do not have a heritage with the future, but we do have an obligation.

Continued adaptation

Few biologists doubt that man, at the time of his emergence from a simian stock and for many millennia thereafter, was shaped physically and behaviorally by the forces of natural selection acting on the heritable diversity within his gene pool. In this sense, his early history is little different from that of any other species; he came to terms with his environment or he ceased to exist. The many human races and subraces indicate not only that man was highly polymorphic, that is, genetically diversified, but also that he was highly adaptable. He survived and maintained a high fertility

In the history of most evolving species a change in the environment is almost always bad. The reason is that, through natural selection in the past, the organism has acquired a set of genes that are well adapted to this particular environment. A change in the environment is almost certain to necessitate some gene replacements. Thus, much of evolution is spent keeping up with what, from the standpoint of any one organism, is a steadily deteriorating environment, the most serious and rapidly changing aspect of which is the improvement of competing species through their own evolution. Man, however, is unique in that most changes in the environment are of his own doing. Therefore, the environment instead of deteriorating is getting better, at least for most genotypes. Consider, for example, the precipitous drop in childhood death rate, with only a slight compensatory rise in adult death from such diseases as cancer.

. . .

As human beings, we are primarily interested, not in the effect of a gene on fitness *per se*, but in its associated effects on health, happiness, intelligence, and other aspects of human well-being. From the standpoint of long-range human welfare, the most beneficial kind of environmental advance is one that reduces the amount of suffering and unhappiness caused by a mutant gene by a greater degree than the increase in fitness. On the other hand, an environmental change that, for example, increases the fertility of persons with a severe or painful disease without a corresponding decrease in the amount of suffering caused by the disease will in the long run cause an increase in human misery.

J. Crow [9]

Through a glass darkly

The most important single change in our world, where life-span is concerned, is that in privileged countries our children grow up and reach old age and our wives no longer die in childbirth. Men have always known the probable limit of their lives. We now know more accurately than ever before when we are likely to die. The most important future change depends on the progress of our understanding of fundamental age processes. If the present trend of medicine continues without such progress, all that will happen is that the commonest age of dying will shift from being nearer 75 to being nearer 85, and the commonest causes may change so that we die of conditions which are not now so common, today's most frequent killers having been removed to uncover the next layer of the onion. If this is all, not many more than the present 2 in 100 born will reach 90, and not many more than the present 1 in 1,000 will reach 100. Those who do will still be the progeny of long-lived stocks, and owe more to their parents' genes than to medical science.

A. Comfort [8]

---

rate in an enormously diversified habitat. In biological terms, his evolutionary success has been unprecedented.

His invention of culture added a new dimension to human life. Through the making of tools and the development of agriculture, through the scientific-technological revolution and the use of symbolic thought and language, man has profoundly altered, and to a large extent controlled, his environment and his way of life. What effect, we may now ask, has this had on his gene pool? Is the human race sufficiently adaptable so that it can accommodate to every created environment without an alteration of its gene pool? Has he, through his culture, escaped the realities of natural selection? Or is man, subtly but inexorably, being molded genetically to the laboratorylike conditions of modern life?

These are not easy questions to answer in an unequivocable manner, and meaningful data are difficult to obtain. It has been argued, for example, that mankind has not changed physically or intellectually for the past 50,000 or 100,000 years. This judgment is based of course on the dead bones and artifacts man has left behind him, not on any knowledge of his genes. It also suggests that the genetic evolution that gives rise to a culture is now a thing of the past, that so far as man is concerned genetic evolution has spent its force, and that cultural evolution itself is the only influence that will affect the future of mankind. But this view implies further that differential fertility rates among different segments of the population, environmental circumstances of order and disorder, and changing patterns of disease, famine, and war have no effect on the total composition of the gene pool, or, if these effects are admitted, that they are without future import to the evolution of man. Biologists find these propositions difficult to accept.

Through a glass darkly

Prolongation of human life has been the goal of almost all Utopias, from Campanella's *City of the Sun* in the sixteenth century to W. H. Hudson's *Crystal Age* in the twentieth. Today, increased longevity of the population in general is no longer a figment of the imagination but a fact and also a hazard. Increased number of individuals reach old age, when they become a more attractive prey for infection. In addition, prolongation of life in subjects suffering from diseases such as cancer, lupus erythematosis, and others creates still another fraction of the population highly susceptible to infections. Since people will continue to live longer and, thanks to new and better drugs, those who suffer from chronic disease will suffer longer, an increase in the spread of infection is to be expected in the future.

H. Koprowski [26]

We need, first of all, to remember that although man's existence on earth as *Homo sapiens* extends backward in time several hundred thousand years, the major cultural impact that led to significant environmental changes has taken place during the past 200 or 300 years, and these changes have come with an accelerated pace. Are the genotypes that were adaptable in a nomadic, hunting era the same as those that are equally adaptable to an agrarian or highly urbanized situation? We can presume that the plasticity of man is great enough to accomplish this change, but we do not know for certain. Culture, in all its forms and degrees of complexity, has created an enormously more diversified environment, but no data suggest that the created environments of today favor certain genotypes in the same manner that the Arctic environment permitted the Eskimo genotype to maintain itself. Time has been too short, and the number of generations too limited, to bring about detectable change, even though such change could possibly be taking place.

There is no debate, however, over whether natural selection has been altered, and perhaps relaxed, in modern time. For example, the infectious diseases that swept through past populations have been brought under general control in many areas of the world. Improved sanitation, antibiotics, and the destruction of disease vectors have permitted millions of individuals, who would otherwise have succumbed, to live to reproductive age. It is unlikely that such past diseases affected all genotypes uniformly. Although we have no definite evidence from human populations, the rabbits of Australia provide a case in point. The myxoma virus wiped out vast numbers of animals, and those that survived were but a minute fraction of the total population. They

I want to deal . . . with the . . . loss of the qualities which have conferred fitness. It seems perfectly obvious that if we eliminate or ameliorate undernourishment, specific dietary deficiencies, the attacks of pathogenic microorganisms, the attacks of predators and all enemies of the species, and if we are no longer exposed to extremes of heat and cold or wet and dry in an air-conditioned world—if we improve the environment in these ways, we are nullifying or discounting the inborn advantages, the alleged genetic virtues, enjoyed by those whose genetic makeups equip them especially well to cope with these various hazards. Therefore, there must be a genetic softening up, a genetic lowering of the defenses. This seems perfectly obvious, and at first sight one feels it must be so; but plausible though the argument seems, I believe it to be completely fallacious. The apparent rightness of the argument depends on the assumption that there is something intrinsically meritorious in possessing the genetic equipment to combat particular hazards even though those hazards are no longer with us. This is not the case. It so happens that the genetic, or inborn, qualities that do confer resistance to particular infections or affections or stresses of one kind or another confer resistance to them alone. They are often achieved by some kind of genetic trick or device which it is a positive drawback to possess in environments in which these particular hazards and perils and challenges no longer exist. The classic demonstration of this argument, the truth of which is conceded by even the gloomiest of our genetic Cassandras, concerns inborn resistance to malaria.

P. B. Medawar [31]

Through a glass darkly

On the simpler Galtonian selective level the development of medical science has, as we have seen, upset the world's population both in quantity and in quality. And the qualitative changes are very diverse. They affect race as compared with race, class as compared with class, and individual as compared with individual. Medical treatment of every kind of genetic disability, except lack of intelligence, enables those who have been treated to survive and to reproduce when they would not otherwise do so. Often those who were saved as children return to the same hospital with their children to be saved. In consequence each generation of a stable society will become more dependent on medical treatment for its ability to survive and reproduce.

This is a process by which our control is changing the direction of evolution. We have to weigh its advantages and its disadvantages. Meanwhile let us note a larger principle: every branch of government in its own field controls the evolution of the people it administers. The punishment of crime affects the reproduction of the criminal class. Education affects or even determines the mating group of those who pass through the system. Taxation and subsidies affect the relative numbers of children born in the different social classes and can be adjusted to vary the results over a wide range. All these policies affecting health, crime, education and economy are carried out in unconsciousness of their evolutionary effects.

C. D. Darlington [10]

10.15 Mass inoculation against tuberculosis in Pakistan.

United Nations

were, however, genetically different from the initial population in that they were disease resistant. Furthermore, the disease itself became less virulent with time and provided the right circumstances for the acquisition of a natural immunity through the production of protective antibodies. A similar situation may hold in human populations. Pulmonary tuberculosis, now a less prevalent disease, was rampant at one time, particularly among the young. Resistance to it is inherited, as studies have shown. The gene or genes responsible for resistance would have possessed a selective advantage and would have increased rapidly in a tubercular society and would have led to a progressively increasing degree of resistance. In a more modern society with improved sanitation and medical care, such a gene would not have the same degree of selective advantage, and it is possible that it would drift in the population and eventually be lost.

Modern medicine, on the other hand, by treatment or corrective surgery, can offset or depress the effects of certain deleterious genes and can bring the carriers to reproductive age. This practice will of course perpetuate the genes and increase their frequency in a population. Diabetes is such an inherited disease. The use of insulin keeps blood sugar levels properly maintained, but some forms of diabetes also contribute to blindness in later life. The reproductive fitness of these individuals seems not to be impaired, but as they produce offspring, the inevitable result will be a greater incidence of blindness, and consequently a greater social burden.

The frequency of generally deleterious genes is therefore increasing in the human population; the geneticist would say that the genetic load of the population is becoming

Through a glass darkly

In sum, the problem of inhibiting population growth in the United States cannot be dealt with in terms of "family-planning needs" because this country is well beyond the point of "needing" birth control methods. Indeed, even the poor seem not to be a last outpost for family-planning attention. If we wish to limit our growth, such a desire implies basic changes in the social organization of reproduction that will make nonmarriage, childlessness, and small (two-child) families far more prevalent than they are now. A new policy, to achieve such ends, can take advantage of the antinatalist tendencies that our present institutions have suppressed. This will involve the lifting of penalties for antinatalist behavior rather than the "creation" of new ways of life. This behavior already exists among us as part of our covert and deviant culture, on the one hand, and our elite and artistic culture, on the other. Such antinatalist tendencies have also found expression in feminism, which has been stifled in the United States by means of systematic legal, educational, and social pressures concerned with women's "obligations" to create and care for children. A fertility-control policy that does not take into account the need to alter the present structure of reproduction in these and other ways merely trivializes the problem of population control and misleads those who have the power to guide our country toward completing the vital revolution.

J. Blake [2]

---

larger. The cost to society will become ever more burdensome. This is particularly true because of an increasingly longer average life span, a greater control over the death rate, and an improved medical practice. Many genetic and congenital abnormalities can now be detected in unborn children, and an abortion can be performed. More widespread genetic counseling can appraise prospective parents of the probabilities of healthy versus abnormal offspring. But a major shift in medical problems has emerged in the developed nations. With most infectious diseases under control, the shift has been from factors that cause speedy death to those that cause chronic, disabling ailments. Mortality has been reduced in favor of morbidity. There can be little doubt that these trends have an effect on the genetic nature of a population, but the long-term effects are not readily evaluated, particularly when one considers the rapidity of cultural change today. The problem of evaluation is difficult also because the chronically ill are generally postreproductive, older persons. We only know that the cost of deleterious genes to society is enormous in terms of anguish and resources.

With our increasing populations, with their higher density-levels per unit of space, there is the intriguing question of whether culture is forcing mankind into a situation comparable to that occupied by laboratory animals, and with similar consequences. Laboratory rats and mice have been bred now for nearly 100 years, and they differ appreciably from their wild ancestors. They live in a rodent welfare state; proper food, shelter, and care are provided, and the animals are freed from the forces of natural selection encountered in the wild. The laboratory rat has smaller adrenal glands, a less active thyroid, and a smaller brain than the

. . . In a world where each pair must be limited, on the average, to two offspring and no more, the right that must become paramount is not the right to procreate, but rather the right of every child to be born with a sound physical and mental constitution, based on a sound genotype. No parents will in that future time have a right to burden society with a malformed or a mentally incompetent child. Just as every child must have the right to full educational opportunity and a sound nutrition, so every child has the inalienable right to a sound heritage.

Human power is advancing with extraordinary rapidity in this realm of control over the genetic characteristics of the unborn. . . . Unlimited access to state-regulated abortion will combine with the now perfected techniques of determining chromosome abnormalities in the developing fetus to rid us of the several percentages of all births that today represent uncontrollable defects such as mongolism (Down's syndrome) and sex deviants such as the XYY type. Genetic clinics will be constructed in which, before long, as many as 100 different recessive hereditary defects can be detected in the carriers, who may be warned against or prohibited from having offspring. Preliminary efforts to synthesize genes and to introduce a sound gene by means of a carrier virus into a child or fetus bearing only the defective allele at the same position in the chromosomes are promising. They may make it possible not merely to correct a genetic defect while leaving intact in the individual the defective gene to be passed on, but actually to substitute the sound gene for the defective gene in the reproductive cells of the treated person. . . .

H. B. Glass [17]

Always in big woods when you leave familiar ground and step off alone into a new place there will be, along with the feelings of curiosity and excitement, a little nagging of dread. It is the ancient fear of the Unknown, and it is your first bond with the wilderness you are going into. What you are doing is exploring. Your are undertaking the first experience, not of the place, but of yourself in that place. It is an experience of our essential loneliness, for nobody can discover the world for anybody else. It is only after we have discovered it for ourselves that it becomes a common ground and a common body, and we cease to be alone.

And the world cannot be discovered by a journey of miles, no matter how long, but only by a spiritual journey, a journey of one inch, very ardous and humbling and joyful, by which we arrive at the frond at our feet, and learn to be at home. It is a journey we can make only by the acceptance of mystery and of mystification—by yielding to the condition that what we have expected is not there.

W. Berry [1]

10.16 White mice balance on a turning rod in the psychopharmacology laboratory at the Medical Research Laboratories of Pfizer, Inc., in Groton, Connecticut.

wild variety. It shows less resistance to diseases and environmental stress and is docile and easily handled. It is sexually mature earlier and has a higher fertility rate. It has been suggested that a comparable trend is occurring in human evolution. Is this why Neanderthal and Cro-Magnon men had larger brains than modern man?

Clearly this is a debatable point. The laboratory rat has been rigorously inbred and selected for those behavioral traits that it displays in the environment in which it exists, just as the wild rat behaves differently in the environment in which it must actively contend for its existence. To draw the analogy with a human situation is to suppose that modern society, as compared to those societies existing in the Ice Age, is headed toward a uniform state of existence devoid of individual challenge and opportunities for initiative and that this pressure will drive man toward a state of docility and conformity. Other evidence, however, sup-

Pfizer, Inc.

United Nations

ports the idea that increased diversities, not uniformities, of environments stem from culture, but this will remain so only if population densities are kept within bounds that permit the existence of such differences.

It has been shown, for example, that wild and domesticated rats respond to conditions of crowding in somewhat different ways. The wild rat apparently requires more elbow room. In an enclosed area whose carrying capacity was sufficient for 5,000 individuals, the population stabilized at 150 adults. Adult mortality was low, but infant mortality very high, so that the population had a slow rate of recruitment of young. Domesticated rats, under conditions of more intense crowding, exhibited a behavioral pathology that included interrupted pregnancies, lack of maternal care of the young, cannibalism, and disoriented life styles. It is of course dangerous to translate these findings into human terms; mob behavior is notoriously difficult to predict, but an antisocial, antihumanistic tendency is all too evident to dismiss as unreal. A behavioral pathology is as possible for a society as it is for an individual.

The future gene pool will depend upon those who contribute to it; it cannot be otherwise. Utopian schemes for enriching this pool with the genes of high-placed and noble men through selective and often artificial insemination (positive selection) and the elimination of genes of those judged unfit (negative selection) have always met with opposition, because the rights of the individual are abrogated. Individual choice and opportunity have always taken precedence over social welfare in such matters, and legal and ecclesiastical barriers have been raised as well. Negative selection procedures are genetically ineffective in any event, because most deleterious genes are recessive, and mutations of these genes

The population explosion is making us ask the fundamental question—so fundamental that it is usually not asked at all—what are people for? Whatever the answer, whether to achieve greater efficiency or power, or, as I am suggesting, to find greater fulfilment, it is clear that the general quality of the world's population is not very high, is beginning to deteriorate, and should and could be improved. It is deteriorating, thanks to genetic defectives who would otherwise have died being kept alive, and thanks to the crop of new mutations due to fall-out. In modern man the direction of genetic evolution has started to change its sign, from positive to negative, from advance to retreat: we must manage to put it back on its age-old course of positive improvement.

The improvement of human genetic quality by eugenic methods would take a great load of suffering and frustration off the shoulders of evolving humanity, and would much increase both enjoyment and efficiency.

J. Huxley [22]

Through a glass darkly

If man continues responding in the same way, there is no basis for optimism. His ability to adapt himself to new conditions, which is usually beneficial, may lead this time to disaster, since he easily identifies himself with the spoiled parts of the anthropocosmos. What is wrong with downtown if I close my windows so as not to see the parking lot and breathe its air? And what is wrong with distances if I have my wheels? The stress is so strong that even utopias are now very weak in conception. Characteristically enough, Skinner, in his *Walden Two,* and Huxley himself, just before the end of his life, in *Island,* follow an escapist line—that is, the very small ideal community of one or a few thousand people. One day near Athens I tested this desire on the captain of a small boat. I told him to go to the best place in the Aegean Sea, and he took me to a small island with a village of a few hundred people, not to a city or natural landscape. The wine was very good, but we could find the same wine in the large cities of the islands. The captain, like me, wanted to escape the pressure, not by avoiding human settlements but by selecting small ones. Our real challenge lay behind us in the big port and its hinterland.

C. A. Doxiadis [11]

The greatest spiritual revolutionary in Western history, Saint Francis, proposed what he thought was an alternative Christian view of nature and man's relation to it: he tried to substitute the idea of the equality of all creatures, including man, for the idea of man's limitless rule of creation. He failed. Both our present science and our present technology are so tinctured with orthodox Christian arrogance toward nature that no solution from ecologic crisis can be expected from them alone. Since the roots of our trouble are so largely religious, the remedy must also be essentially religious, whether we call it that or not. We must rethink and refeel our nature and destiny. The profoundly religious, but heretical, sense of the primitive Franciscans for the spiritual autonomy of all parts of nature may point a direction. I propose Francis as a patron saint for ecologists.

L. White, Jr. [49]

cannot be avoided. Nevertheless, it is well known that the poverty-stricken, uneducated, and untrained segments of every population and in every age contribute more heavily to the future gene pool than those more fortunately placed. The place of an individual in society cannot be ascribed to genetic endowment alone; circumstances of birth, timing, location, and opportunity play large roles. However, success within a given environment is more often than not determined by inherited qualities, particularly by intelligence. Does this mean, then, that the level of human intelligence is on the average being eroded? It is an emotionally loaded question, but it is one that the future cannot afford to ignore.

Bread alone?

Lynn White, Jr., in searching for the historical roots of our Western ecological crisis, has focused on the religious ethic as the primary motivating cause. He sees modern science as "an extrapolation of natural theology," and modern technology as stemming from the "Christian dogma of man's transcendance of, and mastery over, nature." This "orthodox Christian arrogance" is contained in the Mosaic writings; the earth was created for man's use and delight, he was to be fruitful and multiply, and he was to exercise dominion over all living things. Use, unfortunately, took precedence over delight, but before placing the total blame on Christian theology, reinforced by a later Puritan interpretation, one needs to be reminded that Christian teachings also indicate that stewardship of the environment is as important as its exploitation for man's benefit. The Old Testament prophet Jeremiah (2:7) knew in his heart that

Through a glass darkly

We must learn to reawaken and keep ourselves awake, not by mechanical aids, but by an infinite expectation of the dawn, which does not forsake us in our soundest sleep. I know of no more encouraging fact than the unquestionable ability of man to elevate his life by a conscious endeavor. It is something to be able to paint a particular picture, or to carve a statue, and so to make a few objects beautiful; but it is far more glorious to carve and paint the very atmosphere and medium through which we look, which morally we can do. To affect the quality of the day, that is the highest of arts. Every man is tasked to make his life, even in its details, worthy of the contemplation of his most elevated and critical hours. If we refused, or rather used up, such paltry information as we get, the oracles would distinctly inform us how this might be done.

I went to the woods because I wished to live deliberately, to front only the essential facts of life, and see if I could not learn what it had to teach, and not, when I came to die, discover that I had not lived. . . . I wanted to live deep and suck out all the marrow of life, to live so sturdily and Spartan-like as to put to rout all that was not life, to cut a broad swath and shave close, to drive life into a corner, and reduce it to its lowest terms, and, if it proved to be mean, to get the whole and genuine meanness of it, and publish its meanness to the world; or if it were sublime, to know it by experience. . . .

H. Thoreau [46]

this was so: "And I brought you into a plentiful country, to eat the fruit thereof and the goodness thereof; but when ye entered ye defiled my land, and made mine heritage an abomination." Granted that the brutalizing effects of starvation and deprivation dull one's appreciation of the beauties and diversity of nature and sharpen one's exploitative tendencies, man, nevertheless, does not live by bread alone. If we are to attain maturity and serenity as a human species, we must recognize that those things that delight the eye and broaden the spirit are as necessary as those that fill the empty stomach.

Man is, of course, a predator, and the range of plants and animals upon which he feeds is more varied than for any other species. His use of them is also more varied: for fibers, timber, and clothing, as well as for food and recrea-

10.17 A small park in the midst of an overcrowded city—a luxury or a necessity? Oases such as this are disappearing from our cities because all available land is needed for housing, but what value is there in providing dwellings for more and more people in the cities when the quality of life for all must be sacrificed?

Burk Uzzle photo, Magnum

Luther C. Goldman photo, U.S. Department of the Interior

tion. Man has domesticated many plants and animals, and these forms have come to dominate large sections of the surface of the earth. The result has been that the diversity and the extent of the natural landscape has diminished, and man's ties to nature have become seriously frayed. There is something most satisfying in the sweep of a wind-rippled field of wheat, in the orderliness of a well-groomed and productive farm with its fenced fields and sleek cattle, and in the beauty of a planned and colorful garden, but such scenes do not replace the untrammeled forests or fields, mountains or seashore. Difficult as it is to put into words, there is a deep and abiding aesthetic and spritual need, indeed a love, in the individual man for the unplanned formlessness, the unexpected beauty, and the unhurriedness of life that exists outside of that area controlled by man. To deny that need, that love, is to diminish each of us, to make us the captives, not the masters, of the technological civilization in which we live.

The glass is dark. Perhaps there is in man a built-in resistance to change, a remembrance that he is of the earth and is tied to it. It is good that this is so, that we retain a clinging grasp to the land that gave rise to us. The heart, Pascal said, has reasons that the stars do not know, and there remains the need—not only for man's physical welfare, but also for his human dignity—to preserve the marsh where the muskrats and the great blue herons feed, to climb the promontory where the trees brush the clouds, to walk the beaches with the sandpipers, to scoop water to drink from a sparkling, tumbling stream, to tramp to exhaustion through fields and forests. These are not luxuries; they are the desperate needs of desperate men who wish to live out their lives with grace and beauty. The Tin Woodsman in

Through a glass darkly

The Wizard of Oz knew whereof he spoke. "To love," he said, "one must have a heart." And that love must encompass all things that release and give expression to the humanity of man. A future in which man replaces all other living things is no future at all.

How can we recapture, or even attain perhaps for the first time, a feel for the sanctity of the earth and its living forms? Before we can answer this question, others come to mind, most of them unanswerable in universal terms. Are we asking the right questions? Do we in fact have a built-in resistance to change, a tie to the earth that tugs at us at all times? The concentration of mankind in urban centers might suggest otherwise. Are we talking about the preservation of unspoiled nature as a luxury for a small segment of the population while the vast remainder of men need the land to produce food to fill their bellies? Are we willing to give up or curtail the automobile and the airconditioner for the sake of cleaner air? Can we permit the forests to remain uncut while homes are desperately needed? Should we prevent the building of dams when the demands for power and water continue to rise? Must we have faster and faster means of travel and communications and more labor-saving, but energy-using, devices to live a more humane and fuller life? Does all of this have any relevance when viewed in terms of urban economy? Is, in fact, an aesthetic rapport with nature and a desire for the *status quo* only a vestige of our evolutionary past, a nostalgic look over the shoulder as we move to new modes of adaptation in a vastly altered world? We need answers, or at the very least alternative options, as we move into an uncertain future, and we can be sure of only one thing, that these answers will come from the heart as well as from the mind of man.

Through a glass darkly

Here he comes, stumbling down
his ten thousand technological
years—the fragmented man;
a thing of bits and pieces
cast upon the mudflats of the
20th Century by wayward
tides and waves too high.
This is a mosaic that walks,
wearing all his yesterdays
like tattoos. Little, or nothing,
in all his ancient heritage fits

him for this moment.
There is always something
coming ashore, and he is doing
so now. He strides into
the spectrum as once the lonely
horseman rode into the sunset
of another time and place.
And no one knows what new
adventures await him now.

D. Fabun [15]

Tomorrow and tomorrow and . . . ?

In the Museum of Fine Arts in Boston is a painting done in Tahiti in 1898 by the French artist Paul Gauguin. Its enigmatic title is *Whence Do We Come? What Are We? Whither Are We Going?* (illustration 10.18). As Gauguin himself said, the title and the content bear, at best, only an allegorical relation to each other, and the title was added, almost as an afterthought, when the work had been completed, and when, in Guaguin's words, "My eyes close in order to see *without understanding* the dream, in the infinite space, that flies ahead of me, and I perceive the mournful procession of my hopes."

We may well ponder these same questions as we view the canvas of the earth and the figures that populate it. We feel that we know the answers to the first two questions;

10.18 Paul Gaugin, Whence Do We Come? What Are We? Whither Are We Going?

we know, with reasonable certitude, our origins and our nature, our animality and our humanity. But we do not see, *with understanding*, whither we are going. Is the future to be a "mournful procession" of our hopes? Bereft of his gods who would sustain and comfort him, alone with himself, unguided by the nature that gave rise to him, man occupies uneasily the seat of dominance. He did not will his coming, but he is here. His answer has been that there is always tomorrow and tomorrow and . . . . But is there?

Man is ever the optimist. As Don Fabun [13] has expressed it:

> Out of the dreaming past, with its legends of steaming seas and gleaming glaciers, mountains that moved and suns that glared, emerges this creature, man—the latest phase in a continuing process that stretches back to the beginning of time. His is the heritage of all that has lived; he still carries the vestiges of snout and fangs and claws of species long since vanished; he is the ancestor of all that is yet to come. Do not regard him lightly—he is you.

Summary

There seems to be no question that the human species has reached a critical stage in its evolutionary history, a crisis stemming, paradoxically, from its unprecedented success as a species. The growing numbers of individuals resulting from a falling death rate and increased longevity; the tapping of the environment for materials, energy, and cultural use, primarily because of the growing use of science and technology; the rising expectation of all peoples to share in the use of the resources of the world; and the philosophy of use-and-discard rather than use-and-reuse—all have com-

Through a glass darkly

377

The world is but a single dewdrop
set trembling on a stem; and yet . . .

and yet . . .

Haiku, by Issa

bined to force man to the realization that he exists in a finite world and that he can escape neither his biological antecedents nor environmental constraints. To think otherwise today is to court future disaster.

Mankind must therefore generate its own future knowingly and with responsibility; it must recognize that the animate and inanimate earth is a single, if tremendously complex, system; and it must develop an assessment capability that will permit change to take place without the continual occurrence of disturbing global crises. The fact that man is aware of the dimensions of these critical problems and can discuss them openly is a necessary first step toward a solution or to alternate routes of action. What is alarmingly portentous is that, because of the interrelatedness of nature and man, no problem can be singled out and dealt with in isolation, and no problems are strictly local in nature. We do not yet possess a global view or, most obviously, a global course of action.

Through a glass darkly

The number that precedes each title corresponds with the bracketed number following the name of the author of each quotation used in the text.

Bibliographic notes

Chapter 1

1. Allen, D. C., ed. *A Celebration of Poets*. Johns Hopkins Press, Baltimore, 1959, pp. 17, 25. © 1959 by Johns Hopkins Press. Reprinted with permission.
2. Beck, W. *Modern Science and the Nature of Life*. Doubleday (Anchor), New York, 1961, pp. 2–3, 14, 17–18. © 1957 by William S. Beck. Reprinted by permission of Harcourt Brace Jovanovich, Inc.
3. Bernard, C. *Introduction à l'etude de la médecine expérimentale* (1865), trans. H. C. Greene.
4. Beston, H. *Outermost House*. Holt, New York, 1971, foreword. Reprinted by permission of Holt, Rinehart and Winston, Inc.
5. Crane, S. *The Blue Hotel*. 1895.
6. Dobzhansky, Th. *The Biology of Ultimate Concern*. New American Library, New York, 1967. © 1967 by Theodosius Dobzhansky. Reprinted by arrangement with New American Library, Inc.
7. Einstein, A. "What I Believe." *Forum*, October 1930.
8. Fabun, D. *Dynamics of Change*. Prentice-Hall, Englewood Cliffs, N.J., 1970, Section I, p. 25. © 1967 by Kaiser Aluminum & Chemical Corporation.
9. Fahs, S. L. *Today's Children and Yesterday's Heritage*. Beacon, Boston, 1952, p. 14. © 1952 by Beacon Press. Reprinted with permission.
10. Fielding, H. *Tom Jones*. 1749.
11. Frazer, J. G. *The New Golden Bough*. Dover, New York, 1959.
12. Fremantle, A. *The Age of Belief*. New American Library, New York, 1954, preface.
13. Gates, L. E. *Studies and Appreciation*. Macmillan, New York, 1900.
14. Gillispie, C. C. *The Edge of Objectivity*. Princeton Univ. Press, Princeton, N.J., 1960.
15. Herbert, G. "Man," 1633, verses 3–6 and 8.
16. Hoebel, E. A. *Man in the Primitive World*, 2nd ed. McGraw-Hill, New York, 1958, p. 8.
17. Howells, W. *The Heathens*. Doubleday, New York, 1948. © 1948 by William Howells. Reprinted by permission of Doubleday & Company, Inc.
18. Huxley, J. *Essays of a Humanist*. Harper & Row, New York, 1964, p. 107.
19. Huxley, T. H. *On the Origin of Species*. Appleton, New York, 1881.
20. Koch, K. "Permanently," in *Thank You and Other Poems*. Grove, New York, 1962. © 1962 by Kenneth Koch. Reprinted by permission of Grove Press, Inc.
21. Krutch, J. W. *The Modern Temper*. Harcourt, Brace, New York, 1929, pp. xi, 7. © 1929 by Harcourt Brace Jovanovich, Inc.; © 1957 by Joseph Wood Krutch. Reprinted by permission of the publishers.
22. Langer, S. *Philosophy in a New Key*. Penguin, New York, 1942.
23. Lavoisier, A. L. *Traité élémentaire de chimie* (1789), trans. J. Lipetz, D. E. Gershenson, and D. A. Greenberg.
24. Lindsay, V. "The Congo," in *Collected Poems*. Macmillan, New York, 1934. © 1914 by The Macmillan Company; © 1942 by Elizabeth C. Lindsay. Reprinted by permission of The Macmillan Company.
25. Linnaeus, C. *Systema naturae*. 1788 edition.
26. Malinowski, B. *Magic, Science and Religion*. Doubleday, New York, 1954.
27. Marcus, J. "The World Impact of the West: The Mystique and the Sense of Participation in History," in *Myth, and Mythmaking*, ed. H. A. Murray. Beacon, Boston, 1959.
28. Montaigne, M. de. *Essays*, Book I. 1580.
29. O'Casey, S. *Sunset and Evening Star*.

30. Oppenheimer, J. R. *Science and the Common Understanding.* Simon and Schuster, New York, 1953, pp. 68–69. © 1953, 1954 by J. Robert Oppenheimer. Reprinted by permission of Simon & Schuster, Inc.

31. Patton, K. L. *"Man Is the Meaning,"* in *Hymns for the Celebration of Life*, Responsive Reading #374. Beacon, Boston, 1956.

32. Ross, F. H., and T. Hills. *The Great Religions.* Beacon, Boston, 1956.

33. Schaller, G. B. *The Year of the Gorilla.* Univ. Chicago Press, 1964.

34. Schorer, M. "The Necessity of Myth," in *Myth and Mythmaking*, ed. H. A. Murray. Beacon, Boston, 1959.

35. Shakespeare, W. *Hamlet*, Act II, scene ii.

36. ———. *Measure for Measure*, Act III, scene iii.

37. Shelley, P. B. *Adonais: An Elegy on the Death of John Keats.* 1822.

38. Shirley, J. *The Contention of Ajax and Ulysses.* 1659.

39. Stevenson, R. L. "Pulvis et Umbra." *Scribner's Magazine*, April 1888.

40. Swenson, M. Untitled. 1971. Reprinted by permission of the author.

41. Thoreau, H. *The Journal.* 1906.

42. Wilford, J. N. "Medicine Men Successful Where Science Falls Short." *The New York Times*, July 7, 1972.

43. Woodberry, G. E. "Man and the Race." *The Torch*, 1905.

44. Wordsworth, W. *Lyrical Ballads.* 1802 edition, Preface.

45. Ziman, J. *Public Knowledge: The Social Dimensions of Science.* Cambridge Univ. Press, Cambridge, 1968.

Chapter 2

1. Ashton, T. S. *The Industrial Revolution, 1760–1830.* Oxford Univ. Press, New York, 1948, pp. 12–13. Reprinted by permission of Oxford University Press.

2. Augustine, St. *Confessions.* 420

3. Bacon, F. *Novum organum.* 1620.

4. Baker, H. *The Image of Man.* Harper, New York, 1947.

5. Beck, W. *Modern Science and the Nature of Life.* Doubleday (Anchor), New York, 1961, p. 64. © 1957 by William S. Beck. Reprinted by permission of Harcourt Brace Jovanovich, Inc.

6. Becker, C. L. *The Heavenly City of the Eighteenth-Century Philosophers.* Yale Univ. Press, New Haven, Conn., 1932.

7. Boyle, R. *Sceptical Chemist.* 1661.

8. Brinton, C. *The Shaping of Modern Thought.* Prentice-Hall, Englewood Cliffs, N.J. 1963, pp. 32, 40, 87.

9. Bronowski, J. *Science and Human Values*, rev. ed. Harper & Row, 1965, p. 21. © 1956, 1965 by J. Bronowski. Reprinted by permission of Julian Messner, a division of Simon & Schuster, Inc.

10. Burton, R. *The Anatomy of Melancholy.* 1651.

11. Butler, S. "The Elephant in the Moon," in *Genuine Remains in Verse and Prose of Mr. Samuel Butler*, ed. R. Thyer. 1759.

12. Copernicus, N. *De revolutionibus orbium coelestium.* 1543.

13. Dingle, H. "Copernicus and the Planets," in *A Short History of Science.* Doubleday, New York, 1951.

14. Donne, J. "The First Anniversary: An Anatomy of the World." 1611.

15. ———. "The Second Anniversary of the Progress of the Soul." 1612.

16. Dryden, J. *Essay on Dramatic Poesie.* 1668.

17. Durand, D. B. "Tradition and Innovation in Fifteenth-Century Italy," in *Studies in Renaissance Science (Toward Modern Science*, II), ed. R. M. Palter. Farrar, Straus, New York, 1961, pp. 26–27.

18. Feuer, L. A. *The Scientific Intellectual.* Basic Books, New York, 1963.

19. Froude, A. Quoted in L. Eiseley, *Mind as Nature.* Harper & Row, New York, 1962.

20. Harvey, W. *An Anatomical Disquisition on the Motion of Heart-Blood in Animals.* London, 1628.

21. Kepler, J. *Harmony of the World.* 1619.

22. Koyré, A. *From the Closed World to the Infinite Universe.* Johns Hopkins Press, Baltimore, 1957, pp. 1–2. © 1957 by Johns Hopkins Press. Reprinted with permission.

23. Lewis, C. S. *The Discarded Image.* Cambridge Univ. Press, Cambridge, 1964, pp. 10–11.

24. Milton, J. *Paradise Lost*, VIII. 1667.

25. Molnar, T. *Utopia: The Perennial Heresy.* © Sheed and Ward, New York, 1967.

26. Morley, H. "Andreas Vesalius," in *Studies in Renaissance Science, (Toward Modern Science*, II), ed. R. M. Palter. Farrar, Straus, New York, 1961, pp. 73–74.

27. Nicolson, M. H. *Science and Imagination.* Cornell Univ. Press, Ithaca, N.Y., 1956.

28. Paracelsus. Quoted in B. Jaffe, *Crucibles: The Story of Chemistry.* Fawcett, New York, 1957.

29. Pascal, B. *Pensées.* 1670.

30. Rossi, P. *Philosophy, Technology and the Arts in the Early Modern Era.* Harper & Row, New York, 1970.

31. Seaborg, G. T. "A Scientific Society—the Beginnings." *Science*, February 16, 1962, pp. 505–9. © 1962 by the American Association for the Advancement of Science.

32. Shakespeare, W. *King Lear*, Act I, scene ii.

33. ———. "Sonnet XV."

34. Sharp, R. L. *From Donne to Dryden: The Revolt Against Metaphysical Poetry.* Univ. North Carolina Press, Chapel Hill, 1940.

35. Singer, C. *A Short History of Anatomy from the Greeks to Harvey.* Dover, New York, 1957.

36. Sprat, T. *The History of the Royal Society.* London, 1722.

37. Swift, J. *Gulliver's Travels.* 1726.

38. Taylor, R. "To Leonardo the Anatomist," in *Anatomical Studies (Sonnets). International Review*, London, 1952.

39. Thoreau, H. *Walden.* 1854.

Chapter 3

1. Akenside, M. *The Pleasures of Imagination.* London, 1744.

2. Arber, A. *Herbals.* Cambridge Univ. Press, Cambridge, 1912.

3. Ben-David, J. "The Scientific Role: The Condition of Its Establishment in Europe." *Minerva*, Autumn 1965.

4. Brown, T. *Religio medici.* 1635.

5. Buffon. *Histoire naturelle*, IX. 1778.
6. Carrol, L. *Alice's Adventures in Wonderland*. 1865.
7. Clark, D. L. *Fossils, Paleontology, and Evolution*. William C. Brown, Dubuque, Iowa, 1968.
8. Darwin, E. *Zoonomia*. 1794.
9. Greene, J. *The Death of Adam*. New American Library, New York, 1959.
10. Haber, F. C. "Fossils and the Idea of a Process of Time in Natural History," in *Forerunners of Darwin: 1745–1859*, ed. B. Glass *et al*. Johns Hopkins Press, Baltimore, 1959, 245. © 1959 by Johns Hopkins Press. Reprinted with permission.
11. Hanson, N. R. "Galileo's Discoveries in Dynamics." *Science*, January 29, 1965, pp. 471–78. © 1965 by the American Association for the Advancement of Science.
12. Hutton, J. *Theory of the Earth*, Vol. II. London, 1795.
13. Koyré, A. *Newtonian Studies*. Harvard Univ. Press, Cambridge, Mass., 1965. © 1965 by the President and Fellows of Harvard College. Reprinted by permission of Harvard Univ. Press and Chapman & Hall Ltd.
14. Lamarck, J. *Hydrogeologie*. Paris, 1802.
15. ———. *Philosophie zoologique*. Paris, 1809.
16. Lanham, U. *Origins of Modern Biology*. Columbia Univ. Press, New York, 1968, pp. 118, 124.
17. Larkey, S. V., and T. Pyles, eds. and trans. *An Herbal*. Scholars Facsimiles and Reprints, 1941.
18. Leibniz, G. Quoted in L. G. Crocker, "Diderot and Eighteenth-Century French Transformism," in *Forerunners of Darwin: 1745–1859*. Johns Hopkins Press, Baltimore, 1959.
19. Linnaeus, C. *The Invisible World*.
20. ———. *Systema naturae*. 1788 edition.
21. Merton, R. K. "Science, Technology and Society in Seventeenth-Century England." *Osiris*, 4, 1938.
22. More, P. E. *Selected Shelburne Essays*. Oxford Univ. Press, New York, 1935.
23. Ovid. *Metamorphoses*, XV.
24. Playfair, J. *Illustrations of the Huttonian Theory of the Earth*. 1802.
25. Pope, A. *An Essay on Man*. 1732.
26. Raven, C. E. *John Ray, Naturalist: His Life and Works*. Cambridge Univ. Press, Cambridge, 1942.
27. Raven, P. H., B. Berlin, and D. E. Breedlove. "The Origins of Taxonomy." *Science*, December 17, 1971, pp. 1210–18. © 1971 by the American Association for the Advancement of Science.
28. Ray, J. *Historia generalis plantarum*. 1688.
29. Sainte-Beuve, C. A. Quoted in C. C. Gillispie, *The Edge of Objectivity*. Princeton Univ. Press, Princeton, N.J., 1960.
30. Shelley, P. B. "Ozymandias."
31. Tennyson, A. *In Memoriam A. H. H.*, LIV, LV, LVI, CXXIII. 1850.
32. Young, E. *Night Thoughts*, VI. 1750.

Chapter 4

1. Adderley, C. Attributed to Adderley by various sources.
2. Arnold, M. "Dover Beach." 1867.
3. ———. *In Harmony with Nature: to a Preacher*. 1850.
4. Carnegie, A. *Autobiography of Andrew Carnegie*. Boston, 1920.
5. Cowley, M. "Naturalism in American Literature," in *Evolutionary Thought in America*. Braziller, New York, 1950, pp. 317–18, 331.
6. Crane, S. "A Man Said to the Universe." 1895.
7. ———. *The Open Boat*. 1898.
8. Darwin, C. *Autobiography*. London, 1887.
9. ———. *The Descent of Man*. London, 1871.
10. ———. *Journal of Researches into the Geology and Natural History of the Various Countries Visited during the Voyage of the H.M.S. Beagle Round the World*. London, 1845.
11. ———. *On the Origin of Species by Means of Natural Selection, or the Preservation of Favoured Races in the Struggle for Life*. London, 1859.
12. Deluc, J. A. *Elementary Treatise on Geology*. London, 1809.
13. Dickens, C. *Hard Times*. London, 1854.
14. Fiske, J. *Essays Historical and Literary*. New York, 1902.
15. Goss, E. *Father and Son*. London, 1907.
16. Gray, A. *Letters*, Vol. II. London, 1893.
17. Himmelfarb, G. *Darwin and the Darwinian Revolution*. Doubleday, New York, 1959, p. 452.
18. Hofstadter, R. *Social Darwinism in American Thought*. Univ. Pennsylvania Press, Philadelphia, 1944.
19. Huxley, T. H. *On the Origin of Species*. 1881.
20. LeConte, J. *Evolution: Its Nature, Its Evidences, and Its Relation to Religious Thought*, 2nd ed. Appleton, New York, 1891.
21. London, J. *Martin Eden*. 1909.
22. Longwell, C. L. Quoted in L. L. Woodruff, ed., *The Development of the Sciences*, second series. Yale Univ. Press, New Haven, Conn., 1941.
23. Lyell, C. *Principles of Geology*. London, 1830–1833.
24. Malthus, T. *An Essay on the Principles of Population*. 1798.
25. Paley, W. *Natural Theology*. London, 1902.
26. Platt, J. R. *The Step to Man*. Wiley, New York, 1966, p. 172.
27. Rockefeller, J. D. Quoted in R. Hofstadter, *Social Darwinism in American Thought*. Univ. Pennsylvania Press, Philadelphia, 1944.
28. Simpson, G. G. *The Meaning of Evolution*. Yale Univ. Press, New Haven, Conn., 1967.
29. Spencer, H. *Illustrations of Universal Progress*. Appleton, New York, 1865.
30. Stone, I. *Clarence Darrow for the Defense: A Biography*. Doubleday, New York, 1941. © 1941 by Irving Stone. Reprinted by permission of Doubleday & Company, Inc.
31. Temple, F. *Essays and Reviews*. 1860.
32. Tennyson, A. "By an Evolutionist," in *Demeter, and Other Poems*. 1889.
33. ———. "Locksley Hall Sixty Years After," in *Locksley Hall Sixty Years After, Etc.* 1886.
34. Wallace, A. R. *On the Tendency of Varieties to Depart Indefinitely from the Original Type*, Linnaean Society, Vol. 3, 1858.
35. Whitman, W. "Chanting the Square Deific," in *Sequel to Drum-Taps*. 1865.

Chapter 5

1. Allen, J. A. "The Influence of Physical Conditions in the Genesis of Species. *Radical Review*, I, 1877–1878.
2. Carson, R. *Silent Spring*. Houghton Mifflin, Boston, 1962, pp. 29–30.
3. Christian, J. J. "Social Subordination, Population Density, and Mammalian Evolution." *Science*, April 3, 1970, pp. 84–90. © 1970 by the American Association for the Advancement of Science.
4. Darwin, C. *On the Origin of Species by Means of Natural Selection, or the Preservation of Favoured Races in the Struggle for Life*. London, 1859.
5. Dickens, C. *Dombey and Son*. 1848.
6. Dobzhansky, Th. *The Biology of Ultimate Concern*. New American Library, New York, 1967, pp. 49–50. © 1967 by Theodosius Dobzhansky. Reprinted by arrangement with New American Library, Inc.
7. Dodson, E. O. *Evolution: Process and Product*, rev. ed. Van Nostrand Reinhold, New York, 1960. © 1960 by Litton Educational Publishing, Inc. Reprinted by permission of Van Nostrand Reinhold, Inc.
8. Dubos, R. *Man Adapting*. Yale Univ. Press, New Haven, Conn., 1965.
9. Eiseley, L. "Freedom of the Juggernaut." *Mayo Clinic Proceedings*, 40 (1965), 7–22.
9a. ———. *The Immense Journey*. Random House, New York, 1956, pp. 171–73. © 1956 by Loren Eiseley. Reprinted by permission of Random House, Inc.
10. Emerson, R. W. *Nature*, 2nd. ed. 1849.
11. Fiske, J. "Herbert Spencer's Service to Religion," in *Essays Historical and Literary*. New York, 1902.
12. Goodwin, D. R. "Darwin on the Origin of Species." American Theological Review, 1860.
13. Haskins, C. P. "Advances and Challenges in Science in 1970." *American Scientist*, 59 (1971), 298–307. Reprinted by permission of *American Scientist*, journal of The Society of the Sigma Xi.
14. Newman, J. H. *Apologia pro vita sua*. 1864.
15. Pearson, K. *The Grammar of Science*, 2nd ed. Black, London, 1900.
16. Reiner, J. M. *The Organism as an Adaptive Control System*. Prentice-Hall, Englewood Cliffs, N.J., 1968, pp. 3–4.
17. Rice, W. N. "Darwinian Theory of the Origin of Species." *New Englander*, 1867.
18. Russell, P. F. "The Eradication of Malaria." *Scientific American*, June 1952, pp. 22–25. © 1952 by Scientific American, Inc. All rights reserved.
19. Simpson, G. G. "Rates of Evolution in Animals," in *Genetics, Paleontology and Evolution*, ed. G. L. Jepson, E. Mayr, and G. G. Simpson. Princeton Univ. Press, Princeton, N.J., 1949.
20. Sinsheimer, R. L. "The Brain of Pooh: An Essay on the Limits of Mind." *American Scientist*, 59 (1971), 20–28. Reprinted by permission of *American Scientist*, journal of the Society of the Sigma Xi.
21. Stebbins, G. L. "Rates of Evolution in Plants," in *Genetics, Paleontology and Evolution*, ed. G. L. Jepson, E. Mayr, and G. G. Simpson. Princeton Univ. Press, Princeton, N.J., 1949.
22. ———. *Processes of Organic Evolution*. Prentice-Hall, Englewood Cliffs, N.J., 1966, pp. 87–88.
23. Thompson, J. P, "Does Silence Tend to Materialism." *New Englander*, XIX, 1861.
24. Wallace, A. R. *On the Tendency of Varieties to Depart Indefinitely from the Original Type*, Linnaean Society, Vol. 3, 1858.
25. Wallace, B., and A. Srb. *Adaptation*. Prentice-Hall, Englewood Cliffs, N.J. 1964.
26. Winchell, A. "Grounds and Consequences of Evolution," in *Sparks from a Geologist's Hammer*. 1881.
27. Whitman, W. "When I Heard the Learned Astronomer."
28. Wordsworth, W. "Lines Written in Early Spring." 1798.

Chapter 6

1. Ardrey, R. *African Genesis*. Atheneum, New York, 1961, pp. 138–40. © 1961 by Literat S. A. Reprinted by permission of Atheneum Publishers and William Collins Sons & Co. Ltd.
1a. ———. *The Territorial Imperative*. Atheneum, New York, 1966, pp. 214–15. © 1966 by Robert Ardrey. Reprinted by permission of Atheneum Publishers and William Collins Sons & Co. Ltd.
2. Bates, M. *Man in Nature*, 2nd ed. Prentice-Hall, Englewood Cliffs, N.J., 1964, pp. 32–33.
3. Berrill, N. J. *Man's Emerging Mind*. Dodd, Mead, New York, 1955, p. 33.
4. Carr, A. "100 Turtle Eggs." *Natural History*, August–September 1967. © 1967 American Museum of Natural History. Reprinted by permission of *Natural History* magazine.
5. Clark, W. E. Le Gros. *History of the Primates*. © Univ. Chicago Press, 1963, pp. 72–73. Reprinted by permission of the University of Chicago Press and the British Museum (Natural History).
6. ———. *Man-Apes or Ape-Men: The Story of Discoveries in Africa*. Holt, Rinehart & Winston, 1967.
7. Congreve, W. *Letter to Dennis*. 1695.
8. Darwin, C. *The Descent of Man*. London, 1871.
9. Disraeli, B. Speech at Oxford Diocesan Conference, November 25, 1864.
10. Dodson, E. O. *Evolution: Process and Product*, rev. ed. Van Nostrand Reinhold, New York, 1960, p. 236 © 1960 by Litton Educational Publishing, Inc. Reprinted by permission of Van Nostrand Reinhold, Inc.
11. Eiseley, L. "Fossil Man." *Scientific American*, December 1953, pp. 65–72. © 1953 by Scientific American, Inc. All rights reserved.
12. Estes, R. D. "Predators and Scavengers." *Natural History*, February–March 1967. © 1967 American Museum of Natural History. Reprinted by permission of *Natural History* magazine.
13. Gamow, G. *Matter, Earth, and Sky*. Prentice-Hall, Englewood Cliffs, N.J., 1958, p. 104.
14. Gilbert, W. S. *Princess Ida*, Act I. 1884.

15. Haeckel, E. H. "Origin and Pedigree of Man," in *The History of Creation*, trans. E. R. Lankester. Appleton, New York, 1868.

16. Homer. *The Iliad*, trans. A. Pope, Book VI, line 181.

17. Hooton, E. A. *Apes, Men, and Morons*. Putnam's, New York, 1937, 1965, pp. 74, 81–82. © 1937 by G. P. Putnam's Sons. Reprinted with permission.

18. Howells, W. W. "Homo Erectus." *Scientific American*, September 1966, pp. 46–53. © 1966 by Scientific American, Inc. All rights reserved.

18a. ———. *Mankind in the Making*. Doubleday, New York, 1967, p. 45 © 1967 by William Howells. Reprinted by permission of Doubleday & Company, Inc.

19. Jepsen, G. L. "Riddles of the Terrible Lizards." *American Scientist*, 52 (1964), 227–46. Reprinted by permission of *American Scientist*, journal of The Society of the Sigma Xi.

20. McAlester, A. L. *The History of Life*. Prentice-Hall, Englewood Cliffs, N.J. 1968, pp. 20–21.

21. Macey, R. I. In W. D. McElroy *et al.*, *Foundations of Biology*. Prentice-Hall, Englewood Cliffs, N.J., 1968, pp. 684, 694.

22. Marais, E. *The Soul of the Ape*. Atheneum, New York, 1969, pp. 104–6. © 1969 by Human & Rousseau Publishers Ltd. Reprinted by permission of Atheneum Publishers and Anthony Blond Ltd.

23. Olson, W. S. "Origin of the Cambrian-Precambrian Conformity." *American Scientist*, 54 (1966), 458–64. Reprinted by permission of *American Scientist*, journal of The Society of the Sigma Xi.

24. Pearson, O. P. "The Metabolism of Hummingbirds." *Scientific American*, January 1953, pp. 69–72. © 1953 by Scientific American, Inc. All rights reserved.

25. Romer, A. S. *Man and the Vertebrates*. Penguin, Baltimore, 1954. © 1933 by A. S. Romer. Reprinted by permission of the University of Chicago Press.

26. ———. *The Procession of Life*. World, New York, 1968.

27. Simons, E. L. "Some Fallacies in the Study of Hominid Phylogeny." *Science*, September 6, 1963, pp. 879–89. © 1963 by the American Association for the Advancement of Science.

28. Sinsheimer, R. L. "The Brain of Pooh: An Essay on the Limits of Mind." *American Scientist*, 59 (1971), 20–28. Reprinted by permission of *American Scientist*, journal of The Society of the Sigma Xi.

29. Smith, H. *Kamongo: or the Lungfish and the Padre*. Viking, New York, 1932, pp. 30–31. © 1932, © 1960 by Homer W. Smith. Reprinted by permission of The Viking Press, Inc.

30. Stebbins, G. L. *The Basis of Progressive Evolution*. Univ. North Carolina Press, Chapel Hill, 1969, pp. 120–21.

31. Twain, M. Quoted in B. De Voto, *Mark Twain in Eruption*. 1940.

32. Tyson, E. *Orang-Outang sive Homo Sylvestris: or the Anatomy of a Pygmie*. London, 1699.

33. Vogt, K. C. "Origin of Organic Nature," in *Lectures on Man. His Place in Creation, and in the History of the Earth*. Longman, Green, Longman and Roberts, London, 1863.

34. Washburn, S. L. "Tools and Human Evolution." *Scientific American*, September 1960, pp. 62–75. © 1960 by Scientific American, Inc. All rights reserved.

Chapter 7

1. Anthrop, D. F. "Environmental Noise Pollution: A New Threat to Sanity." *Bulletin of the Atomic Scientists*, 25 (1969) 11–16. Reprinted by permission of *Science and Public Affairs, the Bulletin of the Atomic Scientists*. © by the Educational Foundation for Nuclear Science.

2. Belloc, H. *A Bad Child's Book of Beasts*. 1896.

3. Beston, H. *Especially Maine: The Natural World of Henry Beston, from Cape Cod to the St. Lawrence*, selected and with introductions by E. Coatsworth. The Stephen Greene Press, Brattleboro, Vt., 1970, pp. 63–64.

4. Bronowski, J., and U. Bellugi. "Language, Name, and Concept." *Science*, May 8, 1970, pp. 669–74. © 1970 by the American Association for the Advancement of Science.

5. Cole, S. *Races of Man*. Natural History Series, British Museum, London, 1963.

6. Comfort, A. *The Nature of Human Nature*. Harper & Row, New York, 1966, pp. 132–33. © 1966 by Alex Comfort. Reprinted by permission of Harper & Row, Publishers, Inc.

7. Conrad, J. *The Many Worlds of Man*. Thomas Y. Crowell, New York, 1964, p. 45. © 1964 by Jack Conrad. Reprinted by permission of Thomas Y. Crowell Company, Inc.

8. Darlington, C. D. "The Control of Evolution in Man." *Eugenics Review*, 50 (1958), 1–10.

9. Dobzhansky, Th. "Evolution—Organic and Superorganic." *Bulletin of the Atomic Scientists*, 20 (1964), 4–8. Reprinted by permission of *Science and Public Affairs, the Bulletin of the Atomic Scientists*. © by the Educational Foundation for Nuclear Science.

10. Eiseley, L. "Freedom of the Juggernaut." *Mayo Clinic Proceedings*, 40 (1965), 7–22.

11. ———. "Mind as Nature," in *The Night Country*. Scribner's, New York, 1971. © 1962 by Loren Eiseley. Reprinted by permission of Charles Scribner's Sons.

12. Garn, S. M. "Culture and the Direction of Human Evolution." *Human Biology*, 35 (1963), 221–36.

13. Geertz, C. "The Impact of the Concept of Culture on the Concept of Man." *Bulletin of the Atomic Scientists*, 22 (1966), 2–8. Reprinted by permission of *Science and Public Affairs, the Bulletin of the Atomic Scientists*. © by the Educational Foundation for Nuclear Science.

14. Gerard, R. W. "Evolution and Man's Progress." *Daedalus*, Summer 1961.

15. Guhl. A. M. "Sociobiology and Man." *Bulletin of the Atomic Scientists*, 21 (1965), 22–24. Reprinted by permission of *Science and Public Affairs, the Bulletin of the Atomic Scientists*. © by the Educational Foundation for Nuclear Education.

16. Guiterman, A. "Ethnological," in *Gaily the Troubadour*. Dutton, New York, 1936.

17. Harrison, R. J., and W. Montagna. *Man*. Appleton-Century-Crofts, New York, 1969, pp. 232–33, 326.

18. Hockett, C. F. "The Origin of Speech." *Scientific American*,

September 1960, pp. 88–96. © 1960 by Scientific American, Inc. All rights reserved.

19. Hoebel, E. A. *Man in the Primitive World*. McGraw-Hill, New York, 1958, p. 539.

20. Hooton, E. A. *Apes, Men, and Morons*. Putnam's, New York, 1937, 1965, pp. 152–54. © 1937 by G. P. Putnam's Sons. Reprinted with permission.

21. Huxley, J. *Evolution in Action*. Harper, New York, 1953, p. 96. Reprinted by permission of A. D. Peters and Company.

22. Lamb, C. "The Two Races of Men," in *Essays of Elia*. 1823.

23. Nunnally, J. C., and R. L. Flaugher. "Psychological Implications of Word Usage." *Science*, May 17, 1963, pp. 775–81. © 1963 by the American Association for the Advancement of Science.

24. "Old in the Country of the Young." *Time*, August 3, 1970, pp. 49–52.

25. Pascal, B. *Pensées*. 1670.

26. Pope, A. *An Essay on Man*. 1732.

27. Potter, V. R. *Bioethics: Bridge to the Future*. Prentice-Hall, Englewood Cliffs, N.J., 1971, pp. 2–3.

28. Sandburg, C. "Wilderness," in *Chicago Poems*, by Carl Sandburg. Harcourt, New York, 1944. © 1916 by Holt, Rinehart and Winston, Inc.; © 1944 by Carl Sandburg. Reprinted by permission of Harcourt Brace Jovanovich, Inc.

29. Schaller, G. *Year of the Gorilla*. © Univ. Chicago Press, 1964, 141–42. Reprinted by permission of the University of Chicago Press and William Collins Sons Ltd.

30. Simpson, G. G. "The Biological Nature of Man," in *Biology and Man*. Harcourt Brace Jovanovich, New York, 1969. Reprinted with permission.

31. ———. *Biology and Man*. Harcourt, Brace & World, New York, 1966.

32. Stevenson, R. L. "Pulvis et Umbra." *Scribner's Magazine*, April 1888.

33. Straus, W. L., Jr. "Fossil Evidence of the Evolution of the Erect, Bipedal Posture." *Clinical Orthopaedics*, 25 (1962).

34. Twain, M. *The Damned Human Race: I. Was the World Made for Man*.

35. U.S. Department of the Interior, *Conservation Yearbook*, No. 4, 1968.

36. Wallace, B. *Essays in Social Biology*, Vol. III. Prentice-Hall, Englewood Cliffs, N.J., 1971, p. 101.

37. Washburn, S. L. "Speculations on the Problem of Man's Coming to the Ground," in *Changing Perspectives on Man*, ed. B. Rothblatt. Univ. Chicago Press, 1968.

38. ——— and I. DeVore. "The Social Life of Baboons." *Scientific American*, June 1961, pp. 62–71. © 1961 by Scientific American, Inc. All rights reserved.

39. Willey, B. *The Eighteenth-Century Background*. Columbia Univ. Press and Chatto and Windus Ltd., 1941, pp. 1–2.

40. Woodberry, G. E. "Man and the Race." *The Torch*, 1905.

Chapter 8

1. Browne, T. *Religio medici*. 1642.

2. Chardin, P. T. de. *The Phenomenon of Man*. Harper & Row, New York, 1959.

3. Correns, C. "G. Mendel's Law Concerning the Behavior of Progeny of Varietal Hybrids." *Berichte der Deutschen Botanischen Gesellschaft*, 18 (1900), 158–68. Translated and reprinted in *Genetics*, 35 (1950), 33–41.

4. Crow, J. "Mechanisms and Trends in Human Evolution." *Daedalus*, Summer 1961.

5. Cummins, H., and C. Midlo. *Finger Prints, Palms and Soles*. Dover, New York, 1967, pp. 150, 292.

6. Dobzhansky, Th. "Genetic Differences Between People Cannot Be Ignored." *Scientific Research*, July 22, 1968, pp. 32–33. © 1968 by McGraw-Hill, Inc.

7. ———. "Genetics and Equality." *Science*, July 13, 1962, pp. 112–15. © 1962 by the American Association for the Advancement of Science.

8. Donne, J. "The Good Morrow."

9. Dunn, L. C. "Mendel, His Work and His Place in History." *Proceedings, American Philosophical Society*, 109 (1965), 189–98.

10. Eiseley, L. *The Immense Journey*. Random House, New York, 1956, p. 209. © 1956 by Loren Eiseley. Reprinted by permission of Random House, Inc.

11. Fabun, D. "You and Creativity." *Kaiser News*, No. 3 (1968), 1–39. Reprinted by permission of Benziger Bruce & Glencoe, Inc., Beverly Hills, Calif., a division of The Macmillan Company. © 1968 by Kaiser Aluminum & Chemical Corporation.

12. Fuller, R. B. *Nine Chains to the Moon*. Lippincott, Philadelphia, 1938. © 1938, © 1966 by Richard Buckminster Fuller. Reprinted by permission of J. B. Lippincott Company.

13. Gedda, L. *Twins in History and Science*. C. C Thomas, Springfield, Ill., 1961, pp. 6–7. Courtesy of Charles C Thomas, Publisher.

14. German, J. "Studying Human Chromosomes Today." *American Scientist*, 58 (1970), 182–201. Reprinted by permission of *American Scientist*, journal of The Society of the Sigma Xi.

15. Hafez, E. S. E. Quoted in D. Fabun, *Dynamics of Change*. Prentice-Hall, Englewood Cliffs, N.J., 1970, section VI, p. 22.

16. Hardin, G. *Nature and Man's Fate*. Rinehart, New York, 1959.

17. Haskins, C. P. "Advances and Challenges in Science in 1970." *American Scientist*, 59 (1971), 298–307. Reprinted by permission of *American Scientist*, journal of The Society of the Sigma Xi.

18. "Interview with Albert Szent-Györgyi." *International Science and Technology*, June 1966.

19. Jukes, T. H. "The Genetic Code II." *American Scientist*, 53 (1965), 477–87. Reprinted by permission of *American Scientist*, journal of The Society of the Sigma Xi.

20. Kennedy, D. *The Living Cell: Readings from Scientific American*. Freeman, San Francisco, 1966, p. 2. © 1966 by Scientific American, Inc. All rights reserved.

21. Krutch, J. W. *The Modern Temper*. Harcourt, Brace, New York, 1929. © 1929 by Harcourt Brace Jovanovich, Inc.; © 1957 by Joseph Wood Krutch. Reprinted by permission of the publishers.

22. Lederberg, J. "Biological Future of Man," in *Man and His Future*, ed. G. Wolstenholme. Little, Brown, Boston, 1963.

23. ———. "Genetic Engineering and the Amelioration of Genetic Defects." *Bioscience*, 20 (1970), 1307–10.

24. La Rochefoucauld, *Maxims*, No. 57. 1665.

25. Libby, W. F. "Man's Place in the Physical Universe." *Bulletin of the Atomic Scientists*, 21 (1965), 12–17. Reprinted by permission of *Science and Public Affairs, the Bulletin of the Atomic Scientists*. © by the Educational Foundation for Nuclear Science.

26. Lwoff, A. *Biological Order*. M.I.T. Press, Boston, 1962, pp. 11–13.

27. McKusick, V. A. "The Mapping of Human Chromosomes." *Scientific American*, April 1971, pp. 104–13. © 1971 by Scientific American, Inc. All rights reserved.

28. Mendel, G. *Experiments in Plant Hybridization*, trans. Royal Horticultural Society of London. 1865.

29. ———. *Letter to Carl Nageli*, December 31, 1866.

30. Merton, R. K. "Making It Scientifically." *The New York Times Book Review*, February 25, 1968. © 1968 by The New York Times Company. Reprinted by permission.

31. Montaigne, M. de. *Of the Resemblance of Children to Their Fathers*.

32. Muller, H. J. *Evolution After Darwin*. Univ. Chicago Press. 1960.

33. ———. "What Genetic Course Will Man Steer?" *Bulletin of the American Scientists*, 24 (1968), 6–12. Reprinted by permission of *Science and Public Affairs, the Bulletin of the Atomic Scientists*. © by the Educational Foundation for Nuclear Science.

34. Neufeld, E. F., and J. C. Fratantoni. "Inborn Errors of Mucopolysaccharide." *Science*, July 10, 1970, pp. 141–45. © 1970 by the American Association for the Advancement of Science.

35. Pelles, G. *Arts, Artists, and Society: Origins of a Modern Dilemma*. Prentice-Hall, Englewood Cliffs, N.J., 1963, pp. 51, 53.

36. Pliny the Elder. *Natural History*, Book VII.

37. Roberts, J. A. F. *An Introduction to Medical Genetics*, 2nd ed. Oxford Univ. Press, New York, 1959.

38. Sinsheimer, R. L. *The Book of Life*. Addison-Wesley, Reading, Mass., 1967, pp. 21–22.

39. ———. "The Prospect for Designed Genetic Change." *American Scientist*, 57 (1969), 134–42. Reprinted by permission of *American Scientist*, journal of The Society of the Sigma Xi.

40. Swanson, C. P. *The Cell*, 3rd ed. Prentice-Hall, Englewood Cliffs, N.J., 1969.

41. Watson, J. D. *The Double Helix: A Personal Account of the Discovery of the Structure of DNA*. New American Library, New York, 1968, pp. 128–29, 131, 133–34, 139, 141. © 1968 by James D. Watson. Reprinted by permission of Atheneum Publishers and Weidenfeld and Nicolson Ltd.

42. Whitman, W. *Song of Myself*.

43. Wiesenfeld, S. L. "Sickle-Cell Trait in Human Biological and Cultural Evolution." *Science*, September 8, 1967, pp. 1134–40. © 1967 by the American Association for the Advancement of Science.

44. Williams, R. J. *Free and Unequal: The Biological Basis of Individual Liberty*. Univ. Texas Press, Austin, 1953.

45. ———. "Heredity, Human Understanding, and Civilization." *American Scientist*, 57 (1969), 237–43. Reprinted by permission of *American Scientist*, journal of The Society of the Sigma Xi.

46. ———. *You Are Extraordinary*. Random House, New York, 1967. © 1967 by Roger J. Williams. Reprinted by permission of Random House, Inc.

Chapter 9

1. Asimov, I. "And It Will Serve Us Right." *Psychology Today*, 2 (1969), 38–41, 64–65. © Communications/Research/Machines, Inc.

2. Beers, R. F., Jr. "'Open' Economics and a 'Closed' Ecology." *Baltimore Sun*, December 9, 1970.

3. Benedict, R. "The Growth of Cultures," in *Man, Culture and Society*, ed. H. L. Shapiro. Oxford Univ. Press, New York, 1971, p. 187. © 1956 by Oxford University Press, Inc. Reprinted with permission.

4. Binford, S. R., and L. R. Binford. "Stone Tools and Human Behavior." *Scientific American*, April 1969, pp. 70–72 © 1969 by Scientific American, Inc. All rights reserved.

5. Borlag, N. E. "The Green Revolution: For Bread and Peace." *Bulletin of the Atomic Scientists*, 27 (1971), 6–9. Reprinted by permission of *Science and Public Affairs, the Bulletin of the Atomic Scientists*. © by the Educational Foundation for Nuclear Science.

6. Boulding, K. E. "The Scientific Revelation." *Bulletin of the Atomic Scientists*, 26 (1970), 13–18. Reprinted by permission of *Science and Public Affairs, the Bulletin of the Atomic Scientists*. © by the Educational Foundation for Nuclear Science.

7. Brown, H. "Human Materials Production as a Process in the Biosphere." *Scientific American*, September 1970, pp. 195–208. © 1970 by Scientific American, Inc. All rights reserved.

8. Carrington, R. *A Million Years of Man*. New American Library, New York, 1964, p. 173.

9. Chesterton, G. K. *Orthodoxy*. 1908.

10. Clark, C. "Agricultural Productivity in Relation to Population," in *Man and His Future*, ed. G. Wolstenholme. Little, Brown, Boston, 1963.

11. Clark, G. *The Dawn of Civilization*, ed. S. Piggott. Thames and Hudson, London, 1961.

12. Coleman, E. "Encore." 1965. Reprinted by permission of the author.

13. Conrad, J. *The Many Worlds of Man*. Thomas Y. Crowell, New York, 1964, pp. 107–8. © 1964 by Jack Conrad. Reprinted by permission of Thomas Y. Crowell Company, Inc.

14. Coon, C. S. "Growth and Development of Social Groups," in *Man and His Future*, ed. G. Wolstenholme. Little, Brown, Boston, 1963.

15. Cozart, W. R. "Human Imagination in the Age of Space." *Motive*, March–April 1967.

16. Darwin, C. *On the Origin of Species by Means of Natural Selection, or the Preservation of Favoured Races in the Struggle for Life*. London, 1859.

17. Doxiadis, C. A. "Ekistics, The Science of Human Settlements." *Science*, October 23, 1970, pp. 393–404. © 1970 by the American Association for the Advancement of Science.

18. Dubos, R. "Humanistic Biology." *American Scientist* 53 (1965), 4–19.

19. ———. *So Human an Animal*. Scribner's, New York, 1968; p. 128. © 1968 by Rene Dubos. Reprinted by permission of Charles Scribner's Sons.

20. Fabun, D. "Ecology: The Man-Made Planet." *Kaiser News*, No. 1 (1970), 1–15. Reprinted by permission of Benziger Bruce & Glencoe, Inc., Beverly Hills, Calif., a division of The Macmillan Company. © 1970 by Kaiser Aluminum & Chemical Corporation.

21. ———. "Energy: Transactions in Time." *Kaiser News*, The Markets of Change Series, No. 3 (1970). Reprinted by permission of Benziger Bruce & Glencoe, Inc., Beverly Hills, Calif., a division of The Macmillan Company. © 1970 by Kaiser Aluminum & Chemical Corporation.

22. ———. "Food: An Energy Exchange System." *Kaiser News*, The Markets of Change Series, No. 4 (1970), 1–36. Reprinted by permission of Benziger Bruce & Glencoe, Inc., Beverly Hills, Calif., a division of The Macmillan Company. © 1970 by Kaiser Aluminum & Chemical Corporation.

23. ———. "The Corporation as a Creative Environment." *Kaiser News*, No. 2 (1967), 1–31. Reprinted by permission of Benziger Bruce & Glencoe, Inc., Beverly Hills, Calif., a division of The Macmillan Company. © 1967 by Kaiser Aluminum & Chemical Corporation.

24. ———. "You and Creativity." *Kaiser News*, No. 3 (1968), 1–39. Reprinted by permission of Benziger Bruce & Glencoe, Inc., Beverly Hills, Calif. a division of The Macmillan Company. © 1968 by Kaiser Aluminum & Chemical Corporation.

25. Glikson, A. "Man's Relationship to his Environment," in *Man and His Future*, ed. G. Wolstenholme. Little, Brown, Boston, 1963.

26. Handler, P., ed. *Biology and the Future of Man*. Oxford Univ. Press, New York, 1970, pp. 163–64. © 1970 by Oxford University Press. Reprinted with permission.

27. Hardin, G. "Blueprints, DNA, and Abortion: A Scientific and Ethical Analysis." *Medical Opinion and Review*, February 1967.

28. Harlan, J. R., and D. Zohary. "Distribution of Wild Wheats and Barleys." *Science*, September 2, 1966, pp. 1074–79. © 1966 by the American Association for the Advancement of Science.

29. Harris, R. "The Origins of Agriculture in the Tropics," *American Scientist* 60 (1972), 180–93. Reprinted by permission of *American Scientist*, journal of The Society of the Sigma Xi.

30. Hoijer, H. "Language and Writing," in *Man, Culture and Society*, ed. H. L. Shapiro. Oxford Univ. Press, New York, 1956.

31. Huxley, T. H. *Evolution and Ethics, and Other Essays*. Appleton, New York, 1896.

32. Mayr, E. "Taxonomic Categories in Fossil Hominids." *Cold Harbor Symposia on Quantitative Biology*, 15 (1951) 109–17.

33. Morison, E. E. *Men, Machines, and Modern Times*. M.I.T. Press, 1966, pp. 15–16.

34. Muller, H. J. "Should We Weaken or Strengthen Our Genetic Heritage?" *Daedalus*, Summer 1961.

35. Munro, T. *Evolution in the Arts*. Cleveland Museum of Art.

36. Nef, J. U. *The Conquest of the Material World: Essays on the Coming of Industrialism*. Univ. Chicago Press, 1964, pp. 3–4. Reprinted by permission of the University of Chicago Press.

37. Oppenheimer, J. R. "On Science and Culture." *Encounter*, 1963, pp. 3–10.

38. Potter, V. R. "Society and Science." *Science*, November 20, 1964, pp. 1018–22. © 1964 by the American Association for the Advancement of Science.

39. Rappaport, R. A. "Flow of Energy in an Agricultural Society." *Scientific American*, September 1971, 116–32. © 1971 by Scientific American, Inc. All rights reserved.

40. Rosenfeld, A. *The Second Genesis: The Coming Control of Life*. Prentice-Hall, Englewood Cliffs, N.J., 1969. © 1969 by Albert Rosenfeld. Reprinted by permission of Prentice-Hall, Inc., and Ann Elmo Agency, Inc.

41. Shaw, G. B. *Back to Methuselah*. Penguin, Baltimore, 1961, preface. Reprinted by permission of the Society of Authors, on behalf of the Bernard Shaw Estate.

42. Smith, L. *The Journey*. Norton, New York, 1954. © 1954 by Lillian Smith. Reprinted by permission of W. W. Norton & Company, Inc., and McIntosh and Otis, Inc.

43. Spilhaus, A. "The Next Industrial Revolution." *Science*, March 27, 1970, p. 1673. © 1970 by the American Association for the Advancement of Science.

44. Stebbins, G. L. "Pitfalls and Guideposts in Comparing Organic and Social Evolution." *Pacific Sociological Review*, 8 (1965), 3–10.

45. Steward, J. H., and D. B. Shimkin. "Some Mechanisms in Sociocultural Evolution." *Daedalus*, Summer 1961.

46. Swenson, M. "Three Models of the Universe," in *Half Sun Half Sleep*. Scribner's, New York, 1967. Reprinted by permission of Charles Scribner's Sons. First printed as "Models of the Universe," in *Poetry in Crystal*. © 1963 by Steuben Glass.

47. Ubbelohde, A. P. *Man and Energy*, Penguin, Baltimore, 1963.

48. Ward, L. F. *The Psychic Factors of Civilization*, 2nd ed. Ginn, Champaigne, Illinois, 1902.

49. Webster, D. *Remarks on Agriculture*. January 13, 1840.

50. Wertime, T. A. "Man's First Encounters with Metallurgy." *Science*, December 4, 1964, pp. 1257–67. © 1964 by the American Association for the Advancement of Science.

51. White, L. A. *The Science of Culture: A Study of Man and Civilization*. Farrar, Straus & Giroux, New York, 1969, pp. 14, 153. © 1949, 1969 by Leslie A. White. Reprinted by permission of Farrar, Straus & Giroux, Inc.

52. Wiesenfeld, S. L. "Sickle-Cell Trait in Human Biology." *Science*, September 8, 1967, pp. 1134–40. © 1967 by the American Association for the Advancement of Science.

Chapter 10

1. Berry, W. "The One-Inch Journey." *Audubon*, 73 (1971), 4–11. Reprinted by permission of *Audubon*, the magazine of the National Audubon Society. © 1971.

2. Blake, J. "Population Policy for Americans: Is the Government Being Misled." *Science*, May 2, 1969, pp. 522–29. © 1969 by the American Association for the Advancement of Science.

3. Borgstrom, G. A. "The Dual Challenge of Health and Hunger—A Global Crisis." *Population Bureau Reference Selection* No. 31, 1970.

4. Bradley, C. C. "Human Water Needs and Water Use in America." *Science*, 1962, pp. 489–91. © 1962 by the American Association for the Advancement of Science.

5. Brooks, H. National Academy of Sciences *News Report*, 20 (1970), 1–12.

6. Carson, R. *The Edge of the Sea*. Houghton Mifflin, Boston, 1955, pp. 11–12, 14.

7. Coale, A. J. "Man and His Environment." *Science*, March 19, 1970, pp. 132–36. © 1970 by the American Association for the Advancement of Science.

8. Comfort, A. "Longevity of Man and His Tissues," in *Man and His Future*, ed. G. Wolstenholme. Little, Brown, Boston, 1963.

9. Crow, J. "Mechanisms and Trends in Human Evolution," in "Evolution and Man's Progress." *Daedalus*, Summer 1961.

10. Darlington, C. D. "The Control of Evolution in Man." *Eugenics Review*, 50 (1958), 1–10.

11. Doxiadis, C. A. "On the Measure of Man: Challenge and Response in the Anthropocosmos." *Mayo Clinic Proceedings*, 49 (1965), 71–89.

12. Elton, C. E. *The Ecology of Invasions by Animals and Plants*. Methuen, London, 1958.

13. Fabun, D. *Dynamics of Change*. Prentice-Hall, Englewood Cliffs, N.J., 1970, section I, p. 15. © 1967 by Kaiser Aluminum & Chemical Corporation.

14. ———. "Ecology: The Man-Made Planet." *Kaiser News*, No. 1, 1970. Reprinted by permission of Benziger Bruce & Glencoe, Inc., Beverly Hills, Calif., a division of The Macmillan Company. © 1970 by Kaiser Aluminum & Chemical Corporation.

15. ———. *Dynamics of Change*. Prentice-Hall, Englewood Cliffs, N.J., 1970, section III, p. 29. © 1967 by Kaiser Aluminum & Chemical Corporation.

16. Ford, H. Quoted in *The New York Times*, December 3, 1969.

17. Glass, H. B. "Science: Endless Horizons or Golden Age?" *Science*, January 8, 1971, pp. 23–29. © 1971 by the American Association for the Advancement of Science.

18. Gustafsson, A. "Gregor Mendel and 100 Years of Genetic Research." *Acta Agriculturae Scandinavica, Supplement*, 16 (1966), 27–32.

19. Hardin, G. "The History and Future of Birth Control." *Perspectives in Biology and Medicine*, 10 (1966), 1–18.

20. ———. "Nobody Ever Dies of Overpopulation." *Science*, February 12, 1971, p. 527. © 1971 by the American Association for the Advancement of Science.

21. Howard, W. E. "The Population Crisis Is Here Now." *BioScience*, 19 (1969), 779–84.

22. Huxley, J. "The Future of Man—Evolutionary Aspects," in *Man and His Future*, ed. G. Wolstenholme. Little, Brown, Boston, 1963, pp. 9–10, 17, 20. Reprinted by permission of Little, Brown and Company and Ciba Foundation, London.

23. Kantrowitz. A. "The Test: Meeting the Challenge of New Technology." *Bulletin of the Atomic Scientists*, 25 (1969), 20–22. Reprinted by permission of *Science and Public Affairs, the Bulletin of the Atomic Scientists*. © by the Educational Foundation for Nuclear Science.

24. Kendeigh, C. S. "The Ecology of Man, the Animal." *BioScience*, 15 (1965), 521–23.

25. Kiefer, D. M. "Population: Technology's Desperate Race with Fertility." *Chemical & Engineering News*, 46 (1968).

26. Koprowski, H. "Future of Infections and Malignant Disease," in *Man and His Future*, ed. G. Wolstenholme. Little, Brown, Boston, 1963.

27. Krantz, G. S. "Human Activities and Megafaunal Extinctions." *American Scientist*, 58 (1970), 164–70.

28. McElroy, W. D. "Biomedical Aspects of Population Control." *BioScience*, 19 (1969), 19–23.

29. MacLeish, A. "The Great American Frustration." *Saturday Review*, July 13, 1968. Reprinted by permission of Saturday Review, Inc., and Houghton Mifflin Company.

30. Marks, P. L. "A Vision of Environment." *American Scholar*, 40 (Summer 1971), 421–31. © 1971 by United Chapters of Phi Beta Kappa. Reprinted by permission of the publishers.

31. Medawar, P. B. "Do Advances in Medicine Lead to Genetic Deterioration?" *Mayo Clinic Proceedings*, 40 (1965), 23–34.

32. Miller, G. A. "Some Psychological Perspectives on the Year 2000," in *Toward the Year 2000: Work in Progress. Daedalus*, Summer 1967, 885–86.

33. Mills, S. "O and All the Little Babies in the Alameda Gardens Yes," in *Ecotatics*, ed. J. G. Mitchell and C. L. Stallings. Simon & Schuster, 1970, pp. 79–80, 82–83. © 1970 by the Sierra Club. Reprinted by permission of Pocket Books, a division of Simon & Schuster, Inc.

34. Momaday, N. S. "An American Land Ethic," in *Ecotatics*, ed. J. G. Mitchell and C. L. Stallings. Simon & Schuster, New York, 1970, p. 101. © 1970 by the Sierra Club. Reprinted by permission of Pocket Books, a division of Simon & Schuster, Inc.

35. Moran, W. E., Jr. "Brazil: A Prodigy of Growth." *Population Bulletin*, 25 (1969), 89–90.

36. Newman, J. R. Book review in *Scientific American*, January 1959, pp. 149–54. © 1959 by Scientific American, Inc. All rights reserved.

37. Osler, W. *Aequanimitas and Other Addresses*. 1904.

38. Pimentel, D. "Population Regulation and Genetic Feedback." *Science*, March 29, 1968, pp. 1432–37. © 1963 by the American Association for the Advancement of Science.

39. Quarton, G. C. "Deliberate Efforts to Control Human Behavior and Modify Personality," in *Toward the Year 2000: Work in Progress. Daedalus*, Summer 1967, pp. 837–53.

40. Roberts, W. O. "Science, A Wellspring of Our Discontent." *American Scientist*, 55 (1967), 3–14. Reprinted by permission of *American Scientist*, journal of The Society of the Sigma Xi.

41. Rosenfeld, A. *The Second Genesis: The Coming Control of Life*. Prentice-Hall, Englewood Cliffs, N.J., 1969, p. 3. © 1969 by Albert Rosenfeld. Reprinted by permission of Prentice-Hall, Inc., and Ann Elmo Agency, Inc.

42. Seami, M. *Aya no Tsunami* (Japanese Noh play).

43. Shakespeare, W. *The Merchant of Venice*, Act I, scene i.

44. Shapley, H. "The Scholar's Scratch Pad: Some Music From

the Spheres." *American Scholar*, 27 (Spring 1959), pp. 218–21. © 1959 by the United Chapters of Phi Beta Kappa. Reprinted by permission of the publishers.

45. Stycos, J. M. "The Outlook for World Population." *Science*, December 11, 1964, pp. 1435–40. © 1964 by the American Association for the Advancement of Science.

46. Thoreau, H. *Walden.* 1892.

47. Von Fritz, K. "Relativism and Absolute Value." Quoted in D. Fabun, *Dynamics of Change*. Prentice-Hall, Englewood Cliffs, N.J., 1970, Section VI, p. 12.

48. Weinberg, A. M. "In Defense of Science." *Science*, January 9, 1970, pp. 141–45. © 1970 by the American Association for the Advancement of Science.

49. White, L., Jr. "The Historical Roots of Our Ecologic Crisis." *Science*, March 10, 1967, pp. 1203–7. © 1967 by the American Association for the Advancement of Science.

50. Wynne-Edwards, V. C. "Self-regulating Systems in Populations of Animals." *Science*, March 26, 1965, pp. 1543–48. © 1965 by the American Association for the Advancement of Science.

51. Zucker, A. "Coming to Grips with Technology." *Oak Ridge National Laboratory Review*, Spring 1970, pp. 6–8.

*Italicized page numbers indicate illustrations. Boldface
page numbers indicate references to marginal quotations.*

Index